The Wines of Alsace

Having written on wine since the mid-1970s, Tom Stevenson was asked by Telegraph Publications to devise an annual wine publication for ordinary, everyday consumers, and in 1982 he conceived *The Sunday Telegraph Good Wine Guide*, which he edited for a further five years. The recipient of numerous awards, he was voted Wine Writer of the Year in 1986 and Wine Trade Writer of the Year in 1990 and 1993. His books include *Champagne* and *Sotheby's World Wine Encyclopedia*. He writes a regular column in *Wine* magazine and is a freelance contributor to more than a dozen major publications.

FABER BOOKS ON WINE
General Editor: Julian Jeffs
Bordeaux (new edition) by David Peppercorn
Burgundy by Anthony Hanson
French Country Wines by Rosemary George
German Wines by Ian Jamieson
Italian Wines (new edition) by George Robertson
Port (new edition) by Julian Jeffs
The Wines of Alsace by Tom Stevenson
The Wines of Australia (new edition) by Oliver Mayo
The Wines of Greece by Miles Lambert-Gocs
The Wines of Portugal (new edition) by Jan Read
The Wines of the Rhone (new edition) by John Livingstone-Learmonth

THE WINES OF ALSACE

TOM STEVENSON

faber and faber
LONDON · BOSTON

First published in 1993
by Faber and Faber Limited
3 Queen Square London WC1N 3AU

Photoset by Parker Typesetting Service, Leicester
Printed in Great Britain by
Clays Ltd, St Ives plc

© Tom Stevenson 1993

Tom Stevenson is hereby identified as author of this work in
accordance with Section 77 of the Copyright, Designs and
Patents Act 1988

A CIP record for this book is available from the British Library

ISBN 0–571–14952–9 (cased)
0–571–14953–7 (pbk)

2 4 6 8 10 9 7 5 3 1

To Aileen Trew, MW,
an intelligent and gentle person who had
a passion for Alsace and loved to pass her knowledge on.

Contents

＿＿＿＿

Introduction and Acknowledgements   xi

1 The Evolution of Alsace Wines   1
    The First Vineyards   1
    The Emergence of Alsace   3
    Golden Era   3
    Start of the Long Decline   7
    The Renaissance   10

2 Viticulture and Vinification   16
    Phylloxera in Alsace   17
    Grafting   19
    Rootstock Varieties   21
    Vine Training   24
    The Viticultural Cycle   24
    Varietal Growth Characteristics   32
    Grape Reception   38
    Fermentation   38
    Malolactic Fermentation   39
    Racking, Fining and Filtering   40
    Red Wines   41
    Sparkling Wines   43

3 Le Terroir   46
    Location, Topography and Climate   46
    Viticultural Alsace   49
    Rhine Wine?   50
    The Real Rivers of Alsace   50
    Soil   52
    Lexicon of Soil Types   56

4 The Wine Villages of Alsace   64
   Village Profiles   65

5 The *Grands Crus*   147
   Establishing the *Grand Cru* system in Alsace   147
   The Delimitation Process   150
   The Anti-*Crus*   151
   An Alternative Classification   153
   AOC Alsace *Grand Cru*: Facts and Figures   154
   Grand Cru Profiles   156

6 Chateaux, *Clos* and Other Named Sites   225
   Alsace Châteaux   225
   The *Clos* of Alsace   227
   The *Côtes* and *Coteaux* of Alsace   238
   The *Lieux-Dits* of Alsace   241

7 The Styles of Wine   260
   AOC Alsace and AOC Vin d'Alsace   261
   The Varietal Concept   262
   One *Appellation*, Nine Varietals   263
   Alsace Varietals   265
   Alternative Designations   302
   Blended Wines   305
   Speciality Wines   312
   The *Vins de Pays* of Alsace   334
   AOC Crémant d'Alsace   335
   AOC Alsace *Grand Cru*   340
   Medals, Gongs and Competition Wines   342

8 The People and Their Wines   344
   Trade Structure   344
   Infrastructure of Vineyard Holdings   349
   Producer Profiles   350

Appendices
  1 Vintage Assessments   481
  2 Earlier Classifications   517
  3 Production Analysis   520
  4 Sales and Export Statistics   529

5 AOC and EC Regulations   543
6 Linguistic Analysis   547

Glossary   549
Bibliography   574
Index   577

Introduction and Acknowledgements

As a good friend in Alsace once told me, 'There are more than enough books on the folklore, food and storks of Alsace, but a real reference book – now that would be something.'

Well Philippe (why are half the people in Alsace called Philippe?), I hope this is real enough for you. It certainly is not about storks, although the slow, graceful flight of a solitary stork across balmy evening skies is one of the most evocative memories of Alsace. There is no chapter on the food of Alsace, but wine is inseparable from food and the cuisine of Alsace is so rich and varied that the subject crops up here and there, especially when the combinations are made in heaven. As for folklore, that is the lightest ingredient in this book's recipe; a smattering can be found, but the historical chapters try to be pure history, not fantasy, although I try to make them lively, not dense. What folklore does exist in this book is confined to the wine village profiles, where I could not resist repeating a few of the more far-fetched stories.

It is meant, however, to be essentially a reference work, as complete as I can make it, to the wines of Alsace and the often colourful characters who make them. I have tried to attack the subject as comprehensively as possible, with over 300 producer profiles and, of course, every wine style defined, including the ancient *vin de paille*, which is making a reappearance and the recently designated *vins de pays*, as well as the expected varietal wines. All 118 wine villages have their own separate portraits, as do the 50 *grands crus*, 84 *lieux-dits* in current use, 28 *clos* and 4 wine-producing châteaux of Alsace. The idea is that the reader may look up the wines recommended for a specific village or *grand cru*, as well as a producer. This should give you a quick overview of the depth of information this book contains, which I hope not only satisfies the most demanding Alsace wine enthusiast, but also manages, within the constraints of the Faber & Faber format, to be sufficiently compartmentalized in its information to allow free and easy access by the more casual reader, who merely wishes to dip in and out of it.

INFATUATION

My interest in Alsace is now almost obsessive, but not oppressive I hope. It is an infatuation that began more than 20 years ago, but it was not until October 1983 that I first set foot in the region. On that initial visit, I was lucky enough to be accompanied by Aileen Trew, a bright and unassuming Master of Wine whose first and all-consuming passion was Alsace.

Aileen conveyed her affection for these wines in her many lectures on the subject to young wine trade students sitting their Higher Certificate and Diploma examinations. In the late 1970s I was one such student, though it is only now I can consider myself to have been young at the time. At that juncture I thought 27 to be the age of a very mature student indeed.

When I was lucky enough to be asked by Telegraph Publications to create an annual wine publication, I came up with the idea of the *Sunday Telegraph Good Wine Guide*, and it was Aileen who helped me put together its first tasting panels. I had a pretty good idea how the mechanics of such events should work, but they were the very first tasting panels in the UK regularly to tackle in excess of a thousand wines and to cope I needed an almost inexhaustible supply of expert tasters. I had some contacts, but not enough. Enter Aileen. She knew all the right people, the most experienced tasters in the trade, especially those who held flexible enough jobs to donate their time and services. Even then, we soon ran out, but Aileen was also chairman of the Education Committee for the Institute of Masters of Wine and thus began to recommend the most talented tasters among what turned out to be a future generation of MWs. Totally unknown then, most today hold prestigious positions within the trade and are respected for their expertise.

The task of putting together tasting panels has become so well established that it is difficult to describe just how valuable Aileen's contribution was in 1982, but the simple fact is that the *Sunday*

Telegraph Good Wine Guide would not have existed without her efforts. I ran this publication for five years and by combining its tastings with *WINE* magazine's Annual Wine Challenge, its current editor, Robert Joseph, has built the event into the largest and most respected of its kind in the world.

During my time on the *Guide*, Aileen and I crossed paths on numerous occasions and I do not think that on any one of these meetings we did not discuss Alsace. Certainly she continued to feed me with stories of a fairy-tale land and colourful winemakers. It was not, however, until almost exactly six years to the day since we first met that she realized I had not visited the Alsace and this puzzled her. She knew how mesmerized I was by the wines; how then could I be content simply tasting them? Why had I not bothered to visit the region, taste in greater depth, talk to the producers and learn more? Exactly my thoughts at the time – why indeed? The solution was simple, but as I began to organize the trip, I thought: why not go with Aileen? No sooner had I asked than we were on our way to Strasbourg airport.

What better way to visit Alsace for the first time than with such a knowledgeable and bubbly guide as Aileen Trew? The trip was a dream. Alsace was every bit the fairy-tale place I imagined it to be; villages like Ribeauvillé and Riquewihr immediately sprang to medieval life with their cobbled streets and half-timbered buildings. It was suddenly so real, yet more than make-believe in appearance. Trimbach, Hugel, Beyer and others were once merely names on bottles, but now became personalities as individual as the wines they produce. It became impossible for me to drink a glass of Alsace wine without seeing its producer in the back my mind. If I was not already besotted with Alsace, I was from that point on and no matter how many times I return, no matter how long I stay or how hard I work, it remains hypnotically charming and never loses its spell.

Aileen Trew died of cancer before I could complete this book, but her contribution to my love and understanding of this region is alive on every page of *The Wines of Alsace*. We both shared a passion that has really become an infatuation. An infatuation for the most picturesque wine region in the world, the unique culture of the people who live there and the beautifully expressive wines they make. For me, Alsace has a touch of magic that I will always associate with dear Aileen.

THE BIRTH OF A BOOK

That is how my infatuation for the subject grew. It was essentially responsible for igniting the fire inside me to write *The Wines of Alsace*, but the book was not even a thought, let alone a reality, until one day in the spring of 1986.

I had just arrived at Paddington station as the train I intended to catch was pulling away. Naturally I began to chase after it: naturally because it was six years ago and, of course, I was a little younger and a fair bit slimmer. In those days, I ran to catch trains. Nowadays, I do not. It was a good job, therefore, that this little episode occurred when it did. Had it happened merely a year or two later, I would not have entered into an unfair race with a diesel locomotive, would not have caught the train and thus the opportunity to write the book would not have existed. Not by my pen anyway. I ran, flung the door open and, as the train gathered momentum, hurled my briefcase inside and leapt aboard. As I burst breathlessly (I was never slim, just slimmer) into the first compartment available, I discovered it to be occupied by a solitary person, Julian Jeffs. We had both been to the same tasting, but Julian had sensibly left half an hour before me, was sitting comfortably and not out of breath.

We managed to catch the same train and, coincidentally, end up in the same compartment. Fate or coincidence? I certainly thought it opportune, as I closed the compartment door and saw Julian's wise-owl face. He raised his head, switched on an instant smile and declared 'Well, hello there' in that precise yet inimitable way of his. As regular readers of Faber & Faber wine books will know, Julian Jeffs is the author of the definitive work on Sherry and editor of the entire Wine Series. A crazy thought fluttered across my mind; I said, 'Julian, there's something I've been meaning to ask you' and by November of that year, terms had been agreed and a contract signed. I hardly dare admit this, but the deadline for the manuscript in that contract was December 1987, which should have seen this book published more than four years ago!

So many obstacles kept cropping up that I initially began to wonder whether I was destined ever to finish it. The first, biggest and longest running of these hindrances concerned the vexed issue of *grands crus*. To include maps of each and every *grand cru* was fundamental to my concept of this book, but at the time of signing the contract, less than half of these vineyards had actually been delimited. It was not as foolhardy as it may seem, agreeing to finish the book by December 1987, as I had already been told by CIVA (the Comité Interprofessionnel du Vins d'Alsace) that the remainder of the *grands crus* would be delimited and maps made available to me three months prior to my deadline.

It was not CIVA's fault that the growers and INAO (Institut National des Appellations d'Origine) committees could not agree where the boundaries for these sites should go, so I suppose it was not my fault that I was unable to complete the book, but a contract is a contract and Faber & Faber could legitimately have torn ours up. The more recent delays could be fairly and squarely blamed on me. Perhaps at that point Faber should have torn up the contract. In any case, I finally knuckled down and agreed to complete the manuscript by January 1991. This I duly achieved by 30 June 1992, thus my eternal thanks go to Julian Jeffs and everyone at Faber for maintaining their faith in me throughout. (Author's note, March 1993: Ironically, the remaining *grand crus* were delimited in December 1992, although no official maps have as yet emerged.)

It almost goes without saying that an author of a wine book is grateful for the help and hospitality of all the producers he visits, but an author of a book on the wines of Alsace is – I fear – in even more debt. This is because of the multitude of Alsace wines. There are so many varietals and within each of these numerous *cuvées* of various qualities that the number of wines to taste for each vintage is considerably greater than for any other region of France. Multiply that by the span of vintages that must be analysed and the numbers become almost as staggering as the author's gait. Anyone who has tasted at Paul Blanck's will know the extremes to which this can go. The first time I was simply unprepared. I gave up after a hundred wines, asked them to re-cork the rest and told them I would return the next day to finish the job. I would not have missed that opportunity for anything and have been a glutton for such punishment more than once, but thank goodness all producers are not like the Blancks, for otherwise I would still be tasting.

Every producer I have ever visited has my sincere thanks, but to name them all would result in a list spreading over several pages. It could be done, but who would read it? I suspect that most readers are, like me, loath even to open the acknowledgements pages, let alone read it, which is why I decided to write a combined

Introduction and Acknowledgements that did not include anything so impenetrable as a list of names. Doing away with this list is not intended to offend any of the producers who would have been on it. Readers of this book will take it for granted that I am truly indebted to each and every producer included in **Producer Profiles**, Chapter 8, as indeed I hope the producers will themselves.

CERTAIN PEOPLE TO THANK

There are certain people including producers, of course, to whom for various reasons I am especially indebted without diminishing my gratitude to everyone else. In no particular order they include:

Martine and Philippe Becker of Jean Becker in Zellenberg, for letting me take over their house, home and even winery on my last sojourn in Alsace. Although, prior to this trip, Pierre-Étienne Dopff and others had told me that I had already visited more wineries and tasted in greater depth than anybody before me, there were still many smaller growers I had not got around to seeing. I wrote to these producers, explaining that I would be in the region for the very last time before completing my book and that if they would like to send any samples to the Becker establishment, together with any appropriate details, I would be very interested to taste their wines.

Obviously I hoped to discover some intriguing wines upon arrival in Zellenberg, but in no way was I prepared for the 900 different wines that were waiting for us. Martine Becker vacated her flat adjacent to the winery and Pat (my wife) and I moved in, so that we could literally sleep on the job. The Beckers magnanimously stored the wines of their competitors in their deepest cellars, which provided the perfect tasting temperature. We took over more than half of the ground floor of the building that houses the Beckers' administration offices for an almost non-stop series of tastings. The parents of Philippe (the winemaker) and Martine live above these offices and had to put up with the noise and activity of our tastings until 8 or 10 p.m. every day, yet they treated us as if we were part of their family. As one of Philippe's passions is *eau-de-vie*, he distilled the remains of these 900 bottles after the tastings, rather than waste it. This was then matured in new oak. Unlike Philippe, I am no lover of spirits, but it must be the only Eau-de-Vie d'Alsace distilled from a blend of *grand cru*, Vendange Tardive and Sélection de Grains Noble wines. So, if you come across a bottle of Jean Becker Eau-de-Vie d'Alsace 'Cuvée Tom Stevenson', you now know what it is.

I must thank Marcel Blanck of Paul Blanck in Kientzheim, for being the most forthcoming head of all exporting houses when it came to revealing names of little-known growers. He not only gave me a list of growers I should visit, but also offered to drive me to any of them, almost at the drop of a hat. I took him up on this one Saturday afternoon, disturbing him during an afternoon nap. When he opened the door, he was in a string vest with no trousers and a big, sleepy grin on his face, but within three minutes he was driving me along the country roads, full of enthusiasm, and would hear nothing of my apologies for disturbing him. Most other shippers told me that no relatively unknown growers were worth seeking out because if they were any good they would not be unknown. Put into this sort of perspective, Marcel Blanck comes over as a big and charitable man. His wife also happens to make the most delicious *tarte flambée* in all Alsace. His son Philippe also deserves special mention for tracking down certain statistics that the authorities in Alsace had for five years claimed simply did not exist.

Johnny Hugel and David Kirby Ling of Hugel et Fils in Riquewihr receive my special thanks for processing a four-page list of last-minute queries. Johnny even went back to the Bibliothèque in Colmar to check the source of his own statistics after I had questioned them. As the only Englishman employed in the Alsace wine trade and one of very few foreigners to perfect the Alsace dialect, David has been an invaluable source over the years and I confess to having shamelessly ripped off some of his puns on the grounds that faxes are not covered by the copyright laws.

I am indebted to Guy Dopff of Dopff & Irion in Riquewihr, for finding a *gîte* for us on one of our extended stays, letting us utilize Dopff & Irion for certain office facilities and even allowing us to cash Visa vouchers when our cash ran out!

Pierre Bouard of CIVA deserves thanks for patiently supplying information and statistics since 1979, only to update it every year my researches were extended, Monsieur Rayer of ONIVINS (Office National Interprofessionnel des Vins) in Dijon for the speed and efficiency in supplying statistics and other specific information it had been impossible to obtain in the region itself.

Louis Vézien, the Colmar-based representative of the INAO until his promotion in 1991, provided statistics not available from CIVA, and I am most grateful to him for the reference material presented to his committee for consideration of the delimitation of the second batch *grands crus*. Although the maps we have produced from these unofficial presentations might not necessarily correspond in the tiniest detail with the final December 1992 delimitations, they do represent the only visual reference to the 25 *grands crus* still awaiting delimitation at the time of writing. Until I received these, the book was caught in a deadlock, so it was a relief to find a link in the bureaucratic chain that was prepared to push aside official red tape for the sake of a mutually beneficial solution.

Which leads me to Peter Markley of Lovell Johns Limited, near Oxford, who produced all *grand cru* maps over the 1991 Christmas period. Although Louis Vézien broke the deadlock, I still needed one set of maps from two totally different types of map reference. CIVA had promised colour separations for the delimited *crus*, while Louis Vézien had supplied rough photocopies of accurate, but very crude, hand-drawn boundaries on various scales of map. I needed uniform cartography in a rush and Peter Markley provided this.

Although it is not customary to express thanks to dining establishments in a wine book (especially ones where the author has not received a free meal!), Jean-Marie Stoeckel's Winstub le Sommelier was such a welcome retreat that its existence became instrumental to our survival in Alsace and thus vital to the completion of this book. If I had my way, Stoeckel would be awarded the Legion d'honneur for his heavenly *winstub* in Bergheim. He serves Alsace wines by the glass or carafe that are vastly superior to vintaged wines sold by the bottle in many other supposedly superior establishments and his wife produces some of the finest unpretentious food in the region. And it should be borne in mind that I say that fully aware that Alsace itself is one of the most exciting culinary areas in the world. If you like the thought of traditional Alsace cuisine, but find the real thing a bit heavy going, then eat at the Winstub le Sommelier. It is not *cuisine nouvelle*, but the traditional food is cooked with an extremely light hand and presented in the most appealing fashion. However much anyone is in love with the food and wine of Alsace, if you taste in excess of a hundred Alsace wines a day for a month or two and dine regularly on the rich local food, the Winstub le Sommelier will be a blessed relief. In addition to a magnificent list of Alsace, there are great wines from many other areas, as one might expect from an ex-world champion *sommelier* (Stoeckel won the title in 1972 and has been learning ever since). After all those white wines, it is a relief to consider a Burgundy from Tollot-Beaut, a fine Rhône wine by Paul Jaboulet and all the others in Stoeckel's treasure trove. Absolute bliss!

Last, but not least, I have to thank Pat, who accompanied me on most of my trips to Alsace. During one sustained period of visits, which averaged five producers a day, seven days a week, for six weeks, there were times when I did not know whether I was coming or going. I would not have got to many appointments but for Pat's organization. On those days she did not act as navigator, she provided me with a map with the most appropriate route from one producer to another drawn on it, put a pen in my jacket, a tasting book in my hand, pointed me in the right direction and sent me on my way. After the first hundred wines, there were many days I would not have found my way home but for those maps.

JUST ONE REGRET

I confess to one lingering regret that frustrated the writing of this book: that most of you who read it will already be converts. Delighted as I am that anyone at all should read my books, I want my words to inspire as much as edify. I want people to discover the joy of Alsace wine, but if they are not already fascinated by it, how do you entice them to read a book on the subject? Well, if you are daft enough about Alsace to read not just this book but its acknowledgements too, you might just be crazy enough to accept a challenge. I dare you to convert just one person a year to Alsace wine and to pass the dare on to each of your converts. It is not much to ask and, although by the laws of chance very few of you will accept the challenge, according to the theory of multiplicity of universes, a parallel earth must exist where so many of you take it up that the entire population of the world becomes aware of Alsace and enjoys its wines.

MOSELLE

Bitche

Wissembourg

▲356

Sarre-Union

▲353

Reichshoffen

▲192

Wingen-
sur Moder

▲414

Hatten

Rastatt

▲247

Drulingen

Bouxwiller

BAS

Haguenau

▲143

Bischwiller

▲216

Hochfelden

Zorn

Brumath

▲125

Saverne

RHINE

▲565

Mossig

▲165

Marlenheim

Dahlenheim

STRASBOURG

Bergbieten

Wolxheim

Molsheim

▲1010

Bruch

Rosheim

Obernai

▲375

Ste-Odile

Barr

Erstein

GERMANY

▲1026

St.-Blaise-
la-Roche

Andlau

Mittelbergheim

Eichhaffen

Nothalten

Blienschwiller

▲161

Dambach-la-Ville

Giessen

Sélestat

Châtenois

Orschwiller

VOSGES

Roderne

St-Hippolyte

Canal du Rhône au Rhin

Rhine

▲1228

Ribeauvillé

Bergheim

Hunawihr

Riquewihr

Zellenberg

Kaysersberg

Beblenheim

Kientzheim

Mittelwihr

Marckholsheim

Katzenthal

Bennwihr

Niedermorschwihr

Sigolsheim

▲976

Tarckheim

Colmar

Gerardmer

Wintzenheim

Wettolsheim

Munster

Eguisheim

Breisach

Voegtlinshoffen

Hattstatt

Gueberschwihr

Neuf-Brisach

▲1267

Pfaffenheim

Soulzmatt

Rouffach

▲196

Orschwihr

Westhalten

▲503

Guebwiller

▲209

Bergholtz

Fellering

Ill

Wuenheim

HAUT RHINE

Thann

▲1191

Rhine

Müllheim

Masevaux

Vieux-
Thann

Cernay

▲222

BELFORT

Doller

MULHOUSE

● Villages containing at least
one vineyard classified as a
'Grand Crus' d'Alsace

Intensive Vine-growing
zone (areas)

Delimited AOC Region
of Alsace

Department boundary

▲161 Height above sea level

Scale
0   5   10   15   20   25
Kilometres

Paris

I

The Evolution of Alsace Wines

We know that grape-bearing vines grew in the forests of Alsace long before the art of winemaking reached northern Europe. From fossilized pips we also know that prehistoric man gathered the fruit of these wild plants, but whether, perhaps by accident, he ever fermented the juice into some sort of crude wine is a matter of conjecture.

In any case, it is the deliberate cultivation of the vine that marks the true beginnings of winemaking history for any region and in Alsace this commenced in the first century BC, with the arrival of the Romans.

THE FIRST VINEYARDS

Among the very first sites to be cultivated by the Romans were those of Kastelberg and Moenchberg in Andlau, and Mandelberg in Mittelwihr, although, of course, they did not acquire these names until much later on. Nobody can be sure of the original varieties planted and the style or quality of wines that were produced.

By the second century AD, most of the lower foothills of the Vosges had been cleared and cultivated with vines, using a sophisticated trellising system that the Romans had acquired from the Greeks centuries before. In the fourth century, however, this viticultural heritage began to diminish as the Roman Empire declined and a Germanic tribe, the Alemanni, invaded Alsace with increasing regularity.

When the Alemanni were pushed back into Germany in 496 by Clovis, his baptism that very year indirectly led to the revival of viticulture in Alsace. This was because he encouraged Christianity to flourish, which prompted numerous religious orders to settle in Alsace, which had to be self-sufficient, and as wine was a staple of diet, they cultivated the vine, thus expanding the region's vineyards. By the sixth century, 40 abbeys had been established in Alsace.

Chronology of Named Sites in Alsace

The following is by no means complete, as it necessarily leaves out *lieux-dits* or *crus* with origins that cannot be fixed although they may well be just as ancient:

GALLO-ROMAN: Kastelberg (Andlau); Moenchberg (Andlau); Mandelberg (Mittelwihr)

6TH CENTURY: Steinklotz (Marlenheim)

8TH CENTURY: Engelberg (Dahlenheim); Goldert (Gueberschwihr); Mambourg (Sigolsheim, known originally as Sigolttesberg)

9TH CENTURY: Hengst (Wintzenheim); Praelatenberg (Orschwiller & Kintzheim)

11TH CENTURY: Altenberg de Bergbieten; Altenberg de Wolxheim

12TH CENTURY: Altenberg de Bergheim; Eichberg (Eguisheim); Muenchberg (Nothalten); Ollwiller (Wuenheim); Steinert (Pfaffenheim, known originally as Steiner)

13TH CENTURY: Bergweingarten (Pfaffenheim); Pfingstberg (Orschwihr & Kintzheim); Saering (Guebwiller); Sommerberg (Niedermorschwihr & Katzenthal); Wineck-Schlossberg (Katzenthal & Ammerschwihr)

14TH CENTURY: Bruderthal (Molsheim); Furstentum (Kaysersberg); Geisberg (Ribeauvillé); Kessler (Guebwiller); Kirchberg de Ribeauvillé; Clos du Schlossberg (Ribeauvillé, known originally as the Halde); Zotzenberg (Mittelbergheim, known originally as Zoczenberg)

15TH CENTURY: Rosacker (Hunawihr); Schenkenberg (Obernai); Schlossberg (Kaysersberg & Kientzheim); Sporen (Riquewihr); Steingrubler (Wettolsheim); Zahnacker (Ribeauvillé)

16TH CENTURY: Pfersigberg (Eguisheim)

17TH CENTURY: Kitterlé (Guebwiller)

THE EMERGENCE OF ALSACE

The name Alsace or, to be precise, *Alesia* (or *Alesacius* or *Alisatius*) was used from 610, which was, therefore, the earliest juncture from which the region itself could build a reputation for its wines. This began in earnest when the Frisians navigated the Rhine in Alsace for the first time and the Bishop of Strasbourg, who was the largest proprietor of vineyards in the region, hired these highly skilled sailors to transport his wines and those of various monasteries. Thus it was that from the seventh century, the fame of Alsace wines began to spread through Central Europe, to the Low Countries, England and Scandinavia, making viticulture the region's richest asset, according to Adam the Monk in 780.

By the ninth century, there were 119 wine-growing villages in Alsace, and Ermoldus Nigellus, a poet from Aquitaine, compared the wines of one of these (Sigolsheim) with those of Falernium, the most famous *cru* of antiquity.

By the fourteenth century, 300 abbeys had been established in Alsace, which encompassed 172 wine-making villages of some repute. Vineyards stretched almost unbroken from Wissembourg in the north to Mulhouse in the south, which is far beyond the limits of viticulture today. At that time, the wines of Alsace had become known as Aussay, Osey, Ossey or Osoy (the Old French *Aussay* comes from the Latin *Alisatius*). These wines were mostly white (although the proportion of red was considerably higher than that today) and were among the most celebrated and expensive in all Europe, consequently the wine-growers of Alsace were rich, respected and influential.

GOLDEN ERA

Alsace reached its viticultural pinnacle in the fifteenth and sixteenth centuries. By 1400, there were as many as 430 wine-growing villages, according to the famous Alsace historian, Monseigneur Médard Barth (1886–1976). Colmar alone was exporting 100,000 hectolitres of wine, a total that after the decline of the Thirty Years War (1618–48) would not be matched until 1975 and, even then, only through the efforts of the entire region, not just Colmar.

With the exception of wines from vineyards in the very south of

Alsace (which were mostly exported by road to Switzerland via Mulhouse), all wines were transported northwards by river. Everything that had to pass through Strasbourg paid duty there, thus the city's trade registers would give us an almost complete overview of Alsace exports during the region's most prosperous period. Unfortunately, the archives no longer exist and we must therefore make do with individual town records. As already indicated, those of Colmar have survived and as this town was one of only two ports on the river Ill, the sole commercial route to Strasbourg for many of the region's most famous wine villages, we can be sure that its annual flow of 100,000 hectolitres represented a major proportion of the region's total exports. By 1481, Alsace was exporting over 600,000 hectolitres, nearly twice the current level of exports, according to Johnny Hugel's treatise *Reasons for the Renaissance of Alsace Wines* (1991).

The Church no longer monopolized the vineyards and the unprecedented wealth generated by wine soon created a bourgeoisie, which began to assert control over its own wine trade, rather than allow itself to submit to aristocratic or clerical authority. It was due to this political struggle that the Confrérie St-Étienne was founded. Originally called the *Herrenstubengesellschaft*, it was controlled by a democratically elected body of local experts and their objective was to determine the quality of all wines produced within the commune of Ammerschwihr. Its success encouraged other flourishing wine communities to establish similar organizations.

At this juncture, selling wine was not an individual occupation, but a collective concern organized by the town council, which appointed an impartial official called a *Weinsticher* to conduct tastings for customers. The *Weinsticher* received his commission in both wine (*Stichwein*) and cash (*Stichgeld*), added to which all purchases carried a duty that went straight into the community coffers. The lowest quality wines were known locally as *Hüntsch* and were not allowed to be exported. Only the finest wines, called *vinum nobile* by the monks and *Edelwein* or *vin noble* by local traders, were permitted to be sold outside the region. This self-imposed discipline greatly enhanced the quality image of Alsace, and contemporary sources described these noble wines as 'smooth and agreeable on the palate, often sweet and an excellent accompaniment to seasoned food'. Such wines would have been a blend of several grape varieties because the vineyards were a hotchpotch of varieties. The reason for this was twofold.

Firstly, the science we know as ampelography, which is the study of the vine in order to name and describe its different species and cultivated varieties, did not begin in earnest until the second half of the nineteenth century, when this knowledge was needed to combat the diseases and parasites plaguing Europe's vineyards at the time (powdery and downy mildew, phylloxera and black rot). In the fifteenth and sixteenth centuries, however, the basic concept that one species, *Vitis vinifera*, consisted of thousands of different varieties, some of which were closely related, while others were not, was non existent. A single variety often had numerous different names in neighbouring villages, whereas different varieties were sometimes known by the same name and there was no collective knowledge through which the truth could be sifted. Considering that simple errors are still made today, it is certain that even those who were studying the vine at the time would have been relatively inept at identifying vines and would accidentally mix up varieties.

Secondly, different vine varieties may have been deliberately cultivated together because they possess varying tolerances to the vagaries of climate and the onset of disease or disorder. A detailed study of these characteristics was almost half a millennium away, but growers would have noticed the various reactions of different vine varieties, whether or not they could identify them properly and would thus have realized that the greater the mix, the safer it was.

The Earliest Varietal Wines

It is perhaps curious that the oldest identifiable vine known to have been cultivated in Alsace should be the Pinot Noir because that is a black grape, of course, and everyone knows that this region has always been considered a white wine region. But Pinot Noir it was and legend has it that it was brought to the region from Italy in the eighth century by a man called Fulrade. It was Fulrade who brought back the remains of Saint Hippolytus of Rome (AD170–235) to the village named after him and certainly the locals credit him with introducing the Pinot Noir to St-Hippolyte, but it is almost certain that this variety was growing in Alsace long before Fulrade and its origins were probably much closer to home. Certainly, the Pinot Noir was cultivated in Burgundy from at least the fourth century, possibly earlier, if the *Vitis allobrogica* described by Pliny in the first century was in fact Pinot Noir, as some ampelographic historians believe. As it was the Romans who introduced viticulture to this part of France and they controlled both Burgundy and Alsace, the suspicion is that its existence in the latter province preceded Fulrade by several centuries.

It was not, however, until 1477 that the first varietal wine in Alsace, the Riesling or, to be precise, *Rissling*, began to carve out its own reputation. Mention of Muscat and Traminer wines began to appear around 1500. The Muscat wines of Wolxheim were first mentioned in 1523 and appear to be the first of this variety to acquire any significant fame. Pinot Blanc was documented in Alsace by Jérôme Bock in the mid-sixteenth century and legend has it that its grey cousin, the Pinot Gris or Tokay d'Alsace, was brought back to Alsace from Hungary by Baron Lazare de Schwendi, who led an expedition against the Turks between 1564 and 1568. In 1565, Schwendi attacked the fortress town of Tokay, drove the Turks out and seized 4,000 vats of Tokay wine as booty. He was so smitten by the wine that he took back cuttings of the Tokay vine. Fact or fiction? The Tokay d'Alsace is, in fact, the Pinot Gris, which is why it must now be either Pinot Gris or Tokay-Pinot Gris. Tokay is made today from Furmint and Hárslevelu, neither of which bears any relationship or resemblance to the Pinot Gris, and although in the sixteenth century several other varieties were used for the production of Tokay, there is no record that one of them was Pinot Gris or any of its synonyms. It is possible that Pinot Gris was an unrecorded constituent of Tokay wine or, even if it was not, it could have been growing in the region in Schwendi's time and he simply took a cutting from the wrong vine. This is, however, very tenuous and what makes it acutely improbable is that the first documented evidence of the grape in Alsace came almost a hundred years later in a document from Riquewihr dated 1644. And even this revealed no mention of the word Tokay, just *Grauklevner*, which is a German synonym for Pinot Gris. The first use of the name Tokay in Alsace came even later, around 1750, a good two centuries after Schwendi was supposed to have brought it back from Hungary. To seal the fate on poor Schwendi's reputation as champion of the Pinot Gris grape, ampelographers are now certain this variety came to the region via Burgundy.

The introduction of Klevener (not Klevner, which is the synonym for Pinot Blanc) is more meticulously recorded in documents dated 1742 (*See* 'Klevener de Heiligenstein' in Chapter 7 and the Heiligenstein entry in Chapter 4). The first distinction between 'noble' and other varieties came in 1575, when a decree was issued by an association of growers in Riquewihr, which imposed fines on the use of unauthorised vines such as Elbling. Although widely planted since at least the end of the eighteenth century, the earliest recorded mention of Sylvaner as a pure varietal wine was not until 1870. Even though the Chasselas has good claim to be one of the most ancient varieties known to man, its cultivation in Alsace probably did not commence until the mid-eighteenth century.

START OF THE LONG DECLINE

Most vineyards in Alsace were destroyed in the latter part of the Thirty Years War and by 1681 membership of the guild of *Weinsticheren* had dropped from a healthy 160 to just 86. Under the sovereignty of France, these official winetasters also became known as *gourmets*, which is the true origin of the word (whereas a *gourmand* was a true connoisseur of food and wine, rather than a gluttonous pig). The vineyards were slowly renewed by various Swiss, German, Tyrolean and French settlers, who had been attracted to Alsace through the royal edicts of Louis XIV, which offered the devastated lands free to anyone willing to restore them.

Before the Thirty Years War, when only the finest wines of Alsace could be exported, viticulture had been restricted to the slopes, which were more labour intensive to work, but provided the best-quality wines. Afterwards, however, the decline in population, which created a shortage of labour, led to the plains being cultivated. They were not only easier to tend, they also possessed a rich and fertile soil that yielded far larger crops. Thus, although the wines were inferior in quality, they were much cheaper in price and consequently hampered the sales of wines grown on the slopes. Despite a royal edict forbidding the cultivation of vines on the plain in 1731, this habit spread. In 1748, Louis XV signed a commercial treaty with Holland, the oldest and largest customer of Alsace wines. This actually favoured the older French provinces at the expense of Alsace. It is round about this time that some of the wines exported to Germany were blended with low-quality German wines to provide more backbone and smooth out the harsh flavours. By 1750 both the population and the vineyards of Alsace had just about returned to normal, but the quality was not as consistent and the reputation inevitably began to slide. Another royal edict was issued in 1766. This was supposed to reinforce the earlier ban, but it too was ignored.

The popular notion today is that the reputation of Alsace wine was deliberately lost by the Germans after the Franco-Prussian War, but it is clear that the rot set in much earlier and it was in fact the French who were initially responsible.

In the late eighteenth century, three-quarters of Alsace was planted with Elbling – or Burger, as it has always been known in Alsace (and Switzerland). Although today its neutral, acidic wine is considered fit only for *Sekt*, modern viticulture has enabled the naturally prolific variety to yield up to 200 hectolitres per hectare, making it no surprise that any wine it produces has so little flavour. In the late eighteenth century, however, the Elbling was held in high esteem and, at more modest yields, who is to say they were wrong? Two other varieties made up the bulk of the remaining quarter of Alsace vineyards at this time, the Sylvaner in the north and Chasselas in the south.

After the Revolutionary government abolished restrictive commercial practices, the communally organized wine trade in Alsace gradually transformed into the crude beginnings of the industry we know today, as various *gourmets* established their own independent businesses. The Revolutionary government also seized many seigneurial and ecclesiastical estates, auctioning them off in hundreds of minute plots, making Alsace a region of smallholders. As even *vin ordinaire* fetched a good price from the thirsty troops stationed in the province, the vineyards rapidly expanded to cope with the demand, going from 23,000 hectares in 1808 to 30,000 hectares in 1828. In 1821, however, the French government had imposed high taxes on all goods imported from Germany and in 1826 the Germans retaliated by levying similar taxes on French goods. A total collapse of trade between the two countries ensued, dropping the price of Alsace wine from ten to three francs a measure. The gallant troops did their best, but not even the entire French army could heave its way through the equivalent of what Alsace was exporting to Germany every year. Consequently, the cellars of Alsace overflowed with the glut of excess and the wine trade had to endure a dwindling income in addition to their tarnished image.

As if the situation was not bad enough, Alsace continued to expand its vineyards at an alarming rate, which only exacerbated the problem of overproduction. So many of these new vineyards were planted with Knipperlé (also known as the Kliener Riesling, though it bears no relation to that classic variety) that it accounted for four-fifths of the total crop by 1850, just 60 years after the Elbling had occupied three-quarters of Alsace vineyards. By the start of the Franco-Prussian War, 65,000 hectares of vines were in production, proof positive it was Gallic madness, not German vindictiveness, that precipitated the decline of Alsace wine. When Alsace came under German sovereignty, French wine names were dispensed with. *Vin noble* disappeared and was replaced by its Germanic equivalent, *Edelwein*, while the Alsace term *Zwicker* was adopted for lesser quality blends. The duty war with Germany had ruined the export of Alsace wine from the 1820s on, but being annexed by the country was no magical cure as some had desperately hoped. In addition to the commercial aspect of its viticultural problems, Alsace was to face the heaviest attacks in recorded history of oidium and mildew (between 1880 and 1890) and cochylis and eudemis (between 1910 and 1917). Phylloxera appeared in 1904, but in Alsace it was less of a problem than these other disorders, which were not comprehensively checked until as late as the 1930s.

In France, where phylloxera was perceived to be far more dangerous and long-lasting, the dominant school of thought determined that the only permanent solution would be to graft every single vine in the country on to phylloxera-resistant American rootstock. In Germany, however, where phylloxera found it difficult to penetrate the steep and unwelcoming, hard slate slopes of the Rhine and Mosel, oidium and mildew were perceived to be the greater and more immediate problem. German viticulturists thus took a different approach, with crosses and hybrids specifically developed to survive virtually anything that nature could hurl at a vineyard. It was an equally successful solution in many ways, but, if taken to its extreme, it would have meant the demise of classic varieties and, indeed, it was during this period that the cultivation of Riesling in Germany began to decline.

This is merely a précis of the extremely diverse thinking that was going on in a very hectic era of viticultural history and as such, it runs the risk of oversimplification. There were, of course, both schools of thought in each country, plus many other theories, but this overview is adequate for the purpose of explaining why Alsace, which had only just come under German sovereignty, planted so many of the highly resistant varieties that its new masters were developing.

There was stubborn resistance from those who wanted to retain traditional varieties, but less scrupulous growers were soon enticed by the heavy cropping qualities of many German crosses and hybrids. Some classic varieties survived, of course, but the German authorities prohibited grafting and the only permitted remedy against phylloxera was chemical purification of the soil and that turned out to be ineffective.

It was not long before most of Alsace was infested with inferior varieties and the larger the merchant, the more difficult it was to avoid using these in most of its wines. Some producers, however, decided to highlight the main constituent of their finest blends by labelling them as 'Riesling-Zwicker', 'Traminer-Zwicker', etc. This might seem reasonable, desirable even, conveying as it did the different style of each blend to potential customers, but the distinction between pure varietal wines and blends gradually eroded.

THE RENAISSANCE

After the First World War, Alsace became French once again and the emphasis of its wine-labelling swung back to Gallic. The old term *Gentil* (which also means 'noble') was revived for the best-quality blends, but *Zwicker* would not go away, particularly in Germany where most of the region's cheaper wines were sold. The term *Edelzwicker* was adopted, therefore, to distinguish a noble or quality blend from very ordinary ones.

In 1925, the newly formed Association des Viticulteurs voted to rid its vineyards of hybrid vines, replacing them with traditional

Alsace varieties and cultivating only the slopes, not the plains. According to Hugel's *Reasons for the Renaissance of Alsace Wines*, this was very much the result of the efforts and influence of Paul Greiner, a winegrower from Mittelwihr, and his friends. It was from this point that Alsace began to reorganize the administration of its vineyards in line with the new French AOC system. In 1932, the Association des Viticulteurs forbade certain foreign grape varieties and in 1935 the *Code du Vin* printed a list of hybrid vines that were banned throughout France. In 1939, the French Ministry of Agriculture approved the Association's proposals for the strict limitation of Alsace wines, but the Second World War intervened and the Germans occupied Alsace before the process was complete. Thus it was not until after the Second World War that the quest for AOC could be resumed. On 2 November 1945, the Ministry of Agriculture issued a decree based on the 1939 proposals. This outlined the area of cultivation, permitted grape varieties, harvesting date and certain winemaking practices for wines that were entitled to use the regional designation Vin d'Alsace, but it was another seventeen years before the winegrowers' ambition for full AOC status was realized. In 1942 hybrids still accounted for a third of all Alsace vineyards and, even when the AOC laws for Alsace were laid down in 1962, a special dispensation had to be granted to thousands of winegrowers still cultivating Abondante, Bouquettraube, Burdin 7705, Elbling, Goldriesling, Landot 244, Léon Millot, Maréchal Foch, Müller-Thurgau, Seibel 5455 and Seyval Villard 5276.

When Alsace rose to the ranks of AOC, the area under vine was already beginning to level off at 10,000 hectares and it remained thereabouts for many years to come, as good vineyards growing undesirable varieties were gradually replanted with more classic vines. Yet the Knipperlé, Goldriesling (a *Riesling x Muscat* cross), Pinot Meunier and Müller-Thurgau were allowed in blended wines until as recently as January 1980.

Alsace, French or German?

Although modern-day Alsace is very much a part of France, even first-time visitors immediately sense that its medieval towns, with their cobbled streets and timbered buildings, are more German than French. The origin of Alsace and the roots of its people explain the unique character of their wine, food, culture, architecture and language.

The immediate impression is correct: Germany has the longer and stronger claim to the sovereignty of Alsace. The oldest traces of human life in Alsace are the scattered remains of dwellings and burial places that date back to the Neolithic period, 10,000 years ago. It is quite possible, however, that man roamed Alsace almost half a million years ago, as the very earliest evidence of human life in Europe is the *Homo erectus* jaw-bone of so-called Heidelberg Man. This was found at Mauer, just south of Heidelberg, only 30 miles north of Alsace. Although circumstantial, it is hard to imagine that human beings did not wander a mere 30 miles in the 390,000 years between the appearance of Heidelberg Man and the Neolithic period.

The remains of Neolithic man are few and far between, as indeed are those of the Proto-Celts, who inhabited the region *c.*1500 BC. The Proto-Celts represent the earliest identifiable roots of the ancient Gauls or the original French people (as well as being the earliest forebears of other Celtic populations such as the Welsh, Scottish, Irish, etc.), while the contemporaneous Proto-Germanics were to become the German people. Before this embryonic French-German divide, both proto-groups had exactly the same origins, the Proto-Indo-Europeans. Those that eventually became Proto-Germanic were, however, cut off from all contact with other Proto-Indo-Europeans for some considerable time. How, why, where and for how long are intriguing questions not yet answered, but that it happened is evident from the phonetic sound shift that turned the Proto-Indo-European dialect into a totally new Germanic language group, as this could only have occurred through complete isolation over a historically substantial period of time. Considering that the first Proto-Indo-European settlements were in and around the middle reaches of the Rhine, it can be argued that both the French and the German people originated in what is now known as Germany. And, as time progressed, the paradoxical truth is that the ultimate French identity was gradually fashioned through further Germanic influences, primarily from the Franks.

In the first century BC, a Celtic tribe called the Sequani occupied the territory between the Saône, Rhône and Rhine rivers, including the area we recognize as Alsace. To the south-west, another Celtic tribe, the Aedui, lived in a region approximately equivalent to Burgundy. The Aedui gradually began to encroach upon the Sequani's land. Unable to stop them, the Sequani hired a wily mercenary by the name of Ariovistus, whose mixed band of Germanic warriors, the Suebi, easily defeated the Aedui in 61 BC. Rather than simply collect his reward and depart, Ariovistus settled on lands belonging to both tribes.

Compelled to conspire against Ariovistus, the two former enemies appealed to the Romans for help. Julius Caesar realized that a push into this part of Gaul suited his military and political needs, and seized the opportunity. The Suebi were fierce but undisciplined fighters and stood little chance against Caesar's ruthlessly efficient legions. The Romans swept up the Rhône Valley, over the Jura mountains and through the Vosges, to make a surprise attack on Ariovistus's flank, forcing him back over the Rhine at the decisive battle of Cernay in 58 BC. Caesar insisted the Sequani and Aedui revert to and remain in their former lands, which he incorporated in the province of Germania Superior.

Both Germania Superior and, to the north, Germania Inferior were part of Roman Gaul and separated from the heartland of Germanic tribes by the Rhine. It is on this use of the Rhine as the border between Gaul and Germany that France would later base its claim of sovereignty over Alsace, although Germanic tribes had settled both sides of the river centuries before Julius Caesar intervened. Furthermore, this Roman boundary did not last long, as both Germania Superior and Germania Inferior were extended well east of the Rhine under Augustus.

In the fourth century AD, Alsace was gradually occupied by the Alemanni, a Germanic tribe that had invaded the region with increasing regularity during the decline of the Roman Empire. They were pushed back into Germany, however, by Clovis, the Frankish chieftain, in a battle near Wissembourg in 496. The Franks are credited with establishing the boundaries of France, but it should be remembered that they were also a Germanic people. And, even under the Franks, the southern part of Alsace was still known as Alemannia, which proved to be the etymological origin of Allemagne in the French language.

The geopolitical identities of France and Germany start to

emerge after the Frankish empire was divided by the Treaty of Verdun in 843, with what would eventually be France forming the major part of Francia Occidentalis and the future Germany occupying most of Francia Orientalis. At the same time, however, the question of the sovereignty was complicated when Alsace was included in Francia Media, a long swathe of land separating the two larger, more powerful kingdoms on either side. This was settled by Louis the German and Charles the Bald (ruler of the French kingdom), who agreed that Alsace would go to Francia Orientalis (Germany) upon the death of Lothair II, the ruler of Francia Media, because Lothair had no male heir. Charles, however, reneged on this agreement, annexing Lotharingia and forcing Louis to invade. So began the battles for possession of Alsace and the constant arguments over its sovereignty.

Alsace was thus not only German by origin, it was German in the earliest political agreement between the two emerging countries and the first attempt to wrest this sovereignty by force was made not by Germany, but by France, under Charles the Bald.

The cultural identity of Alsace is not, however, simply a combination of things French and German. With two powerful and defiantly different nations bordering a fertile land, the dispute over its sovereignty was inevitable and obviously contributed to the composition and character of its people, but this itself was embroidered by other foreign influences, due to its strategic position at the crossroads of Europe. And this was irrevocably changed when the population was halved by the Thirty Years War and the melting pot of people was further altered by the flood of foreign settlers attracted by the royal edicts of Louis XIV. In *Reasons for the Renaissance of Alsace Wines* Hugel states that Riquewihr had a population of 2,245 in 1610, but only 74 in 1632, while Bergheim had 2,600 inhabitants in 1610 and just 20 in 1650. The Treaty of Westphalia gave France sovereignty of Alsace and in a desperate bid to bolster the population, Louis XIV issued royal edicts in 1662, 1682 and 1687, proffering free land to anyone willing to restore it. This attracted many people, particularly rich landowners and various wealthy religious orders, but also ordinary working people – farm workers, tradesmen and labourers –

from Switzerland, Germany, the Tyrol, Lorraine and southern France. By 1750, the population had doubled and by the Revolution it had tripled. There is no doubting the strong Germanic influence that still exists, but if Alsace was never French, after this influx of diverse nationalities it is no longer German either.

2

Viticulture and Vinification

The earliest, most widespread viticultural practice in Alsace was to plant the vineyards with a mixture of vine varieties that were harvested and pressed together, to vinify a blended, not varietal, wine.

Of course, until the late nineteenth century, many things were different from how they are now. Vines were not grafted, but grown *en foule*, which literally means 'in a crowd' or 'crowded'. This was merely a haphazard method of keeping in check the vine's natural inclination to creep along the ground and reproduce itself by suckering. Nowadays, due to phylloxera, all vines have to be grafted on to foreign rootstock and trained off the ground. The density of an ungrafted vineyard growing *en foule* was 25,000 vines per hectare, whereas with grafted vines employing a more sophisticated training system, this was reduced to between 7,000 and 8,000, but since mechanization, when the space between rows had to be widened, this has fallen to 4,500. Those 25,000 pre-phylloxera vines used to average 40 hectolitres, while the 4,500 now commonly churn out 80 hectolitres; thus, in addition to the average production per hectare doubling, the yield per vine has increased more than elevenfold. Understandably, the less burdened pre-phylloxera vines had much longer lives, averaging 50 to 60 years and often living well beyond a hundred. The working life of a grafted vine is considered to be between 25 and 35 years, with a current tendency to keep to the lower limit, as a grafted vine is at its most productive between 7 and 25 years of age. As the yield declines, so the quality and intensity of fruit and varietal character increase. The more quality-conscious a grower, the longer he will keep the vine growing and even volume-minded growers must take into consideration the cost of uprooting a vineyard and the time it takes to get it back into production. A well-regulated domaine, however, will run smoothly on a programme that ensures the uprooting and replanting of a tiny proportion of vines every year, thus ensuring the minimum frustration to overall production. This can be set to achieve any desired average age, so the economic question will be a relatively minor consideration on a well-run estate.

PHYLLOXERA IN ALSACE

The vine louse *Phylloxera vastatrix* first appeared in Alsace in 1904. Although dreaded throughout France, it was considered less of a problem by the province's German masters, who also had a different philosophy when it came to tackling this insect, and it was certainly less damaging than oidium and mildew, which struck Alsace with devastating effect between 1880 and 1890. Oidium and phylloxera came from the USA on experimental vines imported via London. Unknown outside that continent, European vines had no natural defence, thus destruction was wreaked on an epidemic scale. Attempts to eradicate the phylloxera included chemical fumigation and flooding of vineyards, but all were unsuccessful. The brilliant idea of deliberately introducing phylloxera's natural enemy, *Tyroglyphus phylloxera*, which was not harmful to the vine, but unfortunately unable to adapt to the European climate, also failed. The inability to bring about the downfall of *Phylloxera vastatrix* had nothing to do with the relatively crude technology of the time, as this mite has consistently rebuffed all attempts to destroy it to this day, and infests virtually every major viticultural region in the world, except for sandy and schistous areas, where the little mite is reluctant to tread.

When Alsace was under attack by phylloxera, the most effective solution was already well under way in France, for it soon became evident to the French that every vineyard in the country would have to be planted with vines grafted on to naturally resistant American rootstock, a massive, but necessary undertaking. Germany's unwelcoming, hard, schistous or slaty soil was less easily penetrated by phylloxera, thus its viticultural scientists were more concerned with oidium, mildew and other cryptogamic diseases. Understandably they took what appeared to be the most pragmatic view at the time, which was to develop hardy, rot-resistant crosses, and they were so sure that this would be the best and most economic approach that they forbade growers in Alsace to graft their vines. It was not until 1918, therefore, when Alsace was returned to French sovereignty, that grafting on to foreign rootstock was actually permitted. A full-scale programme did not get under way until the 1920s, when the growers decided to replant all their vineyards with classic varieties. Consequently Alsace was not completely under grafted vines until the 1930s.

Phylloxera vastatrix

The most feared of all the vine's enemies, phylloxera derives its name from the Greek *phyllon* (leaf) and *xeros* (dry), which describe the dry-leaf symptom of a vine attacked by this parasite, which lives only on the vine and cannot survive on any other host. The first signs of phylloxera damage are that the affected vines cease summer growth sooner than healthy vines, and the leaves have a dull, drier look and quickly turn yellow.

The flexibility within the complex 18-stage life cycle of this insect has made it impossible to eradicate so far. The easiest way to come to terms with this multi-staged life-form is to divide it into four distinct variants: the sexual form, the leaf form, the root form and the winged form.

The **sexual form** originates from eggs laid (by the winged form) on the under-surface of young leaves. They have no digestive system and after mating both the male and female die. Before dying, however, the female lays one winter egg in the dead bark of the vine's trunk. It is from this winter egg that the **leaf form** emerges and begins to suck the lower surface of its birthplace (the young leaf), causing the formation of a hollow gall, into which the leaf form lays a number of eggs by parthenogenesis (self-propagation). These numerous eggs hatch into **root forms**, which look like the leaf form, only smaller. They crawl down the vine, enter the soil and seek out the roots, which they puncture for nourishment. While sucking out this nourishment, the root form infects the root wound with a poisonous secretion that prevents it from healing. This is to keep open the root form's source of sustenance, but it also infects the vine, eventually killing it. The root form is also able to reproduce itself by parthogenesis, not just once, but several times throughout the spring and summer, laying eggs in clusters around the root. These hatch in the autumn into larvae (all previous forms emerge from their eggs as wingless insects), which hibernate in the roots, not emerging until the following spring, when the temperature rises above 10° Celsius and the sap begins to rise. As the sap rises from the roots to the vine above, so the larvae mature into the **winged form** and follow it to the surface; many of them then go off in search of other vines to live off. The winged form's eggs, laid on the underside of young leaves, become the sexual form and thus the cycle is complete.

The more complex the life cycle, the easier it should be to eradicate an insect by cutting a vital link in its chain of reproduction, but each link in the chain of phylloxera's life cycle appears to be infinitely adaptable and intrinsically capable of regenerating a modified cycle. In the mid-west United States, for example, where phylloxera originated, none of the above-ground life-forms occur, yet the cycle still thrives.

GRAFTING

There are two basic methods of grafting: bench grafting and field grafting. They both have the same aim – to present the largest possible growing surface between the two canes to be organically bonded to each other. A grafted vine consists of three fundamental elements:

1 The **stock** (underground): essentially the roots, hence the vine types used for this are called rootstock.
2 The **scion** (above ground): the rest of the vine, including trunk, leaf and fruit-bearing parts. As the fruit it bears will be of this variety (i.e., not of the rootstock), the vines reared for this part of the grafting process are known as vinestock.
3 The **union** (ground-level): where the stock and scion are joined.

Whatever method is employed, it is vital for the growth cycle of the stock to be in advance of that of the scion, otherwise the latter will begin to leaf before the union is complete. In all such cases, the graft will die for lack of water and nourishment. A successful graft can be achieved only if the vine forms a protective callus around the union while the two plants seek compatibility. The greater the surface area exposed to each plant, the more likely that they will achieve compatibility, hence the various fancy cuts utilized, especially for bench grafting: Omega (an omega-shaped cut), Jupiter (cut like a lightning flash or two-thirds of a 'W'), Saw-type or Hengl (intermeshing squared-teeth), etc.

Bench grafting takes place indoors, usually with a purpose-built cutting machine, and simply looks like somebody joining two wooden sticks – which is exactly what happens. Cuttings of both stock and scion are taken during the autumn and stored until mid- or late winter, when they are cut and jointed (the most popular technique I have witnessed during bench grafting has been Omega). At this stage, the stock is usually about 10 inches long and the scion between one and three inches. The joints are dipped into a special paraffin wax, usually with fungicide added to reduce the possibility of infection, and stored in hot-room callusing boxes. When a protective skin or callus has developed, the grafts are planted into nursery beds and are then available for purchase by growers the following spring. Large viticultural estates often operate their own bench grafting nurseries. The two advantages are that the grower gains one year because the vines are one year old when planted, and that the rate of failure of these vines taking in the vineyard is just under 2 per cent.

Field grafting requires the rootstock to be planted in the vineyard in the autumn, on to which mature buds are grafted the following spring, just before the sap is due to rise. The simplest method is for the scion to be so cut that it has a wedge of wood exposed beneath the bud and for the grower to cut a steeply angled downward slit in the stock, slot the scion into this and bind the two firmly together. This particular technique is known as Cadillac. There are other more sophisticated methods, such as Mayorquine, which involves a sort of dovetail cut, although the more complicated the cut, the more labour intensive it becomes and the higher the level of skill it requires, thus defeating the main advantage of field grafting, its cheapness. Disadvantages of field grafting include high failure rates (15–20 per cent), the longer period for the graft to take and its labour intensiveness, which makes it not so cheap in areas where labour costs are high.

A variant of field grafting is chip-bud grafting or cleft grafting, where the grower can change the variety of vinestock in an established vineyard almost overnight by simply removing the old and slotting one or two chip-buds (similar to the wedge-shaped buds used for Cadillac, above) of the new. Gewurztraminer today, Riesling tomorrow! With a mature root system, it is possible to produce fruit the following autumn and an almost normal size of crop within 18 months. Another variant is air grafting, whereby the new variety is grafted on while the old variety remains, which provides the grower with a fallback should the graft fail to take (95 per cent success rate) and another graft can be attempted at a later date.

ROOTSTOCK VARIETIES

Since phylloxera made it necessary to graft all European vines on to American rootstock, literally hundreds of rootstock varieties have become available. The initial purpose of the rootstock was, of course, to prevent the European variety from touching the ground, where its natural tendency to send down roots of its own made the vine prone to phylloxera, but it soon became obvious that rootstock varieties would have to be developed for virtually every permutation of vinestock and growing condition. As these became available and were tested, it emerged that not only was it possible to select rootstocks that were more compatible with certain varieties of vinestock and suited to specific conditions of soil and climate, but the choice of rootstock could affect the vigour of the vine and the quantity and quality of the grapes it produced.

Although no official statistics exist, it is 'simply known' that between 50 and 60 per cent of Alsace vines are grafted on to SO_4, with numerous others making up the balance. Since the three most effective phylloxera-resistant species are *Vitis berlandieri*, *Vitis rupestris* and *Vitis riparia*, most rootstock crosses and hybrids (crosses between different species) are derived from these. Vigorous rootstocks are usually preferred in European wine regions such as Alsace, where there are seldom any excess foliage problems. Most resistances quoted are self-explanatory, but some readers may benefit from an explanation of those for nematodes and active-lime.

Nematode resistance is increasingly viewed as an important factor in determining the selection of rootstock, as some nematodes can either cause the vine direct physical damage (e.g. root-knot) while other ectoparasitic nematodes transmit various viral diseases (e.g. fan-leaf). Some vineyards have a high lime content, which can lead to iron deficiency or induce chlorosis. The active-lime content of soil is therefore important, as is knowing what active-lime resistance a rootstock has.

so4

Origin: Vitis berlandieri x *Vitis riparia* (*c.*1900) *Soil suitability:* humid, clayey *Resistances:* nematode (good); active-lime (17 per cent); drought (very poor) *Characteristics and aptitudes:* a vigorous rootstock that gives higher production levels than 161-49 Couderc and 41B, but lower than 5BB, the SO4 encourages a good fruit set and advances ripening. SO stands for Selection Oppenheim.

5BB SELECTION KOBER

Origin: Vitis berlandieri seedling (*c.*1904) *Soil suitability:* humid, clayey *Resistances:* nematode (good); active-lime (20 per cent); drought (poor) *Characteristics and aptitudes:* a vigorous rootstock that has a shorter vegetative cycle than 161-49 Couderc, it roots well, but can be problematic to graft in the field, where the scion has a tendency to root in preference to the stock.

41B MILLARDET ET DE GRASSET

Origin: Vitis vinifera (Chasselas) x *Vitis berlandieri* (1882) *Soil suitability:* very flexible *Resistances:* nematode (none); active-lime (40 per cent); drought (good) *Characteristics and aptitudes:* this rootstock has a very short vegetative cycle, good fruit set and high yields, thus rapidly ripens large crops of grapes, but does not root well and its resistance to phylloxera is only just sufficient. It does, however, have the highest resistance to active-lime of any rootstock.

161-49 COUDERC

Origin: Vitis riparia x *Vitis berlandieri* (1888) *Soil suitability:* flexible *Resistances:* nematode (highly susceptible); active-lime (25 per cent); drought (poor) *Characteristics and aptitudes:* exceptional resistance to phylloxera, the 161-49 is troublesome to bench graft, but field grafting is acceptable. Its rooting capability is merely average and its vigour is initially slow, but this increases once firmly established. It fruits well.

110 RICHTER

Origin: Vitis berlandieri x *Vitis rupestris* (1889) *Soil suitability:* shallow, clayey *Resistances:* nematode (slight); active-lime (17 per cent); drought (excellent) *Characteristics and aptitudes:* a very vigorous rootstock that roots and bench grafts poorly, but field grafts well. It delays the ripening process, therefore is ideal in warmer microclimates, where it yields grapes of a good must weight as well as high yield.

5C TELEKI

Origin: Vitis berlandieri x *Vitis riparia* (1922) *Soil suitability:* humid, clayey *Resistances:* nematode (good); active-lime (20 per cent); drought (poor) *Characteristics and aptitudes:* a vigorous rootstock that has a shorter vegetative cycle than 161-49 Couderc, 5C Teleki crops earlier than other *Vitis berlandieri* x *Vitis riparia* hybrids and roots well, but can be problematic to graft in the field.

3309 COUDERC

Origin: Vitis riparia x *Vitis rupestris* (1881) *Soil suitability:* fresh, deep *Resistances:* nematode (good); active-lime (11 per cent); drought (poor) *Characteristics and aptitudes:* not recommended for either drought or humid conditions, this vigorous rootstock does, however, root and graft easily. It also has an exceptional resistance to phylloxera.

VINE TRAINING

From the *laissez-faire* of growing ungrafted wines *en foule*, various systems of vine training were developed. These systems were initially developed to keep the European vinestocks well away from the ground, where the menace of phylloxera lurked and, just like rootstocks, other advantages were discovered. Vines can be trained high, for example, to avoid frost or low to hug any heat that may be reflected by stony soils at night. They may be cultivated close together, so that they compete with one another and thus produce less wine of higher quality, or further apart, if quantity or mechanization is of prime importance. This is why the vines on the frost-prone, machine-harvested plains of Alsace are trained to a height of 90 centimetres in rows that are relatively far apart, whereas those on the slopes are trained to a height of just 60 centimetres and planted much closer together.

There are two basic schools of vine training: cane training and spur training, on which there are many local variations. Cane-trained vines have no permanent branch because all the canes are pruned back each year to provide a vine consisting of entirely new growth. With spur training, there is no annual replacement of the main branch, thus a solid framework is formed. Most Alsace vines are cane trained, with either one or two canes arched over the wire. A maximum of 12 buds per square metre is permitted, which, with 4,500 vines per hectare, allows just over 26 buds per vine, which is far too many for even the least quality conscious producer, hence the average of eight buds per cane on a double-cane vine and 15 for a single-cane plant. Some spur-trained vines are found in Alsace, particularly on the steeper slopes.

THE VITICULTURAL CYCLE

The vine's annual routine starts and finishes with the end and approach of winter, but human activity in the vineyard cannot stop.

SAP RISING

February

This is the vine's first external sign of its awakening after its winter dormancy. When the soil temperature at a depth of 25 centimetres (10 inches) reaches 10.2°C (50°F), the roots begin to collect water and the vine pushes its sap up to the very limits of its branch system, oozing the sap out of the winter-pruned cane-ends in a manifestation called weeping.

> **Activity in the vineyard** This is the signal to prune for the spring growth, but it poses a problem for the grower because the vine, once pruned, is at its most vulnerable to frost. To wait, however, for the danger of frost to subside would be to waste the vine's preciously finite energy and retard its growth. This would in turn delay both the flowering and the ripening of the vine's fruit by as much as ten days, thus risking exposure to late spring and autumn frosts.

BUD-BREAK

March

Some 20 to 30 days after the vine starts weeping, the buds start opening. This is known as the bud-break and different varieties bud-break at different times; there are early bud-breakers (Chardonnay, for example), mid-season bud-breakers (Pinot Noir) and late bud-breakers (Riesling). Bud-break usually happens towards the end of March, but may not sometimes occur until early April. The same grape variety can bud-break at different times in some years due to climatic changes. The type of soil also affects the timing of bud-break: clay, which is cold, will retard the process, while sand, which is warm, promotes it. Early bud-break varieties are susceptible to frost, while the fruit of late-ripeners is prone to autumn frosts.

> **Activity in the vineyard** Pruning continues into March, the vines are secured to their wires and the protective mound of earth ploughed over the grafting wound to protect it in the winter is ploughed back, aerating the soil and levelling off the ground between the rows.

EMERGENCE OF EMBRYO BUNCHES

April–May

In mid-April, after the fourth or fifth leaf has appeared, which is usually 10 to 15 days after bud-break, miniature green clusters are formed. These are the vine's flowers, but they have yet to bloom. In their berry form they look very much like and are thus called embryo bunches, which is an appropriate term because each successful blossom develops into a grape. They are the first indication of the size of each bunch and therefore represent the earliest guide to the maximum potential of the crop.

Activity in the vineyard Spraying begins in May, to ward off or cure various vine pests, diseases and other disorders and continues until the harvest. Some sprays are combined with systemic fertilizers to feed the vine directly through its foliage. These operations are normally done by hand or tractor, but may be carried out by helicopter, if the slopes are very steep. At this time of year the vine can be affected by coulure or millerandage.

Coulure and Millerandage: the difference

Coulure: A physiological disorder of the vine that occurs as a result of alternating periods of warm and cold, dry and wet conditions after the bud-break. If this culminates in a flowering during which the weather is sunny, the sap rushes past the embryo bunches to the shoot-tips, causing vigorous growth of foliage, but denying the clusters an adequate supply of essential nutrients and the barely formed berries dry up and drop to the ground. While no grower likes imperfect flowering, its yield-reducing effect has had its positive effects: coulure combined with a crop-cutting spring frost and a long, hot, dry summer created the legendary 1961 vintage in Bordeaux, for example. Without coulure it would have been merely excellent, but with it 1961 was one of the three greatest Bordeaux vintages of all time.

Millerandage: This is also a physiological disorder, but one that occurs after cold or wet weather at the time of the flowering (as opposed to coulure, which requires a burst of sunshine and warmth at this point). The cold or wet weather makes fertiliz-ation very difficult, consequently many berries fail to develop and remain small and seedless even when the rest of bunch is full-sized and ripe.

To summarize, coulure is when the berries drop off and requires a sunny flowering, while millerandage occurs after a cold or wet flowering and its small, shot berries remain on the bunch.

FLOWERING OF THE VINE

June

The embryo bunches break into flower after the fifteenth or six-teenth leaf has emerged on the vine, which is usually 10 or 11 weeks after the bud-break and involves pollination and fertilization. This means the flowering will start between 15 and 24 June. It lasts for about ten days, during which time it is essential for the weather to be dry and frost-free, but temperature is the most critical require-ment. A daily average of at least 15 °C (59°F) is required to enable a vine to flower and 20–25°C (68–77°F) is considered ideal. Heat summation, however, is far more important than daily temperature levels, so the length of day has a great influence on the duration of the flowering and, as soil temperature is more significant than air temperature, the soil's heat-retention capacity is another contribu-tory factor (organically poor, mineral-rich, south-facing rocky slopes like Rangen in Thann being an example of great heat-rentention capacity, while north-facing cold clay vineyards are at the other extreme).

Activity in the vineyard Frost is the greatest hazard to the flowering vine, and many vineyards are equipped with stoves or sprinkling systems. Stoves can make the one-degree difference between survival and destruction, while sprinklers force the frost to expend its energy freezing the water, not the vine.

FRUIT SET

July

Some ten days after flowering, the embryo bunches evolve into true clusters, as each fertilized berry expands into a recognizable grape. This is the first visible sign of actual fruit, or rather the embryo bunch's potential fruit, and the process is called fruit-set. The number of grapes per embryo bunch varies from variety to variety, as does the percentage that actually set into grapes. For example, an average Riesling embryo bunch has some 189 unflowered berries per cluster, while the Sylvaner has only 95, yet barely more than 32 per cent of the Riesling's flowers go through a successful fruit-set most years, typically yielding a cluster of about 61 grapes, while the fruit-set success rate for the Sylvaner is almost 53 per cent, which provides 50 or so berries.

Activity in the vineyard Spraying continues, while summer pruning, which concentrates the vine's energy on making fruit, commences. In some vineyards this is the time for weeding, but in others the weeds are allowed to grow as high as 50 centimetres (20 inches) before they are mowed and ploughed into the soil to break it up and provide the vines with an excellent green mulch.

RIPENING OF THE GRAPES

August

As the grape develops its fleshy fruit, little chemical change takes place inside the berry until its skin starts to turn a different colour, which is called the *véraison*. Throughout the grape's green stage, the sugar and acid content remains the same, but during August, usually about the last two weeks of the month, the ripening process begins in earnest and, as the skin changes colour, so the sugar content dramatically increases and the hard malic acid diminishes in direct relation to the riper tartaric acid, which builds up. The tartaric acid content then begins to decline after about two weeks, but it always remains the primary acid. It is at this stage that the grape's tannins are gradually hydrolysed, which is crucially important because only hydrolysed tannins are capable of softening as a wine matures.

Activity in the vineyard Spraying and weeding the vineyard continue, and the vine's foliage is thinned to facilitate the circulation of air and thus reduce the risk of rot. Care has to be taken not to remove too much foliage as it is the effect of sunlight upon the leaves that ripens the grapes.

THE MAIN HARVEST

September–October
White grapes ripen before black grapes and must in any case be harvested relatively earlier to achieve a higher acidity balance; this is even more so for sparkling wine production.

Activity in the vineyard The harvest usually begins mid- to late September and may last for a month or more, picking grapes for Crémant d'Alsace first, then those vineyards usually relegated to generic wine production, followed by the better sites with higher ripeness levels for *grands crus* and premium *cuvées*. Mechanical harvesting is increasing on the flatter vineyards, although much of the harvest is still picked by hand and, due to the topography of certain top sites, a proportion always will be.

Alsace Grape Variety Cycle

The order of growth in Alsace is first the Pinots (Blanc, Gris, Noir) and Chardonnay, then Riesling, Gewurztraminer, Muscat, Sylvaner and, lastly, Chasselas. Chasselas is, therefore, the last to bud-break, flower, etc., yet it is the first to be harvested, while the Riesling is one of the first to begin its vegetative cycle, but the very last to be picked. The length of vegetative cycle is thus a very good indicator of quality; the longer it is, the better. This is especially true when it comes to the *véraison*, although neither the vegetative cycle in general, nor the *véraison* in particular, can be used blindly to determine quality.

LATE HARVEST

November–December

In November the sap retreats to the protection of the vine's root system. As a result of this, the year-old canes begin to harden and any remaining grapes, cut off from the vine's metabolic system, start dehydrating. The concentrated pulp that they yield is subject to severe cold and, occasionally, the warmth of an Indian summer, which induces complex chemical changes in a process known as *passerillage* (*see also* 'Vendange Tardive' under Speciality Wines in Chapter 7), which is a quality-enhancing experience. In certain vineyards with suitable climatic conditions, growers pray for the appearance of *Botrytis cinerea* or noble rot, but it is less prevalent in Alsace than other botrytized wine areas.

Activity in the vineyard Since the introduction of Vendange Tardive and Sélection de Grains Nobles (SGN) designations, an increasing number of these specialist wines are being produced, but because *Botrytis cinerea* is less common than in other specialist botrytis wine areas, and when it does attack seldom spreads as rampantly, the habit had developed whereby SGN is harvested *before* Vendange Tardive wines. This is because it is necessary to harvest botrytized grapes in consecutive sweeps through the vineyards, known as *tries*, selecting only the most affected bunches, after which the remaining crop is collected en masse and vinified to produce Vendanges Tardives, which might well have developed a bit of noble rot from botrytized bunches that have either been missed or were not sufficiently botrytized at the time to warrant picking. Thus in years like 1983 and 1989, many of the Vendanges Tardives had more botrytis character than some so-called SGNs in inferior vintages, particularly from less conscientious growers. The last vineyard operation of the year is to cut away the longer shoots, which conserves the plant's energy for the cold winter months ahead, allows the vigneron easier access to the vineyard and prevents excessive weeping when the sap rises.

A Lot of Rot!

Botrytis literally means 'rot', which is a negative term that generically refers to various cryptogamic disorders such as grey rot, brown rot, etc., but has a positive connotation in English-speaking countries because of its contracted usage from the term *Botrytis cinerea*, which literally means noble rot (*pourriture noble* in French). The fungus *Botrytis cinerea* does not miraculously just appear. In the first place, the spores have to be indigenous to the area (the recent increased interest in these wines is building up the local stock of these spores, which will make the rot more rampant in future and thus the wines should be easier to produce in greater quantities), where they remain dormant in the vineyard soil and on vine bark until they are activated by suitable atmospheric conditions. These conditions are an alternation of moisture and heat; the early-morning mist being followed, day after day, by hot mid-morning autumn sunshine. The spores latch on to the skin of each grape, replacing its structure with a fungal growth and feeding on moisture from within the grape. There are two basic stages to this infection. In the first, the skin goes pink or brown and the grape is rotten but full, whereas when the process is complete (which may take anything from three days to three weeks, depending on conditions), the grape is a shrivelled raisin and its cluster may either be dotted with such grapes or, in extreme cases, one rotten, revolting mass. By this time, *Botrytis cinerea* has devoured one-third of the grape's sugar and a significant amount of its acidity, but as between one-half and two-thirds of the amount of water is consumed (and dehydrated by sun and wind) and a substantial quantity of a new acid, gluconic, is also created, the effect is to concentrate the juice into a sticky, sugar-rich pulp with a relatively high acidity. A healthy, ripe grape with a potential of 13 per cent alcohol is thus converted into a mangy-looking mess with a potential of between 17.5 per cent and 26 per cent. Apart from the relatively straightforward effects of concentration, a botrytis wine has a very special and inimitable character that is said to be primarily the result of three by-products: gluconic acid, dextrin and botrycine.

VARIETAL GROWTH CHARACTERISTICS

The following viticulturally based varietal profiles include area and yield statistics also found in their corresponding entries under 'Alsace Varietals' in Chapter 7, as this information is pertinent to both sections and I believe it preferable to repeat it here rather than constantly refer the reader to another chapter.

Pinot Blanc

Synonyms: Klevner or Clevner (Alsace); Weissburgunder or Weisser Burgunder (Germany and Austria); Feherburgundi (Hungary); Pinot Bianco (Italy).

Area and yield: The Pinot Blanc occupies 2,644 hectares or 19.6 per cent of AOC Alsace, having increased by 25 per cent over the last ten years (2,118 hectares in 1982, when this represented 17.6 per cent of the 12,052 hectares then planted in the region as a whole), with the yield currently averaging 93 hectolitres per hectare.

Soil preference: Deep and damp, light and fertile, which makes it ideal for silty alluvial sites on the plain, especially if deposited on or with any calcareous elements, the active-lime content of which helps intensify varietal aroma.

Recommended rootstock: SO4, 5C Teleki, 161-49 Couderc and 5BB Sélection Kober.

Typical must analysis: 76° Oechsle or 170g/l sugar, which is a potential alcoholic strength of 10.1 per cent by volume; 7.6g/l total acidity expressed as tartaric (4.9g/l as sulphuric).

Viticultural characteristics: Pinot Blanc is resistant to most pests, diseases and disorders, except for viral (particularly leaf-roll) and, due to its compact cluster, common rot. Its low vegetative vigour enables the vine to maintain fairly high yields with the minimum of varietal attenuation. Levels of up to 100 hectolitres per hectare are ideal for sparkling wine production.

Auxerrois

Synonyms: Pinot Auxerrois (Lorraine).

Area and yield: No statistics exist because this variety is officially included with Pinot Blanc above, but informed sources reckon that at least half the 2,644 hectares attributed to that variety are in fact

Auxerrois (some suggest that it is closer to two-thirds). Thus the area under vine is probably somewhere between 1,300 and 1,750 hectares. It is a moderately high-yield variety.

Soil preference: Heavy, marly-clay.

Recommended rootstock: SO4 and 41B Millardet et de Grasset.

Typical must analysis: 76° Oechsle or170g/l sugar, which is a potential alcoholic strength of 10.1 per cent by volume; 6.7g/l total acidity expressed as tartaric (4.3g/l as sulphuric).

Viticultural characteristics: Resistant to most pests, diseases and disorders, moderately high yields, preferable to Pinot Blanc in cooler parts of Alsace.

Tokay-Pinot Gris

Synonyms: Pinot Gris, Pinot Beurot, Malvoisie, Fromentot or Auvernat Gris (France); Rülander, Grauer Burgunder or Grauklevner (Germany); Grauer Mönch or Szürkerbarat (Hungary); Pinot Grigio (Italy); Klevanka (former Yugoslavia); Rulanda (Romania).

Area and yield: The Tokay-Pinot Gris occupies 884 hectares or 6.6 per cent of AOC Alsace, having increased by 58 per cent over the last ten years (was 559 hectares in 1982, representing 4.6 per cent of the 12,052 hectares then planted), with the yield currently averaging 75 hectolitres per hectare.

Soil preference: Deep, minerally-rich, silty-clay or volcanic rock.

Recommended rootstock: SO4 and 41B Millardet et de Grasset, 125AA and SO4.

Typical must analysis: 83° Oechsle or 187g/l sugar, which is a potential alcoholic strength of 11.1 per cent by volume; 6.4g/l total acidity expressed as tartaric (4.2g/l as sulphuric).

Viticultural characteristics: Resistant to most pests, diseases and disorders, but prone to rot, the plus side of which is that it makes its fruit suitable for botrytis wines. Yields must be restricted to an average of less than 60 hectolitres per hectare before wines of classic complexity can be produced. Most recent plantations of new clones do not possess the potential richness, class and style of the old Tokay à Petits Grains.

Pinot Noir

Synonyms: Blauer Spätburgunder (Austria); Spätburgunder, Blauburgunder or Blauer Klevner (Germany); Pinot Nero (Italy); Klevner (Switzerland).

Area and yield: Occupies 1,016 hectares or 7.5 per cent of AOC Alsace, having increased by 43 per cent over the last ten years (712 hectares in 1982, representing 5.9 per cent of the 12,052 hectares then planted), with the yield currently averaging 83 hectolitres per hectare.

Soil preference: Well drained, deep, sandy or calcareous.

Recommended rootstock: SO4, 3309 Couderc, 5BB, 161-49 Couderc and 41B Millardet et de Grasset.

Typical must analysis: 80.5° Oechsle or 184g/l sugar, which is a potential alcoholic strength of 10.9 per cent by volume; 5.9g/l total acidity expressed as tartaric (3.9g/l as sulphuric).

Viticultural characteristics: Susceptible to rot, downy and powdery mildew, and leaf-roll, the Pinot Noir is a delicate plant that requires very careful site selection.

Riesling

Synonyms: Rheinriesling or Weisser Riesling (Austria); Rajnai Rizling (Hungary); Riesling Renano or Reno (Italy); Johannisberg Riesling or White Riesling (USA); Rajinski Rizling (former Yugoslavia).

Area and yield: Occupies 3,015 hectares or 22.4 per cent of AOC Alsace, having increased by 28 per cent over the last ten years (2,364 hectares in 1982 representing 19.6 per cent of the 12,052 hectares then planted), with the yield currently averaging 89 hectolitres per hectare.

Soil preference: Granitic, limestone or marly-limestone.

Recommended rootstock: 3309 Couderc, 5BB, SO4 and 5C Teleki.

Typical must analysis: 71.5° Oechsle or 158g/l sugar, which is a potential alcoholic strength of 9.4 per cent by volume; 8.2g/l total acidity expressed as tartaric (5.3g/l as sulphuric).

Viticultural characteristics: For a vine that is so sensitive to site selection in terms of varietal quality and finesse and provides wine that is so easy to spoil if not handled with absolute care, the Riesling is a surprisingly hardy vine that is capable of very high yields, although it will not produce classic wines unless restricted to less than 50 hectolitres per hectare from fully ripened grapes.

Gewurztraminer

Synonyms: Traminer (France); Clevner, Klavner or Roter Traminer (Germany); Traminer Aromatico, Traminer Rose or Traminer Rosso (Italy); Tramini (Hungary); Red Traminer (USA).
Area and yield: Occupies 2,503 hectares or 18.6 per cent of AOC Alsace, having increased by just 2 per cent over the last ten years (2,453 hectares in 1982 representing 20.4 per cent of the 12,052 hectares then planted), with the yield currently averaging 67 hectolitres per hectare.
Soil preference: Deep and marly with some lime content.
Recommended rootstock: SO4, 5C Teleki and 3309 Couderc.
Typical must analysis: 86° Oechsle or 198g/l sugar, which is a potential alcoholic strength of 11.7 per cent by volume; 5.3g/l total acidity expressed as tartaric (3.5g/l as sulphuric).
Viticultural characteristics: Susceptible to coulure, powdery mildew and very low temperature, Gewurztraminer's natural inclination is to give moderate yields only.

Muscat

Muscat Ottonel synonyms: Muskat-Ottonel (Austria); Muskateller Ottonel (Germany); Muskotoly (Hungary); Muscadel Ottonel (South Africa).
Muscat Blanc à Petit Grains synonyms: Muscat d'Alsace, Muscat de Frontignac or Frontignac (France); Frontignac or Brown Muscat (Australia); Muskateller, Gelber Muskateller, Weisse Muskateller or Weisse Muscketraube (Germany); Moscato d'Asti, Moscato di Canelli or Moscato Bianco (Italy); Muscatel Branco (Portugal); Muskadel (South Africa); Muscat Canelli, White Muscat (USA).
Muscat Rosé à Petit Grains synonyms: Muscat d'Alsace (France); Roter Muskateller (Germany).
Area and yield: Occupies 371 hectares or 2.8 per cent of AOC Alsace, having *decreased* by 11 per cent over the last ten years (417 hectares in 1982, representing 3.5 per cent of the 12,052 hectares then planted), with the yield currently averaging 82 hectolitres per hectare.

35

Soil preference: Silty-sand with some lime content.
Recommended rootstock: 41B Millardet et de Grasset.
Typical must analysis: 72° Oechsle or 159g/l sugar, which is a potential alcoholic strength of 9.5 per cent by volume; 5.3g/l total acidity expressed as tartaric (3.5g/l as sulphuric).
Viticultural characteristics: Both Muscat Blanc and Muscat Rosé à Petit Grains are vigorous but low-yielding varieties that have an early bud-break and ripen fruit by mid-season. They are very susceptible to powdery and downy mildew, fan-leaf can be a problem and the aromatic character of the grapes attracts damage from wasps, bees and the grape berry moth. The Muscat Ottonel is an earlier-ripening variety that is less susceptible to powdery mildew, but more prone to wet weather conditions.

Sylvaner

Synonyms: Silvaner (Germany); Gros Rhin (Switzerland).
Area and yield: occupies 2,367 hectares or 17.5 per cent of AOC Alsace, having *decreased* by 5 per cent over the last ten years (2,497 hectares in 1982, representing 20.7 per cent of the 12,052 hectares then planted), with the yield currently averaging 97 hectolitres per hectare.
Soil preference: Deep and sandy or calcareous.
Recommended rootstock: SO4, 5BB Sélection Kober and 5C Teleki.
Typical must analysis: 69° Oechsle or 155g/l sugar, which is a potential alcoholic strength of 9.2 per cent by volume; 7g/l total acidity expressed as tartaric (4.6g/l as sulphuric).
Viticultural characteristics: Susceptible to both powdery and downy mildew, sensitive to frost (but overcrops in warm microclimates) and prone to chlorosis, the Sylvaner bud-breaks just a few days before Riesling and ripens fruit mid-season.

Chasselas

Synonyms: Valais (France); Gutedel (Germany); Fendant, Dorin or Perlan (Switzerland).
Area and yield: Occupies 230 hectares or 1.7 per cent of AOC Alsace, having *decreased* by 43 per cent over the last ten years (403 hectares in 1982, representing 3.3 per cent of the 12,052 hectares

then planted), with the yield currently averaging 87 hectolitres per hectare.

Soil preference: Various soils of medium fertility.

Recommended rootstock: 3309 Couderc.

Typical must analysis: 70° Oechsle or 157g/l sugar, which is a potential alcoholic strength of 9.3 per cent by volume; 5.9g/l total acidity expressed as tartaric (3.9g/l as sulphuric).

Viticultural characteristics: A vigorous, early-ripening variety that is susceptible to hail, spring and winter frosts, powdery and downy mildew, and the grape berry moth. If grown on very fertile soil, the grape clusters can become too compact, which prevents some of the berries from fully ripening. Although the Chasselas needs to be fully ripe to provide a wine of any interest, it is also subject to low acidity, thus this close-clustering effect could be utilized to provide a better, natural acid balance to the main crop of fully ripened grapes. With the predilection of Alsace producers for spicy, aromatic varieties, I am surprised that the few Chasselas specialists left in the region have not thought of trying the Chasselas Musqué variant.

Chardonnay

Synonyms: Although this grape is known by many names in every winemaking country of the world, it is virtually always sold under its highly bankable correct name, the only exception being Pinot Chardonnay, which is still surprisingly used both inside and outside France, despite it being well known that this grape bears no relation to the Pinot family.

Area and yield: The Chardonnay occupies 15 hectares, or barely more than 0.1 per cent of AOC Alsace, having increased by 33 per cent in 1991-92. Its yield is currently averaging 87 hectolitres per hectare.

Soil preference: Very flexible, but particularly well suited to limestone and other calcareous soils.

Recommended rootstock: Various.

Typical must analysis: Not available.

Viticultural characteristics: A moderately vigorous, hardy variety, which buds early, making it susceptible to spring frosts. Chardonnay is also prone to powdery mildew and rot, although it has some resistance to downy mildew and ripens fruit early, thus avoiding any autumn freeze.

GRAPE RECEPTION

As the various grape varieties ripen at different times and some bunches may be left for the late-harvest wines Vendange Tardive and SGN, the winemaker receives a steady flow of grapes for the first four weeks after the official commencement date and may get dribs and drabs for another four.

After de-stemming and a light crushing, followed by pressing, the grape juice, or must as it is called, will be pumped into either a vat or *foudre*, if indigenous yeasts are used for the fermentation. Should the winemaker opt for dried or cultured yeast, the juice will undergo a light fining and/or filtration to remove unwanted solids. Most pre-fermentation filtrations are accomplished by centrifuge these days. Hugel, for instance, the first to use a centrifuge in Alsace, in 1953, always put the must through a centrifuge as well as fining it with bentonite.

FERMENTATION

Fermentation can commence within 12 hours of the juice being pumped into the fermentation vessel, especially if selected yeast culture of a vigorous variety is added to cleaned-up juice, but the process can take as long as several days to get going. Fermentation, or more correctly alcoholic fermentation, is the biochemical process that transforms fresh grape juice into wine. Yeast cells excrete enzymes that convert natural fruit sugars into almost equal quantities of alcohol and carbonic gas. This process ceases when the supply of sugar is exhausted or when the alcoholic level reaches a point that is toxic for the yeast enzymes (15–16 per cent normally, although certain strains can survive 20–22 per cent).

In Alsace this traditionally takes place in large, oval, wooden *foudres*, although I have seen every shape, size and type of fermentation vessel in the region. Bigger establishments often have glass-lined concrete tanks, although stainless steel is creeping in at all levels from some of the better equipped growers through to Wolfberger, the largest producer in Alsace. Some have various types and sizes of vessel. One such producer, Hugel, likes to retain the best of tradition and yet keep up with technology; thus it is not so surprising that this firm pioneered the introduction of temperature-control facilities within its ancient wooden *foudres*. When controlled, most producers in Alsace favour a fermentation temperature between 20 and 25°C, which is not so-called cool or cold fermentation, so the fruity varietal aromas dominate, rather than the pear or banana amylic character that dominates a wine fermented at lower temperatures (the banana found in youthful Tokay-Pinot Gris and Gewurztraminer is a primary varietal aroma, not a ferment-induced secondary one).

MALOLACTIC FERMENTATION

The malolactic fermentation is sometimes described as the secondary fermentation, but this is inappropriate because, unlike the main fermentation, it does not involve yeast, nor does it produce alcohol. The malo, or MLF, as it is sometimes called, is a biochemical process that converts the 'hard' malic acid of unripe grapes into two parts 'soft' lactic or 'milk' acid (so-called because it is the acid that makes milk sour) and one part carbonic gas. Malic acid is a very strong-tasting acid that is reduced during the fruit's ripening process, but a quantity persists in ripe grapes, and, although reduced by fermentation, in wine.

The quantity of malic acid present in a wine may be considered too much and the smoothing effect of replacing it with just two-thirds the quantity of the much weaker lactic acid is often desirable. Malo is considered vital for all red wines and wine of any colour that is matured in new oak (to 'marry' the wine to the wood, according to generations of growers, although scientists have only just discovered the chemical exchange that takes place when the malo occurs in the presence of new wood, which supports the old belief), but the process is only optional for white, rosé and sparkling wine. In Alsace, it is often said that there are two schools of winemaking: those who always put their wines through malo and those who never do. But there is a considerable overlap of producers who use the malo, in whole or in part, for all or some of their wines and the decision as to which will depend upon the characteristics of each vintage.

To ensure that the malo can take place, it is essential that specific bacteria be present. These are found naturally on grape skins among the yeasts and other micro-organisms. To undertake their task, they require the wine to be of a certain warmth, a low level of sulphur, a pH between 3 and 4 and a supply of various nutrients (found naturally in the grapes).

RACKING, FINING AND FILTERING

Draining the clear wine off its lees, or sediment, into another vat or cask is known as 'racking' because of the different levels, or racks, on which the wine is run from one container to another. In modern vinification, this operation is usually conducted several times throughout the maturation period in vat or cask, often utilizing pumps, although some producers still achieve these operations by gravity. Gradually the wine throws off less and less of a deposit.

After fermentation, the wine may not look hazy to the eye, yet still contain suspended matter that could threaten cloudiness in the bottle. Fining usually assists the clarification of wine at this stage, and special fining agents may be employed to remove unwanted characteristics. When a fining agent is added to wine, it adheres to cloudy matter by physical or electrolytic attraction, creating tiny clusters, known as colloidal groups, which drop to the bottom of the vat in the form of sediment. The most commonly encountered fining agents are egg white, tannin, gelatine, bentonite, isinglass and casein. Winemakers have their preferences and different fining agents have their specific uses, thus positively charged egg white fines out negatively charged matter (for example, unwanted tannins or anthocyanins), while negatively charged bentonite fines out positively charged matter (for example, protein haze and other organic matter).

Cold stabilization will be carried out by many of the producers who export their wines. This subjects the wine to low temperatures, precipitating a crystalline deposit of tartrates, which might otherwise form in the bottle. It really should not be necessary, but the average consumer does not realize that not only are such crystals entirely harmless, but also their presence is an indication that the wine has been naturally produced, rather than heavily processed.

Sulphur dioxide (SO_2) is used in winemaking from the time the grapes arrive at the winery until just before the wine is bottled. It has antioxidant, aseptic and other qualities that make it essential for commercial winemaking. Oxidation is an integral part of winemaking; all wines start to oxidize from the moment the grapes are pressed and the juice is exposed to the air, but the rate of oxidation must be controlled. Occasionally a winemaker claims that SO_2 is superfluous, but wines produced without it are either totally oxidized or downright filthy. Organically produced wines are made with a minimum of SO_2, as every wine should be. The methods for reducing the level of SO_2 are well known, the most important being to leave the sulphuring for as long as possible in the winemaking process and to make the initial dose a very cautious one, because a resistance to sulphur builds up and subsequent doses have to be proportionately larger. Wet weather, rampant rot and sulphur sprays in the vineyard can, however, frustrate the most green-minded winemaker.

Most Alsace wines are cold-sterile bottled, which entails the removal of yeast by filtration and the provision of scrupulously clean conditions at every point from the vat to the bottle. Traditionally, the cheaper, generic wines are bottled in the spring following the vintage, while better *cuvées* are not bottled until September.

RED WINES

Although red wine is one of the oldest recorded styles in Alsace, its level of production in this region has been less than 5 per cent for well over a century. This lack of experience held back the development of red wine to such an extent that the sight of a well-coloured Rouge d'Alsace can now be classed as a very recent phenomenon indeed. Such an achievement can be attributed to the adoption of certain winemaking techniques, although the choice of more suitable Pinot Noir clones and better vineyard sites has also had an effect.

On arrival at the winery the grapes nearly always go through a crusher and usually a de-stemmer, although the practice of leaving a proportion of the grapes on their stems is now on the increase. The juice is often heated prior to and during fermentation, which extracts more colour and the softer tannins. In normal vinification vats, the juice is pumped from the bottom of the vat to the top and sprayed over the *manta* to keep the juice in contact with the grape skins to extract colour pigment. In the cruder facilities that the smaller growers possess, the methods will entail a manual submerging of the *manta* by pushing it under the fermenting juice with poles. Cruder, yet sometimes the best red wines in Alsace have been made this way, although it is true to say that the one cause of deeper, darker, better Alsace reds has been the introduction of the Vinimatic, a rotating fermentation tank that works on the cement-mixer principle. This has enabled producers to extract the maximum amount of colouring pigment under totally anaerobic conditions to produce exceptionally well-coloured wines of enhanced fruitiness.

With or without a rotor-vinificator such as the Vinimatic, the higher the temperature during fermentation, the greater the extraction of colour and tannin; the lower the temperature, the better the bouquet, freshness and fruit. The optimum temperature for the fermentation of red wine is 29.4°C (85°F). If too hot, certain substances (decanoic acid, octanoic acids and their corresponding esters) are produced by yeasts that inhibit their own ability to feed on nutrients and so the yeasts die. It is, however, far better to ferment hot fresh juice than to wait two weeks (which is normal in many cases) to ferment cool but stale juice. The fuller, darker Rouge d'Alsace wines remain in contact with the skins for anything between 10 and 15 days, while lighter reds and rosé style wines are separated from the skins after merely a day or two.

The moment the skins are separated from the juice the wine is divided into two: free-run (or *vin de goutte*) and press wine (or *vin de presse*). The free-run juice is, as its name implies, freely run out of the vat when the tap is opened. What remains, that is to say the *manta* of grape skins, pips and other solids, is put into a press that extracts a very dark-coloured and extremely tannic juice called the press wine. The free-run wine and the press wine are pumped into separate containers, either vats or casks depending on the style of the wine to be produced. These wines then undergo their malolactic conversion separately and are then racked several times, fined, racked again and, in most regions, a certain amount of the press wine would be blended with the free-run, then it would receive a final fining and racking before being lightly filtered and bottled. In Alsace, however, the press wine has seldom been utilized, even in small amounts, although some producers have begun to experiment with this.

SPARKLING WINES

Crémant d'Alsace is produced in exactly the way Champagne is, although the grape varieties allowed differ of course. It is, however, classic *méthode champenoise* and there are no mysteries about how it is made. The grapes allowed are Pinot Blanc, Auxerrois, Pinot Noir, Tokay-Pinot Gris and Chardonnay. They are harvested earlier than Alsace's still wine grapes (*See* Appendix I, Vintage Assessments, for official dates) and the yield, technically set at a maximum of 100 hectolitres per hectare, has been annually restricted to 80, which compares with the *champenois* legal maximum of 13,000 kilograms per hectare (which is the equivalent of 86.7 hectolitres per hectare) and, although this too is subject to annual restrictions that are supposed to be lower, they have in fact been higher in some exceptional cases. The Crémant d'Alsace grapes are pressed by exactly the same rules as apply to Champagne, namely to within a maximum yield of 100 litres for every 150 kilos (at the time of writing, this was expected to be tightened up to 100 litres per 160 kilos, which will effectively cut out the *deuxième taille*).

The initial fermentation of these grapes is a normal alcoholic fermentation that results in a dry still wine that is relatively neutral and more acid to taste than the average generic varietal, but otherwise quite unremarkable in character. Although most Champagnes go through malo, the majority of Crémants d'Alsace do not, but that is in tune with the general winemaking traditions of Alsace. There is nothing right or wrong about malolactic fermentation for sparkling wines, as it depends very much on the base wines, which are different each year, and the fundamental style requirement of the producer. Suffice to say, however, that malolactic fermentation does not simply concern freshness and longevity, it can also add complexity and reduce the amount of *dosage* that might be necessary. I would not like to see Crémant d'Alsace lose its *vif* style, but I suggest that experiments could be made with the malolactic by some producers who seem to be opposed to it but could be surprised by the benefits. Even the use of a fully malo base wine for the final *dosage* could be played with to great effect.

Perhaps the biggest learning curve in the future will concern the blending or *assemblage*, which I believe is crucial to the creation of any classic sparkling wine, even when it comes from a single vineyard (when you have to vinify different plots within the vineyard in small *barriques* in order to have enough building blocks to effect a proper blend). It is a highly skilled and painstaking task that takes place in the first few months of the new year following the harvest. Included within the component parts of a non-vintage blend (and up to 15 per cent of a vintage Crémant d'Alsace) will be any reserve wines, another area ripe for development, although it will take time to build these up.

After the final blend has undergone its last racking, the *liqueur de tirage* (a mixture of wine, sugar, selected yeasts and, usually, a fining agent such as bentonite) is added. The ratio of sugar to liquid is carefully adjusted to control the degree of effervescence it creates. Too much and the bottles will explode, too little and the fizz will soon fade. The wines are then stored in the deepest, coolest cellars to undergo a very slow second fermentation (10–12°C is ideal), which creates not only an additional amount of alcohol, but also an equal quantity of carbonic gas, which remains imprisoned in the wine. This gas cannot escape until the bottle is opened, when it rushes to the surface in the form of a stream of bubbles. When the yeasts have been used up, they die, but their greatest task has yet to be accomplished. After their death, these yeast cells undergo an enzymatic breakdown known as autolysis, which significantly contributes to the 'champagney' character of a sparkling wine.

Autolysis brings finesse to the complexity of a sparkling wine and although not the be all and end all, it is one of the most essential, if elusive, qualities associated with any classic product of this type, whether Crémant d'Alsace, Champagne or something from the New World. Just one of its many functions is to create acetal, which helps the Pinot Noir (essentially) to develop its biscuity complexity. Another aspect of autolysis is that it releases reducing enzymes, which inhibit oxidation, thus Crémant d'Alsace needs significantly less SO_2 than the region's other wines. Autolysis also absorbs certain yeast nutrients that are essential for fermentation, which is one reason Champagne does not re-ferment when the final *dosage* of sugar is added. It is the primary reason why base wines must be relatively neutral and this explains why all Crémant d'Alsace grapes (with the single exception of the Riesling), are excellent for sparkling wine. The influence of autolysis is very subtle and easily overwhelmed by varietally aromatic characteristics, which is why I am strongly opposed to the use of any significant amount of Riesling in a Crémant d'Alsace (for an exception, *See* Muré under the Producer Profiles, Chapter 8), although a judicious amount can be very effective in expressing the fresh, lively character of Alsace, without actually dominating the wine.

When the second fermentation is over, which may take between ten days and three months (but must be left for at least nine months by law and quality-conscious producers will leave the wine in contact with its autolysing lees for two years or more), the bottles are ready to undergo *remuage*, which means the riddling of sediment down to the bottom of the neck (when the bottle is inverted), ready to be disgorged. As most Crémant d'Alsace is produced by larger houses or cooperatives, *remuage* is usually carried out by computerised *gyropalette* system, whereby 500-bottle pallets are riddled clear in just eight days.

After *remuage* some producers allow their wines to undergo a certain ageing before disgorgement, when the sediment is removed. The method used today, known as *dégorgement à la glâce*, was invented at the end of the nineteenth century. It involves the immersion of the bottle neck in a shallow bath of freezing brine, which causes the sediment to adhere (but not fully freeze) to the inner surface of the bottle neck, thus enabling the bottles to be turned upright without disturbing the sediment. When the crown-cap is then removed, the sediment is ejected by the internal pressure of the bottle. A little wine may be lost, but not much.

Before corking, the bottles are topped up with the *liqueur d'expédition*, which essentially includes a suitable base wine plus a small amount of sugar. The younger the wine the greater the *dosage*, as more sugar will be needed to balance the tart effect of youthful acidity, but this rounds out with age, thus the more mature the Crémant d'Alsace, the less sugar required.

3
Le Terroir

The *terroir* literally means 'earth' in French, but in a viticultural sense it refers to the complete growing environment of soil, aspect, altitude, climate and any other factor that may affect the life of the vine.

The same grape grown in the same area can make two radically divergent wines, yet two different grapes grown apart may produce two wines that are very similar. A gardener will tell you how certain varieties of flower and vegetable prefer specific soil types, and that if one variety is planted side by side in different blocks of soil (clay, loam, calcareous, sandy, etc.) the blooms or vegetables produced will be markedly different in quantity and quality. If the same variety is planted in exactly the same soil, but in different parts of the garden, perhaps beside a sunny wall, in a shaded area or exposed to north winds, the results will again differ. This is, then, an example of how *terroir* can have a dramatic effect on plant life in your own garden and how it is possible to discern different microclimates within a few paces of one another (for the opposite argument of how impossible it is to discern a *terroir* or a microclimate, *see* 'The Delimitation Process' in Chapter 4).

LOCATION, TOPOGRAPHY AND CLIMATE

The location of a region basically determines its climate, but this can be influenced by the topography or physical terrain, which determines the aspect and height of the vineyards and introduces other factors that can affect quality, such as the proximity of forests and large masses of water, which may abate or enhance conditions locally through transpiration, evaporation, air currents, reflection, etc.

Alsace is a long, thin strip territory located at between 47.5 and 49 degrees north of the Equator, in the north-eastern corner of France. The most outstanding feature and climatically influencing factor of its geographical situation is that this little fairy-tale land is cut off from the rest of the country by the Vosges mountain range. No mountain range in the classic sense of soaring, snow-capped peaks, the Vosges vary in height from just 500 metres in the north to about 1,200 metres in the south, with summits above this so exceptional that they are called *ballons* (from *ballonné*: swollen or distended), and the 1,424-metre Grand Ballon that overlooks Guebwiller is the highest of these. The crest of the Vosges is not jagged or peaked, but rounded and clad in forest and in parts possible to drive along. It is not the height of these granite and sandstone hills that is important, it is their length and breadth. Standing in one of the pretty little wine villages, they make an impressive backdrop, a daunting one even, with their ghostly ruined castles perched on the odd steep escarpment, but it is impossible to get any impression of their depth. They look as if they might be merely a few miles deep, but in fact stretch westwards for more than 40 miles (the *département* on the other side is actually called Vosges). With a north to south length of some 70 miles, the Vosges are a formidable climatic barrier.

The most noticeable and certainly the most commonly stated climatic effect of the Vosges is their influence over rainfall, which is 1,200–1,500mm on the western side, 2,000mm in the heart of the Vosges, yet only 650mm in the vineyards and as little as 500mm in Colmar (which is less than for Marseilles!).

As the Atlantic rainclouds approach from the west, drawn eastward by the continental mass, they are broken up over the Vosges, where they shed most of their load, climbing over the range. The higher the peaks and the deeper the range, the colder it gets, causing the super-saturated air within the clouds to condense in the form of precipitation. Although this ensures that Alsace has a generally dry climate, some isolated areas are better protected and thus drier than others, but this rainfall effect is too simple and too confined to illustrate the full climatic input of the Vosges. Perhaps the best way to summarize it is to say that the Vosges mountains enable Alsace to have the warmth, dryness and stability of a continental climate that might otherwise be a 100 miles further inland, although being relatively closer to the Atlantic does enable the vineyards to benefit

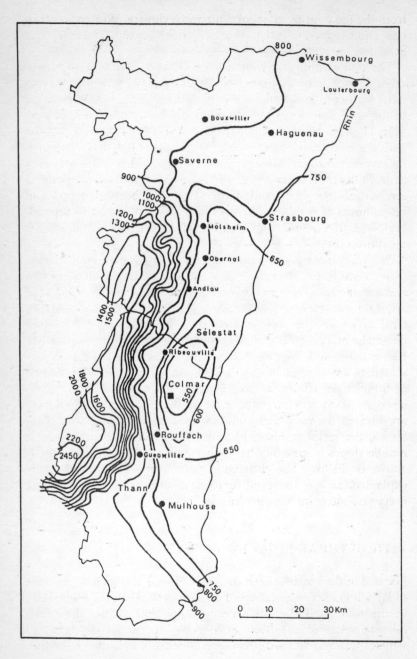

from the moderating effect of a maritime climate. Winters are thus cold and summers warm and sunny, but fresher and less oppressive than they are further inland.

The semi-continental climate gives Alsace a colder winter than other French wine regions, but not as harsh as it would be 100 miles further inland. Although January has an average temperature of just 1.9°C, it drops below freezing for only two weeks in the year. The vine needs to switch off once a year and is perfectly happy with the cold snap of an Alsatian winter, although it brings down the average annual temperature to 10.5°C. This is theoretically beneath the ideal mean of 14–15°C, but the summers and autumns are particularly warm and sunny. There are between 1,700 and 1,800 hours of sunshine (1,100–1,300 between April and September) and the south and south-east aspect of the vineyards maximizes these.

The vineyards of Alsace nestle on the lower slopes of the Vosges, their foothills and the plains beneath, at a height of between 170 and 420 metres. Those in the foothills are usually found at between 200 and 360 metres, while those on the actual mountain slopes tend to be at 250 to 360 metres. A few, such as Furstentum (Kientzheim & Sigolsheim), Sommerberg (Niedermorschwihr & Katzenthal) and Wineck-Schlossberg (Katzenthal & Ammerschwihr), are as high as 400 metres, and Zinnkoepflé (Westhalten & Soultzmatt) climbs to 420 metres. Notwithstanding the excellence of these particular sites, most of the best vineyards in Alsace are located between 220 and 350 metres. According to Claude Sittler, the eminent Alsatian geologist, the temperature of these middle slopes is generally between 1 and 1.5°C higher than those above or below. The difference on the upper slopes is easily explained, as it is universal for temperatures to drop by 1°C for every 100-metre increase in altitude.

VITICULTURAL ALSACE

Located in the north-eastern corner of France, the ancient province of Alsace is today comprised of two *départements*, the Haut-Rhin in the south and the Bas-Rhin to the north. Within these two *départements*, 20,245 hectares are classified as AOC Alsace, of which 13,487 hectares are actually planted (8,076 in the Haut-Rhin and 5,411 in the Bas-Rhin). There appear to be thousands of hectares of non-AOC vineyards in Alsace, although officially there are just 284 (50 in the Haut-Rhin and 234 in the Bas-Rhin) because these statistics include only those vineyards that are registered for the commercial production of *vins de pays* or *vins de table*.

RHINE WINE?

One of the most misunderstood aspects of Alsace wine is its connection with the river Rhine. The effects of a river on the slopes of vines that lead down to it are real, if sometimes overstated, but when it is 20 kilometres away, as the Rhine is from the nearest AOC Alsace vineyards, its influence on the vine can be measured only by those who believe that the flapping of a butterfly's wings can have some direct relationship to a liner being sunk by an iceberg on the other side of the world. There is another river that runs parallel to the Rhine a good 12 kilometres closer and flows into the Rhine just north of Strasbourg. It would be more rational to ascribe the wines of Alsace to this river, rather than the Rhine, but who has heard of the river Ill and would it be very healthy for sales in English-speaking countries?

THE REAL RIVERS OF ALSACE

The only rivers that have a direct influence on the vineyards are those that rise in the Vosges and cut laterally across the region. There are literally dozens of small rivers and streams, but only seven relatively important ones. Starting close to Strasbourg and working south, these are:

1. The river **Mossig** rises near the tiny hamlet of Windsbourg in the hills above Wangenbourg and flows east through Wasselonne before cutting south through some of the vineyards of Marlenheim, Kirchheim, Odratzheim, Traenheim, Scharrachbergheim-Irmstett, Dahlenheim, Dangolsheim, Soultz-le-Bains and Wolxheim. Some of the wines in these villages are sold under the generic geographical designation of Coteaux du Mossig.

2. The river **Bruche** rises in Bourg-Bruche (24 kilometres (15 miles)

west of Epfig) and flows north to Heiligenberg before cutting west through the vineyards of Mutzig and Molsheim, then north again to Avolsheim and Wolxheim, where it is fed by the Mossig and flows west once more through Ergersheim and then Strasbourg, where it joins the Ill.

3. The river **Giessen** comes into being at Urbeis and Bas d'Urbeis (15 kilometres (9 miles) west of Dambach-la-Ville), where it is fed by several streams and flows east-west by east through the vineyards of Villé, then turns south-east to Sélestat.

4. The river **Weiss** or **Weissbach** rises in les Basses Huttes (12 kilometres (7.5 miles) west of Turckheim) and flows north-east through Orbey and Hachimette before looping west through the vineyards of Kaysersberg, Kientzheim, Sigolsheim and Ammerschwihr before joining the Fecht a few kilometres north of Colmar's Hardt.

5. The river **Fecht**, which is perhaps the most important of all Alsace rivers, comes into being just west of Metzeral (15 kilometres (9 miles) west of Gueberschwihr) at the confluence of the Kolbenfecht and several smaller streams and flows north-east to Munster, where it is fed by the Petit Fecht, then through the vineyards of Wihr-au-Val, Walbach, Zimmerbach, Turckheim and Ingersheim and eventually joins the Ill at Illhaeusern.

6. The river **Lauch** starts life as the Lac de la Lauch (12 kilometres (7.5 miles) west of Guebwiller) and flows east to Lautenbachzell before curving south-west through the vineyards of Buhl and Guebwiller. This charming stretch of the Lauch is a picturesque walking route that has been called Florival or Valley of Flowers since 1041, due to the beauty of its flora. From Guebwiller the Lauch loops north, cutting just east of Rouffach and beside the vineyards of Pfaffenheim, Hattstatt and Herlisheim, through Colmar itself to the confluence of the Ill and the Colmar canal.

7. The river **Thur** rises in the lakes area just south of a *ballon* called the Grand Artimont (22 kilometres (14 miles) west of Husseren-les-Châteaux) and runs south to feed the Lac de Kruth-Wildenstein and out of the hydro-dam two kilometres south, to flow gently southeast past the vineyards of Thann and Vieux-Thann, then west to Cernay before looping back north to join the Ill north of Mulhouse.

Of the smaller streams and rivers, the ones you are most likely to come across are the **Auchbach**, which flows through Scherwiller; the **Eckenbach**, which flows half-way between Rodern and St-Hippolyte; the **Bergenbach**, which flows through Bergheim; the **Strengbach**, which flows through Ribeauvillé; the **Sembach**, which flows through Riquewihr, past Beblenheim and through Mittel-wihr; the **Langgraben**, which flows half-way between Eguisheim and Obermorschwihr to feed the large reservoir just north of Herrlisheim; the **Fallbach**, which flows half-way between Voegtlinshof-fen and Gueberschwihr; the **Rimbach**, which flows through Jungholtz and Soultz; the **Wuenheimerbach**, which flows through Wuenheim; the **Fluhbaechle**, which flows through Wattwiller; the **Egelbach**, which flows through Uffoltz; and the **Walbach**, of which there are two, one of which flows through Ammerschwihr and the other through Walbach itself.

SOIL

Does the answer really lie in the soil and, if so, what exactly is the interaction between soil and vine? They say 'a little bit of sand gives a lot of fruit' and I would not take that with a pinch of a crystalline rock, even if it is called sodium chloride. I have come to learn that so much of the perceived wisdom of growing vines and making wine that has been passed down from father to son over many generations has first been ridiculed by science, then proven by it. There is definitely something to the concept of growing certain vines in specific soil types and it is more than the theory of drainage that is so prevalent in the USA (although not adhered to by many of those who actually have to work the soil).

Drainage

The drain-brains consider soil to be merely a medium in which vines grow, which could be replaced by any inert material, as long as it provided the correct drainage. Then all that need be done would be to supply the correct levels of nutrient, temperature, light, etc. If that were true, it would be possible to produce at will the wines of Clos Ste-Hune, Château Margaux, Romanée-Conti *et al.* from vines growing next to one another in hydroponics farms. I can just see the magnificent computerized control board with all the famous names on it. The operator receives a call from the sales director: 'We need more Margaux, man, the Mouton's sticking and Haut-Brion just isn't in any more.' A couple of taps at the keyboard and the computer calculates the number of vines of different varieties that should be pulled out from the production of such passé wines and added to the Margaux program. Computerized instructions go out to kick-in the Margaux formula of nutrients, light, temperature, etc. and the vines will have to undergo a booster course, if they were making entirely different château wines until that moment.

The Complexity of Other Soil Properties

After contemplating such flights of fancy, the mystical union between soil and plant must seem very down to earth. The truth is that we know many reasons why some varieties behave differently in certain soils. The metabolism of the vine is well known, and the interaction between it and the soil is generally understood (although we could always know more!). The ideal medium in which to grow vines for wine production is one that has a relatively thin topsoil and an easily penetrable (therefore well-drained) subsoil with good water-retention characteristics, but which should not be overly humid. The vine does not like 'wet feet', so drainage is vital, yet it needs access to moisture, so access to a soil with good water retention is also important. The temperature potential of a soil, its heat-retaining capacity and heat-reflective characteristics affect the ripening period of grapes: warm soils (gravel, sand, loam) advance ripening, while cold soils (clay) retard it. Chalk falls between these two extremes, and dark, dry soils are obviously warmer than light, wet soils. The soil is seldom purely of one type, it might be sandy-clay or clayey-gravel and there is a difference of emphasis between, for example, sandy-clay and clayey-sand, so the whole business of working out the overall effect of the soil on a vine starts to become complicated. Then bring in just one other factor – aspect. What about a cold soil in a fully south-facing situation, a warm soil in a north-facing situation and all the different combinations in between? Now think of every possible mix of soil and the potential permutations with all the other factors of *terroir* that can affect quality, and the result is a complex matrix of cause and effect for just one vine growing in one situation.

Soil pH

High pH (alkaline) soils (such as chalk) encourage the vine's metabolism to produce sap and grape juice with a relatively low pH (high acid content), which is highly desirable in ripe fruit. Unfortunately, the continual use of fertilizers has lowered the pH level of some viticultural areas in France, and consequently these are now producing wines with less acidity. The pH of a soil, therefore, is not constant: it can be increased or decreased by natural and artificial means. And the pH at any one time is not absolute. Various factors can affect it, the most common being water, which increases the pH. The opposite is also true, as dry conditions dilute the pH. This means that the pH alters not only according to the weather, but also in relation to the drainage and water-retaining properties of the soil itself.

Topsoil and Subsoil

Centuries of constant cultivation alter the topsoil. This happens not only through the addition of fertilizers, but also by the physical working of the soil, which mixes and moves it from its original composition and situation. The subsoil, however, always remains geologically true.

Topsoil is of primary importance to the vine because it supports most of the root system, including most of the feeding network. Main roots penetrate several layers of subsoil, the structure of which influences drainage, the root system's potential depth and its ability to collect minerals.

Mineral Requirement of the Vine

Certain minerals essential to plant growth are found in various soils. Apart from hydrogen and oxygen (supplied as water) the most important soil nutrients are: nitrogen, used in the production of a plant's green matter; phosphate, which directly encourages root development and indirectly promotes an earlier ripening of the grapes (an excess inhibits the uptake of magnesium); potassium, which improves the vine's metabolism, enriches the sap and is essential for the development of the next year's crop; iron, which is necessary for photosynthesis (lack of iron will cause chlorosis);

magnesium, which is the only mineral constituent of the chlorophyll molecule (lack of magnesium also causes chlorosis); and calcium, which feeds the root system, neutralizes acidity and helps create a friable soil structure (though an excess of calcium restricts the vine's ability to extract iron from the soil and thus causes chlorosis).

Soil Influence

Having described, to quote myself, the 'complex matrix of cause and effect' that applies to 'just one vine growing in one situation', it would be foolish of me to say that clay does this and gravel does that, but not to do this would disappoint readers who would like to have a basic framework of the effects of soil. I would love to provide a chart with grape varieties going down and soil types going across, just run your finger down and, hey presto, there is the answer, but the following little table is about as irresponsible as I can get. It should not be taken as gospel, but seen as a very fragile overview. If you can imagine that complex matrix of cause and effect to have an infinite number of cells, every one of which can be either input or output, here then are just seven output cells to dot around it. I leave you to fill in the rest.

Clay – gives body and structure to extrovert varieties and a certain nervosity to the fruit of more delicate ones.
Gravel – restrained but fine characteristics.
Limestone – elegant fruit, early appeal.
Glacial moraine – restrained but fine characteristics.
Sand – fresh and light-bodied, but very fruity.
Schist – delicate fruit, often floral aromas.
Granite – full-bodied, long-lived.

The last thing I would want to do is to defend any of these statements – they should be taken very loosely – but for those willing to do this I should just add that it is easier to see such differences on low-cropped Riesling.

Alsace Soil Divisions

The vineyards can be split into three broad categories: the **mountain slopes**, where the soil is generally siliceous; the **foothill slopes**, which are mainly calcareous; and the alluvial **plains**. This is, however, an oversimplification and the soil divisions within these three categories can be further subdivided.

MOUNTAIN SLOPES

Approximately 25 per cent of Alsace vineyards
The geological formations here are immense, and consequently the soils are far more homogeneous than on the geological faults that comprise the Vosges foothills. The largest cultivation of mountain vineyards is found at Andlau, Reichsfeld, Bernardsvillé, Nothalten, Blienschwiller and Dambach-la-Ville, whereas the vineyards of Eichhoffen and Itterswiller (located between Andlau and Nothalten) are both in the foothills. The mountain soils can be broken down into four basic types: granitic, schistous, volcanic and sandstone.

FOOTHILL SLOPES

Approximately 50 per cent of Alsace vineyards
These vineyards are essentially comprised of the five complex geological faults of Saverne (Cléebourg to Marlenheim), Barr (Heiligenstein to Mittelbergheim), Ribeauvillé (Bergheim to Turckheim), Rouffach-Guebwiller (Wintenheim to Gueberschwihr) and Than (Hartmannswiller to Vieux-Thann). The foothill soils can also be broken down into four basic groups: calcareous, calcareous-sandstone, calcareous-marl and marly-clay.

THE PLAINS

Approximately 25 per cent of Alsace vineyards
The soils here, which are deep and uniform, can be broken down into two basic types: alluvium (mostly sandy-clay or gravelly) and calcareous loess or loam.

LEXICON OF SOIL TYPES

In various parts of this book, especially the next two chapters, I refer to various types of soil, for which the following lexicon acts as a reference. Because Alsace is a geologist's dream, reference to its soil often gets bogged down in geological terms. Although I have included some of the more important below, they are primarily to explain references you might come across elsewhere, as I have tried to simplify things in the main text of this book, where I refer to the basic soil types, rather than their geological origin. The geological origin of rocks is vital, of course, to geologists, but not to the wine amateur. Does it matter whether two clay soils were laid down in two different eras if the soil is similar in both cases? I think not. If one clay soil is heavier, or more silty, sandy or calcareous, then that should be said, but in plain English. I am too well aware of the jargon that crops up when discussing wine, to think of mixing it with rock-speak. There are a few geological finer points that should be adhered to, of course, such as distinguishing between soft, porous chalk and the numerous hard limestone rocks that do not possess the same physical properties of drainage, water retention, root penetration or active lime content. It is important, therefore, that the difference is understood between limestone generally and specific types of limestone, which can range from chalk to marble. Especially as there is no chalk in Alsace, so far as I am aware. Or, at least, those areas I have been told are chalk have not turned out to be so upon examination. Most published references to chalk are erroneous, due either to mistranslation (when originally written in French by geological experts) or ignorance (when written by non-geologists). Some rocks or soils not found in Alsace are briefly mentioned in order to complete the circle of an explanation of one or more that is.

Aeolian soil Sediments deposited by wind (e.g. loess).

Alluvial deposits Material that has been transported by river and deposited. Most alluvial soils contain silt, sand and gravel, and are highly fertile.

Alluvium The noun for alluvial deposits.

Aqueous rocks One of the three basic rock forms. Also called sedimentary or stratified.

Arenaceous rocks Formed by the deposits of coarse-grained particles, usually siliceous and often decomposed from older rocks (e.g., sandstone).

Argillaceous soils A group of sedimentary soils, commonly clays, shales, mudstones, siltstones and marls.

Argille French for clay.

Agilo-marneux French for marly-clay.

Agrilo-limoneuse French for silty-clay.

Basalt Material that accounts for 90 per cent of all lava-based volcanic rocks. It contains various minerals, is rich in lime and soda, but not quartz (the most abundant of all minerals), and it is poor in potash.

Boulder *See* 'Particle size'.

Calcareous clay Argillaceous soil that has carbonate of lime content that affects the clay's intrinsic acidity and can even neutralize it. The cold temperature of this type of soil also delays ripening, and so the wines produced on it tend to have more acidity.

Calcareous soil Any soil, or mixture of soils, with an accumulation of calcium and magnesium carbonates. Essentially alkaline, it promotes the production of acidity in grapes, although the pH of each soil will vary according to its level of active-lime. Calcareous soils are cool, with good water retention. With the exception of calcareous clays (see above), they allow the vine's root system to penetrate deeply and provide excellent drainage.

Calcaro-gréseux The French for calcareous-sandstone.

Carbonaceous soil Derived from rotting vegetation under anaerobic conditions. The most common carbonaceous soils are peat, lignite, coal and anthracite.

Chalk A specific type of limestone, chalk is a soft, cool and porous alkaline rock that encourages the production of grapes with a relatively high acidity level. It also allows the vine's roots to penetrate and provides excellent drainage, yet retains sufficient moisture for nourishment.

Clay A fine-grained argillaceous compound with malleable, plastic characteristics and excellent water-retention properties. It is, however, cold, acid, offers poor drainage and, because of its cohesive quality, is hard to work. An excess of clay can stifle the vine's root system, but a proportion of small clay particles mixed with other soils can be advantageous.

Clay-loam A very fertile version of loam, but heavy to work under wet conditions, with a tendency to become waterlogged.

Cobble *See* 'Particle size'.

Colluvial deposits Weathered material transported by gravity or hill-wash.

Crystalline May be either igneous (e.g. granite) or metamorphic.

Dolomite A calcium-magnesium carbonate rock. Many limestones contain dolomite.

Feldspar or **Felspar** One of the most common minerals, feldspar is a white or rose coloured silicate of either potassium-aluminium or sodium-calcium-aluminium and is present in a number of rocks, including granite and basalt.

Ferruginous clay Iron-rich clay.

Glacial moraine A gritty scree deposited by glacial action.

Gneiss A coarse-grained form of granite.

Granite A hard, mineral-rich rock that quickly warms up and retains its heat. Granite contains 40–60 per cent quartz and 30–40 per cent potassium feldspar, plus mica or hornblende and various other minerals. It has a high pH that reduces wine acidity. It is important to note that a soil formed from granite is a mixture of sand (partly derived from a disintegration of quartz and partly from the decomposition of feldspar with either mica or hornblende), clay and various carbonates or silicates derived from the weathering of feldspar, mica or hornblende.

Gravel A wide-ranging term that covers siliceous pebbles of various sizes. This soil is loose, granular, airy and affords excellent drainage. It is also acid and infertile and encourages the vine to send its roots down deep in search of nutrients, so gravel beds located above limestone subsoils produce wines with markedly more acidity than those above clay subsoils.

Grès or **Gréseux** French for sandstone.

Gypsum Highly absorbent, hydrated calcium-sulphate that was formed during the evaporation of sea-water.

Gypsiferous marl A marly soil permeated with Keuper or Muschelkalk gypsum fragments, which improve the soil's heat-retention and water-circulation properties.

Hornblende A silicate of iron, aluminium, calcium and magnesium, it constitutes the main mineral found in many crystalline rocks, such as basalt, and is a major component of some granite, gneiss, etc.

Humus Organic material that contains bacteria and other micro-organisms that are capable of converting complex chemicals into simple plant foods. Humus makes soil organically fertile; without it soil is nothing more than finely ground rock.

Igneous rock One of the three main groups of rock, igneous rocks are formed from molten or partly molten material. Most igneous rocks are crystalline.

Keuper A stratigraphic name for the Upper Triassic period, it is often used in Alsace, but can mean marl (varicoloured, saliferous grey or gypsiferous grey) or limestone (ammonoid).

Lehm French for loam.

Limestone Any sedimentary rock consisting essentially of carbonates. Its hardness and water retention vary, but as an alkaline rock it generally encourages the production of grapes with a relatively high acidity level.

Limon French for silt.

Loam A warm, soft, crumbly soil with roughly equal proportions of clay, sand and silt. It is perfect for large-cropping mediocre-quality wines, but too fertile for fine wines.

Loess An accumulation of wind-borne material, mainly silty in nature, that is sometimes calcareous, but usually weathered and decalcified. It warms up quickly and has good water-retention properties.

Marl A cold, calcareous clay (technically mudstone) that delays ripening and adds acidity to wine.

Marlstone A clayey limestone that is similar to marl in its effect on the vine.

Marne French for marl.

Marno-calcaire French for calcareous-marl.

Metamorphic rocks One of the three basic categories of rock.

Mica A generic name encompassing various silicate minerals, mica is a component of granite and may become part of the topsoil when weathered out from granite base material.

Millstone Siliceous, iron-rich, sedimentary rock.

Muschelkalk A stratigraphic name for the Middle Triassic period, it is often used in Alsace, but can mean sandstone (shelly, dolomitic, calcareous, clayey, pink, yellow or millstone), marl (varicoloured or fissile), dolomite, limestone (crinoidal or grey) and shingle.

Oolite A type of limestone.

Oolith Small, round, calcareous pebbles that have grown through fusion of very tiny particles.

Particle size The size of a rock determines its descriptive name. No handful of soil will contain particles of a uniform size, unless it has been commercially graded, of course, so all such descriptions can only be guestimates, but it is worth noting what they should be, otherwise you will have nothing to base your guestimates on. According to the Wentworth-Udden scale, they are: boulder (greater than 256mm), cobble (64–256mm), pebble (4–64mm), gravel (2–4mm), sand (1/16-2mm), silt (1/256–1/16mm) and clay (smaller than 1/256mm). Notice that even by this precise scale, Wentworth and Udden have allowed overlaps, thus a 1/16mm particle might be either sand or silt and, of course, sub-divisions are possible within each group, as there is such a thing as fine, medium or coarse sand and even gritty silt.

Pebble *See* 'Particle size'.

Perlite Fine, powdery light and lustrous substance of volcanic origin with similar properties to diatomaceous earth.

Precipitated salts A sedimentary deposit. Water charged with acid or alkaline material, under pressure of great depth, dissolves various mineral substances from rocks on the sea-bed, which are then held in solution. When the water flows to a place of no great depth or is drained away or evaporates, the pressure is reduced, the minerals are no longer held in solution and precipitate in deposits that may be just a few inches or several thousand feet deep. There are five groups (oxides, carbonates, sulphates, phosphates and chlorides).

Quartz The most common and abundant mineral found in various sizes and in almost all soils, although sand and coarse silt contain the largest amount. Quartz has a high pH, which reduces wine acidity, but pebble-sized quartz, or larger, stores and reflects heat, increasing alcohol potential.

Rock A rock may be loosely described as a mass of mineral matter. There are three basic types of rock: igneous, metamorphic and sedimentary (or aqueous or stratified).

Sable French for sand.

Sableuse French for sandy.

Sand Tiny particles of weathered rocks and minerals that retain little water, but constitute a warm, airy soil that drains well and should be phylloxera-free.

Sandstone A sedimentary rock composed of sand-sized particles that have either been formed by pressure or bound by various iron minerals.

Sandy-loam Warm, well-drained, sand-dominated loam that is easy to work and suitable for early-cropping grape varieties.

Schist Heat-retaining, coarse-grain, laminated, crystalline rock that is rich in potassium and magnesium, but poor in nitrogen and organic substances. *See* also Steige and Villé.

Scree Synonymous with colluvium deposits.

Sedimentary rock One of the three basic rock forms, it includes arenaceous (e.g. sandstone), argillaceous (e.g. clay), calcareous (e.g. limestone), siliceous (e.g. quartz), carbonaceous (e.g. peat, lignite or coal), and precipitated salts, of which there are five groups (oxides, carbonates, sulphates, phosphates and chlorides). Sedimentary rocks are also called aqueous or stratified.

Shale Heat-retaining, fine-grain, laminated, moderately fertile sedimentary rock. Shale can turn into slate under pressure.

Shingle Pebble- or gravel-sized stones rounded by water action.

Siliceous soil A generic term for acid rock of a crystalline nature. It may be organic (flint) or inorganic (quartz) and may be either hard nodules (flint or quartz) or soft and powdery, such as kieselguhr, otherwise known as diatomaceous earth. All siliceous soils have good heat retention, but no water retention unless found in a finely ground form in silt, clay and other sedimentary soils.

Silt A very fine deposit, with good water retention. Silt is more fertile than sand, but is cold and offers poor drainage.

Slate Hard, dark grey, fine-grain, plate-like rock formed under pressure from clay, siltstone, shale and other sediments. It warms up quickly, retains heat well and is responsible for many fine wines, most notably from the Mosel.

Steige A type of schist found on the north side of Andlau, which has metamorphosed with the Andlau granite and is particularly hard and slaty. It has mixed with the granitic sand from the top of the Grand Cru Kastelberg and makes a dark, stony soil.

Stone This word should be used in conjunction with rock types (limestone and sandstone, for example), but 'stone' is often used synonymously with pebble.

Stratified rock One of the three basic rock forms. Also called sedimentary or aqueous.

Tufa Various vent-based volcanic rocks.

Villé A special type of friable, grey, clayey schist that is found in Villé and further east on the south side of Andlau.

Volcanic soils Derived from two sources, volcanic soils are lava-based (the products of volcanic flow) and vent-based (material blown into the atmosphere). Some 90 per cent of lava-based rocks and soils are comprised of basalt, while others include andesite, pitchstone, rhyolite and trachyte. Vent-based matter has either been ejected as molten globules, cooled in the air and dropped to earth as solid particles (pumice), or ejected as solid material and fractured through the explosive force with which it was flung (tufa).

4

The Wine Villages of Alsace

Although Alsace has been the focal point of a titanic power struggle between French and German forces for its sovereignty and the subject of much pillage and plunder besides, time seems to have stood still in its 118 wine villages, which still appear as medieval and well preserved as anyone could wish them to be.

As early as the ninth century, there were 119 wine villages in Alsace, almost exactly the same as today. Ermoldus Nigellus, a poet of the times from Aquitaine, compared the wines of just one of these (Sigolsheim) with those of Falernium, which of course was the most famous *cru* of antiquity. By the fourteenth century, 300 abbeys had been established and vineyards extended through 172 villages in a virtually unbroken ribbon from Wissembourg in the north to Mulhouse in the south, which is far beyond the limits of AOC Alsace today, although viticulture of an unclassified ilk still does exist in all these areas. According to the most famous Alsace historian, Monseigneur Médard Barth (1886–1976), the total number of wine villages had increased to as many as 430 by the year 1400, which explains why there are as many tales today of 'lost' villages as there are existing ones.

The delimitation of 118 wine communities in Alsace was revised in October 1990, when the area of land classified as AOC rose minutely from 20,201.18 hectares to 20,244.84 (an increase of just 0.2 per cent). Although not important in total, the change of AOC area in certain villages has been quite substantial (*see* Balbronn, Bergholtz-Zell, Herrlisheim, Osenbach and Vieux-Thann). Of the area classified as AOC Alsace, the amount of land actually under vine is 13,487 hectares. Of the 11,310.34 hectares of AOC-classified land in the Haut-Rhin 8,076 hectares are cultivated and 5,411 of the 8,934.50 hectares in the Bas-Rhin (for a year by year evolution of the area under vine and breakdown by grape varieties, *See* Appendix 3, Production Analysis).

VILLAGE PROFILES

The reader will find all 118 wine-growing villages of Alsace listed below. Obviously, the more important the village the more comprehensive the entry. Some are not merely less significant than others, however; quite a few are so obscure in terms of any sort of reputation, let alone a winemaking one, that there is hardly anything to report. They are included, with whatever detail is available, for the sake of completeness.

Explanatory notes

1. The primary distances indicated under *Location* are an approximate guide as the crow flies, but any reference to nearby villages indicates distance by road with preference given to the Route du Vin wherever possible. No distances under *Location* should be taken as precise; they are provided simply to help the reader zero in on any of the 118 villages.

2. The soil situation indicated under each village is merely a simplistic overview. For more detailed information refer to Chapters 3, 5 and 6.

3. Only cooperatives that actually sell wine under their own label are included.

4. Under *Annual festivals*, the mention of a 'Kilbe' refers to a sort of popular festival of yesteryear, often located under trees, where song and dance flows as liberally as the food and wine.

Albé, Bas-Rhin

Location: 15 miles north of Colmar, just east of Epfig and next to Villé
Area classified as AOC: 89.19 hectares
AOC area under vine: 17 hectares
Grands crus: None
Other vineyard names in use: Clos du Sonnenbach (René & Gilbert Beck); Galgenrain (René & Gilbert Beck)
Soil: Schist

Although more kirsch country than viticultural, Albé's immaculate vineyards, interspersed by orchards, are well worth the trouble of seeking out. This is a picturesque, half-timbered village that also has an interesting museum called the Maison du Val de Villé. Best for Pinot Noir and Auxerrois. René & Gilbert Beck's Domaine du

Remparts has just over two hectares in this village, all of which is planted with Pinot Noir.

Ammerschwihr, Haut-Rhin

Location: 4 miles north-west of Colmar, between Kaysersberg and Ingersheim
Area classified as AOC: 551.59 hectares, including 66.23 hectares (or 12 per cent) of *grand cru* vineyards
AOC area under vine: 452 hectares
Grands crus: Kaefferkopf (60 hectares); Wineck-Schlossberg (6.23 hectares in Ammerschwihr, 17.94 hectares in Katzenthal)
N.B. The classification of Kaefferkopf was not inluded in the decree of 17 December 1992 due to resistance by some growers who fear with some justification that the delimitation and traditional practices recognized by Law in 1932 will not be honoured. As far as this book is concerned, however, Kaefferkopf is not just a *grand cru*, but one of the greatest Alsace *grands crus*.
Other vineyard names in use: Clos Meywihr (part of Grand Cru Kaefferkopf, Roger Klein)
Soil: Granite and limestone
Producers located in the village: Les Caves JB Adam, Domaine Pierre Adam, Henri Ehrhart, Marcel Freyburger, H & J Heitzmann & Fils, Vins d'Alsace Kuehn, André Mercklé & Fils, Domaine Martin Schaetzel, René & Bernard Schneider, Albert Schoech (part of Kuehn), Maurice Schoech, P. Sick-Dreyer, Jean-Paul Simonis, Domaine de la Sinne, GAEC André Thomas & Fils, André Wackenthaler
Others also owning vines in, or making wines from, the village: Maison Léon Baur, Lucien Brand, Claude Dietrich, André Ehrhart, Geschickt, CV Ingersheim, CV Kientzheim-Kaysersberg, Roger Klein, Ringenbach-Moser, Salzmann-Thomann, Bernard Schwach, François Schwach, Pierre Sparr
Annual festivals: Fête du Vin (April, which makes it the first Fête du Vin of the year); Fête du Kaefferkopf

The origins of this village go back to at least 869, when it was first recorded as Amalricivilare or Amalrici's villa. It has always been an important winemaking centre and its Kaefferkopf is perhaps the most famous of all Alsace vineyards. Although it was the fifty-first to claim *grand cru* status, this was due to a political wrangle with local growers who naturally wished to preserve the traditional winemaking practices of Kaefferkopf, which involved the blending and inclusion of varieties not covered by the *grand cru* legislation. Whilst Kaefferkopf was the last to join the ranks of *grand crus* it was, with Beblenheim's Sonnenglanz, the first of two vineyards to be officially recognized (Colmar Tribunal, 1932). Although now housed in the Château de Kientzheim, it was in Ammerschwihr that the Confrérie St-Étienne was founded sometime prior to 1440, when it was known as the *Herrenstubengesellschaft*. In 1951, the Confrérie became a regional organization with chapters all over the world. Regular banquets are held at the Château de Kientzheim, where the food is of an astonishingly high standard given the several hundred people served, but then the Confrérie is surrounded by the greatest concentration of Michelin-rated restaurants in the world and so can call upon an unrivalled level of expertise. The wines served at these dinners always bear the Confrérie St-Étienne's label, which reveals the grape variety and vintage, but never the producer, although the identity will be known to members of the organizing committee and it can sometimes slip out.

Ammerschwihr was one of less than a dozen villages in Alsace to have a reputation for *vin de paille* in the nineteenth century and, as the history of Kaefferkopf and the Confrérie St-Étienne demonstrates, it was also the centre of efforts to improve and maintain the quality of all Alsace wines. It should therefore be little surprise to discover that some of the region's best wines have always been made here. It is also fitting that Riesling and Gewurztraminer, the two grapes that are most synonymous with Alsace, are Ammerschwihr's most successful varieties. When grown on limestone, which forms almost 90 per cent of this village, these wines are mild, delicately rich and full of immediate charm, but when grown on granite they can be as austere as the rock itself. This is, however, only in their youth, for these are the wines of the Kaefferkopf and they are long-lived, with great potential intensity and, after enough bottle-age, are capable of a richness, smoothness and length that might be matched by other great *grands crus*, but is never surpassed. Adam and Sick-Dreyer are the best producers here.

Andlau, Bas-Rhin

Location: 20 miles north of Colmar, just south of Barr
Area classified as AOC: 167.16 hectares, including 10.45 hectares (or 6 per cent) of *grand cru* vineyards
AOC area under vine: 82 hectares
Grands crus: Kastelberg (5.82 hectares); Moenchberg (2.63 hectares in Andlau, 9.2 in Eichhoffen); Wiebelsberg (12 hectares)
Other vineyard names in use: Brandhof (Domaine André & Rémy Gresser); Clos Rebgarten (Marc Kreydenweiss); Clos du Val d'Eléon (Marc Kreydenweiss); Klusterhof (Domaine Mattern); Lerchenberg (Marc Kreydenweiss)
Soil: Shist and granite, with gravel deposits in the foothills, limestone outcrops and areas of clay and of marl
Producers located in the village: CV Andlau, André Durrmann, Domaine André & Rémy Gresser, Jean-Pierre Klein, Marc Kreydenweiss, Domaine Mattern, Jean Wach, Gérard Wagner
Others also owning vines in, or making wines from, the village: Boeckel, Roger & Roland Geyer, Domaine Klipfel, CV Obernai, Meyer, Charles Moritz, Julien Rieffel & Fils, Marcel Schlosser, Guy Wach, Ch. Wantz
Annual festivals: Fête du Vin (organized by the Confrérie des Hospitaliers du Haut d'Andlau, it is possible to taste every grape variety from every *grand cru* at this event in May)

Built around the Abbey de Ste-Richarde, which was founded by Ste Richarde, the wife of Charles the Fat. After 10 years of unconsummated marriage, Charles claimed to have 'caught' her kissing the cross of a bishop and thus accused her of adultery. To prove her innocence, she was forced to walk through fire in a wax-sodden dress, which apparently she did and emerged unscathed. Seeking a place of asylum, this legendary character came across a mother bear and her cubs in the valley of Andlau. The bear drew a plan on the ground, which Richarde immediately recognized as a building and took to be an architectural sign from God and built a convent to this design on the very spot, but try telling this to young people today and they just won't believe you.

The Kastelberg has been planted since Roman times and other Andlau wines also gained early fame. Those from the St-André vineyard, for example, were sufficiently well reputed to be mentioned in a charter dated 926 (the Chapelle St-André is located south-east of the town, between the Moenchberg and Andlau itself). In the fifteenth century, Frederick III, the German king and Holy Roman Emperor, authorized Sophie d'Andlau to appoint *Weinsticheren*, independent wine tasters whose duty it was to ensure the quality of wine for buyers. This service, which helped Andlau to build its reputation, endured until the Revolution.

Unlike most vineyards, those of Andlau are situated on Vosges bedrock, rather than its escarpment faults. The best have very hot and dry microclimates, which with the hard, rocky soil, should be ideal for long-lived Rieslings. In their youth, however, I find Andlau Riesling to have a fennel-like character that is quite boring, unless given the benefit of a few years in bottle, after which it develops a special, rather gentle, floral richness. Gewurztraminer and Tokay-Pinot Gris can also be more floral than spicy and show surprising elegance. This *terroir* is, of course, ideal for Vendanges Tardives and Marc Kreydenweiss wrings every ounce of potential out of this style. Kreydenweiss is certainly the most talented winemaker here, but Klipfel (from Barr) is underrated and André Gresser can sometimes strike gold. The local confrérie is very active and puts on one of the most informative tastings in the region each year when wines from every *grand cru* can be sampled.

Avolsheim, Bas-Rhin

Location: 10 miles west of Strasbourg, between Molsheim and Soultz-les-Bains
Area classified as AOC: 82.71 hectares
AOC area under vine: 32 hectares
Grands crus: None
Other vineyard names in use: None
Soil: Sandstone
Producers owning vines in, or making wine from, the village: Bernard Becht

Site of the eleventh-century Dompeter or Domus Petri, the oldest church in Alsace, and an absolute haven of peace and quiet, but the only pure Avolsheim wine I have tasted has been Bernard Becht's Riesling Finkenberg, which is a fine and rich wine with a touch of spiciness in the aroma. Most of the rest of this village's production is processed by local cooperatives.

Balbronn, Bas-Rhin

Location: 14 miles west of Strasbourg, via Traenheim
Area classified as AOC: 186.94 hectares
AOC area under vine: 110 hectares
Grands crus: None
Other vineyard names in use: Westerweingarten (Anstotz)
Soil: Calcareous clay
Producers located in the village: GAEC Anstotz & Fils

I know very little about the viticultural attributes of this old fortified village, despite its significant viticultural holding, apart from the fact that it is supposed to be specially suited to Riesling. If that is true, I do not think they promote the product very well. I have tasted only one pure Balbronn wine so far as I am aware, a Riesling Westerweingarten from Anstotz & Fils, and that was merely acceptable. It is also claimed that the best hillsides of Balbronn (and those of Westhoffen) were historically considered part of Bergbieten or, at least, that it was the wines produced from these hillsides that helped Bergbieten build up its reputation for Riesling. During the recent reassessment of the communal delimitation of Alsace, the area classified as AOC underwent a modest increase from 160 hectares to its current 187.

Barr, Bas-Rhin

Location: 25 miles north of Colmar, between Obernai and Andlau
Area classified as AOC: 218.60 hectares, including 40 hectares (or 18 per cent) of *grand cru* vineyards
AOC area under vine: 118 hectares
Grands crus: Kirchberg de Barr (40 hectares)
Other vineyard names in use: Clos Gaensbroennel (part of Grand Cru Kirchberg de Barr, Willm and Domaine Héring), Clos Zisser (part of Grand Cru Kirchberg de Barr, Klipfel)
Soil: Clay and limestone
Producers located in the village: CV Andlau, Domaine Hering, Domaine Klipfel, Charles Stoeffler, Ch. Wantz, Willm
Others also owning vines in, or making wines from, the village: E. Boeckel, Jean Heywang, Julien Rieffel, Wolfberger
Annual festivals: Fête du Vin (mid-July); Fête des Vendanges (first two weeks in October)

Barr is a lovely old terraced town that was initially settled in the pre-Roman era. Vines have been growing here since Roman times and it is now an important wine community. Barr's name probably derives from the Celtic *barra*, which means barrier. In the past, this town was known for Pinot Blanc and Sylvaner, but has since developed something of a reputation for Gewurztraminer, particularly on the Kirchberg, where it produces a wine of a more restrained character than those of the Haut-Rhin. This does not mean they are in any way attenuated. Gewurztraminer de Barr are, in fact, quite rich in extract, but they are never fat, although they can develop a liquorice-like intensity after just a few years in bottle. Other varieties sometimes have a smoky style, a distinguishing mark of wines grown in nearby Mittelbergheim and, to a lesser extent, Heiligenstein. Being owned by Wolfberger, the giant cooperative at Eguisheim, has not harmed the quality of Willm, which still rates as one of the best producers in Barr, together with the estate wines of Klipfel, especially Clos Zisser, which is exclusively planted with Gewurztraminer.

Beblenheim, Haut-Rhin

Location: 5 miles north of Colmar, between Bennwihr and Zellenberg
Area classified as AOC: 224.80 hectares, including 32.8 hectares (or 15 per cent) of *grand cru* vineyards
AOC area under vine: 160 hectares
Grands crus: Sonnenglanz (32.8 hectares)
Other vineyard names in use: None
Soil: Limestone
Producers located in the village: CV Beblenheim, Maison Bott-Geyl, André Mauler & Fils
Others also owning vines in, or making wines from, the village: Domaine Marcel Deiss, Jean-Paul Hartweg, Jean Huttard, CV Ribeauvillé, Jean-Paul & Denis Specht
Annual festivals: Fête du Sonnenglanz (last weekend but one in July)

First mentioned in documents dated 1249, when Beblenheim belonged to the Graf von Horbourg, later becoming the property of the dukes of Württemberg. Chrétien Oberlin, the great Alsace ampelographer who founded Colmar's Viticultural Institute, was born in Beblenheim in 1831. This village's Sonnenglanz and

Ammerschwihr's Kaefferkopf were the first two vineyards to be officially recognized, in 1932, when the tribunal in Colmar defined their boundaries and protected the wines produced by law. Sonnenglanz was later confirmed as a sub-appellation in the region's first AOC legislation. Its name, which means 'sunny hill', is a reminder of how long Beblenheim's exceptionally warm microclimate has been known. Indeed, almond trees have blossomed here, just as they have on the Mandelberg in nearby Bennwihr.

While the normally neutral Sylvaner often has a good bouquet when grown in this village, the naturally aromatic Gewurztraminer has a fine, but surprisingly discreet, character – traits that also occur in Mittelwihr and Bennwihr, two nearby villages that share very similar soils. In the good old, bad old days, Beblenheim had a reputation for producing a decent Zwicker. Bott-Geyl is the best producer.

Bennwihr, Haut-Rhin

Location: 4 miles north of Colmar, immediately next to Mittelwihr
Area classified as AOC: 314.12 hectares, including 38.4 hectares (or 12 per cent) of *grand cru* vineyards
AOC area under vine: 280 hectares
Grands crus: Marckrain (38.4 hectares in Bennwihr, 7 hectares in Sigolsheim)
Other vineyard names in use: None
Soil: Limestone
Producers located in the village: CV Bennwihr
Others also owning vines in, or making wines from, the village: Domaine Marcel Deiss, Jean Huttard, Ringenbach-Moser, Maison Wiederhirn
Annual festivals: Fête du Vin (includes open-air chess, second weekend in August)

First mentioned in records dated 777, Bennwihr is now inseparable from Mittelwihr; you can drive into one looking for the start of the other and be out of both before you realize it! Until the 1970s, nearly half of Bennwihr's vineyards were planted with Chasselas. As mentioned under Beblenheim, the Sylvaner here often has a good bouquet, while the Gewurztraminer remains very discreet, traits that also occur in Mittelwihr, all three villages being neighbours and possessing similar soils.

Bergbieten, Bas-Rhin

Location: 12 miles west of Strasbourg, following the Route du Vin from
Soultz-les-Bains through Dagolsheim
Area classified as AOC: 188.85 hectares, including 29 hectares (or 15 per
cent) of *grand cru* vineyards
AOC area under vine: 123 hectares
Grands crus: Altenberg de Bergbieten (29 hectares)
Other vineyard names in use: Glintzberg (Roland Schmitt)
Soil: Marl
Producers located in the village: Roland Schmitt
Others also owning vines in, or making wines from, the village: Gilbert
Leininger, Frédéric Mochel, GAEC Mochel-Lorentz, CV Traenheim

Winemaking in this village dates back to at least the eleventh
century, when Bergbieten attained some reputation for its Riesling,
particularly from the Altenberg. Bergbieten is a good, but not
outstanding village, with the Altenberg de Bergbieten more of a
premier cru than a truly *grand cru*, with Riesling and Gewurztraminer as the best varieties. In the hands of Frédéric Mochel, the
Altenberg almost assumes true *grand cru* status, with his tangy
Gewurztraminer and spicy-ripe Riesling. CV Traenheim makes
softer, less intense wines, which are marketed under the 'Les Vins
du Roi Dagobert' label.

Bergheim, Haut-Rhin

Location: 9 miles north of Colmar, between Ribeauvillé and Rorschwihr
Area classified as AOC: 451.78 hectares, including 38.29 hectares (or 8 per
cent) of *grand cru* vineyards
AOC area under vine: 352 hectares
Grands crus: Altenberg de Bergheim (35.06 hectares); Kanzlerberg (3.23
hectares)
Other vineyard names in use: Burg (Marcel Deiss & Louis Freyburger);
Burlenberg (Marcel Deiss); Engelgarten (Marcel Deiss); Grasberg (Marcel
Deiss); Pflaenzerreben (Rolly Gassmann)
Soil: Marly-limestone
Producers located in the village: Domaine Marcel Deiss, Louis Freyburger
& Fils, Gustave Lorentz, Jean-Martin Spielmann
Others also owning vines in, or making wines from, the village: CV

Beblenheim, Fernand Engel, Jean Halbeison, Koeberlé-Kreyer, Charles Koehly & Fils, Rolly Gassmann, Domaine Jean Sipp, Louis Sipp, Domaine Sipp-Mack, F.E. Trimbach
Annual festivals: Fête du Gewurztraminer (fourth Sunday in July)

The earliest known name of this village was Perchaim. This evolved into Bergheim sometime after it was fortified in the fourteenth century and one still has to drive through the Port Haute of the old fortified wall to gain access today.

Although gastronomy in general is beyond the scope of this book and I certainly do not intend to recommend restaurants, I urge every reader who visits the region to have at least one meal at the Winstub le Sommelier (*see* **Introduction and Acknowledgements**). It is just a few doors down the road from Gustave Lorentz and, if you have been visiting, they will probably lock up shop and join you!

Back to the wine: Bergheim produces elegant wines and is most famous for its Gewurztraminer, which can be extremely reserved in its youth, but develops into magnificent style after a few years in bottle. The Riesling produced in this village also ages very well and even the Sylvaner is well worth trying, although its fresh, lively fruit is definitely best when consumed young. Marcel Deiss is by far the best producer, but Gustave Lorentz comes close with certain wines.

Bergholtz, Haut-Rhin

Location: 12 miles south-south-west of Colmar, between Guebwiller and Bergholtz-Zell
Area classified as AOC: 58.50 hectares, including 12 hectares (or 21 per cent) of *grand cru* vineyards
AOC area under vine: 47 hectares
Grands Crus: Spiegel (12 hectares in Bergholtz, 6.26 hectares in Guebwiller)
Other vineyard names in use: Meissenberg (Eric Rominger)
Soil: Limestone, sandstone and sandy-clay
Producers located in the village: Vins Dirler, Domaine Joseph Loberger, Eric Rominger
Others also owning vines in, or making wines from, the village: Domaines Schlumberger, Wolfberger

Various named vineyards in Bergholtz are mentioned in records dating from the thirteenth century, but most of this village used to be planted with Sylvaner and Chasselas. Not now, of course, and from the expressive quality of wines made by growers like Dirler, Bergholtz obviously has significant potential for the production of Riesling and possibly other classic varieties. Rominger's Meissenberg Riesling is exciting and, of course, part of Schlumberger's Spiegel is located in the village, as its most southerly vineyards are, after all, merely an extension of Guebwiller's.

Bergholtz-Zell, Haut-Rhin

Location: 12 miles south-south-west of Colmar, just up the road from Bergholtz and contiguous with Orschwihr
Area classified as AOC: 55.80 hectares
AOC area under vine: 62 hectares
Grands crus: None
Other vineyard names in use: None
Soil: Limestone
Producers owning vines in, or making wines from, the village: Dirler, Wolfberger

As the Zell part of its name indicates (*see* Zellenberg), Bergholtz-Zell grew out of a monastic settlement and was in fact established by Irish monks in the eighth century. Apart from those vines that literally extend across the boundary with Bergholtz, which is a good mile away, the viticultural worth of these two villages cannot be compared and although Bergholtz-Zell is almost part and parcel of Orschwihr, its vineyards are certainly not. The vineyards of Bergholtz-Zell face north-east and at one time used to be almost entirely planted with Sylvaner and Pinot Blanc, whereas those of Orschwihr are across the valley, consequently face south and west, and have always had a greater reputation. Since the recent reassessment of the communal delimitation, when the area of Bergholtz-Zell classified as AOC dropped from 74.8 to 55.8 hectares, there would seem to be more land planted than actually classified. According to ONIVINS and INAO, as these vineyards were planted prior to the reassessment in October 1990, there is nothing to prevent their use for AOC wines. I agree that it would be most unfair to classify land as AOC, allow a grower to plant vines there and then announce that it is no longer classified, but why, in that case, bother to declassify it?

Bernardswiller, Bas-Rhin

Location: 25 miles north of Colmar, between Obernai and St-Nabor or Heiligenstein
Area classified as AOC: 303.28 hectares
AOC area under vine: 137 hectares
Grands crus: None
Other vineyard names in use: None
Soil: Limestone
Producers owning vines in, or making wines from, the village: GAEC Seilly

I know very little of this village or its vineyards, apart from the fact that it is typically picturesque, with narrow streets and old houses, and its vines are located on the lower slopes of St-Nabor, which is beneath Mont Ste-Odile. As much as 50 per cent of these vineyards were planted with Sylvaner as recently as the early 1970s and, in the old days, Traminer (*sic*) used to have a modest reputation.

Bernardvillé, Bas-Rhin

Location: 15 miles north of Colmar, down a dead-end track up in the hills, off the road from Itterswiller to Reichsfeld (also a dead-end)
Area classified as AOC: 82.85 hectares
AOC area under vine: 43 hectares
Grands crus: None
Other vineyard names in use: None
Soil: Clayey-schist and sedimentary volcanic rock
Producers owning vines in, or making wines from, the village: Domaine Kieffer

Lovely village set off the beaten track in a beautiful valley, over-looked by the Forêt d'Andlau. Bernardvillé is a mountain vineyard village and 90 per cent of it used to be planted with Sylvaner until as recently as the early 1970s.

Berstett, Bas-Rhin

See Gimbrett-Berstett

Berrwiller, Haut-Rhin

Location: 17 miles south-south-west of Colmar, via Hartmannswiller
Area classified as AOC: 34.37 hectares
AOC area under vine: 6 hectares
Grands crus: None
Other vineyard names in use: None
Soil: Limestone

A wine village set on the plain just south of Guebwiller, Berrwiller produces an insignificant amount of wine of very modest quality.

Bischoffsheim, Bas-Rhin

Location: 30 miles north of Colmar, between Obernai and Molsheim
Area classified as AOC: 199.12 hectares
AOC area under vine: 20 hectares
Grands crus: None
Other vineyard names in use: None
Soil: Limestone

Situated on the eastern slope of the Bischenberg, which has excellent views over the plains of Alsace and the Vosges, the best vineyards here are on the south-facing slopes of the Immerschenberg, but they in fact belong to Obernai.

Blienschwiller, Bas-Rhin

Location: 18 miles north of Colmar, between Nothalten and Dambach-la-Ville
Area classified as AOC: 145.91 hectares, including 5 hectares (or 3 per cent) of *grand cru* vineyards
AOC area under vine: 112 hectares
Grands crus: Winzenberg (5 hectares)
Other vineyard names in use: Oberberg (Oscar Schwartz)
Soil: Granite, sand and marl

Producers located in the village: René Kientz, Hubert Metz, Oscar Schwartz, Pierre Sperry, Spitz & Fils, Domaine de la Tour
Others also owning vines in, or making wines from, the village: André Dussourt, Louis Hauller, François Meyer

An attractive village with a fifteenth-century fountain and various historical monuments. I have tasted very good Tokay-Pinot Gris from the Domaine de la Tour of Joseph Straub & Fils, especially the Vendange Tardive, and a fat, extremely fruity Pinot Noir from Pierre Sperry, but locals reckon that Riesling and Gewurztraminer are the most appropriate varieties, particularly on the Winzenberg, where the wines can have some finesse. Some of the wines from these vineyards have helped to make the reputation of neighbouring Dambach-la-Ville and both villages are essentially comprised of mountain vineyards. As with most mountain vineyards, their granite soil was once deemed Sylvaner country.

Boersch-St-Léonard, Bas-Rhin

Location: 13 miles south-west of Strasbourg between Rosheim and Ottrott
Area classified as AOC: 144.31 hectares
AOC area under vine: 25 hectares
Grands crus: None
Other vineyard names in use: None
Soil: Limestone

I have never tasted a wine produced in Boersch-St-Léonard, but the village is old and charming, with three gates, a beautiful Renaissance well and a fresco that dates back to the twelfth century, so it makes a pleasant diversion to keep looking for one.

Bourgheim, Bas-Rhin

Location: 25 miles north of Colmar, between Barr and Obernai, on the D706
Area classified as AOC: 43.38 hectares
AOC area under vine: 31 hectares
Grands crus: None
Other vineyard names in use: None
Soil: Limestone

This modest wine village set on the plain west of Barr has its best vines cut in a wedge out of what appears to be the middle of Heiligenstein's fine, east-facing slopes. There have never been many hectares cultivated here, but Sylvaner and Gewurztraminer have been historically preferred.

Buhl, Haut-Rhin

Location: 13 miles south-south-west of Colmar, just beyond Guebwiller
Area classified as AOC: 47.57 hectares
AOC area under vine: 1 hectare
Grands crus: None
Other vineyard names in use: None
Soil: Sandstone and limestone

Buhl is better known for the fifteenth-century painting that hangs in the altar of its nineteenth-century church than for its one hectare's worth of wine, for it is believed to be the work of Colmar's Martin Schongauer. It is certainly worth visiting Buhl just to see this altarpiece, which has not lost its humorous appeal in the 400 years since it was painted.

Cernay, Haut-Rhin

Location: 20 miles south-south-west of Colmar, between Thann and Mulhouse
Area classified as AOC: 14.80 hectares
AOC area under vine: 1 hectare
Grands crus: None
Other vineyard names in use: None
Soil: Shale & loess

Known primarily because this is where the Route des Crêtes starts, most of Cernay was destroyed in the First World War and 50 per cent of its vineyards were planted with hybrids and the remainder with a melange of Zwicker varieties until as recently as the early 1970s. They have since been uprooted, almost 200 hectares of them. Now only one hectare is in production and less than 15 are classified, which puts into perspective the intrinsic quality of the considerable area of vineyards once cultivated here.

Châtenois, Bas-Rhin

Location: 12 miles north of Colmar, between Scherwiller and Kintzheim
Area classified as AOC: 280.91 hectares
AOC area under vine: 169 hectares
Grands crus: None
Other vineyard names in use: Hahnenberg (Dontenville); Domaine
Weingarten (Bernhard-Reibel)
Soil: Granitic gravel
Producers located in the village: Cécile Bernhard-Reibel, Gilbert
Dontenville
Others also owning vines in, or making wines from, the village: Paul Beck,
Louis Gisselbrecht, Willy Gisselbrecht, J. Hauller & Fils

A Tokay-Pinot Gris from Bernhard-Reibel and a Riesling from
Dontenville, both very ripe and amazingly intense, would seem to
confirm the character of this granitic *terroir* and to suggest its
excellent potential for at least these two varieties. I have little else to
make a thorough judgement on, except many good generics from
several producers owning vines in the village, but who knows the
role each variety from Châtenois plays in any of those wines?

Cléebourg, Bas-Rhin

Location: 4 miles south-west of Wissembourg, in the extreme north of the
region, some 35 miles north of Strasbourg
Area classified as AOC: 75.82 hectares
AOC area under vine: 44 hectares
Grands crus: None
Other vineyard names in use: Keimberg (CV Cléebourg), Reiffenberg (CV
Cléebourg)
Soil: Sand and loess
Producers located in the village: CV Cléebourg

Vineyards were planted here by the monks of Wissembourg's Benedictine abbey shortly after it was established in 630, but by the
Second World War most had either fallen into disuse or were
planted with hybrids. It was on the initiative of Georges Rupp, a
local grower, that 300 hectares in this and surrounding villages
were reclaimed during that war. Under Rupp's guidance, Cléebourg

became one of the first villages in Alsace to replant *en masse* with recommended classic varieties. He founded the local cooperative in 1946 and its members today also grow vines in the neighbouring villages of Rott, Oberhoffen and Steinseltz. Hubrecht Duijker rightly points out in *The Loire, Alsace and Champagne* (Mitchell Beazley, 1983) that Cléebourg is very good for all Pinot varieties. CV Cléebourg is one of the most underrated, value for money producers in Alsace. Perhaps it is so far away from the mainstream that it is simply forgotten.

Colmar, Haut-Rhin

Location: 40 miles south-south-west of Strasbourg, 23 miles north of Mulhouse
Area classified as AOC: 521.55 hectares
AOC area under vine: 347 hectares
Grands crus: None
Other vineyard names in use: Harth (Robert Karcher and Domaine Schoffit)
Soil: Sand, clay and gravel
Producers located in the village: Domaine Viticole de la Ville de Colmar, Domaine Jux, Robert Karcher & Fils, Domaine Schoffit
Others also owning vines in, or making wines from, the village: Domaine Barmès-Buecher, Paul Blanck & Fils, Paul Buecher, Joseph Cattin, Théo Cattin, Claude Dietrich, Dopff Au Moulin, Pierre Freudenreich, Jean Halbeizen, CV Ingersheim, Albert Mann, Domaine Aimé Stentz, Wolfberger
Annual festivals: Foire Régionale des Vins d'Alsace (first two weeks in August); Journées de la Choucroute et des Produits Regionaux (last weekend of August and first weekend of September)

Originally known as Villa Columbaria, Colmar was the most visible centre of viticultural Alsace until industrialization, when its vineyards covered close to 600 hectares. Barely half of this survives today and Colmar, like any sizable French town, has been ruined by the unsightly commercial developments of garish colour and design that litter its outskirts.

Thankfully, much of its beautiful old centre has been preserved. This is quite miraculous, considering that the so-called Colmar Pocket was the focal point of one of the most bitterly fought battles of the Second World War.

Today Colmar is officially the wine capital of Alsace, although its own vineyards do not rank among the best. Historically, only the Hardt vineyard has a reputation of any significance and even that was for a light and rather robust Zwicker, although it is also famous for Chasselas, and Domaine Schoffit produces medal-winning Chasselas from this site (spelt Harth). But those wines that have excelled in the past are not necessarily the only ones that will create reputations in the future. Domaine Schoffit also turns out a Gewurztraminer Harth that is almost too easy to drink and Domaine Jux (purchased by Wolfberger in 1989) could eventually produce the best overall range of Harth wines. Domaine Viticole de la Ville de Colmar also specializes in Colmar wines, but, although they are very acceptable and consistent wines, they are not really special. Dopff Au Moulin has almost as many hectares in Colmar as the Domaine Viticole and most are specifically planted with Pinot Blanc for Crémant. The increasing success that Dopff Au Moulin has experienced with grapes from these vine-yards leads me to suspect that if the plains and Colmar are good for anything, it must be Crémant, which almost brings us full circle back to the Hardt's reputation for light but robust Zwicker because such wines would not be inappropriate base material for a secondary fermentation. Domaine Jux is Colmar's best overall producer.

Dahlenheim, Bas-Rhin

Location: 7 miles west of Strasbourg on the D818 between Scharrachbergheim and Osthoffen
Area classified as AOC: 165.88 hectares, including 11 hectares (or 7 per cent) of *grand cru* vineyards
AOC area under vine: 94 hectares
Grands crus: Engelberg (11 hectares)
Other vineyard names in use: None
Soil: Limestone and marl
Producers located in the village: Domaine Jean-Pierre Bechtold
Annual festivals: Fête du Vin (last weekend in September)

Vineyards have been tended here since at least the ninth century. Grand Cru Engelberg is obviously Dahlenheim's best vineyard and it certainly favours Riesling, although the village once had a name for Chasselas. I have also enjoyed simple village Gewurztraminer from Jean-Pierre Bechtold. The vineyards of this village come within the generic geographical designation of Coteaux du Mossig.

Dambach-la-Ville, Bas-Rhin

Location: 17 miles north of Colmar, between Scherwiller and Blienschwiller
Area classified as AOC: 494.50 hectares, including 53 hectares (or 11 per cent) of *grand cru* vineyards
AOC area under vine: 401 hectares
Grands crus: Frankstein (53 hectares)
Other vineyard names in use: Breitstein (Hubert Metz)
Soil: Granite
Producers located in the village: Pierre Arnold, Jean-Claude Beck, Paul Beck, Beck Hartweg, CV Dambach-la-Ville, Laurent Dietrich, Domaine J-L Dirringer, Charles Frey, Louis Gisselbrecht, Willy Gisselbrecht, J. Hauller & Fils, Louis Hauller, Michel Nartz, Domaine du Rempart, GAEC Ruhlmann-Dirringer, Schaeffer-Woerly
Others also owning vines in, or making wines from, the village: Guy Mersiol, Hubert Metz
Annual festivals: Nuit du Vin (first Saturday in July); Fête des Vins de France (second weekend in August)

This commune used to be surrounded by fir trees and owned by the noble house of Bärenstein, hence the bear and conifer on the town's coat-of-arms, which is prominently positioned over the entrance to this old fortified village. Dambach has been considered by some critics to be the best winemaking village in the Bas-Rhin for Riesling, Sylvaner and even Knipperlé (of which there is no more today, of course). Riesling is now the principal variety and can be long lived. Gewurztraminer is also important for quality, providing a very spicy, classically assertive wine. Auxerrois is often used to plump up the Pinot Blanc, which can be a bit thin here, and a substantial amount of Sylvaner is still grown, although mostly confined to vineyards on the plains. J. Hauller is the best producer of Grand Cru Frankstein, both for Riesling and Gewurztraminer, and is generally underrated for his entire range of wines. This firm and Willy Gisselbrecht are the best producers of Dambach *per se*. I have tasted some remarkably good value wines from Louis Hauller and Hubert Metz makes a full, spicy Gewurztraminer from the *lieu-dit* Breitstein. The vineyards of Dambach-la-Ville are on Vosgien mountain slopes, not the foothills.

Dangolsheim, Bas-Rhin

Location: 12 miles west of Strasbourg, between Bergbieten and Soultz-les-Bains
Area classified as AOC: 126.16 hectares
AOC area under vine: 54 hectares
Grands crus: None
Other vineyard names in use: None
Soil: Marl and limestone

Dangolsheim, which was bequeathed by Count Ruthaud to the Schwarze Abbey in 758, has always been more famous for cider than for wine because, no doubt, the vines have to make do with entirely north-facing slopes. The vineyards of this village come within the generic geographical designation of Coteaux du Mossig.

Dieffenthal, Bas-Rhin

Location: 16 miles north of Colmar, between Scherwiller and Dambach-la-Ville, just north of Sélestat
Area classified as AOC: 75.10 hectares
AOC area under vine: 46 hectares
Grands crus: None
Other vineyard names in use: None
Soil: Granite
Producers owning vines in, or making wines from, the village: Paul Beck, Louis Gisselbrecht, Willy Gisselbrecht

A peaceful village in a beautiful setting. In the nineteenth century the start of the harvest for all of Alsace was proclaimed from Dieffenthal. Overlooking the village is the Edesberg, but although it truly dominates Dieffenthal and includes its closest vineyards, these do in fact come within the communal boundary of Dambach-la-Ville. Dieffenthal's vineyards, which are considered to be good for Pinot Noir and once also had a name for Pinot Blanc, are located south and south-west of the village. The former *lieu-dit* of Neubruch in this village was of sufficient worth for J. L. Stoltz to rank it in 1828 as one of the 17 best vineyards in Alsace.

Dorlisheim, Bas-Rhin

Location: 10 miles west of Strasbourg, just south of Molsheim on the N240
Area classified as AOC: 226.48 hectares
AOC area under vine: 168 hectares
Grands crus: None
Other vineyard names in use: None
Soil: Limestone
Producers located in the village: Bernard Becht, Pierre Becht

A small village with beautiful Baroque houses and fairly important vineyards, Dorlisheim used to be known for its Sylvaner, but now produces a rather exotic style of Riesling, especially on the Finkenberg, where it can even have a touch of musk. Bernard Becht is the best producer.

Eguisheim, Haut-Rhin

Location: 3 miles south-south-west of Colmar
Area classified as AOC: 437.48 hectares, including 113.6 hectares (or 26 per cent) of *grand cru* vineyards
AOC area under vine: 354 hectares
Grands crus: Eichberg (57.6 hectares); Pfersigberg (56 hectares)
Other vineyard names in use: Coteaux d'Eguisheim (Maison Léon Baur); Clos Jean-Philippe Sturm (Wolfberger)
Soil: Limestone
Producers located in the village: Charles Baur, Maison Léon Baur, Léon Beyer, Luc Beyer, Paul Buecher, Joseph Cattin, Joseph Freudenreich, Pierre Freudenreich, Paul Ginglinger, Pierre-Henri Ginglinger, Joseph Gruss, Jean-Victor Hebinger & Fils, Albert Hertz, Bruno Hertz, Domaine Edouard Leiber, Paul Schneider, Michel Schoepfer, Bruno Sorg, Wolfberger
Others also owning vines in, or making wines from, the village: Domaine Barmès-Buecher, Pierre Frick, Alphonse Kuentz, Kuentz-Bas, Albert Mann, Scherer, Gérard Schueller, Gérard Stintzi, Emile Schwartz & Fils
Annual festivals: Présentation des Vins Nouveaux (last Sunday in March); Fête des Vignerons (last Sunday in August)

The oldest recorded mention of the village was in the form of 'Agaisheim' in 720, when Eberhard, the first count of the village, built a castle here, but settlements on the site are known to have existed since the earliest times, archaeological excavations having unearthed traces of Cro-Magnon Man (c.35,000-10,000 BC). Like Gueberschwihr in the hills to the west, Eguisheim is presumed to have been named after Eberhard, who was the grandson of Aldaric, the father of Ste-Odile (see Obernai). Eberhard was not, however, its most famous inhabitant. That honour has gone to a descendant of Eberhard's called Bruno. He was born in Eberhard's castle in 1002, when the family's aristocratic title had become the Graf von Eguisheim und Dagsburg. His rank in the history of Alsace was assured when he became the only citizen of the province to become pope (Leo IX, 1049-54).

Only Guebwiller has more hectares of *grand cru* vineyard. Generally speaking, Eguisheim is most famous for its Riesling, yet it is also considered by many to be at the very heart of the greatest area for growing Gewurztraminer. Certainly few other villages can match Eguisheim for the finesse of this grape, especially when grown on the Eichberg, the reputation of which has been built upon the Gewurztraminer. Léon Beyer's Gewurztraminer 'Cuvée des Comtes d'Eguisheim' is 100 per cent Eichberg, although no mention of this can be found on the label. Charles Bauer and Paul Ginglinger make the finest Eichberg Rieslings, but the best Rieslings in Eguisheim invariably come from Pfersigberg and the greatest exponents of these wines include Paul Ginglinger and Léon Beyer (the classic bone-dry Riesling 'Cuvée Particulière' is pure Pfersigberg). Kuentz-Bas makes Gewurztraminer on Pfersigberg that can rival Eichberg, and Charles Baur, Pierre Freudenreich, Alphonse Kuentz and the underrated cooperative at Eguisheim (Wolfberger's wine is spelt 'Pfirsigberg') come not far behind. Bruno Sorg makes a superb, peach-laden Muscat with quite exceptional acidity. Tokay-Pinot Gris is perhaps Eguisheim's least lauded wine, yet it can stand shoulder to shoulder with the best Tokay-Pinot Gris produced anywhere in Alsace. Eguisheim's vineyards are also well placed for the production of Vendange Tardive and Sélection de Grains Noble, with Kuentz-Bas probably the finest exponent of these two late harvest styles. This village is filled with top-performing producers, but at the very pinnacle I would place Léon Beyer, Paul Ginglinger, Kuentz-Bas, Bruno Sorg and Wolfberger – yes,

Wolfberger. I could preface this by advising you to stick to Wolfberger's *grand cru* and other special *cuvées* only, but that would insult its basic Pinot Noir, which is the most consistent red wine in Alsace.

Eichhoffen, Bas-Rhin

Location: 23 miles north of Colmar, between Mittelbergheim and St-Pierre
Area classified as AOC: 175.65 hectares, including 9.2 hectares (or 5 per cent) of *grand cru* vineyards
AOC area under vine: 110 hectares
Grands crus: Moenchberg (9.2 hectares in Eichhoffen, 2.63 hectares in Andlau)
Other vineyard names in use: Kritt (Marc Kreydenweiss and Domaine André & Rémy Gresser)
Soil: Granite
Producers located in the village: Albert Maurer
Others also owning vines in, or making wines from, the village: E. Boeckel, Domaine André & Rémy Gresser, Domaine Kieffer, Marc Kreydenweiss, Gérard Landmann

Eichhoffen is a *Dinghofrecht*, which means that its inhabitants still have the feudal right to be tried in their own court-leet, a form of manorial court. The vines here are dominated by the Muenchberg (*sic*), even though barely more than nine hectares of it are classified Grand Cru Moenchberg, which means that much of the village wine is exceptionally good. Best known for Riesling, Eichhoffen also produces great Tokay-Pinot Gris. Marc Kreydenweiss and Domaine André & Rémy Gresser are the finest producers here. Some great wines are produced in the *lieu-dit* Kritt.

Epfig, Bas-Rhin

Location: 20 miles north of Colmar, between Sélestat and St-Pierre
Area classified as AOC: 655.63 hectares
AOC area under vine: 505 hectares
Grands crus: None
Other vineyard names in use: Fronholz (Domaine Ostertag and Jean-Claude Beck)
Soil: Granite

Producers located in the village: Yves Amberg, Patrick Beyer, Domaine Ostertag
Others also owning vines in, or making wines from, the village: Jean-Claude Beck, André Dussourt, Domaine André & Rémy Gresser, Louis Hauller, Domaine Kieffer, Gérard Landmann

Not one of the most attractive villages, Epfig is unfortunately situated on a busy stretch of the N422 between Sélestat and Obernai. To make matters worse, there is a virtual right-angled bend in the centre of the town, which causes the traffic to slow down just enough to double the amount of exhaust emission. The vision thus impressed on the minds of most people who travel through Epfig is one of grubby, fume-stained buildings. Although I do not know Epfig very well, the village does becomes tranquil as soon you turn off the main road, but if one town in Alsace deserves a by-pass, this is it.

With over 500 hectares of vineyards, it is obviously a very important wine-growing community, but I find it difficult to express an opinion as to its true potential or typicity. Not only is it a vast viticultural area, but it also houses one of the region's largest producers, Arthur Metz, yet who has heard of the firm? It is as unknown as Marne & Champagne, yet like Marne & Champagne, Arthur Metz is the third largest in its region. Many people have drunk its wines dozens of times without realizing it because, like Marne & Champagne, Arthur Metz churns out its production under countless labels. It can be very respectable own-label wine, and I do not criticize that, but does it tell us about Epfig? What percentage of any of these wines comes from this vast viticultural village? It is impossible to say, so we have to look to other more specific growers for the character of Epfig's wines and considering the importance of its vineyards, there are strangely few to be found.

There are Amberg and Patrick Beyer, whose wines I have tasted infrequently, and which have never excited me. A grower called Jean Stumof was listed as 161st in a list of the 175 largest producers in Alsace in 1986, and I have seen a reference to R. & G. Schmitt, but I have never come across their wines, do not know where in the village they live or even if they still exist. So far as I am aware, others who own vineyards in Epfig (André Dussourt of Sherwiller, Domaine André & Rémy Gresser of Andlau, Louis

Hauller of Dambach-la-Ville, Domaine Kieffer of Itterswiller, Gérard Landmann of Nothalten, for example), include their wines in the melting-pot of their respective blended generics, although Jean-Claude Beck of Dambach-la-Ville has produced a fabulous Gewurztraminer from 70 year old vines in Epfig's *lieu-dit* Fronholz.

And that is it, so far as I can tell, except that Domaine Ostertag with young André Ostertag is, of course, Epfig's best producer and in a totally different class from the others. From the quality of his wines, it is as if he really lives somewhere between Eguisheim and Bergheim. His best wines, I must say, come from Nothalten's Grand Cru Muenchberg, but two-thirds of his vineyards are located within Epfig, so the village must have good potential. Most of Epfig's considerable vineyards are located south-west of the village, radiating out from the tiny community of Fronholz, where both Beck and Ostertag have produced some of their most exciting wines.

Ergersheim, Bas-Rhin

Location: 6 miles west of Strasbourg, between Wolxheim and Osthoffen
Area classified as AOC: 118.71 hectares
AOC area under vine: 93 hectares
Grands crus: None
Other vineyard names in use: Kefferberg (Lucien Brand)
Soil: Limestone and marl
Producers located in the village: Lucien Brand

Winemaking in this village dates from at least 916, when the aptly named Bishop Richwin of Strasbourg donated some of Ergersheim's vineyards to the chapter of St-Thomas. In the twelfth century, Herade de Landsberg, the abbess of Hohenbourg (now Mont Ste-Odile, *see* Obernai) and author of the famed *Hortus Deliciarum*, issued a charter obliging the community of Ergersheim to supply all the wine requested by the monks of the neighbouring priory of St-Jorgom. The best wines come from the large swathe of vines growing west of the village, on either side of the old Celtic road, now the D45, which leads to Strasbourg. This includes the Kefferberg, on the south of the road, where Lucien Brand, among others, makes some very nice wines (particularly the Gewurztraminer).

Flexbourg, Bas-Rhin

Location: 15 miles west of Strasbourg on the D118 via Bergbieten
Area classified as AOC: 5.36 hectares
AOC area under vine: 2 hectares
Grands crus: None
Other vineyard names in use: None
Soil: Marl

An insignificant wine village in terms of production, but I am told its soils best suit Riesling.

Furdenheim, Bas-Rhin

Location: 6 miles west of Strasbourg, two-thirds of the way along the N4 *Route Nationale* to Marlenheim
Area classified as AOC: 49.77 hectares
AOC area under vine: 24 hectares
Grands crus: None
Other vineyard names in use: None
Soil: Limestone

I have nothing of significance to report about this modest wine village, except that 25 per cent of its vineyards used to be planted with hybrids until as recently as the early 1970s.

Gertwiller, Bas-Rhin

Location: 25 miles north of Colmar, between Bourgheim and Barr
Area classified as AOC: 168.48 hectares
AOC area under vine: 101 hectares
Grands crus: None
Other vineyard names in use: None
Soil: Sandstone
Producers located in the village: G. Zeyssolff

Historically best known for Sylvaner and Gewurztraminer, the second of which I can vouch for. I have also tasted a splendid Pinot Noir from Zeyssolff.

Gimbrett-Berstett, Bas-Rhin

Location: 9 miles north-west of Strasbourg, taking the D31 and turning
right at Pfettisheim for Berstett, or just before Gougenheim for Gimbrett,
the two villages being connected by the D61 via Rumersheim
Area classified as AOC: 25.56 hectares
AOC area under vine: 4 hectares
Grands crus: None
Other vineyard names in use: None
Soil: Limestone and marl

These two villages are always lumped together for statistical purposes and I have nothing interesting to comment about their insignificant combined production.

Goxwiller, Bas-Rhin

Location: 25 miles north of Colmar, just south of Obernai
Area classified as AOC: 87.99 hectares
AOC area under vine: 67 hectares
Grands crus: None
Other vineyard names in use: None
Soil: Limestone

This wine village set at the foot of Mont Ste-Odile (*see* Obernai) is
of little qualitative note, although fairly important for generic production. It once had a modest reputation for Sylvaner, Pinot and
Traminer.

Gueberschwihr, Haut-Rhin

Location: 6 miles south-south-west of Colmar, in the hills immediately
south of Voegtlinshoffen
Area classified as AOC: 202.25 hectares, including 45.35 hectares (or 22
per cent) of *grand cru* vineyards
AOC area under vine: 152 hectares
Grands crus: Goldert (45.35 hectares)
Other vineyard names in use: Gaentzbrunnen (shared with Pfaffenheim;
CV Pfaffenheim); Rebgarten (CV Pfaffenheim); Clos St-Imer (part of
Grand Cru Goldert, Maison Ernest Burn)

Soil: Sandstone and limestone
Producers located in the village: Maison Ernest Burn, Bernard Humbrecht, Marcel Humbrecht, E. Schillinger
Others also owning vines in, or making wines from, the village: Lucien Gantzer, Marcel Hertzog, CV Pfaffenheim, Domaine Rieflé, Georges Scherb, Maurice Schueller, Domaine Zind Humbrecht

This village was first recorded in 728, when it was called Vila Eberhardo, after the grandson of Aldaric, the father of Ste Odile (*see* Obernai). Gueberschwihr has been justifiably famous for its winemaking since at least the eighth century. Village wines such as Marcel Humbrecht's Muscat are delicious. Bernard Humbrecht also makes a lovely Muscat, but his best wine – and, with the exception of Goldert, Gueberschwihr's – is his scintillating Riesling. The *grand cru* wines are deep in colour and packed with flavour. Muscat and Gewurztraminer are Goldert's favoured varieties, and Domaine Zind Humbrecht and Ernest Burn (Clos St-Imer) their greatest exponents. The cooperative at Pfaffenheim also makes a superb Gewurztraminer.

Guebwiller, Haut-Rhin

Location: 13 miles south-south-west of Colmar
Area classified as AOC: 188 hectares, including 87.3 hectares (or 46 per cent) of *grand cru* vineyards
AOC area under vine: 130 hectares
Grands crus: Kessler (28.5 hectares); Kitterlé (25.79 hectares); Saering (26.75 hectares); Spiegel (6.26 hectares in Guebwiller, 12 hectares in Bergholtz)
Other vineyard names in use: Rebgarten (CV Pfaffenheim)
Soil: Sandstone and limestone
Producers located in the village: Domaine Schlumberger
Others also owning vines in, or making wines from, the village: Domaine Lucien Albrecht, Vins Dirler, Léon Hell-Cadé, Rominger
Annual festivals: Foire aux Vins (Ascension Day)

When the Armagnacs raided Alsace in 1439 and again in 1444–5, they were mostly unopposed, but evidence of at least one unsuccessful attack still exists in Guebwiller. On the night of 14 February 1445, a band of Armagnacs infiltrated Guebwiller. The town had strong walls and a fine moat, allowing the inhabitants to sleep soundly in their beds, but on this night the moat froze, which allowed the Armagnacs to place scaling-ladders against the ramparts. As they scrambled over the fortification, they were heard by a woman called Brigitte Schick, who was simply unable to sleep that particular night. She raised such a racket that the Armagnacs lost the advantage of surprise and, fearing the entire population of Guebwiller would be upon them, called off the attack and retreated with such speed that they left their scaling-ladders behind. These ladders can still be seen in Guebwiller's St-Léger church.

Guebwiller is the gateway to Florival (Valley of Flowers), a long and pretty valley that follows the river Lauch, a tributary of the Ill, which received its poetic name in 1041 from a monk who was struck by the beauty of its flora. A walk along this long and charming valley is thoroughly recommended and those who shy from the effort can always visit Guebwiller's Florival museum. Calling Guebwiller the gateway to Florival could give the reader the wrong impression, for it is not a particularly pretty Alsace village; it is a busy, bustling town with some depressing industrial areas. There are some superb architectural attractions, such as the sixteenth-century Hôtel de Ville and, of course, the Romanesque church of St-Léger, which houses the scaling-ladders abandoned by the Armagnacs, but the town of Guebwiller is a long way from the fairy-tale image of Alsace, although its vineyards are some of the most beautiful and dramatic in the region.

Guebwiller has more *grands crus* than any other Alsace village. Ribeauvillé comes second with three *grands crus*, but only half the 87.3 hectares covered by Guebwiller's four. Eguisheim is, however, number one in terms of surface area, with its 113.6 hectares of *grand cru* vineyards. In truth, Guebwiller could easily have had at least one other *grand cru*, as there are seven *crus* that have historically been responsible for the great fame of this wine village, the other three being Heissenstein (not to be confused with the Heissenstein *lieu-dit* of Nothalten), Schimberg and Wanne. Many believe Wanne and Kitterlé to be Guebwiller's two greatest growths. It seems that it would be politically impossible to grant Guebwiller one more *grand cru*, even if it were acknowledged to be the greatest vineyard in the universe, but it does surprise me that Wanne is not utilized as a *lieu-dit*, especially as J. L. Stoltz ranked it as one of the very best vineyards in Alsace as long ago as 1828.

The wines of Guebwiller were once called 'leg breakers', due to their high alcoholic strength, and Schlumberger, which owns almost 75 per cent of Guebwiller's vineyards, has historically broken the most legs here. As Schlumberger excels in Gewurztraminer and Tokay-Pinot Gris, it is not unreasonable to assume that these are the two most favourable varieties for Guebwiller as a whole, but Schlumberger also grows Riesling of great finesse on Kitterlé and Saering, the second of which can produce excellent Muscat. But Schlumberger does not totally dominate Guebwiller: its truly greatest Riesling is neither Kitterlé nor Saering but Kessler – and it is made by Jean-Pierre Dirler.

Hartmannswiller, Haut-Rhin

Location: 16 miles south-south-west of Colmar, just off the D5, between Wuenheim and Wattwiller
Area classified as AOC: 23.66 hectares
AOC area under vine: 10 hectares
Grands crus: None
Other vineyard names in use: None
Soil: Stony loess

This village lies in the shadow of the Hartmannswillerkopf, which French troops in the First World War renamed Viel Armand because they were unable to pronounce the name of the native land they were told to defend. Viticulturally speaking, however, there has never been much to defend in the vineyards of Hartmannswiller.

Hattstatt, Haut-Rhin

Location: 5 miles south of Colmar, between Eguisheim and Pfaffenheim
Area classified as AOC: 139.16 hectares including 27.06 hectares (or 20 per cent) of *grand cru* vineyards
AOC area under vine: 108 hectares
Grands crus: Hatschbourg (27.06 hectares in Hattstatt, 20.3 hectares in Voegtlinshoffen)
Other vineyard names in use: None
Soil: Limestone and calcareous-marl
Producers owning vines in, or making wines from, the village: Joseph

Cattin, Théo Cattin, Domaine Kehren, Lucien Meyer, CV Pfaffenheim, Gérard & Serge Hartmann, Wolfberger, Domaine Zind Humbrecht

This old market town once had a certain reputation for Clevner (Pinot Blanc), but Gewurztraminer is undoubtedly its finest variety today, especially on the Hatschbourg, where Tokay-Pinot Gris and Riesling also excel and Vendange Tardive seems easy. The best producer here is Joseph Cattin, Roland Guth's *grand cru* selections from Wolfberger coming a close second, then Théo Cattin.

Heiligenstein, Bas-Rhin

Location: 25 miles north of Colmar, between Barr and Obernai
Area classified as AOC: 146.86 hectares
AOC area under vine: 82 hectares
Grands crus: None
Other vineyard names in use: None
Soil: Stony-sandy-clay, clay and limestone
Producers located in the village: Jean Heywang
Others also owning vines in, or making wines from, the village: CV Andlau, Ch. Wantz
Annual festivals: Fête du Klevener de Heiligenstein (second Sunday in August)

The first recorded mention of this village was in charters of 1277 and 1357, when it was known as Hailengenftein, after which it was spelt as Helgenstein, then Heyligenstein, until 1460, since when its name has taken the definitive form of Heiligenstein. As is common throughout much of Alsace, the vineyards of this village date back much further than its mere name, having been planted sometime in the third century.

Heiligenstein is, of course, famous for its Klevener, which has given this village its unique sub-*appellation*. Unique because, of all the other village *appellations* of some repute (Rouge d'Ottrott, Rouge de Rodern, Rosé de Marlenheim, etc.), only Klevener de Heiligenstein has been specifically defined in, and permitted by, AOC regulations. The Klevener, which must not be confused with Klevner (a synonym for Pinot Blanc and never spelt with a middle 'e'), was first brought to Heiligenstein in 1742 by Ehrhardt Wantz, the village burgomaster. With the introduction of this new vine, the vineyards of Heiligenstein underwent a significant expansion, but it was no *fait accompli*. Heiligenstein and its three neighbouring villages had been subject to an agreement drawn up between the lords of Barr and the city of Strasbourg since 1568; there was considerable opposition to this viticultural initiative and Wantz had to wage a legal and bureaucratic battle for its acceptance. In 1742, however, the Council of the Echevins des Strasbourg authorized Heiligenstein to plant Klevener and it was from this that the winemaking reputation of this village blossomed.

The Klevener de Heiligenstein is like a lighter-bodied Gewurztraminer with a restrained aroma and a flowery, slightly smoky hint to the fruit. Indeed, most varieties grown in this village have a more flowery than spicy character and the best share something of the Klevener's restraint and smoky finesse. The best are CV Andlau, Jean Hewang, Eugène Klipfel (though it is not their own production) and Ch. Wantz. In addition to its uniquely famous village wine, Heiligenstein is also one of less than a dozen villages in Alsace that managed to establish something of a reputation for *vin de paille* in the last century. Unlike those of the Haut-Rhin, Heiligenstein's was essentially Muscat-based – a pity they do not make it any more.

Herrlisheim, Haut-Rhin

Location: 5 miles south of Colmar, on the D45, linking the N422 and N83, the two major roads leading south from Colmar
Area classified as AOC: 202.58 hectares
AOC area under vine: 148 hectares
Grands crus: None
Other vineyard names in use: None
Soil: Alluvial topsoil over limestone
Producers located in the village: Pierre Freudenreich
Others also owning vines in, or making wines from, the village: Théo Cattin, Albert Hertz, CV Pfaffenheim, Wolfberger

Although Herrlisheim itself is on the plains, its vineyards are actually on the Vosgien slopes beneath Obermorschwihr and abut those of Hattstatt. This village has some beautifully situated vineyards but the increase of AOC land under the recent reassessment of the communal delimitation is nothing short of astonishing. Prior to the new delimitation, the area classified as AOC was just 93 hectares, but in October 1990 this more than doubled to 202.58 hectares, which is an unprecedented and alarming level of increase. With 148 hectares already under vine, the growers obviously did not stand still, as that is 55 hectares more than originally classified. If the wines of Pierre Freudenreich are anything to go by, Riesling is the best wine here.

Houssen, Haut-Rhin

Location: Just north of Colmar, near the airfield, but on the right side of the N83 going north
Area classified as AOC: 32.80 hectares
AOC area under vine: 18 hectares
Grands crus: None
Other vineyard names in use: None
Soil: Alluvial deposits

You could have knocked me over with a feather when I discovered that vines grow in this village, which is a stone's throw from the D4 turning to Sigolsheim or Bennwihr, when leaving Colmar by the northern route. Few ever think of taking a look at Houssen. I did once, by mistake, and found myself on a quiet back road that returned me to the centre of Colmar. On that accidental encounter with Houssen, I did not see any vines, but I have since returned deliberately to locate them and found a small patch in the north of the village, just before the cemetery, but on the opposite side of the road. It did not look like 18 hectares, so I suppose there must be more elsewhere. Frankly I cannot see the qualitative point of growing any vines here.

Hunawihr, Haut-Rhin

Location: 6 miles north-north-west of Colmar, between Riquewihr and Ribeauvillé
Area classified as AOC: 245.70 hectares, including 26.18 hectares (or 11 per cent) of *grand cru* vineyards
AOC area under vine: 204 hectares
Grands crus: Rosacker (26.18 hectares)
Other vineyard names in use: Clos Ste-Hune (Trimbach); Muehlforst (CV

Hunawihr); Clos du Windsbuhl (J. Meyer by Domaine Zind Humbrecht)
Soil: Marl, limestone and sandstone
Producers located in the village: David Ermel, CV Hunawihr, Mader,
Frédéric Mallo & Fils, Domaine Mittnacht Frères, Domaine du Moulin de
Dusenbach, François Schwach & Fils, Paul Schwach, Domaine Sipp-Mack
Others also owning vines in, or making wines from, the village: Jean
Becker, Maison 'Bott Frères', Dopff & Irion, Dopff Au Moulin, Philippe
Gocker, Jean Huttard, Roger Jung & Fils, Domaine Mittnacht-Klack,
Louis Sipp, F.E. Trimbach, Domaine Zind Humbrecht
Annual festivals: Kilbe (mid-July); Fête des Vendanges (first two weeks in
October)

Mentioned in records dated 1114, Hunawihr was named after
Huna (now Ste-Hune), who lived in the seventh century and
washed the clothes of the ill and elderly in a fountain. After a
disastrous harvest, the water in this fountain is supposed to have
turned into wine. The fountain has survived and is adorned with
flowers every year in memory of Huna's charitable deeds and, no
doubt, in the hope that it may once more flow with wine. Huna and
her husband, Hunon, built a church, which is still standing,
although most of the present structure is relatively recent, dating
from the fifteenth and sixteenth centuries. It is a remarkable building in many ways, not least in that both Catholics and Protestants
worship there.

Hunawihr has a well-established reputation for delicate racy
wines made from Riesling and Gewurztraminer. Even the Knipperlé
and Chasselas, which accounted for more than half the vineyards
until well into the twentieth century, were highly rated. The best
village wines are mostly Gewurztraminer, which can be refreshingly
mild in aroma and have a gentleness of fruit rarely encountered
elsewhere with this variety. I have occasionally tasted a good, albeit
fat and precocious, Pinot Noir, but the phenomenal class of one
variety, Riesling, grown in just one tiny vineyard, Clos Ste-Hune, is
such that it totally dominates the reputation of the entire village.
Owned by Trimbach, Clos Ste-Hune is technically part of Grand
Cru Rosacker, but the firm stubbornly refuses to recognize the fact
on the label (*See* 'Rosacker' entry in Chapter 5 and the 'Trimbach'
profile in Chapter 8). To imagine Clos Ste-Hune the norm, rather
than an exception, would be like expecting every producer in
Margaux to produce Château Margaux, although Domaine Zind

Humbrecht is starting to do very exciting things with its Clos Windsbuhl. With Clos Ste-Hune, Trimbach is far and away the greatest producer here, but Domaine Zind Humbrecht is a super second and excellent wines are also made by Frédéric Mallo, Mader and Sipp-Mack.

Husseren-les-Châteaux, Haut-Rhin

Location: 4 miles south-west of Colmar, in the hills above Eguisheim
Area classified as AOC: 55 hectares
AOC area under vine: 36 hectares
Grands crus: None
Other vineyard names in use: None
Soil: Sandstone and granite
Producers located in the village: Lucie Colombain, Alphonse Kuentz, Kuentz-Bas, Domaine Edouard Leiber, François Lichtlé, André Scherer, Gérard Schueller, Emile Schwartz & Fils, Fernand Stentz
Others also owning vines in, or making wines from, the village: Paul Buecher & Fils, P. Sick-Dreyer, Wolfberger
Annual festivals: The Fête des Guinguettes d'Europe in July is, as its name suggests, a celebration of food, drink, song and dance, the origin of which is not restricted to Alsace, but may come from anywhere in Europe

The 'châteaux' in the name Husseren-les-Châteaux refers to the three ruined and rather eerie castle towers that dominate not only the village, but also the landscape for miles around, yet these are rather confusingly called the Tours d'Eguisheim. There has been a tiny settlement here since Roman times, when an observation post was built here. Anyone who has sipped a glass of wine on the patio of Kuentz-Bas and witnessed the magnificent panorama below will have no difficulty understanding why, but despite this early beginning, viticulture did not start in Husseren-les-Châteaux until well after the Thirty Years War (1618-48), since when it has become known for its Gewurztraminer, Riesling and Pinot Blanc. I have also tasted some well-structured Tokay-Pinot Gris and fresh, flowery Muscat. The luxuriant quality of the wines from Kuentz-Bas make it far and away the greatest producer. André Scherer is next best and both Lucie Colombain and Domaine Edouard Leiber should figure somewhere in the rankings.

Ingershcim, Haut-Rhin

Location: on the western outskirts of Colmar
Area classified as AOC: 378 hectares, including 15 hectares (or 4 per cent) of *grand cru* vineyards
AOC area under vine: 258 hectares
Grands crus: Florimont (15 hectares)
Other vineyard names in use: Dorfburg (CV Ingersheim); Letzenberg (CV Ingersheim); Steinweg (CV Ingersheim, this *lieu-dit* is shared with Wintzenheim and Turckheim, although the vast majority of its considerable vineyards are located in Ingersheim)
Soil: Limestone and marl
Producers located in the village: René Fleith, CV Ingersheim
Others also owning vines in, or making wines from, the village: Les Caves JB Adam, Domaine Pierre Adam, Paul Buecher & Fils, Henri Ehrhart, Ringenbach-Moser, Bruno Sorg

This historic village, which is situated between the Munster and Kaysersberg valleys, was first documented in 768, when it was known as Anngehizeshaim, and has been cultivating the vine since the Middle Ages. It was severely damaged in the Second World War, but some elegant Renaissance houses remain and its rue Josephine Steinlé is famous, having been named after a remarkable former inhabitant who was the oldest woman in France at one time. The local cooperative makes excellent wines across the board under the Jean Geiler label and René Fleith produces fine Auxerrois and Tokay-Pinot Gris, but Ingersheim's single greatest wine is Florimont Riesling and its supreme exponent is Bruno Sorg.

Irmstett, Bas-Rhin

See Scharrachbergheim-Irmstett

Itterswiller, Bas-Rhin

Location: 19 miles north of Colmar, between Andlau and Nothalten
Area classified as AOC: 90.44 hectares
AOC area under vine: 69 hectares
Grands crus: None
Other vineyard names in use: Fruehmess (Domaine Kieffer)

Soil: Sandy-gravel, silty-loess and marl
Producers located in the village: Domaine Kieffer, Jean-Luc Schwartz,
Justin Schwartz
Others also owning vines in, or making wines from, the village: E.
Boeckel, Louis Gisselbrecht, Domaine Ostertag

With such obviously excellent vineyards situated on the south-
facing slopes of an outcrop known locally as the Kirchberg (upon
which the village itself is perched), plainly some very good wines
should be produced here. However, the only pure Itterswiller
wines I have tasted have been from Justin Schwartz and Domaine
Kieffer, which, although decent, were not in any way special.
Kieffer seems to be better overall, but the most successful individual wine was a fruity Pinot Noir from Schwartz, which was
made in a rosé style.

Jungholtz, Haut-Rhin

Location: 15 miles south-south-west of Colmar, via Soultz
Area classified as AOC: 25 herctares
AOC area under vine: 9 hectares
Grands crus: None
Other vineyard names in use: None
Soil: Marly-limestone

From the point of view of soil and topography, there would seem
ample potential here, but I have never knowingly drunk a pure
Jungholtz wine, therefore I cannot comment about the wines. The
former *lieu-dit* of Schauenberg in 1828 was ranked by J. L. Stoltz
as one of the 17 best vineyards in Alsace, which would seem to
support the notion of there being potential.

Katzenthal, Haut-Rhin

Location: 4 miles north-west of Colmar, between Ammerschwihr and the
Ingersheim to Niedermorschwihr road
Area classified as AOC: 211 hectares, including 19.24 hectares (or 9 per
cent) of *grand cru* vineyards
AOC area under vine: 163 hectares
Grands crus: Sommerberg (1.3 hectares in Katzenthal, 26.7 hectares in

Niedermorschwihr); Wineck-Schlossberg (17.94 hectares in Katzenthal, 6.23 hectares in Ammerschwihr)
Other vineyard names in use: None
Soil: Clay and limestone
Producers located in the village: Jean-Marc Bernhard, Jean-Paul Ecklé, Henri Klée, Victor Klée & Fils, Klur-Stoecklé
Others also owning vines in, or making wines from, the village: Domaine Pierre Adam, Albert Boxler, René Fleith, CV Ingersheim, André Mercklé & Fils, Marcel Mullenbach, René & Bernard Schneider, P. Sick-Dreyer, CV Turckheim
Annual festivals: Fête des Vendanges (first two weeks in October)

There are numerous theories about the etymological origin of Katzenthal. Some believe it to be named after a Frankish lord called Kazo, others that it evolved from 'Caïdenthalo', which means 'Valley of the Hills', or 'Kastelthal', which would refer to the eleventh-century Wineck castle, the ruins of which dominate the slopes above the village today, whilst yet another school of thought believes it to be a variation of Katharinenthal, which is a local convent founded in the thirteenth century.

Whatever its origins, it is difficult to believe that Katzenthal was totally destroyed during the winter of 1944–5, but it was meticulously restored in authentic medieval style after the war, along with its vineyards, which accounts for their orderly fashion today. Johann Fischart (1546–1590), the Strasbourg satirist, was among the first to praise the wines of Katzenthal, although both its *grands crus* had been known since the thirteenth century. The vineyards of Katzenthal are best suited to Riesling and Wineck-Schlossberg is, of course, its true *grand cru*, as barely more than one hectare of Sommerberg is actually located within the communal boundaries of this village. The most successful wine is Jean-Paul Eckle's Wineck-Schlossberg Riesling, whereas the best village wine is Victor Klée's straight Riesling, although there are several other fine producers owning vineyards in or producing wines from Katzenthal.

Kaysersberg, Haut-Rhin

Location: 5 miles north-west of Colmar, via either Ammerschwihr or Kientzheim

Area classified as AOC: 107 hectares, including 0.5 hectares (or 0.5 per cent) of *grand cru* vineyards
AOC area under vine: 35 hectares
Grands crus: Schlossberg (0.5 in Kaysersberg, 79.5 hectares in Kientzheim)
Other vineyard names in use: None
Soil: Granite to the north; alluvial plain to the south
Producers located in the village: Salzmann-Thomann, Domaine Weinbach
Others also owning vines in, or making wines from, the village: Paul Blanck & Fils, Claude Dietrich, CV Kientzheim-Kaysersberg, Jean Halbeizen, Albert Mann

The site of this village was strategically placed on Rome's most important route between Gaul and the Rhine Valley, which is why it became known as *Caesaris Mons* or Caesar's Peak and, thus, Kaysersberg. It has other claims to fame. By 1354 the village was important enough to be a member of the decapolis, a military and commercial alliance formed to free Alsace from the control of the Hapsburg princes. By the end of the next century, however, Kaysersberg was firmly under the control of Maximilian I (1459–1519), who was Holy Roman Emperor from 1486. It is believed that Maximilian installed Baron Schwendi as the bailiff of Kaysersberg, but the truth is not clear. Schwendi owned the village of Kientzheim, less than a mile away and nearby Wintzenheim was his fief, so it is quite possible that this village was also his domain. Kaysersberg is also famous for being the birthplace of Albert Schweitzer (1875–1965) and was one of less than a dozen villages in Alsace to have a genuine reputation for *vin de paille* in the nineteenth century. The steep slopes of the Bixkoepflé have long been considered the village's best vineyards, but although most of Schlossberg is situated very close to Kaysersberg on the slopes of the Bixkoepflé, virtually all of this *grand cru* falls within the communal boundaries of Kientzheim. Ironically, most of what little of Bixkoepflé does fall within Kaysersberg is not actually classified as *grand cru*. It is, however, on these very steep, west-facing slopes that Kaysersberg produces its best wine from Gewurztraminer vines. Schlossberg Gewurztraminer excels in less sunny years, but in truly great years it is the Gewurztraminer grown in this little viticultural enclave of Kaysersberg that is best.

Kienheim, Bas-Rhin

Location: 9 miles north-north-west from Strasbourg, taking the D31 and turning left just before Gougenheim
Area classified as AOC: 46.69 hectares
AOC area under vine: 5 hectares
Grands crus: None
Other vineyard names in use: None
Soil: Limestone and marl

This village is of very minor importance.

Kientzheim, Haut-Rhin

Location: 4 miles north-west of Colmar, between Sigolsheim and Kaysersberg
Area classified as AOC: 293.80 hectares including 93.8 hectares (or 32 per cent) of *grand cru* vineyards
AOC area under vine: 216 hectares
Grands crus: Furstentum (14.3 hectares in Kientzheim, 11.35 hectares in Sigolsheim); Schlossberg (79.5 hectares in Kientzheim, 0.5 in Kaysersberg)
Other vineyard names in use: Altenbourg (Paul Blanck and Claude Dietrich); Clos des Capucins (Faller's Domaine Weinbach); Grafreben (Paul Blanck and CV Kientzheim-Kaysersberg); Patergarten (Paul Blanck, Alphonse Gueth and CV Kientzheim-Kaysersberg); Coteaux du Haut-Koenigsbourg (Domaine Siffert and Bernhard-Reibel)
Soil: Granite to the north-west; sandy-shingle alluvial plain to the east and west; limestone, marl and sandstone to the north
Producers located in the village: André Blanck, Paul Blanck & Fils, Claude Dietrich, CV Kientzheim-Kaysersberg
Others also owning vines in, or making wines from, the village: Domaine Pierre Adam, Dopff & Irion, Dopff Au Moulin, Alphonse Gueth, Albert Mann, Jean-Paul Mauler, Ringenbach-Moser, Salzmann-Thomann, André Thomas & Fils, Domaine Weinbach, Maison Wiederhirn
Annual festivals: Fête du Vin (last weekend in July)

Winemaking was of sufficient importance to be mentioned in the first documented evidence of this village in 785, when it was known as Cönesheim. The castle, now the home of the Confrérie St-Étienne, was built by the counts of Lupfen, who owned the village for several centuries. It was later owned by Baron Lazare de Schwendi, who is buried in the local church. Kientzheim was one of less than a dozen villages in Alsace to have a reputation for *vin de paille* in the nineteenth century and, in November 1975, its Schlossberg vineyard became the first *grand cru* in Alsace to be officially recognized. Schlossberg Gewurztraminer is Kientzheim's most famous wine, even though it actually fares best in poorer years. It is Schlossberg Riesling, however, that is currently the most exciting wine this village produces, as the superb examples from Paul Blanck and Madame Faller of Domaine Weinbach demonstrate. When grown on the fertile plain of the Weiss valley, Gewurztraminer makes an appealing, fruity wine that is easy to drink and best when young. In really sunny vintages, the finest Gewurztraminer generally comes from the slopes of the Mont de Sigolsheim north of the village and the best of these are grown on the *grand cru* of Furstentum, where Riesling and Tokay-Pinot Gris fare even better.

Kintzheim, Bas-Rhin

Location: 11 miles north of Colmar, between Châtenois and Orschwiller
Area classified as AOC: 199.98 hectares, including 11.9 hectares (or 6 per cent) of *grand cru* vineyards
AOC area under vine: 125 hectares
Grands crus: Praelatenberg (11.9 hectares in Kintzheim, 0.1 hectares in Orschwiller)
Other vineyard names in use: None
Soil: Granite
Producers located in the village: Jean-Marie Koehly
Others also owning vines in, or making wines from, the village: Jean Becker, Raymond Engel, Domaine Siffert
Annual festivals: Fête de St-Urbain (nearest Saturday to 25 May)

Kintzheim is known for its Montagne des Singes or Monkeys' Mountain, where hundreds of monkeys of various species roam an open-air reserve. Even more famous is its Volerie des Aigles, a spectacular outdoor display where eagles swoop so close overhead that the viewing public feels the slipstream. This village once had a reputation for Chasselas and Traminer (*sic*), but I have had a superb oak-aged Pinot Noir from Jean-Marie Koehly. Most of the grapes grown closest to the village end up in generic blending vats, but its best vineyards are to be found a mile away, overlooking Orschwiller. The *grand cru* slope of Praelatenberg is so close to Orschwiller that it actually abuts the buildings of that village, but the communal boundary of Kintzheim extends right to the outlying buildings of Orschwiller and appropriates all of its best vineyards. Having said that, Praelatenberg has yet to make its mark as a serious *cru*, let alone a genuine *grand cru*. The only wine of true *grand cru* quality made here has been a Gewurztraminer from Jean Becker in 1990 and that firm does not even own any vines here, which means the locals need to pull up their socks!

Kirchheim, Bas-Rhin

Location: 9 miles west of Strasbourg on the N4 *Route Nationale*, turning left just before Marlenheim
Area classified as AOC: 35.57 hectares
AOC area under vine: 22 hectares
Grands crus: None
Other vineyard names in use: None
Soil: Limestone

Residences in Kirchheim were once owned by Dagobert, the Merovingian king, and Charles the Fat, Holy Roman Emperor. The vineyards of this village come within the generic geographical designation of Coteaux du Mossig. I have no idea whether I have tasted a pure Kirchheim wine. I certainly have not come across a wine that claimed to be one.

Leimbach, Haut-Rhin

Location: 23 miles south-south-west of Colmar, just south of Thann & Vieux-Thann
Area classified as AOC: 23 hectares
AOC area under vine: 1 hectare
Grands crus: None
Other vineyard names in use: None
Soil: Gravel and limestone

If not for a small spur of Vosgien foothill, this small community would merely be a southern suburb of Thann and Vieux-Thann, although its classified area is nowhere near the vineyards of those great wine villages. Leimbach is really better suited to orchards.

Marlenheim, Bas-Rhin

Location: 9 miles west of Strasbourg on the N4 *Route Nationale* just before Wasselone
Area classified as AOC: 155.23 hectares, including 24 hectares (or 15 per cent) of *grand cru* vineyards
AOC area under vine: 75 hectares
Grands crus: Steinklotz (24 hectares)
Other vineyard names in use: None
Soil: Limestone
Producers located in the village: Romain Fritsch, Maison Michel Laugel
Annual festivals: Fête des Vendanges (third Sunday in October)

In 589 Bishop Georgius Florentius, otherwise known as St-Gregory of Tours, praised the wines of Marlenheim. He also recorded that Childebert II sentenced one of his lords to forced labour in the royal vineyards at Marlenheim. Best known for Pinot Noir and originally famous for *Vorlauf*, a light red wine that must have been similar in style to the Rosé des Riceys from the Aube, in that it was betwixt and between a light red and a dark rosé. The virtues of *Vorlauf* were first extolled in 1582 and although the wine can still be found today, the village is now known for its Rosé de Marlenheim, a fresh and fruity wine made in an authentic rosé style. Commercially, this village is dominated by Laugel, an underrated producer that is often misjudged due to the large scale of its production. Good and bad come in all sizes. Laugel might be a large producer, but definitely has the capacity to be a good one, as its Riesling Grand Cru Steinklotz demonstrates. From the same *grand cru*, I have had good Tokay-Pinot Gris from Romain Fritsch. The vineyards of this village generally come within the generic geographical designation of Coteaux du Mossig.

Mittelbergheim, Bas-Rhin

Location: 22 miles north of Colmar, between Barr and Andlau
Area classified as AOC: 208.89 hectares, including 34 hectares (or 16 per cent) of *grand cru* vineyards

AOC area under vine: 150 hectares
Grands crus: Zotzenberg (34 hectares)
Other vineyard names in use: Brandluft (Christian Dolder, Haegi and
Seltz); Côte des Amandiers (Jean Greiner, Greiner-Schleret and Edgard
Schaller)
Soil: Mostly heavy calcareous-clay, but also lighter sandy soil mixed with
limestone and clay, while some areas have a deep sandstone scree over marl
and others are more limestone
Producers located in the village: E. Boeckel, Christian Dolder, Armand
Gilg, GAEC Bernard & Daniel Haegi, Julien Rieffel & Fils, Pierre &
Jean-Pierre Rietsch, Alsace Seltz, André Wantz, André Wittmann
Others also owning vines in, or making wines from, the village: Ed. Hering
& Fils, Ch. Wantz
Annual festivals: Fête du Vin (last weekend in July)

The vineyards here date back to 388 and records of the quantity,
quality and outstanding characteristics of every vintage since 785
have survived in the local archives. Mittelbergheim is justifiably
famous for Sylvaner, a variety that once claimed more than 70 per
cent of its vineyards. Although Zotzenberg Sylvaner, which can
have a resinous complexity but cannot claim *grand cru* status, has
the greatest reputation as a *vin de garde*, Sylvaner on the pure
limestone Stein vineyard immediately south of the village has more
finesse and is probably superior. When this variety is grown on the
lower slopes of the Crax to the west of the village in an area known
as the Forst, it produces light wines that are low in alcohol, high in
acidity and can even taste like Sauvignon Blanc when young, which
is exactly when these wines should be drunk. Other varieties can be
quite smoky, a characteristic shared with vines growing in Barr
and, to a lesser extent, Heiligenstein.

Mittelwihr, Haut-Rhin

Location: 5 miles north-north-west of Colmar, immediately adjacent to
Bennwihr
Area classified as AOC: 208 hectares, including 12 hectares (or 6 per cent)
of *grand cru* vineyards
AOC area under vine: 172 hectares
Grands crus: Mandelberg (12 hectares)
Other vineyard names in use: None

Soil: Gravel over limestone

Producers located in the village: Baumann-Zirgel, Frédéric Berger, Philippe Gocker, Jean Greiner, GAEC Greiner-Schleret, Ernest Horcher & Fils, Jean-Paul Mauler, J. C. Preiss-Henny, Edgard Schaller & Fils, Philippe Scheidecker, J. Siegler Père & Fils, Jean-Paul & Denis Specht, Bernard Wurtz, W. Wurtz, J-J Ziegler-Mauler

Others also owning vines in, or making wines from, the village: Domaine Pierre Adam, CV Beblenheim, Maison Bott-Geyl, Domaine Marcel Deiss, Dopff Au Moulin, Jean Huttard, Frédéric Mallo & Fils, André Mercklé & Fils, CV Ribeauvillé, Maison Wiederhirn

Annual festivals: Fête des Amandiers (first Sunday in August)

Known locally as the 'sud de France de l'Alsace' because almond trees can blossom and flourish (hence Mandelberg), Mittelwihr has been in existence since at least the third century, when the Romans called it Flaviacum, the origins of the name stemming from Mittenwihr or 'middle village', which was first documented in 974. After 17 centuries of continued existence, Mittelwihr was totally destroyed in the Second World War, although few can believe it. Looking at the half-timbered buildings of seemingly medieval origin, it is impossible to imagine that except for a small chunk of the village church, nothing of the original Mittelwihr was left standing after the battle of the Colmar Pocket. Every house was faithfully replicated, although the local castle, which used to belong to Preiss-Henny, was not rebuilt. Mittelwihr and Bennwihr are like one village without any hint of a join. You can drive into one looking for the start of the other and be out of both before you realize it.

Mittelwihr was well reputed for its Chasselas at one time and, curiously, produces Sylvaner that often has a fine bouquet while its Gewurztraminer can be very discreet indeed, traits that also occur in Bennwihr and Beblenheim, both of which share the same soil. The exception is Jean-Paul Mauler's Grand Cru Mandelberg Gewurztraminer, which seems to be supercharged in both intensity and acidity, but Riesling is the true king of the Mandelberg and Edgar Schaller is its greatest exponent. There are, however, more than enough excellent growers both on the *grand cru* specifically and in the village generally to make it easy to seek out excellent wines here.

Molsheim, Bas-Rhin

Location: 10 miles west of Strasbourg, east of Mutzig and north of Obernai
Area classified as AOC: 186.98 hectares, including 19 hectares (or 10 per cent) of *grand cru* vineyards
AOC area under vine: 88 hectares
Grands crus: Bruderthal (19 hectares)
Other vineyard names in use: Finkenberg (Bernard Becht and Bernard Weber)
Soil: Limestone
Producers located in the village: Gérard Neumeyer, Bernard Weber
Annual festivals: Foire Régionale aux Vins (1 May); Reconstitution du Mariage de l'Ami Fritz (14 and 15 August); Fête des Vendanges (third Sunday in October)

The most intriguing architectural attraction of this ancient university town is the *Metzig*, a sixteenth-century meat market in the town square, with magnificent voluted gables, yet dominated by a double staircase that rises on the outside of the building to a first-floor entrance beneath an ornate clock tower. Riesling and Gewurztraminer are reputed to be the best varieties: the latter is supposed to be very floral and I have tasted good, fruity Riesling from this village, including an elegant wine from the Grand Cru Bruderthal by Bernard Weber. Otherwise very little has impressed me. Several redundant *lieux-dits* in Molsheim used to be famous for Sylvaner and I suspect that was its true limit.

Mutzig, Bas-Rhin

Location: 14 miles west of Strasbourg, just west of Molsheim
Area classified as AOC: 99.57 hectares
AOC area under vine: 37 hectares
Grands crus: None
Other vineyard names in use: None
Soil: Limestone

This old fortified town situated at the opening of the Bruche Valley has always been more famous for beer than wine. Alsace makes more than a third of all the beer produced in France and the Mutzig brand is one of the best known.

Niedermorschwihr, Haut-Rhin

Location: 4 miles west of Colmar, in the hills above Turckheim
Area classified as AOC: 96.50 hectares, including 26.7 hectares (or 28 per cent) of *grand cru* vineyards
AOC area under vine: 52 hectares
Grands crus: Sommerberg (26.7 hectares in Niedermorschwihr, 1.3 hectares in Katzenthal)
Other vineyard names in use: None
Soil: Limestone
Producers located in the village: Albert Boxler, Justin Boxler, Marcel Mullenbach
Others also owning vines in, or making wines from, the village: CV Ingersheim, Bruno Sorg, Domaine Aimé Stentz, CV Turckheim
Annual festivals: Fête des Vendanges (first two weeks in October)

This village used to be a haven for Chasselas, but is best known now for Riesling, especially from the steep slopes of Sommerberg. I used to think the vines here were too high, but the erratic genius of Albert Boxler has forced me to change my mind. Marcel Mullenbach produces excellent village Gewurztraminer, and neither CV Ingersheim nor Domaine Aimé Stentz should be ignored.

Nordheim, Bas-Rhin

Location: 7 miles west of Strasbourg, just north of Marlenheim
Area classified as AOC: 119.41 hectares
AOC area under vine: 60 hectares
Grands crus: None
Other vineyard names in use: None
Soil: Limestone and marl

I do not know anyone who owns vines here and have never knowingly tasted a pure Nordheim wine, but the vineyards look well sited for quality, particularly on the Zahlberg to the north of the village and Schoenenberg (*sic*) to the west, both of which have south-east facing slopes of excellent exposition.

Nothalten, Bas-Rhin

Location: 18 miles north of Colmar, between Blienschwiller and
Itterswiller
Area classified as AOC: 172.73 hectares, including 18 hectares (or 10 per
cent) of *grand cru* vineyards
AOC area under vine: 157 hectares
Grands crus: Muenchberg (18 hectares)
Other vineyard names in use: A360P (Domaine Ostertag for 'subversive'
vinification of Tokay-Pinot Gris from Muenchberg); Heissenberg
(Domaine Julien Meyer, Domaine Ostertag); Heissenstein (Domaine Julien
Meyer); Zellberg (Domaine Julien Meyer)
Soil: Marly-colluvium over granite
Producers located in the village: Roger & Roland Geyer, Gérard
Landmann, Domaine Julien Meyer
Others also owning vines in, or making wines from, the village: Willy
Gisselbrecht, Domaine Ostertag, Jean-Luc Schwartz
Annual festivals: Fête du Vin (first Sunday in July)

Well over half of these mountain vineyards were once planted with
Sylvaner and Domaine Julien Meyer is one producer today who is
keeping up the tradition with his superb Sylvaner from the *lieu-dit*
of Zellberg. This village nestles under the protective bulk of the
Undersberg, a 901-metre peak, which is very high this end of the
Vosges mountains. Sylvaner apart, Nothalten is obviously a
Riesling village, the best coming from its Grand Cru Muenchberg
and the greatest Riesling Grand Cru Muenchberg is made by Domaine Ostertag, especially young André Ostertag's Vieilles Vignes.
He makes fabulous Tokay-Pinot Gris from this vineyard too.
Gérard Landmann produces a fat and juicy Riesling that is
immensely enjoyable, although not in the same class as Ostertag's,
nor as exceptional for its variety as Landmann's own Sylvaner.

Oberhoffen, Bas-Rhin

Location: 2 miles south of Wissembourg, in the extreme north of the
region, some 35 miles north of Strasbourg
Area classified as AOC: 9.09 hectares
AOC area under vine: 8 hectares
Grands crus: None

Other vineyard names in use: Karchweg (CV Cléebourg)
Soil: Silty-sandy clay

The entire production from this village is utilized by the CV
Cléebourg. More than half of Oberhoffen's vineyards fall within
the south-facing *lieu-dit* Karchweg, where Tokay-Pinot Gris is supposed to excel. *See* Cléebourg.

Obermorshwihr, Haut-Rhin

Location: 5 miles south-south-west of Colmar, half-way up the slopes from
Hattstatt to Voegtlinshoffen
Area classified as AOC: 148 hectares
AOC area under vine: 118 hectares
Grands crus: None
Other vineyard names in use: Bildstoeckle (Laurent Bannworth)
Soil: Limestone, sandstone and calcareous-clay
Producers located in the village: Laurent Bannwarth & Fils
Others also owning vines in, or making wines from, the village: Théo
Cattin, Kuentz-Bas, CV Pfaffenheim, Gérard Schueller, Wolfberger

I have not knowingly tasted a pure Obermorschwihr wine, but its
vineyards, which face south-east south of the village and south and
east in the north, are beautifully situated, owned by some excellent
producers and hemmed in by the vines of Hattstatt, Voegtlinshoffen and Eguisheim, so I can only presume they are as prime as they
look.

Obernai, Bas-Rhin

Location: 27 miles north of Colmar, 15 miles south-west of Strasbourg
Area classified as AOC: 363.16 hectares
AOC area under vine: 128 hectares
Grands crus: None
Other vineyard names in use: Clos Ste-Odile (CV Obernai); Schenkenberg
(Seilly)
Soil: Sandy
Producers located in the village: CV Obernai, GAEC Seilly
Annual festivals: Fête des Vendanges (third Sunday in October)

Established by Celts, Obernai is one of the oldest towns in Alsace. It was well known in Gallo-Roman times, prosperous under the Franks, provided residence for the dukes of Alsace in the Middle Ages and boasted the privileges of an imperial city during the seventeenth century. The first viticultural mention of Obernai was in 788, when the town was called Ehinhaim, which then became Ehenheim and finally Ober Ehenheim before adopting its current usage, but this town is most famous for Ste-Odile. Born in the seventh century blind, ugly and mentally defective, Odile was unwanted by her father, Adalric, who was a Merovingian lord and the Duke of Alsace. He longed for a son and heir and was so depressed by the arrival of a child who was not only the wrong sex, but also seemed defective in every other way that he ordered her killed. Odile was saved, however, by her nurse and the legend is that when she was baptized, her sight and intellect were not only miraculously restored, but she also transformed instantly into a woman of great beauty. She founded a convent on top of what is now Mont Ste-Odile, the Holy Mountain of Alsace, and this convent owned Obernai until the twelfth century. There is even a 10.5 hectare Clos Ste-Odile in Obernai, the wine of which is made and marketed through the local cooperative.

Another plausible story concerns Obernai's celebrated 'Vin de Pistolet', which carries a label bearing an old flintlock pistol. This one is set in 1562 when the Emperor Ferdinand was passing through the village. He was invited by the mayor to taste the town's wines and, having found them excellent, informed the mayor of this fact. Flattered by the compliment, the mayor enthusiastically revealed to the emperor that the town's people had an even better wine, but it was so good that they reserved it strictly for themselves. Indignant that these small town folk had the effrontery to deny their emperor their best wine, yet fully cognizant of the dignity of his own position, Ferdinand handed the mayor his pistol and told him that should he ever encounter anyone more insolent than himself, the mayor had permission to shoot that person. If true, Ferdinand had more style then than the 'Vin du Pistolet' has now. The best yardstick for Obernai is, however, the cooperative's wines, of which Clos Ste-Odile is the most famous: not a great wine, but a good one certainly. From this vineyard, it is Tokay-Pinot Gris that excels, followed closely by the Gewurztraminer, with Riesling a definite third. Under the cooperative's own label, which accounts for 98 per cent of its total production, CV Obernai currently makes Gewurztraminer of some finesse and has in the past been quite successful with a very fruity Riesling and a lively, floral Muscat.

Odratzheim, Bas-Rhin

Location: 8 miles west of Strasbourg, between Kirchheim and Scharrachbergheim
Area classified as AOC: 41.63 hectares
AOC area under vine: 25 hectares
Grands crus: None
Other vineyard names in use: None
Soil: Limestone

The vineyards of this village come within the generic geographical designation of Coteaux du Mossig, but I have not knowingly tasted a pure Odratzheim wine.

Orschwihr, Haut-Rhin

Location: 12 miles south-south-west of Colmar, just up the road from Bergholtz and contiguous with Bergholtz-Zell
Area classified as AOC: 230.40 hectares, including 28 hectares (or 12 per cent) of *grand cru* vineyards
AOC area under vine: 193 hectares
Grands crus: Pfingstberg (28 hectares)
Other vineyard names in use: Bollenberg (Château d'Orschwihr and Vignobles Reinhart); Clos Himmelreich (Lucien Albrecht); Lippelsberg (Matterne Haegelin)
Soil: Limestone
Producers located in the village: Domaine Lucien Albrecht, Camille Braun & Fils, François Braun, Joseph Gsell, M. Haegelin, Château d'Orschwihr, Raymond Rabold, Vignobles Reinhart, Jean-Michel Welty
Others also owning vines in, or making wines from, the village: Théo Cattin, Wolfberger
Annual festivals: Fête du Crémant (first weekend in July)

First recorded in 728, when it was called Otaleswilre in documents donating the village to Murbach Abbey by Eberhard, the first Duke of Eguisheim. This terraced village with its splendid Renaissance houses is bounded by the Bollenberg and was a fief of the Hapsburgs from the thirteenth to fifteenth century. It still possesses the remains of a fine baronial hall. Orschwihr used to be known for its Pinot Blanc and Tokay-Pinot Gris and some of the best wines in my experience have certainly been from the latter grape, especially when grown on the Grand Cru Pfingstberg, but I also rate Gewurztraminer, which can have real richness and some class. Lucien Albrecht makes the best Tokay-Pinot Gris and one of the best Gewurztraminers. François Braun makes a comparable Gewurztraminer and the finest Riesling, which has such finesse that Orschwihr must be well suited to this variety. His generic Muscat is attractively fresh and floral, with crisp fruit. Camille Braun produces a brilliant Klevner Vieilles Vignes Cuvée Marguerite-Anne, which supports Orschwihr's history of this grape, and a deliciously fruity Gewurztraminer Cuvée St-Nicolas. Matterne Haegelin makes a fabulously rich Tokay-Pinot Gris Cuvée Elise. Of the *lieux-dits*, the Bollenberg has historically grown Gewurztraminer of some note and is by far the most famous, but Lippelsberg also has an authentic reputation.

Orschwiller, Bas-Rhin

Location: 11 miles north of Colmar, between Kintzheim and St-Hippolyte
Area classified as AOC: 93.19 hectares, including 0.1 hectares (or just over 0.1 per cent) of *grand cru* vineyards
AOC area under vine: 66 hectares
Grands crus: Praelatenberg (0.1 hectares in Orschwiller, 11.9 hectares in Kintzheim)
Other vineyard names in use: Coteaux du Haut-Koenigsbourg (Domaine Siffert and Bernhard-Reibel)
Soil: Limestone
Producers located in the village: Allimant-Laugner, Claude Bléger, Raymond Engel, CV Orschwiller, Domaine Siffert, A. Zimmermann
Others also owning vines in, or making wines from, the village: Domaine Muller-Koeberle

Vines have been cultivated in this most southerly village of the Bas-Rhin since at least the eighth century. Stand back and admire the lovely slope of vines that totally dominates this village. That is Praelatenberg. It is a *grand cru* and although it has yet to prove itself with any consistency, it is obviously the best site for vines in the area. When you look at the hill above Orschwiller, it is impossible to imagine why it should come within the communal boundary of Kintzheim, which is a mile away, around the corner, where it is impossible to glimpse Praelatenberg even with a telescope! But Kintzheim's it is, only the bottom couple of rows actually wandering into Orschwiller's official domain, so we must judge the quality of this village on the vineyards located to the east on much flatter ground, and a small spur of steeper vineyards to the west, although I dare say that historically the wines of Praelatenberg played a large part in creating the reputation of Orschwiller, which was once famous for its Gewurztraminer. Within this restriction, however, there is a surprising potential for Tokay-Pinot Gris and Pinot Noir, while the Riesling can have an aromatic elegance.

Osenbach, Haut-Rhin

Location: 10 miles south-south-west of Colmar, in the hills, via Soultzmatt
Area classified as AOC: 49.29 hectares
AOC area under vine: 9 hectares
Grands crus: None
Other vineyard names in use: None
Soil: Limestone

What few vineyards there are here are tucked away to the west of Osenbach itself in an area known as Holtzberg (although I have never seen it used as a *lieu-dit*), just south of a small holiday village called Waldacker. These south-facing vineyards appear to be better situated for viticulture than a couple of thousand hectares on the plains are, but in the recent reassessment of the communal delimitation of Alsace, the area classified as AOC was dropped by more than half from its previous total of 104.1 hectares, so no doubt other interests are at work. Another holiday development, perhaps?

Osthoffen, Bas-Rhin

Location: 5 miles west of Strasbourg, between Furdenheim and Egersheim
Area classified as AOC: 48 hectares
AOC area under vine: 29 hectares
Grands crus: None

Other vineyard names in use: None
Soil: Limestone

I know nothing about this village or its wines.

Ottrott, Bas-Rhin

Location: 13 miles south-west of Strasbourg, between Boersch-St-Léonard and St-Nabor
Area classified as AOC: 57.64 hectares
AOC area under vine: 23 hectares
Grands crus: None
Other vineyard names in use: None
Soil: Scree-covered grey limestone
Producers owning vines in, or making wines from, the village: Ch. Wantz

Set at the foot of Mont Ste-Odile (*see* Obernai), Ottrott has been famous for its red wines since medieval times, but really does not deserve its reputation, the best such wine today being simply an enjoyable fruity red from Ch. Wantz that has more to do with winemaking technique than *terroir*. If the truth be known, far more of Ottrott's vineyards were traditionally planted Sylvaner than Pinot Noir. It was also one of less than a dozen villages in Alsace to establish a reputation for *vin de paille* in the last century and, unlike those of the Haut-Rhin, Ottrott's was essentially Muscat-based. Perhaps they should have another try?

Pfaffenheim, Haut-Rhin

Location: 7 miles south of Colmar, between Rouffach and Hattstatt
Area classified as AOC: 316.13 hectares, including 38 hectares (or 12 per cent) of *grand cru* vineyards
AOC area under vine: 256 hectares
Grands crus: Steinert (38 hectares)
Other vineyard names in use: Bergweingarten (CV Pfaffenheim and Pierre Frick); Gaentzbrunnen (shared with Gueberschwihr, CV Pfaffenheim); Schneckenberg (part of Steinert, CV Pfaffenheim)
Soil: Brown calcareous
Producers located in the village: François Flesch, Pierre Frick, CV Pfaffenheim, Domaine Rieflé, François Runner, E. Schaeflé, Pierre-Paul Zink

Others also owning vines in, or making wines from, the village: Domaine
Zind Humbrecht

This village has always had a reputation for Pinot Blanc, which is
fatter than that found just a few kilometres north or south, yet has
fine acidity. Pfaffenheim is now also appreciated for Tokay-Pinot
Gris and for its Crémant, made from either Pinot Blanc or Tokay-
Pinot Gris or a combination of the two. Sylvaner responds well
here, providing a wine that is not without a certain complexity,
although it is in no way a *vin de garde*. This is one of the most
underrated wine villages in Alsace, with an excellent cooperative
and an up-and-coming *grand cru*. With producers such as Pierre
Frick, Domaine Rieflé and, especially, Domaine Zind Humbrecht,
growing vines here, Pfaffenheim needs no further endorsement of
its viticultural potential.

Reichsfeld, Bas-Rhin

Location: 15 miles north of Colmar, down a dead-end track up in the hills,
turning off the D35 between Eichoffen and Itterswiller, on to the D253,
then the D202
Area classified as AOC: 102.95 hectares
AOC area under vine: 14 hectares
Grands crus: None
Other vineyard names in use: None
Soil: Schist and volcano-sedimentary rock
Producers located in the village: A. Ruhlmann

A visit to this relatively unknown, but charming village at the foot
of the Ungersberg and overlooked by the Forêt d'Andlau is well
worth the detour. Reichsfeld is mountain vineyard country and
Sylvaner used to dominate here until as recently as the early 1970s.
Good acid levels obviously helped to make Ruhlmann's splendid
1988 Crémant d'Alsace, although I cannot comment in any depth
about the full wine potential of this village.

Ribeauvillé, Haut-Rhin

Location: 7 miles north-north-west of Colmar, between Bennwihr and
Bergheim

Area classified as AOC: 455.40 hectares, including 43.93 hectares (or 10 per cent) of *grand cru* vineyards
AOC area under vine: 326 hectares
Grands crus: Geisberg (8.53 hectares); Kirchberg de Ribeauvillé (11.4 hectares); Osterberg (24 hectares)
Other vineyard names in use: Clos du Schlossberg (Jean Sipp); Clos du Zahnacker (CV Ribeauvillé); Côtes de Ribeauvillé (Louis Sipp); Trottacker (Jean Sipp)
Soil: Marl and sandstone
Producers located in the village: Robert Faller & Fils, André Kientzler, CV Ribeauvillé, Domaine Jean Sipp, Louis Sipp, F.E. Trimbach
Others also owning vines in, or making wines from, the village: Jean-Pierre Baltenweck, Maison Bott-Geyl, Jean Huttard, Mader, Frédéric Mallo & Fils, Domaine Mittnacht Frères, Domaine Sipp-Mack, Jean-Paul & Denis Specht
Annual festivals: Fête de Kugelhopf (June: crowded but fun); Fête du Vin (July); Fête du Vin (last-but-one weekend in July); Fête des Ménériers or *Pfifferdaj* (first Sunday in September)

The first mention of Ribeauvillé was in 759, when it was known as Ratbertovilare, or Ratberto's villa, just a few years before the earliest documented evidence of local viticulture in 768. After ownership by various dukes, counts and archbishops, the village became the fief of the counts of Ribeaupierre, who were *ménétriers* or wandering minstrels. The Ribeaupierres lived in three castles, St-Ulrich, Giersberg and Haut-Ribeaupierre, whose famous ruins dominate the steep, rocky escarpment that rises from the dense forest behind the village. Ribeauvillé is definitely one of the most attractive and well-preserved villages in Alsace, although so many tourists make a beeline for it that it is also one of the busiest. Nearby is the famous Carola mineral water spring. If, like me, you do not like your water to be tainted with a minerally flavour, preferring it to taste clean and crisp, then Carola is for you. Not that you will have the choice of anything else in restaurants and winstubs the length and breadth of Alsace.

Guebwiller has more *grands crus* than Ribeauvillé, but the three growths of Ribeauvillé are at least their equal in reputation and produce stunning wines that rank with the very best in all Alsace. Riesling is perhaps the greatest variety and F.E. Trimbach's Cuvée Frédéric Émile is consistently the finest produced. F.E. Trimbach and André Kientzler are Ribeauvillé's top producers, but you cannot ignore some of the superb wines made by the two Sipps. Robert Faller & Fils should also be considered, particularly for its wines from the *grands crus* Geisberg and Kirchberg de Ribeauvillé. Mader has more vineyards in Hunawihr, of course, but Ribeauvillé does represent one-third of his domaine and his quality is exciting and on the up. I do not include the top-performing Frédéric Mallo & Fils in my round-up of best producers because he owns only 0.3 hectares in Ribeauvillé, his reputation being built more on Mittelwihr and Hunawihr. There can be no denying the quality of Ribeauvillé generally for all the noble varieties, and a classic blend of exceptional quality is produced by CV Ribeauvillé from its ancient Clos du Zahnacker. Half of the vines planted in this village were Chasselas until as recently as the 1970s, but it should be remembered that this modest grape helped to make Ribeauvillé one of less than a dozen villages in all Alsace that can claim to have been truly famous for the *vin de paille* nectar of the nineteenth century.

Riedseltz, Bas-Rhin

Location: 3 miles south of Wissembourg, in the extreme north of the region, some 35 miles north of Strasbourg
Area classified as AOC: 14.50 hectares
AOC area under vine: 6 hectares
Grands crus: None
Other vineyard names in use: None
Soil: Loess, sand and sandy-clay.

I have no knowledge of this village or its wines.

Riquewihr, Haut-Rhin

Location: 5 miles north-north-west of Colmar, via Bennwihr
Area classified as AOC: 323 hectares, including 62 hectares (or 19 per cent) of *grand cru* vineyards
AOC area under vine: 257 hectares
Grands crus: Schoenenbourg (40 hectares); Sporen (22 hectares)
Other vineyard names in use: Birgele (J-J Baumann)
Soil: Sand and marl
Producers located in the village: J-J Baumann & Fils, Ernest Bronner,

Dopff & Irion, Dopff Au Moulin, Hugel & Fils, Roger Jung & Fils,
Domaine Mittnacht-Klack, Preiss-Zimmer, Maison Wiederhirn
Others also owning vines in, or making wines from, the village: CV
Beblenheim, Jean Becker, Paul Blanck & Fils, Maison 'Bott Frères', Maison
Bott-Geyl, Domaine Marcel Deiss, Jean Halbeizen, Ernest Horcher & Fils,
Jean Huttard, Mader, Jean-Paul Mauler, J. C. Preiss-Henny, CV
Ribeauvillé, Edgard Schaller & Fils, René Schmidt, Bernard Schwach, CV
Turckheim
Annual festivals: Fête du Riesling (first weekend in October)

Alsace is full of beautiful villages, but Riquewihr is my favourite.
First documented as Richovilare in 1094, this vllage is thought to
have derived its name from a Frankish lord called Richo. This
delightful place, with its narrow cobbled streets and old half-
timbered buildings, has somehow avoided much of the commercial
exploitation that has made nearby Ribeauvillé such a thriving yet
far less intimate place. Ribeauvillé may still beguile the first-time
visitor and there are many attractions to lure regulars back, but it
does not have quite the same charm as Riquewihr. On the other
hand, Riquewihr closes its shutters very early, even in the height of
summer, and if you try to spend an evening there out of season, it
can seem quite deathly.

Riquewihr is best known for its Riesling, which is supposed to
have the aroma of angelica when young and can achieve superb
honeyed-petrolly perfection after ten or more years in bottle. It also
has a well-established reputation for its rather delicate style of
Gewurztraminer and is just beginning to carve out a name for
Muscat, but we should not forget its classic blended wines, for
which Sporen was once famous. You have only to glimpse the great
names that own vines here to understand its universal acclaim.
Hugel & Fils has produced the greatest number of the most scintillating *cuvées* from this village, but lacks strength in its most basic
range of generics and it is impossible to pin down the geographical
origin of the most outstanding *cuvées* (with the exception of its
classic Sporen blended wine, of course; the renaming of which its
fans, which include me, anxiously await). Marcel Deiss has made
some equally stunning wines, but with less than one hectare, or 5
per cent, of his vines on the Grand Cru Schoenenbourg, the number
of these spectacular wines has been relatively small. Other top
exponents of Schoenenbourg include Domaines Dopff Au Moulin

and Baumann & Fils. Dopff & Irion's vineyard-based *cuvées* of Les Amandiers, Les Sorcières and Les Maquisards can provide delightful wines, although this needs qualifying (*See* Dopff & Irion entry under 'Producer Profiles', Chapter 8).

Rodern, Haut-Rhin

Location: 10 miles north of Colmar, via Rorschwihr
Area classified as AOC: 90.16 hectares, including 23 hectares (or 26 per cent) of *grand cru* vineyards
AOC area under vine: 86 hectares
Grands crus: Gloeckelberg (23 hectares in Rodern, 0.4 hectares in St-Hippolyte)
Other vineyard names in use: None
Soil: Granite with patches of sandstone, shale and even coal!
Producers located in the village: François Ehrhart & Fils, Koeberlé-Kreyer, Charles Koehly & Fils
Others also owning vines in, or making wines from, the village: CV Ribeauvillé, Rolly Gassmann, E. Schaeflé, Domaine Siffert, Domaine Jean Sipp
Annual festivals: Fête du Pinot Noir (third weekend in July)

A famous winemaking village since the Middle Ages, Rodern's origins go back to at least the eighth century. Its claim to have been the first place in Alsace to grow Pinot Noir a good few centuries before the grape was first documented in the region can, I think, be dismissed along with similar claims by St-Hippolyte. Both villages were, however, the first to attract an authentic reputation for the grape and its Pinot Noir today is an attractive, light red wine with a very pure aroma of cherries. Tokay-Pinot Gris and Gewurztraminer are also grown. Like St-Hippolyte, Rodern does not have to depend on Pinot Noir for its past claim to fame, for it was one of less than a dozen villages in Alsace to have established a reputation for *vin de paille* in the nineteenth century.

Rorschwihr, Haut-Rhin

Location: 10 miles north of Colmar, between Bergheim and St-Hippolyte
Area classified as AOC: 227.90 hectares
AOC area under vine: 177 hectares

Grands crus: None
Other vineyard names in use: Kapelweg, Moenchreben, Oberer-Weingarten, Pflaenzerreben, Silberberg (all Rolly Gassmann)
Soil: Marly clay and limestone
Producers located in the village: Fernand Engel & Fils, Willy Rolli-Edel, Rolly Gassmann
Others also owning vines in, or making wines from, the village: CV Beblenheim, Domaine Marcel Deiss, Koeberlé-Kreyer, Domaine Muller-Koeberle

Originally called Chrodoldesvilare, or Chrodolde's villa, wine-making in this village dates back to at least 742. Historically best known for its Gewurztraminer, Rorschwihr also had something of a reputation for Chasselas, but the outstanding grower in this village, Rolly Gassmann, produces stunning Muscat and fat, con-centrated Auxerrois. His Moenchreben, which should not be con-fused with the *grand cru* of Andlau and Eichhoffen, is by far the best *lieu-dit* and superior to some *grands crus*. I have had good Tokay-Pinot Gris from Willy Rolli-Edel and Koeberlé-Kreyer makes fat, juicy, easy-to-drink Pinot Blanc.

Rosenwiller, Bas-Rhin

Location: 13 miles south-west of Strasbourg, via the D435 from Rosheim
Area classified as AOC: 69.19 hectares
AOC area under vine: 35 hectares
Grands crus: None
Other vineyard names in use: Westerberg (Einhart)
Soil: Limestone
Producers located in the village: Einhart

This village used to be part of the Sylvaner heartland, but my only experience of a pure Rosenwiller wine is Tokay-Pinot Gris from the *lieu-dit* Westerberg, where Einhart produces a splendidly rich and expressive wine.

Rosheim, Bas-Rhin

Location: 12 miles south-west of Strasbourg, half-way between Molsheim and Obernai, turning of the D422 on to the Route du Vin

Area classified as AOC: 329.88 hectares
AOC area under vine: 162 hectares
Grands crus: None
Other vineyard names in use: None
Soil: Limestone
Producers owning vines in, or making wines from, the village: Domaine Klipfel
Annual festivals: Fête des Vendanges (first two weeks in October)

The so-called *Heidehaus*, or Pagan House, is the only Roman building that has survived in Alsace. Rosheim is an ancient village, whose limestone soil was inevitably planted with much Sylvaner in times gone by, but also had a name for its Gewurztraminer in the nineteenth century. I have never knowingly drunk pure Rosheim wine and the only grower I have come across with vines here is Domaine Klipfel, but as they own just five hectares out of 162, there must be a lot of people out there that I have missed!

Rott, Bas-Rhin

Location: 2 miles south-west of Wissembourg, in the extreme north of the region, some 35 miles north of Strasbourg
Area classified as AOC: 50.88 hectares
AOC area under vine: 40 hectares
Grands crus: None
Other vineyard names in use: None
Soil: Clay, sand and sandstone over marl

The entire production from this village is utilized by the CV Cléebourg. *See* Cléebourg.

Rouffach, Haut-Rhin

Location: 9 miles south-south-west of Colmar, between Pfaffenheim and Westhalten
Area classified as AOC: 602.34 hectares, including 68.21 hectares (or 11 per cent) of *grand cru* vineyards
AOC area under vine: 455 hectares
Grands crus: Vorbourg (68.21 hectares in Rouffach, 3.7 hectares in Westhalten)

Other vineyard names in use: Bollenberg; Clos St-Landelin (part of Grand Cru Vorbourg, Muré); Côte de Rouffach (Bruno Hunold, Muré and Domaine Rieflé); Rot-Murlé (Pierre Frick)
Soil: Sandstone and limestone
Producers located in the village: Domaine de l'Ecole, Bruno Hunold, Muré
Others also owning vines in, or making wines from, the village: Domaine Lucien Albrecht, Camille Braun & Fils, Pierre Frick, CV Pfaffenheim, Domaine Rieflé, François Runner, Domaines Schlumberger, CV Westhalten

First recorded in 720, Rouffach was then known as Rubeaquam, or 'Red Water', due to the local water being tainted by red-clay-infused sandstone. Feminists might be interested to know that the women in Rouffach have had a special standing in official ceremonies since the twelfth century. The story is quite amusing. It concerns the German Emperor Henry V, who apparently tried to abduct a young girl as she was leaving church. When none of the local men dared to intervene, some women seized what weapons they could find and chased Henry off. He was in such a hurry to flee, it is said, that he left his crown behind, though nobody seems to know what happened to it. Part fact or all fiction, the women of Rouffach take pride of place over the men at ceremonies today.

This town, which has many fine Renaissance buildings, including the twin-gabled former Hôtel de Ville, is overlooked by the Château d'Isenbourg, which is now a hotel. The château's vineyards supply grapes for its own label wine, which is also marketed by Dopff & Irion, who make the wine. There is also the Lycée Regionale d'Agriculture et Viticulture. Muré is the best producer, and Pinot Noir, Riesling and Tokay-Pinot Gris all grow well here, with Gewurztraminer excelling in the bigger, hotter years. Schlumberger has extended its domaine quite extensively into Rouffach, around the Bollenberg.

St-Hippolyte, Haut-Rhin

Location: 10 miles north of Colmar, between Rorschwihr and Orschwiller
Area classified as AOC: 364.13 hectares, including 0.4 hectares (or 0.1 per cent) of *grand cru* vineyards
AOC area under vine: 262 hectares
Grands crus: Gloeckelberg (0.4 hectares in St-Hippolyte, 23 hectares in Rodern)

Other vineyard names in use: Burgreben (Muller-Koeberle); Clos des Aubépines (Muller-Koeberle); Coteaux du Haut-Koenigsbourg (René Klein and Muller-Koeberle); Geisberg or Geissberg (Muller-Koeberle); Schlossreben (Jacques Iltis, René Klein and Muller-Koeberle)
Soil: Granite to the west, gravel-covered marl to the east.
Producers located in the village: Armand Fahrer, Jacques Iltis, Georges Klein, René Klein & Fils, Domaine Muller-Koeberle
Others also owning vines in, or making wines from, the village: Paul Blanck & Fils, Domaine Marcel Deiss, Koeberlé-Kreyer, Charles Koehly & Fils, CV Ribeauvillé
Annual festivals: The Fête de Pinot Noir in July and a Fête du Vin Nouveau in September.

The most northerly winemaking village in the Haut-Rhin, St-Hippolyte was named after St-Hippolytus of Rome (AD170–235), a Christian martyr and the first anti-Pope. His remains were brought back to the village from Rome in the eighth century, by a man called Fulrade, who locals also credit with introducing the Pinot Noir from Italy. This variety was, however, almost certainly brought to Alsace, not from Italy, but from Burgundy, where it is thought to have been cultivated as early as the fourth century, possibly as early as the first century, if the *Vitis allobrogica* described by Pliny was in fact Pinot Noir, as some ampelographic historians believe. Nevertheless, St-Hippolyte is well known for its Pinot Noir today, which is usually made in a soft, gently rich style, although Muller-Koeberle excels with a red wine that shows some spicy-cherry finesse. Pinot Noir is not, however, its only claim to fame, as this village was also one of less than a dozen in Alsace to have a real reputation for *vin de paille* in the nineteenth century. The vines are prone to a lack of moisture, which makes St-Hippolyte superior in wetter years, as the rain drains away very quickly. Marcel Deiss is making a name with Riesling and Muller-Koeberle leads with the more traditional Pinot Noir.

St-Nabor, Bas-Rhin

Location: 14 miles south-west of Strasbourg, via either Ottrott or Bernardswiller
Area classified as AOC: 8.05 hectares
AOC area under vine: 4 hectares

Grands crus: None
Other vineyard names in use: None
Soil: Sandstone, volcanic sedimentary deposits and tufa

This small winemaking village is off the Route du Vin at the foot of Mont Ste-Odile (*See* Obernai).

St-Pierre, Bas-Rhin

Location: 23 miles north of Colmar, between Stotzheim and Eichhoffen
Area classified as AOC: 102.06 hectares
AOC area under vine: 77 hectares
Grands crus: None
Other vineyard names in use: None
Soil: Limestone

More than 60 per cent of St-Pierre's vineyards were planted with Sylvaner until as recently as the early 1970s, but I know nothing about the wines made here today.

Scharrachbergheim-Irmstett, Bas-Rhin

Location: 8 miles west of Strasbourg, turning off the D422 at the CV Traenheim on the junction with the D225
Area classified as AOC: 151 hectares
AOC area under vine: 70 hectares
Grands crus: None
Other vineyard names in use: Coteaux du Mossig (CV Traenheim blends this village with other Mossig villages under its Roi Dagobert label)
Soil: Sandy-clay and marly-limestone
Producers owning vines in, or making wines from, the village: Domaine Jean-Pierre Bechtold

The Romans grew vines on the steep slopes of the Scharrach in the third century, but it was not until the sixth century that this village began to carve out any reputation for its wines. By the fifteenth century these vineyards were flourishing, but like many Alsace villages fell into disuse after the Thirty Years War. The traveller who reaches Scharrachbergheim and does not climb to the top of the vine-clad Scharrach will miss one of the most magnificent views in Alsace. My only significant tasting of wines I knew to be from this village was from Domaine Jean-Pierre Bechtold in 1990, but nothing stood out, although I have been impressed by other wines from this producer. The vineyards of this village come within the generic geographical designation of Coteaux du Mossig.

Scherwiller, Bas-Rhin

Location: 15 miles north of Colmar, between Châtenois and Dambach-la-Ville
Area classified as AOC: 431.26 hectares
AOC area under vine: 293 hectares
Grands crus: None
Other vineyard names in use: Rittersberg (Paul Beck)
Soil: Sandy-granitic
Producers located in the village: André Dussourt
Others also owning vines in, or making wines from, the village: Paul Beck, Louis Gisselbrecht, J. Hauller & Fils
Annual festivals: Fête du Riesling in mid-August.

Overlooked by the ruins of Ortenbourg and Ramstein castles, the growers of this pretty little village pride themselves on their Riesling, even to the point of proclaiming Scherwiller '*la capitale du Riesling*', but of the few I have tasted, none stood out. However, in 1828 the former *lieu-dit* of Ortenbourg (presumably close to, or part of, Rittersberg, which is just beneath the ruins of Ortenbourg castle) was ranked by J. L. Stoltz as one of the best vineyards in Alsace. The only producer I rate who has vines here is J. Hauller & Fils, but I have not knowingly tasted a pure Scherwiller wine. Nearly half of Hauller's own vineyards are situated in this village, so they must consider it worthy, but Hauller's entire vineyards provide barely 8 per cent of its total production, so it could well get lost in the blending vat.

Sigolsheim, Haut-Rhin

Location: 4 miles north-west of Colmar, just east of Kientzheim
Area classified as AOC: 370.49 hectares, including 83.35 hectares (or 22 per cent) of *grand cru* vineyards
AOC area under vine: 323 hectares
Grands crus: Furstentum (11.35 hectares in Sigolsheim, 14.3 hectares in

Kientzheim); Mambourg (65 hectares); Marckrain (7 hectares in
Sigolsheim, 38.4 hectares in Bennwihr)
Other vineyard names in use: Vogelgarten (Claude Dietrich)
Soil: Sandy-shingle alluvial plain to the west and east; limestone, marl and
sandstone to the north
Producers located in the village: Ringenbach-Moser, Pierre Schillé, CV
Sigolsheim, Pierre Sparr
Others also owning vines in, or making wines from, the village: Paul
Blanck & Fils, Claude Dietrich, Albert Mann, Salzmann-Thomann, René
& Bernard Schneider, P. Sick-Dreyer, André Thomas & Fils

Founded in the sixth century by Sigwalt, a Frankish warrior, vineyards have been in existence since at least 783, when winemaking
was mentioned in an old deed. In the ninth century Ermoldus
Nigellus, a poet from Aquitaine, compared the wines of Sigolsheim
with those of Falernium, the most famous *cru* at the time. It was
just outside Sigolsheim at the Champ du Mensonge (or Field of
Deceit) that Charlemagne's successor Louis the Pious was abandoned by his own forces and captured by his sons in 833. It is hard
to believe that this pretty little village was totally destroyed in
January 1945, but it has been completely rebuilt in the most auth-
entic and obviously loving way. Sigolsheim has long had a reputation for Riesling, Gewurztraminer and Muscat, particularly on the
Mambourg, where contemporary experience suggests that Tokay-
Pinot Gris fares equally well. The best producers here are Paul
Blanck on Grand Cru Furstentum, and Pierre Sparr and André
Thomas on Grand Cru Mambourg.

Soultz, Haut-Rhin

Location: 14 miles south-south-west of Colmar, between Guebwiller and
Wuenheim
Area classified as AOC: 142.80 hectares
AOC area under vine: 74 hectares
Grands crus: None
Other vineyard names in use: None
Soil: Limestone
Producers located in the village: Raymond Schmitt
Others also owning vines in, or making wines from, the village: CV
Westhalten, Vieil Armand

Situated in the extreme south of Alsace's vineyards, Soultz is often called Soultz-Haut-Rhin to avoid confusion with Soultz-les-Bains, near Strasbourg, in the Bas-Rhin. I have not knowingly tasted any pure Soultz wines.

Soultz-les-Bains, Bas-Rhin

Location: 10 miles west of Strasbourg, north of Molsheim on the Route du Vin between Avolsheim and Dangolsheim
Area classified as AOC: 103.79 hectares
AOC area under vine: 46 hectares
Grands crus: None
Other vineyard names in use: None
Soil: Limestone

Tucked away in the small and beautiful Mossig Valley, Soultz-les-Bains literally means 'Spa baths', the efficacy of which were lauded by Ste-Odile. The vineyards of this village come within the generic geographical designation of Coteaux du Mossig, but I have not knowingly tasted any pure Soultz-les-Bains wines.

Soultzmatt, Haut-Rhin

Location: 10 miles south-south-west of Colmar, between Westhalten and Orschwihr
Area classified as AOC: 297.69 hectares, including 34.56 hectares (or 12 per cent) of *grand cru* vineyards
AOC area under vine: 206 hectares
Grands crus: Zinnkoepflé (34.56 hectares in Soultzmatt, 27.87 hectares in Westhalten)
Other vineyard names in use: Vallée Noble (Léon Boesch)
Soil: Clay, limestone or sandy
Producers located in the village: Léon Boesch, Raymond & Martin Klein, Seppi Landmann, Landmann-Ostholt, Joseph Klein & Fils, Jules & Rémy Zimmermann
Others also owning vines in, or making wines from, the village: Camille Braun & Fils, CV Westhalten
Annual festivals: Soiré Alsacienne (August); Kilbe (end of August, beginning of September); Fête du Vin Nouveau (October); Bal des Vendanges (October)

A Roman settlement on the site of Neolithic remains, Soultzmatt means 'salt-water meadow', which refers to the local *eau de source naturelle*. A visit to this beauty spot in the Noble Valley to see some of the highest vineyards in Alsace is well worth the effort. Gewurztraminer is probably the best variety here, producing wines that are typically exotic and fruity, often hinting of mango or pawpaw, except on the Grand Cru Zinnkoepflé, where the Gewurztraminer gives a stronger wine of more classic structure, with a distinctive spicy character of pepper, clove and, sometimes, coriander. Other village wines of Soultzmatt include Pinot Blanc, which is usually grown on sandy-clay soil, where it produces fresh and fruity wines with a mild and supple finish that evolve quickly and are easy to drink. Riesling, grown on sandy-calcareous soil is normally fresh and light, with a musky nuance. There are a few good producers here, but Seppi Landmann stands out.

Steinbach, Haut-Rhin

Location: 20 miles south-south-west of Colmar, via Cernay
Area classified as AOC: 68.84 hectares
AOC area under vine: 1 hectare
Grands crus: None
Other vineyard names in use: None
Soil: Gravel and limestone
Producers owning vines in, or making wines from, the village: CV Westhalten

Presumably the one hectare under vine in this insignificant wine village belongs to CV Westhalten. I know nothing about Steinbach.

Steinseltz, Bas-Rhin

Location: 3 miles south of Wissembourg, in the extreme north of the region, some 35 miles north of Strasbourg
Area classified as AOC: 68.16 hectares
AOC area under vine: 39 hectares
Grands crus: None
Other vineyard names in use: Huettgasse (CV Cléebourg), Brandhof (CV Cléebourg)
Soil: Clay and sand over marl

The entire production from this village is utilized by the CV Cléebourg. Best for Pinot grapes, the *lieu-dit* Huettgasse for Pinot Noir and Brandhof for Tokay-Pinot Gris. *See* Cléebourg.

Stotzheim, Bas-Rhin

Location: 23 miles north of Colmar, just south of Zellwiller
Area classified as AOC: 26.42 hectares
AOC area under vine: 17 hectares
Grands crus: None
Other vineyard names in use: None
Soil: Limestone

I know nothing about this village.

Thann, Haut-Rhin

Location: 23 miles south-south-west of Colmar, just beyond Vieux-Thann, going west
Area classified as AOC: 14.33 hectares, including 12.81 hectares (or 89 per cent) of *grand cru* vineyards
AOC area under vine: 7 hectares
Grands crus: Rangen (12.81 hectares in Thann, 6 hectares in Vieux-Thann)
Other vineyard names in use: Clos St-Théobold (part of Grand Cru Rangen, Domaine Schoffit); Clos St-Urbain (part of Grand Cru Rangen, Domaine Zind Humbrecht)
Soil: Volcanic
Producers owning vines in, or making wines from, the village: Bruno Hertz, Domaine Schoffit, Domaine Zind Humbrecht
Annual festivals: Fête du Vin (July)

Until the recent reassessment of the communal delimitation, it could be said that Thann and Vieux-Thann were the only 100 per cent *grand cru* villages in Alsace. Historically, of course, the reputation of Thann has always been synonymous with that of Rangen. The most southerly wine village of Alsace, Thann has been famous for its hillside wines since at least the twelfth century. In 1548 Thann passed a law that prevented the wines of Rangen from being blended with any others and, in 1581, issued another law that was effectively the precursor to the region-wide decision taken by growers some 350 years later, whereby only noble varieties were allowed to be planted and all other varieties had to be pulled up. The power and potency of Thann wines are legendary. In 1776, the anonymous author of *Petite Chronique de Thann* wrote 'Take note that no one can drink a tankard of this generous nectar without getting roaring drunk and rolling on the floor', an obvious reference to the high alcoholic degree that is easily achieved on the full south-facing, steep slopes of hard, heat-retaining volcanic soil.

The reputation of Thann today is almost entirely due to Léonard Humbrecht, who replanted its abandoned steep slopes in the early 1970s, but Domaine Schoffit, the next best producer, has very quickly achieved standards here that would put the domaine firmly at the top of the quality ladder in most other Alsace villages. The gap between them, however, is still profound and is particularly noticeable when comparing Rieslings. Tokay-Pinot Gris is the equal of Riesling here and can attain immense richness, power and structure, yet retains classic balance and finesse.

Traenheim, Bas-Rhin

Location: 12 miles west of Strasbourg, between Westhoffen and Scharrachbergheim-Irmstett
Area classified as AOC: 116.54 hectares
AOC area under vine: 74 hectares
Grands crus: None
Other vineyard names in use: Coteaux du Mossig (CV Traenheim blends this village with other Mossig villages under its Roi Dagobert label)
Soil: Marl
Producers located in the village: Frédéric Mochel, CV Traenheim

If anywhere in Alsace is the cradle of Germanic identity, it must be Traenheim, where the Teutonic heroes of the epic poem *Nibelungenlied* were supposedly born, yet the village is also inextricably linked to Dagobert, the Merovingian king, who owned an estate close by. The local cooperative is capable of producing some good wines, but Frédéric Mochel is obviously in a much higher class. The vineyards of this village come within the generic geographical designation of Coteaux du Mossig.

Turckheim, Haut-Rhin

Location: 3 miles west of Colmar
Area classified as AOC: 536.53 hectares, including 57 hectares (or 11 per cent) of *grand cru* vineyards
AOC area under vine: 339 hectares
Grands crus: Brand (57 hectares)
Other vineyard names in use: Heimbourg (CV Turckheim and Domaine Zind Humbrecht); Herrenweg (Barmès-Buecher and Domaine Zind Humbrecht); Clos Jebsal (Domaine Zind Humbrecht); Côtes du Val St-Grégoire (CV Turckheim); Steinweg (CV Ingersheim, this *lieu-dit* is shared with the village of Ingersheim, where the vast majority of its considerable vineyards are located, and Wintzenheim)
Soil: Limestone, granite and marl
Producers located in the village: François Baur Petit-Fils, Charles Schleret, CV Turckheim
Others also owning vines in, or making wines from, the village: Domaine Barmès-Buecher, Albert Boxler, Paul Buecher & Fils, Dopff Au Moulin, Henri Ehrhart, René Fleith, Auguste Hurst, JosMeyer, Marcel Mullenbach, Bruno Sorg, Pierre Sparr, Domaine Zind Humbrecht
Annual festivals: Fête du Vin (first weekend in August)

Wine growing has been a staple of this village since Roman times. Turckheim still has its old fortified wall with three gates intact and, at Christmas and every night throughout the summer, you can see a man dressed in fourteenth-century garb and clutching a lantern walk through each one of the entrances, stopping at various street corners within the town to shout out a strange old warning in the local dialect. This is Turckheim's official watchman. He and his predecessors have carried out this duty for 600 years, shouting out the same warning 'Watch your fires and your lamps'. Tens of thousands of times those words have echoed through Turckheim's streets. This town is, if nothing else, steeped in tradition and mystery and there is no greater local legend than the duel of the dragon of Brand (*See* the profile of Grand Cru Brand in Chapter 5). Turckheim was once planted entirely with black varieties and famous for a red wine known as Turks' Blood. Although the vineyards are now mostly planted with other varieties, some Pinot Noir remains and Turckheim still produces one of the best Pinot Noir wines in Alsace. The excellent local cooperative's 'Cuvée à l'Ancienne' is as classic an example of Turckheim's Pinot Noir as you will find, with its light and soft yet gently rich flavour. It is, however, another member of the Pinot family that excels here, the Tokay-Pinot Gris, and CV Turckheim makes excellent *cuvées* of this too. Riesling and Gewurztraminer are very nearly as successful on the Brand itself; Domaine Zind Humbrecht is without doubt the best producer on the Brand and thus Turckheim. Other top-performing producers are Domaines Dopff Au Moulin, JosMeyer, Pierre Sparr, Albert Boxler and, last but not least, we should not forget Charles Schleret, the 'bachelor of Turckheim', who does not specify the origin of his medal-winning wines and rarely gives anything away, but I imagine his sensationally rich Tokay-Pinot Gris could come from nowhere other than this particular village. Turckheim was one of the ten villages in Alsace to have a reputation for *vin de paille* in the nineteenth century.

Uffolz, Haut-Rhin

Location: 19 miles south-south-west of Colmar, just north of Cernay
Area classified as AOC: 52 hectares
AOC area under vine: 8 hectares
Grands crus: None
Other vineyard names in use: None
Soil: Gravel and limestone

I know nothing about this minor wine village.

Vieux-Thann, Haut-Rhin

Location: 23 miles south-south-west of Colmar, just to the east of Thann
Area classified as AOC: 25.56 hectares including 6 hectares (or 23 per cent) of *grand cru* vineyards
AOC area under vine: 1 hectare
Grands crus: Rangen (6 hectares in Vieux-Thann, 12.81 hectares in Thann)
Other vineyard names in use: None
Soil: Volcanic

Until the recent reassessment of the communal delimitation, when the area of Vieux-Thann classified as AOC rose from 6 to 25.56 hectares, it could be said that Thann and Vieux-Thann were the only 100 per cent *grand cru* villages in Alsace. A fourfold increase in the area of land suitable for *appellation contrôlée* wine should normally be viewed with great scepticism, if not actual alarm, but the amount of land involved (less than 20 hectares) and the supreme suitability of the original area of classified land in this village is such that few eyebrows will be raised. *See* Thann.

Villé, Bas-Rhin

Location: 18 miles north of Colmar, on the road from Sélestat to St-Blaize
Area classified as AOC: 2.10 hectares
AOC area under vine: 1 hectare
Grands crus: None
Other vineyard names in use: None
Soil: Schist

Villé is in Kirsch country. It is far better suited to orchards than vineyards, which are minuscule mountain slopes.

Voegtlinshoffen, Haut-Rhin

Location: 5 miles south-south-west of Colmar, in the hills immediately south of Husseren-les-Châteaux
Area classified as AOC: 87.25 hectares, including 20.3 hectares (or 23 per cent) of *grand cru* vineyards
AOC area under vine: 67 hectares
Grands crus: Hatschbourg (20.3 hectares in Voegtlinshoffen, 27.06 hectares in Hattstatt)
Other vineyard names in use: None
Soil: Clay over sandstone
Producers located in the village: Joseph Cattin, Théo Cattin, André Hartmann, Gérard & Serge Hartmann, Domaine Kehren
Others also owning vines in, or making wines from, the village: CV Pfaffenheim, Ginglinger-Fix, Lucien Meyer, Wolfberger

The height of this village's vineyards is such that they are seldom subject to spring frosts. It is famous primarily for Muscat, but Pinot Blanc and Gewurztraminer are also of some repute, except on the Grand Cru Hatschbourg, where Gewurztraminer is the best variety, but Tokay-Pinot Gris and Riesling can be very exciting too. The top producer here is Joseph Cattin, but cousin Théo, Wolfberger and both Hartmanns are well worth seeking out.

Walbach, Haut-Rhin

Location: 6 miles west of Colmar, between Zimmerbach and Wihr-au-Val
Area classified as AOC: 81.60 hectares
AOC area under vine: 42 hectares
Grands crus: None
Other vineyard names in use: Côtes du Val St-Grégoire (A. Gueth & Fils and CV Turckheim); Felsen (A. Gueth & Fils)
Soil: Granite
Producers located in the village: A. Gueth & Fils
Others also owning vines in, or making wines from, the village: CV Turckheim

I know very little about the wines of this charming little village in the Munster Valley, except that its mountain vineyards were once considered fine for Chasselas, Pinot Blanc and Tokay-Pinot Gris.

Wangen, Bas-Rhin

Location: 10 miles west of Strasbourg, between Westhoffen and Marlenheim
Area classified as AOC: 148.20 hectares
AOC area under vine: 74 hectares
Grands crus: None
Other vineyard names in use: None
Soil: Limestone and marl
Annual festivals: Fête du Vin (first Sunday after 3 July)

Wangen is dominated by the Wangenbourg, which protects the vineyards clinging to its south-east-facing slopes. The vines run up to the wooded top of the Wangenbourg and are interspersed with orchards, although it looks very much like vine country to me. I have not knowingly tasted a pure Wangen wine, although I hear that the village fountain actually flows with the stuff for four hours every 6 July!

Wattwiller, Haut-Rhin

Location: 18 miles south-south-west of Colmar, between Wuenheim and Uffoltz
Area classified as AOC: 22.48 hectares
AOC area under vine: 1 hectare
Grands crus: None
Other vineyard names in use: None
Soil: Shale and loess

One of the last bastions of the hybrid, Wattwiller did not uproot these inferior vines until as recently as the early1970s and is insignificant in wine terms today.

Westhalten, Haut-Rhin

Location: 10 miles south-south-west of Colmar, between Soultzmatt and Rouffach
Area classified as AOC: 485.73 hectares, including 31.57 hectares (or 7 per cent) of *grand cru* vineyards
AOC area under vine: 291 hectares
Grands crus: Vorbourg (3.7 hectares in Westhalten, 68.21 hectares in Rouffach); Zinnkoepflé (27.87 hectares in Westhalten, 34.56 hectares in Soultzmatt)
Other vineyard names in use: Bollenberg; Grosstein (Pierre Frick); Côte de Rouffach (Heim); Strangenberg (CV Westhalten)
Soil: Limestone and sandstone
Producers located in the village: GAEC Dirringer, SA Heim, CV Westhalten, A. Wischlen
Others also owning vines in, or making wines from, the village: Domaine Lucien Albrecht, Pierre Frick, Seppi Landmann, Domaine Rieflé, François Runner
Annual festivals: Echo du Strangenbourg (a sort of *fête du vin* with food, music and dancing, which takes place in the first week of June); Apéritif Concert et Fête Champêtre (June); Fête du Vin (first weekend in August)

First mentioned in 1101, the village was then known as Westhaulda. Unusually for Alsace, its vineyards are located on three hills. Two of these, Zinnkoepflé and Vorbourg, are either side of the opening to the Vallée Noble, which is the norm for Alsace, as most villages are situated at the head of a valley. The third hill, however, is the Bollenberg, which faces the other two across the Ombach river. The best wines of Westhalten, which can have an almost exotic character, are generally agreed to be Pinot Blanc and Tokay-Pinot Gris; these can be very good and other varieties also thrive here and can share characteristics that can be attributed only to the *terroir*. The Auxerrois and Sylvaner, for example, two wildly different varieties, both show above their station and share a restrained, but distinctive, smoky-floral character.

Westhoffen, Bas-Rhin

Location: 12 miles west of Strasbourg, between Wangen and Traenheim
Area classified as AOC: 250.56 hectares
AOC area under vine: 129 hectares
Grands crus: None
Other vineyard names in use: None
Soil: Marl

It is claimed that the best hillsides of Westhoffen (and those of Balbronn) were historically considered part of Bergbieten or, at least, that it was the wines produced from these hillsides that helped Bergbieten build up its reputation for Riesling. I have not knowingly tasted pure Westhoffen wines, most of which I imagine end up in cooperative blending vats.

Wettolsheim, Haut-Rhin

Location: 2 miles south-west of Colmar, just south of Wintzenheim
Area classified as AOC: 223.61 hectares, including 19 hectares (or 8 per cent) of *grand cru* vineyards
AOC area under vine: 178 hectares
Grands crus: Steingrubler (19 hectares)
Other vineyard names in use: Leimenthal (Domaine Barmès-Buecher); Pfleck (Albert Mann)
Soil: Limestone, with small patches of gravel, granite and sandstone
Producers located in the village: Domaine Barmès-Buecher, Paul Buecher, Claude Dietrich, François Ehrhart & Fils, Albert Mann, Jean-Louis Schoepfer, Domaine Aimé Stentz, Wunsch & Mann
Others also owning vines in, or making wines from, the village: Domaine

Viticole de la Ville de Colmar, Robert Dietrich, Wolfberger
Annual festivals: Fête du Vin (end of July)

Christianity flourished in Wettolsheim as early as the fourth century, when it is known that viticulture had already been firmly established. More than half of the vineyards in Wettolsheim were planted with Chasselas until as recently as the mid-1970s, although it has always been most famous for its Muscat, which used to be prescribed as a tonic for the ill and infirm, according to folklore. Gewurztraminer stands out today and not just on the Grand Cru Steingrubler, where Tokay-Pinot Gris excels and Riesling can be nearly as good. The top producers in this village are Domaine Barmès-Buecher, Albert Mann, Wunsch & Mann and Wolfberger (Grand Cru Steingrubler).

Wihr-au-Val, Haut-Rhin

Location: 10 miles west of Colmar, just beyond Walbach
Area classified as AOC: 114.30 hectares
AOC area under vine: 33 hectares
Grands crus: None
Other vineyard names in use: Côtes du Val St-Grégoire (CV Turckheim)
Soil: Granite
Producers owning vines in, or making wines from, the village: Domaine Pierre Adam

The south-facing mountain slopes of this village can produce very pleasant, fresh-tasting Pinot Blanc.

Wintzenheim, Haut-Rhin

Location: 2 miles west of Colmar
Area classified as AOC: 420.15 hectares, including 75.78 hectares (or 18 per cent) of *grand cru* vineyards
AOC area under vine: 296 hectares
Grands crus: Hengst (75.78 hectares)
Other vineyard names in use: Clos Hauserer (Domaine Zind Humbrecht); Rotenberg (Domaine Zind Humbrecht); Steinweg (CV Ingersheim, this *lieu-dit* is shared with the village of Ingersheim, where the vast majority of its considerable vineyards are located, and Turckheim)

Soil: Limestone, granite, gravel, marl and sandstone
Producers located in the village: JosMeyer, Bernard Staehlé, Domaine Zind Humbrecht
Others also owning vines in, or making wines from, the village: Domaine Barmès-Buecher, Braunheizen-Fink, Paul Buecher, Claude Dietrich, André Ehrhart, René Fleith, Hubert Krick, Albert Mann, Meyer-Brauneizer, Domaine Aimé Stentz, CV Turckheim, Wolfberger, Wunsch & Mann

This village was first mentioned in 786, when it was known as Wingisheim, although its vineyards were established several centuries earlier. In the sixteenth century Wintzenheim became the fief of Baron Lazare de Schwendi, who was buried not too far away in Kientzheim church. The easiest judgement to make about this very important wine village is the top producer, which can only be Domaine Zind Humbrecht, even though there are other truly excellent ones, but to specify the best varieties is much harder. Even the best site is difficult, despite the obvious supreme situation of the Hengst, which is one of the most famous vineyards in Alsace. What about Rotenberg and Clos Hauserer? They are both Domaine Zind Humbrecht properties, of course, which helps to explain why it is so easy to pluck that name out as the top producer, if any explanation is necessary. Rotenberg is cooler than the Hengst, yet still makes fabulously fat Tokay-Pinot Gris with powerful aromatic qualities, which are literally ripe for Sélection de Grains Nobles in good vintages. Clos Hauserer is located at the foot of the Grand Cru Hengst, where it produces magnificent Riesling from well-aged vines. On the Hengst itself, of course, Domaine Zind Humbrecht has to face competition from numerous talented producers. JosMeyer, for example, can be its equal for Riesling. Barmès-Buecher and Wolfberger are both excellent. André Ehrhart makes one of the finest Tokay-Pinot Gris on this *grand cru* and Albert Mann one of the most exciting, yet terribly underrated Gewurztraminers. The generic village wines must be legion, or at least Wintzenheim-dominated generic *cuvées* are, but as often as not they are difficult to pin down.

Wissembourg, Bas-Rhin

Location: 35 miles north of Strasbourg, in the extreme north of the region
Area classified as AOC: 60 hectares

AOC area under vine: 2 hectares
Grands crus: None
Other vineyard names in use: None
Soil: Sandstone and limestone

Surely the most bizarre relics of the centuries-old struggle for sovereignty of Alsace are the German vineyards that still exist within this city's limits. There are only two hectares of AOC Alsace vines in Wissembourg, yet no less than 130 hectares of 'sovereign' German vineyards are located here. In the north, east and west outskirts of this French city can be found vineyards planted with typically Palatinate varieties, such as Müller-Thurgau, Portugeizer, Scheurebe and Huxelrebe. They belong to, and are still tended by, their German owners, who harvest the grapes and trundle them over the border every year. What sort of wine do they make with this crop? An EC blend of table wine, perhaps? No. A German *Tafelwein* that must state clearly that it has been made from French grapes? No, nothing of the sort. It is officially classified as German Qualitätswein from the Bereich Südliche Weinstrasse!

Wolxheim, Bas-Rhin

Location: 7 miles west of Strasbourg on the D45 between Ergersheim and Soultz-les-Bains
Area classified as AOC: 183 hectares, including 28 hectares (or 15 per cent) of *grand cru* vineyards
AOC area under vine: 142 hectares
Grands crus: Altenberg de Wolxheim (28 hectares)
Other vineyard names in use: Clos Philippe Grass (part of the *lieu-dit* Rothstein, Muhlberger); Horn de Wolxheim (Muhlberger); Rothstein (Muhlberger); Clos Roth-Stein (part of the *lieu-dit* Rothstein, Jean Arbogast)
Soil: Limestone
Producers located in the village: Jean Arbogast, Charles Dischler, François Muhlberger, Laurent Vogt
Others also owning vines in, or making wines from, the village: Lucien Brand, CV Traenheim
Annual festivals: Fête du Riesling (early September)

Wolxheim's Altenberg, which is a *grand cru* of course, provided Napoleon with one of his favourite wines, which might well have been a *vin de paille*, as this village was one of the ten in Alsace to gain a reputation for this style of wine in the nineteenth century. Unlike the *vins de pailles* of the Haut-Rhin, Wolxheim's was essentially Muscat-based. Charles Dischler makes fine village Riesling, Muhlberger flowery Gewurztraminer and an interesting blend of Pinots from the *lieu-dit* Horn de Wolxheim.

Wuenheim, Haut-Rhin

Location: 15 miles south-south-west of Colmar, between Soultz and Hartmannswiller
Area classified as AOC: 145.83 hectares, including 35.86 hectares (or 25 per cent) of *grand cru* vineyards
AOC area under vine: 79 hectares
Grands crus: Ollwiller (35.86 hectares)
Other vineyard names in use: Château Ollwiller (part of Grand Cru Ollwiller, Cave du Vieil Armand); Clos de la Tourelle (part of Grand Cru Ollwiller, Cave du Vieil Armand)
Soil: Limestone
Producers located in the village: CV Vieil Armand
Others also owning vines in, or making wines from, the village: Château Ollwiller, Raymond Schmitt, CV Turckheim, Wolfberger
Annual festivals: Fête du Vin (last weekend in September)

Wuenheim has been growing vines since at least the twelfth century and used to be appreciated for its Chasselas. The best wines are found, not unnaturally, on the Grand Cru Ollwiller, although I can comment only on Rieslings, the best of which have come from Château Ollwiller, CV Vieil Armand and Raymond Schmitt.

Zellenberg, Haut-Rhin

Location: 6 miles north-north-west of Colmar, between Bennwihr and Ribeauvillé
Area classified as AOC: 217 hectares, including 13 hectares (or 6 per cent) of *grand cru* vineyards
AOC area under vine: 189 hectares
Grands crus: Froehn (13 hectares)

Other vineyard names in use: Burlenberg (Jean Huttard); Hagenschlauf (Jean Becker); Kronenbourg (Roger Jung); Rimelsberg (Jean Becker)
Soil: Marl and limestone
Producers located in the village: Jean Becker, Jean Huttard, Edmond Rentz
Others also owning vines in, or making wines from, the village: CV Beblenheim, Maison Bott-Geyl, Dopff & Irion, Dopff Au Moulin, Hugel & Fils, Mader, Edgard Schaller & Fils

Uniquely in Alsace, Zellenberg is situated on a hilltop. There are other large mounds, such as the Bollenberg, but only one with a village perched on its top. It was established in the ninth century, when monks cleared the hill of its forest. The name 'Zell' means a monk's cell. The wines of Zellenberg are the forgotten wines of Alsace (at one time the Riesling and Gewurztraminer ranked among the best in the region). For some reason they became unfashionable and only now are they slowly regaining recognition, albeit for Muscat from Grand Cru Froehn, first and foremost. I predict that Hagenschlauf, rather than Froehn, will resurrect the reputation of Zellenberg's great Rieslings of the past with its ultra-ripe, peachy-musk fruit and fine acidity, while Rimelsberg will not only breathe life back into the reputation of this village's Gewurztraminer, with its equally exotic rendition of this grape, but will also create a new one for its smoky-rich Tokay-Pinot Gris. The quality and style of these wines will not be established immediately, but Jean Becker is showing remarkable progress and I look forward to others in the village giving him rather stiffer competition.

Zellwiller, Bas-Rhin

Location: 25 miles north of Colmar, between Stotzheim and Barr
Area classified as AOC: 55 hectares
AOC area under vine: 41 hectares
Grands crus: None
Other vineyard names in use: None
Soil: Limestone

I know nothing about this village.

Zimmerbach, Haut-Rhin

Location: 5 miles west of Colmar, just before Walbach, on the road from
Turckheim to Wihr-au-Val
Area classified as AOC: 53.34 hectares
AOC area under vine: 32 hectares
Grands crus: None
Other vineyard names in use: Côtes du Val St-Grégoire (CV Turckheim)
Soil: Granite

Headquarters of the resistance movement during the Second World
War, Zimmerbach was also one of the last outposts of hybrid vines,
which accounted for one in every two vines as recently as the
mid-1970s, but its south-facing hillside is now mostly planted with
Pinot Blanc and capable of producing a fresh, zesty style of wine.

5
The Grands Crus

━━━━

While it is true that very few individual site names have been traditionally used to commercialize Alsace wines, the best *terroirs* have always been known locally. Even the biggest merchants have consistently sourced certain of their best wines from these specific sites and if you analyse their holdings today, you will find a good concentration of *grands crus*. Many of the most famous Alsace wines have thus been single-vineyard wines in all but name.

ESTABLISHING THE *GRAND CRU* SYSTEM IN ALSACE

It was the growers, not merchants, who pushed for *grands crus*, as it was the growers who would gain most from a system that focuses attention on the idea that wines of superior quality are produced from individually named sites. The belief, however, that merchants were solidly against the *grand cru* concept is a myth. The only merchants who still do not market *grand cru* wines are Beyer, Hugel and Trimbach, and it is because of the importance of these three houses, particularly on export markets, that their views and actions have been taken as the official stance for all Alsace merchants. Yet it is by no means a black and white issue for even these firms and their views have been over-simplified and grossly misinterpreted in recent years.

Johnny Hugel's views on *grands crus* have been quoted more than anyone else's, which is probably due to the fact that he talks more than anyone else, but how often do we read that he was president of the first commission set up to advise INAO on *grands crus*, for example? It is true that he is passionately rebellious about the subject now, but he actually sat on committees to delimit some of the *grand crus*, so his views have been shaped over a considerable number of years and deserve more than a few blunt statements quoted in the press.

The idea of *grands crus* was first mooted in the AOC regulations of 1962. At this time, *grand cru* was not an *appellation* in its own right, but merely an expression that could be used in conjunction with the basic AOC Vin d'Alsace to indicate a wine of superior quality. There was no mention whatsoever of any sort of limitation to specific sites or *lieux-dits*, although the entire ethos of European *appellations*, whether issued directly by INAO in France or part of the EC wine regime dictates of Brussels, is that they are geographically based; thus when *grand cru* moved from being just an expression to a fully-fledged AOC, the delimitation of suitable sites was inevitable. At the time, however, the expression *grand cru* was simply restricted to five varieties, which included Pinot Noir in addition to the four that qualify today (Riesling, Muscat, Gewurztraminer and Tokay-Pinot Gris) and a slightly higher technical specification (minimum natural alcoholic degree of 10 per cent by volume for Riesling and Muscat, 11 per cent for the others). Hugel was in fact using the term *grand cru* on some of its best wines, but as the official limits were far lower than the levels the firm had set itself, they stopped the practice. Not that this was the reason Hugel gave. They thought it prudent to explain to customers that the name had to be changed due to legislation, which made the firm appear to be morally scrupulous, as they were not yet obliged to do so and commercially it was a very expensive step to take. It was, no doubt, the right course of action; had Hugel merely changed the label without reference to any reason, their customers would have spotted it and wondered what the company had been caught doing. One paradox about the great public is that it is very difficult to make them (us?) take notice of something important, yet they pick up the silliest little details. Drouhin, for example, will never forget the time they revamped their Clos des Mouches label, as numerous American customers noticed there were less flies printed on the new one and were convinced the wine was not as good as it used to be with more flies on the label. Several customers apparently wrote to Drouhin demanding a reinstatement of the original number of flies!

Well, the fly in the *grand cru* ointment for Hugel encouraged him to take a leading role in how the forthcoming legislation would be enacted. In 1975 a list of no less than 94 *lieux-dits*, or named sites, was proffered by the growers for consideration; the fact that this was reduced to just 25 when it was officially published in 1983 was due in no small part to the efforts of Hugel and his *Comité de Délimitation des Grands Crus*, even though he was not entirely happy with the size of many of those *grands crus* and his committee had been disbanded, some say sacked, five years earlier.

The committee that Hugel had presided over between 1975 and 1978 was certainly one of the most prestigious and expert bodies ever asked to contemplate the concept of Alsace *grands crus*. In addition to Hugel, whose vast experience cannot be disputed, there were two extremely knowledgeable growers, François Muhlberger and Marcel Humbrecht, not to mention Robert Marocke, the eminent INRA (Institut Nationale Recherche Agricole) geological expert and co-author (with Claude Sittler) of *Terroirs et Vins d'Alsace*. Hugel believed in a real *grand cru* system and thought the only way it could be achieved was to be right there in the middle of it, arguing his case, but after three years he realized the impossibility of the task. Informed sources say that his committee was disbanded because of Schlossberg, the very first *grand cru* to be delimited (to illustrate the forthcoming regulations for the new AOC). The committee could find only 20 hectares and thought they were being generous at that, but the committee that replaced Hugel's found 80 hectares, which led to jokes about the Hanging Gardens of Kientzheim and the theory of multi-layered viticulture whereby the vines are planted on top of one another.

Hugel became so disillusioned by the whole system that he began speaking out and has been constantly quoted about it ever since. He has said, for example, that he has serious reservations about the Germanic-sounding names of these *crus*. After a lifetime of telling people that Alsace is French, he reckons that a blitzkrieg of new Alsace wines bearing Germanic names only makes matters worse. I disagree with him. There is a French-German confusion, but not among those consumers knowledgeable enough to seek out these more expensive wines, which even now account for barely 5 per cent of Alsace wines. Where the identity problem does exist is among the base of wine drinkers, who see the Germanic looking Flûte d'Alsace bottle (so beloved that its use is enforced by law) and naturally think it is German. If they take the trouble to examine the label, they will see Germanic names for the producer and villages. Even the French *département* names make them think they are drinking a Rhine wine, which of course they are, but it's all part of the confusion that is present at the grass-roots of the market, not the top.

Hugel has worried unnecessarily about the Germanic-sounding names of the *grands crus*, but I sympathize with him over their delimitation. The whole process of proposing, examining and delimiting these *grands crus* has proved to be too ridiculously democratic. That, of course, is how things must be in the Liberty, Equality and Fraternity of the French republic, but democracy in this case merely means that growers propose their own sites, agree their authenticity and delimit them themselves. For various reasons, some growers did not want to propose their own sites (see Kaefferkopf, for example), which has resulted in no recognition for a few of the most famous names of Alsace, while fictitious sites have been conjured up. This is not proper delimitation, it is creative classification.

Some growers lumped several different *crus* into one super-site in the belief (probably correct) that they would be allowed only one or perhaps two *grands crus* for their particular village. There was also the mentality that every village must have at least one *grand cru*, whatever the reputation (or lack of reputation) of its vineyards.

THE DELIMITATION PROCESS

After much discussion, research and haggling, the growers draw up a map of their *grand cru* and present it to INAO. That is just the beginning, however, as other growers now get a chance to see the proposed delimitation and those on the periphery of a *cru* naturally demand to know why their vines, which adjoin those proposed for a *grand cru*, should not be of the same status. It is like standing between two vines in a vineyard, one of which is classified, while the other is not and asking why this should be so? Any grower could ask the question and when you get down to such specific details as two vines growing next to each other, there can be no satisfactory answer.

All *terroirs* are defined by various factors, such as soil, aspect, drainage, microclimate, but none of them are so clear cut that you can differentiate between two neighbouring vines. The topsoil is dragged this way then that way by man or tractor and altered by various practices, natural or chemical fertilization being the least of them. The subsoil and drainage? Nobody can be that precise about where faults occur beneath the surface without removing the topsoil and physically chipping away at the base rock. Like the topsoil, you can say that it runs here or there, but the dividing lines are even less easy to determine accurately and it is impossible to say which way a specific vine's roots have gone. The roots of two rows of vines probably intermingle anyway, even if one row belongs to a *grand cru* and the other does not. As for aspect, the curve of even the steepest slope is such that it is impossible to distinguish between the effects on two vines next to each other, unless there is something as physically abrupt as a cliff, but then there would be no second vine to discuss. As to microclimate, it is even more difficult to draw a line through thin air and say what the weather is like either side.

So there you have it. Those growers who view the proposed delimitation and realize their own vines are right next door have every right to feel unjustly penalized and so the real haggling begins. This could go on for ever and sometimes almost does, as plots two or three removed from the boundary originally proposed eventually border it and then clamour for inclusion. There has to be a cut-off point somewhere, otherwise the first plot in a continuous strip of vines stretching the length and breadth of France could claim to be part of the same *lieu-dit* as the last! It is possible to draw the approximate borders of an authentic *terroir* because of the reaction of the vines, which can be discernible every year in the foliage or fruit. Growers may be fond of saying that it stops at such and such a row and, indeed, when it does affect the foliage, it is possible literally to see these distinct boundaries from a distance, but if you farm that land year after year, the grower knows that the limits shrink and expand by two or three rows (or the equivalent) according to annual conditions. It is the outer limit of these boundaries that should be drawn, but by somebody totally oblivious to who owns what.

THE ANTI *CRUS*

Hugel has no intention of marketing a *grand cru*, either now or at any time in the foreseeable future. He is understandably disenchanted, but remains true to his initial enthusiasm, which explains why he still maintains that 'a seriously delimited *grand cru* system would be perfect'. After Hugel, the firm of F.E. Trimbach is most often quoted in these matters, as they steadfastly refuse to put Rosacker on their Riesling Clos Ste-Hune. I am sure, however, that Trimbach would love to put the term *grand cru* on their label (as indeed they did 50 years ago), providing this referred to Clos Ste-Hune, not Rosacker, that Rosacker would not be mentioned on the label and, equally important, that the term *grand cru* was not debased by so many undistinguished, fictitious and oversized *lieux-dits*. It goes without saying that Clos Ste-Hune does not need the name Rosacker on its label to justify its status. It is not just the most outstanding Riesling in Alsace, it is one of the world's greatest white wines and in such circles where does the name Rosacker figure? Although some famous *clos*, such as Clos Gaensbroennel, have begun to label their wines with the name of their respective *grands crus*, Trimbach would have nothing to gain. There are some fine wines produced elsewhere in Rosacker and I doubt the Trimbachs would deny this, but there is a world of difference between one of many fine Rieslings and Clos Ste-Hune, so why stretch the global fame of this tiny 1.25 hectare vineyard to Rosacker's 26.18 hectares?

Only the house of Léon Beyer seems to be unconditionally and philosophically opposed to the *grand cru* concept and whereas I would fight for Marc Beyer's right to say what he believes, I can only follow his reasoning, not agree with it. He told me, 'Of course the *terroir* is vital to the character of a wine, but we believe that it is the winemaker who achieves the reputation, hence the ups and downs of some of the great Bordeaux châteaux.' It is his last clause I cannot accept. We agree that the *terroir* is vital, which is why Beyer's Riesling 'Cuvée Particulière' is always sourced from the Grand Cru Pfersigberg, just as his Gewurztraminer 'Cuvée des Comtes d'Eguisheim' is always from Grand Cru Eichberg, even if neither wine indicates this origin on the label. And, of course, we agree that the winemaker is vital, as he either maximizes or minimizes the intrinsic quality of the grapes he receives. When it comes to reputation, however, the 1855 classification has proved to be remarkably resilient. The exceptionally well informed consumer might well know the ups and downs in quality of certain illustrious Bordeaux châteaux, but this has not prevented these very same wines achieving prices far higher than they deserve. If the sovereignty of Alsace had not bounced backwards and forwards between France and Germany and the region had had the foresight to create its own 1855 classification based on vineyard origin, Alsace wines would be much more famous now, the house of Beyer would have a much greater profile and its wines would fetch twice their current price (even though they are relatively upmarket in terms of Alsace wines).

A *grand cru* system, even a flawed one (as they all inevitably are), serves to focus the mind of the consumer wonderfully. The sovereignty of Alsace did bounce back and forth, there was no *grand cru* inspiration in the nineteenth century and the industry has irrevocably changed. Alsace wine, its makers and its consumers, have become too sophisticated to be restrained by the simplicity of one basic AOC defined in 1962 and the day of the *grand cru* was bound to arrive. Some sort of classification was inevitable, whatever Marc Beyer thinks, and it will stay, even if it takes a while to shape up.

AN ALTERNATIVE CLASSIFICATION

My only regret is that they started with *grands crus*, instead of something a little more modest, such as *premiers crus*, and that they created too many of them, far too quickly. There are probably more proposals of how this could have been better achieved than there are variations of proportional representation, but my own pet solution would have started out far more liberalized and ended up far more restricted. I would have allowed any number of named sites (could be hundreds or even thousands, as far as I am concerned; *see* introduction to 'The *lieux-dits* of Alsace' in Chapter 6 for the absolute potential number of such sites) to filter on to the market with the status of *cru exceptionnel*, not *grand cru*. With time, the best of these would rise to the top of the pile, attracting critical acclaim and receiving higher prices, thus after, say, 15 or 20 years, it would be possible to upgrade the top 50 to *premier cru exceptionnel*. After another similar period, the very best of these (maybe only 20 in number) could be promoted to *grand cru exceptionnel*.

One of the major defects of the current system is its inability to recognize that some sites have been historically famous for producing the highest quality blended wines (see Kaefferkopf and

Sporen) or the finest versions of varieties not now permitted for *grand cru* (see Hengst, Kitterlé, Sonnenglanz, Steinert, Zinnkoepflé and Zotzenberg), while the regulations blindly allow Riesling, Gewurztraminer, Tokay-Pinot Gris and Muscat for every classified growth, when all four varieties do not excel in every site.

Had they followed a slower process, such as the one I suggest, the true *grands crus* to emerge after 30 to 40 years could be restricted to the wine styles that have specifically excelled, whether that be one variety or eight, pure varietal wine or blended, or Crémant. The proper way to reach the most objective decisions would be for the growers and merchants to elect a panel of impartial experts with no political axes to wield, then give them the power to impose their delimitation, classification and future upgrading of sites on the trade.

It is all very well for anyone to be clever with hindsight, to declare that the process should have been evolutionary, rather than revolutionary, but you can't squeeze the paste back into the tube. After the first 25 *grands crus* were delimited in 1983, an additional 23 *leux-dits* were awarded *grand cru* status in 1985 subject to an official delimitation of their borders, which was expected to be finalized by 1987, but was still under negotiation between the grower and INAO when in March 1988 Florimont and Bruderthal were added. And finally, if that word can be used in the context of this region's *grand cru* legislation, the number rose to 51 in 1990 with the long overdue inclusion of Kaefferkopf, although still only 25 had been officially delimited and this did not change until the decree of 17 December 1992, when all but one (Kaefferkopf) of Alsace's *grands crus* were eventually classified.

So now they exist, that is a fact, and whatever Beyer, Hugel, Trimbach *et al.* do or think, the *grand cru* system will remain intact, although the market will ultimately determine the truly great growths from those that are merely *premier cru* in all but name by virtue of the prices they fetch.

AOC ALSACE *GRAND CRU*: FACTS AND FIGURES

Of the 20,245 hectares classified as AOC Alsace, 1,610 hectares have been delimited (or in the case of Kaefferkopf, are under consideration) as AOC *grand cru*. This represents less than 8 per

cent of the total available viticultural surface, although not all of
this is actually cultivated with vines. Indeed, as there were only
13,487 hectares of AOC Alsace vineyards in 1991, for example, so
only 585 hectares of *grand cru* vineyards were in production, which
represents an even smaller proportion of just over 4 per cent. A
good part of the reason why less than half the area classified as
AOC Alsace Grand Cru is actually in production is because some of
the land in question is not even planted with vines. However, other
factors include certain proprietors who do not market their best
wines as *grands crus* (F.E. Trimbach, Hugel, Léon Beyer, etc.), or
those who do, but also like to cultivate varieties such as Pinot Noir,
Pinot Blanc, Auxerrois, Chasselas and Sylvaner in part of their best
vineyards and thus cannot claim *grand cru* status (such as
JosMeyer). There are those who produce classic blends, which also
do not qualify for *grand cru* status (e.g. Hugel and the ongoing
quandary over Kaefferkopf) and, finally, there are some growers
who prefer not to be restricted by the *grand cru* yield, but as that is
not very strict, they should have their vineyards confiscated, be
locked in a medieval dungeon and left to survive on bread and
cheap Edelzwicker.

To qualify as AOC Alsace Grand Cru, the yield must be restricted to 70 hectolitres per hectare, which quality conscious Alsace
growers agree is far too high for a basic *appellation*, let alone one
that claims *grand cru* status. Since 1987 the authorities have fixed a
temporary limit of 65 hectolitres per hectare, which is better, but
certainly nowhere near good enough. Only four varieties are
allowed: Riesling, Muscat, Gewurztraminer and Tokay-Pinot Gris.
The wine must be 100 per cent pure varietal and 100 per cent from
the vintage indicated on the label. The Riesling and Muscat grapes
must possess a natural alcoholic potential of at least 10 per cent
alcohol by volume, while the higher ripening varieties of Gewutz-
traminer and Tokay-Pinot Gris must achieve 12 per cent. Until
December 1992, the minimum must weights for these two varietal
divisions of *grand cru* were 170 and 186 grams per litre of sugar
respectively, but a decree then dropped the first of these to 153 g/l,
which is the equivalent of just 9 per cent alcohol and thus allows
the producer to increase the much needed acidity in his Riesling and
Muscat *grand cru* wines without sacrificing richness. (Because the
average must weight will still have to be at least 170 grams per litre
in order to achieve a minimum natural alcoholic content of 10 per

cent, the winemaker has to balance any underripe grapes with overripe grapes.) There being less of a perceived problem concerning preferred levels of acidity in Gewurztraminer and Tokay-Pinot Gris, the minimum must weight for these two varieties was not dropped, but actually increased, albeit by an irrelevant one gram to 187g. This was a mistake because it never harms to allow the winemaker any flexibility that could improve his or her wines, because no one is forced to use it and the overall richness and strength of the product is guaranteed.

GRAND CRU PROFILES

The following profiles are based on six years of tasting and research, having taken this long to dig out examples from many of the grands crus. Some grand cru wines I have discovered only in the last year or so, as more and more producers have begun to market their wines from these sites. The 1990s should be a golden era for anyone who has enjoyed Alsace wine in the past, as there is a new generation of winemakers, who are eager to express themselves and have taken up the grand cru challenge with an enthusiasm unprecedented in this conservative corner of France. We know which are the truly great grands crus, or most of them anyway, but it will take thirty years or more of continuous production by numerous growers before we have a clear picture of the full potential of many of the lesser known growths. In the meantime, we can all enjoy the differences.

Altenberg de Bergbieten
Bergbieten, Bas-Rhin
29 hectares

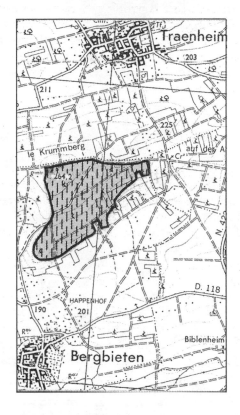

South-east-facing, steep, middle slope, 210–265m; marly-clay soil permeated with highly absorbent Keuper gypsum fragments, which improve the soil's heat-retention and water-circulation properties.

Of the several Altenbergs in Alsace, only three have been classified. The reputation of Bergbieten's has been documented since 1050 (Pope Leo IX archives), but it is merely an exceptional growth, not a truly great one. The wines have a very floral character and immediate appeal, yet can improve for several years in bottle.

Frédéric Mochel has always been the top performer in this *cru*, producing tangy-fruity Gewurztraminer and spicy-rich Riesling with lots of ripe acidity and vanilla, cloves and cinnamon complexity (no, they are not the wrong way around!), but recent vintages have seen very serious competition from a rapidly improving Roland Schmitt, who now makes classy Gewurztraminer and very intense Riesling. The CV Traenheim makes a soft, floral Gewurztraminer under its 'Les Vins du Roi Dagobert' label. Other growers with vines on the *grand cru* include Gilbert Leininger and GAEC Mochel-Lorentz.

Altenberg de Bergheim
Bergheim, Haut-Rhin
35.06 hectares

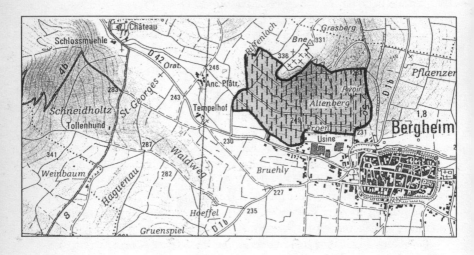

Mostly south facing, fairly steep slope, 220–320m; thin topsoil of very stony, red-coloured, fossil-rich calcareous-marl over limestone bedrock.

The combination of its marly limestone soil, warm and temperate microclimate, very regular rainfall and well drained slopes has made this Altenberg a true *grand cru* since the twelfth century. Altenberg de Bergheim is particularly famous for its Gewurztraminer, which is tight and austere in youth, but gains in depth and bouquet with ageing. It is fascinating to compare these wines with those of neighbouring Kanzlerberg, which also has a marly soil, but a much heavier type and the wines produced are distinctly fatter.

The most expressive wines are those of Marcel Deiss, made by the son Jean-Michel, who has a passion for wine that verges on the manic. To see him in full flow, with his wild brown curly locks, obsessed eyes and cutting smile, as he extols the contrasting virtues of his different *terroirs* is an experience not to be missed by any wine-lover. By reducing yields and harvesting late, Jean-Michel manages to extract the richest of all Altenberg de Bergheim's Gewurztraminers. Not the fatness of Kanzlerberg, but a richness of extract that is expressed as a liquorice intensity that develops great complexity in bottle. Altenberg also produces fine Riesling and Marcel Deiss again provides the yardstick, making wines that acquire the classic honeyed-petrolly character. One of the best Altenberg Rieslings I have tasted was the 1976 from Gustave Lorentz, yet the wine was originally refused its AOC and had to be resubmitted! Gustave Lorentz are definitely the second best producers for this *cru*. They achieve the same intensity of flavour in the Gewurztraminer as Deiss, but not quite the finesse or complexity (which is not to deny the great class of the wine). Charles Koehly makes a good Gewurztraminer Vendange Tardive. Other producers of varying success include Fernand Engel, Louis Freyburger, Halbeizen and Jean-Martin Spielmann (exceptionally fine Gewurztraminer in 1988). The CV Beblenheim also has members with vineyards in this *cru*, but did not produce a pure Altenberg de Bergheim wine until relatively recently (a fine 1990 Riesling with ripe tropical fruits on the palate turning into definitive pineapple on the finish). Muscat grown on this *grand cru* is supposed to have a minty character, but I have not noticed. The best Altenberg de Bergheim Muscats I have tasted have been from Marcel Deiss and Gustave Lorentz, but both were far too discreet to show any mint and, frankly, not worthy of *grand cru* status.

Altenberg de Wolxheim
Wolxheim, Haut-Rhin
Approximately 28 hectares

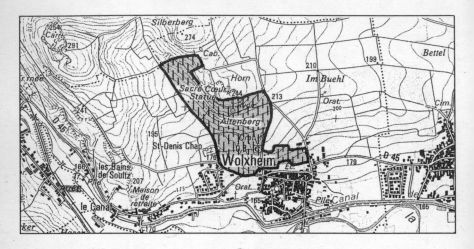

*At the foot of the Rocher du Horn, south-east facing, modest incline,
200–250m; very stony calcareous-marl, extremely dry microclimate.*

Historical records show that various religious orders have had a
predilection for this Altenberg since 1003. It was appreciated by
Napoleon, but cannot honestly be described as one of the greatest
growths of Alsace, although it has a certain reputation for its
Riesling wines.

Charles Dischler and Muhlberger both make the best this *cru* can
offer, albeit in different styles, Dischler being richer, Muhlberger
more elegant (his Gewurztraminer is flowery rather than spicy).
The Altenberg de Wolxheim produced by the CV Traenheim under
its 'Les Vins du Roi Dagobert' label falls between the two.

Brand
Turckheim, Haut-Rhin
57 hectares

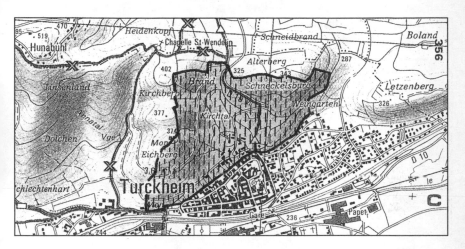

Steep, south-south and east facing slope, 260–343m; with very diverse soils, ranging from silty colluvium or mica over granite in the north, where the original Brand hill lies, to granitic sand over limestone and marl in the eastern section formerly called Schneckelsburg or Schneckenberg.

This *cru* might legitimately be called 'Brand new'. The original Brand was a tiny *cru* – little more than 3 hectares – with an ancient history and a truly authentic reputation. In 1924, however, substantial sections of various surrounding sites (Steinglitz, Kirchthal, Schneckenberg, Weingarten and Jebsal) were incorporated, so that by the time Hubrecht Duijker published his book, *The Loire, Alsace and Champagne* (1981), it had already swollen to 30 hectares. Since then, much of Turckheim's Eichberg has been added, so that Brand now comprises almost 60 hectares.

Visually it remains one of the most magnificent sights in the entire region and the wines from this confederation of *crus* consistently excite me with their quality, the only pity is that they cannot claim their authentic names and retain their status. The original Brand site was a suntrap where, so the legend goes, a battle took place between the sun and a local dragon in the Middle Ages. The dragon lost and was burnt to the ground, leaving the brand and infusing the soil with a heat so fierce that grapes would always have great colour and extraordinary ripeness. This is supposed to explain why all of Turckheim was once planted entirely with black varieties and famous for a red wine known as Turks' Blood (honestly!). Another version of the legend maintains that the dragon survived after losing the battle with the sun and took refuge in a cave beneath the Brand, where it still breathes fire and warmth into the soil.

The excellent local cooperative still produces one of the best Pinot Noir wines in Alsace ('Cuvée à l'Ancienne'), but few black grapes are to be found on the Brand itself today and it is in fact another member of the Pinot family that excels here, the Tokay-Pinot Gris. Riesling and Gewurztraminer are very nearly as successful, although the former suffers in the original Brand site in the best years, preferring an average or damp one, when the wine will have enough acidity to balance the Brand's intrinisic fruitiness. As the price in such 'off' years will be lower, it is the knowledgeable consumer who ends up with both the best and cheapest Riesling wines from this *cru*. On Brand's satellite sites, where calcareous soils are more in evidence, the Riesling is more reliable, yet it never quite matches the intensity of fruit found in a true Brand wine. It is on these soils, however, that the Gewurztraminer shows best, with abundant acidity and often possessing a super citrussy or grape-fruity finesse. Domaine Zind Humbrecht is without doubt the best producer on the Brand, although superb wines are also produced by Domaines Dopff Au Moulin, JosMeyer, Pierre Sparr and the CV Turckheim (particularly Gewurztraminer and Vendanges Tardives). Albert Boxler is somewhat erratic in quality, but sometimes produces something stunning. On a more modest level, François Baur and Auguste Hurst can also be recommended.

Bruderthal
Molsheim, Bas-Rhin
Approximately 19 hectares

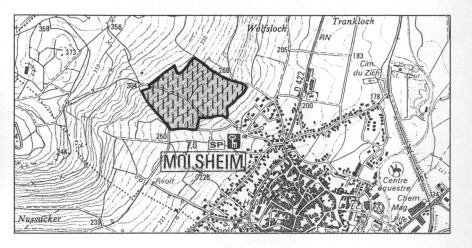

*South-east facing, up to 300m; calcareous-marl over grey limestone, very
stony on the upper slopes.*

Named by Cistercian monks, the first mention of Bruderthal was in
1316 in Molsheim's archives. It was one of two growths (the other
being Florimont) that were singled out for *grand cru* status in
March 1988, which, with the second tranche of 23 sites on the
statute books from the year before, brought the total of *grands crus*
up to 50. The exposure and drainage of Bruderthal encourage
higher levels of maturity than can be found in surrounding vineyards. Riesling and Gewurztraminer occupy most of this *cru* and
are reputed to be the best varieties. Gewurztraminer is supposed to
be very floral, with scents of acacia and roses. I have tasted a good
and fruity Riesling from Bernard Weber, which was elegant in style,
but not really top stuff and the Riesling, Tokay-Pinot Gris and
Gewurztraminer of Domaine Neumeyer have not impressed me at
all.

Eichberg
Eguisheim, Haut-Rhin
57.6 hectares

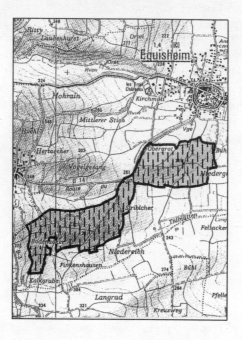

South-east facing, gentle slopes, 220–240m; calcareous-marl subsoil covered with a pebbly scree of limestone, marl, sandstone and gravel.

The Eichberg vineyard was taxed by the abbey of Murbach as long ago as the eleventh century. It has a warm microclimate with the lowest rainfall in the Colmar area and produces very aromatic wines of exceptional delicacy, yet great longevity. Genuinely famous for Gewurztraminer, which is potentially the finest in Alsace, Eichberg is also capable of producing superb Riesling and Tokay-Pinot Gris.

Kuentz-Bas produces the most sublime of all Grand Cru Eichberg wines with its Gewurztraminer Vendange Tardive, which combines sensational fruit and great power with remarkable finesse. Charles Baur produces a fine, elegant Riesling, while Paul Ginglinger's Riesling is richer and more aromatic. Ginglinger also makes a good

Gewurztraminer. Albert Hertz makes a Gewurztraminer that develops a pungent spiciness. It is good, but no better than his excellent generic Gewurztraminer. His Riesling is rich and enjoyable, but lacks finesse. Although the house of Léon Beyer is philosophically opposed to the *grand cru* system, its Gewurztraminer 'Cuvée des Comtes d'Eguisheim' is none the less 100 per cent pure Eichberg. The CV Eguisheim, which sells its wines under the Wolfberger label, is one of the most underrated producers of Grand Cru Eichberg. Others include Pierre-Henri Ginglinger, Alphonse Kuentz, Domaine Edouard Leiber, André Scherer and Gerard Stintzi.

Engelberg
Dahlenheim, Bas-Rhin
Approximately 11 hectares

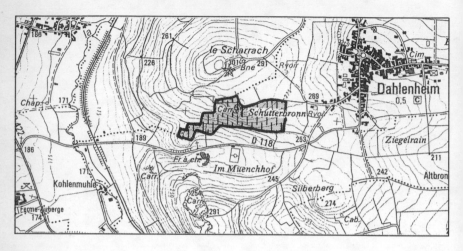

Half a hectare is actually in neighbouring Scharrachbergheim; fully south-facing, fairly steep, 250–300m; shallow stony calcareous-marl soil, rich in fossils, particularly in the extreme west.

The wines of Engelberg were first mentioned as early as 884, but most historical references are the result of its ownership by various religious orders and not due to any sustained reputation for quality. This vineyard receives long hours of sunshine and is supposed to favour Gewurztraminer and Riesling, but it is impossible for me to make any judgement about the contemporary worth of this *cru* when I have tasted only two examples, both from Domaine Jean-Pierre Bechtold. One was a Riesling that was so unexciting I forgot to write down the vintage, the other was a 1987 Gewurztraminer that had the strange aroma of a cold ashtray intermingled with mint, although it had fine minerally fruit on the palate and a flattering vanilla aftertaste.

Florimont
Ingersheim, Haut-Rhin
Approximately 15 hectares

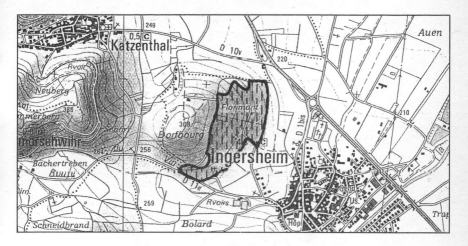

South and east facing and fairly steep, 250–280m; pre-Vosgian limestone butte with a relatively stony, calcareous-marl topsoil.

Florimont means 'hill of flowers' and refers to the Mediterranean flora found on its sun-blessed slopes (the only other being on the Zinnkoepflé and Strangenberg slopes of Westhalten). The wines of Ingersheim have been well known since the Middle Ages and although Florimont, which dominates the main slope above the town, was greatly appreciated by the Baron Schwendi, it has not yet really established a name for itself. Except, perhaps, in the hands of Bruno Sorg, one of the lesser-known growers of Alsace, but consistently the greatest producer of Florimont. He makes a fine Gewurztraminer, which is the widest plant variety and generally considered the best variety for the *terroir*, but it is Sorg's stunning Riesling that achieves and surpasses the sort of quality one expects from a true *grand cru*. The CV Ingersheim produces big but well-balanced Gewurztraminers with plenty of smoky fruit. Florimont was one of two growths (the other being Bruderthal) singled out for *grand cru* status in March 1988, which, with the second tranche of 23 sites from the year before, brought the total of *grands crus* up to 50.

Frankstein
Dambach-la-Ville, Bas-Rhin
Approximately 53 hectares

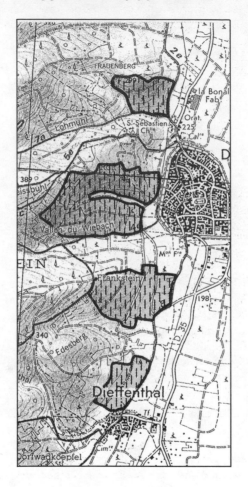

*Four separate plots proposed, east and south-east facing, fairly steep,
220–310m; deep colluvial topsoil, granitic and acid from decomposed
twin-mica granite bedrock.*

The warm, well-drained, granite soil of this *cru* is best suited to
Riesling and Gewurztraminer. The Riesling is delicate and racy,

while the Gewurztraminer is elegant and floral. J. Hauller is by far the best producer of Grand Cru Frankstein, both for Riesling and Gewurztraminer. Hauller is generally underrated for his entire range of wines. Other producers include Pierre Arnold, Louis Gisselbrecht (a surprisingly good Riesling in 1988), Willy Gisselbrecht (better than cousin Louis), Beck-Hartweg, Jean-Claude Beck, Louis Hauller, Guy Mersiol, Schaeffer-Woerly and the CV Dambach-la-Ville.

————

Froehn
Zellenberg, Haut-Rhin
Approximately 13 hectares

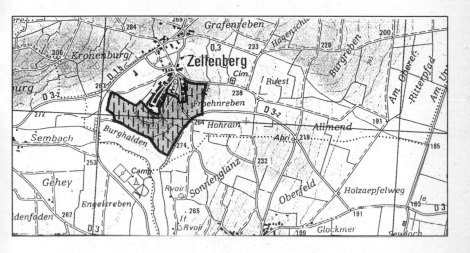

South-south-east facing, fairly steep slopes, 270–300m; dark grey, clayey and schistous marls, with beds of white limestone and carboniferous and ferruginous concretions.

Unusually for an Alsace wine village, Zellenberg sits on a hill. It is the vines that sweep up the southern half of the hill that are today classified as Froehn, a vineyard that has long been known to produce rich and long-lived Gewurztraminer, Tokay-Pinot Gris and Muscat, but it has my respect only for Gewurztraminer and, particularly, Muscat and even that was earned as recently as 1988 and from the wines of one house: Jean Becker. It was in that year that young Philippe Becker first put his mark on his family's wine business and what he did was to prune savagely his Muscat vines. As a result, he reduced his yield in the Froehn to the lowest for all *grands crus* in Alsace for the year. He went even further, however, and attempted to produce the rarest of Alsace wines, a Muscat Sélection de Grains Noble (only three ever made to my knowledge), by a method that is only theory these days. He picked the grapes individually to ensure that every one was botrytis affected and soon found that he had to use an escargot fork to achieve it! The resultant must contained no less than 405 g/l of sugar, almost double that required for Sauternes. Tasted from cask, it was so sensational that I placed an order for a case there and then. This illustrates that the potential of even the finest *cru* ultimately lies in the hands of the grower and winemaker, which is why a true *grand cru* takes many generations to establish. At its best, Becker's Riesling is elegant and slightly exotic in style, but does not have the Muscat's consistency. His Gewurztraminer has the consistency of the Muscat, but comes nowhere near it in terms of quality, although it is a most enjoyable, mellow-spicy wine.

Furstentum
Kientzheim & Sigolsheim, Haut-Rhin
27.65 hectares

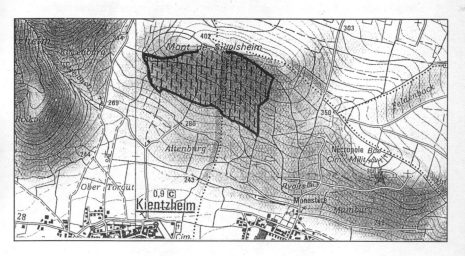

South-south-east facing, fairly steep slopes, 300–400m; brown calcareous, magnesium-rich, pebbly-marl topsoil over grey magnesium-rich limestone and calcareous-marly-sandstone bedrock.

Well protected in the heart of the beautiful Kaysersberg valley, Furstentum has an excellent exposure to the sun, is well drained and retains heat, maximizing its ability to ripen grapes. Despite this, and the fact that its origins can be traced back to at least 1330, Furstentum was not recognized as a true *grand cru* until relatively recently. Until Marcel Blanck pushed for its classification many people in Alsace itself had not even heard of it and it was not until his firm, Paul Blanck, actually began to promote the wines of Furstentum that anyone outside the area could make an objective judgement about the potential of this *cru*.

If its reputation is to rest – initially at least – on the wines of Paul Blanck, it must be seen as one of the most dramatic successes of the fledgling *grand cru* system in Alsace. If I have tasted one Furstentum wine from Paul Blanck, I have tasted fifty, such have been its efforts to understand this *cru* and exploit all its potential. In my assessment, it is best for Riesling, although the vines have to be well established to take full advantage of the *terroir*. Gewurztraminer can also be fabulous in an elegant, more floral, less spicy style, and Tokay-Pinot Gris excels even when the vines are very young. It should also be noted that Pinot Noir works well, providing wines of exceptional colour and structure, although I do not think that the Blancks have always been successful in their vinification and maturation of this style and, of course, it is not a *grand cru* variety, so cannot claim the *appellation*.

—

Geisberg
Ribeauvillé, Haut-Rhin
8.53 hectares

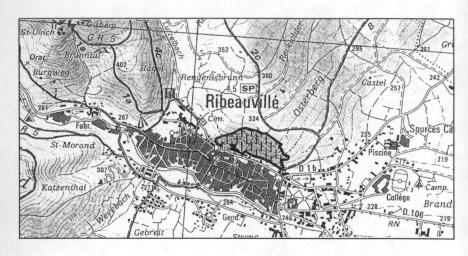

South facing with steep, terraced slopes, 250–350m; stony-clay over multicoloured sandstone layered with marls and Keuper gypsum.

Geisberg has been well documented since 1308 as Riesling country *par excellence*. The wines are fragrant and have great finesse, yet they are also powerful and long lived. These are true *grands crus*, not widely available and highly sought after.

André Kientzler is the greatest exponent of Geisberg Riesling. His regular selection is classic, his Vendange Tardive a notch higher and his SGN simply sensational. Robert Faller (not to be confused with Faller of Domaine Weinbach) produces several interesting bottlings, some of which can be quite exotic. Jean-Pierre Baltenweck is another producer, but I have not tasted his wine. Trimbach own vines here and the wine produced forms a large part of its superb 'Cuvée Frédéric Émile'.

Gloeckelberg
Rodern and St-Hippolyte, Haut-Rhin
23.4 hectares

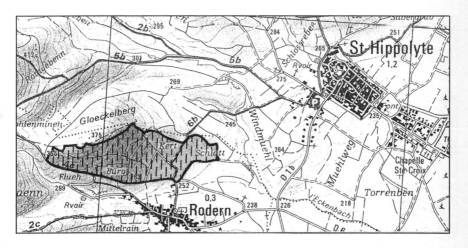

South and south-east facing, gentle slope leading up to steep slopes, 250–360m; topsoil of coarse brown sand with varying amounts of clay and carboniferous or schistous sandstone over granite bedrock.

This *cru*, which has a history dating back to the Middle Ages, is known for producing wines that are light, elegant and yet persistent. Charles Koehly occasionally disappoints, but he is certainly the top producer of Gloeckelberg. His Gewurztraminer is classic, particularly in the Vendange Tardive style, and his Tokay-Pinot Gris has tremendous acidity. The CV Ribeauvillé makes a charming, delicate Gewurztraminer that retains its youth for many years and a lush, easy to drink Tokay-Pinot Gris. François Ehrhart, Metz-Bleger and Koeberlé-Kreyer are also worth trying.

———

Goldert
Gueberschwihr, Haut-Rhin
45.35 hectares

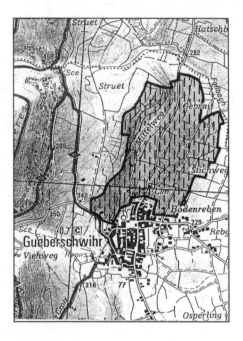

Mostly east facing with gentle slopes, but some very steep, especially on the Mittelweg in the north-west of the cru, 230–330m; calcareous soils mixed with clay and sandstone over limestone subsoil.

The reputation of Goldert dates back to 750 and this was recognized on export markets as long ago as 1728. Its name derives from the colour of its wine, the most famous of which, not surprisingly, is the naturally golden Gewurztraminer, but Muscat also excels, particularly in the hands of this *cru*'s two top growers: Domaine Zind Humbrecht and Ernst Burn (Clos St-Imer). Burn's Tokay-

Pinot Gris la Chapelle is Goldert's top-performing version of this variety. Very close behind comes the excellent CV Pfaffenheim, which makes a typically rich, spicy Gewurztraminer with a luscious creamy aftertaste. Of the rest, I would single out Bernard Humbrecht and I have had very good wines from Marcel Hertzog, Fernand Lichtlé, Louis Scherb and Clément Week. Other wines I have either seldom or never tasted, but which, on the basis of the general quality of Goldert should be worth looking out for, include Lucien Gantzer, Gérard Hertzog, Marcel Humbrecht (fine Muscat), Georges Scherb and Maurice Schueller.

Hatschbourg
Hattstatt and Voegtlinshoffen, Haut-Rhin
47.36 hectares

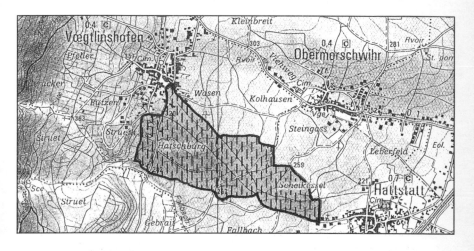

South-south-east facing with a moderate slope, 220–330m; heavy, deep but well-drained topsoil comprising colluvial deposits and gravelly loess over calcareous-marl subsoil.

Mentioned as early as the Middle Ages, Hatschbourg achieved a considerable reputation by the sixteenth and seventeenth centuries, when its wines demanded and received much higher prices than the norm, according to invoices of the time. Gewurztraminer excels, but Tokay-Pinot Gris and Riesling are also excellent. Whereas Théo Cattin does make good wines, including Grand Cru Hatschbourg, his cousin Joseph is far more talented. Next I would place the CV Eguisheim (Wolfberger), whose gifted winemaker Roland Guth takes his *grand cru* selections very seriously, and André Hartmann. Gewurztraminer and Tokay-Pinot Gris from Gérard and Serge Hartmann can be well worth the search. Other growers include Ginglinger-Fix, Domaine Kehren, Lucien Meyer and the CV Pfaffenheim.

——

Hengst
Wintzenheim, Haut-Rhin
75.78 hectares

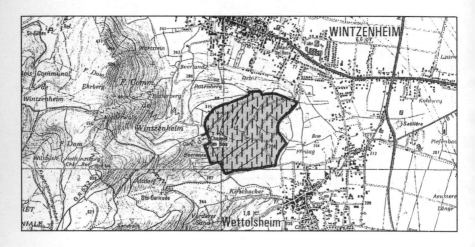

South-east facing, fairly steep slopes, 270–360m; sedimentary scree, dark and calcareous, over calcareous-marl base.

Mentioned as early as the ninth century, when the abbot of Murbach purchased some vineyards here, the Hengst was under feudal ownership of the lords of Haut-Landsbourg and Kaysersberg until the Revolution, since when its plots have been very sought after. If there were a *grand cru* for Auxerrois, then this would surely be it, as the wines from this grape have a very fine verbena aroma and a certain raciness that is not experienced elsewhere. Hengst Gewurztraminer is also very special. A complex wine, it seems to combine the most classic qualities found in the best Gewurztraminers with the orange zest and rose petal aromas that are characteristic of the Muscat. But Hengst is a very flexible *cru*, as top quality Riesling, Muscat and Tokay-Pinot Gris are also produced and Jean Meyer of JosMeyer would like to be able to put the Hengst name on the Chasselas he grows in this *grand cru*. Because he cannot, it is we who suffer, as the wine is consumed locally by people in the know. His most consistent Hengst wine is, ironically, another non-classic variety, the Pinot-Auxerrois 'H'. Domaine Zind Humbrecht consistently makes the finest Hengst, but JosMeyer can be its equal for Riesling, although less reliable for the other classic varieties, which frankly range from stunning to merely mediocre. Next comes Barmès-Buecher and Wolfberger. Henri Ehrhart makes one of the finest Hengst Tokay-Pinot Gris and Albert Mann produces a succulently rich Gewurztraminer that is grossly underrated. I would also single out Paul Buecher. Albert Mann produces Gewurztraminer and a serious Pinot Noir (but cannot put Hengst on the label, of course). Wunsch & Mann also produce a Gewurztraminer and I have heard of Hubert Krick's wines, but not tasted them. Brauneisen-Fink, Meyer-Brauneizer and Domaine Aimé Stentz all own vines on the Hengst, but have not yet produced a pure *grand cru* wine as far as I know, whereas the CV Turckheim has just begun to do so and the wines demonstrate excellent potential, particularly the Tokay-Pinot Gris.

Kaefferkopf†
Ammerschwihr, Haut-Rhin
Approximately 60 hectares

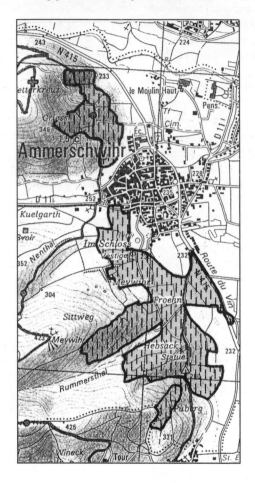

East facing, mostly gentle slopes, although quite steep high up, 240–320m;
diverse topsoils over granite bedrock.

† Although a question mark hangs over this *cru*'s official status, it is a *grand cru* as
far as I am concerned.

The greatest irony of the *grand cru* system is that Kaefferkopf, the most famous of all Alsace vineyards, was the last to receive recognition in the *grand cru* legislation (1990). It was officially delimited in 1932 by a tribunal in Colmar, which declared that only wines from Gewurztraminer, Riesling, Tokay, Muscat and Pinot Blanc – or a blend of any of these varieties – could be sold as Kaefferkopf. These conditions were enforced by AOC regulations in 1966, when Kaefferkopf was awarded its own sub-*appellation*. As *grand cru* legislation permits only pure varietal wine and limits these to just four of those allowed for Kaefferkopf, its producers were not keen to be restricted in such a way and pushed for acceptance on its own unique terms, based on historical precedence, which was, after all, the basis of all AOC regulations.

It seems unfair that they should not have been successful in forcing through acceptance of these high-quality blended wines on exclusively historical grounds. There has, after all, been a more extreme precedent set. INAO long ago agreed that pink Champagne could be blended from red and white wines, despite the fact that this is specifically forbidden for any quality wine. INAO made the ruling, however, because the *champenois* had always made pink Champagne by this method and it was endorsed by Brussels for precisely this reason. Pink Champagne remains totally unique in the entire gamut of EC quality wines. The growers of Kaefferkopf asked for much less on the same grounds and yet were refused for reasons that are contrary to the principles of the French AOC system. Furthermore, I was reliably informed that the growers of Kaefferkopf had no hope of having the tribunal's decision endorsed by INAO purely because of the diversity of its *terroir*, which is another injustice. The original delimitation in 1932 was based on custom and practice, with little or no regard to the geological integrity of the soil and subsoil, resulting in the variation of soils found today. The issue of *terroir* was to be expected, but geological uniformity has not been rigorously applied to all other *grands crus*, which makes a nonsense of using this as an objection. In the first place, geology can only be true to the subsoil, not the topsoil, and all of the Kaefferkopf classified by the tribune is situated on pure granite, whereas the rest of Ammerschwihr's vineyards are limestone. Secondly, many *grands crus* have diverse soils: Brand is the obvious example, though certainly not the only one. The third and most ironic reason is that the majority of *grands crus* are not true to the history of their *terroir*, but have been the result of compromise and finally delimited on few strict criteria of any kind, whereas the Kaefferkopf is probably the best documented *cru* in Alsace. It seems that bureaucracy and democracy have conspired to ignore the very real history of Kaefferkopf, while it has conveniently invented reputations elsewhere. Mind you, if the delimitation of every *grand cru* was faithful to its historical origin and the clock on Kaefferkopf was turned back prior to its classification in 1932, it would be one of the tiniest *grands crus* in Alsace, just 1.8 hectares in total and wedged between the *lieux-dits* of Hebsack and Purberg, just above the most southerly island of vines in the map above.

The wines of Kaefferkopf are well-structured, austere in their youth and require greater ageing than those grown on the surrounding limestone vineyards. Producers of Riesling only include Kuehn. Producers of Gewurztraminer only include Pierre Adam (good), Léon Baur, Marcel Freyburger (some spicy finesse), Domaine Martin Schaetzel (pleasant stuff, but the bottle is far more interesting), Bernard Schwach (very good), François Schwach & Fils, André Thomas (good wines sometimes spoilt by sweetness) and the CV Kientzheim-Kaysersberg (good). Producers of both Riesling and Gewurztraminer include J.B. Adam (excellent Riesling), Lucien Brand (good Gewurztraminer), André Ehrhart (both very good), Henri Ehrhart (delicately rich Riesling of great finesse and soft, ripe, liquorous Gewurztraminer), Geschickt (elegant Riesling, but the Gewurztraminer is sometimes a bit too sweet), René & Bernard Schneider (good Riesling), Sick-Dreyer (excellent Riesling, particularly 'Cuvée Joseph Dryer') and André Wackenthaler (good Riesling, excellent Gewurztraminer). J.B. Adam and Pierre Sparr were well known for their Kaefferkopf blends, which can no longer be sold under the name of the *cru*, so if you have not tasted them, you had better hurry. Other producers include Maurice Schoech.

Kanzlerberg
Bergheim, Haut-Rhin
3.23 *hectares*

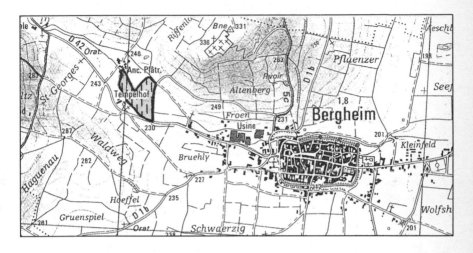

South and south-west facing, steep slopes, 250m; heavy calcareous, grey and black marls with Keuper gypsum, which improve the soil's heat-retaining and water-circulation properties, over limestone base.

This tiny *cru* adjoins the western edge of Altenberg de Bergheim, but the wines are so different that the vinification of these two sites has always been kept separate. If anything, the wines of Grand Cru Kanzlerberg are much more similar to those of the *lieu-dit* Burg than they are to its neighbouring *grand cru*. First mentioned in 1312, this *cru* was originally known as Tempelhof, being the former property of the Templars. Kanzlerberg has a truly great reputation for both Riesling and Gewurztraminer, but the ample weight of these wines can be at odds with their varietal aromas when young and require plenty of bottle-age to achieve harmony. Tokay-Pinot Gris also fares well. Two producers own most of this tiny *cru*: Gustave Lorentz (by far the best) and Jean-Martin Spielmann (variable Riesling that can be fresh and zesty and a promising Gewurztraminer that shows plenty of spicy finesse).

Kastelberg
Andlau, Bas-Rhin
5.82 hectares

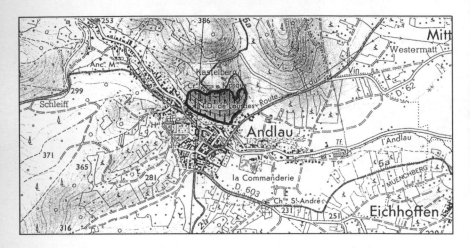

*South-east facing and very steep, 240–300m; dark, stony, mineral-rich,
siliceous soil over very dark, slaty, extremely hard schist rich in quartz,
mica and chlorite.*

Planted since the Roman occupation, this is one of the oldest
vineyards in Alsace. Situated on a small hill next to Wiebelsberg,
Anlau's other *grand cru*, Kastelberg is an excellent site for Riesling,
the wines of which can be racy and delicate, but usually very closed
when young, requiring some bottle-age to develop in bouquet. The
top producer here is Marc Kreydenweiss, whose wines remain
youthful for more than 20 years and show true *grand cru* quality
even in so-called 'off' years. Other fine wines are made by André
Durrmann, Domaine Klipfel, Charles Moritz and Guy Wach.

Kessler
Guebwiller, Haut-Rhin
28.5 hectares

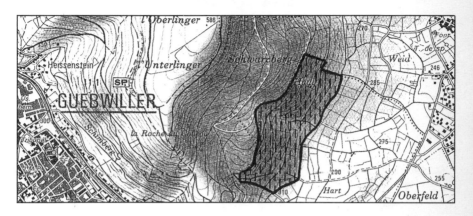

West facing, upper slopes quite steep, lower slopes very gentle, 300–390m; red sandy-clay soil over sandstone and limestone bedrock.

Although mentioned as early as 1394 and commercialized by Schlumberger since 1830, this *cru* is more *premier* than *grand*, Kitterlé and Wanne (which is not classified) being the truly famous sites of Guebwiller. The central part of Kessler would, however, justify *grand cru* status. Here the vines grow in a well protected valley-like depression, one side of which has a very steep, south-south-east facing slope. But everything is relative and the entire Kessler vineyard is certainly superior to many other so-called *grands crus* in Alsace.

Kessler is reputed for its full, spicy, mellow Gewurztraminer and Schlumberger produces the best and most pungent, but if Jean-Pierre Dirler's consistently superb wine is anything to go by, Riesling might well be the optimum variety for Kessler. It is really top stuff and certainly the best Kessler I have ever drunk.

Kirchberg de Barr
Barr, Bas-Rhin
40 *hectares*

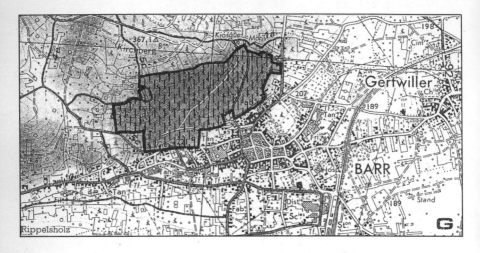

South-east facing, steep slopes, 215–315m; calcareous-marl with slabs and boulders of limestone over limestone bedrock.

The true *grands crus* of Barr are Gaensbroennel and Zisser, but these were incorporated into an enlarged Kirchberg. As the Kirchberg of Barr already has a well established and well deserved name for fine wine, the addition of these two smaller, intrinsically finer sites can only enhance its overall reputation. Kirchberg de Barr is known for full-bodied wines of delicate, spicy fruit. Gewurztraminer is typically fruity with a fine spicy aroma that ages well. Riesling shares this spicy character and Tokay-Pinot Gris can also perform well. Head and shoulders above everything else is the sensational Gewurztraminer 'Clos Gaensbroennel' by Alsace Willm, which is a testament to the integrity of Wolfberger, the owner of Willm since 1984. Willm's Kirchberg de Barr Riesling is very good, but not in the same class. A good notch down, yet still excellent is Klipfel's Gewurztraminer 'Clos Zisser', followed by a good but not stunning Kirchberg Riesling. Domaine Hering makes a good Riesling *vin de garde* and a very good Gewurztraminer 'Gaensbroennel' (this domaine owns half an hectare of this 6.5

hectare site). Gewurztraminer from Jean Heywang is elegant, understated and ages gracefully. The firm of E. Boeckel did not produce a pure Grand Cru Kirchberg until relatively recently (a Gewurztraminer that was four-square in 1988, yet a very elegant, not too spicy 1989). André Kleinknecht also owns vines on the Kirchberg de Barr.

———

Kirchberg de Ribeauvillé
Ribeauvillé, Haut-Rhin
11.4 hectares

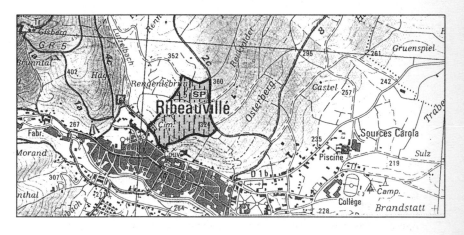

South and south-west facing, initially steep, smoothing out higher up, 270–350m; clayey soils, often stony, over marl, with the marl subsoil on the lower slopes layered with sandstone and Keuper gypsum.

Kirchberg was first mentioned in 1328 and is one of the few *lieux-dits* that has been regularly used to commercialize Alsace wine over the centuries. It is famous for Riesling, which typically is firm, totally dry and long lived, developing intense petrolly characteristics with age. Kirchberg also produces great Muscat with a discreet, yet very specific, orange and musk aroma, excellent acidity and lots of finesse.

Kirchberg should be judged on its Riesling, which means that

Jean Sipp and Louis Sipp vie for premier position in this *cru*. Both are powerful and long lived, but Jean Sipp's wines show more charm in their youth, while Louis Sipp's eventually achieve great depth and petrolly finesse. Robert Faller makes the best Gewurztraminer I have tasted and ties with André Kientzler for the most expressive Muscat. The CV Ribeauvillé also makes good Riesling, which is tight and compact in its youth and capable of ageing gracefully.

Kitterlé
Guebwiller, Haut-Rhin
25.79 hectares

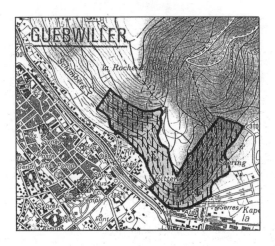

Two sides of a spur extending from the Unterlinger massif, the slopes are steep and face south-east through south-west, 270–360m; sandy topsoil derived from quartz-rich sandstone bedrock, which is exposed throughout much of this cru. Towards the top there is mica-clay sandstone, while on the western extremity the sandstone is greywacke (fine, with volcanic elements) with schist and volcanic andesite.

First mentioned in 1699 and commercialized by Schlumberger since 1830, this is one of the great vineyards of Guebwiller. Ironically,

Kitterlé built its fame on the Clevner (Pinot Blanc), a variety that must not be used for any *grand cru* wine. Of the noble varieties, however, it is the crisp, petrolly Riesling that shows greatest finesse, yet Gewurztraminer and Tokay-Pinot Gris can also be very good in a gently rich, supple and smoky-mellow style.

I always imagined that Schlumberger was the sole producer of Kitterlé and thus the descriptions above refer exclusively to the wines from this domaine, but I have recently heard of a small grower by the name of Léon Hell-Cadé, who makes Kitterlé Gewurztraminer, although I have not yet tasted it.

———

Mambourg
Sigolsheim, Haut-Rhin
Approximately 65 hectares

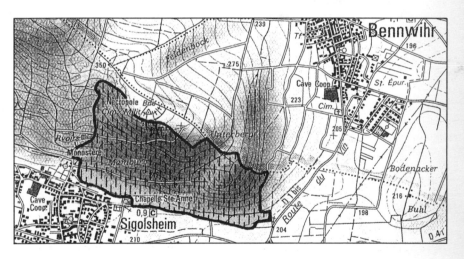

Fully south facing, quite steep, 240–360m; magnesium-rich, pebbly-marl topsoil over limestone and marl.

The reputation of the wines of 'Sigolttesberg' (later called Mambourg) has been documented since 783. A limestone *coteau*, it stretches for almost a mile, penetrating further into the plain than any other spur of the Vosges foothills. Its vineyards are supposed to be the warmest in Alsace and the wines produced tend to be rich and warm, mellow and liquorous. I have enjoyed good Tokay-Pinot Gris from Ringenbach-Moser. Pierre Sparr makes smoky-rich Tokay-Pinot Gris that has excellent acidity and a Vendange Tardive type character even in ordinary vintages. Sparr also knocks out an excellent Gewurztraminer with supremely rich, turbo-charged spicy-fruit and, in 1983, produced a sublime SGN wine from this variety. André Thomas made a wonderful Gewurztraminer 1989 Vendange Tardive that had more botrytis character than some SGN. I have recently tasted a good Gewurztraminer from Pierre Schillé & Fils.

Mandelberg
Mittelwihr, Haut-Rhin
Approximately 12 hectares

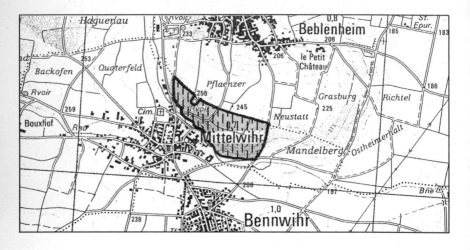

South-south-east facing, 200–240m; calcareous-marl over limestone.

The Mandelberg, or 'almond tree hill', has been planted with vines since Gallo-Roman times and commercialized as an *appellation* since 1925. Its reputation has been built on Riesling, although more Gewurztraminer is planted today. High quality Tokay-Pinot Gris and Muscat can also be produced.

Preiss-Henny was once the most famous producer of Mandelberg wines, but has long since sold its vineyards and merged with Léon Beyer. Unless you are lucky enough to try an old bottle from the firm's original, semi-abandoned cellars in Mittelwihr, you will just have to take my word that they were soft, gentle, delicious wines that just honeyed and never aged. Frédéric Mallo makes his Gewurztraminer in a similar, delicate style, while Edgard Schaller is uncompromising in the severity of its style, producing a Riesling Mandelberg Vieilles Vignes that positively shocks the system and demands considerable ageing. Wine produced from young Riesling vines grown on the Mandelberg is sold under Schaller's 'Les Amandiers' label, while other growers, such as Jean Greiner and Greiner-Schleret, indicate 'Côte des Amandiers' on their *grand cru* wines. Jean-Paul Mauler makes a super-spicy Gewurztraminer with lots of acidity. Other producers include Baumann-Zirgel, Daniel Wiederhirn and Bott-Geyl. The cooperative at Ribeauvillé produced a tremendous Riesling in 1990. It was their first Grand Cru Mandelberg and what a classic too.

Marckrain
Bennwihr & Sigolsheim, Haut-Rhin
Approximately 45 hectares

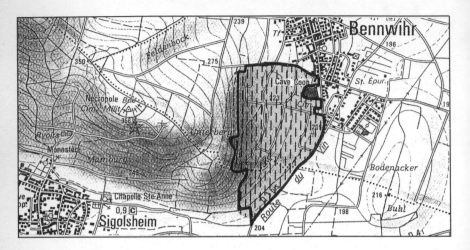

East and south-east facing, gentle slope, 200–250m; calcareous-marl over limestone layered with marl.

Not one of the most famous names in Alsace! Marckrain is supposed to be best for Gewurztraminer and Tokay-Pinot Gris. I have tasted only wines from the CV Bennwihr (which included a Muscat), but frankly none stood out. Soft and easy to drink, they would have been perfectly acceptable as generic wines, but as a *grand cru* I found them undistinguished and lacking.

Moenchberg
Andlau & Eichhoffen, Bas-Rhin
11.83 hectares

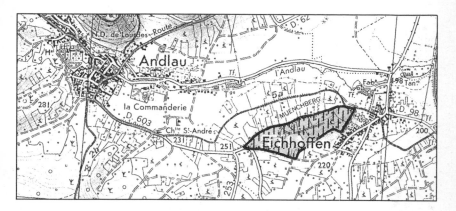

*South-east facing, gentle slope, 230–260m; fine-textured, silty-clay, with
lime content on the upper slopes, over granite.*

Planted with vines during the Roman occupation, Moenchberg, or
'monk's hill', was owned by a Benedictine order until 1097, when it
was taken over by inhabitants of Eichhoffen. Do not be confused by
this Moenchberg and Nothalten's Muenchberg. They are two completely different *grands crus*.

With its excellent exposure to the sun and a very hot, dry microclimate, this *cru* has built up a reputation for its firm, fruity and
racy Riesling, but the finest wines I have tasted have been Tokay-
Pinot Gris and Marc Kreydenweiss makes the best. His Vendange
Tardive is a monstrous wine of great vinosity and complexity, yet
beautifully balanced with lots of finesse. Domaine André & Rémy
Gresser makes the best Riesling. Good examples can also be found
by Armand Gilg, Charles Moritz and Guy Wach (Domaine des
Marroniers). Marcel Schlosser also makes an elegant Gewurztraminer and the firm of E. Boeckel owns vines here, but has not
produced a pure Grand Cru Moenchberg.

Muenchberg
Nothalten, Bas-Rhin
Approximately 18 hectares

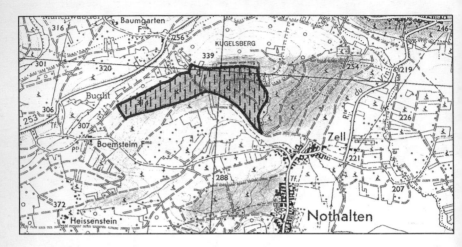

South facing, fairly steep slopes, 260–300m; ancient stony and sandy soils
250 million years old, rich in volcanic debris, including tufa and weathered
lava cinders.

Belonging to the abbey of Baumgarten, whose monks used to tend
vines in the twelfth century, this *cru* has similar etymological
origins to Moenchberg and also means 'monk's hill'. On local and
Institut Géographique National maps, the Moenchberg of Andlau
and Eichhoffen is actually spelt Muenchberg, whereas there is no
trace of a 'monk's hill' of any spelling in Nothalten. There might be
a map somewhere with the name Muenchberg on it, but on all the
ones I have studied, the authentic name of this *grand cru* would
appear to be Kugelsberg. I do not know why it was not called
Kugelsberg. It seems to be an admirable name for a crescent-shaped
vineyard, but Muenchberg it is and I suppose Muenchberg we will
have to call it.

This vineyard is a suntrap that nestles under the protection of the
Undersberg, a 901-metre peak in the Vosges mountains, creating a
special microclimate, which together with Muenchberg's unique
and ancient soil accounts for the striking style of its wines. The soil

heats up quickly, cools down slowly and, after a rare rainfall, drains away very fast. This forces the vine's roots to dig down deep, something it has to do anyway in such poor soil, as the vine needs to seek out the preciously few fertile elements. The combined effect is a naturally restricted, thus concentrated, yield. Under these conditions, this vineyard has become the realm of Riesling. Most Muenchberg Riesling is intense and powerful, but André Ostertag's is the most intense and most powerful. If this is the realm of Riesling then young Ostertag must be king and Domaine Ostertag's Muenchberg Riesling Vieilles Vignes the jewel in his crown. He is flawed by his own enthusiasm and thus his Muenchberg Riesling Vieilles Vignes can go awry, but when it is singing it is one of the very greatest wines of Alsace and his Muenchberg Tokay-Pinot Gris rivals it. Gérard Landmann produces a good Riesling, but in a much fatter style and nowhere near the same class. Other producers include Willy Gisselbrecht, Jean-Luc Schwartz and Roger & Roland Geyer.

Ollwiller
Wuenheim, Haut-Rhin
35.86 hectares

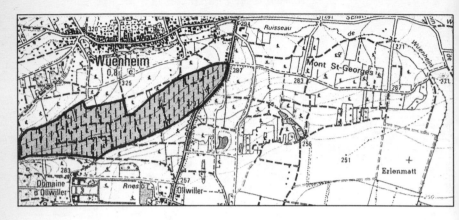

South-east facing, gentle slope, 260–320m; red sandy-clay, heavier when
over marl subsoils, deeper and with more sand when mixed with colluvium
on the lower slopes.

The first vineyards here were planted in the twelfth century. Ollwiller's annual rainfall is just 40 cm, which is one of the lowest in
France and yet another contradiction to accepted wisdom because
the vine is supposed to require at least 67.5 cm of precipitation per
year. Riesling and Gewurztraminer are supposed to fare best,
although I have tasted only Riesling. The best have been Château
Ollwiller and CV Vieil Armand, both of which are bottled and
marketed by the cooperative of Soultz-Wuenheim, which in turn
belongs to the Wolfberger group. Raymond Schmitt makes a good
Riesling, but it is not exceptional and also grows Gewurztraminer,
but I have not tasted it. The CV Turckheim owns a couple of
hectares, but has only just begun producing its own Grand Cru
Ollwiller. Other growers include Schwendemann-Haegelen (also
Riesling).

Osterberg
Ribeauvillé, Haut-Rhin
Approximately 24 hectares

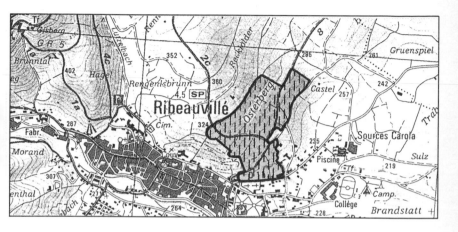

East-south-east facing, steep slopes, 250–350m; stony, clayey soil over marl, with multicoloured, calcareous marls in the eastern extremity of the cru.

Once the property of the Seigneurs de Ribeaupierre, Osterberg was first mentioned in documents dating back to the Middle Ages. This growth abuts Geisberg, another Ribeauvillé *grand cru*, and is superb Riesling country. The wines age very well, developing the famous 'petrolly' nose of a fine old Riesling. Gewurztraminer and Tokay also fare well.

André Kientzler produces exceptional Riesling in Vendange Tardive and SGN categories and has twice harvested a *vin de glace* (sort of French equivalent of a German *Eiswein*). The CV Ribeauvillé makes a rich Riesling with fine acidity, which just lacks the touch of finesse that would propel it into the top flight. Louis Sipp produces intense Gewurztraminer in true *vin de garde* style. Trimbach owns vines in this *cru*, but does not market a pure Osterberg wine.

Pfersigberg
Eguisheim, Haut-Rhin
Approximately 56 hectares

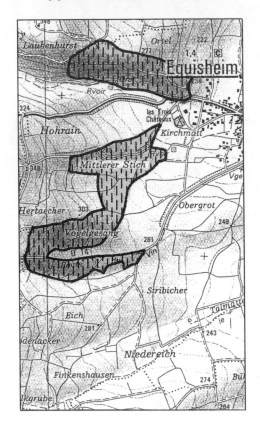

Two separate plots proposed, the largest just beneath Husseren-les-Châteaux, east-south-east facing, modest slope, 230–340m; topsoils of calcareous marl, magesium-rich limestone and rendzina, which is dark and very calcareous, over a bedrock of limestone, either grey and very hard or yellow and soft.

First mentioned in sixteenth-century documents, Pfersigberg is well known for its full, aromatic and long-lived Gewurztraminer. Tokay-Pinot Gris, Riesling and Muscat also grow well. All wines benefit from fruity acidity and possess exceptional aromatics.

Kuentz-Bas make the best Gewurztraminer – pure quality and concentration – but Charles Baur comes a close second and other fine Gewurztraminers come from Pierre Freudenreich (spelt Pfersichberg), Alphonse Kuentz and the underrated Wolfberger CV Eguisheim (spelt Pfirsigberg). Bruno Sorg makes the finest Muscat, of that there can be no doubt; its vivacious, peach-laden fruit, mouthwatering ripe acidity and sheer exuberance make it one of the greatest Muscats of the region. Paul Ginglinger makes good but not exceptional Tokay-Pinot Gris, yet manages to excel with Riesling. It is probably the finest in Pfersigberg, although it should be remembered that Léon Beyer's classic, bone-dry Riesling 'Cuvée Particulière' is also pure Pfersigberg, even if it is not stated on the label. Other good Rieslings are made by André Scherer and Gérard Schueller. Emile Schwartz & Fils also grows vines here, but I have not tasted the wine.

Pfingstberg
Orschwihr, Haut-Rhin
Approximately 28 hectares

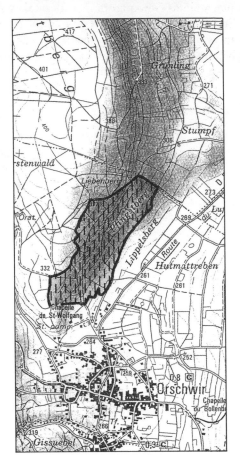

South-east facing, fairly steep slopes, 250–350m; calcareous and micaceous sandstone on the high ground, clayey-sandstone lower down.

The reputation of this *cru* dates back to 1299, when it was handed over as a gift to the convent at Unterlinden by a nobleman called Richard d'Epfig. All four *grand cru* varieties grow well here, producing wines of typically floral aroma, but the greatest single wine is Lucien Albrecht's fabulously rich Tokay-Pinot Gris, which has great finesse, especially his Vendange Tardive. Albrecht's apricot and marmalade Gewurztraminer also takes some beating, but his Rieslings wax and wane between cumbersome and richly honeyed. François Braun's Gewurztraminer rivals Albrecht's, but his Riesling has no peers in this *cru*, with its extraordinary depth, extract and finesse, which give it more class than the good to very good Rieslings from Raymond Rabold and Château d'Orschwihr.

Praelatenberg
Orschwiller & Kintzheim, Bas-Rhin
Approximately 12 hectares

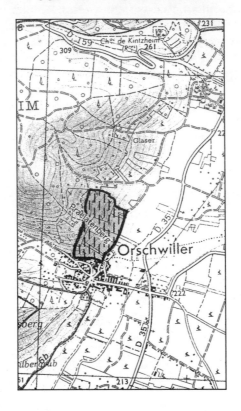

East-south-east facing, fairly steep slopes, 250–350m; heavy stony,
siliceous soil, rich in iron and quartz, more friable, gravelly and richer in
various minerals on the lower slopes.

Although not one of the most famous names of Alsace, Praelatenberg was recorded as early as 823, in the documents of the abbey
of Ebersmunster. Praelatenberg dominates the north side of Orschwiller so effectively that it looks as if it belongs entirely to this
village, but virtually all of the *cru* actually comes within the communal boundary of Kintzheim, which is a mile away. The locals

today say all four varieties grow to perfection. Well they would, wouldn't they? The best Praelatenberg I have tasted was a rich and honeyed Tokay-Pinot Gris by Raymond Engel (Domaine des Prélats). Riesling would appear to be the next best variety, with Engel and Domaine Siffert producing pretty good examples. I am in print as saying that it would take some serious bribery for me to slip Praelatenberg into my classification of *premiers crus*, let alone *grands crus* and my general opinion has not changed, although I have since tasted a super-charged 1990 Gewurztraminer from Jean Becker, which is far and away the best wine I have come across from this *cru*.

Rangen
Thann and Vieux Thann, Haut-Rhin
18.81 hectares

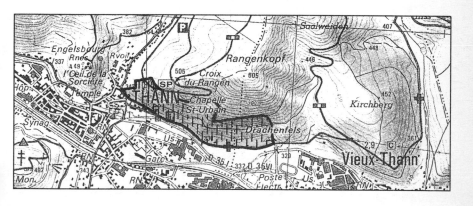

Fully south-facing, very steep slopes, 330–480m; hard, dark, very poor but mineral-rich soil, very stony and covered with greywacke (fine sandstone with volcanic elements), andesite (fine-grained volcanic rock), tufa ash, and various lava-based volcanic rocks hardened by metamorphism.

The wines of Rangen have been famous since the twelfth century. In 1291 the Dominican convent of Basle purchased vineyards in the Rangen and the following year the convent of St-Ursitz in Einsden and the abbots of Masmunster and Haute Seille became fellow proprietors of neighbouring vineyards that were also part of Rangen. With the cathedral of St-Théobold attracting pilgrims from Germany, England and Scandinavian countries to Thann, it was always easy to sell the wines of Rangen. Sebastian Brant, the fifteenth-century satirist, when writing about the little-known travels of Hercules through Alsace, reveals that this mythical strongman drank so much Rangen that he fell asleep and was so ashamed when he woke up that he ran away leaving his bludgeon behind. This club today forms part of Colmar's Coat of Arms. In 1628 Dr Claudius Deodatus recorded in his *Pantheum Hygisticum* the best wines of Alsace, which included Rangen. At the time of Empress Maria Theresa (1717–80, Empress of the Holy Roman Empire from 1745), the wines of Rangen were regularly served at the court and enjoyed an exceptional reputation.

Until the October 1990 revision of the AOC delimitation, it was possible to say that most of Rangen is in Thann and all of Thann is Rangen, which made Thann the only entirely *grand cru* village in Alsace. Since the new delimitation, however, they have found a few more hectares to plant in Thann, so now it can boast only that 89 per cent of its vineyards are classified *grand cru*. The Thur river runs immediately beneath Rangen, moderating the climate, helping to protect its vines from spring frosts and encouraging noble rot on late-harvested grapes. Rangen is so steep that it can be cultivated only when terraced. Although the soil is very poor in organic terms, it is extremely fertile minerally. It also drains very quickly and its dark colour makes it almost too efficient in retaining the vast heat that pours into the Rangen's sweltering suntrap. This fierce heat and rapid drainage are essentially responsible for the regular stressing of the vine, which gives the wines their great power and pungency, the characteristics that have made Rangen famous for so many centuries and enable it to produce great wines in even the poorest years. It is a true *grand cru* in every sense of the title and if a genuinely unbiased classification took place, there is little doubt that Rangen would be in an élite *premier grand cru* category with no more than half a dozen other, strictly delimited, vineyard sites (and not all of those are even granted *grand cru* today).

That said, the current reputation of Rangen is almost entirely due to Léonard Humbrecht, who replanted its abandoned steep slopes in the early 1970s. He is indubitably the most passionate of growers when it comes to restricting yield, and his son Olivier, who now makes the wines, was the first Frenchman to qualify as a Master of Wine. This formidable combination can only add to the already exceptional prestige of Rangen, which is historically famous for Tokay-Pinot Gris (although equally reputed for its blended wine), but is now well known for its equally exciting Riesling and Gewurztraminer. There is such a large gap between the standard set by Domaine Zind Humbrecht and that of Domaine Schoffit, the next best producer, that it would be embarrassing but for the fact that everyone recognizes that the Humbrechts are in a class of their own. The quality difference is particularly noticeable when comparing Rieslings, but Rangen is a true *grand cru* and Schoffit does make fine wines that stand up to some of the best *grands crus* produced elsewhere, particularly his Tokay-Pinot Gris (in 1989, he harvested Tokay-Pinot Gris grapes at 216° Oechsle or a natural potential alcoholic strength of 31 per cent!). Bruno Hertz, who produces an interesting Gewurztraminer, should not be forgotten.

Rosacker
Hunawihr, Haut-Rhin
26.18 hectares

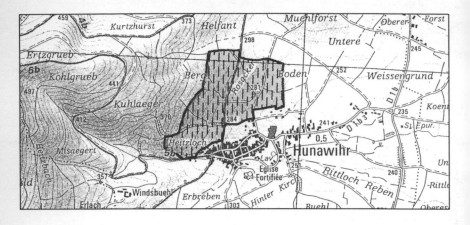

East-south-east facing, gently sloping, 260–330m; heavy, stony, calcareous marly-clay soil, rich in magnesium, over a limestone bedrock with marl and sandstone strata.

Named after the wild rose bushes that used to border this vineyard, Rosacker is situated north of Hunawihr, half-way between Ribeauvillé and Riquewihr. First mentioned in the fifteenth century, this *cru* has built up a fine reputation for its Riesling, but one wine, Trimbach's Clos Ste-Hune, is in a class of its own. Almost every year, Clos Ste-Hune is far and away the finest Riesling in Alsace. Occasionally other producers make an exceptional vintage of Riesling that may challenge Clos Ste-Hune, but none have matched its excellence over a two-year period, let alone on a regular basis. Of course, Trimbach makes no reference to Rosacker on its label. The Trimbachs rightly consider that much of Rosacker should not be classified as a *grand cru*, but also acknowledge that exceptional *terroir* does exist beyond the boundaries of Clos Ste-Hune and there certainly are other wines produced in Rosacker that can be compared with the best that other Alsace *grands crus* can offer. The three most successful Rieslings after Trimbach Clos Ste-Hune are the soft-styled wines of Frédéric Mallo, the richer wines of Mader and the firmer, more intense wines of Sipp-Mack. Other Rosacker Rieslings are made by Philippe Gocker, Domaine Mittnacht, Mittnacht-Klack and the CV Hunawihr, the last two of which make much better Gewurztraminer. I have also come across Gewurztraminer from David Ermel, which was round and fruity.

Saering
Guebwiller, Haut-Rhin
26.75 hectares

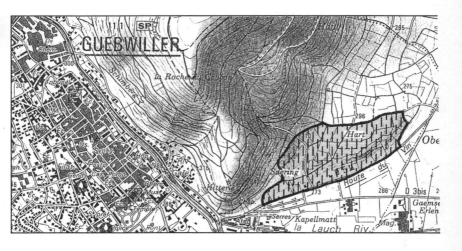

East and south-east facing, most softly sloping, steepish beneath the Hart, 260–300m; deep, stony, sandstone soil with sandy-marl deposits over calcareous-marl subsoil.

Situated beneath Kessler and Kitterlé, Guebwiller's other two *grands crus*, is the Saering vineyard, which was first documented in 1250 and has been commercialized by Schlumberger since 1830. Like Kessler, this *cru* is more *premier* than *grand* yet is still better than many other so-called *grands crus*. The floral, fruity and elegant Riesling is best, especially in hot years, when it becomes exotically peachy, but Muscat and Gewurztraminer can also be fine.

Domaine Schlumberger is consistently the best producer, but

Dirler is very good, occasionally produces an even finer Riesling and also makes a very attractive Muscat. Eric Rominger's Riesling is also worth trying.

———

Schlossberg
Kaysersberg & Kientzheim, Haut-Rhin
80 hectares

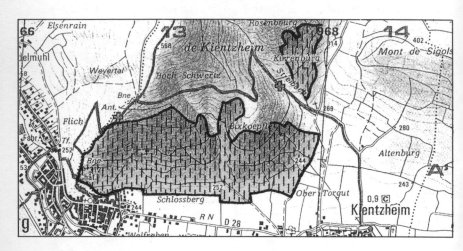

South and south-east facing, mostly quite steep, terraced, 200–300m; colluvial, rough, alluvial clayey-sand, rich in minerals, over a magmatic and granitic bedrock.

Cited from the fifteenth century on, the production of Schlossberg was voluntarily controlled by charter in 1928 and in 1975 became the very first Alsace *grand cru*. Although this *cru* looks from the ground as if it is almost equally shared between Kaysersberg and Kientzheim, the communal boundary is such that all but a tiny section, less than half a hectare, actually belongs to Kientzheim. A small section is separated from the rest of Schlossberg in the north-eastern extremity of this *cru*, but the terrain is of the same geological origin. Schlossberg is best for Riesling, as evidenced by the wines of Paul Blanck and Domaine Weinbach: two entirely different styles, yet both have the same concentration and great extract, which is the mark of Schlossberg. The Gewurztraminer from this *cru* can be exceptionally successful in so-called 'off' vintages, with Salzmann-Thomann producing a most elegant wine that shows classic banana finesse in its youth.

Some of Paul Blanck's wines can be every bit as sensational as Domaine Weinbach's, but the firm produces so many variations on each theme through the age of the vines, their exact location and alternative vinification techniques, that there is inevitably some variation in quality and style. It is, however, part of Blanck's continuous quest fully to understand Schlossberg and thus it may one day exploit far more of the potential of this *cru* than any other grower. Only time will tell. Salzmann-Thomann can be regarded on the same quality level for his Gewurztraminer, the regular bottlings of which often have more concentration than most Vendange Tardive, although his Rieslings are merely average, not special. Other exceptional Rieslings include André Blanck, followed in order by Pierre Sparr, Albert Mann and the CV Kientzheim-Kaysersberg.

Schoenenbourg
Riquewihr, Haut-Rhin
Approximately 40 hectares

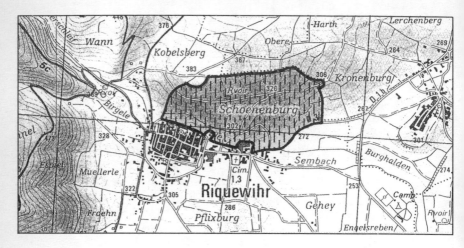

Fully south facing, fairly steep, 265–380m; stony, siliceous soil, rich in Keuper gypsum and nutrients, over marl, limestone and sandstone, with calcareous-marl subsoil in the extreme east.

Voltaire once owned part of this vineyard, which was renowned in the Middle Ages and gained fame throughout Europe by the sixteenth century. Riesling and Muscat are historically the most successful grapes here, although modern wines show Riesling to be supreme and Tokay-Pinot Gris now vies with Muscat for the number two spot. All Schoenenbourg wines are rich, strong and aromatic; ideal potential for Vendange Tardive and SGN styles in appropriate vintages.

Marcel Deiss, Domaines Dopff Au Moulin and Baumann & Fils are consistently the best for Riesling, but in recent years Deiss has excelled itself and is now producing one of the finest Rieslings not just in this *cru* but in all of Alsace. Mittnacht-Klack makes excellent, intensely flavoured, petrolly-citrus Vieilles Vignes. Less consistent, but capable of equally fine quality are René Schmidt and Daniel Wiederhirn. Dopff & Irion produce an inconsistent Riesling and have just introduced a Muscat. Hugel own vines here, but do not market *grand cru* wines. I have been disappointed by CV Turckheim's Riesling.

———

Sommerberg
Niedermorschwihr and Katzenthal, Haut-Rhin
28 hectares

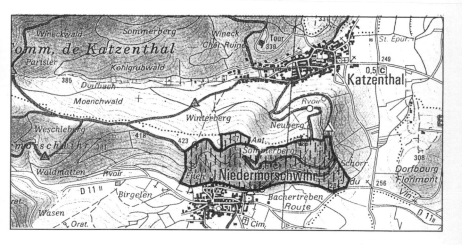

Fully south facing, steep slopes, 265–400m; mineral-rich, granitic sand over granite and mica.

Known since 1214, the fame of this *cru* was such that a strict delimitation was in force by the seventeenth century. It is situated in the foothills leading up to Trois-Epis and some people have suggested that the etymological origin of this town might be that its vineyards were once planted with three grape varieties. Certainly those who work Sommerberg today claim it is equally suitable for each of the four classic *grand cru* varieties. I can comment only on the Riesling, however, as that is the only Sommerberg I have tasted, and when it has been from Albert Boxler it has proved to be a fine and aristocratic wine indeed. Domaine Aimé Stentz makes a fatter, spicier Riesling and the CV Ingersheim can even rival Boxler in certain years. CV Turckheim's Riesling is a deliciously succulent contrast to this cooperative's efforts with the same grape on the Schoenenbourg.

———

Sonnenglanz
Beblenheim, Haut-Rhin
32.8 hectares

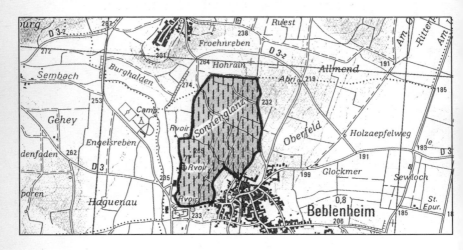

South-east facing, moderate slope, 220–270m; marl soil, heavy but very stony and well structured, over limestone with marl strata; extremely low rainfall.

In 1935, two years after Kaefferkopf was defined by tribunal at Colmar, Sonnenglanz received a similar certification, but unlike Kaefferkopf, producers failed to exploit the *appellation* until the local cooperative was formed in 1952 and, even then, it was merely Sonnenglanz Edelzwicker that was promoted! The Sonnenglanz vineyard, which extends from the outskirts of Beblenheim village to the rural border of Zellenberg, was once reputed for its Sylvaner. As this is not a *grand cru* variety and the Edelzwicker saga is best forgotten, we are now told that Sonnenglanz is really best suited to Gewurztraminer and Tokay-Pinot Gris, the wines of which are reputed to be very ripe and golden in colour. The best producer of these varieties is Bott-Geyl. Jean-Paul Hartweg, Frédéric Berger and the local cooperative all make soft, easy, eminently drinkable Gewurztraminer. The CV Ribeauvillé produced a rich and succulent Tokay-Pinot Gris with its first vintage in 1990.

Spiegel
Bergholtz and Guebwiller, Haut-Rhin
18.26 hectares

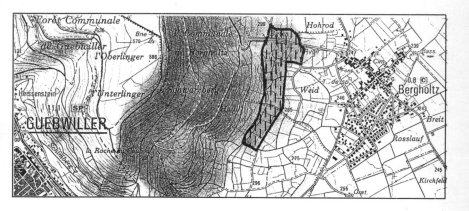

*East facing, gently sloping, 260–315m; heavy scree of sandy-clay
colluvium over sandstone and marl.*

Known for only 50 years or so, this is not one of the great *grands crus* of Alsace, but Dirler produces a fine, racy Riesling with a delicate bouquet and good, but not great, Gewurtztraminer and Muscat. Domaine Loberger makes pretty successful Riesling, while Eugène Meyer and the CV Eguisheim (Wolfberger) make rich Gewurztraminer that manages to avoid being blowzy. Joseph Lorberger-Hell also grows vines here.

Sporen
Riquewihr, Haut-Rhin
Approximately 22 hectares

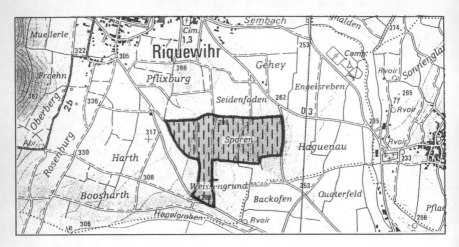

East facing, gentle slope, 275m; deep, decalcified marly-clay over marly-clay subsoil, colder and more clayey on the lower slopes.

Cited in 1432 in the archives of the dukes of Württemberg and classified by Fischart in 1580 as the best wine in Alsace, Sporen is indeed one of the truly great *grands crus*. Capable of producing wines of remarkable finesse, it is historically famous for Gewurztraminer and Tokay, the two vines that today occupy virtually all of its vineyard. Vines grown on the lower slopes produce wines of immediate appeal, but less ageing potential.

The greatest Sporen is Hugel's, a classic blended wine, which was originally called Sporen 'Gentil'. Capable of ageing 30 years or more, this was no mere Edelzwicker, so when they outlawed the name Gentil, Johnny Hugel had no intention of putting that bastardized name on the label. When they officially classified Sporen as a *grand cru*, he could no longer use even that name, unless he produced a pure varietal, which would be a totally different sort of wine. So, despite Hugel's declaration that it is the end of Hugel Sporen, I now hear that he will continue to produce the wine and sell it as 'Cuvée SP' or something. Bernard Schwach produces one of the few Sporen Rieslings and an excellent wine it is, with fragrant floral aromas that belie its great longevity. Domaine Dopff Au Moulin and Roger Jung make Gewurztraminer that can sometimes excel, as can Dopff & Irion, who also produce Tokay-Pinot Gris. Daniel Wiederhirn owns vines here, but has not so far produced a pure Sporen. The CV Ribeauvillé made a rich, potentially long-lived Gewurztraminer with its first vintage in 1990.

Steinert
Pfaffenheim, Haut-Rhin
38 hectares

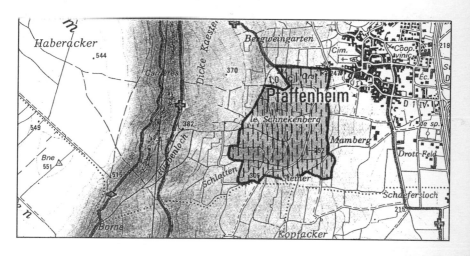

East facing, modestly steep, 240–310m; dry, stony, colluvium over limestone base, sandy on the upper slopes.

Vines have been grown here since at least 1150, when the land was owned by the Swiss Benedictine Abbaye de Muri. The name should in fact be Steiner, but no doubt the locals thought it too Prussian and stuck a 't' on the end. Tokay-Pinot Gris is the king of this *cru*, although historically, Pfaffenheim generally and Schneckenberg (now part of Steinert) specifically have always been renowned for producing a style of Pinot Blanc that tasted more like Tokay-Pinot

Gris. The local cooperative still produce Pinot Blanc Schnec-kenberg, but it is not a *grand cru*, of course, and it is the stunning Tokay-Pinot Gris that steals the show. A great concentration of mouth-filling flavour and superb acidity. Gewurztraminer fares best on the lower slopes, while Riesling prefers the higher, more sandy slopes. The cooperative's Gewurztraminer is also very good, but I think it is slightly less successful with Riesling. On the other hand, organic wine producer Pierre Frick makes a fine Riesling. His Muscat has obvious finesse, but the Gewurztraminer is some-times spoilt by sweetness. Rieflé Gewurztraminer has a wonderful grapy-spicy complexity with lots of refreshing acidity. François Runner also owns vines here.

Steingrubler
Wettolsheim, Haut-Rhin
Approximately 19 hectares

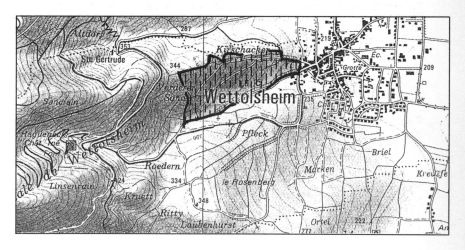

South-east facing, gentle slopes, 280–350m; stony, calcareous-marl and sandy-clay over marl and limestone, partially covered with granitic, sandy scree.

This *cru* dates back to 1487, when the vineyard was owned and run by a monastic order. Although it has not created a reputation as one of the truly great names of Alsace, I have tasted some excellent wines, particularly Tokay-Pinot Gris, which can be very rich, yet show great finesse. This is certainly one of the better 'unknowns' and could well be a great *grand cru* of the future. Wunsch & Mann is one of the specialists of this *cru* and, of the range produced, I am most impressed by the Riesling 'Collection Joseph Mann', a wine of great concentration that can develop an amazingly complex bouquet. The Tokay-Pinot Gris 'Collection Joseph Mann' is also good, but not in the same class. Barmès-Buecher produce the best Gewurztraminer and Robert Dietrich the best Tokay-Pinot Gris. The Riesling and Gewurztraminer sold by the CV Eguisheim under its Wolfberger label are well made and represent excellent value for money.

Steinklotz
Marlenheim, Bas-Rhin
24 *hectares*

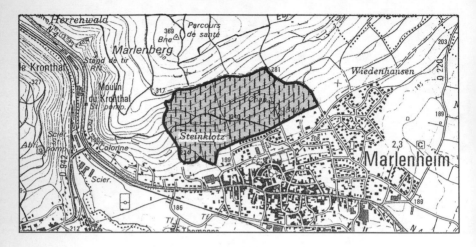

South-south-east facing, fairly steep slopes, 200–300m; light, calcareous
magnesite scree of brown rendzine soils on an uplifted rock base of grey
limestone and sandy limestone.

One of the oldest vineyards in Alsace, Steinklotz (or 'block of stone') was part of the estate of the Merovingian King Childebert II in 589. It is from this vineyard that Marlenheim built up its reputation – still strong today – for Pinot Noir wines of red and rosé style. Since it has flown the *grand cru* flag, Steinklotz is supposed to be good for Tokay-Pinot Gris, Riesling and Gewurztraminer. I have tasted a rich, honey-spiced Tokay-Pinot Gris from Romain Fritsch, but do not know this grower's wines very well, so cannot comment on its consistency. The Riesling from Laugel is indeed superior for this producer (whose real talent is Crémant d'Alsace), with very pure, rich, ripe fruit flavours, although its Gewurztraminer is much less classy.

Vorbourg
Rouffach and Westhalten, Haut-Rhin
Approximately 72 hectares

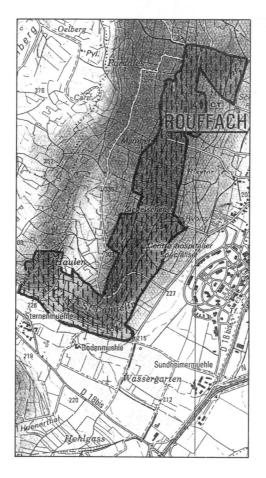

South-south-east facing, moderate slope, 220–300m; calcareous-marl over sandstone and limestone, with loess on the higher ground.

In 762, the Bishop of Strasbourg gave this vineyard to the newly established convent at Ettenheim. At their best, the wines of Vorbourg are *grand cru* in quality, but some varieties can disappoint in certain years, which used to make me think of it more in terms of *premier* than *grand cru*. Clos St-Landelin and a few surrounding plots at the southern end of the Vorbourg are, however, definitely *grand cru*, as their occasional disappointments can be traced to the failure of man, not *terroir*, so it must be concluded that a good part of Vorbourg is of the status claimed and that this is merely another instance of the 'ballooning' effect of self-delimitation. All four varieties are supposed to excel here and each is said to develop a bouquet of peaches, apricots, mint and hazelnut. I cannot pretend to have found all of these characteristics in any wine, but I have noted mint in some well-ripened Pinot Noir wines (that do not claim *grand cru* status, of course). The Vorbourg certainly is well adapted to Pinot Noir, catching the full glare of the sun from dawn to dusk, consequently the skins of this variety are exceptionally heavy with pigment. I have also noted orange-flower and peaches in the best Muscats, but they are, after all, characteristics of the grape rather than of the soil. Generally, Riesling and Tokay-Pinot Gris are the best, but Muscat is also good and benefits in warmer vintages, when it positively explodes with flavour. Gewurztraminer excels in some good years but not others, although this may have more to do with the random effect of man – the grower or winemaker – as no other influencing factor seems discernible. The best and most important producer of all varieties is Muré, from their Clos St-Landelin estate. I have also tasted a good but not exceptional Gewurztraminer from Bruno Hunold and the CV Westhalten has vineyards here, although it has not yet marketed a pure Grand Cru Vorbourg.

Wiebelsberg
Andlau, Bas-Rhin
12 hectares

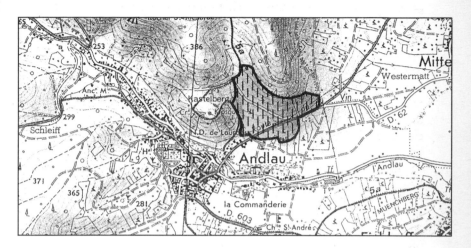

South and south-east facing, steep slopes, 250–300m; siliceous topsoil,
mostly quartz, with ferruginous elements over sandstone bedrock.

Overlooking the smaller *grand cru* of Kastelberg, which occupies
the neighbouring hill, Wiebelsberg has a very good sun exposure,
retains heat and drains well. It is particularly favourable to the
Riesling, the wines of which can be very fine, floral and delicate,
with ripe-peachy fruit, especially from a gifted grower such as Marc
Kreydenweiss. Wiebelsberg Riesling is one of the very best wines
produced by E. Boeckel and Ch. Wantz (who buy from contracted
growers), but they do not compare with Kreydenweiss's Vendanges
Tardives. I have also had good Rieslings from André Durrmann,
Domaine André & Rémy Gresser, Jean-Pierre Klein and Marcel
Schlosser. Other producers include Charles Moritz and the CV
Obernai (Divinal). In 1987 six growers owning some 10 hectares of
this growth (Marcel Schlosser, Domaine Mattern, Roger & Roland
Geyer, André Durrmann, André & Rémy Gresser and E. Boeckel),
together with INRA (Institut Nationale Recherche Agricole), were
the first in France to control the larvae of the *Cochylis* and *Eudemis*
by natural means. These grape moths lay their eggs in spring and

summer, usually on the buds of the vine and, depending when they hatch, the larvae will feed on the tender shoots, the flowers or the fruit. INRA suggested using a little wasp-related insect called *Trichogramma minutum* to eat the eggs of the moths before they hatch. *Trichogramma* has been successfully employed against various agricultural pests, but this was the first application in viticulture and the results so far have been significantly better than those achieved by chemical insecticides.

Wineck-Schlossberg
Katzenthal and Ammerschwihr, Haut-Rhin
Approximately 24 hectares

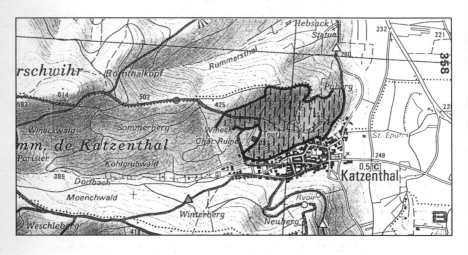

South and south-east facing, fairly steep, 280–400m; mineral-rich, granitic and micaceous soils similar to Sommerberg on the next Vosgien spur south.

Mentioned as early as 1264, Wineck-Schlossberg is situated at the end of a valley. Closed in on three sides, it enjoys a sheltered microclimate and is supposed to be ideal for Riesling followed by Gewurztraminer. I have tasted mostly Riesling, which has always been light and delicate, with a fragrant aroma. The wines from Klur-Stoecklé show most finesse, but Jean-Paul Ecklé's have a little more body, while one vintage of Domaine de la Sinne (1989) is really quite racy for the year.

———

Winzenberg
Blienschwiller, Bas-Rhin
Approximately 5 hectares

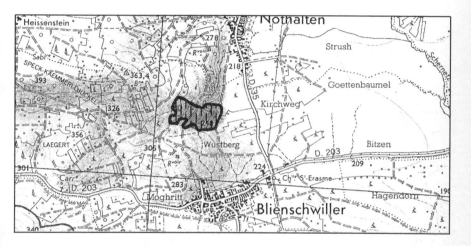

South-south-east facing, gentle slopes, 240–320m; granitic and miceous soil over twin-mica and granite bedrock.

Locals make the vague claim that this *cru* is cited in 'old documents' and that Riesling and Gewurztraminer fare best. I have had a fine, fresh Gewurztraminer with a refined spiciness and some complexity from Hubert Metz and a light but charming Riesling from François Meyer.

———

Zinnkoepflé
Westhalten and Soultzmatt, Haut-Rhin
Approximately 62 hectares

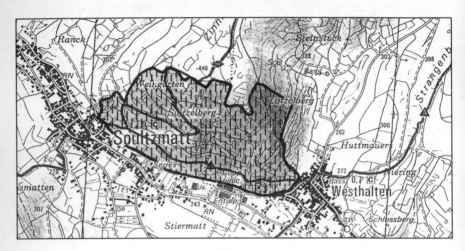

South and south-east facing, steep slopes, rising up to 420m; sandy and calcareous clay over sandstone and limestone.

With its unique exposure, this hillside was celebrated in pagan times by sun-worshipping cults. Sheltered by the Petit and Grand Ballon d'Alsace, Zinnkoepflé is uniquely hot and dry. This has given rise to a rare concentration of Mediterranean and Caspian fauna and flora near the summit and, a little lower down, provides the vine with just 27 cm of rain during the vegetative cycle. It is the stressing caused by this arid microclimate that gives Zinnkoepflé its reputation for producing a strong, spicy and fiery style of Gewurztraminer and Tokay-Pinot Gris. Zinnkoepflé Riesling appears to be a delicate and most discreet wine when young, yet has hidden depths of bouquet, flavour and power that require long slow ageing in bottle to release. A perfectly matured Zinnkoepflé Riesling is a big wine that can stand shoulder to shoulder with this *cru's* other two wines. This special microclimate also gave Zinnkoepflé Sylvaner the exceptional reputation of being a true *vin de garde*, but it is not a *grand cru* variety and can no longer be sold as such.

The supreme examples of Zinnkoepflé are Riesling and Gewurztraminer from Seppi Landmann. These are wines that show great
extract and acidity, particularly in the Vendange Tardive style. He
also produces fine SGN wines (although they should be thought of
more as super-concentrated Vendanges Tardives than the full botrytis style) and in 1990 even brought in a *vin de glace*, although it
lacked the intensity of an authentic *Eiswein*, even taking into consideration this producer's essentially drier style. I have also had
good Riesling and super Gewurztraminer from Landmann-Ostholt.
Other Rieslings I can recommend are Schlegel-Boeglin (especially
Vendange Tardive) and the CV Westhalten. I have not tried the
wines of Léon Boesch (although I have tasted a fine Gewurztraminer Vendange Tardive that did not claim *grand cru* status) or
Armand Gilg.

Zotzenberg
Mittelbergheim, Bas-Rhin
Approximately 34 hectares

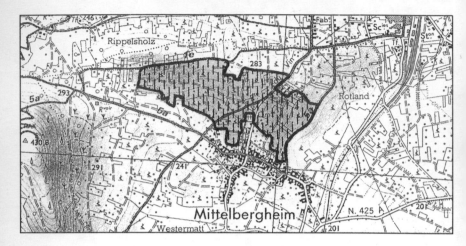

Basin-shaped, east and south facing, gentle slope, rising up to 320m;
limestone and marl.

First mentioned in 1364 by the name of Zoczenberg, this *cru* has
been commercialized under its *lieu-dit* since the beginning of this
century. It has good exposure and the limestone soil drains well, yet
retains sufficient moisture to resist very dry weather. Zotzenberg is
one of the most famous of those *grands crus* that make mockery of
the restriction on grape varieties that may be used because it is
historically the finest site in Alsace for Sylvaner!

E. Boeckel produce good Gewurztraminer and a rapidly
improving Riesling that shows a lovely creamy richness of fruit and
gives every impression of being one of the world's eternally youthful wines. Time will tell. Other Rieslings I have enjoyed come from
Bernard & Daniel Haegi and André Wittmann. I have not been
impressed by either the Riesling or Gewurztraminer from Julien
Rieffel and have not tasted the wines of Pierre & Jean-Pierre
Rietsch.

6

Châteaux, Clos and other Named Sites

ALSACE CHÂTEAUX

The châteaux of Alsace more often describes the numerous castles and towers, often in ruins and eerie, that are perched high on the slopes of the Vosges. The three towers of Husseren-les-Châteaux are a prime example. In viticultural terms, however, there are a few château vineyards that warrant mention.

Château d'Isenbourg

Rouffach
Soil: sandstone and limestone
Dopff & Irion rent this vineyard from the château, which was rebuilt in the nineteenth century and more recently converted into a luxury hotel that has become a favourite haunt of rich Americans. This superb, east-facing, terraced vineyard is an authentic *clos*, although not sold as such, with substantial walls enhancing its already privileged microclimate. It certainly has the greatest potential of all Alsace châteaux and should be producing wines to match the best *clos*, but under the auspices of Dopff & Irion, Château d'Isenbourg has produced inconsistent Gewurztraminer, Riesling and Pinot Blanc wines. They tend to be attenuated in style, lacking in all but the biggest years the richness and body that could be expected from this vineyard. Tasting back over the vintages, exceptional years such as 1989, 1983, 1976 and 1964 all stood out (the last two of which will age gracefully for at least another ten years). Dopff & Irion bottle much of the wine for the hotel itself, so that its pampered customers may enjoy them while dining in the restaurant, which looks out over the vineyard. There seems to be

insufficient incentive for Dopff & Irion to promote the wines of this property, which must filter back to the vineyard. A new deal should be struck (either with Dopff & Irion or another producer) in a bid to extract the full potential of these wines, which can be realized only by severely restricting yields and expressing the *terroir*.

Best varieties: judgement reserved

Château du Moulin

At one time, Dopff Au Moulin used to sell château-bottled wines under this name, the label of which featured the present day 'Au Moulin' property and claimed *grand cru* status.

Château Ollwiller

Wuenheim
Soil: sandy
This château is owned by J-H Gros & Ses Fils, who also own Clos de la Tourelle, but the wines are made and sold by the CV Vieil Armand (part of the Wolfberger group). I have little experience of the wines, apart from a very pale rosé, which was light and delicate, with charming fruit, and a very fine Riesling.

Best varieties: Riesling & Pinot Noir

Château d'Orschwihr

Orschwihr
Soil: limestone
This château was known in 1049, when visited by Pope Leo IX, and was owned by the Hapsburgs from the thirteenth to fifteenth century. The present owner, Hubert Hartmann, planted a vineyard on this property, which is situated on the Bollenberg, but extends into Grand Cru Pfingstberg, where he makes his best wine, a decent Riesling. Gewurztraminer and Pinot Noir under the Bollenberg label are not as good.

Best varieties: judgement reserved

Château de Riquewihr

This is not a wine-producing château, but the offices and winery of Dopff & Irion in Riquewihr.

Château Wagenbourg

Soultzmatt
Soil: limestone
Owned by Joseph Klein & Fils, whose family have been wine-growers since 1605, but did not acquire this property until 1905. I have little experience of these wines, apart from a delicately fruity rosé, restrained Riesling and passable Gewurztraminer.
Best varieties: judgement reserved

THE *CLOS* OF ALSACE

These include some of the greatest vineyards in Alsace, which may be part of a *grand cru* and utilize both *appellations* (such as Willm's Clos Gaensbroennel) or prefer not to because the owners believe their own name to have a much greater reputation (e.g. Trimbach's Clos Ste-Hune), but some are not part of any official *grand cru*. A number of the *clos* not situated within a *grand cru* are unclassified for good reason. It has even been decided that no exclusively owned *clos* will be granted *grand cru* status, which is just the sort of petty-minded politics that will undermine the *grand cru* system in Alsace. Denying Clos des Capucins its due status, for example, simply because it is owned by one person, Madame Faller, is not only illogical, it is unjust and devalues the reputation of those vineyards that are granted *grand cru* status. Any suggestion to include such a *clos* in a larger *grand cru* encompassing other surrounding vineyards would be entirely fictional and equally unjust. If the same rule were to be applied in Burgundy, there would be no such thing as Romanée Conti. I wonder what sort of reply INAO would get if they told Lalou Bize-Leroy that she could no longer use the title *grand cru*, unless she wanted to include her two hectares with 20, 40 or even 60 hectares of surrounding vines in a newly created designation called, say, Romanbourg?

Clos des Aubepines

St-Hippolyte, 0.4 hectares
Grand cru: None
Soil: Granite
A tiny *clos* situated within the *lieu-dit* of Geissberg and part of Domaine Muller-Koeberle, which exclusively produces an oak-aged Pinot Noir from this vineyard.
Best varieties: Pinot Noir

Clos des Capucins

Kientzheim, 5.2 hectares
Grand cru: None
Soil: Silty-alluvium over gravel
Exclusively owned by the redoubtable Mme Colette Faller, this *clos* is actually situated in the front garden of the impressive Faller residence and represents just 20 per cent of Domaine Weinbach, yet the Clos des Capucins neck label appears on every bottle of wine the domaine produces. How can this be so? According to the Fallers, it is because the name of the *clos*, the house, the winery and the whole domaine have become synonymous over the years. Labelling the entire production as Clos des Capucins is a pity, as genuine *clos* wines are a rarity these days and the Faller's front garden, the original Clos des Capucins, is an authentic wall-enclosed *clos*. It is a pity that customers are unable to distinguish the exclusively Clos des Capucins wines (Cuvée Théo Riesling and Gewurztraminer and Tokay-Pinot Gris Ste-Cathérine) from the other excellent wines of Domaine Weinbach, but at the moment that is impossible. Like many genuine *clos*, Clos des Capucins is flat, but its enclosed environment regularly enables it to produce some of the greatest wines of Alsace, making it one of the most highly-prized vineyards ever to be found on an alluvial plain. If monopolies were allowed to be classified as *grands crus*, Clos des Capucins would certainly be one. In real terms it ranks as one of the very finest vineyards in Alsace.
Best varieties: Riesling and Tokay-Pinot Gris, followed by Gewurztraminer

Clos Gaensbroennel

Barr, 6.5 hectares
Grand cru: Kirchberg de Barr
Soil: Calcareous-clay
Owned by Domaine Willm (6 hectares) and Domaine Hering (0.5 hectares), the south-facing slopes of this *clos* are located at the bottom of the Kirchberg de Barr.
Best varieties: Gewurztraminer, followed by Riesling (used to be famous for 'Gentil Gaensbroennel', a high quality blend of Gewurztraminer, Tokay-Pinot Gris and Sylvaner that, sadly, is no more).

Clos des Gourmets

Hunawihr, 0.4 hectares
Grand cru: None
Soil: Calcareous clay
Exclusively owned by Domain Mittnacht Frères.
Best varieties: Unknown

Clos Philippe Grass

Wolxheim, 2 hectares
Grand cru: None
Soil: Light, sandy and stony, over red sandstone, light sandy-rocky topsoil over red sandstone
This *clos*, which is situated on the Rothstcin (*see* Rothstein under 'The *Lieux-Dits* of Alsace' below) is planted entirely with Riesling and belongs cxclusivcly to Muhlberger.
Best varieties: Riesling

Clos Hauserer

Wintzenheim, 1.3 hectares
Grand cru: None
Soil: Marly-limestone
Exclusively owned by Domaine Zind Humbrecht, Clos Hauserer is located at the foot of the Grand Cru Hengst and its south-east-facing slope is planted entirely with mature Riesling vines. These

were planted in 1972 and are just beginning to settle down, producing wine that has fine acidity and is sherbetty and zesty when
young, attaining great petrol complexity after five to eight years or
so.
Best variety: Riesling

Clos Himmelreich

Orschwihr, 1.6 hectares
Grand cru: None
Soil: Limestone
Situated next to the Grand Cru Pfingstberg, but not quite as well
favoured by sun and warmth, this *clos* is exclusively owned by
Lucien Albrecht and planted entirely with Riesling.
Best variety: Riesling

Clos du Jardin

I have come across this *clos*, but all I know about it is that it is
commercialized by Bott Frères for Gewurztraminer.

Clos Jebsal

Turckheim, 1.4 hectares
Grand Cru: None
Soil: Gypsum-rich marly-limestone
Owned by Domaine Zind Humbrecht, this very steep, completely
terraced vineyard is located next to Grand Cru Brand on a
geological cliff. Fully south facing and well protected from cold
northerly winds, this *clos* has a very hot microclimate, which combines with the rich soil to provide Tokay-Pinot Gris with exceptionally high levels of both sugar and acidity. The vines were only
planted in 1983, and thus did not produce their first real crop until
1987 and it will no doubt be a decade or so before this vineyard
begins to reveal its true potential, although the wines made so far
show exciting promise.
Best variety: Tokay-Pinot Gris

Clos de Meywhir

Ammerschwihr, 0.06 hectares
Grand Cru: Kaefferkopf
Soil: Limestone
I have never seen this vineyard, nor visited its owner, Roger Klein, but this is supposed to be the smallest officially recognized *clos* in Alsace. Its name alludes to the 'long lost' village of Meywihr, it is south facing and planted entirely with Gewurztraminer.
Best variety: Gewurztraminer

Clos Rebgarten

Andlau, 0.3 hectares
Grand cru: None
Soil: Sandstone, sand and glacial debris
Exclusively owned by Marc Kreydenweiss, this south-facing slope is planted entirely with Muscat Ottonel and consistently produces one of the most exquisite, orange-flower scented wines of this varietal it is possible to find.
Best varieties: Muscat

Clos Roth-stein

Wolxheim, 7 hectares
Grand cru: None
Soil: Calcareous-clay
Apart from a Riesling and Pinot Noir tasted just once, neither of which was very impressive, I have little experience of this *clos*, which is exclusively owned by Jean Arbogast. *See* also Rothstein under 'The *Lieux-Dits* of Alsace' below.
Best varieties: unknown

Clos St-Imer

Gueberschwihr, 5 hectares
Grand cru: Goldert
Soil: Stony calcareous
Exclusively owned by Ernest Burn, who produces excellent Gewurztraminer, superb Muscat and stunning Tokay-Pinot Gris.

Special *cuvées* of the Tokay-Pinot Gris labelled 'la Chapelle' can be even more exciting.
Best varieties: Tokay-Pinot Gris and Muscat, followed by Gewurztraminer

Clos St-Jacques

Colmar, 4.5 hectares
Grand cru: None
Soil: Silty-stony alluvium
Owned and commercialized by Domaine Viticole de la Ville de Colmar as a blended wine, this *clos* is planted 40 per cent Riesling, 20 per cent Tokay-Pinot Gris, 20 per cent Gewurztraminer, 15 per cent Auxerrois and 5 per cent Muscat. Only a small part of the production of Clos St-Jacques is utilized for this wine, which is comprised of 80 per cent Auxerrois, 10 per cent Gewurztraminer and 10 per cent Muscat, the balance going into the domaine's generic varietal wines and Crémant d'Alsace *cuvées*.
Best varieties: Judgement reserved.

Clos St-Landelin

Rouffach, 16 hectares
Grand cru: Vorbourg
Soil: Limestone
Landelin takes its name from the son of an Irish prince, who came to Rouffach to spread the gospel in the early eighth century. He died in 843 and a monastery was built next to his grave. This *clos* is exclusively owned by Muré, who produce exceptionally intense Riesling and Tokay-Pinot Gris on Landelin's stony-limestone terraces at the southern end of the Grand Cru Vorbourg. Muscat always excels in warmer vintages, while Gewurztraminer can be very good, but is not consistent. Some tremendous Pinot Noir grapes have been produced here, but the wine has not always been crafted in the best style.
Best varieties: Riesling and Tokay-Pinot Gris for consistency, Muscat for absolute quality, but perhaps Pinot Noir has the most potential of all?

Clos St-Theobold

Thann, 3.2 hectares
Grand cru: Rangen
Soil: Hard, dark and volcanic
This *clos* is named after Thann's cathedral of St-Théobold, which used to attract thousands of pilgrims in the Middle Ages. Clos St-Théobold was formerly the property of Charles Hippler, the president of the Syndicat du Viticole de Thann, but was acquired by Domaine Schoffit in 1986. At the time of writing just 1.2 hectares of old vines were in production on this *clos*'s precipitous, heat-baked slopes, with 1.5 hectares just replanted.
Best varieties: Tokay-Pinot Gris & Riesling

Clos St-Urbain

Thann, 5 hectares
Grand cru: Rangen
Soil: Granite and volcanic rock
Exclusively owned by Domaine Zind Humbrecht, this *clos* takes its name from the small chapel in the middle of the vineyard, which was built in the fifteenth century. St-Urbain is the local patron of the winegrowers and each year a procession would march from Thann to the chapel singing songs and praying for a good crop. The chapel was completely destroyed during the French Revolution, but later rebuilt, only to be severely damaged during the First World War and rebuilt once more in 1934. Domaine Zind Humbrecht produces magnificently powerful, intensely flavoured Riesling of great potential longevity on these south-east-facing precipitous slopes (an incline of almost 70 per cent) and Gewurztraminer and Tokay-Pinot Gris of almost the same superb quality.
Best varieties: Riesling, followed closely by Gewurztraminer and Tokay-Pinot Gris

Clos Ste-Hune

Hunawihr, 1.3 hectares
Grand cru: Rosacker
Soil: Calcareous-clay
Exclusively owned by Trimbach and entirely planted with Riesling,

Clos Ste-Hune is without doubt the greatest site for this grape variety in Alsace. Clive Coates once told me he thought Clos Ste-Hune to be the greatest Riesling in the world, and frankly I have no inclination to argue the matter. It probably is. Solitary vintages from various producers in the region might rival Clos Ste-Hune now and again, but I cannot think of any Alsace Riesling that could match its performance year-in, year-out over a span of, say, 40 vintages. It is the consistency of performance that establishes the greatness of a growth. *See* 'Trimbach Clos Ste-Hune – In a Class of its Own' under the Riesling section of Chapter 7.
Best varieties: Riesling

Clos Ste-Odile

Obernai, 10.5 hectares
Grand cru: None
Soil: Calcareous-clay
These wines are made and bottled by CV Obernai, which markets them in conjunction with S.A. Ste-Odile, which is owned by Michel Weiss, the proprietor of this *clos*.
Best varieties: Gewurztraminer and Tokay-Pinot Gris

Clos du Schlossberg

Ribeauvillé, 1.2 hectares
Grand cru: None
Soil: Siliceous and pebbly soil over marl
Located at the north-western end of the village, this *clos* is exclusively owned by Jean Sipp. It was originally called 'Halde' in 1352, when it was first mentioned as a vineyard in a document, but by the beginning of the seventeenth century it had become 'Hagel' (as it is still referred to on IGN maps of the area) before acquiring the name by which its wine is currently commercialized.

Jean Sipp first exploited this *clos* in 1965, since when he has maintained the tradition of planting its steep, south-east-facing slope with the following *mélange* of noble grapes: 50 per cent Riesling, 20 per cent Gewurztraminer, 20 per cent Tokay-Pinot Gris and 10 per cent Muscat, which records show have been growing there since at least 1610. The vines are tended by hand as

even the simplest mechanization is impossible (although, paradoxically, this sometimes means that the vineyard will be sprayed
by helicopter to prevent oidium and mildew spreading, as indeed it
would by the time the job could be completed manually), the yield
is severely restricted, averaging just 30 hectolitres per hectare, and
all the varieties are harvested and vinified together to produce a
classic blend.
Best varieties: mixture.

Clos du Sonnenbach

Albé, 4 hectares
Grand cru: None
Soil: Calcareous clay and schist
For many years this *clos* was not cultivated due to its height
(380-465 metres – only Rangen is higher), steep incline, intrusion
of game and the fact that it comprised more than 100 separately
owned parcels of land. In 1978, however, René & Gilbert Beck
formed a group to buy up these parcels and reconstruct the *clos*
before replanting it. Beck now cultivate 1.6 hectares, including it
within their Domaine du Rempart. Clos du Sonnenbach is often
shrouded in fog for two or three weeks before the normal harvest
date, after which it is favoured by the sun. With its south and
south-east exposure, this climatic peculiarity encourages exceptional ripeness in the grapes, hence its cultivation with Alsace's only
black variety.
Best varieties: Pinot Noir

Clos Jean-Philippe Sturm

Eguisheim, 1.5 hectares
Grand cru: None
Soil: Calcareous-clay
Exclusively cultivated with Tokay-Pinot Gris, this wine is made and
marketed by the Wolfberger group.
Best varieties: judgement reserved

Clos de la Tourelle

Wuenheim, 4.5 hectares
Grand cru: Ollwiller
Soil: Limestone
Owned by J-H Gros & Ses Fils, who are also proprietors of Château Ollwiller, this *clos* is planted with 2.5 hectares of Pinot Blanc and 2 hectares of Pinot Noir, from which CV Vieil Armand (part of the Wolfberger group) exclusively produces a Crémant d'Alsace.
Best varieties: judgement reserved

Clos du Val d'Eléon

Andlau, 1.5 hectares
Grand cru: None
Soil: Schist
This steep, south-facing hillside vineyard was recently acquired by Marc Kreydenweiss and four other partners, including New York lawyer Bob Wade. Purchased in 1986, it was cleared and replanted the following year with equal proportions of Riesling and Tokay-Pinot Gris. According to local archives, buyers in the early part of this century would come from other cities and the first wine they purchased was always from this *clos,* which many considered to be the best vineyard in Andlau. Marc Kreydenweiss produced his first Clos du Val d'Eléon in 1990 from a blend of 70 per cent Riesling and 30 per cent Tokay-Pinot Gris and an excellent, slow-maturing wine it seems to be.
Best varieties: Riesling and Tokay-Pinot Gris

Clos du Vicus Romain

Wintzenheim, 0.5 hectares
Grand cru: Hengst
Soil: Dark calcareous scree over calcareous marl
A small, south-facing vineyard where they found the remains of a Roman inn, including the walls, bones and assorted jewellery. Owned by Domaine Aimé Stentz.
Best varieties: Tokay-Pinot Gris

Clos Windsbuhl

Hunawihr, 6 hectares
Grand cru: None
Soil: Limestone
First planted at the end of the seventeenth century, when viticulture
on the plains was strictly controlled by royal decrees and the wines
of this *clos* enjoyed a great reputation. In more recent times, this
vineyard was owned by Bérangère Meyer, but the wines were made
and marketed by CV Hunawihr (I tasted the 1983s and 1985s at
the cooperative, sold as Domaine de Windsbuhl, but they were not
in the least special) before Domaine Zind Humbrecht rented the
property. They farmed it for three vintages (1987, 1988 and 1989),
before making the decision to purchase it outright.

Clos Windsbuhl's terraced, south-facing, limestone slopes are
covered with clay and calcareous stones. The site is well protected
from north winds and enjoys a warm microclimate. All Alsace
varieties were once cultivated here, but after three years of practical
study, the Zind Humbrechts are convinced by the nature of its soil
and subsoil that Tokay-Pinot Gris is ideal for Clos Windsbuhl.
Consequently, they have begun to replace many of the lesser
varieties with Tokay-Pinot Gris, although existing old vines of all
four *grand cru* grapes will also be retained. Furthermore, they are
currently conducting experiments with Chardonnay.

The very first wines vinified by the Zind Humbrechts were from
the 1988 vintage, since when the *clos* has more than proved its
worth for both Tokay-Pinot Gris and Gewurztraminer, which give
fabulously rich, powerful and spicy wines that appear to have the
potential to benefit enormously from several years in bottle. The
Riesling has been surprisingly successful, especially the SGN, which
many believe to be the most sensational wine Domaine Zind Humbrecht has ever produced.
Best varieties: Tokay-Pinot Gris, Gewurztraminer and Riesling

Clos du Zahnacker

Ribeauvillé, 1.2 hectares
Grand cru: None
Soil: Calcareous-clay
Produced and marketed by the CV Ribeauvillé from equal parts of

Tokay-Pinot Gris, Riesling and Gewurztraminer, Clos du Zahnacker is not part of any *grand cru*, but is situated immediately
next to Osterberg on the Côte de Ribeauvillé and its classic blended wine is *grand cru* in all but name. This *clos* has been known
and referred to since it was first planted by Benedictine monks
from the monastery of St-Morand in the ninth century, although it
did not get its present name until a few centuries later. Records
show that three different varieties have been grown in equal proportions in this triangular-shaped vineyard since the twelfth century, when a certain ennobled monk by the name of Martin Zahn
was in charge, although it is impossible to discern the identity of
those vines. Zahn's influence was such that documents dated 1491
refer to it as Martin Zahn's *acker* or 'field', a fact that is com-
memorated by a stone set into the vineyard wall. The blended
wine of Clos du Zahnacker has been famous since at least 1673,
when it was served by the Seigneur de Ribeaupierre to Louis XIV
during in his passage through Ribeauvillé. The wine today is a
credit to its history and to the expertise of the local cooperative.
Best varieties: Tokay-Pinot Gris, Riesling and Gewurztraminer

Clos Zisser

Barr, 5 hectares
Grand cru: Kirchberg de Barr
Soil: Calcareous-clay
Part of Domaine Klipfel, the vines of this *clos* are second only to
those of Clos Gaensbroennel on the Kirchberg de Barr. It is
planted entirely with Gewurztraminer, with which it excels,
especially when late harvested, as has long been the tradition of
Domaine Klipfel.
Best varieties: Gewurztraminer.

THE *CÔTES* AND *COTEAUX* OF ALSACE

A sort of intermediate designation between the generic wines of
Alsace and the up and coming *lieux-dits* are the various *côtes* and
coteaux. These can refer to a relatively small area within one
village or a series of hills spread across several communes.

Côte des Amandiers, Mittelwihr (Haut-Rhin): term used by some growers, such as Jean Greiner and Greiner-Schleret, in conjunction with the Grand Cru Mandelberg for some wines.

Côtes de Barr, Barr (Bas-Rhin): a generic term used for all varieties grown by Domaine Klipfel on the slopes that surround the town of Barr.

Coteaux d'Eguisheim, Eguisheim (Haut-Rhin): a range of limestone slopes to the west of the village, Coteaux d'Eguisheim has been commercialized by Maison Léon Baur for its Riesling Cuvée Elisabeth Stumpf, but appears to have dropped it during a change (for the better) of its label design.

Coteaux du Haut-Koenigsbourg, St-Hipolyte-Orschwiller-Kintzheim (Bas-Rhin): these *coteaux* extend across the many slopes, hills and little vales that spread beneath Haut-Koenigsbourg, which is indubitably the most imposing castle of Alsace; most of the vineyards here are either granite or limestone; wines using this name are commercialized by Domaine Siffert and Bernhard-Reibel. (*See also* Burgreben, under 'The *Lieux-Dits* of Alsace'.)

Coteaux du Mossig, Wasselonne to Ergersheim (Bas-Rhin): a string of vine-clad hills and dales along the basin of the peaceful Mossig river, which in viticultural terms runs from Wasselonne south to Soultz-les-Bains and Wolxheim. Depending where you draw the boundary, these *coteaux* could be said to encompass four *grands crus* (Steinklotz in Marlenheim, Altenberg de Bergbieten, Engelberg in Dahlenheim and Altenberg de Wolxheim) and 22 *lieux-dits* (including the following active names: Finkenberg in Dorlisheim, Glintzberg in Bergbieten, Horn de Wolxheim, Kefferberg in Ergersheim, Rotstein in Wolxheim and Westerweingarten in Balbronn). The Coteaux du Mossig have an average annual rainfall of 650 mm and a minimum of 1800 hours of sunshine, face all points of the compass, with soil that is predominantly calcareous-clay, although extremely varied in places. These vineyards were planted as early as the third century, assumed some recognition by the sixth and were flourishing in the fifteenth. The term 'Mossig', whether Vignobles de la Mossig or Coteaux du Mossig, has been a recognized geographic designation since the turn of the century for the vineyards of Marlenheim, Wangen, Wasselonne, Wolxheim, Dan-golsheim, Soultz-les-Bains, Traenheim, Scharrachbergheim and Westhoffen, according to diplomas for its award-winning wines; all varieties of Alsace vines are grown in its many vineyards today and wines of this denomination are commercialized by CV Traenheim under the Roi Dagobert label.

Côtes de Ribeauvillé, Ribeauvillé (Haut-Rhin): 7.5 hectares of south, south-east and south-west-facing slopes of calcareous-sandstone and clayey-calcareous soil encompassing one-third of a hectare of Grand Cru Kirchberg de Ribeauvillé, plus the *lieux-dits* of Rengelsbrunn, Oberturnert and Weinbaum. Planted primarily with Pinot Blanc, which usually accounts for 40 per cent of the excellent wine commercialized by Louis Sipp under this denomi-nation, the remainder of the blend consisting of Sylvaner, Riesling and Gewurztraminer.

Côte de Rouffach, Rouffach-Pfaffenheim-Westhalten (Haut-Rhin): this denomination could almost be called the Côtes du Haut-Rhin, as it currently covers no less than 150 hectares and, if negotiations with Soultzmatt, Gueberschwihr and Hattstatt go well, could double in size. There is understandable resistance from some growers in these villages, who do not see why the name Rouffach should be on the label of their wines, which do not come from that village, but it should be pointed out that the Vosges foothills from Hattstatt down to Rouffach are one big slope, rather than a series of hills, and the concept of naming a large all-encompassing area after one village is not new, although perhaps they should follow the Burgundian example and call it Côtes de Rouffach-Villages. Whatever form it finally takes, the concept itself, as originally conceived by Jean-Claude Rieflé, is eminently sensible, as it has been predicted that there will be 'thousands' of Alsace *lieux-dits* (*see* introduction to 'The *Lieux-Dits* of Alsace' below) confusing the consumer in the coming years, thus the only salvation would be 'umbrella' denominations, such as the Côte de Rouffach, under which all the various growths could be marketed. This does not rid the market of the range and diversity of so many individual wines, but it makes their number easier to grasp, as the label would have two levels of information and it would be up to each consumer what to digest; all the wines carry the Côte de Rouffach denomination lightly superimposed over a map of the *côte* itself and beneath this comes the name of the *lieu-dit* (if indeed the wine comes from one), village (either with or without the *lieu-dit*) or just the grape variety. The first to commercialize this denomination was in fact Domaine Rieflé with their 1988 vintage, but I have also seen the term used by Bruno Hunold, and Muré (who say that 'the reputation of Côte de Rouffach dates back to the eighth century', although they make no claim that it has been used to commercialize the wines), Heim (CV Westhalten) and others unknown to the author who took part in the original discussions.

Côtes du Val St-Grégoire, Munster Valley (Haut-Rhin): a series of south and south-east-facing, granitic hills at the beginning of the Munster Valley and close to the forest, encompassing the villages of Zimmerbach, Walbach, Wihr au Val and a small part of Turckheim. The topsoil is partly sandy-granitic and partly sandy-clay and planted for the most part with vines of the Pinot family, the majority of which are Pinot Blanc and Auxerrois, but also include Pinot Noir and Tokay-Pinot Gris. About 54 hectares of vineyards centring on, but not totally confined to, Walbach are considered to be the true heart of the Val St-Grégoire, where the soil is deepest and the climate driest. Wines labelled Côtes du Val St-Grégoire are commercialized by A. Gueth & Fils and CV Turckheim. *See* also Felsen, under 'The *Lieux-Dits* of Alsace'.

THE *LIEUX-DITS* OF ALSACE

What follows refers to those *lieux-dits* (literally named sites) in current use, with the exception of the *clos, côtes, coteaux* and châteaux profiled above and the *grands crus* featured in the previous chapters. There are thousands of *lieux-dits* in Alsace. A look at any map from the IGN Blue Series will reveal a dozen or more for each village, yet such maps merely scratch the surface. Go to the *mairie* of a village and look at the communal map, which shows every single plot of vines. Well over 120,000 of these are spread across that part of AOC Alsace which is currently cultivated (and there is potential to plant almost half as much again) and the vast majority of them are named. Indeed, if you look closely, you can see the 'original' size of every so-called *grand cru* and *lieu-dit,* and they are tiny indeed. Of course, with time, some of these have become better known than others, locally, and the use of those names has historically spread from their minute, authentic origins to somewhat larger areas. Go back to the IGN Blue Series and you will see that some have even shifted position, but even when expanded through usage and repositioned with time, they are still a fraction of the size claimed today. This is understandable on a grower-by-grower basis (though should not be pandered to, when deliminating something as potentially prestigious as a *grand cru*), as nobody produces a greater range of products every year than an Alsace winegrower. If this range of wines were to be multiplied by a factor of 15 (the average number of plots per grower) or 50 (which is the average for most growers who actually commercialize their own wines), the number of different wines soon becomes impractical to make and impossible to market, which is why the name of perhaps one or two of the very best *lieux-dits* might be used to market the wines that come from those general areas.

Other growers with vines neighbouring a *lieu-dit* of increasing fame might then consider their wines to come from the same slope and start marketing them as such – hence the ballooning and shifting effect. Complicate this by the historical breaking-up of family domaines as each grower's *patrimoine* is divided among the next generation and then compound it as other families are united through marriage and their respective vineyards amalgamated, and the relevance of individual *lieux-dits* becomes confused if not questionable. Even though such wines are increasingly fashionable, in the wake of the *grand cru* revolution, only a relatively small number of those that exist will be utilized. From a potential, therefore, of tens of thousands, the number of *lieux-dits* might eventually run into hundreds. There are probably between 100 and 150 of these names in current use, although fewer than 80 are listed below. This section is not as complete as I would have liked it to be, but there are obviously some producers commercializing wines that I have never encountered, especially the smaller growers whose wines may be available on a very local scale.

A360P, Nothalten (Bas-Rhin): codename used by Domaine Oster-tag for 'subversive' Tokay-Pinot Gris grown on Grand Cru Muen-chberg.

Altenbourg, Kientzheim (Haut-Rhin): situated on the lower slopes of the Mont de Sigolsheim, just beneath Furstentum, immediately above Grafreben and to the east of Schlossberg, the rich, calcareous-clay soil of this south-south-west-facing vineyard is planted with Muscat, Gewurztraminer and Tokay-Pinot Gris, the wines being commercialized by Claude Dietrich and Paul Blanck.

Bergweingarten, Pfaffenheim (Haut-Rhin): mentioned since the thirteenth century in records of the Swiss Benedictine Abbaye de Muri, the soil is brown, calcareous and sometimes clayey (the best parts are said to be those that are stony) on east-and south-east-facing slopes of the Coteau de Pfaffenheim, immediately north of and contiguous with the Grand Cru Steinert and the *lieu-dit* of Schneckenberg. Bergweingarten is about 20 hectares in size, planted predominantly with Gewurztraminer and commercialized by CV Pfaffenheim, but Pierre Frick also has a tiny plot of Sylvaner, which often achieves a natural alcoholic strength of 12 per cent by volume, which is remarkable for this variety. François Runner and Domaine Rieflé both produce a Gewurztraminer.

Bildstoeckle, Obermorschwihr (Bas-Rhin): small, calcareous-clay vineyard commercialized by Laurent Bannworth.

Birgele, Riquewihr (Haut-Rhin): sand and marl vineyard commercialized by J-J Baumann.

Bollenberg, Orschwihr-Rouffach-Westhalten (Haut-Rhin): a massive limestone mound separated from the foothills of the Vosges by the vale of Orschwihr, the Bollenberg stretches from the eastern outskirts of Orschwihr to the south-western edge of Rouffach. Throughout its enigmatic history, the Bollenberg's impressive site has attracted religious cults, satanists and practitioners of the black arts to perform the most bizarre rites on its summit; these mysterious events have been spoken about since the earliest times (witches regularly initiated their apprentices on the Bollenberg and, in 1886, Abbot Braun claimed that all the witches in the country rendezvoused there each year). Although it encompasses parts of three different communes, I have seen only the wines from the Orschwihr section sold under the Bollenberg name. About 100 hectares of this *lieu-dit* lie within Orschwihr, where its slopes face south, south-east and south-west, which is unusual in itself; there are very few vines on the full south-facing slope. The south-eastern slope is calcareous-clay, has a special microclimate that enables rare and protected species of flora to grow and is primarily planted with Riesling and Gewurztraminer; the south-western slope has a very deep, heavy clay soil, in which the Gewurztraminer and all three varieties of Pinot fare especially well. In fact, all varieties of Alsace grapes grow on these slopes, having found and adapted to a par- ticular niche of suitable soil, and, according to Pierre Reinhart, it is this variation in soil types that prevents Bollenberg from claiming *grand cru* status because it goes against the geological homogeneity expressed in the regulations, which is true enough, but has not prevented Brand and others from successfully convincing the *grand cru* commission otherwise. The wines are commercialized by Théo Cattin, Château d'Orschwihr and Vignobles Reinhart.

Brandhof, Andlau (Bas-Rhin): a 14-hectare calcareous and sandy vineyard in a predominantly granite area, Brandhof has a south- south-east exposure. It was classified by ampelographer J. L. Stoltz in 1824 as one of the best sites in Alsace and first used as an *appellation* for wine in 1933. The wines, which typically have generous yet elegant fruit, are commercialized by Domaine André & Rémy Gresser, who have planted its south-south-east-facing slope with Tokay-Pinot Gris, Muscat and Pinot Noir. Riesling is also commercialized by Julien Rieffel & Fils.

Brandhof, Steinseltz (Bas-Rhin): barely more than 2.5 hectares, this silty-clay vineyard has grown vines since the Middle Ages. It is situated at an altitude of between 180 and 200 metres, and faces south-south-east. Planted for the most part with Tokay-Pinot Gris, but with some Gewurztraminer, Auxerrois and a smattering of Sylvaner (new plantations will be exclusively Tokay-Pinot Gris), it has provided CV Cléebourg with some of its best wines since 1962, although only sold under this name since 1986.

Brandluft, Mittelbergheim (Bas-Rhin): calcareous vineyard with high active-lime content, which enables elegant Riesling with elevated acidity levels to be produced; commercialized by Christian Dolder, Haegi, Seltz and André Wantz.

Breitstein, Dambach-la-Ville (Bas-Rhin): granite vineyard around which the Route du Vin makes a right-angled bend north of the village, just before Blienschwiller. A full, spicy Gewurztraminer is marketed under this *lieu-dit* by Hubert Metz.

Burg, Berghcim (Haut-Rhin): gently sloping, south-facing vineyard, situated at between 250 and 280 metres in height, Burg is 13.6 hectares in size and has a heavy, lime-rich marly soil with gypsum nodules, which improve the soil's heat-retaining and water-circulation properties. This combination of situation, aspect and soil tends to stretch out the vine's ripening process: the soil's water-retention peaks in the summer, dropping to its lowest point in September, with a very slow build-up in the autumn – if all other factors combine to provide healthy fruit, this can result in really splendid, absolutely authentic, Vendanges Tardives of true *vin de garde* quality. Riesling and Gewurztraminer are especially well suited. Wines utilizing the Burg *lieu-dit* are commercialized by Marcel Deiss and Louis Freyburger.

Burgreben, St-Hippolyte (Haut-Rhin): granite vineyard over-looking the upper reaches of the Eckenbach at the southern end of the Coteaux du Haut-Koenigsbourg. Four hectares of Burgreben are owned by Muller-Koeberle, who grows 1.6 hectares of Riesling, 1.2 hectares of Pinot Noir, 0.8 hectares of Gewurztraminer and 0.4 hectares of Pinot Blanc. René Klein also produces Riesling. *See* also Coteaux du Haut-Koenigsbourg in 'The *Côtes* and *Coteaux* of Alsace' above.

Burgreben, Zellenberg (Haut-Rhin): south and south-east-facing, clayey-marl slope beneath Hagenschlauf on the eastern side of the village, commercialized by Jean Huttard.

Burlenberg, Bergheim (Haut-Rhin): heat-hardened limestone vine-yard ideal for Pinot Noir; commercialized by Marcel Deiss.

Dorfburg, Ingersheim (Haut-Rhin): rich calcareous-marl soil vine-yard at the foot of Grand Cru Florimont, commercialized by CV Ingersheim.

Engelgarten, Bergheim (Haut-Rhin): light gravelly vineyard capable of producing fine, elegant Riesling, but quite fat and exotic in big years; commercialized by Marcel Deiss.

Felsen, Walbach (Haut-Rhin): very steep, 7-hectare, sandy-granitic *lieu-dit* on the Côtes du Val St-Grégoire, planted with Tokay-Pinot Gris (best), Riesling and Gewurztraminer, wholly-owned and commercialized by A. Gueth & Fils.

Finkenberg, Molsheim (Bas-Rhin): some of this limestone vineyard, which, in 1828, was ranked as one of the best vineyards in Alsace by J. L. Stoltz, forms part of the *grand cru*, but it is also commercialized as a *lieu-dit* by Bernard Becht and Bernard Weber.

Frieberg, Barr (Bas-Rhin): north-facing vineyard south of Barr on the opposite side of the village to the Grand Cru Kirchberg de Barr, which produces light and lacking wines most years, although the drawbacks in the situation of this *lieu-dit* enable it to come into its own in very hot and sunny years like 1976, 1983 and 1989, when its wines are truly great and often have a better balance than those of Kirchberg de Barr; commercialized by Domaine Klipfel.

Fronholz, Epfig (Bas-Rhin): granite vineyard that takes its name from the small community of Fronholz, which comes within the communal boundaries of Epfig, being situated just south-west of the village on the D703 towards Blienschwiller. Although on the plain, the Fronholz mound, which rise from 220 to 260 metres, is in fact geologically part of the Vosges, being connected to the mountain range by an umbilical cord of solid rock. Its situation provides exceptional sunlight while at the same time its vines are exposed to cool currents from the Rhine valley. The epicentre of Epfig's finest vineyards, Fronholz can be divided into three geologically different areas:(1) the summit and south, with its white siliceous sandy soil, which is broken up by pebbly quartz and planted with Riesling; (2) the south-east flank, which is marly-clay and favours Gewurztraminer or Tokay-Pinot Gris; and (3), the south-east-facing lower slope, which is marl and best suits Muscat or Pinot Noir. The wines of this *lieu-dit* are typically strong, minerally and long-lived, with an exceptional combination of high sugar and excellent acidity. Commercialized by Domaine Ostertag and Jean-Claude Beck.

Fruehmess, Itterswiller (Bas-Rhin): this gently inclined, north-east-facing *lieu-dit* is situated behind the Kirchberg (not to be confused with the Kirchberg *grands crus*) that dominates the village and has sandy soil. Commercialized by Domaine Kieffer and Justin Schwartz.

Gaentzbrunnen, Pfaffenheim (Haut-Rhin): a vast viticultural area extending from the heart of Pfaffenheim to the centre of Gueberschwihr, its east-and south-east-facing slopes are uniformly covered with gravelly-clay and sandstone-derived deposits of loess and produce excellent Pinot Noir with a marked cherry character that is commercialized by CV Pfaffenheim. Riesling is also commercialized by Rieflé from an area within the *lieu-dit* of calcareous-marl soil.

Galgenrain, Albé (Haut-Rhin): very stony calcareous clay with schist, this vineyard is planted with Auxerrois and commercialized by René & Gilbert Beck.

Geisberg or *Geissberg*, St-Hippolyte (Haut-Rhin): south-south-east-facing granite vineyard situated between St-Hippolyte and Orschwiller. A Rouge de St-Hippolyte Geisberg is commercialized by Muller-Koeberle and Tokay-Pinot Gris by René Klein.

Glintzberg, Bergbieten (Bas-Rhin): situated on a western extension of the Grand Cru Altenberg de Bergbieten, this vineyard has excellent exposure to the sun, facing south, south-west and south-east. This, together with its ruddy-coloured, calcareous-clay soil, which like the Altenberg is permeated with highly absorbent Keuper gypsum fragments, improving the soil's heat-retention and water-circulation properties, makes Glintzberg particularly suitable for late-ripening varieties such as Riesling, which accounts for 47 per cent of the area planted (Gewurztraminer represents 24 per cent, Sylvaner 19 per cent, Muscat 6 per cent and Pinot Noir and Tokay-Pinot Gris account for the remaining 4 per cent); these wines are apparently commercialized by several growers, but I have only come across those of Roland Schmitt.

Grafreben, Kientzheim (Haut-Rhin): small vineyard situated on the lower slopes of the Bixkoepflé, between the Grand Cru Schlossberg and the *lieu-dit* Altenbourg, the wines of Grafreben (which means 'lord's vines') have a minerally finesse and good potential longevity. They are commercialized by Paul Blanck for Tokay-Pinot Gris and CV Kientzheim-Kaysersberg for Gewurztraminer.

Grasberg, Bergheim (Haut-Rhin): limestone vineyard commercialized by Marcel Deiss.

Grosstein, Westhalten (Haut-Rhin): an 8-hectare, east-facing vineyard with a siliceous-clay soil dominated by large sandstone rocks (from whence its name derived), just under half an hectare of which is planted with Sylvaner and Pinot Noir. Owned and commercialized by Pierre Frick.

Hagenschlauf, Zellenberg (Haut-Rhin): east and south-east-facing, 8.9-hectare vineyard of clayey conglomerate soil, some 90 per cent planted with Riesling. This site is capable of producing very ripe, fruity wines with an exotic peachy-musk character and good acidity, which makes it naturally suited to Vendanges Tardives. Approximately 1.6 hectares are owned by Jean Becker, who have commercialized the wine under this name since 1960.

Hahnenberg, Chatenois (Bas-Rhin): small, 1.2-hectare, granitic gravel vineyard commercialized by Dontenville and J. Hauller & Fils.

Hardt or *Harth*, Colmar (Haut-Rhin): the Hardt is located in a vast expanse of vines north-west of Colmar, bordered by the N83 south and east, the N415 south-west and the river Fecht and its surrounding forest north and north-west. Over the years, this has been divided into the Grosshardt to the north, Mittelhardt, not surprisingly in the middle and south, and Oberhardt, which is even further south. The soil is entirely alluvial, comprised of sand, clay and gravel, and warms up rapidly in even meagre sunlight. Most of these vineyards are cultivated by Domaine Jux (which was purchased by Wolfberger in 1989), although there is no indication of the name, be it Harth or Hardt, on the labels, which I think is a pity. Hardt wines generally do not have the structure to promise much longevity, but they have more finesse than most wines of the plain, have the capacity of overt fruitiness at reasonable yields and are perfect for most modern consumers. If it is famous for anything, the Hardt is famous for Chasselas, so perhaps it is no coincidence that Domaine Schoffit is virtually the only producer to make medal-winning Chasselas as its wine comes from the Hardt vines that are over 60 years old. Schoffit also turns out a Gewurztraminer Harth that easily flatters. Robert Karcher and Albert Mann also commercialize wines from this *lieu-dit*.

Heimbourg, Turckheim (Haut-Rhin): the wines from this *lieu-dit* used to be sold as Brand until that *grand cru*'s delimitation, although Heimbourg's soil is a magnesium-rich, hard limestone called Muschelkalk, whereas the heart of the original Brand is granite; this west-facing vineyard has a fairly steep slope, which faces the opening of the Munster valley and gets the best of the evening sun, but is essentially a late-ripening site. Various grapes are grown here, including Sylvaner, Pinot Blanc, Riesling, Tokay-Pinot Gris and Gewurztraminer, the wines of which often reach Vendange Tardive and SGN standard. The size of this *lieu-dit* is about six hectares, of which Domaine Zind Humbrecht own four, equally divided between Tokay-Pinot Gris and Gewurztraminer. Heimbourg wines are also commercialized by CV Turckheim.

Heissenberg, Nothalten (Bas-Rhin): approximately 15 hectares of south-facing vineyards, situated at 250 to 280 metres in altitude on the steep slope behind Nothalten church, Heissenberg literally means 'hot mountain' and its baking-hot, stony, silty-sandy, brown acid soil over twin-mica granite, sandstone and tufa encourages over-ripeness in even late varieties and is thus ideal for Riesling, which typically has high sugar levels and a distinctive minerally taste. The *lieu-dit* also produces fine Gewurztraminer and Pinot Noir. These wines are commercialized by Domaine Ostertag and Domaine Julien Meyer.

Heissenstein, Nothalten (Bas-Rhin): despite the unfavourable north-east aspect of this 10-hectare site, Heissenstein is well suited to certain precocious varieties, such as Pinot Blanc and Pinot Noir, due to the stony structure of its soil, which stores the heat received during the day, dissipating it very slowly into the vine at night (Heissenstein means 'Hot Stones'). These wines are commercialized by Domaine Julien Meyer.

Herrenweg, Turckheim (Haut-Rhin): situated on flat alluvial land south of Turckheim, between the Fecht and the outskirts of Wintzenheim, Herrenweg enjoys exceptionally long hours of sunshine, particularly in the evenings. It is very dry (just 525–600 mm of rain per year) and the soil, consisting of granite, silt and loess over pebbly siliceous-gravel and clay, quickly warms up, ripening fruit eight to ten days in advance of that on nearby slopes. Typical of alluvial soils, these wines evolve relatively rapidly; if, however, the yield is severely restricted, wines of much greater longevity can be produced, although they still mature relatively quickly. The Riesling is particularly successful, providing wines of truly expressive aroma and delightful lime-fruit flavour. This *lieu-dit* is commercialized by Barmès-Buecher, JosMeyer and Domaine Zind Humbrecht.

Horn de Wolxheim, Wolxheim (Bas-Rhin): dominated by the Sacré Coeur statue, which divides this substantial 25-hectare vineyard from the Grand Cru Altenberg de Wolxheim on the other side of the hill, the Horn de Wolxheim faces south and south-east, is covered with calcareous-marl and limestone over loess-enriched limestone, and planted predominantly with all three Pinot grapes, which are considered ideal for this soil and situation. A good blended wine is made and commercialized from these varieties by Muhlberger.

Huettgasse, Steinseltz (Bas-Rhin): this 2.5-hectare vineyard is situated at an altitude of between 200 and 235 metres, has full southerly exposure and its silty soil is planted almost entirely with Pinot Noir (Tokay-Pinot Gris, Gewurztraminer and Sylvaner account for less than half a hectare and new plantations will be exclusively Pinot Noir). Its wines are commercialized by CV Cléebourg.

Kapelweg, Rorschwihr (Haut-Rhin): just over one hectare of this 5.7-hectare, east-facing, *lieu-dit* is owned by Rolly Gassmann, who grows Riesling and Gewurztraminer on its brown clayey soil that is marly in patches.

Karchweg, Oberhoffen (Bas-Rhin): just over 5 hectares in size, this silty-sandy clay vineyard is situated at an altitude of between 200 and 235 metres and has a full southerly exposure. Just over half the vineyard is planted with Tokay-Pinot Gris (the balance being Riesling, Sylvaner, Auxerrois, Pinot Noir and Gewurztraminer, with new plantations exclusively reserved for Tokay-Pinot Gris). The wines are commercialized by CV Cléebourg.

Keimberg, Clécbourg (Bas-Rhin): some 3.3 hectares in size, this silty-sandy-clay vineyard has been cultivated with vines since the Middle Ages. It is situated at an altitude of between 210 and 240 metres, with a south-south-east aspect and more than two-thirds planted for the most part with Auxerrois, the balance being Riesling, Tokay-Pinot Gris, Gewurztraminer and Sylvaner (new plantations will be exclusively Auxerrois). These wines are commercialized by CV Cléebourg, which has produced medal-winning wines from this *coteaux* since 1962.

Kefferberg, Ergersheim (Bas-Rhin): this south-facing vineyard is located east of the Altenberg de Wolxheim, covers 27 hectares and has a very dry microclimate, but the vines easily penetrate the brown calcareous soil, digging deep into the calcareous marl subsoil for moisture. Riesling, Tokay-Pinot Gris and Gewurztraminer fare extremely well in this *lieu-dit*, the last being particularly capable, even in lesser years, a quality attributed in part to the specific selection of this variety growing in the Kefferberg. These wines are commercialized by Lucien Brand, who own 3.5 hectares.

Klusterhof, Andlau (Bas-Rhin): granite vineyard commercialized by Domaine Mattern.

Kritt, Eichhoffen (Bas-Rhin): this 42-hectare vineyard consists of clayey, gravelly and sandy alluvium on its south-south-east-facing slopes located at the foot of the Brandhof, close to Andlau, although technically in Eichhoffen. Most of this *lieu-dit* is commercialized by Domaine André & Rémy Gresser, who grow Pinot Blanc and Gewurztraminer (the latter being well suited to Vendanges Tardives and SGN when grown on clay), although Marc Kreydenweiss cultivates 4 hectares with Pinot Blanc (the late-picked wines of which are labelled Klevner), Gewurztraminer and the relatively recent addition of Chardonnay. Marc used to produce a fascinating *barrique*, aged Kritt Sylvaner, but alas no more.

Kronenbourg, Zellenberg (Haut-Rhin): although situated within the commune of Zellenberg, this lovely south-east-facing slope is in fact a continuation of Riquewihr's Schoenenbourg. The marly soil has an active-lime content of some 40 per cent, which gives wines of very favourable acidity. Riesling is very floral on the nose, with peachy fruit; commercialized by Roger Jung and Jean Becker.

Leimenthal, Wettolsheim (Haut-Rhin): situated to the west of Wettolsheim, at a height of about 300 metres above sea-level, this vineyard has calcareous-clay with a very high pH and vast water-retention capacity, thus being capable of producing wines of exceptionally fine acidity in the very hottest years. Leimenthal is also well-suited to Vendanges Tardives and SGN. Less than half a hectare of this *lieu-dit* is commercialized by Barmès-Buecher and it is planted entirely with Riesling.

Lerchenberg, Andlau (Bas-Rhin): small 0.9-hectare vineyard next to Moenchberg, east-facing, with a soil composed of clayey glacial deposits. It is planted with Tokay-Pinot Gris and commercialized by Marc Kreydenweiss.

Letzenberg, Ingersheim (Haut-Rhin): this raised, limestone plateau has a slight north-east-facing slope and is located west of Colmar, between Ingersheim and Turckheim. Approximately 40 hectares in size, 30 of which are cultivated with Gewurztraminer and Riesling for the most part. Some seven hectares are commercialized by CV Ingersheim under the name of this *lieu-dit*. This is a particularly good source in very hot years.

Lippelsberg, Orschwihr (Haut-Rhin): this *lieu-dit* has south-east-facing slopes and could be described as the lower extension of the Grand Cru Pfingstberg. Commercialized by Matterne Haegelin.

Meissenberg, Bergholtz (Haut-Rhin): a small, sandy-clay vineyard that often produces Riesling with a distinctly musky character and is commercialized by Eric Rominger.

Moenchreben, Rorschwihr (Haut-Rhin): there are numerous Moenchrebens, which means 'monk's hill', in Alsace due to the many religious orders that established themselves in the region from the Middle Ages on, but this one should not be confused with the Grand Cru Moenchreben of Andlau and Eichhoffen. This south-east-facing *lieu-dit* is located east of the village and covers some six hectares, of which 2.36 hectares are owned by Rolly Gassmann, who grow Auxerrois, Pinot Noir and Muscat on its brown clayey and sandy-gravelly soil. Rolly Gassmann's Moenchreben Auxerrois is excellent, but it is his Moenchreben Muscat that truly excels, with its expressive aroma and extravagantly rich fruit, which has a little residual sugar and is all the better for it; it is undoubtedly one of the two greatest Muscats in Alsace.

Muehlforst, Hunawihr (Haut-Rhin): a large, south-south-east-facing vineyard that extends for almost 55 hectares, culminating at a height of 311 metres, close to the boundary with Ribeauvillé, to the north of Hunawihr. First documented in 1284 and cultivated with vines since at least the fourteenth century, Muehlforst was mentioned for its Riesling by Charles Grad in *L'Alsace* (1889). Its heavily fossilized calcareous-clay soil is today planted with every Alsace variety, although most of the wine produced is blended into various generic varietals by the CV Hunawihr, but both the cooperative and Domaine Mittnacht Frères commercialize Riesling and Gewurztraminer under this *lieu-dit*.

Oberberg, Blienschwiller (Bas-Rhin): granite, sand and marl vineyard commercialized by Oscar Schwartz.

Oberer-Weingarten, Rorschwihr (Haut-Rhin): almost eight hectares in size, 1.75 of which belong to Rolly Gassmann, who grows Gewurztraminer on its marly-limestone, east-facing slope.

Patergarten, Kientzheim (Haut-Rhin): situated on the alluvial flat ground immediately west of Kientzheim, where the soil is warm (but the heat quickly dissipates at night), the vines ripen early and the wines, which also mature quickly, are commercialized by Paul Blanck for Riesling and Tokay-Pinot Gris, by A. Gueth for Riesling and by CV Kientzheim-Kaysersberg, also for Riesling.

Pflaenzerreben, Rorschwihr and Bergheim (Haut-Rhin): situated half-way between Rorschwihr and Bergheim, on the eastern side of the Dɪbis, this is effectively a combination of the east-facing

Pflaenzer in Bergheim and the northeast-facing Runtzmatt in Ror-schwihr. Just over one hectare is owned by Rolly Gassmann, who grows Riesling and Tokay-Pinot Gris on its silty-clay and marl over limestone soil.

Pfleck, Wettolsheim (Haut-Rhin): this *lieu-dit* is situated just south of the Grand Cru Steingrubler and commercialized by Albert Mann, who grows Riesling on its sandy soil.

Rebgarten, Bennwihr (Haut-Rhin): located to the north-east of Bennwihr, this *lieu-dit* covers an area of 24.2 hectares and is comprised of numerous small parcels (Hasenhaut, Kaufstueckel, Gaensweide, Altwaesch, Gaessel, Sendel, Neubrunnen, Ober Rebgarten and, to the very east of these, the original Rebgarten itself), which undulate in a generally east-facing fashion and have various soil types, although silty and siliceous colluvium over a granitic gravel base dominates. Rebgarten is mentioned in various old village documents, and wines were commercialized under this *lieu-dit* before the Second World War. Since the formation of the local cooperative, these wines have been vinified separately and, according to CV Bennwihr, it is the very diversity of the soils that enables Rebgarten to produce such well-balanced wines. I can certainly vouch for the Rieslings on occasions, although I am not so sure about the Muscat.

Rebgarten, Gueberschwihr (Haut-Rhin): adjoining the eastern bor-ders of Grand Cru Goldert, this well-known *lieu-dit* has sandy soil, is east facing, favours Riesling and is commercialized by CV Pfaf-fenheim.

Reifenberg, Cléebourg (Bas-Rhin): almost 7.5 hectares in size, this silty-clay vineyard has been cultivated with vines since the Middle Ages, but replanted with classic varieties just after the Second World War. It is situated at an altitude of between 200 and 235 metres, is south-south-east facing, and planted for the most part with Tokay-Pinot Gris, Gewurztraminer, Riesling and Auxerrois (Sylvaner, Pinot Noir and Muscat account for less than a fifth of a hectare and new plantations will be exclusively Tokay-Pinot Gris or Gewurztraminer). The wines have been commercialized under this name by CV Cléebourg only since as recently as the 1986 vintage.

Rimelsberg, Zellenberg (Haut-Rhin): this 6.4-hectare vineyard is south-east facing, with a very heavy, clayey soil that is rich and marly and planted with 70 per cent Gewurztraminer, 10 per cent Tokay-Pinot Gris and the balance a *mélange* of varieties. It is capable of producing exotic Gewurztraminer and smoky-rich Tokay-Pinot Gris, both of which are well suited to Vendanges Tardives. Just under 2.3 hectares are commercialized by Jean Becker.

Rittersberg, Scherwiller (Bas-Rhin): dominated by the still impressive ruins of Ortenbourg castle, this steep hillside vineyard is on a mineral-rich, granite and mica soil and enjoys a hot and dry climate. Paul Beck and J. Hauller each own about 1.5 hectares of Rittersberg (which means 'the lord's mountain') and commercialize wines under this *lieu-dit*.

Roemerberg, Bennwihr (Haut-Rhin): located to the east of Bennwihr, this *lieu-dit* covers an area of 21.7 hectares on the east- and south-east-facing, calcareous-clay slopes of a hill called Bodenacker and encompasses the parcels of Buehl, Entenlachbuehl and Higerst. It is commercialized by the CV Bennwihr for Gewurztraminer, which is supposed to be particularly spicy when grown here, with plenty of body and good potential longevity.

Rosenberg, Wettolsheim (Haut-Rhin): limestone vineyard commercialized by Domaine Aimé Stentz.

Rotenberg, Wintzenheim (Haut-Rhin): approximately 5 hectares in size, this *lieu-dit* is the western slope of the Hengst, although does not fall within the boundary of that *grand cru*. The soil is similar to that found on the Hengst, but richer in calcareous rocks and mineral elements, especially iron, which accounts for its red colour and explains the name Rotenberg, or 'red hill'. The organic paucity of this soil makes it possible to produce only small yields (20-25 hectolitres per hectare), thus the wines are naturally big, fat and powerful with emphatic aromatics. Rotenberg's climate is cooler than that of the Hengst, but particularly well suited to the development of noble rot in late-harvest wines, which make it Domaine Zind Humbrecht's favourite vineyard for Sélection de Grains Nobles in good vintages, hence the record-breaking (at the time) 1986

Tokay-Pinot Gris, which had the equivalent of 425g/l of sugar prior to fermentation and 230g/l after, which is enough to qualify easily for Sauternes on the residual sugar alone!

Rothmuerlé or *Rothmüerle*   *See* Rot-Murlé.

Rothstein, Wolxheim (Bas-Rhin): originally called Rothsteingrube, this south-and south-west-facing vineyard comprises approximately 12 hectares of light, sandy-rocky soil over a solid base of red sandstone (from where this *lieu-dit* gets its name). From this site rocks were quarried and transported by the old Bruche canal (now abandoned) to Strasbourg for the construction of that city's fortifications in the seventeenth century and the cliffs created by this quarrying provide a unique protection for the vineyards today. They are planted exclusively with Riesling and commercialized by Muhlberger. *See* also Clos Philippe Grass in 'The *Clos* of Alsace' above.

Rot-Murlé, Rouffach (Haut-Rhin): situated on the summit of a hill just south of Steinert, this 10-hectare vineyard (also spelt Rothmuerlé) derives its name from the red colour of its iron-rich stony soil and is bathed in sun from dawn to dusk, enabling the grapes grown there to ripen well in advance of those on the foothills below, although its exposure on all sides can be a risk. Some 1.5 hectares are cultivated with Pinot Noir, Tokay-Pinot Gris and Gewurztraminer by Pierre Frick. Domaine Rieflé also produces a Pinot Noir Rotmüerle (*sic*) de Rouffach.

Schenkenberg, Obernai (Bas-Rhin): the origin of this *lieu-dit*'s name dates from the Schenk d'Ehenheim (Ehenheim was one of the earliest forms of the town's name) family, who are mentioned in local documents from 1178 and who by the fifteenth century were in the service of the emperor. Records show they owned five arpents (approximately two hectares) of vines on a slope that by then had already acquired the name Schenkenberg. This *lieu-dit* today consists of 22 hectares, located 265 metres above sea-level, with a south and south-east exposure, its limestone soil planted with 60 per cent Gewurztraminer, 25 per cent Riesling, 5 per cent Muscat, 5 per cent Tokay-Pinot Gris and 5 per cent mixed (for 'Vin de Pistolet' – *see* the Edelzwicker entry in Chapter 6). Wines are commercialized under the Schenkenberg *lieu-dit* by Seilly.

Schlossreben, St-Hippolyte (Haut-Rhin): stony-sandy granite vineyard situated on the foothill slopes of Haut-Koenigsbourg, at an altitude of between 250 and 350 metres. Commercialized by Jacques Iltis, René Klein and Muller-Koeberle.

Schneckenberg, Pfaffenheim (Haut-Rhin): the name of this site is derived from the type of brown calcareous soil, which contains fossilized snail-shells (Schneckenberg means 'mountain of snails'). It is situated on the Coteau de Pfaffenheim immediately west of Pfaffenheim itself, west of and contiguous with the Grand Cru Steinert (which actually contains part of the original Schneckenberg) and, like that growth, also favours a Pinot grape, but Pinot Blanc, not Gris, which produces a rich, spicy wine with an almost musky character. These wines are commercialized mostly by CV Pfaffenheim.

Silberberg, Rorschwihr (Haut-Rhin): according to the map, this *lieu-dit* is located in Rodern, on the border with Rorschwihr, but definitely Rodern; according to Rolly Gassmann, who own less than half a hectare of its total of 20 hectares, it is definitely Rorschwihr. Perhaps just a bit of the *lieu-dit* overlaps, who knows, but certainly the 40 ares of Riesling that grow in the north-western corner of this village overlooking a tiny reservoir are responsible for the wine sold by Rolly Gassmann as Riesling Silberberg.

Steinweg, Ingersheim-Wintzenheim-Turckheim (Haut-Rhin): this *lieu-dit* means 'road of stones', a reference to its very stony soil, which warms up quickly, retains this heat throughout the night and is different from the limestone and marl soil of surrounding vineyards. Its road-like appearance is due to this gravelly material having been deposited by the river Fecht in the distant past. The Steinweg is significantly drier than the norm for Alsace, which is exceptionally dry anyway, and with its intrinsically warmer soil, this encourages the grapes to ripen earlier than those in neighbouring vineyards. The total area of Steinweg is 83 hectares, of which 70 are located in Ingersheim and the balance almost equally split between Wintzenheim and Turckheim. For the most part, this *lieu-dit* is planted with Gewurztraminer and Riesling, the latter being the more successful, producing a spicy, full-bodied wine. Fifty hectares of Steinweg are commercialized by CV Ingersheim.

Strangenberg, Westhalten (Haut-Rhin): the south-and south-east-facing limestone slopes of this *lieu-dit* have an exceptional climate that enables Mediterranean fauna and flora to flourish (and found elsewhere in Alsace only on the nearby Zinnkoepflé and on the sunny Florimont slopes of Ingersheim). Some 7 hectares of vineyards are planted with Pinot Blanc, Riesling and Tokay-Pinot Gris, and commercialized by CV Westhalten.

Trottacker, Ribeauvillé (Haut-Rhin): the presence of this *lieu-dit* has been recorded under various guises since 1319, assuming the name *im Trottehuse ze Hagenach* in the seventeenth century and appearing in local documentation as 'Trottacker' as from 1665. It is situated north-east of Grand Cru Osterberg, just along the slope from Clos du Zahnacker, on east-south-east-facing slopes at an altitude of between 250 and 350 metres. Its brown, very stony, clay, calcareous clay and marly soil is planted for the most part with Tokay-Pinot Gris, but also some Gewurztraminer and Riesling, and is commercialized by Jean Sipp.

Vallée Noble, Soultzmatt (Haut-Rhin): this valley is a sort of geographical basin at the foot of two peaks of the Vosges, the Petit Ballon (1,267m) and Grand Ballon (1,424m), which protect it from rain clouds blown from the west; consequently the vineyards here receive the same amount of sunshine as Bordeaux and rainfall equivalent to that of Perpignan. The soils are either clayey, limestone or sandy. Wines utilizing this denomination are commercialized by Léon Boesch.

Vogelgarten, Sigolsheim (Haut-Rhin): a lime-rich, calcareous-clay vineyard of 56 hectares, most of which are owned by members of the Sigolsheim cooperative, who have shown no interest in commercializing the *lieu-dit*, although a tiny amount of Pinot Noir grown by Claude Dietrich is sold under this name.

Weingarten, Domaine, Chatenois (Bas-Rhin): granitic gravel vineyard formerly belonging to the Archbishop of Strasbourg, now the monopoly of Bernhard-Reibel, who commercialize Riesling, Gewurztraminer and Tokay-Pinot Gris under this property name.

Westerberg, Rosenwiller (Bas-Rhin): limestone vineyard, half a hectare of which is commercialized by Einhart, who produces a well-flavoured Pinot and an exquisitely rich Tokay-Pinot Gris under this *lieu-dit*.

Westerweingarten, Balbronn (Bas-Rhin): calcareous-clay vineyard commercialized by Anstotz.

Zellberg, Nothalten (Bas-Rhin): this *lieu-dit* covers some 20 hectares, but it is the heart of Zellberg that is the most interesting, the 5 to 6 hectares of south-and south-east-facing mid-slope vineyards in the stony-colluvial foothills of the Vosges where the soil is brown calcareous sandy-clay. These wines are commercialized by Domaine Julien Meyer, who makes an exceptional Sylvaner.

7

The Styles of Wine

The essence of Alsace is the purity of its fruit, which should always be expressed, whatever the variety of grape or method of vinification. It is the clarity of style and vivid varietal definition of these wines that sets Alsace apart from other classic wine areas. Alsace is quintessentially an elegant, beautifully focused wine; it can also be complex, but it is not necessary for it to be so. It is equally well suited to food as it is to drinking on its own, a rare quality that applies to all varietal forms, which are so varied and appealing that there should be at least one style to please everybody. It is this panoply of styles that has made Alsace unique and so appealing.

More than three-quarters of the vineyards are now planted with just six classic vines: Riesling, Gewurztraminer, Tokay-Pinot Gris, Muscat, Pinot Noir and Pinot Blanc (which statistically includes Auxerrois). These varieties produce the region's best wines, yet such has been the radical change in Alsace that in 1918 they represented less than 10 per cent of the vines planted. Sylvaner is also widely planted, although very much on the decline, as is Chasselas. There is also a very small, but slowly increasing, amount of Chardonnay. This completes the list of varieties currently cultivated in the region. Alsace is often regarded as having an unusually extensive range of grape varieties, but nine (or ten, if Auxerrois is considered a separate variety) is not that many. Bordeaux has seventeen, after all. No, it is the fact that a different wine is produced from each one, whereas the wines are usually blended in those regions that actually have a greater number of varieties.

Alsace Wine at a Glance

Alsace wine represents a quarter of the region's agricultural output and 20 per cent of all French AOC white wines. For the historical development of the figures below, please refer to *Appendix III* at the end of the book.

AOC AREA UNDER VINE	13,487 hectares
AVERAGE PRODUCTION	1.1 million hectolitres
AVERAGE YIELD	86 hectolitres per hectare
WHITE WINE	95 per cent
RED OR ROSÉ	5 per cent
AOC ALSACE	86 per cent
AOC ALSACE GRAND CRU	4 per cent
AOC CRÉMANT D'ALSACE	10 per cent

Note:
Because of climatic differences experienced each year, it would be meaningless to provide average figures for the production of late-harvested wines, but as a good rule of thumb in prolific late-harvest vintages, it would be unrealistic to expect the production of these wines to exceed 2 to 2.5 per cent for Vendanges Tardives or 1 to 1.5 per cent for Sélection de Grains Nobles.

AOC ALSACE AND AOC VIN D'ALSACE

Prior to the acquisition of AOC status for Alsace, the very first commonly used, official designation was Vin d'Alsace, a regional *appellation* authorized by ministerial decree in 1945. When AOC regulations were established in 1962, the term Alsace plain and simple was also introduced, but this was merely synonymous with Vin d'Alsace.

AOC Alsace or Vin d'Alsace is still the region's basic *appellation* and, in fact, this was the only Alsace AOC until as recently as 1976, when Crémant d'Alsace was introduced. There are now three appellations: **AOC Alsace** or **AOC Vin d'Alsace**, which encompasses both varietal and blended wines; **AOC Alsace Grand Cru**, which is restricted to the varietal wines of four specific grapes grown in any one of 51 individual sites; and **AOC Crémant d'Alsace**, which is for the region's bottle-fermented sparkling wines.

The maximum yield allowed in the regulations for these wines is

100 hectolitres per hectare for AOC Alsace and Crémant d'Alsace, and 70 hectolitres per hectare for AOC Grand Cru. Since 1987, however, the Comité Régional d'Experts has implemented an annual self-regulatory control of 80 hectolitres per hectare for AOC Alsace and 65 hectolitres per hectare for AOC Grand Cru. Similarly, the maximum yield for AOC Crémant d'Alsace has been fixed annually at 80 hectolitres per hectare since 1990. These annual limits need to be much stricter and there is some indication that they will be, but they were probably obliged to make these restrictions when *départemental vins de pays* began to appear on the market with a maximum yield of 90 hectolitres per hectare. After an official rebuke by the EC for the high yield of 1982, Alsace could not allow itself to be ridiculed by the press, which could easily have asked what worth the AOC Alsace is when most of its wines would not pass the criteria for *vins de pays*.

THE VARIETAL CONCEPT

Contrary to the traditions of either France or Germany, Alsace has an authentic history of selling some of its most famous wines by their varietal names and this has now become the tradition. The earliest documented evidence of this practice dates back to 1477 (*see* 'The Earliest Varietal Wines' in Chapter 1), but its widespread commercial use did not really take off until the mid-1920s, when a collective decision was taken by a new and ambitious generation of winegrowers to rid themselves of hybrids, crosses and other grapes they considered undesirable.

Their aim was to replant the entire region with just a handful of lower-cropping, classic varieties, which was either a brave and noble cause or a foolish and suicidal venture because it required an enormous investment and the commitment of virtually every grower. And, even if this were to be achieved, their survival would thenceforth depend on receiving significantly higher prices for the new varietal wines they produced. Increased prices could be attained only if potential customers perceived the intrinsic superiority of these specific varieties, yet the average consumer in the 1920s was nowhere near as sophisticated as today's customers. They had little perception that grape varieties even existed, let alone the relative differences that might be discerned between them. It was very much like the current lack of consumer awareness of varieties of potato. Why bother enquiring about the variety when they are going to be mashed anyway? Consumers in the 1920s probably realized that wine was made from grapes, just as whisky was obviously made from grain, but the difference in the character and quality of individual wines would have been attributed not to anything as esoteric as grape variety but, quite plainly, to their geographical origin; thus Bordeaux was Bordeaux and Burgundy inevitably Burgundy.

This presented the growers of Alsace with a major problem: how to ask higher prices for wines made from superior grape varieties when to most people a grape was just a grape? The solution was brilliantly simple: to market the wines by their grape names and invent the not totally fictitious 'noble variety' concept, which would put these particular wines at the top of the varietal hierarchy. Thus, the world's first varietal wine region was born, not by the slow birth of accumulated custom and practice, but by a deliberate decision to solve an immediate communications problem. It was perhaps the first generic marketing initiative of any wine region, although New World producers have since proved themselves far more adept at using it as a marketing tool because, if anything, the varietal concept is commonly believed to be a Californian invention.

ONE *APPELLATION*, NINE VARIETALS

Under the *appellation* of Alsace or Vin d'Alsace, eight varietal denominations are allowed: Pinot (which may also be labelled Pinot Blanc, Clevner or Klevner), Tokay-Pinot Gris (which may also be labelled Pinot Gris), Pinot Noir, Riesling, Gewurztraminer, Muscat, Sylvaner and Chasselas (which may also be labelled Gutedel). Although not officially sanctioned by AOC laws, a ninth varietal category has emerged, for Auxerrois. This is one of the varieties permitted for the production of Pinot wine, but Auxerrois makes such a distinctly different wine that it has often been labelled separately, a practice that is currently waxing, rather than waning.

Varietal Wines at a Glance

Varietal wines represent 86 per cent of total Alsace production. For the historical development and a further breakdown of the figures below, refer to *Appendix III* at the end of the book.

PINOT (including AUXERROIS)	18 per cent	Fresh, deliciously fruity, barest hint of spice
TOKAY-PINOT GRIS	4 per cent	Rich, creamy, fine acidity, spicy-complexity
PINOT NOIR	6 per cent	Elegant, perfumed, pure and succulent
RIESLING	20 per cent	Crisp and racy, the best require ageing
GEWURZTRAMINER	14 per cent	Big, fat and spicy, touch of sweetness
MUSCAT	3 per cent	Dry, with a musky-flowery fragrance
SYLVANER	19 per cent	*Should be* dry and fresh with sappy fruit
CHASSELAS	2 per cent	*Can be* fresh and delicate, but most dull
BLENDS	4 per cent	Most neutral, but some are rich and complex
CRÉMANT D'ALSACE	10 per cent	Crisp, fresh, classic *méthode champenoise*

Notes:
The percentages above differ from those indicated for each varietal entry below because they refer to wines and are average figures for production, whereas the entries below relate to the actual area under vine and, of course, each variety has a different yield per hectare. Additionally, some of the production from certain varieties will be utilized for the production of blended wines and Crémant d'Alsace and these are accounted for separately above.

ALSACE VARIETALS

Every producer in Alsace, from the smallest grower to the largest *négociant* or cooperative, makes at least one range of varietal wines. This is generally referred to as the generic range. In addition to this, most producers market various higher quality varietals. These are often referred to as *réserve, réserve exceptionnelle, réserve personnelle*, etc. (there is no regulatory control over such terms, therefore they might mean everything or nothing) and, with the advent of *grands crus*, many producers have added another tier of varietal wines, albeit restricted to the four permitted varieties. Although such wines may be referred to in this chapter, they are dealt with separately and in more detail in Chapter 5. The *grand cru* phenomenon has created an interest in wines from specific locations, which has led to numerous village and single-site or *lieux-dits* wines coming on to the market, creating yet another tier. Again, some are mentioned below, but they are also covered more comprehensively in Chapter 5, as well as Chapter 4.

Explanatory notes

1. Synonymous commercial designations are indicated immediately after the principal varietal name.

2. *Common youthful descriptors* are the most frequently found aromas and flavours that are associated with youthful examples of the variety in question (obviously they are not always present and other less common aromas may dominate individual wines).

3. *Common bottle-aged descriptors* are the most frequently found aromas and flavours associated with bottle-aged examples of the variety in question (obviously they are not always present and other less common aromas may dominate individual wines).

4. If no specific *cuvée* is indicated for a wine described under 'In a totally different class' and 'Other Top Performers', it can be assumed that it is the basic generic of the producer in question. Please remember that these varietal wines do not include Vendanges Tardives or SGN, which cannot be compared with essentially dry styles of wine and are found under their respective entries within the 'Speciality Wines' section of this chapter.

5. As a rule, only wines – not vintages – are recommended because for me to say 'you can rely on such-and-such wine', its producer must have established a certain track record for it over several years. There is thus less need to be specific about a certain vintage, especially in a book intended to have several years' shelf life, and the vintage in question will inevitably become unavailable sooner or later. There are two disadvantages to my own rule, as far as I can see; the first is that the relative differences between different vintages of a specific *cuvée* cannot be discerned and the second is that exceptional wines of bargain quality from otherwise under-performing producers are not singled out. In part, the vintage assessments, producer profiles and the occasional deviation from my own guidelines will make up for this, but I accept that it will not totally satisfy these missing areas of recommendation. There are, however, two good reasons why this does not bother me. First, assessing specific vintages of individual *cuvées* and digging out the bargains and exceptions are the job of annual guides, monthly magazines and weekly wine columns. Second, Alsace is not Bordeaux; if I did cover every vintage of every *cuvée* for just one producer for, say, the last ten years, that would be at least 150 tasting notes on average, but up to 400 for many other firms, which produce as many as 40 different wines every year. There are more than 300 producer profiles in this book, which would mean a minimum of 45,000 tasting notes, requiring Faber to put wheels and a handle on the book just to push it around!

6. For further information about the *grands crus*, See 'The *grands crus*' in Chapter 5.

Pinot

Also sold as Pinot d'Alsace, Pinot Blanc, Pinot Blanc d'Alsace, Clevner, Clevner d'Alsace, Klevner and Klevner d'Alsace

Area under vine: 2,699 hectares or 20 per cent of AOC Alsace
Ten-year trend: Pinot vineyards have increased by 26 per cent compared to a general increase of 15 per cent for the whole AOC Alsace region
Average yield: 93 hectolitres per hectare
Grape varieties permitted: Pinot Blanc, Tokay-Pinot Gris, Pinot Noir and Auxerrois
Common youthful descriptors: apples, flowery, creamy
Common bottle-aged descriptors: buttery, honeyed

Background: *I used to think of this wine as a Pinot Blanc wine that could also be labelled Pinot, but it is really the other way round: a generic Pinot wine that may be labelled Pinot Blanc if the wine is 100 per cent of that variety. Historically, producers have used any variety belonging to the Pinot family for this wine and consequently the regulations clearly indicate this is merely a white wine made with any permitted Pinot grapes. Pinot Blanc is just one member of the large and varied Pinot clan, hence the numerous varieties that are allowed for the production of this wine.*

Most of these wines, whatever their designation, tend to be a mixture of Pinot Blanc and Auxerrois, with a distinct inclination for producers south of Colmar to use more Pinot Blanc in the blend, while those further north use more Auxerrois. Pinot Blanc is thought to produce the finer wine, while Auxerrois is fatter and spicier. Bergheim is Pinot Blanc's Watford Gap. North of this charming old village, this grape begins to lack depth, fruit and character, virtually compelling the addition of Auxerrois. Get up as far as Cléebourg and the Auxerrois in its pure form can display an astonishing amount of finesse for what is often thought of as a fat and blowzy variety.

In most classic Alsace villages, however, it is the skilful blending of these two grapes that produces the best results, typically capable of providing rich, but well balanced wines with more elegance, immediate appeal and interest than any pure example of either variety can achieve.

But what is the role of Tokay-Pinot Gris and Pinot Noir in the blending of a Pinot wine? Occasionally both these varieties have the equivalent enrichment function of the Auxerrois, but the frequency of their use is determined by other considerations. Ordinarily, Tokay-Pinot Gris is utilized only when the wine is not rich enough to produce a respectable quality of its own varietal style. Although such a wine might be somewhat disappointing for Tokay-Pinot Gris, it will add some fat, spice and a touch of class to a lightweight Pinot blend. Similarly, due to climatic conditions, the Pinot Noir in some locations can possess insufficient colour pigment in the skins to make a decent rosé, let alone a red wine, yet will add a delightfully perfumed, black Pinot aroma and a certain succulence of fruit, while at the same time giving a wishy-washy white Pinot blend an edge, some structure and body. In the case of both Tokay-Pinot Gris and Pinot Noir, the result depends, of course, on the composition of the grapes in question, as some can be so neutral that they would dilute the lightest Pinot Blanc.

As the trend for lighter and drier wine has developed, this fast-expanding varietal has begun to replace Gewurztraminer as the first wine that consumers new to Alsace are likely to taste. This is good news, not because Gewurztraminer is a bad wine, but because it is so distinctive that people either love it or hate it. If you have already discovered the vast range of wines available from Alsace, this is no problem, but for the uninitiated who dislike Gewurztraminer's spicy extravagance, such an experience can turn them off Alsace for life. Pinot's immediate appeal is thus the ideal introduction to the fascinating and ultimately rewarding myriad of Alsace wines.

Quality and character: Not very long ago, too many of these wines were so light and neutral that an honest Edelzwicker was preferable. Now they are probably the fastest-rising stars in Alsace, thanks to Chardonnay. Why thanks to Chardonnay? Well, when nearly every wine region in the world was busily planting and marketing Chardonnay, producers in Alsace saw the opportunity to improve the quality of Pinot and present it to potential new customers as a real, affordable alternative to the more classic, yet decidedly ubiquitous Chardonnay. Through reduced yields, stricter selection of *cuvées* and improved vinification techniques, the quality of Alsace Pinot has dramatically increased and Alsace now has an authentic Chardonnay alternative with its own, refreshingly different character.

As a result, Pinot has enjoyed a huge boom in sales since the late 1980s and those who were making boring examples of this variety have had radically and rapidly to improve their product, if they wanted to share in its success. Some disappointing wines do exist, of course, but the chances of encountering them are rapidly receding. Achieving the right degree of richness and balancing it with just enough ripe acidity has totally transformed a wine that was once renowned for its boring character and thankfully short finish, into one of immediate charm. The most successful Pinots have a delightful plumpness, rich, ripe, juicy fruit with apple or floral overtones and a lovely long, rich and creamy finish.

At the top end of the quality scale, the best Pinots approach Tokay-Pinot Gris for richness and depth, although few can aspire to any great height in the classic wine stratosphere. Alternatively, even the most modest Pinots are good gulping wines. They are for the hedonist, an absolute joy on their own, yet astonishingly flexible with food. Many times I have drifted from drinking mode to the table with a glass of Pinot in my hand, not thinking about what might best accompany the food, only to be entranced by the combination to hand. Pinot ranks as the best value and most improved varietal wine in Alsace.

Comment on new oak for fermentation and/or ageing: Although I prefer my Pinots straight, I have to refute the view of some producers that this grape does not have the body to stand up to new oak. This is unquestionably not true. It merely depends on selecting a wine of sufficient size and acidity to withstand the intended duration in cask and then it will not be overwhelmed. The simple fact is that of all the region's varietals, Pinot has proved to be the most successful for oak. For the sake of balanced argument, I must also add that part of this success could be due to the fact that Pinot is the most pervasive of oak-aged varieties, but even this begs the question why so many producers considered this grape such a likely candidate. Domaine Ostertag has produced excellent Pinot Blanc Barriques, but has not been consistent and there has been a tendency to over-oak. The best wine I have tasted so far has been from Paul Blanck. This was a 1988 Klevner that had been aged for six months in two-thirds new oak.

Prime drinking: Within two to four years (exceptional wines and the best oak-aged examples may improve for up to six years).

IN A TOTALLY DIFFERENT CLASS

None

OTHER TOP PERFORMERS

J.B. Adam: rich with superb acidity. **Léon Beyer:** absolutely dry and correct, capable of ageing and makes an ideal food wine. **Paul Blanck:** exotic oaky *Klevner Réserve* with tropical fruits and a real creamy finesse. **Camille Braun:** the rich *Klevner*

Vieilles Vignes Cuvée Marguerite-Anne is so succulent that it is almost sweet, but is usually beautifully balanced by excellent acidity. **Paul Buecher:** an interesting rather than exciting *Robinson*, which is oak-aged with half the casks new. **Théo Cattin:** rich and ripe, often with a touch of sweetness, but usually well balanced. **CV Cléebourg:** the *Kiemberg Pinot Blanc Auxerrois* is another with lovely acidity. **Marcel Deiss:** a fresh, light flowery *Bennwihr* and a classic, much creamier *Bergheim.* **JosMeyer:** the elegant *Pinot Les Luttins* has lots of creamy finesse. **Roger Jung:** *Les Préludes* is a fresh and zesty wine that has attractive crunchy fruit and may sometimes be lifted by a slight spritz. **Hugel & Fils:** the basic *Blanc de Blancs* (labelled *Les Amours* or *Les Vignards* on some markets) was not very special until the splendid 1987 vintage, since when it has been consistently one of the region's most classic examples of this grape. **Koeberlé-Kreyer:** very rich and succulent, best for early drinking. **Charles Koehly:** has almost startling acidity in some years, but this makes the wine potentially long-lived and provides a welcome finesse in riper vintages. **Gustave Lorentz:** soft and tasty generic. **Albert Mann:** intense *Pinot Blanc Auxerrois* with honeyed fruit and smoky complexity. **CV Pfaffenheim:** the *Schneckenberg* is an excellent wine with lots of crisp fruit and refreshing acidity. **Rolly Gassmann:** typically fat and rich with sweet fruit finish. **Jean Sipp:** capable of a good generic, particularly when the wine has a little noble rot and is quite exotic with peach and pineapple fruit flavours. **Martin Spielmann:** a rich, fine and aromatic wine that sometimes exhibits youthful honey, but always remains fresh. **CV Traenheim:** soft and creamy *Klevner*, hinting of Auxerrois, but with finer acidity. **CV Turckheim:** easy to drink generic, richer, well-balanced *Val St-Grégoire*, lovely ripe-mellow *Klevner*, particularly in good but not great years. **Domaine Zind Humbrecht:** an exotically perfumed wine with a great intensity of flamboyant fruit that seems to be packed with youthful complexity as soon as it is bottled.

Note: Unless otherwise stated, all the wines referred to above are labelled simply Pinot or Pinot Blanc.

Auxerrois

Also sold as *Auxerrois d'Alsace, Pinot Auxerrois* and *Pinot Auxerrois d'Alsace*

Area under vine: included in Pinot above
Ten-year trend: included in Pinot above
Average yield: included in Pinot above
Grape varieties permitted: Auxerrois (although any wine labelled Pinot Auxerrois could be a blend of any of the varieties permitted for Pinot, above, they are usually dominated by Auxerrois and many are 100 per cent pure)
Common youthful descriptors: musky, buttery, spicy, honeyed, apricot, orange blossom, tangerine peel
Common bottle-aged descriptors: fatter, exaggerated youthful characteristics

Background: *In theory, Auxerrois is not a permitted designation, but the inclusion of this grape in the production of the Pinot designation is allowed, thus its own denomination is 'officially tolerated' according to CIVA. Alsace growers have traditionally embraced Auxerrois in Pinot blends, <u>believing it to be a member of the Pinot family</u>. Whether it is nobody knows. Ampelography – or the study of the vine – is a precise science, but the subject is so vast that great gulfs of ignorance exist. If there is no financial justification for certain time-consuming areas of research, they will be the last to be tackled, and whereas Auxerrois is important to Alsace, its cultivation on a worldwide basis is minuscule, thus providing little incentive to solve its deeper mysteries. The pity is that no one in Alsace itself has bothered to put Auxerrois under the microscope. They do not even know how much is growing in the region, let alone its ampelographic origins and without solid research, the experts are naturally divided on the issue.*

In the misty grey area of opinion, ampelographers assume the role of theatre critics or, dare I say, wine writers. Their opinion becomes a matter of trust. Pierre Galet is the ampelographer I trust most and he believes the Auxerrois to be an entirely separate variety, therefore I shall categorize it as such until, and if, future research yields evidence to the contrary.

As to the most important characteristic of Auxerrois, the style of wine it produces, in Alsace it most definitely falls between that of Pinot Blanc and Tokay-Pinot Gris. This is surely a good enough reason why the generations of growers who have cultivated the vine and fermented its juice believed it to be a member of the Pinot family. The raison d'être *of the AOC system was to codify traditional practices within a legal framework that would serve to protect the reputation of the various wine styles that have evolved. Whether this is more for the benefit of the producer than of the consumer is a different question, but it provides ample justification for including Auxerrois in the AOC regulations for wines with the Pinot designation. Where they did go a little too far, however, was to refer to the Pinot Blanc as the 'true Auxerrois', which is patently not true and merely confuses the whole issue of the latter grape's true identity.*

Quality and character: Auxerrois is fatter than Pinot Blanc, with more buttery, honeyed and spicy character to the fruit. Its greatest asset is its natural richness and immediate appeal, but it is inclined to low acidity and can become too fat and blowzy, unless grown in a perfect situation. When too ripe, Auxerrois can be positively flabby and prone to an overkill of muskiness. The worst examples are so musky they are almost foxy.

Comment on new oak for fermentation and/or ageing: I also prefer my Auxerrois unoaked, but it is, with Pinot Blanc, the most suitable variety for oak-ageing, although its use with oak has been less prolific. André Kientzler has developed the finest example so far.

Prime drinking: Within three to five years (exceptional wines up to ten years).

IN A TOTALLY DIFFERENT CLASS

André Kientzl
Pure Auxerrois of this degree of finesse is very rare indeed.

Mark Kreydenweiss
The rich, stylish *Kritt Klevner* is pure Auxerrois, full of lush, honeyed, spicy-apricot fruit with floral hints and a touch of tangerine-peel on the finish.

JosMeyer
The 'H' in JosMeyer's *Pinot Auxerrois 'H' Vieilles Vignes* reveals the Hengst origin of this classic, complex and well-structured wine.

OTHER TOP PERFORMERS

Pierre Frick: it is merely a matter of coincidence and positioning that we are only on the second varietal entry in this chapter and I am already bucking my own rule of avoiding vintages of specific wines (*see* explanatory note 5 above), but the extraordinary quality and circumstances of Frick's *Pinot Blanc 1988 N.C. Eudémis* require it. This intensely rich wine is the product of an attack by the Eudémis moth, which almost halved the vine's potential yield, concentrating the grapes and donating to the wine its Vendange Tardive character. **Note** – this wine is 100 per cent Auxerrois despite its name. (N.C. indicates no chaptalization.) **Landmann-Ostholt:** more class and less fat than most Auxerrois. **André Kientzler:** the well-structured *Auxerrois Vin Élevé en Futs de Chêne* was one of the first of oak-aged

Alsace wines not to be over-oaked. **Julien Rieffel**: another pure Auxerrois despite the Pinot Blanc synonym on the label, the *Klevner Vieilles Vignes* is packed with the tangy smack of ripe fruit that is immediate in appeal, yet manages to remain fresh and youthful for many years in bottle. **Rolly Gassmann**: a big, fat, spicy *Auxerrois Moenchreben* that becomes very honeyed shortly after bottling. **Bruno Sorg**: superbly rich and well balanced

Tokay-Pinot Gris

Also sold as *Tokay-Pinot Gris d'Alsace, Pinot Gris* and *Pinot Gris d'Alsace*

Area under vine: 884 hectares or 6.6 per cent of AOC Alsace
Ten year trend: vineyards have increased by 58 per cent compared to a general increase of 15 per cent for the whole AOC Alsace region
Average yield: 75 hectolitres per hectare
Grape varieties permitted: Tokay-Pinot Gris
Common youthful descriptors: banana, sometimes smoky, little or no spice, pineapple in precocious wines
Common bottle-aged descriptors: increasingly spice, honeyed, smoky, toasty, creamy, nutty (walnuts, brazils)
Additional blind tasting note The spiciness of some examples can be confused with Gewurztraminer or Auxerrois on the nose, but the amount of acidity on the palate is the key. Tokay-Pinot Gris has relatively high acidity, while Auxerrois is lowish and Gewurztraminer very low indeed. If you have an Auxerrois and a Tokay-Pinot Gris of similar acid levels, the Auxerrois will probably be fatter with a hint of musk, while the Tokay-Pinot Gris should have an extra notch of class.

Background: *Whereas a great Riesling is often considered superior to a great wine from this grape, it is the Tokay-Pinot Gris that many of the younger generation of winemakers consider to be the* classic Alsace variety. *Certainly superlative examples of Tokay-Pinot Gris are far more prolific than those of Riesling. It is so well suited to Alsace that in years like 1989 virtually all the generic wines reached Vendange Tardive levels. The same could be said for Gewurztraminer, of course, but the best Tokay-Pinot Gris have excellent acidity, which prevents them from becoming as fat and blowzy as the average Gewurztraminer, let alone a super-rich example from a really big year. For the opposite of reasons, the Gewurztraminer is almost as picky as Riesling when it comes to classic examples, whereas the Tokay-Pinot Gris has so much* *natural class, it is often difficult not to produce a great wine.*

Originally called the Grauklevner, this grape has been known as Tokay d'Alsace (see mention of Baron Schwendi under 'The Earliest Varietal Wines' in Chapter 1) for more than 250 years, but EC legislation in 1980 prohibited the term, forcing producers to utilize the correct ampelographic name of Pinot Gris. Some growers complained that they would lose business because their regular customers had no idea what a Pinot Gris is, while others simply ignored the new law and continued their traditional practice of labelling these wines Tokay d'Alsace. If the Euro-bureaucrats had been resident in Strasbourg rather than Brussels, more than a few Alsace growers would have demonstrated their French inclination by dumping manure on the Commission's doorsteps. It did not get that far, however, as the EC relented a little, allowing the old Tokay designation to be tagged on to the new (or true, one should say) name, thus creating the Tokay-Pinot Gris. A good 90 per cent of these wines are so named, but now that the fuss has died down, there is an increasing tendency to use the authentic Pinot Gris name, plain and simple, without any mention of Tokay, which is proof positive of just how Gallic Alsace is becoming. A very few growers of indubitably French lineage still stubbornly refuse to call their wine anything except Tokay d'Alsace and illegal examples of this can be found. They seldom find their way out of the region itself, so nobody makes a fuss, not even the EC, which is probably one of its more sensible policies, unless it wants a doorstep full of dung.

Quality and character: Like all Alsace wines, Tokay-Pinot Gris is produced in a dry style, but some styles are drier than others. This varietal traditionally has more residual sugar than all other designations with the exception of Gewurztraminer. When such wines, whether Tokay-Pinot Gris or Gewurztraminer, are well balanced, they can be utterly delicious and there is no earthly reason why we should not admit this, although the wine snob inevitably attaches a certain stigma to wines that possess a little residual sugar. I find bone-dry examples of Tokay-Pinot Gris more useful with food, but I cannot deny my appreciation of some sweeter renditions. My only criticism is that any wine that is noticeably sweet to one degree or another (as opposed to those that possess so much acidity that most people perceive them as dry) should say so on the label. Apart from that, I think we should let the wines do the speaking.

Most Tokay-Pinot Gris have excellent acidity, thus many wines are capable of retaining fairly high levels of natural sweetness yet remain relatively dry to taste. Being the most luscious of Alsace grapes, even generics can come across as decadently rich, but with the correct balance of acidity they rarely tire on the palate. Some Tokay-Pinot Gris can be quite big and fat, but good quality examples are never blowzy and, with a little bottle-age, develop great complexity. The distinguishing characteristic of a truly great Tokay-Pinot Gris is that no matter the size and intensity of the wine, it will have tremendous finesse.

Comment on new oak for fermentation and/or ageing: There is no doubt that Tokay-Pinot Gris has the body to take wood and its excellent acidity prevents it from turning flabby after a year or two in bottle, but this grape provides such a complete and satisfying wine on its own, what could it possibly gain from a marriage with oak? Nothing, in my experience. Most oak-aged Tokay-Pinot Gris merely swap their smoky-spicy finesse for more obvious oaky overtones. The only exception is oak-aged SGN (*see* the Sélection de Grains Nobles entry under 'Speciality Wines' later in this chapter).

Prime drinking: Within five to ten years (I prefer most Tokay-Pinot Gris nearer five than ten years, although great examples can last several decades).

IN A TOTALLY DIFFERENT CLASS

Maison Ernest Burn
Simply stunning combination of exotic fruit, tremendous creamy-richness, yet great finesse: *Clos St-Imer Grand Cru Goldert* and *Clos St-Imer Grand Cru Goldert La Chapelle*

Domaine Zind Humbrecht
Great classic wines at generic level, with the following *cuvées* of even more superior quality completing the role of honour: *Vieilles Vignes Grand Cru Rangen*, *Clos St-Urbain Grand Cru Rangen* and *Clos Jebsal*

OTHER TOP PERFORMERS

Lucien Albrecht: lush, creamy *Réserve du Domaine* and a fabulously rich, absolutely classic *Grand Cru Pfingstberg*. **Léon Beyer:** the beautifully structured *Cuvée Particulière* is proof that a Tokay-Pinot Gris can be exquisitely rich without any residual sugar. **Barmès-Buecher:** fresh, succulent and underrated. **Bott-Geyl:** ripe and zesty *Grand Cru Sonnenglanz*. **Théo Cattin:** classic *Grand Cru Hatschbourg*. **Marcel Deiss:** the smoky-spicy *Bergheim* has great elegance, even in poor years. **Claude Dietrich:** full of youthful vigour and finesse. **Robert Dietrich:** exquisitely rich *Grand Cru Steingrubler*. **Dopff & Irion:** a *Grand Cru Sporen* of great elegance and breeding. **Raymond Engel:** his *Domaine des Prélats Grand Cru Praelatenberg* is the best wine of any variety from this *cru*. **Pierre Frick:** the rich, complete and satisfying *Rot-Murlé* can have a distinctive smoky-marmalade complexity some years. **Einhart:** rich and stylish *Westerberg*. **Ehrhart:** one of the finest *Grand Cru Hengst*. **Domaine André & Rémy Gresser:** *Andlau Brandhof* is very restrained, remaining young and relatively closed for many years before blossoming into a classic Tokay-Pinot Gris. **Haegelin:** rich, spicy and beautifully structured *Cuvée Elise*. **Hugel & Fils:** *Cuvée Tradition* always good, but *Jubilée* has the edge, with its delicate richness and undeniable finesse – a wine that ages gracefully and is well worth the extra. **CV Hunawihr:** capable of producing a stunning *Réserve* quality. **André Kientzler:** basic generic is often better than the *Réserve Particulière*, but the *Vendange Tardive* always shows great banana finesse and potential. **Koeberlé-Kreyer:** deeply flavoured, intensely expressive *Grand Cru Gloeckelberg*. **Charles Koehly:** a *Grand Cru Gloeckelberg* with a tremendous capacity for acidity. **Marc Kreydenweiss:** the finest *Grand Cru Moenchberg*. **Kuentz-Bas:** the *Cuvée Tradition* has luxuriant, creamy fruit, while the *Réserve Personnelle* is even richer, with a fine smoky, buttery-nutty intensity. **Landmann-Ostholt:** delightfully pure. **Landmann Seppi:** brimming with delicious, refreshing fruit. **Gustave Lorentz:** rich *Réserve* and a *Cuvée Particulière* has noticeable finesse, but the *Grand Cru Altenberg de Bergheim* is weightier and has more finesse than either. **Frédéric Mallo:** fat, sweet and spicy medal-winner. **Mittnacht Frères:** the *Cuvée Ste-Cathérine* is packed with exotic fruit and rich apricot-spice even in poor years. **Muller-Koeberle:** an intense *Vieilles Vignes* that has perfect balance and great potential longevity. **Domaine Ostertag:** a stunning *Grand Cru Muenchberg* that shows a multiplicity of blazing fruit flavours. **CV Pfaffenheim:** the *Cuvée Rabelais* has great finesse, a very long and rich flavour and is almost Vendange Tardive in style, but it is CV Pfaffenheim's *Grand Cru Goldert* and *Grand Cru Steinert* that truly excel. **Rieflé:** elegant *Côtes de Rouffach*. **Ringenbach-Moser:** fine, well-balanced *Grand Cru Mambourg*. **Domaine Martin Schaetzel:** a fresh and lively *Cuvée Réserve*. **Edgard Schaller:** elegantly rich generic. **Charles Schleret:** capable of amazing richness. **Domaine Schlumberger:** recent vintages of the generic have shown the creamy richness of a much higher quality than has been the norm in the past and the *Cuvée Clarisse Schlumberger* is an extraordinary medium-sweet botrytis wine that is produced once every 25 years or so (1989 is the current vintage,

1964 the previous one). **Domaine Schoffit:** great *Grand Cru Rangen* that suffers only in comparison with the stratospheric offerings of Domaine Zind Humbrecht. **Jean Sipp:** rich but firm *Trottacker* of great potential longevity. **Bruno Sorg:** classy and well-constructed. **Pierre Sparr** massively rich *Tête de Cuvée*. **CV Turckheim:** excellent generic, other top *cuvées* even better and just beginning to fashion a luscious *Grand Cru Hengst*. **Bernard Webber:** concentrated wine of some finesse. **Domaine Weinbach:** exquisite at all levels. **Wolfberger:** most vintages of the generic are very good, but some, like the 1989, are sublime. The *Vins Armoriés* are rich and classy and this cooperative is also one of the most underrated producers of *grand cru* wines, the availability of which varies from year to year, but I have tasted excellent Gewurztraminer Hengst and Steingrubler. **Bernard Wurtz:** excellent, traditionally vinified, generic with well-focused fruit. **W. Wurtz:** concentrated generic Tokay-Pinot Gris that shows exceptional finesse. **Zimmermann:** luxuriantly rich *Réserve Exceptionnelle* which can have a seductive touch of sweetness.

Pinot Noir

Also sold as *Pinot Noir d'Alsace, Rouge d'Alsace* and *Rosé d'Alsace*

Area under vine: 1,016 hectares or 7.5 per cent of AOC Alsace
Ten-year trend: vineyards have increased by 43 per cent compared to a general increase of 15 per cent for the whole AOC Alsace region
Average yield: 83 hectolitres per hectare
Grape varieties permitted: Pinot Noir
Common youthful descriptors: strawberry, raspberry, redcurrant, cherry, black cherry
Common bottle-aged descriptors: mellowed youthful characteristics

Background: *Ten years ago most of these wines were made in a rosé style and few Alsace aficionados could see any real potential for the wine, but Burgundy began pricing itself out of the inexpensive end of the market at the very time that local restaurants started demanding true red Alsace wines to satisfy their tourist trade.*

From an unimportant varietal with a dwindling following, Pinot Noir soon begun to acquire a fashionable reputation and new plantations of the vine were cropping up everywhere. It took some time, however, before a significant number of producers were regularly able to produce the sort of red wine the restaurateurs were calling for. Although wines such as Rouge d'Ottrott and Rouge de Rodern had been famous for centuries, a great gulf existed between rouge *the name and red the colour. The Pinot Noir in Alsace does not possess a very thick skin, consequently a relatively small amount of pigment is available to colour the wine; hence one person's Rouge d'Alsace was often lighter in style than someone else's Rosé d'Alsace, absurd though it may sound.*

Well-coloured Rouge d'Alsace is a recent phenomenon, its consistent production due entirely to the introduction of the Vinimatic, a rotating fermentation tank that works on the cement-mixer principle. This enabled producers to extract the maximum amount of pigment under totally anaerobic conditions. Other methods, including heating the must during a pre-fermentation maceration period and hotter temperatures during the fermentation itself, have enabled others to achieve a similar density without going to the expense of purchasing a Vinimatic. Suffice to say, however, that the Vinimatic solved the problem for the larger producers and thus proved to be the catalyst for all the others. The only way to improve on current colour levels is by planting Pinot Noir in only the hottest of favourable sites, pruning to cut yields, and separating the free-run juice to produce a rosé wine, which then provides a greater proportion of skins to juice for the coloration of the red. Various growers are already employing some or all of these techniques. Maturing in small casks with 25–50 per cent new oak is now commonly practised.

Alsace Pinot Noir will always be at its most popular in the region itself, particularly amongst tourists in the local restaurants and winstubs. However, it is doubtful if it will ever be a commercial success in any major export country, as the Germanic flûte d'Alsace is simply not perceived as a red wine bottle. This is an aesthetic matter. It just seems odd seeing red wine being poured out of something so tall and slender. We are just not conditioned to expect it. Unless, therefore, Alsace switches to, say, a Burgundy-shaped bottle, Pinot Noir will always face sales resistance on international markets. The problem is that the use of the flûte d'Alsace is protected by law, a law that many who try to sell Alsace wines abroad would like to see rescinded for all the region's wines. Certainly it should be for Pinot Noir.

Red wine quality and character: Some producers make a deep-coloured red wine, but refuse to mature the wine in new oak. They point out that the essence of Alsace is the purity of its varietal character, not new oak. They are right, of course. Many of the most expressive winemakers have failed to produce an interesting red, let alone an exciting one. They will one day, no doubt, but until they do I prefer to make my choice between the simple delight of a delicate rosé and the fine complexity of an oak-aged red, although too many of producers of the latter style tend to over-oak their wines.

Comment on new oak for fermentation and/or ageing red wine: Oak often transforms the fruity characteristic of Pinot Noir to a black cherry flavour, even when the pre-oaked fruit hints more of strawberry or redcurrant. It is all too easy to put too much oak on any Pinot Noir and Alsace Pinot Noir is more susceptible to this than most. Over-oaked wines may taste bitter and often appear dried out because it takes little effort for the astringency of just a little oak tannin to overwhelm such delicate fruit. More often than not, over-oaked examples are also tough, over-extracted and atypically dark in colour because the grower has pushed the colour extraction beyond sensible limits. Such wines will never soften. On the other hand, the judicious use of a little press wine to correct the structure and balance of a wine is not widely appreciated. Too many oaked Pinot Noirs have caramelized aromas, lack elegance and tend to oxidize rather rapidly.

The ageing period of the most consistent Alsace Pinot Noir I have come across is a bare six months and the amount of new oak applied to the wine is restricted to 60 per cent. The wine in question is no great Burgundy, but it is definitely red, delightfully soft and fruity, dominated by varietal character, rather than wood, and is caressed on the finish with the gentlest hint of creamy oak. Which small grower is producing this attractive wine do I hear you ask? None. It is not a grower at all, but rather a cooperative and a big one at that. It is Eguisheim, the biggest cooperative in Alsace, and the wine I am referring to is its Wolfberger Rouge d'Alsace. Not one of its supposedly superior *cuvées*, merely a generic Pinot Noir (the one bearing the traditional Noak cartoon label that is sold in supermarkets).

Red wine: prime drinking: Within two to six years (perhaps as much as 12 years for really exceptional *cuvées*).

Rosé quality and character: At its best, this wine has a deliciously fragrant aroma with oodles of soft, strawberry fruit (less often the raspberry, redcurrant or cherry found in red wine styles of Alsace) on the palate. It is the lightness of body found in such wines that belies the richness of flavour and although made in a true dry style, the very succulence of the fruit can seem off-dry or almost sweet.

The village of Marlenheim is particularly noted for this style of wine, which traditionally used to be sold as *Vorlauf*, an Alsace term indicating a wine produced from the first and thus best pressing. This wine was nearer to a *vin gris* than a full rosé and like many Alsace Pinot Noir wines today tasted of cherries, according to nineteenth-century descriptions.

Comment on new oak for fermentation and/or ageing rosé wines: No rosés as such have been matured in new oak, although many delicately coloured reds have.

Rosé wine: prime drinking: Best within one to two years, but a few exceptional examples may last five years or more.

ALMOST IN A TOTALLY DIFFERENT CLASS

There are indeed Pinot Noir wines that are head and shoulders above the rest, but they have not been established long enough at a sufficiently high international standard to warrant true classic wine status, thus the somewhat amended heading to this section.

Marcel Deiss
Only since 1989 and only with one wine, the *Bergheim Burlenberg Vieilles Vignes*, has the frenetic, expressive Jean-Michel Deiss managed to bring Pinot Noir up to the level of his other stunning varietals. This is a very rich, well structured wine with powerful Pinot character and a high toast, smoky complexity.

Albert Hertz
At a blind tasting of more than 70 Alsace Pinot Noir from three vintages, this producer's nicely coloured, beautifully balanced and

elegantly fruity wine was easily the best red wine the region produced in both 1988 and 1989.

CV Pfaffenheim

The *Cuvée des Dominicains* is a superb selection from old vines that is so full of fruit, it hardly ages and merely mellows.

CV Turckheim

This cooperative's *Rosé de Turckheim* is as voluptuous as Alsace Pinot Noir comes, with more class and finesse than one should expect in such an unpretentious style.

Wolfberger

The Noak *cuvée* is singled out as the most consistent and best value Pinot Noir in Alsace.

OTHER TOP PERFORMERS

J.B. Adam: the *Cuvée Jean-Baptiste* is a well-coloured wine with a deep aroma of cherries and strawberries. **Allimant-Laugner**: only tasted once, but the 1989 was so deliciously rich and seductive, it must merit inclusion. **Léon Baur**: a fruity rather than oaky *Vielli en Fûts de Chêne* with a distinctly perfumed bouquet. **René Beck**: a *Domaine du Remparts Clos du Sonnenbach* that is full of youthful fruit and promise. **Jean Becker**: a *Rouge d'Alsace* to watch since the 1988 vintage, when Philippe Becker achieved his most successfully balanced Pinot Noir with the inclusion of just 15 per cent new wood to give beautiful precision to this fruit-driven red, underpinning with hardly noticeable oak. **Paul Buecher**: very youthful with good redcurrant-pastille varietal aroma. **Joseph Cattin**: rich, soft and well-perfumed Pinot Noir. **CV Cléebourg**: the *Huettgasse Steinseltz* is surprisingly fruity with exceptional varietal character for the most northerly Pinot Noir in France. **Robert Faller**: rich and fruity with some elegance. **René Fleith**: soft and fruity, with plummy-raspberry-blackberry aromas and above average tannin content. **Hugel & Fils**: the *Jubilée Réserve Personnelle* is a wine that builds in the glass and has a varietal intensity that deepens with each vintage. **CV Hunawihr**: a Pinot Noir *vinifié en fûts de chêne* that is light in colour, but teems with exuberant oak-kissed fruit. **Jacques Iltis**: very fruity, easily accessible *Rouge de St-Hippolyte*. **Roger Jung**: usually nicely perfumed Pinot aromas with almost sweet, redcurrant-pastille fruit and enough tannin to require a couple of years to develop. **Georges Klein**: tasted only once, but this producer's 1989 *Rouge de St-Hippolyte* was as rich and classy as you could expect from Alsace. **Kuentz-Bas**: has been gradually crafting a very smooth and elegant style of Pinot Noir under its *Réserve Personnelle* label. **Landmann-Ostholt**: a *Vallée Noble cuvée* that may not be very deep in colour, but has a lovely Pinot nose and lots of ripe fruit, with a fine varietal aftertaste. **Albert Mann**: deep coloured, serious wine with a touch of oak. **Hubert Metz**: the *Vieilles Vignes* is always young, fresh and makes good food wine due to its nice edge of supple tannin. **Muller-Koeberle**: a fine, spicy-cherry *Rouge de St-Hippolyte Geissberg* with a touch of tannin and a *Rouge de St-Hippolyte Burgreben, Coteaux du Haut-Koenigsbourg*, which tries to be more serious, but does not always succeed. **Muré**: when it works, the *Clos St-Landelin 'Vielli en Pièce de Chêne'* is a firmly structured wine with plenty of fruit and ripe acidity to absorb the significant influence of oak vanillin, but some vintages are more successful than others. **Siffert**: very fruity *Coteaux du Haut-Koenigsbourg* with good, raspberry-pastille varietal aromas. **Domaine Aimé Stentz**: usually provides a good mouthful of flavour. **Turckheim**: the *Cuvée à l'Ancienne* is consistently fine in a delicately fruity style that will with time in bottle show a little caramel and coffee on the aftertaste. **Ch. Wantz**: fruity *Rouge d'Ottrott*.

Riesling

Also sold as *Riesling d'Alsace*

Area under vine: 3,015 hectares or 22.3 per cent of AOC Alsace
Ten-year trend: vineyards have increased by 28 per cent compared to a general increase of 15 per cent for the whole AOC Alsace region
Average yield: 89 hectolitres per hectare
Grape varieties permitted: Riesling
Common youthful descriptors: apple, fennel, soapy, grassy, steely, flinty, floral, hints of citrus and peach
Common bottle-aged descriptors: so-called petrolly or kerosene, honey, more intense forms of citrus and peach

Background: *This grape originated in Germany and was first recorded as the* Rissling *in Alsace in 1477, when the land was part of Germany not France. As such, the Riesling was the first Alsace vine to develop its own identity and is considered by most today as the region's most classic variety.*

To produce a great Riesling necessitates harvesting fully ripe fruit. Early-drinking wine of a modestly pleasant character can be made from relatively unripe grapes and good to (sometimes) even excellent quality can originate from grapes that are almost ripe, but truly great Riesling requires the very ripest of grapes. The sugar level and acidity balance of such grapes will vary according to the vintage, but only fully ripe fruit has the potential to make wines of

*the intensity of aroma, penetrating flavour and great longevity
that has made classic Riesling so legendary.*

*Riesling is more susceptible to different soils than any other
Alsace variety. Other vines are affected by a change of soil type, of
course, but it is the extreme sensitivity of the Riesling plant itself
combined with the delicate varietal characteristics of the wine it
produces that results in such clearly defined divergences of style
when cultivated on different soils. Clayey soils produce fat wines
of marked richness; granite makes for a firmer structure and great
intensity, though this can be so restrained that the wine may seem
quite austere when young and will always be slower than clay
wines to evolve and ultimately capable of more petrolly finesse;
limestone has obvious finesse from the outset, though less
richness; sandy soils produce the lightest wines, but can have a
minerally elegance; gravel wines have much more body than sandy
soils produce, but less acidity and are more inclined to develop
petrolly finesse.*

*A late-ripening variety, Riesling naturally benefits from being
planted in a soil that remains warm right through the* véraison
*period until late autumn. This is why the greatest Alsace Rieslings
invariably grow on hard rock soils, such as granite or schist,
which quickly warm up in the sun and yet retain their heat well
into the cool of night. A similar level of quality (albeit totally
different in style) can be achieved in cooler soils, although there
has to be a sufficiently warm microclimate to redress the balance
of temperature. No better example of such a situation exists than
Trimbach's Clos Ste-Hune, a site that consists of cool calcareous-
clay, yet it, not granite, regularly produces the greatest Riesling in
Alsace. It is the exception that proves the rule and this is borne
out by the vineyard's predilection for the hottest years, when it
manages to produce wines of seemingly eternal youth.*

Quality and character: Trimbach of Ribeauvillé is one of the
greatest exponents of the ultra-dry style of Riesling. All its
Riesling *cuvées* are as dry as they come and made in an uncompromising style that requires a considerable amount of bottle-age
to mature. It is also a style that is best appreciated with food, but
it is so distinctive that consumers passionately love it or hate it.
Those who hate it protest that a Riesling does not have to be

mouth-puckering, nor need it be as hard as rocks, to be fine. That is certainly true, but it does not alter the fact that the best ultra-dry Rieslings are fine wines. There are other truly dry Rieslings that seem soft and appealing from the moment they are bottled. That is another style and the best are also fine wines. And there are, of course, those wines that are deliberately made with a little residual sugar. The best of these are fine wines too.

If neither the producer nor the consumer is prepared to age the wines (and that is hard enough to achieve for the red wines of Bordeaux, let alone the whites of Alsace), then there are only so many methods that can be applied to smooth out the Riesling's youthful character. The first is to put the wine through malolactic, which is something that Trimbach avoids, some producers religiously practise, and most use as a fine-tuning tool that may be required in part or whole, or not at all, as the varying effects of vintage require. Tartrate precipitation through cold stabilization also has its effect on the acidity of a wine, though less dramatic-ally. Almost all other methods of de-acidifying leave a noticeable effect on the taste or texture of a wine. Apart from these practices, the only other way of softening a wine that promises to be austere in its youth is to stop the fermentation while a little sweetness remains.

The amount of residual sugar found in some so-called dry Rieslings, can be quite alarming and this is particularly so if the wines have been deliberately fashioned for entering competitions. Even the *Sigillé de Qualité*, which unquestionably has the highest standards of any Alsace competition, has bestowed its prestigious award on apparently dry Rieslings (i.e., not Vendange Tardive) with almost 10 g/l of residual sugar. If the wines are so well balanced that they seem dry, I have no objection. My only arbiter is quality and such examples are surely fine wines. Where I do take exception is when a wine of *noticeable* sweetness gives no indication of this on the label. I enjoy all styles of Riesling, from bone dry to intensely sweet, but I do like to know what it is I am opening, otherwise it could be a wasted bottle.

Because of the sensitivity of this grape in the vineyard and in the winery, it is also the easiest varietal to get wrong. If the grower overcrops, overpresses or makes any mistake at all, he will be punished for it in the wine he produces. Good value Riesling can be found, but it is relatively rare and as a general rule it is better

to pay a premium for these wines than to risk something dull and
insipid at best, mean and acidic at worst.

Comment on new oak for fermentation and/or ageing: This has
been attempted more in Germany than in Alsace and in neither has
it been successful, although there is good argument for only
fermenting, not ageing, Riesling in new oak, to add an extra dimension to the complexity of the wine without exposing it to any
obvious oaky overtones.

Prime drinking: Within four to 20 years

THE PREMIER GRAND CRU OF ALSACE

Trimbach Clos Ste-Hune
The quintessential Riesling.

IN A TOTALLY DIFFERENT CLASS

Marcel Deiss
A superb set of *lieux-dits*, from the light but elegant *Bergheim
Engelgarten*; through the *Bergheim Grasberg*, which is the fullest,
firmest and youngest in style; the *Bergheim-Burg*, a fatter wine that
often has a little residual sweetness; to the *Bergheim Grasberg*,
which definitely has the best acidity and most finesse; yet, head and
shoulders above all these, come the *Grand Cru Altenberg de
Bergheim* and *Grand Cru Schoenenbourg*, wines of unbelievable
succulence and immaculate balance that simply ooze class.

F.E. Trimbach
The *Cuvée Frédéric Emile*, which comes from part of the *grand cru*
Osterberg vineyard that overlooks Trimbach's distinctive *maison*,
is a wine of such outstanding quality that I wonder whether I might
not rank it alongside*Clos Ste-Hune* if it came from any other
producer? As it is, there are all too many chances to compare the
two wines and after a while it becomes clear that *Clos Ste-Hune* has
that extra touch of class and finesse, which separates it from all
other Alsace Rieslings. Anyone tasting these wines for the first time,

however, could be forgiven for thinking *Cuvée Frédéric Emile* not just the equal of *Clos Ste-Hune*, but its superior. The truth is *Cuvée Frédéric Emile* is a shade fatter and inclined to be further forward in its development than*Clos Ste-Hune*, thus charms at a much younger age.There is no shame in being one of the second greatest Rieslings in Alsace.

Domaine Weinbach
Where does Madame Faller find the moon-dust to go in her beautifully floral *Grand Cru Schlossberg Cuvée Ste-Cathérine* with its utterly ravishing, yet refined and complex fruit? And surely the *Cuvée Théo*, which is more intense and a real *vin de garde*, is more than enough evidence that Clos des Capucins is top *grand cru* material?

Domaine Zind Humbrecht
Herrenweg has a delightfully precocious aroma and delicious, zesty-sherbetty fruit, hinting of limes.*Clos Hauserer* is stunning and zesty when young and capable of great finesse and petrolly complexity with age.

OTHER TOP PERFORMERS

J.B. Adam: excellent *Kaefferkopf*. **Barmès-Buecher:** one of the best producers of *Grand Cru Hengst*. **Baumann & Fils:** rich and aromatic *Grand Cru Schoenenbourg*. **Léon Baur:** very intense *Cuvée Elizabeth Stumpf* and a most elegant *Grand Cru Eichberg*. **CV Beblenheim:** now making delicious, tropical fruit *Grand Cru de Bergheim*. **Jean Becker:** fresh, lively *Hagenschlauf* with a minerally complexity that develops peachy richness. **Léon Beyer:** the absolutely dry, impeccably crisp *Cuvée Particulière* and *Les Escaliers* are wines of great and graceful longevity. **André Blanck:** exceptional *Grand Cru Schlossberg*. **Paul Blanck:** fine *Grand Cru Furstentum*, intense *Grand Cru Schlossberg*. **E. Boeckel:** relatively recently introduced *Grand Cru Zotzenberg* is showing superb creamy fruit and promises to remain youthful for many years. **Bott Frères:** richly flavoured *Réserve Personnelle*. **Albert Boxler Fils:** ripe and fruity generic and a much finer *Grand Cru Sommerberg*, a wine of obvious class and breeding. **François Braun:** *Grand Cru Pfingstberg* of great extract. **Théo Cattin:** very dependable generic and fine *Grand Cru Hatschbourg* that is capable of ageing well. **Marcel Deiss:** fine, varietally expressive generic, but the village wines are a notch up and well worth the extra, especially the *St-Hippolyte*. **Dirler:** fine and stylish even at generic level, but his stunning *Grand Cru Kessler* is well worth the extra, the *Grand Cru Saering* can sometimes outperform Schlumberger's excellent wine and the *Grand Cru Spiegel* is a masterful wine of great delicacy and finesse; intensely aromatic *Hahnenberg* of great potential longevity. **Dopff & Irion**: the potentially outstanding *Les Murailles* does justice to itself only in the ripest years (e.g., 1976, 1983, etc.), when its extremely dry, underrated varietal finesse and high acidity require at least seven years to come together in bottle. **Dopff Au Moulin**: currently making excellent, flinty-petrolly generic wine, but watch out for the excellent *Grand Cru Schoenenbourg* under its Domaines Dopff label. **Henri Ehrhart**: extraordinarily rich generic. **René Fleith**: not great wines, but there is a deft feel to this grower's basic Rieslings that gives the impression that he has fashioned a silk purse out of a sow's ear and that is meant to be a compliment. **Pierre Freudenreich**: deliciously fresh and sherbetty Riesling of real depth and finesse that benefits from mid-term ageing. **Pierre Frick**: fine, organic *Grand Cru Steinert*. **Geschickt**: perfumed, elegant and stylish *Kaefferkopf Réserve*. **Paul Ginglinger**: rich, aromatic *Grand Cru Eichberg* and *Grand Cru Pfersigberg*. **Domaine André & Rémy Gresser**: the finest *Grand Cru Moenchberg*. **André Hartmann**: rich, fruity *Armoirie Hartmann* of some class. **Domaine Hering**: cool fermented *Kirchberg de Barr* with a youthful banana aroma that persists for a couple of years, but usually has the extract and acidity to develop. **Albert Hertz**: award-winning wines that combine richness and freshness with petrolly finesse. **Marcel Humbrecht**: brilliant village Riesling from Gueberschwihr. **CV Hunawihr**: super-fresh and tangy *Muehlforst* that sometimes has a little late crop sweetness. **Jacques Iltis**: strong, ripe and potentially long-lived *Schlossreben*. **CV Ingersheim**: a *Grand Cru Sommerberg* that sometimes rivals Albert Boxler's. **CV Kientzheim-Kaysersberg**: nicely balanced *Grand Cru Schlossberg* of some richness. **Kientzler**: generic of great class and finesse, yet the *Grand Cru Geissberg* and *Grand Cru Osterberg* are a measurable step up. **Klur-Stoecklé**: fine Riesling *Grand cru Wineck-Schlossberg*. **Marc Kreydenweiss**: racy *Grand Cru Kastelberg* that is capable of acquiring a fine petrolly aroma in bottle. **Gérard Landmann**: fat and juicy *Grand Cru Muenchberg*. **Seppi Landmann**: a *Grand Cru Zinnkoepflé* of great extract and acidity. **Gustave Lorentz**: a *Cuvée Particulière* of some precocious, petrolly elegance and a rich, fulsome *Grand Cru Altenberg de Bergheim* capable of graceful old age. **Mader**: fine generic and richly flavoured *Grand Cru Rosacker*. **Frédéric Mallo**: fine, soft-styled *Grand Cru Rosacker*. **Albert Mann**: rich and fulsome *Grand Cru Schlossberg*. **JosMeyer**: *Grand Cru Hengst* that can rival Domaine Zind Humbrecht, but needs time to reveal its full potential. **Mittnacht-Klack**: intense, petrolly-citrus *Grand Cru Schoenenbourg*. **Frédéric Mochel**: spicy-rich *Grand Cru Altenberg de Bergbieten*. **Muhlberger**: elegant *Grand Cru Altenberg de Wolxheim*. **Muré**: firm, serious, long-lived *Grand Cru Vorbourg Clos St-Landelin*. **Château Ollwiller**: refined Riesling. **Domaine Ostertag**: *Fronholz* is too fat to have real class, but *Vignoble d'Epfig* shows obvious class from an early age and will benefit from a few years in bottle, but of all his Rieslings *Grand Cru Muenchberg* is Ostertag's flagship wine. **Preiss-Zimmer**: now producing a very well-flavoured *Réserve Comte Jean de Beaumont* that shows some citrus complexity. **CV Ribeauvillé**: firm, slow maturing

Grand Cru Kirchberg de Ribeauvillé. **Rolly Gassmann:** like all Rolly Gassman *cuvées*, the *Réserve Millésime* is very rich with some residual sweetness, but it also has plenty of mellow-ripe acidity and benefits from a few years bottle-age. **Edgar Schaller:** fine Riesling in the classic, ultra-dry style, which can quickly show a petrolly finesse on the nose, but has steely fruit and needs time to mellow, his *Grand Cru Mandelberg Vieilles Vignes* is superb and *Les Amandiers*, made from young vines growing on the Mandelberg, is a more approachable wine for those just beginning to discover this classic style of Alsace Riesling. **Philippe Scheidecker:** fine, fruity-floral *Cuvée Prestige*. **Domaine Schlumberger:** crisp, petrolly *Grand Cru Kitterlé*, elegant peachy-floral *Grand Cru Saering*. **Roland Schmitt:** outstanding *Grand cru Altenberg de Bergbieten* and *Grand Cru Altenberg de Bergbieten Sélection Vieilles Vignes* (though not necessarily any more outstanding than the 'ordinary' Altenberg), but also a truly delicious *Glintzberg lieu-dit* that is superior to many *grands crus*. **Domaine Schoffit:** an outstanding *Grand Cru Rangen, Clos St-Théobold* that is very rich and absolutely correct. **Bernard Schwach:** a rare (for Riesling, that is) *Grand Cru Sporen* of mystifyingly fragrant floral aromas, which belie the great longevity of the wine. **Sick-Dreyer:** well concentrated *Kaefferkopf*, particularly the *Kaefferkopf Cuvée Joseph Dreyer*. **Jean Sipp:** classic long-lived *Grand Cru Kirchberg de Ribeauvillé*. **Louis Sipp:** used to be firm structured wines of austere character that developed intense, petrolly finesse and complexity over a period of eight to ten years and lasted twice as long, but now the wines are more accessible in their youth, gaining honeyed richness relatively quickly – not quite the class they once were, but superior varietals nevertheless, especially the *Grand Cru Kirchberg de Ribeauvillé*. **Sipp-Mack:** very attractive, superior generic Riesling that often has a touch of spritz to lift the finish and a *Grand Cru Rosacker* of exceptional intensity. **Bruno Sorg:** beautiful balanced generic with deliciously ripe, peachy fruit and a fabulous *Grand Cru Florimont* that some years can rival some of Marcel Deiss's wines for its succulence and class. **Pierre Sparr:** rich and easy *Grand Cru Schlossberg*. **Bernard Staehlé:** very attractive, fresh and floral *Cuvée Dame Blanche*. **Domaine Aimé Stentz:** fat, spicy *Grand Cru Sommerberg*. **CV Turckheim:** succulent *Grand Cru Sommerberg*. **André Wackenthaler:** good *Kaefferkopf*. **Ch. Wantz:** fine, petrolly-inclined *Grand Cru Wiebelsberg*. **Domaine Weinbach:** glorious generic Riesling that would knock spots off many a *grand cru*. **Wiederhirn:** a rich *Réserve* with plenty of extract, tending to have some residual sweetness in riper years like 1989. **Willm:** made by Wolfberger, but in a fuller, softer, slightly sweeter style, this generic also has a clever touch of spritz to lift the wine for immediate consumption, but the *Grand Cru Kirchberg de Barr* is made to lay down. **Wolfberger:** the generic is a clever commercial blend made with easily accessible fruit of good varietal character and a slight spritz; also very fine *Vins Armoriés* and this cooperative is also one of the most underrated producers of *grand cru* wines, the availability of which varies from year to year, but I have tasted excellent Riesling Eichberg, Hatschbourg, Hengst and Steingrubler. **Wunsch & Mann:** a *Grand Cru Steingrubler Cuvée Joseph Mann* of fabulous richness and potential complexity.

Gewurztraminer

Also sold as *Gewurztraminer d'Alsace*

Area under vine: 2,503 hectares or 18.6 per cent of AOC Alsace
Ten-year trend: vineyards have increased by just 2 per cent compared to a general increase of 15 per cent for the whole AOC Alsace region
Average yield: 67 hectolitres per hectare
Grape varieties permitted: Gewurztraminer
Common youthful descriptors: banana, grapefruit, capsicum, vanilla, smoky bacon
Common bottle-aged descriptors: lychees (though not as often as some people seem to think), gingerbread (in the very finest examples that have aged gracefully), smoky bacon (if present in youth, becomes more intense with age)

Background: *This used to be the first Alsace wine people encountered, but although its voluptuous, up-front style is immediately appealing to many, it is by no means appreciated by all. It is a variety that cannot be ignored. Either you like it or you don't, and some people obviously hate it. Maybe one in three newcomers to Alsace wine finds the Gewurztraminer's distinctive spicy character too extrovert and exotic, even in the most restrained examples, which is why the Pinot Blanc is taking over the role of varietal vanguard for the region. Perhaps the most puzzling aspect of the entire Gewurztraminer issue is that almost one in five vines is of this variety. Over the last ten years, its sales have dropped considerably and producers have begun to grumble about growing stocks of unsold wine, yet the area of Gewurztraminer continues to expand. This growth might be only 2 per cent compared to 15 for Alsace vineyards in general, but any increase at this time will only exacerbate the overstock situation. It is now time to cut back the cultivation of this variety, restrict it to the most suitable terroirs and sell only the finest examples as a speciality to the cognoscenti, rather than cheap generics for the uninitiated.*

It may no longer be a fashionable variety, but, for those who love the grape, its wine is difficult to shake off. While even its most ardent admirers inevitably move on to other varieties, very few of us can forget the Gewurztraminer's early pleasures and happily accept a glass whenever the opportunity arises. When it comes to wines of finesse, however, the Gewurztraminer is almost as fussy as Riesling in where it should be grown, although the climatic effects are quite the reverse. It does not take much fine weather for this

grape to slip into Vendange Tardive gear, which can result in fat
and blowzy wines, even at the generic level, so if you prefer a more
restrained style of Gewurztraminer, avoid the hyped-up vintages
and go for a medium-good year or less. There is evidence to suggest
that the ideal vintage for refined Gewurztraminer is one that has a
rainy June and July prior to a balmy August and September.

Quality and character: The fattest and most aromatic of Alsace wines, classic renditions of this grape have the aroma of banana when young and can develop into one of two basic styles, either strong and spicy or fragrant and floral. The spice in great Gewurztraminer can mature with such pungency that it will be a shock to the system of anyone not accustomed to these wines. Some people never get used to it. The very finest Gewurztraminer has such a refined quality of spice that it will acquire the aroma of fresh-baked gingerbread after eight or so years in bottle.

Gewurztraminer is a grape that has an intrinsically low level of acidity, but this can go unnoticed in the best examples, whose intensity of spice, high degree of alcohol and perceptible phenolic content (from the skins) blaze the flavour on to the palate, giving it a length that would otherwise be impossible in such a wine. Traditionally all Alsace varietals are dry wines, but some styles are drier than others and Gewurztraminer is the least dry of all. Many examples today have a surprisingly high level of sugar that, together with their low acidity, makes them far too fat and blowzy.

Classic Gewurztraminer has almost legendary potential longevity, which might at first seem impossible for a low-acid wine, but we tend to think too simplistically about the ageing capacity of wine. For reds, for example, we concentrate on tannin, commonly forgetting acidity, which is equally crucial, while for whites we usually think of acidity as the only preservative, yet sugar, tannin and alcohol all have their part to play and, for Gewurztraminer, one or all of these components will sustain the wine.

Comment on new oak for fermentation and/or ageing: No known attempts have been made and it is doubtful that new wood could have any perceptible effect without killing off the wine first.

Prime drinking: Within three to ten years (great examples will continue for 20 or 30 years).

IN A TOTALLY DIFFERENT CLASS

Kuentz-Bas
Delicious wines of voluptuous texture, great concentration and finesse, particularly the *Grand Cru Eichberg and Grand Cru Pfersigberg*.

Domaine Ostertag
Vignoble d'Epfig has great banana finesse and retains it for several years in bottle before blossoming into a truly classic Gewurztraminer.

F.E. Trimbach
The *Cuvée des Seigneurs de Ribeaupierre* is a wine that should be aged ten or more years to reveal the true pungency of its spice-shocking quality.

Domaine Weinbach
A fat, but stylish and succulent *Cuvée Laurence* that simply bursts with exotic fruit, flowery-spice and smoky-honeyed complexity; *Cuvée Théo* is usually bigger, bolder and perhaps has a touch more class.

Willm
The huge, rich and concentrated *Grand Cru Kirchberg de Barr Clos Gaensbroennel* has always been one of the region's most brilliant, if sometimes eccentric flavoured, wines.

Domaine Zind Humbrecht
Wines of astonishing complexity and finesse from:*Herrenweg, Grand Cru Hengst, Grand Cru Rangen, Grand Cru Goldert* and *Clos Windsbuhl*.

OTHER TOP PERFORMERS

Pierre Adam: well balanced *Kaefferkopf*. **Lucien Albrecht:** apricot-marmalade

Grand Cru Pfingstberg. **Charles Baur**: beautifully crafted *Grand Cru Pfersigberg*. **François Baur**: capable of generous *Grand Cru Brand* in better vintages. **Barmès-Buecher**: generic with excellent banana finesse that is drier than most and the best Gewurztraminer on the *Grand Cru Steingrubler*. **Jean Becker**: fine quality *Rimelsberg* with well stated spice and a touch of exotic fruit and a nice, mellow-spicy *Grand Cru Froehn*. **Léon Beyer**: when the *Comtes d'Eguisheim* is singing, it is a magnificently rich and spicy wine of impeccable dryness and fragrance, which would a few years ago have been included with the other Gewurztraminers that are in a 'totally different class', but sadly (and unusually for Maison Beyer) this wine lacks consistency and can be strangely out of tune. **Paul Blanck**: although it may be restrained on the nose, the *Réserve Spéciale* is a wine of some class with extrovert spicy-fruit on the palate. Blanck's *Grand Cru Furstentum* is strikingly elegant with charming floral-spice. **Bott Frères**: underrated *Réserve Personnelle* with fragrant rose-petal and grapefruit aromas and fine, spicy complexity. **Bott-Geyl**: a powerful, spicy *Grand Cru Sonnenglanz*, with great acidity and intensity of fruit. **Lucien Brand**: unusual but interesting peppery-spicy wine that excels in off-years, but it pays to search out the *Kefferberg*. **Camille Braun**: long, intense *Cuvée St-Nicolas*. **François Braun**: exquisitely rich and honeyed *Grand Cru Pfingstberg*. **Joseph Cattin**: discreet yet powerful *Grand Cru Hatschbourg*. **Théo Cattin**: good *Grand Cru Hatschbourg*, but a finer, even more delicious *Bollenberg*. **Marcel Deiss**: a *Grand Cru Altenberg de Bergheim* of great extract and liquorice intensity. **Claude Dietrich**: super-banana finesse, but lacks the acidity of a truly exceptional Gewurztraminer. **Dopff & Irion**: the excellent *Les Sorcières* is the richest of the three *terroir*-based *cuvées* that have historically made the reputation of this house. **Dopff Au Moulin**: a generic that can normally be relied upon to provide a pungently spicy style, but look out for the distinctly classier *Grand Cru Brand* under the Domaines Dopff label. **Robert Faller**: ties with André Kientzler for the best *Grand Cru Kirchberg de Ribeauvillé*. **René Fleith**: lively, rich-flavoured *Eschard* with plenty of sherbetty banana potential. **Pierre Freudenreich**: a *Grand Cru Pfersichberg* (*sic*) with a fine balance of spicy extract and fragrance. **W. Gisselbrecht**: rich, spicy and flavoursome with good acidity. **J. Hauller**: fine, floral *Grand Cru Frankstein*. **Albert Hertz**: firm, pungently spicy generic and *Grand Cru Eichberg*. **Bruno Hertz**: characterful *Grand Cru Rangen* with well-charged spice. **Jean Heywang**: an elegant, understated *Grand Cru Kirchberg de Barr* that ages very gracefully. **Hugel & Fils**: a better generic than most, but it is the *Jubilée* that takes the honours for its fine, warm pungency of spice with hints of vanilla and banana. **CV Hunawihr**: delicately rich and spicy *Grand Cru Rosacker*. **CV Ingersheim**: big, smoky-rich *Grand Cru Florimont*. **André Kientzler** superb *Grand Cru Kirchberg de Ribeauvillé*, which regularly ranks as the best of its growth. **Klein aux Vieux Remparts**: fine generic with spicy aroma, mellow fruit and crisp structure. **Domaine Klipfel**: truly excellent *Grand Cru Kirchberg de Barr Clos Zisser* even if it does suffer in comparison with Willm's *Clos Gaensbroennel*. **Charles Koehly**: top producer of *Grand Cru Gloeckelberg*. **Marc Kreydenweiss**: the *Kritt* has exceptional strength and style. **Alphonse Kuentz**: well flavoured *Grand Cru Pfer-*

sigberg with good spicy finesse. **Kuentz-Bas**: truly splendid *Cuvée Tradition*, with deliciously rich fruit and a ripe, spicy finish. **Seppi Landmann**: strong, fiery *Grand Cru Zinnkoepflé*. **Landmann-Ostholt**: *Grand Cru Zinnkoepflé* of huge extract and grip. **Gustave Lorentz**: the basic *Réserve* is always a firm, forthright wine with fine spicy fruit that ages well, but the *Cuvée Particulière* is much richer, yet more elegant and has a real spicy finesse, while the *Grand Cru Altenberg de Bergheim* is very full on the nose, yet another couple of notches richer on the palate with a few grams of sugar to make the fruit seem really succulent, but needs the sweetness if kept ten years or more to balance the spice, which gains in intensity. **Frédéric Mallo**: soft and delicate *Grand Cru Mandelberg*. **Albert Mann**: a certain residual sweetness makes the generic more medium-dry than dry, but together with a slight spritz, the wine has a good, crisp balance; look out for the much finer, more luscious *Grand Cru Hengst*. **Jean-Paul Mauler**: super-spicy *Grand Cru Mandelberg*. **Hubert Metz**: fresh and refined *Grand Cru Winzenberg* of some complexity. **JosMeyer**: consistently fine *Les Archenets*. **Mittnacht-Klack**: fine, fragrantly spicy *Grand Cru Rosacker*. **Frédéric Mochel**: an elegant generic with fine sherbetty-banana finesse and a deliciously tangy *Grand Cru Altenberg de Bergbieten*. **Muhlberger**: elegant, flowery *Grand Cru Altenberg de Wolxheim*. **Mullenbach**: spicy-banana finesse. **CV Obernai**: currently making an exquisitely well-balanced wine that shows superb banana finesse in its youth. **CV Pfaffenheim**: rich, creamy-spicy *Grand Cru Goldert*. **Preiss-Zimmer**: under the auspices of CV Turckheim this has grown into a wine of exceptional acidity and varietal intensity for a generic. **CV Ribeauvillé**: ever-youthful *Grand Cru Gloeckelberg* of infinite charm and fragrance. **Rieflé**: very good *Grand Cru Steinert* with fine grapy-spicy aroma and some complexity. **Rolly Gassmann**: typically tending to the medium-sweet side, but has real richness of flowery-spice with lovely acidity. **Salzmann-Thomann**: extremely elegant *Grand Cru Schlossberg*. **Edgard Schaller**: the rich, sweet, luscious apricot and vanilla *Vendanges de la St-Nicolas* has true Vendange Tardive intensity, even if it does not claim the AOC designation. Otherwise Schaller's Gewurztraminers are as unrelenting in their dryness as this producer's scintillating Riesling. **Charles Schleret**: a very good, sweet fragrance of spice, softly rich fruit, sometimes with a smoky-bacon complexity. **Marcel Schlosser**: an elegant *Grand Cru Moenchberg*. **Domaine Schlumberger**: the *Princes Abbés* has a full, spicy nose with rich, mellow fruit on the palate, sitting neatly on fine balancing acidity; a *Grand Cru Kessler* of wonderfully mellow pungency and a supple, smoky-spicy *Grand Cru Kitterlé*. **Roland Schmitt**: a fresh, varietally pure, delightful, easy-drinking wine. **Gérard Schueller**: tremendously expressive generic, lots of spice on the nose and rich, well-balanced fruit with a spice-tingling finish. **Bernard Schwach**: rich, well-balanced *Kaefferkopf*. **CV Traenheim**: fine, expressive Altenberg de Bergbieten. **Jean Sipp**: stylish medium dry wine of some finesse and capsicum-spice on the finish; much richer, firmer *Réserve Personnelle*. **Louis Sipp**: firm and long-lived generic and an intensely flavoured *Grand Cru Osterberg* that requires ageing. **Bruno Sorg**: even the most basic *cuvée* is classic. **Pierre Sparr**: rich and classy *Grand Cru Mambourg Cuvée Centenaire*, finely balanced *Grand Cru Brand Cuvée Réserve*, both having a citrussy-spicy finesse. **Jean-Martin Spielmann**: full-flavoured generic with fruity-spice and often a touch of spritz to lift the finish, but try the spicy-finesse of *Grand Cru Altenberg de Bergheim* or *Grand Cru Kanzlerberg* for a real treat. **CV Turckheim**: excellent *Grand Cru Brand*. **Wolfberger**: rich and classy *Vins Armoriés*, this cooperative is also one of the most underrated producers of *grand cru* wines, the availability of which varies from year to year, but I have tasted excellent Gewurztraminer Pfirsigberg (*sic*) and Hengst. **Domaine Zind Humbrecht**: a generic that is vastly superior to many *grand cru* wines.

Muscat

Also sold as *Muscat d'Alsace*

Area under vine: 371 hectares or 2.8 per cent of AOC Alsace
Ten year trend: vineyards have *decreased* by 11 per cent compared to a general increase of 15 per cent for the whole AOC Alsace region
Average yield: 82 hectolitres per hectare
Grape varieties permitted: Muscat Blanc à Petit Grains, Muscat Rosé à Petit Grains and Muscat Ottonel
Common youthful descriptors: gloriously floral, rose petals, orange, tangerine, peach, citrusy (Muscat d'Alsace)
Common bottle-aged descriptors: general intensification causing a blurring of the crisply defined, youthful characteristics
Additional blind tasting note: Generally, Muscat is flowery and Gewurztraminer spicy, but there can be an overlap, so how do you discern the difference between a spicy Muscat and a flowery Gewurztraminer? Unlike the choice between Gewurztraminer and a very spicy Tokay-Pinot Gris, where the latter's relatively high acidity plays a vital role in identifying the wines, both Muscat and Gewurztraminer are notoriously low in acidity, so no help there. From the same vineyard in the same year, however, a Muscat wine will be considerably lighter in colour and alcohol, whereas the Gewurztraminer will have a distinctly golden colour and heady alcoholic degree. Furthermore, Muscat is normally made as a bone dry wine, while Gewurztraminer traditionally has at least a little residual sugar. It is possible, of course, to get a heavy Muscat (particularly as growers are encouraged by Oechsle-based prices to harvest Muscat grapes far too ripe for ordinary generic wine), just as it is possible to find a light and fragrant Gewurztraminer (as many of the better producers who do not like the big and blowzy style deliberately aim for a Gewurztraminer of elegance and finesse) and there is no reason why wines presented in a blind tasting have to come from the same year, let alone vineyard. So how do you tell the difference? If all the logic previously expressed fails, see if you can perceive orange or tangerine in one of the wines because, if you can, the chances are that the wine is Muscat. If you cannot,

then do not bother trying to work out the impossible; you're not expected to be a magician!

Background: *Some growers believe that the best Muscat wine is made by the so-called Muscat d'Alsace, which is a synonym that covers both the white and pink versions of Muscat à Petit Grains, while a similar number of growers are equally convinced that the Muscat Ottonel is best, but most believe that a blend of the two is preferable. Muscat Ottonel originated in eastern Europe, while Muscat à Petit Grains is the same variety as used for Muscat de Beaumes de Venise. In many ways, the choice of Muscat in Alsace is very much like the choice for Pinot Blanc and Auxerrois, as it involves options of blending and balancing a wine, but, unlike those two grapes, there is no northern divide for the different varieties of Muscat, which are equally easy (or difficult) to grow throughout the region. The viticultural difference between the two is the contrasting size of their crops. The oenological preference, however, is not necessarily based on the variety that has the lower yield because their opposing organoleptic characteristics have little to do with yield. Muscat d'Alsace is an unreliable and small cropper, which gives a less aromatic but stronger, fuller-flavoured wine that is capable of greater longevity. Muscat Ottonel is an early ripener, a reliable cropper and gives a sizeable yield of very fragrant and aromatic wines. This is not to say that yield has no effect on quality, because overcropping the naturally generous Muscat Ottonel simply results in an attenuation of its delicate flavour and aroma. And it is both pointless and virtually impossible to force the Muscat d'Alsace to give a large yield, when it is far easier to cultivate Muscat Ottonel for larger crops and still maintain a certain quality.*

As a general guideline, both these grape varieties are better in average or modestly fine years, which stretch the ripening process, enhancing the wine's meagre potential acidity, rather than truly 'great' vintages, when the wines are too flabby, lack freshness and are inclined to oxidize rapidly in the bottle. For dry generic wines, Muscat grapes benefit from a relatively early (but not unripe) harvest. Unfortunately, many growers who sell their grapes in bulk wait until the harvest is too ripe because increasing the sugar level amplifies their income.

Quality and character: These are dry, aromatic wines with fine floral characteristics that often smell or taste of ripe peaches or zesty oranges. When harvested correctly, they are naturally low in alcohol and make wonderful apéritifs, but must be drunk young, fresh and lively. Early harvesting gives a crisper acidity to the wine, but naturally produced Muscat can never have a true ripe-acid tang and must rely on the freshness and liveliness of the product to create the illusion. Muscat Ottonel is lighter, fresher and more fragrant, while Muscat d'Alsace is fuller, richer and often has a generally citrus (rather than specifically orange) character. A skilful blending of the two can provide a wine of wonderfully fragrant aroma and a deep, delightful richness of fruit. An interesting comparison of these two Muscats can be tried at Dopff & Irion, whose fresh, up-front, floral-rosewater *Seigneur d'Alsace* is 100 per cent Muscat Ottonel, while the more discreet *Les Amandiers*, which builds in the glass and has fine peachy fruit underneath is 100 per cent Muscat d'Alsace (in fact 50 per cent each Muscat Blanc à Petit Grains and Muscat Rosé à Petit Grains).

Exceptional Muscats can last 20 or 30 years, but, however great the wines may be, they neither start out, nor end up, classic Muscat. Great Muscat is not necessarily classic Muscat. Classic Muscat is fresh and young, has a smouldering beauty, but cannot wait to seduce you with it and shamelessly throws itself at you. It is the classic tart of the wine world and everyone secretly loves it. Even the locals furtively hide their affair with this wine, but it is a well-known secret they find Muscat the most delicious accompaniment to fresh asparagus. A classic Muscat of the quality of Bruno Sorg's stunning, peach-laden Pfersigberg is a great wine by any standard, but a Muscat with a potential life of 20 years or more is not classic Muscat, although certainly a great wine *per se*. In its youth, the quality of such a wine is not always obvious. It is not a wine that will be fresh and scintillating, it will mystify most as to its varietal origin and, when mature, it will even baffle the experts. Great old Muscats are a tremendous experience, but they are not classic.

Comment on new oak for fermentation and/or ageing: Apart from the exciting possibility for late-harvest wines, the thought of new oak for this varietal is positively horrifying.

Prime drinking: Immediately.

IN A TOTALLY DIFFERENT CLASS

Rolly Gassmann
It is amazing what a little residual sugar can do (if you have a fine wine to start with) and I am not ashamed to admit it because this producer's *Grand Cru Moenchreben* is a pure delight.

Bruno Sorg
Grand Cru Pfersigberg: simply the best Muscat in Alsace.

OTHER TOP PERFORMERS

Jean Becker: surrounded by prime Muscat vineyards that have often yielded great Muscat in the 20 to 30 year mould, Philippe Becker has only recently tried to consistently craft a classic Muscat of great quality; the undisputed master of Muscat SGN (*see* entry below), his dry varietal *Grand Cru Froehn* will one day join Bruno Sorg's. **Ernest Burn:** very rich *Grand Cru Goldert Clos St-Imer*, capable of ageing well. **Joseph Cattin:** fine, flowery and intensely flavoured with a good musky aftertaste. **Dirler:** attractive, floral *Grand Cru Saering*. **Dopff & Irion:** this firm's *Les Amandiers* is a beautifully discreet wine of great finesse, which does not stand out in clinical tastings, but truly opens up at the table, where it shows its breeding. **Robert Faller:** very expressive *Grand Cru Kirchberg de Ribeauvillé*. **Pierre Frick:** a *Grand Cru Steinert* of obvious finesse. **Marcel Humbrecht:** fine *Grand Cru Goldert*. **André Kientzler:** delicate, fragrant and expressive *Grand Cru Kirchberg de Ribeauvillé*. **Marc Kreydenweiss:** exquisite, orange-flower *Clos Rebgarten*. **Kuentz-Bas:** deliciously fruity *Cuvée Tradition* and somewhat richer, more stylish *Réserve Personnelle*. **Mader:** a generic that can be relied upon for its richness. **Muré:** the *Grand Cru Vorbourg Clos St-Landelin* is always a refreshing relief in those hotter years when it is difficult to find top-quality, dry Muscat. **Domaine Ostertag:** not one of his most consistent varietals, but when *Fronholz* is right it is a truly beautiful and opulent wine. **Rolly Gassmann:** delicious *Réserve Millésime*. **Charles Schleret:** beautifully dry, light-bodied, fresh, fragrant and flowery generic. **Jean-Martin Spielmann:** deliciously rich and honeyed 1988 *Réserve* that had a distinctly Vendange Tardive quality about it, although it did not claim that rare status (which is rare for Muscat, anyway). **CV Traenheim:** fresh, orange-flower style. **Domaine Zind Humbrecht:** classy generic, outstanding *Grand Cru Goldert*, but not in the same class as Sorg.

Sylvaner

Also sold as *Sylvaner d'Alsace*

Area under vine: 2,367 hectares or 17.5 per cent of AOC Alsace
Ten-year trend: vineyards have *decreased* by 5 per cent compared to a general increase of 15 per cent for the whole AOC Alsace region
Average yield: 97 hectolitres per hectare
Grape varieties permitted: Sylvaner
Common youthful descriptors: green, neutral
Common bottle-aged descriptors: tomato

Background: *An early-ripening, heavy-cropping variety, the Sylvaner does not best suit the heat of top vintages. Its current decline will continue because almost one in five of all Alsace vines planted is of this variety and that does not correspond with its unfashionable reputation. This decline will, however, stop at a seemingly high percentage of the vineyard due to its role in the production of Edelzwicker, which is becoming progressively more important as the popularity of pure Pinot varietal wine increases.*

The greatest Sylvaners I have ever tasted have all been from the Granite Belt in Queensland of all places. Alsace could learn a thing or two from Angelo Puglisi of Ballandean Winery, who achieves remarkable results with this intrinsically modest variety by cane-cutting, which severs the canes that support grape clusters from the vine at the end of véraison. This cuts off the fruit from the vine's metabolism, inducing Vendange Tardive-like qualities. With a well-developed, petrolly intensity reminiscent of a great Riesling, Angelo's 1985 was far and away the best vintage until his 1991 was affected by 'noble rot', which propelled it into a completely different class with its succulent fruit and botrytis-rich complexity.

In Alsace, Sylvaner is not permitted to be sold as Vendange Tardive, of course, such is the wisdom of bureaucracy, but there is nothing to stop growers from making a Sylvaner Vendange Tardive and selling it under some obscure name at a dramatically increased price that will intrigue the more inquisitive Alsace consumer and entice them into finding out more about this particular wine. If the odd plot of late-harvested Sylvaner were occasionally affected by noble rot, surely an Alsace version of this wine would be at least as interesting as one from Queensland's Granite Belt? The nearest

attempts so far have been from Albert Seltz and F.E. Trimbach in
1989 and Jean Becker in 1990, but in terms of quality they are
merely interesting compared to Queensland Auslese.

Quality and character: An Alsace Sylvaner has a certain fat-earthiness, but is not as fat as one from the Rheinfalz, nor as earthy-spicy as one from Franconia. Hugh Johnson once described Alsace Sylvaner as the 'local tap-wine' and by the tap is exactly how it should be served: direct from the megalitre stainless-steel vat, with all the zip and zing of natural carbonic gas. Unfortunately, this spritz is usually filtered out during the bottling process, but Sylvaner is such an unpretentious wine with, at best, a mere fragrance rather than a real fruitiness, that the authorities should consider compulsory bottling of this variety *sur lie*! In fact, some of the more attractive Sylvaners do have a little residual gas. Certainly, it is best to drink Sylvaner as young as possible, although, like the Muscat, there are exceptionally long-lived examples that can be found. A 1959 Sylvaner from Klipfel, for example, was quite extraordinary in 1986, showing rich fruit with exotic touches of vanilla and coconut. It was not Sylvaner in any classic sense of the variety, but it was a great wine indeed.

Comment on new oak for fermentation and/or ageing: The only example I have come across has been Marc Kreydenweiss's *Kritt* Sylvaner, which was surprisingly successful, as the variety's relatively neutral aroma and lean structure adapted well to the influence of oak. Regrettably this wine is no longer available. Not a cheap wine to produce, it was impossible to achieve the price it deserved due to the Sylvaner's lowly image, so Marc Kreydenweiss uprooted the vines and replanted with classic varieties. Other attempts would be interesting, if growers would be willing to run the experiment at a loss for a few years!

Prime drinking: Immediately.

IN A TOTALLY DIFFERENT CLASS

None

OTHER TOP PERFORMERS

Christian Dolder: powerful *Zotzenberg*, which is technically illegal, but long may he get away with it. **Dopff Au Moulin**: the *Sylvaner de Riquewihr* is consistently exceptional in riper years, when it can have the aroma of fresh garden mint and a lovely depth of fruit, although the generic can even better it on rare occasions. **J. Hauller**: consistently fine. **Seppi Landmann**: fresh, well-flavoured *Vallée Noble*. **Julien Meyer**: a rich-flavoured *Zellberg* that can be quite exotic in warmer years. **Domaine Ostertag**: has gradually perfected a fine, floral rendition of this variety with his *Vieilles Vignes*, which can be unashamedly ripe and overtly fruity. **Rolly Gassmann**: rich, ripe and tasty. **Domaine Martin Schaetzel**: the *Vieilles Vignes* tends to be quite rich and full, without losing freshness, and its touch of residual sweetness is nicely balanced by good acidity. **Domaine Schoffit**: a *Cuvée Prestige* of real depth and surprising finesse. **Albert Seltz**: classic *Vieilles Vignes* from Grand Cru Zotzenberg (in 1989 he managed to produce a Sylvaner from his Zotzenberg vineyard with an astonishing 126° Oechsle, which is 10° above the minimum required for SGN, but unable to mention either the vineyard or botrytis designation, he called it *Cuvée Z 126*). **F.E. Trimbach**: always straight and correct, but not usually very exciting, Trimbach is not the first name that comes to mind when thinking of Sylvaner, although I have tasted some extraordinarily long-lived examples that have managed to survive centrally heated front-room storage in suburban England, and in 1989 this firm also produced an excellent, exceptionally concentrated, late-harvest wine from the Grand Cru Osterberg (although it cannot be commercialized as such, of course). **Domaine Zind Humbrecht**: a combination of relatively low yield richness and slight *pétillance* from being bottled *sur lie* probably make this the most consistently fine Sylvaner available, with rich, floral-lime aromas and a dazzling array of fruit flavours, but even the masterful touch of Zind Humbrecht does not elevate the wine into a totally different class.

Chasselas

Also sold as *Chasselas d'Alsace, Gutedel* and *Gutedel d'Alsace*

Area under vine: 230 hectares or 1.7 per cent of AOC Alsace
Ten-year trend: vineyards have *decreased* by 43 per cent compared to a general increase of 15 per cent for the whole AOC Alsace region
Average yield: 87 hectolitres per hectare
Grape varieties permitted: Chasselas
Common youthful descriptors: Not enough fine wine made to identify
Common bottle-aged descriptors: Not enough fine wine made to identify

Background: *This is the Swiss Fendant, which produces light and delicately fruity wines in the Valais, but it is really a table grape, not a wine grape, and in France it is in fact the most important variety grown for the production of table grapes. Even in Alsace, it is rarely seen as a pure varietal wine and when it is, it is usually commercialized as Chasselas, not Gutedel and never Fendant. Nobody should mourn the disappearance of the dull, thin and characterless wines this lowly table grape generally provides, but in exceptional circumstances of origin and producer it has been responsible for some uncommonly fine wines, so it would be sad to see it gone for ever. The Chasselas is, however, in rapid decline, with few vines existing today and only a small percentage of these used to produce pure varietal wines, as true exponents of this grape today are few and far between.*

Quality and character: Without doubt most of the best Chasselas wines are not actually bottled, but are sitting in vats of various cooperatives waiting to be blended into anonymous *cuvées* of Edelzwicker. They are neither profound nor complex, but teem with vibrant, mouth-tingling, fresh and fragrant fruit and are an absolute joy to drink.

Comment on new oak for fermentation and/or ageing: It might be interesting to ferment these wines in cask and bottle them *sur lie* without any racking just a few months later, but as to the overt influence of new oak, I doubt anyone would bother, as it would totally overwhelm the richest of these essentially delicate wines.

Prime drinking: Immediately.

IN A TOTALLY DIFFERENT CLASS

None

OTHER TOP PERFORMERS

André Kientzler: this is usually surprisingly ripe and weighty and it is as good as any Chasselas produced today, but, if anything, it is produced in too serious a style and would benefit from a more light-handed (light-hearted?) approach. JosMeyer: a fluffy-light, fresh and fruity *'H' Vieilles Vignes* from the Hengst. **Domaine Schoffit:** the *Vieilles Vignes* is consistently the richest Chasselas produced today, but it has a deft balance, is very open and full of easily accessible fruit.

ALTERNATIVE DESIGNATIONS

The designations listed here relate to varietal wines. More specific varietals, such as certain village wines of historical repute, are to be found with late-harvest varietals under 'Speciality Wines' in this chapter.

AUXERROIS is a grape variety allowed in the production of Pinot wine and, although technically not permitted as its own designation, common practice has made Auxerrois wine so widely available that it has evolved a ninth designation and, as such, has been treated as a separate varietal wine entry (*see* above).

CHARDONNAY came of age in Alsace in 1990, when it was included for the first time in the official harvest statistics. Its then total of just 12 hectares (nine in the Haut-Rhin, three in the Bas-Rhin) was sufficient for this variety to creep in as a rounded-up 0.1 per cent of the total vines planted. There are now 15 hectares of Chardonnay in Alsace, where it is permitted for Crémant d'Alsace only. Indeed, it is permitted as a varietal designation for Crémant, although the only pure Chardonnay Crémants d'Alsace I have come across have been Kuentz-Bas, which stopped production after just two vintages in the early 1980s, and E. Boeckel, which was also from the early-1980s and labelled Pinot Chardonnay. René Klein used to produce a pure Chardonnay Crémant d'Alsace, but this is now 70 per cent Chardonnay and 30 per cent Pinot Blanc from old vines.

Although it is not permitted as a variety for still wines under the AOC Vin d'Alsace, E. Boeckel has produced such a wine (labelled Pinot Chardonnay), but frankly the quality did not warrant running the risk of marketing a technically illegal product. Not that Chardonnay is incapable of producing a fine wine in Alsace; I have tasted an excellent tangy-rich Chardonnay from Klein aux Vieux Remparts, which was simply labelled 'CH' 1986 Réserve Personnelle (aged in oak for as much as two and a half years, yet seemed capable of developing further in bottle when tasted in 1990) and a fresh and tasty one-off bottle of 1991 Chardonnay from Marc Kreydenweiss (surprising potential for the product of three-year-old vines, but whatever might happen in the future – an upmarket *vin de table* has been suggested – the barrel of lightly oaked wine I tasted was destined for the Pinot Blanc melting pot). Domaine Zind Humbrecht has planted a little Chardonnay in its Clos Windsbuhl vineyard, but the experiments will hardly have begun as this book goes to press. Other growers who to my knowledge are cultivating this grape include Barmès-Buecher and Paul Buecher (for their jointly produced Crémant), Albert Hertz (also for Crémant, under the Prince Albert label), Klein aux Vieux Remparts (again for Crémant d'Alsace) and Domaine Aimé Stentz (also Crémant). Currently, the average yield for Chardonnay is 73 hectolitres per hectare (70 in the Haut-Rhin, 82 in the Bas-Rhin).

CLAIRET is specified in the regulations for AOC Alsace as a term that may be used to designate a Pinot Noir wine that has been vinified in the *clairet* style, which is to say deeper than rosé, but not quite red. It is rarely used and, although many Rouges d'Alsace would be more accurately described as Clairet d'Alsace, its employment would probably confuse more than it would clarify. Furthermore, there is no Alsace ring to Clairet. *See* Pinot Noir entry in 'Varietal Wines', above.

CLEVNER is a synonym for Klevner, which is an alternative designation commonly used for the commercialization of Pinot wines. *See* Pinot entry in 'Varietal Wines', above.

GUTEDEL is an alternative, but rarely seen, designation authorized for the commercialization of Chasselas wines. *See* Chasselas entry in 'Varietal Wines', above.

KLEVNER is a commonly used alternative designation that is authorized for the commercialization of Pinot wines. *See* Pinot entry in 'Varietal Wines', above.

PINOT AUXERROIS is sometimes encountered and may be either an erroneous synonym for Auxerrois or a blend of Pinot and Auxerrois. *See* Pinot and Auxerrois entries in 'Varietal Wines', above.

PINOT GRIS is the correct ampelographic name for, and thus given preference in the regulations over, Tokay-Pinot Gris. As the now banned term Tokay d'Alsace has been in widespread use for this variety since 1750, many growers prefer to use the appended reference of Tokay-Pinot Gris, although the use of Pinot Gris is on the increase. *See* Tokay-Pinot Gris entry in 'Varietal Wines', above.

ROSÉ D'ALSACE is an alternative designation for Pinot Noir made in a rosé style. *See* Pinot Noir entry in 'Varietal Wines', above.

ROUGE D'ALSACE is an alternative designation for Pinot Noir and, paradoxically, was more common when red Alsace wine seldom displayed any more colour than rosé. *See* Pinot Noir entry in 'Varietal Wines', above.

SCHILLERWEIN is specified in the regulation for AOC Alsace as a term that may be used to designate a Pinot Noir wine that has been vinified as a rosé. The use of this Germanic name obviously harks back to the time when terms such as *Spätlese* and *Auslese* were in common use, but it is not seen these days. *See* Pinot Noir entry in 'Varietal Wines', above.

TRAMINER has not been permitted since 1973. Prior to this date, wines now sold as Gewurztraminer would have had the choice of using either Traminer or Gewurztraminer. Some authorities suggest that there used to be two varieties, while others say that the Traminer was merely a less spicy version of Gewurztraminer. According to Pierre Galet, the ampelographer I normally defer to, they are two different varieties, and he is adamant that the Traminer is in fact none other than the Savagnin of the Jura. If they are indeed one and the same grape, the Alsace version must have changed beyond all recognition because I have never tasted an old Traminer that was remotely like the Savagnin. One would not expect Alsace Traminer to have the *flor*-induced character of the Jura's deliberately oxidized Vin Jaune, but there ought to be some resemblance to the local table wines made in that region, just south of Alsace itself, yet there is not the slightest hint of similarity.

Obviously the degree of spiciness has something to do with the etymological origins of the name Gewurztraminer, as *gewurz* means 'spicy', thus Gewurztraminer literally means a 'spicy Traminer', which is not to suggest that Traminer wines were not spicy, just that they were less spicy than those wines labelled Gewurztraminer. Every Traminer I have tasted has had a certain spiciness, even if it has been discreet. I am in no position to contradict Galet's scientifically based ampelographic findings, but the subjective appreciation of the wines these varieties make tells me there is no organoleptic connection whatsoever between the Savagnin in the Jura and Traminer in Alsace. Also, as there was no programme to uproot Traminer vines when that variety was officially banned, they must still exist, yet the authorities claim that only Gewurztraminer is cultivated in Alsace nowadays, and all Gewurztraminer wine is spicy to one degree or another.

The aromatic quality of the Gewurztraminer in Alsace has always varied according to its location and soil, from discreet to intense, so it is probable that the choice of designation did originate in the cellar as a means of identifying *cuvées* from the various *terroirs* for commercial purposes. As a footnote, it should be realized that, historically, the reference to Gewurztraminer has been a relatively recent phenomenon. Traminer was the original name, having been introduced around 1500 and its use was more widespread than that of Gewurztraminer right up to and beyond the introduction of AOC regulations in 1962. *See* Gewurztraminer entry in 'Varietal Wines', above.

BLENDED WINES

When Alsace came under German sovereignty in 1871, after the Franco-Prussian War, the Germanic term *Edelwein* was reintroduced for the finest blends and the Alsace term *Zwicker* adopted for blends of a more common quality. After the First World War, when Alsace became French once again, the emphasis on labelling swung back to Gallic. The old term *Gentil*, which also means noble, was initially revived for the best blends, but Zwicker would not go away, particularly in Germany where most of the region's cheaper wines were still sold. Thus the term *Edelzwicker* evolved, literally distinguishing a 'noble blend' from a simple blend or *Zwicker*.

The simplicity and effectiveness of this two-tier classification for blended wines were officially recognized by the AOC statutes. *Zwicker* was defined as a blend of any permitted grape variety, whereas Edelzwicker could be blended only from noble grapes. In 1972, however, the term *Zwicker* was banned, which might not have been such a bad thing if it had actually eliminated the wines that were being sold as *Zwicker*, but as all permitted AOC Alsace vines were effectively ennobled at the same time, *Zwicker* prior to 1972 was merely sold as Edelzwicker after that date. The only thing they had managed to ban was the name and, inevitably, this led to a debasing of Edelzwicker's reputation.

It is obvious, however, that it would have been counter productive to eliminate the lower-quality wines of Alsace, whether they are called *Zwicker* or Edelzwicker. Alsace is no more capable of *exclusively* producing fine wines than is Bordeaux, Burgundy or Champagne. No matter how famous the region, it is impossible for its producers to make cream without milk. In fact, with the increasing emphasis on the *grands crus*, the need for *Zwicker* today is greater than it has ever been, as more and more cream is skimmed off. Unless increasingly larger amounts are also siphoned off the bottom of the pot, it stands to reason that the quality of the products in between will be diluted. In many ways, the products in between are more important than the *grands crus* because they represent the generic ranges, which are the bulk of Alsace wines, and thus the producers' bread and butter, the wines you and I are most likely to drink and the wines all newcomers to Alsace will first encounter.

It is impossible to resurrect the reputation of Edelzwicker, even if *Zwicker* were reintroduced. Its image has been tarnished and the mud always sticks. What is required is a *vin de pays* to mop up these ordinary wines. If the wines sold as Edelzwicker happened to be *vins de pays*, the image would immediately change from boring AOC plonk to cheap and cheerful *vin de pays*, which would not only make an exciting new introduction to the region's finer wines, but would also make it possible to 're-ennoble' the region's truly *edel* ones (*See* 'The Great Blended Wines of Alsace' after 'Edelzwicker née *Zwicker*' below). As I wrote this book, two Alsace *vins de pays* started to appear on the market, but they will have no qualitative impact on the rest of the wines of Alsace, as the *Vin de Pays du Haut-Rhin* and *Vin de Pays du Bas-Rhin* do not come from the same vineyards at all and are simply pure varietal wines (*see* 'The *Vins de Pays* d'Alsace' and 'AOC *Grand Cru*' later in this chapter) made from vines growing in unclassified land east of the river Ill.

Edelzwicker née *Zwicker*

Edelzwicker is also sold as Edelzwicker d'Alsace, although any wine, blended or varietal, may be simply labelled Vin d'Alsace, which is what the finer blended wines of Alsace usually resort to, although that is by no means any guarantee that the lesser quality blends are not also sold as such. There are 402 hectares (or 3.0 per cent of AOC Alsace) under 'mixed varieties' and these vineyards have *decreased* by 24 per cent over the last ten years, compared to a general increase of 15 per cent for the whole AOC Alsace region. These vineyards are mostly cultivated with a mix of Chasselas, Sylvaner and some Pinot Blanc, the grapes of which are harvested and vinified together, but it is impossible to say how much ends up as Edelzwicker (most of which will be an *ad hoc* blend of unwanted, left-over or second pressings of various varietal wines). On the one hand, the most classic blended wines are cultivated and vinified together, as these vines are (Hugel's Sporen, CV Ribeauvillé's Clos du Zahnacker, Jean Sipp's Schlossberg, etc.), but such fine wines are not overcropped, while the average for these vineyards is 110 hectolitres per hectare.

The Edelzwicker *appellation* allows its wines to be blended from two or more of the authorized grape varieties (Pinot Blanc, Auxerrois, Tokay-Pinot Gris, Pinot Noir, Riesling, Gewurztraminer, Muscat Ottonel, Muscat à Petit Grains, Sylvaner and Chasselas). *Edel* means 'noble', *zwicker* means 'blend', thus this should be a 'noble blend', as indeed the history of the wine shows it once was, but since the cosmetic removal of the AOC Zwicker, this *appellation* has become so devalued that many producers prefer to sell their blends as AOC Vin d'Alsace under a brand name, rather than use it. Most cheap blends are sold in litre bottles in Germany, but virtually all producers concede that the name Edelzwicker on the label is the kiss of death in more quality-minded markets.

Decent Edelzwicker blends are dry, light-bodied, clean in flavour and best drunk young. Most are either Sylvaner- or Pinot Blanc-based (although less so, since this variety has come into its own), with the better or slightly more expensive products having a generous touch of good Gewurztraminer or Tokay-Pinot Gris to fatten up the blend. I have tasted only one exceptional (contemporary) example of Edelzwicker and that was the extraordinary 1985 Edelzwicker of Henri Ehrhart in Ammerschwihr. This was a total anomaly, as his vintages both before and after have been nothing special (although as respectable as most in this category).

Classic blended wines of Alsace

It may come as a bit of a surprise after all the varietal wine hype, but Alsace is capable of making blends of the finest quality. And, indeed, it would be most strange if it could not. There is, after all, no intrinsic failing in its grapes, soil or climate and most critics agree that its producers are amongst the best in the world.

Alsace does produce some classic blends, but their number is small and dwindles every year because so few consumers realize their true quality. It is difficult to make potential customers appreciate why some Alsace blends are more expensive than ordinary Edelzwicker, but they should be no more categorized with Edelzwicker than a *cru classé* should be compared to generic Bordeaux.

Occasionally, one Edelzwicker excels here, as does another there, the reason usually being that the producer had an unexpectedly large volume of good Gewurztraminer or Tokay-Pinot Gris surplus to requirements, which then does wonders to the most innocuous and four-square blend. The few classic blends that do exist are the result of design, not accident, as they have to rely on their own individual reputations for survival. Such wines are, however, limited in supply and their fame, consequently, is not very widespread. As they slowly blink out of existence, it becomes evident that these relics of Alsace history are in danger of extinction.

Ennobled with a truly *edel* title, however, all these wines would belong to one category, which could be effectively promoted and the wines might then stand a chance of survival. This would also encourage others to take up the challenge of constructing classic blends, although their numbers would always be small if production were strictly controlled to ensure quality.

If the authorities want to avoid repeating the Edelzwicker née *Zwicker* mistake, they should create a special *appellation* that not only limits yield, but also regulates the content of a blend. It should insist upon a very substantial minimum content of noble varieties, which must be named to avoid the current 'noble' controversy. A strictly limited quantity of other Alsace varieties should be permitted for fine-tuning purposes. It does not matter what this classic quality blended *appellation* is called, although I favour *Gentil d'Alsace*, a term that was banned in 1973 (but a change of law could revive it), as this has an authentic and untarnished reputation that also works well in both French and English, which would be an advantage in export markets.

As AOC laws are essentially a codification of tradition and practice, it might be prudent to insist that all noble varieties are pressed and fermented together, with only the small percentage of lesser varieties allowed to be blended in afterwards to correct the annual balance of a wine. This would certainly help to ensure the quality of the wine, not because blending wines is technically inferior to blending grapes (it is not), but because the producer would have to consider the making of these wines from grape to glass, instead of just mixing up the best compromise from left-overs.

Although many producers now prefer to market their blended wines under brand names, rather than a devalued *appellation*, most of them are no better in terms of quality than those that are sold as Edelzwicker

In preference to brand names, which many consumers consciously shun, two semi-generic terms, *Réserve* and *Côtes du –*, have been adopted by several producers for their best blends. Of the *réserve* wines, Schlumberger is by far the best. In fact, one rung beneath the *Schlumberger Réserve*, this firm's basic Edelzwicker *Cristal-Marée* still ranks as one of the better of its ilk, with its attractive, fresh and lightly aromatic style. The *Réserve* is, however, obviously a more serious wine, with full body and laden with honey and spice-fruit flavour. Neither wine is totally dry, but both are well balanced, tasting richer, rather than sweeter. Both benefit in consistency from being non-vintage blends.

Of the *Côtes du –* wines, Louis Sipp's *Côtes de Ribeauvillé* is the finest I have encountered, with its typically high combination of acidity and extract and, although quite light in body, it is fairly austere in its youth, requiring a few years in bottle to mellow. For more details about this wine, *See* 'The Côtes and Coteaux of Alsace' in Chapter 5.

The following is a selection of Alsace wines that deserve to be called classic blends:

Explanatory note

At the time of writing, there is uncertainty about the future of *grand cru* status for Kaefferkopf. If the various differences are not resolved, it is certain that under the current myopic regulations, the blends that have created one of the truly great site names of Alsace will be prevented from mentioning either Kaefferkopf or the term *grand cru*. It is equally certain, however, that those producers who pride themselves on their Kaefferkopf blends will continue to make the wines and find some way of getting the message across to interested consumers. I have kept to the historically correct *appellations* for these wines below, but I suggest you look out for the appearance of *Cuvée* 'K' or whatever.

Kaefferkopf Kaefferkopf, J.B. Adam
From Caves J.B. Adam, this excellent wine is made from equal
quantities of Riesling and Gewurztraminer. It has a fine floral-spiced
nose, is dominated by soft, fresh, peachy fruit on the palate and has a
smoky-spice complexity on the finish. A superior *Réserve Particulière* version of this *cuvée* was introduced with the 1988 vintage.

Kaefferkopf Kaefferkopf, Kuehn
Considering that this wine is primarily a Gewurztraminer-based
blend, it is surprisingly closed on the nose during the first couple of
years in bottle and can also be quite tight and firm on the palate, with
plenty of assertive acidity. It eventually softens when the spiciness of
the Gewurztraminer shows through.

Kaefferkopf Kaefferkopf, Pierre Sparr
This wine is a perfect reflection of its 80 per cent Gewurztraminer
and 20 per cent Tokay-Pinot Gris composition, with its soft, but
spicy nose and a touch of honey-rich Tokay fruit on the palate. Its
fine balance of acidity makes it an ideal food wine, especially with
duck.

Ribeauvillé Côtes de Ribeauvillé, Louis Sipp
Pinot Blanc usually accounts for 40 per cent of this classy, fresh and
well-balanced non-vintage wine, which Louis Sipp produces from
some 7.5 hectares of south, south-east and south-west-facing slopes
in Ribeauvillé, including a small portion (one-third of a hectare) of
Grand Cru Kirchberg de Ribeauvillé. The other grapes in this blend
are Sylvaner, Riesling and Gewurztraminer.

Schlossberg Clos du Schlossberg, Jean Sipp
On a steep vineyard with an incline in excess of 55 per cent, a
mélange of noble grapes (50 per cent Riesling, 20 per cent Gewurztraminer, 20 per cent Tokay-Pinot Gris and 10 per cent Muscat) are
harvested together at severely restricted yields that average just 30
hectolitres per hectare and vinified *en masse* to produce a truly classic
vin de garde.

Sporen Sporen, Hugel & Fils
This wine was called Sporen 'Gentil' until 1973, which was the last
vintage that was allowed to use the now-banned name. In the spring

of 1990, I had the privilege to taste the 1988, 1981, 1979, 1973, 1964 and 1961 Sporen Hugel. This convinced me that not only can Alsace make the highest quality blends, but, like all great wines, the best need to be perfectly cellared for a considerable amount of time in order to reach their peak. The 1964 was classic Riesling over-laying the rich, honeyed, apricot-spice of Tokay-Pinot Gris. A superb wine that will continue to develop in the ideal conditions of Hugel's cellars in Riquewihr. The 1961 was even better – pure nectar! At the time of this tasting, Johnny Hugel told me he had made his last Sporen Hugel because the vineyard was being delimited as a *grand cru* and this prevented him from using the name on the label of a blended wine. He could always sell it as 'Cuvée SP', I mused, and, later that year, he did produce a 1990 vintage of the wine. As I write this, the wine has not been released (it is Hugel's custom to cellar its wines until they are ready – or beginning to be ready – to drink, which is something very few Alsace producers can claim to do and certainly none can afford to do it on the scale that Hugel does) and no decision had been made about what to call the wine when it eventually is sold. There are enough abbreviated *grand cru* names on wines made from so called modest grapes, so I think Johnny ought to be more original. What about a label featuring a sporran? He could always put a back label on the wine, explaining that Scotsmen wear these fur pouches in front of their kilts, where nobody would dare to rob them of their contents. He could then say that he has been robbed of the right to name the slope where his grapes are grown, but he just wants to assure the consumer that it is a famous name that would be recog-nized by all his loyal customers.

Symphonie Symphonie, Pierre Sparr

The production of a high-quality, classic blend called Symphonie will be music to the ears of most wine lovers, provided that it does not herald the end of Sparr's superb Kaefferkopf. The first vintage of Symphonie was 1989 and comprised of 35 per cent Riesling, 30 per cent Tokay-Pinot Gris, 25 per cent Pinot Blanc and 10 per cent Gewurztraminer.

Val d'Eléon Clos du Val d'Eléon, Marc Kreydenweiss

In 1990 Marc Kreydenweiss made his first classic blend, from 70 per cent Riesling and 30 per cent Tokay-Pinot Gris, which showed tremendous promise for young vines, making this a wine to watch, especially when the vines have time to develop, but the current wines suggest they will develop well in bottle.

Zahnacker Clos du Zahnacker, CV Ribeauvillé
Made from equal parts of Tokay-Pinot Gris, Riesling and Gewurz-traminer, grown in a small triangular-shaped vineyard that adjoins the Grand Cru Osterberg on the Côte de Ribeauvillé. Clos du Zahnacker has been referred to since it was first planted by Bene-dictine monks in the ninth century and has grown these three varieties in equal proportions since the twelfth century. The wine today is a true *vin de garde* that improves for up to 20 years, yet immediately appeals through the honeyed richness of its Tokay fruit. Eventually it matures like a fine old Gewurztraminer, but with the Riesling holding a somewhat firmer balance together.

SPECIALITY WINES

In this section, I have brought together various village wines that have a genuine historical reputation for their particular speciality, late-harvest and botrytis-affected wines that were only rarely pro-duced in this region until the relatively recent introduction of legislation and other wines of a specific nature, both old and new.

Vendange Tardive

Also sold as *Vendanges Tardives* (which is grammatically just as correct for a single wine, indicating the number of harvests, or *tries,* that are required to produce such a wine), the growth of this category of wine cannot be denied, but its very low base ten years ago and the seasonal nature of its production makes it impossible to quantify (*see* graph in Appendix III). A Vendange Tardive must be made as a varietal wine, but only four grape varieties are permitted. With their technical specification, these varieties are:

- **Gewurztraminer and Tokay-Pinot Gris** must have a minimum natural sugar content of 243g/l (equivalent to 105° Oechsle and a potential alcoholic strength of 14.3 per cent by volume).
- **Riesling and Muscat** must have a minimum natural sugar

content of 220g/l (equivalent to 95° Oechsle and a potential alcoholic strength of 13 per cent by volume).

No Vendanges Tardives may be chaptalized, and the wines must be checked and verified at the time of pressing, although they will not be awarded Vendange Tardive status unless they pass a tasting examination conducted after the wines have been commercially bottled. Although no system is perfect, this is no rubber-stamp test (35 per cent failed in 1983). This wine is not an *appellation* in itself, but rather a subordinate designation that may be appended to either the basic AOC or an AOC Alsace Grand Cru. It was pioneered by the late Jean Hugel of the famous Hugel firm, but unlike the SGN, another style officially placed in the statute books through Hugel's efforts, the rules governing Vendanges Tardives are less than satisfactory and, although a good number of truly great Vendanges Tardives are produced, it is generally a style that is inconsistent in quality and character.

This wine should be the product of late-harvested grapes, which have a different chemical composition from normally harvested grapes of the same sugar level, but some producers abuse the spirit of the *appellation*, albeit legally, by making Vendanges Tardives from grapes that have the correct sugar, although they have been picked at the normal harvest time and, sometimes, even at the beginning of the harvest.

The simple solution is to make it illegal to sell an AOC Alsace Vendange Tardive, unless it has been made from grapes harvested on or after a specific, annually adjustable, date. This would involve a certain risk, of course, because the longer grapes are left on the vine, the greater the chance of bad weather, but that is the gamble that must be taken, and part of the reason why the consumer is expected to pay more for these wines. The consumer also has a right to expect that Vendanges Tardives are what they claim to be, i.e. late harvested, as anything less is misrepresentation. Although honesty is as good a reason as any, there is another, equally important, motive for regulating the date when these wines should be harvested and that concerns the intrinsic difference in quality and character that exists between two wines of the same must weight that have been picked at either end of a harvest.

This is due to the complex changes that occur inside a grape that remains on the vine until November or December. As the leaves begin to fall and the sap retreats underground to the confines of its root-system, the grapes are cut off from the vine's metabolic system and start dehydrating in a process known as *passerillage*. The chemical compounds that this produces are in turn affected by the prevailing climatic conditions, thus *passerillé* grapes that have endured progressively colder temperatures (the norm) and those that have enjoyed a late burst of warmth of an Indian summer (not so common, but more Vendanges Tardives should be produced in such years), will render two entirely different wines. Both will be true Vendanges Tardives with a style far removed from that of a wine made from grapes of the same sugar content harvested without the effects of *passerillage*.

It may sound sacrilegious, but when a Vendange Tardive wine is botrytis-affected (as many were in 1989, for example), the *passerillé* character is lost but the result is an infinitely superior wine. I adore great *passerillage* wines and am fascinated by the contrasting characteristics produced by a warm or a cold autumn, but if there is a choice between botrytis or *passerillage* character, botrytis wins every time.

Dry or sweet? Another problem with Vendanges Tardives is the inconsistency in the level of sweetness, and the confusion this causes among consumers. Some producers try to fully-ferment their Vendanges Tardives, but many do not. A number believe the concept of a late-harvest wine demands some residual sweetness and even the dry wine purists find themselves in a quandary when faced with a stuck fermentation because the addition of a selected yeast of much stronger constitution to restart the process often gives a wine a poor balance and can cause an unpleasant bitter aftertaste. The degree of sweetness found in Vendanges Tardives therefore depends not only upon each producer's philosophy, but also upon bacteriological circumstances that vary from year to year.

Place six bottles of Vendange Tardive in front of any Alsace winemaker and ask him which are dry, medium-dry, medium-sweet or sweet and he would be as confused as anyone (unless, of course, he had made one of the wines himself and knew what it tasted like). If the winemakers of Alsace are unable to discern whether these wines are sweet or dry, what chance does the consumer have? There is no right or wrong style, but the confusion over relative sweetness is totally unnecessary, counterproductive to the enjoyment and better understanding of these wines, and could very easily be avoided. It is not a matter of whether a Vendange Tardive should be sweet or dry, but that we should at least have some idea what the wine is before we are expected to buy it.

General quality: Whether dry, medium or sweet, a Vendange Tardive should be a relatively full-bodied and alcoholic wine that has the concentrated and complex fruit aromas and flavours of *passerillage*. The specific characteristics will, of course, depend on the grape variety in question, but the fruit should be literally super-ripe and abundant, with great extract and capable of ageing extremely well. Within this context, a *passerillage* wine from a cooler autumn will be leaner and somewhat *nerveux* in style (firm and vigorous, but takes a long while to settle down), whereas from a warmer autumn it will be more lush and settled. Cooler autumns are capable of creating more complexity than warm-weather Vendanges Tardives, but will never be as voluptuous.

Comment on new oak for fermentation and/or ageing: A very good idea, particularly for Tokay-Pinot Gris, and I would suggest that it might also work wonders for Muscat on the rare occasions that style is attempted (although it would be a grave mistake on regular, fully-fermented Muscat).

Prime drinking: between five and 20 years

Gewurztraminer Vendanges Tardives

The richest and most flamboyant of all Vendanges Tardives, these wines are exotically rich in ripe-creamy banana, vanilla, lychee and apricot flavours. The more slow-forming the spice, the greater the pungency with age in bottle. Gewurztraminer is often cited as one of the few wines that can tackle Eastern food and, of all Gewurztraminer wines, it is Gewurztraminer Vendange Tardive that truly suits such dishes, particularly when from Chinese cookery, which is much fruitier and sweeter than other Eastern cuisines.

IN A TOTALLY DIFFERENT CLASS

Hugel & Fils

This fabulously concentrated wine with great, ripe, spicy extract and exceptional acidity is merely Hugel's third-best Vendange Tardive, yet such is this firm's expertise at this style that it easily ranks in this special category.

Kuentz-Bas

A most sublime *Grand Cru Eichberg Cuvée Caroline*, combining sensational sweet-fruit intensity with great power and remarkable finesse. Always a great wine, but in the ripest years, this is better than many an SGN.

Domaine Weinbach

An exquisitely rich, sweet and elegant wine of great finesse and style.

Domaine Zind Humbrecht

The *Grand Cru Goldert* is probably the best structured and most classic of this producer's Gewurztraminer Vendanges Tardives, but the *Herrenweg, Grand Cru Hengst* and *Grand Cru Heimbourg* are at least of the same stunning quality in a more voluptuous style.

OTHER TOP PERFORMERS

J.B. Adam: sweet and intense, with strong extract and promising great potential longevity. **E. Boeckel:** not the sweetest of styles, but this richly flavoured wine has plenty of candied-peel spicy complexity. **Léon Boesch:** capable of fine generic Vendange Tardive. **Joseph Cattin:** can produce the most striking *Grand Cru Hatschbourg*. **Dopff Au Moulin:** sweet and very fresh with a delightful fruity balance. **René Fleith:** sweet and stylish with super banana finesse in its youth. **Geschikt:** powerful, grapefruity, not too sweet. **Roger Jung:** medium-sweet with velvety texture and mouth-filling concentration of flavour (some botrytis in the 1989). **André Kientzler:** classic, sweet and concentrated *Grand Cru Geisberg*. **Charles Koehly:** a medium-sweet *Grand Cru Altenberg de Bergheim* that shows good, youthful banana character; richer, sweeter *Grand Cru Gloeckelberg* of equal finesse. **Domaine Ostertag:** sweet, concentrated, complex *Epfig*, with plenty of youthful banana finesse. **André Thomas:** sweet, rich and liquorous *Grand Cru Mambourg* (more botrytis in the 1989 than some SGN). **CV Turckheim:** capable of sweet, rich and exciting Vendanges Tardives, particularly from the Brand.

Tokay-Pinot Gris Vendanges Tardives

When young, the fruit will be lush and tropical, concentrated and creamy in texture, taking on an exotic, honeyed-apricot richness with smoky-spicy, buttery complexity after a few years in bottle. The individual nuances and their possible permutations are far to numerous to describe without ending up with a list that is so long and complicated that it would be incomprehensible, but you can often find orange, peach, liquorice and even strawberry (particularly redolent in the Kuentz-Bas 1985). With more acidity than all but the Riesling and capable of a degree of ripeness only Gewurztraminer can match, the amount of residual sugar Tokay-Pinot Gris can soak up in the Vendange Tardive style is such that massively rich examples seldom taste too sweet. It is also the most inclined of all varieties to show the sumptuous and seductive characteristics of botrytis, which effectively makes many of the greatest examples virtually SGN in style and quality. Better, in fact, to buy a great Tokay-Pinot Gris Vendange Tardive at a relatively expensive price than a 'bargain' SGN, which would be more expensive however cheap it might appear to be and bound to disappoint. I would take a Kuentz-Bas Vendange Tardive against an unknown SGN any day.

IN A TOTALLY DIFFERENT CLASS

Hugel & Fils
Plump and honeyed, sweet, spicy-ripe and voluptuously complex wine of immense class and extraordinary longevity.

Kuentz-Bas
The superb *Cuvée Caroline* is always genuinely late-harvest, is never picked before mid-November and is always one of the most expressive of cool-weather or warm-weather *passerillage*.

Domaine Zind Humbrecht
Sensationally rich and sweet wines of tremendous concentration, structure and acidity: *Rotenberg, Grand Cru Rangen, Clos Jebsal, Clos Windsbuhl.*

OTHER TOP PERFORMERS

Lucien Albrecht: fabulously rich *Grand Cru Pfingstberg*, definitely sweet and tremendous finesse. **Joseph Cattin**: has produced excellent *Grand Cru Hatschbourg*, very 'more-ish' indeed, yet exquisitely rich and ripe. **Marc Kreydenweiss**: mega-concentrated *Grand Cru Moenchberg* of great class and finesse. **Domaine Ostertag**: fabulously rich *Grand Cru Muenchberg*, with lots of smoky-spicy buttery fruit. **Vignobles Reinhart**: splendidly rich *Cuvée Charlotte*. **Domaine de la Tour**: well-structured.

Riesling Vendanges Tardives

Because Riesling has a low natural sugar content, the regulations insist on a level of ripeness that makes an exceptionally fine dry wine, but a meagre Vendange Tardive. True Riesling Vendanges Tardives are few and far between and most are probably pretending to be SGN. They should positively explode with rich, concentrated fruit on the palate and have the potential of great complexity.

IN A TOTALLY DIFFERENT CLASS

Hugel & Fils
The arch-master of Vendange Tardive excels with the Riesling like no other, with wonderfully honeyed wines that can age gracefully for 60 years or more.

Domaine Zind Humbrecht
The incomparable *Grand Cru Brand* tops the bill here, yet *Clos Hauserer* deserves to be in this élite category and *Herrenweg*, *Clos St-Urbain*, *Clos Jebsal* and *Clos Windsbuhl* probably have the same potential.

OTHER TOP PERFORMERS

Paul Blanck: a *Grand Cru Schlossberg* of exceptional concentration, yet a fine filigree of finesse. **André Kientzler**: the *Grand Cru Osterberg* is a Vendange Tardive of good ripeness that goes for angular elegance and correct style rather than outright richness. **Marc Kreydenweiss**: *Grand Cru Wiebelsberg* of astonishing richness and raciness, especially as the normally harvested wine hardly ever stands out, while the *Grand Cru Kastelberg* always makes splendid Riesling, whenever it may be harvested (and even in 1984 for Vendange Tardive!). **Domaine Ostertag**: intensely flavoured, beautifully ripe *Grand Cru Muenchberg*. **Schlegel-Boeglin**: has produced some fine *Grand Cru Zinnkoepflé*. **Domaine Weinbach**: beautifully balanced generic of great concentration and complexity.

Muscat Vendanges Tardives

The reason why this is one of the rarest wines in Alsace is probably because of the real difficulty that is experienced trying to retain freshness and good balance in over-ripe grapes of this variety when grown in Alsace. In fact, I have tasted only three wines: a 1985 from Geschickt and a 1983 from Bernard Weber, neither of which justified the status, but the 1989 from Muré Clos St-Landelin was ripe and lusty. I have also tasted three wines that did not claim to be Vendanges Tardives, but deserved to be so classified. Two were modest generics of astonishing quality (*see* André Thomas and Jean-Martin Spielmann in the Muscat entry under 'Alsace Varietals'), but one was hoping to claim SGN status (*see* Ernest Burn under 'Muscat Sélection de Grains Nobles' entry below). Regrettably I have not yet tasted the 1990 Vendange Tardive of Jean Becker. Nobody has anything like a record of making this style of wine, thus there can be no such thing as a top performer.

IN A TOTALLY DIFFERENT CLASS

None

OTHER TOP PERFORMERS

None

Sélection de Grains Nobles

The growth of this category is even more difficult to quantify than for Vendange Tardive. A mere 20 hectolitres were produced in 1981 and, although this jumped to 750 in the beautiful botrytis year of 1983, by the time another comparable vintage occurred, in 1989, Alsace managed to produce 12,275 hectolitres of SGN. Then, in 1990, the region yielded barely more than 40 per cent of the previous year's record and in 1991 it was back down to just 281

Relative ripeness of
Vendanges Tardives & Sélections de Grains Nobles
Minimum Requirements
(Expressed in grammes per litre of sugar, degrees Oechsle
and potential alcohol percentage by volume)

Variety	Vendanges Tardives			Sélections de Grains Nobles		
	G/L	°Oechsle	Alc%	G/L	°Oechsle	Alc%
G'traminer	243	105	14.3	279	120	16.5
Tokay-PG	243	105	14.3	279	120	16.5
Riesling	220	95	13.0	256	110	15.2
Muscat	220	95	13.0	256	110	15.2

Note

As a comparison to the German QmP system in Baden, which is the same latitude as Alsace on the other side of the Rhine, a wine must have a minimum Oechsle of 86° for Spätlese, 100° for Auslese and 128° for Beerenauslese (thus all wines, from the lowest specification for a Vendange Tardive to the highest for a Sélection de Grains Nobles, would be classified as Auslese), while compared to other French limits, almost all these Alsace wines are more than qualified to be Sauternes, which must have a minimum of 221g/l of natural sugar. In practice they all are well qualified because chaptalization, forbidden for Vendange Tardive and above, is not merely permitted for Sauternes but virtually encouraged as the wines must have a minimum *actual* alcoholic strength of 12.5 per cent by volume, which would leave a residual sugar of maybe eight or nine grams per litre, a level exceeded by many so-called dry wines and absurd for an intensely sweet wine like Sauternes. To put all of this into perspective, the minimum levels for any wine are usually well surpassed by quality-conscious producers whatever the region and, in Alsace, the degree of ripeness now being attained through restriction of yield was once considered totally impossible. Johnny Hugel could have told them (and tried to), as he and his predecessors regularly produced wines in excess of 150° Oechsle. The grapes used for all of Hugel's surviving nineteenth-century wines that remained drinkable were at least 150° and Hugel's legendary 1865 Tokay d'Alsace was over 200°. Now that wines are being produced where *the residual sugar alone* (i.e., after fermentation) would qualify as Sauternes, there is a widespread regret that all these minimum levels had not been set considerably higher. They say it cannot now be done, but I say that if everyone wanted to do it, there would be nothing to prevent them, as individual wine *appellations* have the right in EC law to set their own limits as high as they like above any minimum level imposed by the Community itself.

hectolitres (*see* graph in Appendix III)! Also exclusively a varietal wine made from the same four grape varieties permitted for Vendange Tardive:

- **Gewurztraminer and Tokay-Pinot Gris** must have a minimum natural sugar content of 279g/l (equivalent to 120° Oechsle and a potential alcoholic strength of 16.5 per cent by volume)

- **Riesling and Muscat** must have a minimum natural sugar content of 256g/l (equivalent to 105° Oechsle and a potential alcoholic strength of 15.2 per cent by volume)

These rare and sought-after wines are made from botrytis-affected grapes, but unlike Sauternes, Alsace is no haven for 'noble rot'. It occurs far more haphazardly and in much reduced concentrations; thus the wines are made in tiny quantities, even after the great increase in production mentioned above. Consequently they are sold at very expensive prices and rarely seen on export markets. Just a few years ago, the highest Oechsle SGN I knew of was Domaine Zind Humbrecht's 182° 1986 Tokay-Pinot Gris, which had the equivalent of 425g/l of sugar. Just 450 litres of this wine were produced from the domaine's Rotenberg vineyard. It stopped fermenting at 11.5 per cent alcohol with a staggering 230g/l of residual sugar and a no less amazing 11.5g/l of acidity expressed as tartaric. That was such a phenomenal wine for its era that it left its closest Oechsle rival way behind. Now there is (in relative terms) many a Sélection de Grains Nobles that is around this level, although you cannot count quality in grams, of course, and so they are not all necessarily in the same league as Domaine Zind Humbrecht's fabulous wine. With the current tendency to produce super-SGN (which started with Madame Faller's Tokay-Pinot Gris 1983 Quintessence de Grains Nobles, since when Marcel Deiss has also adopted the *Quintessence* designation, Hugel and Blanck have come up with the literally superior designation of *Super* Sélection de Grains Nobles, while F.E. Trimbach prefer the term *Hors Choix*), so the degrees Oechsle have soared and the highest I have encountered so far is Hugel Tokay-Pinot Gris 1989 Super Sélection de Grains Nobles at 214° or 505g/l. These wines have gone so far beyond normal levels that they go off the scale of the equipment that was designed specifically for the purpose of analysing the must weight in the field. New instruments are having to be recalibrated, just as they are having to extend the tables found in technical literature!

In many ways, then, this category of wine has improved by leaps and bounds, which should be particularly impressive considering how sublime they were in the early days of their regulation. There has been a demonstrable learning curve, as producers who are naturally inclined to produce the driest style of wine have discovered that fermenting SGNs as far as they will go is often the worst thing to do when it comes to effecting a well balanced wine, thus with steeply increasing sugar levels, we have gone from monstrous wine with 14.5 per cent alcohol (often 15–16 per cent) and sometimes just 20g/l of residual sweetness to far more exquisite products with around 12 per cent alcohol and well over 100g/l. Yet, contrary to these advances, I now encounter a greater number of more disappointing SGN wines than before. This must simply be due to the vast increase in production, but it does illustrate that even at the high prices these wines cost, you cannot guarantee satisfaction. Bargains are possible, of course, but unless you have been recommended a specific wine (a certain vintage of a particular *cuvée* from a specific producer), it will almost certainly be a false economy to buy the cheaper SGNs.

General quality: It is impossible to generalize the taste and character of a range of totally unique wines, but the finest examples do have one quality in common: the most amazing finesse and balance for wines of such incomparable concentration, complexity and intense sweetness. It is quite extraordinary how delicate they appear to be in the mouth, yet they are almost indestructible and will still be as fresh as a daisy in fifty years' time.

Comment on new oak for fermentation and/or ageing: The very first was Domaine Weinbach Clos des Capucins 1983 Tokay-Pinot Gris Quintessence, a wine that can be compared with Château d'Yquem. I am being serious, although it will be decades before we know quite how well Quintessence shapes up to such prestigious opposition.

Prime drinking: An absolute delight as soon as it has been fermented, but most probably need five to ten years and the best will not peak for several decades.

Gewurztraminer Sélection de grains nobles

Stunningly exotic wines that attain the greatest honeyed succulence of all SGN varieties. Gone are any hints of banana or citrus fruits such as grapefruit, which may be commonly found in other Gewurztraminer wines and in comes a ripe intensity of peach to add to the deep-red rose aroma, the inevitable lychee and fabulously rich, creamy-buttery vanilla and just a wisp of smoke. One of the most inexplicable features of heavily botrytized Gewurztraminer is that there is often no spice as such, yet its intrinsic varietal identity is amplified (as opposed to other grapes, which are totally overwhelmed by the botrytis character itself). You know it is that spicy variety, but cannot discern any spiciness, let alone identify the specific spices they remind you of. Perhaps it is due to the effects of botrytis, which increase acidity, thus these wines (and to a lesser degree, Vendanges Tardives) have a totally different balance that does not depend on phenolics, which serve to enhance the pungency of this variety's spicy character.

IN A TOTALLY DIFFERENT CLASS

Kuentz-Bas
Fabulously rich, but too stylish to be decadent, the *Grand Cru Pfersigberg Cuvée Jeremy* is the epitome of excellence.

F.E. Trimbach
Fabulous concentration, but more structure, less luxurious than the Kuentz-Bas, although the supercharged *Hors Choix* is a distinctive step up and as honeyed and luscious as it is possible to be.

Domaine Weinbach
The *Quintessence*, made only in years like 1983 and 1989, is sensationally sweet and as classy as Gewurztraminer can get.

Domaine Zind Humbrecht
Rangen must be the ultimate combination of sweetness and structure.

OTHER TOP PERFORMERS

Léon Beyer: one of the best producers in 1983 and 1989, but although the quality of this wine wobbled a little in between, it is certainly worth keeping an eye on. **Paul Blanck:** sweet, flamboyantly expressive *Grand Cru Furstentum* and an even more concentrated *Super* Sélection de Grains Nobles. **Albert Boxler:** great power and structure. **Marcel Deiss:** superb *Bergheim Burg* and *Grand Cru Altenberg de Bergheim*; the 200° Oechsle *Quintessence* produced in 1989 was simply too overwhelming to make a coherent judgement, but in a few decades it will either turn into something great or a monstrous oddity. **Dirler:** exotic, complex and intricately fruity wine of considerable finesse. **Hugel & Fils:** always classically structured *vins de gardes* that are extremely sweet and intensely flavoured; a *Super* selection was produced in 1989. **Albert Mann:** sweet rather than intensely sweet, but opulent and truly excellent. **Rolly Gassmann:** rich, sweet and concentrated *Cuvée Anne*. **Sick-Dreyer:** an intense and powerfully structured *Kaefferkopf* with firm sweetness. **Pierre Sparr:** has produced some of the most succulent of this style. **Domaine Weinbach:** excellent straight SGN, but not in the class of the *Quintessence*, or of the straight Tokay-Pinot Gris SGN.

Tokay-Pinot Gris Sélection de Grains Nobles

The skin of this grape is more susceptible to botrytis than any other variety permitted for SGN, which makes the wines it produces potentially the most powerful, exuberant and complex. It is also a grape of relatively high acidity, which in its botrytis-boosted form can soar to extraordinary heights. Combine this power and acidity and the result is a unique balance of firm structure, huge peachy-fruit, great buttery, toffee-apple richness, sublime creamy-spicy complexity and stupendous acidity.

IN A TOTALLY DIFFERENT CLASS

Marcel Deiss
Fabulously rich *Quintessence* 1989 with its intensely sweet, utterly unctuous fruit and scintillating acidity.

Hugel & Fils
Astonishingly rich and complex *Super* 1989.

Marc Kreydenweiss
Dazzling *Grand Cru Moenchberg*.

Kuentz-Bas
Impeccably stylish *Cuvée Jeremy*

Domaine Ostertag
Fabulous *Barrique Sélection de Grains Nobles*

F.E. Trimbach
Lovely concentration, especially the *Hors Choix*.

Domaine Weinbach
Tremendous regular SGN, but the first *Quintessence* in 1983 rivals
Yquem and the 1989 might even be better.

Domaine Zind Humbrecht
Superb straight Sélection de Grains Nobles, but most of it probably
comes from *Clos Hauserer*, which has the greatest potential for
botrytis-affected wine of all Domaine Zind Humbrecht vineyards.

OTHER TOP PERFORMERS

JB Adam: extraordinarily rich wines produced so far in minuscule amounts. **Albert
Boxler**: an immensely rich and concentrated *Grand Cru Brand* with superb acidity
and structure that promises decades of pleasure; and in some years a superb blend of
Boxler's two *grand cru*s (Brand and Sommerberg).

Riesling Sélection de Grains Nobles

Genuine Riesling SGNs should be the most exquisite botrytis wines
of all. They are very rare and treasured indeed, as there is much risk
and difficulty trying to harvest at the right Oechsle (which really
should be well above the minimum required) and it is remarkably
easy to mess up the vinification. A very light hand is required in the
cellar, where the wines should be as naturally produced as possible.
When everything goes right, these are wines of great intensity and
finesse, which remain remarkably fresh in bottle and develop a
honeyed complexity only after many years.

IN A TOTALLY DIFFERENT CLASS

Albert Boxler
A sensationally rich, ripe and stunning *Grand Cru Sommerberg* of
great finesse.

Marcel Deiss
More in the sweet category than intensely sweet, but the emphasis here is on style and it is one of incomparable finesse; the *Grand Cru Altenberg de Bergheim* is vivacious and fairly makes the palate tingle with acidity, while the *Grand Cru Schoenenbourg* is richer and has more body, yet is exquisitely tuned, but is the unbelievably super-concentrated *Quintessence* Deiss made in 1989 the greatest botrytis Riesling ever? This super-succulent wine is beautifully liquorous in the mouth, with true sweetness, yet electrifying with such rip-roaring acidity that it can be compared only to the very best of the most legendary *Eiswein* from Germany.

Hugel & Fils
This famous old house has the longest list of the most splendid vintages of this style in Alsace and continues to honour the tradition.

André Kientzler
Simply sensational *Grand Cru Geisberg* and *Grand Cru Osterberg*.

F.E. Trimbach
The *Cuvée Frédéric Émile* has an established pedigree as an ever-youthful wine of inimitable class.

Domaine Weinbach
Immaculate straight Sélection de Grains Nobles, but in 1989 the very first *Quintessence* was even more phenomenal.

Domaine Zind Humbrecht
The only Sélection de Grains Nobles I have come across is the absolutely divine *Clos Windsbuhl*, but this domaine has the potential to produce the most extraordinary botrytis wines in numerous locations, every one of which I would gamble the cost of a bottle on without a second thought.

OTHER TOP PERFORMERS

J.B. Adam: small amounts of succulently fine, honey-sweet wine. **Domaine Ostertag**: if you can afford to risk the cost of a SGN, you should gamble on the *Grand Cru Muenchberg*, which comes in 'Vieilles Vignes', 'Barrique' and for all we know, 'Raspberry-Ripple' flavour.

Muscat Sélection de Grains Nobles

The rarest of all Alsace wines, I know of just two attempts and although only one of those was successful, its quality was so extraordinary that other fully fledged and genuine attempts should certainly be encouraged. The 'failed' wine was a 1989 made by the otherwise brilliant Ernest Burn, which at 118° Oechsle made a feeble SGN, lacking the botrytis character and velvety texture expected from wines of that category. It would have been very well received with the altogether different expectations of a Vendange Tardive, and, having tasted the wine prior to the official tasting, a Vendange Tardive is what I imagined it would end up as, if the panel in question carried out its duties properly. The reader will understand my surprise, therefore, when I later discovered Monsieur Burn's wine had been granted full SGN status.

IN A TOTALLY DIFFERENT CLASS

Jean Becker

No one-off should get into this category, but Philippe Becker's
1988 Grand Cru Froehn Muscat is literally in a totally different
class from anything that has been made either before or since. He
achieved this by a method that he believed to be universal to all
great Sauternes but is only theory these days: the picking (or
plucking, to be more precise) of each individual grape to ensure that
every one used would be entirely botrytis-affected. When he
discovered that the only way this could be truly accomplished was
with an escargot fork, it soon dawned on Philippe that perhaps
Sauternes is not made quite that way today. Certainly not at the
minuscule six hectolitres per hectare that this wine was harvested
at. The result, however, certainly justified the effort (even though he
is not eager to repeat it!), as the highly concentrated juice squeezed
from such a rotten mass yielded 405g/l of sugar and, tasted from
cask eighteen months later, was so sensational that I placed an
order for a case. It really is special, but its massively rich botrytis
bouquet, great intensity of flavour (boosted no doubt by 204g/l of
residual sugar), exceptionally high acidity and seductively unctuous
texture reminds me more of an ultra-successful Alsace *vin de paille*
than a Sélection de Grains Nobles, although that is what it most
certainly and most literally is.

OTHER TOP PERFORMERS

None

VIN DE PAILLE

A wine that does not officially exist, even though it was the most illustrious wine produced between the eighteenth and nineteenth centuries, *vin de paille* was revived in 1987 by André Ostertag, who produced the first such wine for well over a hundred years. The following year, Hugel made 225 litres of *vin de paille* to celebrate the firm's 350th anniversary the following year, but the first such wines I tasted were those of Marcel Deiss and Domaine Zind Humbrecht, which were from the 1989 vintage and still lethargically fermenting the following spring. At the same time, I tasted a pure Riesling 1988 Cuvée Gilles from André Thomas & Fils, which claimed to be made in the *méthode vin de paille*.

There are *vins de pailles* and *vins de pailles* and in 1990 I saw the evidence in Alsace today. When I visited the cellars of Jean-Michel Deiss, he showed me a demijohn containing a minuscule quantity of 240°Oechsle (which is 570g/l of natural sugar) luscious liquid, which could barely have been half a dozen bottles worth, yet photographs of the entire crop of Riesling, Tokay-Pinot Gris and Gewurztraminer grapes this trifling *cuvée* was pressed from revealed an entire warehouse full of bunches hanging from the rafters. After drying for the requisite length of time, the fruit was so hard and concentrated that more than 90 per cent of its original bulk was lost. The result fairly filled the cellars with its spectacular bouquet, even though Jean-Michel begrudgingly dished out barely a teaspoonful. It was syrupy and liquorous, far above and beyond any common reference to the relative sweetness of a wine, yet beautifully balanced with acidity and a phenomenal extraction of flavour.

André Thomas's Riesling Cuvée Gilles was a deliciously ripe, intensely sweet (165g/l residual sugar) wine, but more in the botrytis style than *vin de paille*.

At Domaine Zind Humbrecht, Olivier Humbrecht showed me a greater quantity of *vin de paille*. He too used a demijohn, but had pressed slightly more grapes than Deiss and, as the excess was so prized, he had half-filled a cider bottle with this nectar and connected it to the mother-container by a transparent umbilical cord so that they would burp in sympathy with each other during the fermentation, which was obviously still following its agonizingly slow progress, according to the burp and bubble emitted every ten minutes or so.

The *vin de paille* from Domaine Zind Humbrecht was every bit as mind-blowingly impressive as the one from Marcel Deiss and it will be a matter of decades before anyone will be able to see which one is better and, of course, that is academic because it will probably be all gone ages before then. I have not tasted Domaine Ostertag, but according to Clive Coates it cannot be anything like the same animal. Neither is Hugel's *vin de paille*, although it is a fine wine indeed and certainly superior to most Jura versions of this wine I have tasted. The difference between Hugel's *vin de paille* and those of Deiss and Zind Humbrecht is, I am sure, purely a matter of yield, which is not to say that the Hugel wine is a lightweight. Far from it: weighing in at a potential alcoholic strength of 24 per cent by volume, it is almost twice the minimum for SGN. It is, however, a good 100 grams per litre of sugar less than the Deiss wine and, although I do not know the exact technical specification of the Zind Humbrecht, I suspect it must be of a similar order. Hugel should perhaps have left the grapes to dry and shrivel up a month or so longer, but then Johnny Hugel might not have had enough to give to all the illustrious people invited from all around the world to his firm's 350th anniversary. Even so, the room required to hang a sufficient quantity of grapes to produce 225 litres must have been enormous, which merely confirms my suspicion that Hugel's cellars under Riquewihr are larger than the village above!

Coincident with Hugel's anniversary celebrations, the firm published a limited edition of 1,000 copies of a translation by David Ling of a treatise entitled *Plan and instruction based on experience, in order to improve the products of the land, in particular the vineyards, dictated by patriotic instinct, its sole purpose being to promote the welfare of mankind*, which was originally published in 1789 by Jean-Michel Ortlieb, a nurseryman and winegrower in Riquewihr. This book is full of gems, the most interesting of which is:

Method of making genuine Vin de Paille,
and observations which ought to be made in this respect

It was in 1774 that I made this wine for the first time, in the following manner: I took 36 baskets of grapes, comprising Gentil, Red Gentil, Chasselas, Kleiner Rauschlinger and Common Muscat, choosing the ripest ones and only those which were in no way damaged. I suspended bunches from strings in a room with hardly any ventilation, after having attached a piece of thick wire to each bunch, in order to suspend the bunch inverted, with its lower part uppermost, so that each grape hung outwards and permitted the air to circulate freely between them. As a further precaution, I suspended the bunches at different heights, to prevent them touching; however, as mentioned above, because there was insufficient air in the room, the grapes began to rot and gave off an unpleasant musty odour, until it was practically impossible to find a single grape which was not so affected. Rats and mice contributed to the untidiness by running along the strings and causing whatever grapes they had not already destroyed by other means, to fall to the floor. The floorboards were covered by bunches and grapes to a depth of four inches, and hardly one grape in thirty was not affected by mould and by rot. In the hope of being able to salvage the very minimum, I resolved to press whatever remained and did so between Christmas and New Year. The must obtained from these mouldy, spoiled grapes was as disagreeable to the eye as it was to the palate, being at the same time green, blue and yellow, and totalled some four and half measures. I put it in a small cask and left it to rest for eighteen months; at the end of this period, I racked it and clarified it for the first time; but it was still impossible to reach the slightest conclusion. Six months later, I repeated the same operation, and perceived that the wine was beginning to improve, and could perhaps at last become drinkable. My hopes were not ill-founded, as having again racked and clarified the wine the following year, I obtained a Vin de Paille of superior quality and unrivalled delicacy.

Ortlieb goes on to explain that while 'it is from the bed of straw, on which the grapes are usually spread, that this particular wine takes its name' it is 'none the less more advantageous' to suspend the bunches in the manner he describes. From this and the inverted nature of this suspension, it is clear that the looser the clusters the more ideal they will be for the purpose, as only loose and dangling grape berries could possibly be 'hung outwards'. Thus tightly clustered grapes such as Riesling are not best suited to this procedure and he does, in fact, go on to discount this variety, recommending the Gentil and Red Gentil (Traminer and Gewurztraminer) as 'by far the best', but points out that a *vin de paille* of these two grapes alone would 'become too strong and possess less sweetness', thus he advises the addition of equal quantities of Muscat and Chasselas. In Ortlieb's very first *vin de paille*, he also used the Kleiner Rauschlinger, which is the Knipperlé and, in fact, this variety is sometimes called the Ortlieber. This was because as a nurseryman, Ortlieb was so impressed by the huge cropping capacity of the Kliener Rauschling vine that he was almost fanatical in selling it to other growers and was so successful that by the end of the next century, it accounted for a quarter of all the vineyards in Alsace. Little wonder, then, that he should make the following note in his treatise 'May I be pardoned my vanity if I dared to express the wish that this Kleiner Rauschlinger be referred to, in preference, as Ortlieber's vine?' Well, his wish came true, the only pity being that someone so passionate about the quality and authenticity of a great *vin de paille* should be remembered for such a common grape variety. Not only is the quality of this grape obviously so poor when cropped so high, but its propensity to rot is just as rampant as its yield.

Back to the present and the *vins de paille* currently produced, those of Marcel Deiss and Domaine Zind Humbrecht are not merely of a completely different order from anything else I have tasted, they are so authentic that such wines will never be commercially available. Even the microscopic amounts that have been available to the privileged few are not wines to drink, being far too viscous and intense for that, but they are profound wonders to behold. If you should get the chance, just sip and be bedazzled.

VIN DE GLACE

This is a recent phenomenon in Alsace, but likely to occur with greater frequency as more grapes are left on their vines to produce Vendange Tardive and SGN wines. *Vin de glace* is the French equivalent of German *Eiswein*. When grapes are left on the vine for late-harvest wines, they run the risk of inclement weather but, should they be frozen by snow or frost, it is possible to harvest the crop quickly and to press the grapes while they are still frozen. Only the water in the grapes freezes, and this rises to the top of the vat in the form of ice. If this is skimmed off, it leaves behind a condensed and concentrated juice that is capable of producing a wine of an equivalent quality to SGN, but in a totally different style. From the disappointing quality of some Alsace *vins de glace*, some producers obviously think that it is merely the novelty of harvesting in the snow that makes these wines, but they have to have the ice skimmed, otherwise the water melts back into the juice, which reverts to its pre-frozen composition and the result is nothing special.

Those produced so far include a Lucien Albrecht 1985 Grand Cru Pfingstberg, which was harvested on 13/14 December at -10°C, but is not that special; Albert Mann produced a Riesling Pfleck 'Cuvée des Premières Neiges' in 1987, which was harvested at 94°Oechsle, although he makes no *vin de glace* claim for this wine, merely stating that it was harvested in snow; the Seppi Landmann 1988 Grand Cru Zinnkoepflé lacked richness, although he is capable of excellent SGN (yet, even these have to be viewed more as sweet Vendanges Tardives than a full botrytis style); but nobody can touch the quality and style of André Kientzler, who has twice harvested a Riesling Grand Cru Osterberg Vin de Glace. The first was in 1985 (106°Oeschle), but it was his second attempt in 1986 (117° Oeschle) that yielded the greatest *vin de glace* Alsace has so far produced. The 1986 is a wine of impeccable quality and finesse, with an excruciatingly high level of acidity when young, which will guarantee its place in oenological history in the decades to come.

HISTORIC VILLAGE *APPELLATIONS*

Most of the village *appellations* that have survived today are based on Pinot Noir, usually famous for red wine, but not exclusively so, and date back to hazy beginnings during the medieval period. Rouge d'Ottrott is perhaps the most well known of these, although the red wines currently produced are rather lightweight products. Those from Ch. Wantz are the best, although they are simply fruity wines of no great claim or complexity. Rouge de Rodern ranks as the second most famous of this group, but its wines are not as commonly encountered as those of Ottrott, although those I have tasted have had a lovely varietal aroma of cherries. Rouge de St-Hippolyte, also known for centuries, has been somewhat in the shadow of Ottrott, but its best wines (Muller-Koeberle) are much finer and have some spicy-cherry complexity. Georges Klein has made wine of the same ilk in 1989, but that is the only vintage I have tasted, so I cannot say whether it is always that good or merely a flash in the pan in a great, rich vintage. Jacques Iltis produces lovely drinking wine, although it does not have the finesse or the complexity of either Muller-Koeberle or Georges Klein and reminds me more of an exceptional Rouge d'Ottrott than a typical Rouge de St-Hippolyte. Another village that has had a reputation for its Pinot Noir wines, although for nothing more pretentious than a simple rosé style, is Marlenheim, but by far the best wine of this ilk made today is the Rosé de Turckheim from the local cooperative.

KLEVENER DE HEILIGENSTEIN

This is an oddity in Alsace for three reasons. First, it is from a grape variety that is apparently native to the Jura further south and certainly not found anywhere else in Alsace. Secondly, of all the famous village *appellations* (Rouge d'Ottrott, Rouge de Rodern, Rouge de St-Hippolyte, Rosé de Marlenheim, etc.), only Klevener de Heiligenstein is specifically defined in the regulations. Thirdly, it is the only grape that is confined by law to a geographical area within Alsace (just 13 hectares within the commune of Heiligenstein, although, according to INAO, this could theoretically be extended to a maximum of 200 hectares in Heiligenstein, Barr, Goxwiller, Gertwiller and Obernai, but this would still amount to a geographical limitation).

Klevener should not be confused with the common synonym for the Pinot Blanc, Klevner or Clevner, which is always spelt without the middle 'e' of Heiligenstein's Klevener. The Klevener de Heiligenstein is supposed to be the Savagnin Rosé, which was introduced to this village in 1742 by Ehrhardt Wantz, whose ancestors run the small *négociant* firm of Ch. Wantz. The Savagnin Jaune or Savagnin Blanc is the grape that makes the famous *vin jaune* of the Jura, the most celebrated of which is the Vin Jaune de Château

Châlon. As some ampelographers are certain that the Savagnin Jaune or Savagnin Blanc is the Traminer, the existence of a pink-berried variant would suggest that this grape is the original Gewurztraminer (*see* the Traminer entry under 'Alternative Designations' for the argument against this). According to local growers, the Klevener is less susceptible to coulure at flowering and less vigorous. As a wine, Klevener de Heiligenstein is not dissimilar to Gewurztraminer, but it is lighter in body and more discreet in character, with a subdued spicy aroma and delicate fruity flavour. The very best are comparable to the more subtle versions of Gewurztraminer and have a certain finesse, but are best drunk within two to four years. They can last ten years or more, particularly if they are from bigger, richer vintages, but they seldom benefit, just mellow. Of the ten producers of this wine, the most consistent examples tasted have come from CV Andlau, Jean Hewang, Eugène Klipfel (not their own production, though) and Ch. Wantz.

THE *VINS DE PAYS* OF ALSACE

The first *vin de pays* in Alsace was a Vin de Pays du Bas-Rhin, produced by Georges Boehler of Kuttolsheim in 1984. He had applied for AOC status for 20 years, but had been denied, so he decided to produce a *départemental vin de pays*, as every French *département* has the right to produce such wines (although they must, of course, be submitted for tasting and analytical tests before being granted *vin de pays* status). No doubt Monsieur Boehler felt hard done by, especially as the next village to Kuttolsheim is Nordheim, where 119 hectares are classified AOC Alsace and more than 60 of these are planted and in production, but he is unfortunately on the periphery of the AOC region and I suppose (because I do not own vines there!) that the line has to be drawn somewhere. Just over the hills to the north-west of Kuttolsheim is the village of Rangen, which also possesses vineyards. Think what a fine old rumpus that would make if the growers were allowed to produce AOC Alsace because there would be nothing to stop them from selling their wines by the village name, as growers in other Alsace villages do, and what would the producers of Grand Cru Rangen make of that? Of course, if the vineyards happen to be suitable (and

I have no idea whether they are), why should they or, indeed, Monsieur Boehler be denied?

The current production of *vins de pays* in Alsace stands at just under 100 hectolitres from just a handful of producers, all but one of whom produce Vin de Pays du Bas-Rhin, and one producer of Vin de Pays du Haut-Rhin (Roger Barbier of Horbourg-Wihr) made his last wine in 1991 and has now retired. To illustrate that these *vins de pays*, as modest as their status is, are not merely rubber-stamped, only 67 hectolitres of Vin de Pays du Bas-Rhin was passed out of the 83 hectolitres proffered in 1991. The pass rate for Vin de Pays du Haut-Rhin was even less, with just 28 hectolitres out of 49 making the grade. The maximum yield is 90 hectolitres per hectare, which was less than AOC Alsace until an annual limit of 80 hectolitres per hectare was introduced in 1987. In addition to Monsieur Boehler, other *vin de pays* producers in Alsace include Liliane Faust, Jean-Paul Heim, Alain North, Michel Stutzmann, Joseph Vierling, Lucie Vierling and, in the Haut-Rhin, Roger Barbier, although he, as has been mentioned, retired after the 1991 vintage.

These *vins de pays* are all varietal wines and all grapes permitted for the production of AOC Alsace are also allowed for the *départemental* country wine *appellations*. Boehler, for example, has produced Pinot Blanc, Riesling and Muscat Ottonel. I have nothing against the production of such wines, but they are not produced from the same vineyards as AOC Alsace and, as argued in the introduction to 'Blended Wines' earlier in the chapter, the increasing production of *grand cru* wines demands a parallel *vin de pays* to redress the effect they are having on the overall quality of generic Alsace wines (see 'AOC Grand Cru' below).

AOC CRÉMANT D'ALSACE

Although small growers such as Dirler of Bergholtz had made Vin Mousseux d'Alsace as early as 1880, it was not until 1900 that Dopff Au Moulin established the sparkling wine industry on a truly commercial scale. Due to a clerical error, however, the designation Vin Mousseux d'Alsace was denied equal status when the AOC laws were drawn up for Alsace in 1962 and this was not rectified until 1976, when AOC Crémant d'Alsace was introduced for the region's *méthode champenoise* wines.

Since 1976, the production of Crémant d'Alsace has increased from less than 1 million bottles to more than 15 million, as the number of producers has risen from just 10 (3 cooperatives, 3 *négociants* and 4 growers) to 438 (18 cooperatives, 16 *négociants* and 404 growers). The quality is already good and getting better, although apart from a small handful of *cuvées*, every time I have conducted comprehensive Crémant d'Alsace tastings, it has been relatively easy to blend infinitely more characterful and noticeably better balanced wines from the mass of wines present than could be found in any of their component parts. This indicates that most sparkling wine producers still have a long way to go in mastering the art of blending and, for some, this could simply be due to their not sourcing grapes from a sufficient number of good sites. For others, it could be that they already do this, but have not vinified each source separately (even *mono-cru* Champagnes are blended from different parts of the vineyard, where maybe the soil, drainage, height, aspect, microclimate, variety or age of the vines make possible a variety of blending ingredients). The level of technical expertise and personal passion is very high in Alsace, but I suppose there must be some who are simply bad blenders and it is no good having a palette of the finest colours if you cannot paint.

The quality of Crémant d'Alsace should obviously continue to improve as the most talented producers gain experience, but specifically as they:

- become willing to grow grapes specifically for Crémant;
- discover where those vineyards are best situated;
- source their grapes from as many areas as possible;
- vinify these components in smaller, separate lots;
- commit investment to building up stocks of mature wines for blending into future non-vintage *cuvées*;
- keep the amount of processing (fining and filtering) to the minimum, prior to bottling for the second fermentation;
- give the wines longer time on the yeast before disgorging (although there is no intrinsic advantage to be gained from allowing a period in excess of three years for every wine, as it depends on the quality and character of each individual *cuvée* how long the autolysis will last and whether the wines will benefit from being kept after that – some wines will not improve after 18 months *sur lie*);

- allow more time between disgorgement and shipping to develop hints of toasty bottle-aromas and endow the wines with a natural mellowness, which will reduce the amount of dosage necessary;
- experiment with the possibilities of utilizing different types, styles and ages of base wine for the dosage, as the tiniest adjustment at this point will have a magnified effect on the character of the finished product.

These procedures are not merely part of the learning curve; most winemakers probably understand each and every one of them, but may be prevented from taking the fullest advantage due to the expense involved. It is a fact that the production of even the most basic *méthode champenoise* wine requires a substantial investment in equipment and stocks, and most of the best producers happen to be large *négociants* and cooperatives. There are, of course, some excellent small producers and, as money cannot replace talent, some of the largest producers have sold some of the lousiest sparkling wines. It is evidently possible for small growers to make a fine quality fizz on a shoestring, but the financial burdens involved will always limit their numbers.

Then there is the question whether the effort is worth it, and this itself can be influenced by the state of the market. When Kuentz-Bas, for example, produced a very fine, pure-Chardonnay Crémant d'Alsace in 1982 and 1983, there was a shortage of Champagne, which had pushed up prices to such an extent that the time, effort and expense of producing a Champagne alternative of this quality was worthwhile. By the time they were ready to be launched on the market, however, there was a glut of large Champagne vintages, which had encouraged the production of inexpensive BOB (buyer's own brand) Champagnes in French supermarkets. Kuentz-Bas found it impossible to obtain anything like the price paid for the poorest quality BOB, which was preferred by consumers to this infinitely superior Crémant d'Alsace because, whatever it tasted like, the supermarket wine bore the famous Champagne *appellation*.

Kuentz-Bas gave up production after only two vintages because the cost of crafting a Crémant of this quality was not recovered in the price it fetched. I think they made the wrong decision, not simply because Champagne prices are as cyclic as their stocks

(which go up and down due to the vagaries of that region's northern climate), but because a firm of Kuentz-Bas' repute could get a
good enough price for a strictly limited production, if it were
offered on a market that appreciated individual wines of quality,
whatever their origin or *appellation*. Kuentz-Bas did not even try to
sell this wine in the UK, for example, and when I approached their
agents to buy a couple of cases, the response I received was 'What
Chardonnay Crémant?' and heard no more. If a wine journalist
who has tasted the wine and wants to buy it cannot lay his hands on
it (I did later by physically collecting the stuff by car), how can
Kuentz-Bas say that it was not possible to sell the wine? If the wine
is good enough and its producer has a sufficiently high reputation,
Crémant d'Alsace will sell at the right price.

Initially, Riesling was the dominant variety for sparkling Alsace
wine, but its character was soon found to be too fruity and aromatic for the classic *méthode champenoise* style and this conflicted
with the subtle influence of autolysis, which gives any sparkling
wine its classic 'champagny' character. In very little time, the somewhat neutral Pinot Blanc was considered far more suitable,
especially because it possessed excellent acidity (though, of course,
nowhere near as much as the Riesling). If the Pinot Blanc had one
major stumbling block for sparkling wine, it was that it can often
lack sufficient richness and several producers have now come to the
conclusion that the Tokay-Pinot Gris, which has both acidity and
richness, should play a far greater role. Auxerrois has also proved
extremely suitable, but is usually preferable in a blend with Pinot
Blanc for very similar reasons to those expressed for the blending of
these two varieties for still wines (*See* the Pinot entry under 'Alsace
Varietals'). More and more of these wines are being sold by the
vintage but, if it is worth purchasing, even a non-vintage Crémant
d'Alsace will improve if kept for a further one to two years. Most
vintage *cuvées* drink well at around three years after the date of
harvest, but will be even better after five and the best will develop
nicely for up to eight. Crémants d'Alsace Rosé are the least appreciated and most underrated of all the region's sparkling wines. These
are really delightful wines that can possess a finer purity of Pinot
Noir perfume and flavour than many pink Champagnes and are
best consumed within three to five years.

Many firms sell Crémant d'Alsace that they have not produced
themselves, but has been fabricated for them by various specialists

such as Dopff Au Moulin and Laugel. Quite often the deal will be to supply the finished wine, but some houses will supply grapes that the specialists convert into Crémant d'Alsace. The vast majority of the smaller grower-producers of sparkling wine will send their wines away to be riddled, disgorged and dosaged. The following firms are those I know for sure produce their own sparkling wine, but in no way does this represent a definitive list (the date in parentheses indicates when they first made/sold sparkling wine): Lucien Albrecht (1972/73), CV Beblenheim (1975/77), Paul Blanck (1982/84), E. Boeckel (1980/82), Joseph Cattin (1980/82), Domaine de la Ville de Colmar (1981/82), Robert Dietrich (1981/83), Dopff Au Moulin (c. 1900), Willy Gisselbrecht (1981/83), CV Ingersheim (1981/82), CV Kientzheim-Kaysersberg (1981/83), Marc Kreydenweiss (1981/83, although no longer in production), Kuentz-Bas (1982/84), Laugel (1981/82), Muré (1982), CV Obernai (1980/81), CV Pfaffenheim (1981/2), CV Ribeauvillé (1981/82), Edgard Schaller (1974/76), Pierre Sparr (1976/77), CV Westhalten (1974/75).

IN A TOTALLY DIFFERENT CLASS

Dopff Au Moulin
Although dressed up to look a bit like an upmarket Italian fizz, the *Cuvée Bartholdi* is a very stylish wine that needs about eight years from the date of harvest to show its full, classy potential. The *Blanc de Noirs* has a noticeably deeper hue than most Crémant d'Alsace, a full body and rich, apricoty fruit that will improve for at least five years after the date of harvest. The *Brut Sauvage* is a complex, biscuity wine of classic, bottle-aroma-enhanced autolytic character that needs eight years to show its true finesse.

Laugel
Although this firm has a 'pile 'em up, knock 'em out' reputation, all its Crémant d'Alsace *cuvées* are at least good and the *Blanc de Blancs* and *Blanc de Noirs* are exceptionally fine, smooth and stylish wines.

OTHER TOP PERFORMERS

CV Bennwihr: very fresh, well-constructed *Cuvée Hansi Réserve* with a commercially well-tuned dosage. **Paul Blanck:** a fine vintage *Domaine des Comtes de Lupfen*, shows its class on the nose. **Robert Dietrich:** a vintage of typically excellent acidity and richness that is capable of fine toasty bottle aromas after four or five years; very good *rosé*, with fine varietal perfume and elegant Pinot fruit. **Dopff & Irion:** noticeably improved in the last few years and now ranks favourably against *Cuvée Julien* from Dopff Au Moulin, who make this wine for Dopff & Irion using Dopff & Irion grapes. **Dopff Au Moulin:** *Cuvée Julien* is above average quality for the *appellation*, but merely acceptable by Dopff Au Moulin's own high standards; the *rosé* has a creamy sauce Anglaise nose and good Pinot fruit, but again, merely relatively acceptable. **W. Gisselbrecht:** refreshing fruit, fine acidity. **CV Hunawihr:** the *Cuvée Calixte II 1123* varies from good to very good. **Kientzheim-Kaysersberg:** fine balance, technically excellent mousse and normally one of the most mature *cuvées* on the market. **Kuentz-Bas:** fine, fresh and fragrant vintage *Réserve Personnelle*, although the intrinsically superior vintage *Brut de Chardonnay* is alas no more. **Landmann Seppi:** the *Brut de Brut Vallée Noble* usually needs an extra 6–12 months in bottle to bring out the bouquet. **Laugel:** all *cuvées* are well made and represent excellent value for money. **Hubert Metz:** the *Réserve de la Dîme* may not be quite the quality of Sorg or Sparr, for example, but it is nevertheless a good, full-bodied, nicely balanced wine that is well above the norm for this *appellation*. **CV Pfaffenheim:** the *Hartenberger Pinot Gris* was one of the first wines that demonstrated the potential of Tokay-Pinot Gris for these wines and it certainly used to be one of the very best *cuvées* of Crémant d'Alsace available, but on its current form can be classified only as good, not outstanding (potentially in a totally different class). **Bruno Sorg:** his *Blanc de Blancs* has fine fruit-acidity balance and autolytic character. **Pierre Sparr:** the *Brut Réserve* stands out due to its fine autolysis on the nose and has the richness of fruit that typifies most Sparr wines. **CV Turckheim:** the *Mayerling* non-vintage brut has an exceptional richness of fruit, balanced by excellent acidity and lifted by autolytic finesse on the nose (potentially in a totally different class). **Wolfberger:** decent non-vintage generic, fine non-vintage *Rosé* (redcurrant Pinot Noir fruit), good vintage in a garish lilac and white transfer bottle, but the non-vintage *Prestige Cuvée*, in its even more garish gold-embossed bottle, is easily the best with extra Tokay-Pinot Gris richness and just enough Riesling to correct the balance and keep the wine lively for a good five years, although the *Riesling* would attract only Sekt lovers.

AOC ALSACE *GRAND CRU*

It is a puzzling fact that while Alsace has a more complex geology than any other region in France, it was not until the 1980s that its first *grands crus* were delimited. The profusion of different soils and microclimates in Alsace produces radically different styles of wine within each grape variety, yet for 30 years the wines have been marketed as nothing more specific than generic varietals.

The expression *grand cru* was introduced with the AOC regulations of 1962, but as merely an adjunct to the one and only *appellation*, Vin d'Alsace, for wines of superior variety and technical specification. The concept of individual sites did not appear on the statute books until November 1975 and the first list of these did not appear until 1983, although the very first *grand cru*, that of Schlossberg in Kientzheim and Kaysersberg, was specially delimited in 1975 to illustrate the law. In 1987 the number of *grands crus* increased to 48, but only 25 had actually been delimited. In March the following year two more were added and, in 1990, Kaefferkopf was proposed, bringing the total of *grands crus* to 51. Although barely 5 per cent of the total volume of Alsace wine, the number and variety of *grands crus* that are progressively becoming available is disproportionately large, due to the increasing number of producers who are making a greater range of these wines. Some of the *grands crus* may be too large to be authentic (*See* 'The Delimitation Process' in Chapter 5), but this will have little immediate effect on consumers, who do not know the size of individual *crus* and do not care. Even if they did come across the size of a *grand cru*, they would not have the faintest idea whether it happened to be too big or too small. What counts for the customer is the availability and quality of the wine itself. If there are too many wines, even if there just appear to be too many, they will lose their élitist value. If the wines are not significantly superior in quality, the term *grand cru* will lose all meaning and further devalue the wines.

In view of this, the fact that the *grand cru* habit is on the increase should be a warning signal for producers in Alsace and the relevant authorities, but it does not seem as if the signal is getting through. These wines more than doubled in just three years (from almost 18,000 hectolitres to well over 37,000 between 1985 and 1988) and although the current production appears to have levelled off, hovering at just under 40,000 hectolitres, this is merely the lull before the storm. The volume of *grand cru* wine is set to explode as new plantations come on stream, as the legislation and the increase in price these wines attract have caused growers to rip up unclassified varieties and replant with noble ones.

With the production of *grands crus* increasing, so the need to introduce a lower *appellation* becomes more apparent, as the greater amount of *grand cru* cream that is skimmed off the generic blends, the more attenuated and less interesting those wines will become. As new Alsace consumers begin with generic wines, the effect on the future base of this region's customers could be catastrophic. It is a little like the ecological future of the world; nothing is happening at the moment, so nobody gives a damn, but if anything has a chance of working it must be introduced now, not when it is too late. It is not as if the problem were a difficult one. When more and more cream is skimmed off the top of the pot, the only way to maintain quality in the middle is by siphoning off equally increasing amounts from the bottom. As already touched on earlier in this chapter, the simplest way to achieve this would be to create a new denomination called Vin de Pays du Côtes d'Alsace, which could be used to blend the lesser quality elements of AOC Alsace. This would not only redress the balance of production and quality, but would add an exciting new dimension to the way Alsace wines are marketed. The resistance to this in the region itself has been that a *vin de pays* would lower the image of Alsace wines, but the opposite is true. *Vins de pays* are seen by young consumers as fresh, unpretentious introductions to the higher-quality AOCs of a wine region, whereas the cheapest Alsace wine currently available is Edelzwicker, a product that is dull, boring and only harms the reputation of Alsace. The consumer is often willing to pay good money for a *vin de pays* and many of these wines are far more expensive than the cheapest Edelzwicker. In a way, the introduction of a Vin de Pays du Côtes d'Alsace would be equally as cosmetic as the banning of Zwicker, but the results could enhance the reputation of Alsace, rather than debasing it and would lead to increased consumer awareness and bigger, more honest, profits.

For specific recommended *grand cru* wines, *see* 'The Grands Crus' in Chapter 5.

MEDALS, GONGS AND COMPETITION WINES

The public's growing awareness of competition medals has meant that such wines are sold off at a premium and this has led many producers actively to pursue the competition circuit with wines made to stand out. These have become known as 'competition' wines and they are made, not by everybody, but by a great many and by every type of producer, from small growers to cooperatives and large shippers. A competition wine is one that easily flatters the judges, even though the judges themselves like to think not. The medals are usually identified by narrow neck labels, but can also be simply part of the main label. Some producers even make a speciality range of medal-winning wines, but are they worth seeking out?

The local **Colmar** medals are the most commonly encountered ones, but **Paris, Mâcon** and the **Sigillé de Qualité** (Confrérie St-Étienne) are also found. To generalize, most of the supposedly dry styles have at least a little residual sugar and are at their exuberantly drinkable peak in the actual year of their awards. I have found that many **Colmar** medal-winning wines tend to fade quickly thereafter. Some break up within a couple of years, others merely lose their spark. Many lose their aromatic attack first of all, then go flabby or flat on the finish. The level of residual sweetness in a well-balanced medal-winner will be less important and such wines should age well, although they definitely are a minority. Having said that, I have found the **Colmar** results more consistent than either **Paris** or **Mâcon**, although the **Sigillé de Qualité** is an infinitely higher grade than all of them. The **Sigillé de Qualité** wines hold up much longer in bottle and tend not to be so obviously fattened up and sweet, but they are by no means free from the 'competition' wine style.

8

The People and their Wines

The people of Alsace are a fascinating amalgam: definitely German, defiantly French and yet definitively neither, which is, in essence, the nature of the wines they tend to produce.

Never have I come across a region packed with so many colourful people. How can one great wine family, such as the Dopffs, produce two such contrasting personalities as cousins Guy and Pierre-Étienne? The discreet and diminutive Guy (Dopff & Irion), who is so precise, Gallic and genteel and the slightly eccentric, big hearted Pierre-Étienne (Dopff Au Moulin), who has smiling eyes and a straight face. From two cousins to two brothers, the Trimbachs: Hubert the extrovert and Bernard the introvert, both utterly charming and totally different. The irrepressible Johnny Hugel. Totally unique, thank God, this one-off can be absolutely enchanting in small doses. He is so packed with facts, figures and opinions that he simply must tell everyone or go pop! Guy, Pierre-Étienne, Hubert, Bernard and Johnny; five such delightfully diverse individuals, yet plucked from just two villages, Riquewihr and Ribeauvillé, which should give you a clue to how many original characters there are in the entire region.

TRADE STRUCTURE

There are in excess of 7,000 vineyard owners in Alsace, which is less than two-thirds of the number there were 20 years ago and a mere fifth of those declaring harvests prior to the advent of AOC. Less than a quarter of the current number of vineyard owners actually sell wine. In terms of actual sales, the twenty most important producers in 1991 were, in order of volume (with their 1986 positions in parentheses):

1. Wolfberger (1)	11. Dopff Au Moulin (14)
2. CV Obernai (2)	12. CV Pfaffenheim (24)
3. Arthur Metz (3)	13. CV Ingersheim (9)
4. CV Turckheim (4)	14. Lucien Freyermuth (18)
5. Michel Laugel (11)	15. CV Ribeauvillé (16)
6. J. Hauller & Fils (13)	16. Dopff & Irion (10)
7. CV Beblenheim (7)	17. CV Hunawihr (15)
8. CV Bennwihr (8)	18. CV Kientzheim (20)
9. Union Sigolsheim (6)	19. Gustave Lorentz (12)
10. Jean Biecher & Fils (19)	20. Eugène Klipfel (32)

Breakdown and Comparison of Alsace Producers				
	Number[1]	Hectares	Production[2]	Sales
Cooperative Members	2,962[3]	4,689	393,417 (35.3%)	39%
Négociants	41	432	31,970 (2.9%)	37%
Vignerons-Récoltants[4]	424	2,877	228,590 (20.5%)	19%
Vignerons-Partiel[5]	874	3,387	286,547 (25.7%)	5%
Vendeurs de Raisins[6]	2,403	1,605	130,531 (11.7%)	–
Vendeurs en Vrac[7]	198	462	41,640 (3.7%)	–
Own consumption[8]	485	35	1,959 (0.2%)	–
TOTAL	7,387	13,487	1,114,654 (100%)	100%

Notes
1 **Number** column represents the number of enterprises or members.
2 **Production** is expressed in hectolitres.
3 2,962 **Cooperative Members** represent 18 producing cooperatives.
4 **Vignerons-Récoltants** sell, in principle, the entire produce of their vineyards under their own label, although there is nothing to stop them selling wine in cask to *négociants* from time to time.
5 **Vignerons-Partiel** or, more correctly, *Vignerons-Récoltants Partiel*, traditionally sell part of their crop under their own label and the rest to cooperatives or *négociants*.
6 **Vendeurs de Raisins** sell all their crop to *négociants*.
7 **Vendeurs en Vrac** make wine and sell it in bulk to *négociants*.
8 **Own consumption** corresponds to those family holdings that are too small to commercialize, the output of which is consumed by the owners.

With cooperatives taking 11 of the top 18 places and, more important, quantitatively, the first, second and fourth positions, they are certainly the most powerful marketing force in Alsace and they are growing, not declining as some sources suggest. Ten years ago, the cooperative membership stood at 2,533, owned 3,511 hectares and yielded 297,000 hectolitres or 33 per cent of total production, whereas today the membership stands at 2,962 (up 17 per cent) and they own 4,689 hectares (up 34 per cent), yielding just over 393,000 hectolitres (up 32 per cent) or 35.3 per cent of total production (which is an increase of 10 per cent in an expanding market). These are the official CIVA figures. The cooperatives themselves claim a slightly higher membership (3,147), which might be explained if some are members of more than one cooperative, but a slightly lower vineyard area (4,582 hectares).

Cooperatives

The commercial growth of the cooperatives can be attributed partly to tax advantages that are not made available to *négociants*. The original reason for such tax advantages (which apply throughout France) was to encourage investment in technology in a bid to raise the quality of wines produced by thousands of family enterprises that were too small and too cut off to purchase vital, but very expensive, equipment for themselves. Nowhere has this strategy worked so well as in Alsace. It is unfair competition, as far as the *négoce* may be concerned, but the consumer has benefited as much as the cooperatives and *négociants* have been forced to respond in terms of quality and value.

Table A shows the relative size of the Alsace cooperatives by their total membership and the number of hectares of vines their members own:

Table A: The Alsace Cooperatives

Cooperative	Members	Cooperative	Hectares
1. Eguisheim[1]	453	1. Eguisheim[1]	638
2. Traenheim[2]	270	2. Dambach[1]	403
3. Turckheim	261	3. Bennwihr	340
4. Dambach[1]	252	4. Traenheim[2]	305
5. Pfaffenheim	203	5. Turckheim	302
6. Bennwihr	202	6. Sigolsheim	285
7. Cléebourg[3]	192	7. Ingersheim	259
8. Ingersheim	181	8. Beblenheim	231
9. Andlau	165	9. Westhalten[5]	230
10. Orschwiller[4]	140	10. Andlau	227
11. Sigolsheim	140	11. Ribeauvillé	217
12. Westhalten[5]	135	12. Obernai[2]	205
13. Beblenheim	125	13. Hunawihr	194
14. Vieil Armand[1,6]	125	14. Pfaffenheim	190
15. Kientzheim	119	15. Kientzheim	170
16. Hunawihr	96	16. Cléebourg[3]	147
17. Ribeauvillé	78	17. Orschwiller[4]	123
18. Obernai[2]	10	18. Vieil Armand[1,6]	116

Note

1 The cooperative of Eguisheim is better known as Wolfberger and includes the cooperatives of Soultz-Wuenheim (Vieil Armand in the table) and Dambach in its group, although the membership and vineyards of all individual cooperatives are recorded separately and not included in Eguisheim's statistics.

2 The cooperatives of Obernai and Traenheim belong to DIVINAL, although their individual membership and vineyards are recorded separately here.

3 This is the cooperative of Cléebourg, Oberhoffen, Rott & Steinseltz.

4 This is the cooperative of Orschwiller-Kintzheim.

5 This is the cooperative of Westhalten-Soultzmatt.

6 This is the trading name of the cooperative of Soultz-Wuenheim.

7 This is the cooperative of Kientzheim-Kaysersberg.

Négociants

There are just 41 *négociants* in Alsace. A *négociant* is a commercial wine producing company that supplements its needs with grapes, juice or wine purchased from other growers. The nearest translation for the term *négociant* is trader or merchant, the name deriving from the traditional practice with growers (to buy wine) and wholesalers or other customers (to sell it). At its highest level, it is an honourable and demanding profession. It is easy enough to buy grapes or wines every year, but to buy or vinify grapes and wines that are of a quality and character that the merchant knows will enable him to blend something his customers will immediately recognize as being, say, the Trimbach, Hugel or Kuentz-Bas style, requires great skill and experience.

Les Grandes Maisons d'Alsace

This is the title of a group of eight top producers that was formed in the 1970s to promote a certain image of Alsace in general and to market their own wines in particular. They obviously hope to assume a reputation and mystique similar to that of the Syndicat de Grandes Marques in Champagne and, like a dozen members of that organisation, the Grandes Maisons have set up an annual school for candidates sponsored by the UK wine trade. Called L'École d'Alsace, its four-day course, launched in 1979, provides an excellent basic grounding in the wines of Alsace and, naturally, a complete introduction to the activities of all eight participating *maisons*. There is an examination at the end of the course with a special prize for the candidate with the highest marks. Again, mirroring the *champenois* example, ex-candidates have formed an association. Called 'The Stork and Glass Club', its slowly swelling membership meets for a prestigious annual dinner attended by the UK importers and their Alsace principals.

The Grandes Maisons d'Alsace are: Léon Beyer, Dopff & Irion, Dopff Au Moulin, Hugel & Fils, Kuentz-Bas, Gustave Lorentz, Domaine Schlumberger and F.E. Trimbach. Domaine Schlumberger replaced Preiss-Zimmer, when the vinification and global marketing of the wines of this firm were taken over by the CV Pfaffenheim. Ironically, the wines are infinitely better now than when Preiss-Zimmer was a member of the Grandes Maisons, but one of the criteria for membership is that each house must be a family company with centuries of experience, although this does raise a question-mark over Dopff & Irion, which is no longer owned by Guy Dopff's family. Other 'rules' insist that they must: be directly managed by descendants of the founder; own large holdings of the finest vineyards in the best sites; be faithful to the traditions handed down from father to son, yet remain attentive to the positive aspects of technological advances; maintain strict quality control from the grape to the bottle; have considerable reserves of bottle-matured stocks to ensure continuity of supply and quality; and, finally, for the head of the firm to be personally involved with all aspects of the business, from the vineyards to the cellars, sales and marketing.

Growers

The mention of *Vigneron-propriétaire* or *Propriétaire-viticulteur* on a label guarantees that the wine has been made from grapes grown in and restricted to vineyards belonging to the producer indicated. The vast majority of such wines will come from small growers, although *négociants* also own vineyards and many of these merchants produce wines exclusively from them. If you are not sure whether a *négociant* wine is from his own domaine, check the label for one of the terms mentioned, although such wines are usually presented with some sort of special emphasis that separates them from the rest of the range. If a range of special *cuvées* is marketed as coming only from the merchant's own vineyards, yet fails to indicate either *Vigneron-propriétaire* or *Propriétaire-viticulteur* on the label, I would take the claim with a pinch of salt, but do not rule out the possibility of the wines being truly special. Single-domaine wines might be capable of being the most express-ive and individual in Alsace, but the term is no guarantee of quality, only origin. There are good and bad growers, just as there are good and bad *négociants*. Most growers whose wines you are likely to encounter, even in the region itself, own in excess of five hectares, although there are relatively few such growers (*See* next section).

INFRASTRUCTURE OF VINEYARD HOLDINGS

There are in excess of 8,000 owners of the AOC vineyards currently cultivated in Alsace, but only 3,000 of these own more than one hectare. The spread of ownership among these 3,000 growers is as follows:

- 60 own vineyards of more than 10 hectares
- 440 own vineyards between 5 and 10 hectares

- 1,400 own vineyards between 2 and 5 hectares
- 1,100 own vineyards between 1 and 2 hectares

Most of the balance of 5,000-plus growers, who own less than one hectare each, are members of cooperatives. Although it is unrealistic to categorize growers by the size of their vineyards, without official statistics (which do not exist in this instance), it is possible to get a rough idea by looking at the average holdings of each category itself: Cooperative Members (1.5 hectares), *Négociants* (7.0), *Vignerons-Récoltants* (5.8), *Vignerons-Partiel* (2.7), *Vendeurs de Raisins* (0.6), *Vendeurs en Vrac* (1.8) and Own consumption (0.1).

PRODUCER PROFILES

If I have said it once, I have said it a thousand times – the human element is the joker in the pack when it comes to wine. The grape might be the single most important element in the entire panoply of factors that affect the taste and quality of wine, but even when the less tangible influences of soil and climate have played their part, humans can either maximize what nature has handed them or totally ruin it; from the grower, who has to make crucial decisions such as how and when to prune and harvest, to the winemaker, who receives grapes that represent 100 per cent of the wine's potential, yet whatever he does that will always be impossible to achieve. Not only that, but whatever he tries is not necessarily right or wrong. Many times I have seen neighbouring winemakers make a different quality and character of wine using virtually the same raw product, equipment and technique, while two very distant winemakers can produce remarkably similar wines from different grapes and contrasting equipment and techniques. Many inferior wines have been made by the misuse of up-to-date technology and I have seen dedicated winemakers produce spell-binding wines using what I would consider to be totally inadequate or inferior equipment and utilizing questionable techniques. At the end of the day it is the commitment and passion of the grower and winemaker that really counts.

Explanatory notes

1. Auxerrois is included with Pinot Blanc in *Grape Varieties*.

2. All measurements of area are rounded up or down to the nearest tenth of a hectare.

3. *Clos*, châteaux and brand names that are given prominence over the name of the producer are cross-referenced to the producer in question. Furthermore, readers may wish to look up separate entries for the *clos* and châteaux of Alsace in Chapter 5.

4. For brevity, CV is used in place of Cave/s Vinicole, Cave/s Viticole, Cave Coopérative Vinicole, Cave Coopérative Viticole and other similar titles in all situations except the full trading name, which is given under the main entry of each Producer Profile.

5. The length of each entry does not necessarily reflect the quality or importance of every producer. In many cases it does, but there are instances where I have come across wines about whose producers I know very little. There are, of course, many small growers whose wines I have never tasted. It is preferable in such cases, I think, to give the name, address and, if possible, a one-line comment than to omit the entry altogether and if I have managed to dig out a telephone number, so much the better. At the very least, it should help you to track down the producer of a wine you have encountered, even if I have not!

6. It is quite common for small growers to trade under the name of their father, grandfather, founder or whatever, yet be referred to within the area itself and in publications by their own names. As there are also many growers sharing the same surname, the multiplicity of titles can be confusing to say the least. Thus such names are cross-referenced to the main entries, where they are referred to as 'Also known as . . .'.

Adam

Les Caves JB Adam
5 rue de l'Aigle,
68770 Ammerschwihr
Telephone: (89) 78.23.21

Established: 1614 by the Adam
family
Production: 120,000 cases
Other labels: Veuve Joseph Pfister,
Schroedel
Vineyards: 13 hectares (10ha
Ammerschwihr, 3ha Ingersheim),
representing about 10 per cent of
total production, the balance
coming from 100 contracted
growers
Grape varieties: 1ha Sylvaner,
0.5ha Chasselas, 3ha Riesling, 4ha
Pinot Blanc, 2ha Tokay-Pinot Gris,
1ha Pinot Noir, 1ha
Gewurztraminer, plus 0.5ha other
varieties

Family enterprise for fourteen
generations, J.B. Adam is a well-
known but seriously underrated
producer of rich, upfront wines that
have been traditionally vinified in
large oak casks and age extremely
well. Delicious Pinot Blanc and very
fruity Pinot Noir, but essentially a
Riesling and Gewurztraminer
house, with a qualitative emphasis
on their Kaefferkopf holdings and
occasional, extremely successful
forays into late-harvest wines.
Cuvée Jean Baptiste is used for
various varietals and is usually
worth the premium charged.

Adam

Domaine Pierre Adam
8 rue Lt Louis Mourier,
68770 Ammerschwihr
Telephone: (89) 78.23.07

Established: 1950
Winemaker or *oenologist:* Rémy
Adam
Production: 7,500 cases
Vineyards: 10 hectares (4ha
Ammerschwihr, 2ha Kientzheim,
2ha Katzenthal, 0.5ha Mittelwihr,
0.5ha Ingersheim, 1ha Wihr-au-Val)
Grands crus: 1ha Schlossberg
(Kientzheim), 0.2ha Mandelberg
(Mittelwihr), 1ha Kaefferkopf
(Ammerschwihr)

The most outstanding wine I have
had from this small, traditional
producer was a Tokay-Pinot Gris
1988 Cuvée Prestige, which stood
out due to its botrytis character, but
it also has a reputation for Riesling
Grand Cru Mandelberg and
Gewurztraminer Kaefferkopf.
There is a Rouge d'Alsace
Sonnenberg, but I have not heard of
this *lieu-dit* and the Crémant
d'Alsace is a Pinot Auxerrois blend.

Albert

Prince Albert
Registered trademark used by
Albert Hertz for Crémant d'Alsace.
See Albert HERTZ

Albrecht

Domaine Lucien Albrecht
9 Grand'rue, 68500 Orschwihr
Telephone: (89) 76.95.18

Established: 1772 by Joseph
Albrecht
Production: 40,000 cases
Vineyards: 26 hectares (22ha
Orschwihr, 2ha Rouffach, 1ha
Guebwiller, 1ha Westhalten),
representing about 40 per cent of
total production; no vineyards are
rented, the balance coming from
non-contracted growers
Grape varieties: 3ha Sylvaner, 6ha
Riesling, 6ha Pinot Blanc, 3ha
Tokay-Pinot Gris, 2ha Pinot Noir,
5ha Gewurztraminer, 1ha Muscat
Rosé à Petit Grains, 1ha Muscat
Ottonel
Grands crus: 7ha Pfingstberg
(Orschwihr)

This producer is best known for his
Riesling Grand Cru Pfingstberg, of
which I have had some good
vintages (particularly 1983 and
1985 and even more especially the
Vendange Tardive style), but I find
the Tokay-Pinot Gris from that
vineyard considerably more
exciting. The *lieu-dit* Himmelreich
Riesling has left me unmoved, but I
have sometimes enjoyed
Gewurztraminer Bollenberg and the
best Sélections de Grains Nobles
have been Gewurztraminer and
Tokay-Pinot Gris.

Allimant-Laugner

Allimant-Laugner
10 Grand'rue, 67600 Orschwiller
Telephone: (88) 92.06.52

Encountered once and only the
1989 Pinot Noir tasted, but it was a
beautifully rich and luscious wine,

so it might not harm to seek out
other examples from this grower.

Alsace Seltz

See SELTZ

Alsace Willm

See WILLM

Amberg

Yves Amberg
19 rue Fronholz, 67680 Epfig
Telephone: (88) 85.51.28

This grower has 10 hectares of
vines and I have tasted a few of his
wines on occasions, but nothing
special stands out.

CV Andlau

Cave Vinicole d'Andlau
15 avenue des Vosges, 67140 Barr
Telephone: (88) 08.90.53

Current Membership: 165
Vineyards: 227 hectares
Part of the Divinal group of
cooperatives. Nothing startling
here, but some good value wines
can be found, the Klevener de
Heiligenstein can be of interest and
the occasional Sylvaner can be
exceptionally fine. *See* also Divinal,
CV OBERNAI and CV
TRAENHEIM

Anstotz

GAEC Anstotz & Fils
51 rue Balbach, 67310 Balbronn
Telephone: (88) 50.30.55

I know very little about this grower, except that he has some ten hectares of vineyards and I have tasted a very decent, but not really exciting, Riesling Westerweingarten.

Arbogast

Jean Arbogast
Clos Roth-stein, 18 rue de Soultz, 67120 Wolxheim
Telephone: (88) 38.17.10

I know very little about Jean Arbogast, apart from the fact that he owns a seven hectares calcareous-clay vineyard called Clos Roth-stein, from which I have tasted a Riesling and Pinot Noir, but they were merely ordinary in quality. *See* also Rothstein under 'Other Named Sites' in Chapter 5.

Arnold

Pierre Arnold
16 rue de la Paix, 67650 Dambach-la-Ville
Telephone: (88) 92.41.70

From a family of growers since 1711, Pierre Arnold farms six hectares today, including a plot of Riesling on Grand Frankstein, which produces his best wine.

Aussay

A second label of Wolfberger used on some export markets and accounting for less than 0.05 per cent of this cooperative's volume sales. *See* WOLFBERGER

Baltenweck

Jean-Pierre Baltenweck
68150 Ribeauvillé

Small grower with three hectares of vines, including just over a quarter of a hectare of Riesling on Grand Cru Geisberg.

Bannwarth

Laurent Bannwarth & Fils
9 route du Vin,
68420 Obermorschwihr
Telephone: (89) 49.30.87

This grower has nine hectares of vineyards, including Bildstoeckle, a *lieu-dit* from which I have tasted Riesling and Tokay-Pinot Gris but they were not special.

Barbier

Roger Barbier
2 route de Neuf Brisach
68180 Horbourg Wihr

A small producer up to and including the 1991 vintage of Tokay-Pinot Gris, Pinot Noir and Gewurztraminer under the Vin de Pays du Haut-Rhin denomination. He was the president of the Syndicat pour le Défense des Vins de Pays du Haut-Rhin, which must have involved a lot of lonely meetings, as he was the only producer. He is now retired and has rented out his vineyards, but to whom and for what remain a mystery.

Barmès-Buecher

Domaine Barmès-Buecher
30-32 rue Ste-Gertrude,
68920 Wettolsheim
Telephone: (89) 80.62.92

Established: 1985
Winemaker or *oenologist:* François
Barmès
Production: 1,000 hectolitres
Vineyards: 15 hectares (6.5ha
Wettolsheim, 1ha Eguisheim, 2ha
Wintzenheim, 3ha Turckheim,
2.5ha Colmar)
Grands crus: 1.2ha Hengst
(Wintzenheim), 0.8ha Steingrubler
(Wettolsheim)

An underrated producer who makes
excellent generic *cuvées* of
Gewurztraminer. Wines also from
the *grands crus* of Hengst (Riesling
especially recommended) and
Steingrubler (including the best
Gewurztraminer in this *cru*) and the
lieux-dits of Herrenweg and
Leimenthal. I have not been
impressed by the Crémant d'Alsace
(80 per cent Pinot Blanc, 15 per cent
Riesling, 5 per cent Chardonnay).

Baron de Hoen

Cooperative label for export
markets, accounting for 25 per cent
of CV Beblenheim's production.
See CV BEBLENHEIM

Baumann

J-J Baumann & Fils
43 rue du Général de Gaulle,
68340 Riquewihr
Telephone: (89) 47.92.47

Winegrowers since the beginning of
the seventeenth century, the current
incumbents are most adept at
Gewurztraminer, particularly from
the Grand Cru Sporen or when late
harvested. Also capable of fine
Riesling Schoenenbourg.

Baumann-Zirgel

Baumann-Zirgel
5 rue du Vignoble, Mittelwihr,
68630 Bennwihr-Mittelwihr
Telephone: (89) 47.90.40

Small grower with five hectares. I
have tasted an attractive, floral
Riesling that showed potential, a
rather forward Gewurztraminer,
and an elegant Tokay-Pinot Gris.

Baur

Charles Baur
29 Grand'rue, 68420 Eguisheim
Telephone: (89) 41.32.49

Consistently elegant Riesling and
beautifully ripe, concentrated
Gewurztraminer from Grand Cru
Eichberg. Sometimes a fine Muscat
too.

Baur

François Baur Petit-Fils
3 Grand'rue, 68230 Turckheim
Telephone: (89) 27.06.62

Again, I have very little experience,
but I have tasted a few excellent
Gewurztraminers, including one
superb Domaine Langehald 1989
Grand Cru Brand. Also known as
Pierre Baur.

Baur

Maison Léon Baur
71 rue du Rempart Nord,
68420 Eguisheim
Telephone: (89) 41.79.13

Established: 1738
Winemaker or *oenologist:* Jean
Louis Baur
Production: 15,000 cases
Vineyards: 10 hectares
(Ammerschwihr, Eguisheim)
Grands crus: 0.5ha Eichberg
(Eguisheim), 0.4ha Pfirsigberg
(Eguisheim), 0.5ha Kaefferkopf
(Ammerschwihr)

The roots of this house go back
seven years before its official
founding, to 1731, when Jean-
Jacques Baur purchased a small
lieu-dit called Stripicher (which
today is part of the Grand Cru
Eichberg) and planted its 48 ares –
just less than half a hectare – with
vines. Today, this vineyard,
together with 37 other parcels or
plots of vines, comprises the ten
hectares of Maison Baur. Seems to
excel with fruit-driven, oak-aged
Pinot Noir.

Baur

Pierre Baur
See François BAUR Petit-Fils

CV Beblenheim

Société Coopérative Vinicole de
Beblenheim
14 rue de Hoen, 68980 Beblenheim
Telephone: (89) 47.90.02

Established: 1953

Current membership: 125
Production: 300,000 cases
Vineyards: 231 hectares
(Beblenheim, Riquewihr,
Zellenberg, Mittelwihr, Bergheim,
St-Hippolyte, Ostheim,
Rorschwihr)
Grape varieties: 20 per cent
Sylvaner, 20 per cent Riesling, 25
per cent Pinot Blanc, 5 per cent
Tokay-Pinot Gris, 5 per cent Pinot
Noir, 20 per cent Gewurztraminer,
5 per cent Muscat
Grands crus: 50ha Sonnenglanz
and Altenberg
Labels: Caves de Hoen (25 per cent
of sales), Baron de Hoen (25 per
cent of sales), the balance being sold
under the cooperative's principal
label

I have tasted, on and off, very good
generic Pinot Blanc, Riesling Cuvée
Baron, Tokay-Pinot Gris Cuvée
Baron and Gewurztraminer Grand
Cru Sonnenglanz, but some years
are definitely better than others and
you cannot always rely on specific
varieties. These wines are very
sensibly priced, however, so it is
worth taking the trouble to taste
through the range and find which
are the bargains. In recent years, the
wines have begun to show more
upfront fruit style and nowhere is
this more noticeable than in this
cooperative's delicious, tropical
fruit Grand Cru de Bergheim.

Becht

Bernard Becht
84 Grand'rue, 67120 Dorlisheim
Telephone: (88) 38.20.37

This grower owns a substantial estate of some ten hectares, including a plot on the *lieu-dit* of Finkenberg in Avolsheim, where he produces a rich and sustaining Riesling with a fine, spicy aroma.

Becht

Pierre Becht
26 fbg des Voges, 67120
Dorlisheim
Telephone: (88) 38.18.22

Only one Pierre Becht wine tasted, a Crémant d'Alsace and, although there was nothing wrong with it, the wine did not grab me.

Bechtold

Domaine Jean-Pierre Bechtold
49 rue Principale, 67310
Dahlenheim
Telephone: (88) 50.66.57

Established: 1959
Winemaker or *oenologist:* Jean-Pierre Bechtold
Production: 9,000 cases
Vineyards: 15.5 hectares (10.5ha Dahlenheim, 5ha Scharrachbergheim)
Grands crus: 2.5ha Engelberg (Dahlenheim)

I have tasted the odd wine from this producer over the years and had been impressed by the Riesling Grand Cru Engelberg on a couple of occasions, but when I tasted a range of Bechtold's wines in 1990 nothing stood out.

Beck

Domaine Didier Beck
See Paul BECK

Beck

Gaston Beck
See Jean BECKER

Beck

Gilbert Beck
See Domaine du REMPART

Beck

Jean-Claude Beck
16 rue Irma-Mersiol, BP 16, 67650
Dambach-la-Ville
Telephone: (88) 92.47.29

Jean-Claude Beck has produced a decent Pinot Auxerrois and, in 1990, an excellent Gewurztraminer Fronholz Vieilles Vignes (from vines almost 70 years old) that was superbly rich and beautifully balanced, with exceptionally good acidity, but his quality is inconsistent. Also owns vines on the Grand Cru Frankstein.

Beck

Paul Beck succ.
1 rue Clémenceau, 67650
Dambach-la-Ville
(Cellars at 10 route du Vin, 67650 Dambach-la-Ville)
Telephone: (88) 92.40.17

Established: 1949 by the Beck family, vinegrowers since 1596

Winemaker or *oenologist:* Didier
Beck
Production: 5,000 cases
Vineyards: 6 hectares (3.2ha
Dambach-la-Ville, 2.5ha
Scherwiller-Châtenois, 0.3ha
Dieffenthal)
Grands crus: 1.6ha Frankstein
(Dambach-la-Ville)

Known variously as Domaine
Didier Beck, Domaine Paul &
Didier Beck and, of course, Paul
Beck succ., I have in no way been
put off by the awful labels (some of
my greatest finds have lurked
behind positively repulsive labels!),
but during my mass tasting of 900
Alsace wines in 1990, I was
alarmed to find that I had
consistently pushed these wines to
the back.

Beck

Domaine Paul & Didier Beck
See Paul BECK

Beck

René Beck
See Domaine du REMPART

Beck

René & Gilbert Beck
See Domaine du REMPART

Becker

J. Becker
See Jean BECKER

Becker

Jean Becker
4, route d'Ostheim, Zellenberg,
68430 Riquewihr
Telephone: (89) 47.90.16

Established: 1610 by George
Beckher
Production: 15,000 cases
Vineyards: 15 hectares (1.1ha
Riquewihr, 0.1ha Hunawihr,
12.4ha, Zellenberg, 0.8ha
Beblenheim, 0.4 Ribeauvillé)
including 0.2ha fallow, plus 4.05ha
rented (Hunawihr, Riquewihr,
Beblenheim and Zellenberg),
representing about 33 per cent of
total production
Grape varieties: 0.6ha Chasselas,
0.5ha Sylvaner, 3.9ha Riesling,
1.7ha Pinot Blanc, 1.4ha Tokay-
Pinot Gris, 2.1ha Pinot Noir, 3.8ha
Gewurztraminer, 0.3ha Muscat
Rosé à Petit Grains, 0.3ha Muscat
Ottonel, 0.2ha Muscat Blanc à Petit
Grains
Grands crus: 2.9ha Froehn
(Zellenberg), 0.4ha Sonnenglanz
(Beblenheim)

Also known as Gaston Beck, J.
Becker and Vignobles de propriété
Jean Philippe Becker, this hilltop
enterprise is run by a charming
family indeed: from the mother,
who is the most charming of all, to
the father, who is a shy and truly
gentle man (and happiest when he
can get lost in his own cellar,
keeping himself busy by lifting and
pushing stock from one corner to
another), the daughter, Martine,
who is by no means shy and lives
out of a suitcase, and last, but not

least, the son, Philippe, who is the winemaker and a man of very placid character indeed. Philippe does smile quite a lot, but you have to get to know him before he drops his guard to reveal the happy fellow behind that silent, reserved mask.

Until 1988, the Becker range of wines was decent and respectable, but not that exciting, except for the odd bottle (usually Muscat) of 20-or 30-year-old wine that could always be pulled from the depths of the cellars. In 1988, it was as though another winemaker had taken over, but it was still Philippe Becker and the change he effected went right across the board, although nowhere was it more noticeable than in his Froehn wines, particularly his Muscat. The onus of making the wine was probably placed on Philippe Becker's shoulders too early and too quickly. The firm is a busy little one and boasts a very strong coach business, so the tasting room is often packed out and Philippe is busy sorting out lots of tiny orders, which probably left him little time to flex his creative muscle. He was too hard pushed just trying to keep a grip on the production and keep the vineyard in order to worry very much about expressing himself. Since 1988, however, there has been a definite trend to more stylish wines of greater concentration and quality and no single wine marks this sea-change more than his incredible Muscat 1988 Sélection de Grains Nobles (see the appropriate entry in Chapter 6).

There can be no doubting that

Philippe Becker has always had the ability to make his mark. He is as well qualified as anyone and was, for example, a classmate of Olivier Humbrecht at wine school in Burgundy, but whereas Olivier and his father Léonard Humbrecht shared duties before finally splitting them down the middle (Olivier in the cellar, Léonard in the vineyard), Philippe's father was that much older and, although he still puts in a full day's work, I think he was relieved to pass the winemaking and viticultural reins of the business to Philippe as soon as his son came back clutching his degree, and the marketing and administration responsibilities to Martine. How did Philippe suddenly realize that he must somehow make his mark when he hardly had time to stop and think? I have my own personal theory. He certainly will not tell you this, but he had a horrific accident in the vineyard; the tractor fell on him and he was literally a hair's breadth away from being turned into natural fertilizer by shiny-bright agricultural blades. He spent, I think, about two months immobilized in bed and for a long time he was in a coma. They did not know whether he would pull through and there is a question about whether Philippe actually wanted to, once he regained consciousness, but I will not dwell on that. There is no way of proving this and Philippe will not thank me for even suggesting it, but I think that as he lay there, day after day, with nothing to think about apart from what he wanted for the future, he made a couple of promises to himself and we have seen the beginnings of one of those promises in the 1988 vintage.

The wines to watch at the moment are Muscat (he is the only master of botrytis Muscat in Alsace and is capable of much greater Grand Cru Froehn in classic dry style than he is currently producing), Rouge d'Alsace (achieving a delicious, fruit-driven, oak-aged essence of Pinot Noir), Riesling (especially his minerally complex Hagenschlauf), Gewurztraminer (both the opulently spicy Rimelsberg and the mellow, rich and spicy Grand Cru Froehn).

Becker

Vignobles de propriété Jean Philippe Becker
See Jean BECKER

Beck Hartweg

Yvette & Michel Beck Hartweg
5 rue Clémenceau, 67650 Dambach-la-Ville
Telephone: (88) 92.40.20

The Beck name is ubiquitous in this part of Alsace and most can claim to descend from the same beginnings in Dambach in 1590. This small grower has vineyards that include a plot of Riesling and Gewurztraminer on the Grand Cru Frankstein, but I have tasted better generic wines, particularly Pinot Noir.

CV Bennwihr

Caves Vinicoles de Bennwihr
BP 6, 68630 Bennwihr
Telephone: (89) 47.90.27

Established: 1946
Current membership: 202
Production: 280,000 cases (about 5 per cent sold in bulk to *négociants*)
Vineyards: 340 hectares
Grands crus: 20ha
Grape varieties: 19ha Sylvaner, 80ha Riesling, 120ha Pinot Blanc, 25ha Tokay-Pinot Gris, 25ha Pinot Noir, 65ha Gewurztraminer, 6ha Muscat (mixed)
Labels: Victor Preiss (5 per cent of sales), Lentz (10 per cent), Caves Klug (5 per cent), plus 20 per cent under various own-labels, the balance being sold under the cooperative's principal label

Also known as Société Coopérative Vinicole de Bennwihr, which is worth pointing out because villages in other regions often have more than one cooperative with slightly different names. When I first started writing this book, I was not very impressed with these wines, but the quality has dramatically improved in the last few years and many of the wines now offer tremendous value. The Pinot Noir Elevé en Fûts de Chêne in its tall, elegant bottle can be too oaky, but is very easy to drink. For Riesling it is best to go for one from the Rebgarten *lieu-dit*, which is the richest of the CV Bennwihr range and often has a touch of *pétillance* to lift the finish. The Cuvée Hansi Réserve Crémant d'Alsace is very consistent and

Pinot Blanc has been attractively fruity with a hint of spice since the 1985 vintage.

Bennwihr

Société Coopérative Vinicole de Bennwihr
See CV BENNWIHR

Berger

Frédéric Berger
8 rue de Riquewihr, 68630 Mittelwihr
Telephone: (89) 47.90.79

Small grower, traditionally vinified wines, best for Riesling, Gewurztraminer and Tokay-Pinot Gris, especially the Grand Cru Sonnenglanz.

Bernhard

Jean-Marc Bernhard
21 Grand'rue, 68230 Katzenthal
Telephone: (89) 27.05.34

A family enterprise since 1802, the Bernhards own some seven hectares of vines in the Katzenthal area.

Bernhard-Reibel

Cécile Bernhard-Reibel
20 rue de Lorraine, 67730 Châtenois
Telephone: (88) 82.04.21

This enterprise is the result of a merger between two long-established families, the Bernhards of Châtenois and the Reibels of Scherwiller. Run by Madame Cécile

Bernhard-Reibel, the combined vineyards now total 12 hectares and stretch from Domaine Weingarten in Châtenois to the hillside vineyards of Haut Koenigsbourg, with just a few vines growing on the plain. One-third of these vineyards is planted Riesling, the remainder being equally divided between Sylvaner, Pinot Blanc, Tokay-Pinot Gris, Pinot Noir and Gewurztraminer. Natural viticultural techniques are employed and the fermentation is temperature-controlled. The Domaine Weingarten wines are definitely the best, particularly Tokay-Pinot Gris Cuvée de la St-Hubert.

Besser

See Robert DIETRICH

Beyer

Léon Beyer
2 rue de la 1ère Armée, BP1, 68420 Eguisheim
Telephone: (89) 41.41.05

Established: Vintner 1580, Company 1867 by Émile Beyer
Production: 65,000 cases
Vineyards: 20 hectares (Eguisheim), representing about 70 per cent of production
Grands crus: 1ha Eichberg (Eguisheim), 3ha Pfersigberg (Eguisheim)

This fine old house has built up a well-deserved reputation for its uncompromisingly dry style, which often gives Beyer wines exceptional elegance in hotter years. Beyer is best known for its crisp and correct Riesling, which is made to accompany food and ages extremely gracefully. The Cuvée des Comtes d'Eguisheim was the most illustrious Gewurztraminer in the region until the mid-1980s, when it became somewhat inconsistent, but it is still top class in some years. Muscat can be Beyer's most underrated wine in rich, heady vintages like 1989 and, although I do not immediately think of Tokay-Pinot Gris when considering Léon Beyer, this producer has a superb Vendange Tardive, but then all of its late-harvest wines are superb.

Fundamentally more opposed to *grands crus* than any other producer, the current head of house, Marc Beyer, believes that man is ultimately responsible for the quality and thus the reputation of any wine and cites the rise and fall, and rise and fall again, of many 'great' Bordeaux châteaux in defence of this view. He is adamant that his firm will never market *grand cru* wines. Famous last words?

Beyer

Luc Beyer
7 place du Château, 68420 Eguisheim
Telephone: (89) 41.40.45

Old-established family of growers with vineyards on the Grand Cru Pfersigberg, but the most pleasant wine I have had here has been its vintage Crémant d'Alsace Cuvée Prestige.

Beyer

Patrick Beyer
27 rue des Alliés, 67680 Epfig
Telephone: (88) 85.50.21

The odd wine tasted occasionally, but nothing special noted.

Biecher

Jean Biecher & Fils
68590 St-Hippolyte

Included for the sake of completeness, I know absolutely nothing about this firm, other than its general location in St-Hippolyte. Although I have not seen these wines, let alone tasted them, I found this producer's name on official statistics, just as I was completing the manuscript for this book and was amazed to discover that it is the third-largest exporter of Alsace wines. It seems that an author's job is never done. Biecher does not even rank in the list of top 71 Alsace exporters to all countries excluding Germany (Germany is excluded because it is not just the largest export market for Alsace wine, but one that is so dominated by cheaper wines, particularly litre bottles of Edelzwicker, that its inclusion in global sales can distort the true picture). This might seem confusing, contradictory even, but it does help to clarify the situation. Biecher is, in fact, the second-largest exporter of Alsace wines to Germany, which pigeon-holes the firm as a bulk wine producer. Nevertheless, I will be hot foot to St-Hippolyte on my next trip to

Alsace because it is the 10th largest producer of all Alsace wines and with such a vast production, I must be optimistic of finding something worthwhile, even if most of it ends up at the lower end of the German market.

Biehler

A *sous marque* used by J. Hauller for Holland.
See J. HAULLER

Blanck

André Blanck
Ancienne cour des Chevaliers de Malte, 68240 Kientzheim
Telephone: (89) 78.24.72

The 'other Blancks' are in fact cousins and also own some impressive vineyards, including a small 1.5-hectare plot of Grand Cru Schlossberg. I have tasted the Riesling Cour des Chevaliers from this *grand cru* in several vintages and it is the lighter, lesser years, such as 1987, which usually excel. Also capable of producing exquisite SGN.

Blanck

GAEC Paul Blanck & Fils
Domaine des Comtes de Lupfen
32 Grand'rue, Kientzheim,
68420 Kaysersberg
Telephone: (89) 78.23.56

Established: 1922 by Paul Blanck
Production: 20,000 cases
Vineyards: 22 hectares (Colmar, St-Hippolyte, Riquewihr,

Ammerschwihr, Kaysersberg, Sigolsheim, Kientzheim), representing about 75 per cent of production, plus 9 hectares rented (Colmar, St-Hippolyte, Sigolsheim, Kientzheim)
Grape varieties: 1ha Sylvaner, 0.2ha Chasselas, 7.8ha Riesling, 3ha Pinot Blanc (including Auxerrois), 2.9ha Tokay-Pinot Gris, 1.7ha Pinot Noir, 4.3ha Gewurztraminer, 0.8ha Muscat (Blanc à Petit Grains & Ottonel), 0.3ha new planting
Grands crus: 2.1ha Schlossberg (Kientzheim), 6ha Furstentum (Kientzheim and Sigolsheim)

The irrepressible Marcel Blanck is gradually giving way to the new generation, with his nephew Frédéric, who is quiet and reserved, in charge of winemaking, and his son Philippe, who is both intense and gregarious, the globetrotting, philosophizing marketer. The biggest problem with this firm is the viti-vinicultural curiosity of the current two generations, which has led to such a multiplicity of wines. If you think there are only 30 or 40 wines here, think again because when you ask to taste a specific wine, there are the young vines and the old vines, the early harvest and the later harvest (and I am not talking about Vendanges Tardives, they come later and, of course, there are the young vines and the old vines of that). It seems to go on *ad infinitum*. The first time I visited the Blancks, it was late afternoon, at the end of a busy day of tasting and the line of wines went up and down trestle tables, in and out of alcoves, disappearing out of sight. After 70 wines, I told Marcel Blanck not to open any more and that I would have to return the next day, well before my first appointment, to finish off!

There are simply too many wines to list here (many are described elsewhere, anyway) or to summarize accurately, so I will just say that the Blancks' strengths are mostly in the *vin de garde* Riesling of Grand Cru Furstentum and Schlossberg. Wines are also sold and known as Domaine des Comtes de Lupfen.

Bléger

Claude Bléger
23 Grand'rue, 67600 Orschwiller
Telephone: (88) 92.32.56

I have tasted a decent Tokay-Pinot Gris and Pinot Noir and a Riesling of some aromatic elegance, but it was from the exceptional 1989 vintage and I do not have sufficient experience of these wines to suggest any sort of consistency.

Boeckel

Vins Fins d'Alsace E. Boeckel
2 rue de le Montagne,
67140 Mittelbergheim
Telephone: (88) 08.91.02

Established: The firm was founded in 1853 by Frédéric Boeckel, but the Boeckels have been winegrowers since 1530
Production: 55,000 cases
Vineyards: 20 hectares (11.6ha

Mittelbergheim, 3ha Andlau, 3ha Eichhoffen, 0.4ha Barr, 1ha Heigigenstein, 1ha Itterswiller), representing about 20 per cent of production; 3 hectares of vineyards (Mittelbergheim) are rented, much of the balance coming from 35 contracted growers
Grape varieties: 2ha Sylvaner, 5ha Riesling, 5ha Pinot Blanc, 3ha Pinot Noir, 4ha Gewurztraminer, 1ha Muscat Rosé à Petit Grains
Grands crus: 3.5ha Wiebelsberg (Andlau), 3ha Zotzenberg (Mittelbergheim), 0.6ha Kirchberg de Barr, 0.7ha Moenchberg (Andlau)

I have to say that I am more in love with Monsieur Boeckel's beautiful reproduction label than I am with the quality of his wines, although there are some wines of interest to be found. Famed for Sylvaner, which has historically excelled on the Grand Cru Zotzenberg, this firm is generally better for Gewurztraminer (Grand Cru Zotzenberg being the richest, but Grand Cru Kirchberg de Barr has the ability to be more elegant, although not so consistent in quality). He has produced quite good Riesling Grand Cru Wiebelsberg in the past (especially as far back as 1976), but recent vintages have not been that special, while the relatively recently introduced Riesling Grand Cru Zotzenberg shows superb, creamy-ripe fruit. His Crémant d'Alsace is crisp and correct, but not special and, although his Pinot Chardonnay Brut Zéro Crémant d'Alsace sounds promising, it delivers nothing of interest whatsoever. The one Boeckel wine I *would* go out of my way to buy is its excellent Gewurztraminer Vendange Tardive. Although not the sweetest of styles, it is packed with rich flavours and carries plenty of candied-peel spicy complexity.

Monsieur Boeckel has always seemed to me a man in a hurry, a man distracted by other thoughts, even though on one of my visits to the firm he took the time to show me some old vintages of Pinot Chardonnay (the still kind, not sparkling), which ranged from an elegant and toasty 1975, to a 1978 that tasted of tinned lychees. Then, after apologizing for not having any really very old wines to taste because 'wines are made to drink, not be museum pieces', he started hunting round for the key to a special locker in his own cellar. 'Where is it?' he kept muttering, as he went through innumerable drawers and cupboards, opening up little tins and jars, poking through the contents for something obviously very small and, when he saw my bemused look, he explained with a shrug of his shoulders that Madame Boeckel keeps the key hidden because every time he opens up the locker, a bottle goes missing. Madame Boeckel is, apparently, a born curator, while Monsieur Boeckel believes all liquid assets should be consumed. The greatest pity to this story is that the nineteenth-century wine he generously opened was so far over the hill that it probably needed drinking before the First World War!

Boehler

Georges Boehler
12 rue des Romains,
67520 Kuttolsheim
Telephone: (88) 87.53.54

The first producer of *vins de pays* in Alsace, Monsieur Boehler's vines are located just north of Marlenheim, north-west of Strasbourg, in an area not classified as AOC Alsace. After 20 years of being refused AOC status, in 1984 he made and marketed a Vin de Pays du Bas-Rhin. He currently produces Pinot Blanc, Riesling and Muscat Ottonel under this denomination and is the president of the Syndicat pour le Défense des Vins de Pays du Bas-Rhin.

Boesch

Léon Boesch
4 rue du Bois, 68570 Soultzmatt
Telephone: (89) 47.01.83

Tasted only recently, and then only occasionally, but I have enjoyed a very fine Gewurztraminer Vendange Tardive from the 1988 harvest.

Bott

Maison 'Bott Frères'
13 avenue du Général de Gaulle,
68150 Ribeauvillé
Telephone: (89) 73.60.48

Established: 1836 by Gaston Bott

Production: 12,000 cases
Vineyards: 10.5 hectares (9.5ha Ribeauvillé, 0.4ha Riquewihr, 0.6ha Hunawihr), which account for its total production

If you look long and hard enough, it is possible to find an occasional good Riesling in the crisp but richly flavoured mould, especially the Réserve Personnelle, fatter, more perfumed Gewurztraminer, an occasional Tokay-Pinot Gris of note and Muscat that is seemingly fresh and very aromatic, but this last variety has not been tasted often enough to make a generalized comment. Réserve Personnelle wines are usually richer than those labelled Cuvée Exceptionnelle. Good Vendanges Tardives. Bott Frères is, however, a good/steady producer, rather than one that excels, and one that 'attaches no importance' to the *grand cru* concept.

Bott-Geyl

Maison Bott-Geyl
1 rue du Petit Château,
68980 Beblenheim
Telephone: (89) 47.90.04

Established: 1947
Winemaker or *oenologist:* Edouard Bott
Production: 10,000 cases
Vineyards: 12.8 hectares (7.8ha Beblenheim, 3.2ha Zellenberg, 1.3ha Riquewihr, 0.2ha Ribeauvillé, 0.3ha Mittelwihr)
Grands crus: 2.2ha Sonnenglanz (Beblenheim), 0.3ha Mandelberg (Mittelwihr), 0.2ha Schoenenbourg (Riquewihr)

This producer can usually be relied upon to produce good, lively Tokay-Pinot Gris and powerful, spicy Gewurztraminer from the Grand Cru Sonnenglanz, particularly in warmer years; otherwise, there is very little to get excited about.

Boxler

Albert Boxler
78 rue des Trois-Epis,
68230 Niedermorschwihr

Production: 6,000 cases
Vineyards: 9.5 hectares (Niedermorschwihr, Katzenthal, Turckheim)
Grands crus: 2.1ha Sommerberg (Niedermorschwihr), 1.4ha Brand (Turckheim)

Boxler is a genius, capable of producing the most stunning wines but occasionally falling flat on his face. This is fine by me, as it means he is always searching, learning and improving in his quest for that impossible dream, the perfect wine, and I would not want to be denied the fabulous wines he makes along the way. When on song, his Brand Tokay-Pinot Gris sizzles with luscious smoky fruit and has a complex creamy-brazilnut finesse. His Riesling from the Brand is classic and steely, while that from Sommerberg is at least as classy, but in a much more accessible style. Boxler's Tokay-Pinot Gris SGN from the Brand is perhaps his greatest potential wine, although the Sommerberg Riesling of the same botrytized style is consistently

his most successful. Give me this
sort of flawed genius in preference
to mechanized consistency any day!

Boxler

Justin Boxler
15 rue des Trois-Épis,
68230 Niedermorschwihr
Telephone: (89) 27.11.07

Just along the road from Albert
Boxler is his lesser known cousin,
who owns 7.5 hectares of
vineyards, including a small plot on
Grand Cru Brand, from which I
have had a couple of fairly good
Rieslings. I have also tasted a
generic Gewurztraminer of some
finesse.

Brand

Lucien Brand
71 rue de Wolxheim,
67120 Ergersheim
Telephone: (88) 38.17.71

Established: 1742
Winemaker or *oenologist:* Charles
Brand
Production: 5,000 cases
Vineyards: 8 hectares (Ergersheim,
Wolxheim)
Grands crus: Kaefferkopf

Lucien Brand utilizes ecological
techniques in the vineyard, such as
cultivating beneficial weeds,
manual picking, preservation of old
vines, etc. This producer's
Gewurztraminer can be interesting
in a peppery-spicy way, especially
in off-years, when it seems to excel,
although his Kaefferkopf

Gewurztraminer is richer and
decidedly superior.

Braun

Camille Braun & Fils
16 Grand'rue, Orschwihr,
68500 Guebwiller
Telephone: (89) 76.95.20

Established: 1800
Winemaker or *oenologist:* Camille
Braun and Christophe Braun
Production: 6,500 cases
Vineyards: 7.5 hectares (3ha
Orschwihr, 3.4ha Rouffach, 1.1ha
Soultzmatt)
Grands crus: 0.5ha Pfingstberg
(Orschwihr)

Although from several generations
of growers, this family enterprise
did not start bottling its own wines
until 1947. The best wines I have
tasted here are the rich and
succulent Klevner Vieilles Vignes
Cuvée Marguerite-Anne and an
exuberantly fruity Gewurztraminer
Cuvée St-Nicolas.

Braun

François Braun
19-21 Grand'rue, 68500 Orschwihr
Telephone: (89) 76.95.13

I have tasted an attractively floral
generic Muscat, but François
Braun's best wines, which come
from the Grand Cru Pfingstberg,
include a Riesling of exceptionally
fine concentration and a
Gewurztraminer that can be
honeyed and succulent.

Brauneisen-Fink

Monique & Gérard Brauneizen-Fink
49 rue Clémenceau, 68000 Colmar

Little known about this small family enterprise except that it includes a plot of Gewurztraminer on Grand Cru Hengst.

Bronner

Ernest Bronner
1 chemin de Beblenheim, 68340 Riquewihr
Telephone: (89) 47.93.91

Not much experience here, either, but a couple of interesting generic wines tasted in the past included a fine, floral Muscat.

Brucke

F. Brucker
See A. GASCHY

Brucker-Gaschy

F. Brucker – A. Gaschy
See A. GASCHY

Buecher

Paul Buecher & Fils
15 rue Ste-Gertrude, 68920 Wettolsheim
Telephone: (89) 80.64.73

Established: end of seventeenth century
Winemaker or *oenologist:* Henri Buecher
Production: 12,500 cases
Vineyards: 19.5 hectares (1.5ha

Husseren-les-Châteaux, 0.5ha Eguisheim, 5ha Wettolsheim, 6ha Wintzenheim, 4ha Turckheim, 0.5ha Ingersheim, 2ha Colmar)
Grands crus: 1.5ha Hengst (Wintzenheim)

This producer prides itself on the diversity of its slope sites, but apart from the occasional bottle here or there, when I have enjoyed Riesling and Gewurztraminer Réserve Personnelle, the only time I have tasted a few together was in 1990 and then just five different wines. The most intriguing was the 1986 Robinson, so named because it comes from a *lieu-dit* of mysterious location called 'Vendredi', but I am not sure if or how its soft vanilla fruit might develop. I have not been impressed by the Crémant d'Alsace.

Burn

J. & F. Burn
See Ernest BURN

Burn

Maison Ernest Burn
14 rue Basse, 68420 Gueberschwihr
Telephone: (89) 49.31.41

Established: 1689
Production: 5,000 cases
Vineyards: 9 hectares
Grands crus: 6ha Goldert

Situated within Monsieur Burn's six hectares of Grand Cru Goldert is the fabled Clos St-Imer, a five-hectare vineyard with a superb south-east-facing aspect and well-drained stony calcareous soil,

planted with 35 per cent
Gewurztraminer, 22 per cent
Riesling, 18 per cent Muscat, 13 per
cent Tokay-Pinot Gris and 12 per
cent Pinot Noir. Clos St-Imer
produces excellent
Gewurztraminer, superb Muscat
and stunning Tokay-Pinot Gris,
with special *cuvées* labelled 'la
Chapelle' even more exciting.
Ernest Burn's daughter, Bernadette
Burn, is co-author of *Alsace Clos et
grands crus* (Jacques Legrand,
1989).

Calixte II

Crémant d'Alsace label.
See CV HUNAWIHR

Capucins

Clos des Capucins
See Domaine WEINBACH

Cattin

Joseph Cattin
18 rue Roger Frémeaux, 68420
Voegtlinshoffen
Telephone: (89) 49.30.21

Established: 1850
Production: 20,000 cases
Vineyards: 21 hectares (9ha
Voegtlinshoffen, 6ha Hattstatt, 1ha
Eguisheim, 5ha Colmar),
representing its total production
Grape varieties: 2ha Sylvaner, 5ha
Riesling, 4ha Pinot Blanc, 3ha
Tokay-Pinot Gris, 1ha Pinot Noir,
5ha Gewurztraminer, o.6ha Muscat
Ottonel, o.3ha Muscat Blanc à Petit
Grains

Grands crus: 5ha Hatschbourg
(Voegtlinshoffen)

For some reason cousin Théo is
better known in the UK than Joseph
(or Jacques, actually), but whereas
Théo makes good wines, including
Grand Cru Hatschbourg, his cousin
is really far more talented. Not that
you would think he could make
wines of such finesse. Our Jacques
is a big lad, looks like a farmer
(which he is, of sorts, of course),
has the ruddy complexion of an
outdoor chap and hands, as they
say, as big as plates. Yet this big,
country lad makes wine with a very
deft touch indeed. His Muscat is
very flowery and intensely
flavoured; he produces a discreet
Gewurztraminer Hatschbourg,
which gradually builds up a rich
and powerful flavour, plus a hugely
successful Vendange Tardive from
the same grape and vineyard. His
Pinot Noir is ripe and well
perfumed with rich fruit and the
only reason there is any
inconsistency in the style of Joseph
Cattin's Crémant d'Alsace is
because he keeps changing the
cépage; it is always an interesting
wine, albeit the most rustic in the
range.

Cattin

Théo Cattin
35 rue Roger Frémeaux,
68420 Voegtlinshoffen
Telephone: (89) 49.30.43

Established: 1947 by Théo Cattin
Production: 15,000 cases
Vineyards: 16.7 hectares (6.7ha

Colmar, 4.3ha Hattstatt, 0.2ha
Obermorschwihr, 2.7ha
Voegtlinshoffen, 2ha Herrlisheim,
0.8ha Orschwihr), which account
for 80 per cent of production, plus
1.6ha rented (Hattstatt,
Obermorschwihr, Orschwihr,
Voegtlinshoffen and Colmar)
Grape varieties: 0.6ha Sylvaner,
0.9ha Chasselas, 5.3ha Riesling,
1.1ha Pinot Blanc, 1ha Tokay-Pinot
Gris, 1.5ha Pinot Noir, 5.5ha
Gewurztraminer, 0.8ha Muscat
Ottonel
Grands crus: 2.6ha Hatschbourg
(Voegtlinshoffen), 1.8ha
Hatschbourg (Hattstatt)

Just down the road from Joseph
Cattin lives Jacques's magnificently
moustached cousin Théo. If Joseph
reminds me of a farmhand, then
Théo resembles one of Kaiser Bill's
lot: stick him in uniform and put a
spiked helmet on his head and he
would make a fortune as a film
extra. As a winemaker, he is not too
bad either, and when I say that his
cousin is far more talented, that is
some compliment because Théo is
very good too. Perhaps best known
for his elegant Riesling Grand Cru
Hatschbourg, which ages into a fine
old petrolly wine, and his Tokay-
Pinot Gris from the same vineyard,
which has classic, creamy-buttery
fruit with fine smoky-spicy
complexity, but I think Théo
Cattin's Gewurztraminer Grand
Cru Hatschbourg is at least as
good, while his theoretically lesser
Gewurztraminer Bollenberg is
decidedly superior and absolutely
delicious. Experiments with new

wood for Pinot Noir have mostly
been too enthusiastic, whereas the
simple generic version is usually a
nice mouthful. I tasted a splendid
1971 Pinot Noir Grand Cru (when
both blended and Pinot Noir wines
were allowed to utilize this
designation) that was brimming
with light, elegant cherry, plum,
vanilla and liquorice fruit with an
exquisitely perfumed aftertaste. It
would have compared very well
with an old Beaune. Théo's Pinot
Blanc is rich and ripe, not always
that dry, but usually delicious.

Châteaux

See the specific name of each
château (e.g. ISENBOURG,
ORSCHWIHR, WAGENBOURG),
except for Château Ollwiller, which
is under CV VIEIL ARMAND

CV Cléebourg

Cave Coopérative Viticole de
Cléebourg
Route des Vosges, Cléebourg
67160 Wissembourg
Telephone: (88) 94.50.33

Established: 1946
Current membership: 192
Production: 110,000 cases (about
25 per cent sold in bulk to
négociants)
Vineyards: 147 hectares
(Cléebourg, Rott, Oberhoffen and
Steinseltz)
Grands crus: None
Labels: Clérostein (Crémant
d'Alsace)

Probably the most underrated

cooperative in Alsace, CV
Cléebourg owes its qualitative
success to Georges Rupp, a local
grower who persuaded his
colleagues to reclaim 300 hectares
of vineyards in Cléebourg and
surrounding vineyards during the
Second World War. Under Rupp's
guidance, Cléebourg became one of
the first villages in Alsace to replant
en masse with recommended classic
varieties and he founded this
cooperative in 1946. CV Cléebourg
is particularly good at all Pinot style
wines, its most excellent being the
Kiemberg Pinot Blanc Auxerrois
from Cléebourg itself, which has
lovely acidity, and the Huettgasse
Pinot Noir from Steinseltz, which is
surprisingly fruity and decently
coloured for the most northerly red
wine in France. Although tasted
only once, and that was a couple of
years ago, the 100 per cent
Auxerrois Crémant d'Alsace, which
is sold under the Clérostein label,
does seem to have the style and
potential to put it above the
mainstream of this *appellation*.

Clerostein

See CV CLÉEBOURG

Clos des Capucins

See Domaine WEINBACH

Clos Gaensbroennel

See Domaine WILLM

Clos Philippe Grass

See MUHLBERGER

Clos Hauserer

See ZIND HUMBRECHT

Clos de Meywihr

See Roger KLEIN

Clos Rebgarten

See Marc KREYDENWEISS

Clos Roth-Stein

See Jean ARBOGAST

Clos St-Imer

See Maison Ernest BURN

Clos St-Jacques

See Domaine Viticole de la Ville de
COLMAR

Clos St-Landelin

See MURÉ

Clos St-Theobold

See Domaine Schoffit

Clos St-Urbain

See ZIND HUMBRECHT

Clos Ste-Hune

See TRIMBACH

/ **Clos Ste-Odile**

See S.A. STE-ODILE and CV
OBERNAI

Clos du Schlossberg

See Jean SIPP

Clos du Sonnenbach

See Domaine du REMPART

Clos de la Tourelle

See CV VIEIL ARMAND

Clos du Val d'Eléon

See Marc KREYDENWEISS

Clos du Windsbuhl

See ZIND HUMBRECHT

Clos du Zahnacker

See CV RIBEAUVILLÉ

Clos Zisser

See Domaine KLIPFEL

Collection Joseph Mann

See WUNSCH & MANN

Colmar

Domaine Viticole de la Ville de
Colmar
2 rue du Stauffen, 68000 Colmar
Telephone: (89) 79.11.87

Established: 1895

Production: 13,000 cases
Vineyards: 20 hectares (13.7ha
Colmar, plus Wettolsheim,
Wintzenheim and Eguisheim)
Grands crus: Hengst
(Wintzenheim), Pfersigberg
(Eguisheim)

This was established by Oberlin
Chrétien (1831–1915), the famous
ampelographer. Known originally
as the Institut Oberlin, the heart of
this viticultural research station is
the Hardt or Harth in Colmar,
where half its domaine and all its
experimental vineyards are located.
It became known by its present
name in 1980. They have
everything from Viognier to Syrah
and Cabernet Sauvignon growing
here on an experimental basis,
though the only wines sold under
this domaine's label are, of course,
exclusively from permitted Alsace
varieties. The last time I had any
sort of comprehensive tasting here
was in 1987, when I tasted the
entire range, plus one or two
slightly older *cuvées*. There were 20
wines in total and the average
quality was good, but not special,
although there were five quite
excellent examples (Riesling 1986,
Riesling 1981 Vendange Tardives,
Tokay-Pinot Gris 1985 Cuvée du
Centenaire, Gewurztraminer 1985
Cuvée du Centenaire and Tokay-
Pinot Gris 1981 Vendange
Tardive). Perhaps the biggest
disappointment here is the Clos St-
Jacques, which is a fresh, clean and
soft blended wine, but not a classic
blend. Instead of selling it at a
premium of just one franc over this

domaine's ordinary Edelzwicker, maybe it should be twice the price, which would allow a much greater flexibility in pumping up its quality to enhance the reputation of this *clos*? The domaine sells three varietal Crémants d'Alsace: a Crémant Brut, which is 100 per cent Pinot Blanc, a Crémant Rosé (Pinot Noir) and a Crémant Riesling. I find them adequate, but nothing more.

Colombain

Lucie Colombain
5 rue Jeanne-d'Arc, 68420
Husseren-les-Châteaux
Telephone: (89) 49.30.39

My experience of this small grower is limited to an attractive, floral-fresh generic Gewurztraminer.

Comte de Sigold

Cooperative label for Crémant d'Alsace.
See CV SIGOLSHEIM

Comtes de Lupfen

Domaine des Comtes de Lupfen
See Paul BLANCK

Cooperatives

See name of village (e.g. the cooperative in Beblenheim will be listed as CV BEBLENHEIM) in all cases except Eguisheim (*See* WOLFBERGER) and Soultz-Wuenheim (*See* CV VIEIL ARMAND)

Dagobert

Les Vins du Roi Dagobert
See CV TRAENHEIM

CV Dambach-la-Ville

Cave Vinicole de Dambach-la-Ville
2 rue de la Gare, 67650 Dambach-la-Ville
Telephone: (88) 92.40.03

Established: 1902
Current membership: 252
Production: 300,000 cases (only about 10,000 cases sold)
Vineyards: 403 hectares
Grape varieties: 80ha Sylvaner, 2ha Chasselas, 190ha Riesling, 54ha Pinot Blanc, 13ha Tokay-Pinot Gris, 19ha Pinot Noir, 42ha Gewurztraminer, 3ha Muscat (mixed)
Grands crus: Frankstein (Dambach-la-Ville)
Labels: Krossfelder

Founded at the same time and by the same seventeen *Darlehnkassen* as the Eguisheim cooperative (*See* WOLFBERGER), this cooperative went its own way until 1976, when it rejoined CV Eguisheim. Most production ends up in Wolfberger blends, but some 10,000 cases are sold under the Krossfelder label, either by mail order or direct retail sales to visitors. I have not visited this cooperative, have rarely tasted its Krossfelder wines and cannot make a realistic judgement, although I have come across a Riesling Grand Cru Frankstein that displayed the sort of fine minerally character expected from a granite *cru*.

See also WOLFBERGER

Deiss

Domaine Marcel Deiss
15 route du Vin, 68750 Bergheim
Telephone: (89) 73.63.37

Established: 1949 by Marcel Deiss
Production: 12,500 cases
Vineyards: 20 hectares (11.2ha
Bergheim, 2.5ha Bennwihr, 1ha
Rorschwihr, 1.8ha Beblenheim,
0.7ha Mittelwihr, 1.8ha St-
Hippolyte, 1ha Riquewihr), which
account for the total production
Grape varieties: 1ha Sylvaner, 7ha
Riesling, 2ha Pinot Blanc, 1.5ha
Tokay-Pinot Gris, 1.5ha Pinot
Noir, 6ha Gewurztraminer, 0.5ha
Muscat Ottonel, 0.5ha Muscat
Blanc à Petit Grains
Grands crus: 2.5ha Altenberg de
Bergheim, 0.7ha Schoenenbourg
(Riquewihr)

What can one say about the
amazingly talented, vociferously
dedicated, frenetic and, indeed,
charmingly eccentric Jean-Michel
Deiss that has not already been
said? Well, he is without doubt one
of the region's greatest winemakers,
but then everyone knows that. His
great mass of curly hair is real (it
would come off otherwise, the way
he throws his head around when he
is in full flow, besides which I've
tugged it!). He flings his hands all
over the place, describes each one of
his wines in language that would
shame a poet, then flashes a huge
smile, his eyes wide and bright,
while waiting for you to make a
comment. But how can you
possibly add anything when he has
already used up the dictionary three
times over? That is the man; his
wines are so often described and
recommended elsewhere in this
book, I dare not add anything in
detail here. I will just say that they
are tremendously expressive, of
both the *terroir* and winemaker.
They are wines that aim for finesse
and balance, rather than size, which
is not to suggest that they lack
intensity, as Deiss has produced
some of the most fabulously rich
and concentrated wines in Alsace,
but they always have such
impeccable balance, the size of the
wines can easily deceive. I often
think that Deiss is best at Riesling,
but I soon remember the Tokay-
Pinot Gris of extraordinary quality
he is constantly producing, then the
stunning Gewurztraminers, the
creamy-rich Pinot, and his Pinot
Noir, for goodness sake. What
about his late-harvest wines, his
extraordinary SGN, the
Quintessence and the *vin de paille*
... ? No, it is impossible to single
out a style.

Dietrich

Claude Dietrich
32 Grand'rue, 68240 Kientzheim
Telephone: (89) 78.25.01

Established: 1987
Winemaker or *oenologist:* Claude
Dietrich
Production: 4,000 cases
Vineyards: 4 hectares, plus 2.3

hectares due to be planted by 1995 (Kientzheim, Kaysersberg, Ammerschwihr, Sigolsheim & Colmar)
Grands crus: 2.3ha Schlossberg (one hectare of Riesling planted, the other due to be planted in 1993)

Relatively new venture jointly run by Claude Dietrich and his young wife, Elisabeth (the sister of Philippe Blanck of Paul Blanck & Fils). So far the Gewurztraminer has stood out, but it is the vibrant generic Tokay-Pinot Gris that has the most finesse.

Dietrich

Laurent Dietrich & Fils
1 rue des Ours, 67650 Dambach-la-Ville
Telephone: (88) 92.41.31

Just one or two wines tasted here, but nothing special to report.

Dietrich

Robert Dietrich
RN 83, Route du Vin, Wettolsheim 68000 Colmar
Telephone: (89) 41.46.75

Production: 30,000 cases
Vineyards: 4 hectares (Wettolsheim, Wintzenheim), representing some 10 per cent of total production
Grands crus: 1.4ha Steingrubler (Wettolsheim)

The quality here is not consistent across the range, but there are some very good odds and ends, well worth searching out. In the generic range, for example, the Muscat is fine and flowery and there is an elegant Gewurztraminer. The Tokay-Pinot Gris from Grand Cru Steingrubler is beautifully balanced and hedonistically rich, but do not forget the terribly underrated Crémant d'Alsace. Wines are sold under Dietrich, Besser and Caves du Kreutzfeld labels.

Dîme

Cave de la Dîme
See Hubert METZ

Diringer

GAEC Diringer
18 rue de Rouffach, 68250 Westhalten
Telephone: (89) 47.01.06

Not to be confused with Dirringer of Dambach-la-Ville in the Bas-Rhin, this one owns just over an hectare of Grand Cru Zinnkoepflé, from which he is supposed to produce good Riesling and Gewurztraminer, although I have never tasted the wines.

Dirler

Vins Dirler
13 rue d'Issenheim, Bergholtz, 68500 Guebwiller
Telephone: (89) 76.91.00

Established: 1871
Production: 5,500 cases
Vineyards: 7 hectares (3.5ha Guebwiller, 3.3ha Bergholtz, 0.2ha Bergholtz-Zell)
Grands crus: 1.4ha Spiegel

(Bergholtz), 0.4ha Kessler
(Guebwiller), 1ha Saering
(Guebwiller)

Although Dopff Au Moulin was responsible for creating the sparkling wine industry in Alsace, Dirler was the first recorded producer of this style, commencing production in 1880. Unfortunately Dirler stopped making sparkling Alsace wine in 1939, so there is no way to judge how successful it was. The current incumbent, Jean-Pierre Dirler, is very passionate about the quality and style of his wines and they are quite often stunning.

Even the generics are fine and stylish, but it is his Riesling from the *grands crus* of Kessler, Saering and Spiegel that are so outstanding for their great delicacy of richness and obvious finesse. Dirler's Muscat from the Saering is another beautiful wine. This grower deserves to be far better known.

Dirringer

Domaine J-L Dirringer
5 rue du Maréchal Foch,
67650 Dambach-la-Ville
Telephone: (88) 92.41.51

Not to be confused with Diringer of Westhalten, I have once come across a simple but attractive Muscat from this producer.

Dischler

Charles Dischler
23 le Canal, 67120 Wolxheim
Telephone: (88) 38.22.55

I have had fine, elegant Wolxheim Riesling from this grower.

Divinal

Divinal and CV Obernai are often used synonymously, but Divinal is in fact a union, of which Obernai is just one cooperative, albeit the biggest and most important. The Divinal group also includes CV Andlau and CV Traenheim, both of which produce and sell wines under their own labels, plus three cooperative *vendangoirs* in Dangolsheim, Dorlisheim and St-Hippolyte, which merely press grapes and neither make nor market wine on their own behalf. Wines sold under the Divinal label are produced by CV Obernai. *See* CV OBERNAI primarily, also CV ANDLAU and CV TRAENHEIM.

Dolder

Christian Dolder
4 rue Neuve, 67140 Mittelbergheim
Telephone: (88) 08.96.08

This grower produces a powerful Zotzenberg Sylvaner that is worth digging out (although the silly regulations attempt to prevent the joining of a lofty *grand cru* name with such a lowly variety as Sylvaner) and a rich, racy and elegantly fruity Riesling Brandluft.

Domaine Ehrhart

See Henri EHRHART

Domaine Engel

See Raymond ENGEL

Domaine Geyer

See Roger & Roland GEYER

Domaine Hering

See HERING

Domaine Kehren

See Domaine KEHREN

Domaine Langehald

See François BAUR Petit-Fils

Domaine des Comtes de Lupfen

See Paul Blanck

Domaine des Marronniers

See MARRONNIERS

Domaine du Moulin de Dusenbach

See Bernard SCHWACH

Domaine de l'Oberhof

See SALZMANN-THOMANN

Domaine du Rempart

See Domaine du REMPART

Domaine du Tonnelier

See Louis HAULLER

Domaine du Vieux Pressoir

See Marcel SCHLOSSER

Dontenville

Gilbert Dontenville
2 route de Kintzheim,
67730 Châtenois
Telephone: (88) 82.03.48

Fifth generation of growers working ten hectares, including just over one hectare of Riesling on the Hahnenberg *lieu-dit*, which produces this producer's finest wine, intensely aromatic and long-lived.

Dopff & Irion

Dopff & Irion
Château de Riquewihr,
68340 Riquewihr
Telephone: (89) 47.92.51

Established: same lineage as Dopff Au Moulin, but this company was formed in 1945 by René Dopff
Production: 300,000 cases
Vineyards: 30 hectares (27.5ha Riquewihr, 1.5ha Zellenberg, 0.5ha Hunawihr, 0.5ha Kientzheim), representing about 10 to 15 per cent of total production, plus the vineyard of Château d'Isenbourg, which is rented, the balance coming from 300 contracted growers
Grape varieties: 0.5ha Sylvaner, 12ha Riesling, 1.5ha Pinot Blanc, 2.5ha Tokay-Pinot Gris, 1.5ha Pinot Noir, 10.5ha Gewurztraminer, 1.5ha Muscat Rosé à Petit Grains
Grands crus: 5ha Schoenenbourg

(Riquewihr), 1.5ha Sporen
(Riquewihr)
Labels: Château d'Isenbourg

Dopff & Irion has not exactly sat on the fence over the *grand cru* question, so it came as quite a surprise when the firm actually started to produce and promote these wines. Like most firms, Dopff & Irion had produced *grands crus* in the early days, when the term referred only to wines of a slightly higher theoretical quality (*see* 'The *grands crus*' in Chapter 5), but like Hugel, Trimbach and Léon Beyer, became bitterly disillusioned with how the system developed. As Guy Dopff once put it to me, 'We are not basically against a *grands crus* system, but we oppose the politically motivated distribution of too many *grands crus* and support the idea of blending *grands crus* from various *grand cru* vineyards, the criterion being quality, not geography.' I found this illogical. There have been too many *grands crus*, of course, and the quality conditions for the *appellation* are insufficient, but a *cru* is a *cru* is a *cru*. How can you have a wine claiming to come from a 'great growth', when it does not even come from a single growth, whatever the quality? The *grand cru* legislation must be tightened up, but you cannot turn the clock back. By all means introduce a superior *appellation* for blended wines (in every respect of the description) and call it anything you like, but not *anything cru*.

Guy Dopff was honest in confessing not to be against the theory of a *grand cru* system, merely its prostitution (my description, not his). How could he be against the concept of superior wines issuing from privileged sites, when Dopff & Irion's best wines have been its *lieux-dits*? The Riesling Les Murailles can be elegant and flowery, although its high acidity and classically dry finish does sometimes make young vintages seem a little austere and reserved, but they usually develop well. For most vintages, Les Murailles needs at least seven years to mature in bottle, but it really excels in hot years, when it can be almost fat and capable of achieving a stunning honeyed-petrol richness, given time in bottle. Gewurztraminer Les Sorcières is the richest and fullest of Dopff & Irion's *lieux-dits*, but it is never blowzy and retains its succulence, however intense it becomes in bottle. While it is true that this producer aims for elegance and finesse in its best wines, rather than power and strength, no one should be fooled into thinking that they do not possess considerable longevity. Most vintages of Les Sorcières are still in their prime at 20 years of age and the bigger the year, the more exotic – yet strangely classic – the wine gets, with capsicum, liquorice and sweet spices commonly found on the aftertaste. Muscat Les Amandiers will disappoint the blind-taster with its discreet style, yet never bores no matter how many glasses you drink as an apéritif, and reveals soft, sensual, peachy fruit with asparagus or other light dishes at the start of a meal. The gently rich Tokay-Pinot Gris Les Maquisards stands out due to its minerally rich complexity, which develops into deep, spicy aromas on the nose and intense, yet refined and elegant liquorice fruit on the palate.

Since Dopff & Irion decided to market *grand cru* wines, it has had an effect on the quantity and labelling of one of its well-established, classic *lieux-dits*. As 3.5 hectares of Les Murailles overlap Schoenenbourg, this has been vinified separately since 1988, which effectively reduces the production of Les Murailles by some 27 per cent. Although Dopff & Irion insist they will make *grand cru* wines only in truly great vintages, I must say that I have not been very impressed with any of the wines produced so far. I have tasted all of them and the Riesling Schoenenbourg has been the most disappointing. It could be that the heart of Les Murailles is even more reserved when vinified separately and, perhaps, might evolve into something special that nobody has the required experience to discern in the first young wines. Another possibility is that it could be due to the age of the vines, some of which were only five years old when Dopff & Irion produced its first *grand cru* wines. Alternatively, the *grand cru* wines might simply be very mediocre. Most of them certainly seem to be lacking, weak and feeble compared to the three special *terroir*-based *cuvées* that have

historically made Dopff & Irion's reputation, even though these wines are themselves restrained rather than upfront.

As Les Amandiers is located entirely within Schoenenbourg, this wine will, in future, simply be relabelled Muscat Grand Cru Schoenenbourg Les Amandiers. No such wine had been released at the time of writing, but when it is, it should surely be its old self. Neither of the other two *lieux-dits*, Les Sorcières and Les Maquisards, are located within any *grand cru*, thus will remain unaltered. Frankly, I do not care for the cheaper wines from this producer, which are made in bulk and deliberately aimed at the most competitive sectors of the market. On the other hand, I have more time for many of this firm's better quality wines than some critics seem to have. The problem (and Les Amandiers is just a prime example) is that all of Dopff & Irion's best wines are made for discreet revelations at the table, not for the immediacy of clinical tastings. Combine that with the unfortunate fact that there are too many, too cheap wines that are just neutral and attenuated at the bottom end of the Dopff & Irion range and it is easy to understand how it is possible to misread the discreet and subtle qualities of its finer wines when so many other wines practically explode out of the glass. When the Cuvée René Dopff range was first introduced, I thought it was a good midway quality, something that bridged the gap from fine to feeble and, perhaps, if the firm could gradually pull itself out from the bottom end of the market, might make a new bottom-line standard of truly excellent quality and value for money. Recent examples have not, however, displayed the nice, understated style that was the hallmark when originally launched. On the other hand, the quality of this firm's Crémant d'Alsace has gone up at the same time as that of Cuvée René Dopff has fallen. Both the Brut and Brut Rosé are made for Dopff & Irion, using the firm's own grapes, by Guy's cousins, the sparkling wine specialists of Dopff Au Moulin, just down the road (which should scotch rumours that these cousins do not speak!). These wines were good, but are now even better and can show a nice creaminess of fruit with some honeyed highlights, if kept a year or so in bottle.

Dopff Au Moulin

Dopff Au Moulin
2 avenue J-Preiss, 68340 Riquewihr
Telephone: (89) 47.92.23

Established: Sixteenth century by Jean Daniel Dopff
Production: 200,000 cases
Vineyards: 58 hectares (14.9ha Colmar, 0.7ha Hunawihr, 0.5ha Kientzheim, 1.9ha Mittelwihr, 6.9ha Turckheim, 4ha Zellenberg, 29.1ha Riquewihr)
Grape varieties: 2.2ha Sylvaner, 1.6ha Chasselas, 10.3ha Riesling, 15.8ha Pinot Blanc, 3.4ha Tokay-Pinot Gris, 4.5ha Pinot Noir, 14.9ha Gewurztraminer, 1ha Muscat Ottonel, 2.8ha Chardonnay, plus 1.5ha under plantation
Grands crus: 1.1ha Sporen (Riquewihr), 8.6ha Schoenenbourg (Riquewihr), 3.2ha Brand (Turckheim)

Can anyone keep a straight face when Pierre-Étienne Dopff is around? I really want to know because I certainly cannot. When this larger-than-life man packs his pipe and begins to puff on it, then looks at you with a slight cock of his head and that glint in his eye, I just crack up. Ask him a serious question and, as often as not, he will take on an innocent little boy look and ask a deliberately naive question in response. He then watches how you react. Pierre-Étienne loves to play games with people, it is his way of measuring them up, although exactly what for I am not sure. Knowing this explains his jovial behaviour, but it is very little help when it comes to interviewing the man. I have learned, for example, that if you take him seriously when he jokes and look for a mischievous twinkle in his eye when he sounds profoundly serious, you will get it right nine times out of ten, but it does not solve the problem of actually getting a straight answer from him.

The wines, therefore, often have to do the talking, and when it comes to sparkling wine, Dopff Au Moulin virtually invented it in commercial terms, as far as Alsace is concerned. This company *was* the Crémant d'Alsace industry for the first seven decades of this century and it still leads the way. As the industry's leader, it should be held to higher standards than the norm, so I will start by being super-critical of two wines that are, in any case, recommended under 'Top Performers' (*see* AOC Crémant d'Alsace entry in Chapter 7). Cuvée Julien is much better than average Crémant d'Alsace, but I really do think that Dopff Au Moulin could be a little cleverer in its construction, particularly in the choice of wine for the base of the dosage, which could turn the *cuvée* around overnight, if one were chosen that gave an immediate succulence and a lasting freshness. With very little difficulty, this *cuvée* could be superior and preferable (two completely different things) to a great many non-vintage Champagnes. A similar comment could be made about the rosé. There is no need to say anything about this firm's Cuvée Bartholdi, Blanc de Noirs and Brut Sauvage, which are adequately acclaimed as three of the five best sparkling wines of Alsace.

The firm's other wines are often ignored due to the dynamism exerted by its sparkling wine side, but it has a large and often overlooked estate of prized vineyards, which provide this firm with some of its very finest wines under the Domaines Dopff label. Of these, I have found the Tokay-Pinot Gris de Riquewihr, Riesling Grand Cru Schoenenbourg,

Gewurztraminer de Riquewihr and Gewurztraminer Grand Cru Brand to be the most consistent. The Sylvaner de Riquewihr has also provided the occasional surprise, especially in riper years, when it can have the aroma of fresh garden mint and a lovely depth of fruit, although twice in my experience even this exceptional wine has been overwhelmed by the generic Sylvaner, the last time being the 1988, which had a late-harvest, botrytis richness, deep, concentrated fruit and excellent balancing acidity. On both occasions, however, I was greatly disappointed with what appeared to be exactly the same *cuvée* later in the year, which can always be a problem with a *négociant*'s generics. My advice therefore is to rely on the Sylvaner de Riquewihr for consistency at a very high level (for the variety) and if and when you come across an outstanding (by any standards) generic Sylvaner, buy it there and then!

Durrmann

André Durrmann
11 rue des Forgerons, 67140 Andlau
Telephone: (88) 08.95.83

Exclusively domaine-produced wines, with good Riesling from the *grands crus* of Kastelberg and Wiebelsberg.

Dusenbach

Domaine du Moulin de Dusenbach
See Bernard SCHWACH

Dussourt

André Dussourt
2 rue de Dambach,
67750 Scherwiller
Telephone: (88) 92.10.27

Established: 1964
Winemaker or *oenologist:* Paul
Dussourt
Production: 7,500 cases
Vineyards: 8 hectares (3.5ha
Blienschwiller, 3.5ha Scherwiller,
1ha Epfig)
Grands crus: None

The Dussourts have been
winegrowers since the eighteenth
century and base their reputation
on a very dry, racy style of Riesling,
although the few I have tasted have
not stood out.

Ecklé

Jean-Paul Ecklé
29 Grand'rue, 68230 Katzenthal
Telephone: (89) 27.09.41

I have restricted experience of this
grower, who owns a small plot of
vines on the Grand Cru Wineck-
Schlossberg, the wines of which I
have tasted a few times and find his
Riesling to be well bodied and full
flavoured. Other wines have
included a well-balanced generic
Muscat, which was pleasantly *vif*
and fruity.

Ecole

Domaine de l'Ecole
8 rue aux Remparts,
68250 Rouffach
Telephone: (89) 49.60.17

This is the private vineyard of the
Lycée Agricole et Viticole de
Rouffach. I would love to describe
the wines as didactic, but I have
absolutely no experience of them.

Ed Hering

See Domaine HERING

Eguisheim

CV Eguisheim
See WOLFBERGER

Ehrhart

André Ehrhart
68 rue Herzog, Wettolsheim,
68000 Colmar
Telephone (89) 80.66.16

Not much experience of these
wines, but I have had the occasional
generic Riesling of some interest
and very good Riesling and
Gewurztraminer from the Grand
Cru Hengst.

Ehrhart

François Ehrhart & Fils
6 rue St-Rémy, 68920 Wettolsheim
Telephone: (89) 80.60.57

The Ehrharts have been *vignerons*
since 1725. I have had fine
Gewurztraminer of welcome grip
(any taster who has had to taste
hundreds of Gewurztraminers will
know how welcome grip is!),
especially from the Grand Cru
Gloeckelberg.

Ehrhart

Henri Ehrhart
2 rue du Romarin,
68770 Ammerschwihr
Telephone: (89) 78.23.74

Production: 30,000 cases
Vineyards: 6 hectares (4ha Ammerschwihr, 1ha Ingersheim, 1ha Turckheim), representing about 15 per cent of total production, the balance coming from 10 contracted growers and other purchases
Grape varieties: 1.6ha Riesling, 0.7ha Pinot Blanc, 0.3ha Tokay-Pinot Gris, 1ha Pinot Noir, 2ha Gewurztraminer, 0.4ha Muscat Ottonel

A family winegrowing enterprise for many generations, Henri Ehrhart is an underrated producer of wines that stand out by their rich, ripe fruit and elegant style. Although not one of his most consistent wines, when performing well the Pinot Noir does have a fine, smoky varietal character. Henri Ehrhart is, however, strongest with his Tokay-Pinot Gris, Gewurztraminer and Riesling. He makes excellent Riesling: his generic is exceptional, and the Réserve is a good step up in richness and elegance, although his finely tuned Grand Cru Kaefferkopf definitely shows the most finesse. The Kaefferkopf Gewurztraminer is a much softer, more luscious style of wine. In 1985, Henri Ehrhart even produced an outstanding Edelzwicker (under that debased *appellation*, as opposed to the classic blends with historic names that avoid the *appellation*) and, although his Sylvaner, Pinot Blanc and Muscat are all decent, they have not excited me like the other varietals. The Crémant d'Alsace, which is made by Joseph Cattin of Voegtlinshoffen, can be worth trying. Henri Ehrhart's wines are also sold simply as Domaine Ehrhart, which can be a bit confusing, as there are at least three different Ehrharts producing wine in Alsace.

Einhart

Einhart
15 rue Principale,
67560 Rosenwiller
Telephone: (88) 50.41.90

This grower owns some eight hectares of vineyards, including a small plot of the *lieu-dit* Westerberg, where he produces an extremely rich, beautifully balanced Tokay-Pinot Gris.

Engel

Fernand Engel & Fils
1 route du Vin, 68590 Rorschwihr
Telephone: (89) 73.77.27

Small family enterprise with vineyards at the foot of Haut-Koenigsbourg, including just over one hectare on the Grand Cru Altenberg de Bergheim, where Fernand Engel grows mostly Gewurztraminer but also a little Tokay-Pinot Gris.

Engel

Raymond Engel
1 route du Vin, 67600 Orschwiller
Telephone: (88) 92.01.83

Domaine Engel comprises some 15
hectares, from which I have tasted a
fine, concentrated Riesling Vieilles
Vignes. I have also come across a
notable Crémant d'Alsace and,
under the Domaine des Prélats
label, a very ripe and honey-rich
Tokay-Pinot Gris Grand Cru
Praelatenberg.

Ermel

David Ermel
30 route de Ribeauvillé,
68150 Hunawihr
Telephone: (89) 73.61.71

Only one wine encountered from
this small grower and that was a
simple, round and fruity
Gewurztraminer Grand Cru
Rosacker.

Fahrer

Armand Fahrer
24 route du Vin, 68590 St-
Hippolyte
Telephone: (89) 73.00.40

This grower has a certain
reputation for Rouge de St-
Hippolyte, although not tasted by
the author.

Faller

Robert Faller & Fils
36, Grand'rue, 68150 Ribeauvillé
Telephone: (89) 73.60.47

Established: Since 1638 by Faller
Production: 11,000 cases
Vineyards: 11 hectares
(Ribeauvillé), representing some 70
per cent of total production, plus
two hectares rented (Ribeauvillé)
and the balance purchased from
non-contracted growers
Grape varieties: 1.5ha Sylvaner,
0.6ha Chasselas, 3ha Riesling,
1.5ha Pinot Blanc, 1.2ha Tokay-
Pinot Gris, 1.9ha Gewurztraminer,
0.3ha Muscat Rosé à Petit Grains
(1ha not planted)
Grands crus: 1.6ha Geisberg
(Ribeauvillé), 0.7ha Kirchberg de
Ribeauvillé

Not to be confused with the Faller
of Domaine Weinbach, Robert
Faller does produce some pretty
nice wines, but not in the same
class. My initial meeting with
Monsieur Faller was hardly
confidence inspiring on either side,
as the first two wines in his range
were corked. One, well okay, but
two? He must have thought I was
trying to be awkward and I
certainly thought he should have
picked the faults up first or at least
be able to recognize them once I
had (which he conceded only after
comparing with a fresh bottle). No
matter, he had some other pretty
good wines, so we ended up on
good terms. Of his generic wines,
the Pinot Noir is usually fat and full
without being sweet; the Muscat
very full on the nose and lifted by a
slight spritz and good acidity; while
the Gewurztraminer has nice, spicy-
soft fruit and a tingly balance. His
best wines are, however, from the

Grand Cru Geisberg, where he usually harvests his Riesling very ripe, yet manages to balance the resulting richness with very racy acidity; and from Grand Cru Kirchberg de Ribeauvillé, where the finesse of his Gewurztraminer compares with that of André Kientzler. He is also capable of producing very expressive Muscat.

Faller

Théo Faller
See Domaine WEINBACH

Faust

Liliane Faust
67520 Kuttolsheim

Small producer of Pinot Blanc and Gewurztraminer under the Vin de Pays du Bas-Rhin denomination.

Fleith

René Fleith
'Lange Matten', Ingersheim,
68000 Colmar
Telephone: (89) 27.24.19

Established: 1970 by René Fleith
Production: 5,200 cases
Vineyards: 8 hectares (0.2ha Turckheim, 0.2ha Wintzenheim, 0.3ha Katzenthal, 6.9ha Ingersheim, 0.4ha Sigolsheim), representing over 80 per cent of total production, plus 1.2 hectares rented (Ingersheim)
Grape varieties: 0.2ha Sylvaner, 2.7ha Riesling, 1ha Pinot Blanc, 0.8ha Tokay-Pinot Gris, 0.9ha Pinot Noir, 2ha Gewurztraminer,

0.4ha Muscat Ottonel

The Fleiths have been *vignerons* for generations and René spent the first 16 years of his working life helping his father grow grapes for the local cooperative before establishing his own vineyard, of just 3.5 hectares, in 1970. He too sold grapes to the cooperative until 1976, when he sold his entire crop to a *négociant*. René Fleith vinified his own wines for the first time in 1977, and won a bronze medal in Paris, despite it not being an auspicious vintage to begin with. His best wines so far have been Pinot (which contains 90 per cent Auxerrois) and Tokay-Pinot Gris.

Flesch

François Flesch
rue du Stade, 68250 Pfaffenheim
Telephone: (89) 49.66.36

No experience whatsoever of this small grower.

Freudenreich

Joseph Freudenreich
3 cour Unterlinden,
68420 Eguisheim
Telephone: (89) 41.36.87

I recently came across a delicious 1989 Muscat from this small producer, who should not be confused with Pierre Freudenreich.

Freudenreich

Pierre Freudenreich & Fils
32 Grand'rue, Eguisheim,

68420 Herrlisheim
Telephone: (89) 41.44.29

Established: 1653
Winemaker or *oenologist:* Jean-Luc
Freudenreich
Production: 3,000 cases
Vineyards: 5 hectares
Grands crus: 1ha Pfersigberg
(mostly Gewurztraminer and spelt
Pfersichberg on the label)

After almost 350 years the
Freudenreichs are still operating
from the same house, which would
be some sort of a record in any area
other than Alsace. As the current
incumbent, Jean-Luc Freudenreich,
hosts his own music show on local
radio during his spare time, he has a
disproportionate number of actors,
dancers, pop stars, musicians and
magicians among his private
customers. Freudenreich's
Gewurztraminer and Tokay-Pinot
Gris are regularly awarded the
Sigillé de Confrérie St-Étienne,
although the wine I have been most
impressed with is his deliciously
fresh and tangy Riesling, which has
a great depth of racy fruit and
shows true finesse with just a few
years' ageing. All Pierre
Freudenreich's wines are
traditionally fermented in old
wooden casks, with no centrifuge
or any of the other bells or whistles
of high-tech vinification. The
Crémant d'Alsace is produced by
his friend Jacques Cattin (of Joseph
Cattin in Voegtlinshoffen).

Frey

Charles Frey
4 rue des Ours, 67650 Dambach-la-
Ville
Telephone: (88) 92.41.04

Not encountered very often, but the
two wines I have tasted were both
generics and both showed very
good richness (Pinot Noir and
Riesling).

Freyburger

Louis Freyburger & Fils
1 rue du Maire-Witzig,
68750 Bergheim
Telephone: (89) 73.63.82

This is a grower of some repute,
although he cannot produce wines
from Bergheim's *lieu-dit* Burg
anywhere near the quality of
Marcel Deiss. However, I have
tasted good, aromatic
Gewurztraminer Grand Cru
Altenberg de Bergheim and equally
fine generic Tokay-Pinot Gris.

Freyburger

Marcel Freyburger
13 Grand'rue,
68770 Ammerschwihr
Telephone: (89) 78.25.72

Little known about this grower,
apart from a fine, spicy
Gewurztraminer Kaefferkopf.

Freyermuth

Lucien Freyermuth
13 rue de la Gare, 67650 Dambach-
la-Ville

Like the entry for Jean Biecher & Fils, this producer is included for completeness, although I know very little about it. I have not seen these wines, let alone tasted them, but found this producer's name on official statistics during the finishing stages of writing this book and was surprised to discover that such a low-profile firm could be the fifth-largest exporter of Alsace wines. Having already experienced the Biecher phenomenon, I immediately turned to the export figures for Germany, where it was placed fourth, and then to the top 71 Alsace exporters to all countries excluding Germany, where, unlike Biecher, it *was* listed, although at the lowly position of 35th. It does not feature anywhere in the top 100 exporters to all countries (i.e., *including* Germany). These statistics, together with the fact that Freyermuth is the 14th largest wine producer in Alsace, firmly establish it as one of the major players in the bulk wine sector. Big is by no means always bad: the larger the production, the greater the chance of selecting something special to market in small quantities, such as the superb quality Dom Pérignon that the huge Champagne house of Moët & Chandon consistently manages to produce. It all depends, of course, on the philosophy, passion, capability and determination of both the owner and the winemaker. Ever the optimist, I intend paying Lucien Freyermuth a visit on my very next trip to Alsace, to see what little vinous gems might be hidden beneath its sea of bulk-produced wine.

Frick

Pierre Frick
5 rue de Baer, 68250 Pfaffenheim
Telephone: (89) 49.62.99

Winemaker or *oenologist:* Jean-Pierre Frick
Production: 5,000 cases
Vineyards: 8 hectares (3ha Pfaffenheim, 4ha Rouffach, 0.6ha Westhalten, 0.4ha Eguisheim)
Grands crus: 1.3ha Steinert (Pfaffenheim), 0.4ha Eichberg (Eguisheim)

This bio-dynamic producer (Demeter) makes wines without any chaptalization and utilizes three *lieux-dits*: Bergweingarten in Pfaffenheim, Grosstein in Westhalten and Rot-Murlé in Rouffach. The last of these has proven to be the best so far, producing a rich, complete and satisfying Tokay-Pinot Gris that some years can have a distinctive smoky marmalade complexity. Monsieur Frick also makes fine, expressive Riesling and Muscat from Grand Cru Steinert and, in 1989, an outstanding Pinot Blanc Eudémis (*See* 'Top Performers' under Pinot Varietal entry in Chapter 7).

Fritsch

Romain Fritsch
49 rue du Général de Gaulle,
67520 Marlenheim
Telephone: (88) 87.51.23

I have had a good Tokay-Pinot Gris Grand Cru Steinklotz but little else from this grower.

Gaensbroennel

Clos Gaensbroennel
See Domaine WILLM

Gantzer

Lucien Gantzer
4 rue du Nord,
68420 Gueberschwihr

Small but well-known grower with just under one hectare of vines (Gewurztraminer, Riesling and Muscat) on Grand Cru Goldert.

Gaschy

A. Gaschy
Caves de la Martinsbourg, 6 rue Edouard Branley, 6800 Colmar
Telephone: (89) 41.08.90

The son of Antoine Gaschy (*see* next profile) developed the family wine business, which could be traced back through the establishment of A. Gaschy in 1912, which stemmed from the founding of F. Brucker in 1812 and Mathias Custer in 1619. Trying to unravel the modern saga of Gaschy is fraught with problems, not the least being that it is a very touchy subject with many people in the trade, even today. When I started visiting the region to research this book, I naturally included A. Gaschy in the first list I gave to CIVA of producers I wished to visit. The firm was, after all, very

important, being the second-largest *négociant* in terms of volume. The name Gaschy was simply ignored when CIVA organized my itinerary, although every other producer on the list was included without problem. Nothing was said, however. The appointment with Gaschy simply was not made. When I specifically requested an appointment, thinking that it had just been missed off the list by accident, I was told it just would not be possible. Naturally I persisted. Why not, I asked, and was rather reluctantly informed that Brucker-Gaschy had not paid its dues, that 'action' was being taken and, until such action was resolved, CIVA obviously could not contact the firm directly. Every interprofessional organization requires its members to pay a levy. The amount charged is per kilo or per bottle, depending on whether the member in question is a grower or a *négociant*. It is a pittance, but such pittances add up and as Gaschy was at that time the largest exporter in Alsace, there were a great many pittances and they added up to a significant proportion of CIVA's income. I could understand why CIVA did not make an appointment, but Gaschy's production was too important to ignore, so I arranged my own visit, to taste the wines and, as my curiosity was aroused, to find out the other side of the story, if indeed there was one. I managed this by going through the UK agent, Michael Harrison of Norwich, and I have to say that I found Jean

Antoine Gaschy to be a charming man. He was very candid about the situation of his firm, agreeing that he had not paid his dues, but asked why he should. He immodestly told me that he was the most successful salesman of wine in Alsace and achieved this by finding the right wine at the right price. What, he asked, did CIVA do to help him sell his wine? Nothing, he claimed. Why, therefore, should he give CIVA a share of his profits? Why indeed? The fact is, however, that the French wine industry is what it is through exercising a certain régime. I was not able to disagree with a word that Gaschy said, but knew that it would result in total anarchy. It would seem that he managed to sell the wines at the 'right' price only by undercutting everyone and the price received did not cover his overheads. After considerable financial difficulties, the inevitable happened and the company went broke. The trademarks were sold to a bulk-bottling firm that specializes in generic French wines primarily for the German market and Jean Antoine Gaschy now works for this firm, whose generic Alsace wines sell under the A. Gaschy and F. Brucker labels.

Gaschy

Antoine Gaschy
1 rue de Château, Wettolsheim, 6000 Colmar
Telephone: (89) 79.99.59

With only one hectare of Riesling

and Gewurztraminer, which Monsieur Gaschy utilizes mostly for himself and his family, plus a few bottles sold to tourists, this grower would not warrant an entry in this book, but for the fact that this is the old address for Brucker-Gaschy, which needs some explaining. This is Antoine Gaschy (the father of Jean Antoine), a gentleman in his seventies. The father has now sold off most of his vineyards and rented out all but one hectare of the rest. He lives here in semi-retirement, his tiny private production merely requiring the small old cellar under the original house. The big bottling plant and cellars at the back of the house, which once belonged to Brucker-Gaschy, have been sold and Monsieur Gaschy's courtyard is sealed off from these production facilities by a wire fence.

Gaschy

Bernard Gaschy Succ.
16 Grand'rue, 68420 Eguisheim

No connection with the preceding two Gaschys, this small grower's vineyards include just under half a hectare of Riesling on Grand Cru Eichberg.

Gassmann

See ROLLY GASSMANN

Geiler

Jean Geiler
Cooperative label accounting for 20

per cent of CV Ingersheim's sales.
See CV INGERSHEIM

Gène

Madame Sans Gène
A cooperative Crémant d'Alsace
label.
See CV WESTHALTEN

Geschickt

Jérôme Geschickt & Fils
1 place de la Sinne,
68770 Ammerschwihr
Telephone: (89) 47.12.54

Good Kaefferkopf Riesling Réserve,
which is quite elegant for the *cru*.
The Kaefferkopf Gewurztraminer is
often a bit on the sweet side, but
can be lifted in some years by a
touch of spritz on the finish, while
the generic Gewurztraminer
Vendange Tardive is strangely not
too sweet and has a tremendous
grapefruity character. Also known
as Domaine de la Sinne (every wine
village once had a *Sinne*, where
every cask of wine had to pass to be
assessed and gauged before it was
allowed to leave the town; after the
Sinne the wine travelled at the risk
of the buyer).

Geyer

Roger and Roland Geyer
148 route du Vin, 67680 Nothalten
Telephone: (88) 92.46.82

Also known as Domaine Geyer, this
family enterprise has eight hectares
of vineyards that include a plot on
the *grands crus* of Muenchberg and

Wiebelsberg, but I have not tasted
these wines.

Gilg

Armand Gilg
2 rue Rotland,
67140 Mittelbergheim
Telephone: (88) 08.92.76

From this producer's 20 hectares of
vineyards, I have tasted good
Riesling Grand Cru Moenchberg.
He also grows Gewurztraminer on
the Grand Cru Zinnkoepflé, but I
have not tasted the wine and have
only occasionally encountered his
generic wines.

Ginglinger

Paul Ginglinger
8 place Charles de Gaulle,
68420 Eguisheim
Telephone: (89) 41.44.25

This grower is the president of the
Eguisheim History Society. His
vineyards include just over 2
hectares of Grand Cru Eichberg (50
per cent Gewurtztraminer, 30 per
cent Riesling, 15 per cent Tokay-
Pinot Gris and 5 per cent Muscat)
and his wines are vinified very
traditionally in wooden *foudre* with
natural wild yeasts. Some good to
very good wines are produced here.

Ginglinger

Pierre-Henri Ginglinger
4 and 33 Grand'rue,
68420 Eguisheim
Telephone: (89) 41.32.55

Small grower with two-thirds of a hectare of Gewurztraminer and Riesling on Grand Cru Eichberg, but not tasted, although I have had the occasional generic of some interest.

Ginglinger-Fix

Ginglinger-Fix
38 rue Roger-Frémeaux,
68420 Voegtlinshoffen

Small grower with 1.5 hectares of Gewurztraminer on Grand Cru Hatschbourg.

Gisselbrecht

Louis Gisselbrecht
5 rue du Sapin, 67650 Dambach-la-Ville
Telephone: (88) 92.41.24

Established: 1936 by Louis Gisselbrecht
Production: 70,000 cases
Vineyards: 12 hectares (6ha Dambach-la-Ville, 0.5ha Châtenois, 2ha Scherwiller, 1ha Itterswiller, 2.5ha Dieffenthal), representing about 12 per cent of total production, plus 4ha rented (Dambach-la-Ville) and contracts with more than 50 growers
Grape varieties: 0.6ha Sylvaner, 6ha Riesling, 2.4ha Pinot Blanc, 0.6ha Tokay-Pinot Gris, 1.2ha Pinot Noir, 1.2ha Gewurztraminer
Grands crus: 2.5ha Frankstein (Dambach-la-Ville)

Until this house produced Riesling Grand Cru Frankstein in 1988, it had stubbornly stuck to a single range of varietal wines, all of which were labelled Grande Réserve, whatever the quality happened to be. There were no special *cuvées* unless a wine happened to win a medal, in which case it would be sold under the designation of that particular award. While this may sound boring as a range, it should really have been extremely effective at boosting the quality of those solitary generic wines, as there were no special wines to cream off the quality from the lower blends. The unfortunate and totally baffling truth is that for no apparent reason, the wines of Louis Gisselbrecht were virtually always lacklustre and foursquare. In fact, they still are. There is nothing overtly wrong with them in terms of identifiable faults, they are all technically sound, but that is all they are – sound. They are so sound they are boring, with nothing special, different or stylish about them at all. Only the extrovert character of Gewurztraminer manages to shine through the dull straitjacket of the Louis Gisselbrecht style, making it the most enjoyable variety of the range. The 1988 Riesling Grand Cru Frankstein turned out to be good and was just developing a little honeyed character in 1992, while the 1989 was a touch finer in quality, with the intensity expected of the year, although atypically restrained on the nose.

Gisselbrecht

Willy Gisselbrecht & Fils
Route de Vin, 67650 Dambach-la-
Ville
Telephone: (88) 92.41.02

Established: 1936 by Willy
Gisselbrecht
Production: 150,000 cases
Vineyards: 15 hectares (8.5ha
Dambach-la-Ville, 2.5ha
Dieffenthal, 3ha Scherwiller, 1ha
Châtenois), representing about 10
per cent of total production, with
the balance coming from contracts
(some written, some merely an
understanding) with more than 250
growers owning 140 hectares
Grape varieties: 2ha Sylvaner, 5ha
Riesling, 2.5ha Pinot Blanc, 1ha
Tokay-Pinot Gris, 2ha Pinot Noir,
2.5ha Gewurztraminer
Grands crus: Frankstein (Dambach-
la-Ville)

The firm of Willy Gisselbrecht is far
bigger in size and yet much better in
quality than cousin Louis
Gisselbrecht just around the corner.
The strange thing is that Willy is far
less well known than Louis in some
markets, particularly the UK, due
no doubt to the varying level of
performance of their respective
importers. Unlike Louis, Willy
Gisselbrecht is typically Alsace in
his production, with numerous
qualities and *cuvées* of wine and to
illustrate how serious they are in
this respect, one has only to look at
the winery. Willy Gisselbrecht has a
large number of small vats and
casks and more were installed in
1987 to ensure the optimum

conditions for the fermentation of
many small *cuvées* of *grands crus*
and Vendanges Tardives, which
were becoming the trend. This firm
is run by two very nice brothers of
totally contrasting character: Jean,
who is small and as quiet as a
mouse, and Léon, who is taller and
more gregarious. There are several
fine wines to be found here, but I
would sum up Willy Gisselbrecht as
an essentially Gewurztraminer
house that can often turn out
exceptional Tokay-Pinot Gris under
its Cuvée Espécial label (and,
frankly superior to its good, but not
exceptional Grand Cru Frankstein).
The 100 per cent pure Auxerrois
Crémant d'Alsace has good, fat
Pinot character, backed up by fine
acidity.

Gocker

Philippe Gocker
24 rue de Riquewihr,
68630 Mittelwihr
Telephone: (89) 47.92.73

Small family enterprise owning
some seven hectares of vineyards.

Goldlinger

A non-AOC vin mousseux sold by
Ch. Wantz.

Grass

Clos Philippe Grass
See MUHLBERGER

Greiner

Jean Greiner
1 rue du Vignoble,
68630 Mittelwihr
Telephone: (89) 47.90.41

The original Jean Greiner established himself as a *vigneron* in Mittelwihr in 1636. Part of the family vineyards today include a good size plot on the Grand Cru Mandelberg, which also claims the Côte des Amandiers denomination, but I have not tasted this or any of his other wines as yet.

Greiner-Schleret

GAEC Greiner-Schleret
22 rue de Riquewihr,
68630 Mittelwihr
Telephone: (89) 47.92.67

Another small grower whose wines I have not tasted, Greiner-Schleret also owns a small plot on the Grand Cru Mandelberg and he too utilizes the Côte des Amandiers denomination for his wines.

Gresser

Domaine André Gresser
See Domaine André & Rémy
GRESSER

Gresser

Domaine André & Rémy Gresser
2 rue de l'Ecole, 67140 Andlau
Telephone: (88) 08.95.88

Established: 1667
Winemaker or *oenologist:* Rémy
Gresser

Production: 5,500 cases
Vineyards: 10 hectares (6ha Andlau, 3.4ha Eichhoffen, 0.6ha Epfig)
Grands crus: 0.2ha Kastelberg (Andlau), 0.8ha Moenchberg (Andlau and Moenchberg), 1ha Wiebelsberg (Andlau)

Also known as Domaine André Gresser and sold as Domaine André-Rémy Gresser until relatively recently, this is one of the most active producers in Andlau. Rémy Gresser is a young and very energetic exponent of *terroir* and proud of the fact that his wine comes from eight different soil types, each being bottled separately. He has established his reputation on Riesling from all three Andlau *grands crus* (including the finest Moenchberg Riesling produced), the Brandhof Pinot Noir (although I prefer his Tokay-Pinot Gris) and Andlau Gewurztraminer. When used by this producer, the term 'Sélection Vieilles Vignes' actually means something because it signifies that the wine has been produced from vines of 65 years or older.

Gresser

Domaine André-Rémy Gresser
See Domaine André & Rémy
GRESSER

Gros

J-H Gros & Ses Fils
The owner of Château Ollwiller and Clos de la Tourelle.
See CV VIEIL ARMAND

Gruss

Bernard Gruss
See Joseph GRUSS & Fils

Gruss

Joseph Gruss & Fils
25 Grand'rue, 68420 Eguisheim
Telephone: (89) 41.28.78

A couple of generic wines from this grower have come my way, the most memorable of which was a charming Pinot Noir, which displayed gentle, round fruit characteristics. Also known as Bernard Gruss.

Gsell

Joseph Gsell
26 Grand'rue, 68500 Orschwihr
Telephone: (89) 76.95.11

Nothing known about this producer.

Gueth

A. Gueth & Fils
5 rue St-Sébastien, 68230 Walbach
Telephone: (89) 71.11.20

Vignerons since 1661, this grower's vineyards include plots on the *lieu-dit* of Felsen in the Côte Val St-Grégoire. Also known as Edgard Gueth.

Gueth

Edgard Gueth
See A. GUETH & Fils

Haegelin

Matterne Haegelin
45-47 Grand'rue, 68500 Orschwihr
Telephone: (89) 76.95.17

The best wine here is Haegelin's tremendously rich, well structured Tokay-Pinot Gris Cuvée Élise, which is very expressive, with its spicy aroma, and has great potential longevity.

Haegi

GAEC Bernard & Daniel Haegi
33 rue de la Montagne,
67140 Mittelbergheim
Telephone: (88) 08.95.80

The best wines I have had from this small grower have both been Riesling (Brandluft and Grand Cru Zotzenberg).

Halbeisen

Jean Halbeisen
43 Grande'rue, 68750 Bergheim

This small family enterprise works 11 hectares of vineyards in Bergheim, Colmar, Kaysersberg and Riquewihr, including just over half a hectare of Gewurztraminer on the Grand Cru Altenberg de Bergheim.

Hartmann

André Hartmann
11 rue Roger Frémeaux,
68420 Voegtlinshoffen
Telephone: (89) 49.38.34

Rich, well-balanced, fruity Riesling

Armoirie Hartmann of some class, but the Tokay-Pinot Gris under the same label is relatively disappointing.

Hartmann

Gérard & Serge Hartmann
13 rue Roger Frémeaux,
68420 Voegtlinshoffen
Telephone: (89) 49.30.27

Seemingly erratic quality, but tasted only occasionally, so I might be unlucky. Nevertheless, I have had some good wines, especially Gewurztraminer and Tokay-Pinot Gris from the Grand Cru Hatschbourg.

Hartmann

Hubert Hartmann
See Château d'ORSCHWIHR

Hartweg

Jean-Paul Hartweg
39 rue Jean-Macé,
68980 Beblenheim

A well-known grower with Gewurztraminer on the Grand Cru Sonnenglanz, but nothing that stands out in my mind.

Hauller

J. Hauller & Fils
18 rue de la Gare, 67650 Dambach-la-Ville
Telephone: (88) 92.40.21

Established: 1956 by Jean Hauller
Production: 200,000 cases

Vineyards: 18.3 hectares (9.4ha Dambach-la-Ville, 7.3ha Scherwiller, 1.6ha Châtenois), representing just 7 or 8 per cent of total production, the balance supplied through purchases from non-contracted growers
Grape varieties: 1.8ha Sylvaner, 9.7ha Riesling, 2.1ha Pinot Blanc, 0.6ha Tokay-Pinot Gris, 0.8ha Pinot Noir, 3ha Gewurztraminer, 0.3ha Muscat Ottonel
Grands crus: 4ha Frankstein (Dambach-la-Ville)
Labels: Wines from this producer are found under various labels, which are restricted to certain markets, such as Hellmuth (France), Biehler (Holland), Roth (Germany) and Willmann (selected markets)

A very large producer (twice the size of Hugel & Fils, for example), but very capable, J. Hauller regularly makes wines of excellent value. Well known for its fine quality Sylvaner of extraordinary longevity in some vintages, this variety represents almost 20 per cent of the firm's total production. The best wine in recent times, however, has been the very elegant Gewurztraminer Grand Cru Frankstein. I have often enjoyed very soft, ripe and easy to drink Klevner; a *bon vin lampant* indeed. Riesling is fresh and peachy in style, and immensely enjoyable at the lowest generic level, but the Cuvée St-Sébastien shows great petrolly intensity and finesse with a few years in bottle. Old vintages of Riesling Vendanges Tardives have been quite exceptional (1976 was fantastic), but I have not tasted this style recently. Of the Gewurztraminer, the Cuvée St-Sébastien shows the finer, crisper-cut varietal character, but the Cuvée du Barillier has more finesse. I strongly recommend that you visit this truly underrated, very friendly producer and taste the wines for yourself.

Hauller

Louis Hauller
Domaine du Tonnelier
92 rue du Maréchal Foch,
67650 Dambach-la-Ville
Telephone: (88) 92.41.19

Established: by 1989 by a family that had been growers and cask-makers (hence Domaine du Tonnelier) since 1786
Winemaker or *oenologist:* Louis Hauller
Production: 5,500 cases
Vineyards: 8.3 hectares (4.3ha Dambach-la-Ville, 3ha Epfig, 1ha Blienschwiller)
Grands crus: 0.5ha Frankstein (Dambach-la-Ville), 0.2ha Winzenberg (Blienschwiller)

My experience of this Hauller is limited to six wines tasted in 1990, when nothing special stood out. Also known as Domaine du Tonnelier.

Hauserer

Clos Hauserer
See ZIND HUMBRECHT

Hebinger

Jean-Victor Hebinger & Fils
14 Grand'rue, 68420 Eguisheim
Telephone: (89) 41.19.90

Apart from one good Gewurztraminer tasted, I know very little about this grower.

Heim

Jean-Paul Heim
2 rue du Meunier,
67520 Kuttolsheim

Small producer of Pinot Blanc, Sylvaner and Riesling under the Vin de Pays du Bas-Rhin denomination.

Heim

SA Heim
Old established producer dating back to 1765, but now merely a *sous marque* of the Westhalten cooperative.
See CV WESTHALTEN

Heitzmann

H. & J. Heitzmann & Fils
2 Grand'rue, 68770 Ammerschwihr
Telephone: (89) 47.10.64

Capable of honey-rich Tokay-Pinot Gris, particularly in the Vendange Tardive style.

Hell-Cadé

Léon Hell-Cadé
14 route de Colmar,
68500 Guebwiller

This grower owns a small plot of

Gewurztraminer at the foot of the Grand Cru Kitterlé.

Hellmuth

A *sous marque* used by J. Hauller for France.
See J. HAULLER

Hering

Domaine Hering
6 rue Sultzer, 67140 Barr
Telephone: (88) 08.90.07

Established: 1858
Winemaker or *oenologist:* Pierre Hering
Production: 6,500 cases
Vineyards: 9 hectares (8.1ha Barr, 0.9ha Mittelbergheim)
Grands crus: 6ha Kirchberg de Barr

Of the several wines I have tasted of late from this producer, the Riesling Grand Cru Kirchberg de Barr certainly stands out as the finest, promising almost eternal youth, but I have not been very impressed with any others. Also known as Pierre Hering and Ed. Hering & Fils

Hertz

Albert Hertz
3 rue du Riesling, 68420 Eguisheim
Telephone: (89) 41.30.32

Established: 1982
Winemaker or *oenologist:* Albert Hertz
Production: 4,500 cases
Vineyards: 5 hectares (4ha Eguisheim, 1ha Herrlisheim)
Grands crus: 1ha Eichberg

(Eguisheim), 1ha Pfersigberg (Eguisheim)
Labels: Prince Albert (Crémant d'Alsace)

One of the best producers of Pinot Noir in Alsace, at a blind tasting of more than 70 of these wines from three different vintages, Albert Hertz came out on top in both 1988 and 1989. These are well-coloured, beautifully balanced and elegantly styled wines that retain youthful fruit and vigour for several years. The generic Riesling combines racy richness with freshness and, after a couple of years in bottle, petrolly finesse. His generic Gewurztraminer can also excel, with its firm, pungently spicy flavour, which is every bit as good as his excellent Grand Cru Eichberg. Unfortunately, the only opportunity I had to taste the Crémant d'Alsace (40 per cent Chardonnay, 40 per cent Pinot Blanc and 20 per cent Auxerrois), the wine was corked. Also known as A. Hertz-Meyer.

Hertz

Bruno Hertz
9 place de l'Église,
68420 Eguisheim
Telephone: (89) 41.81.61

This small grower is capable of producing an exceptional generic Tokay-Pinot Gris in ripe years and characterful Gewurztraminer Grand Cru Rangen that has good grip and well-charged spice.

Hertz-Meyer

A. Hertz-Meyer
See Albert HERTZ

Hertzog

Gérard Hertzog
30 rue des Forgerons,
68420 Gueberschwihr

The Hertzogs have been *vignerons* since 1612, with vineyards that include just over half a hectare of Gewurztraminer on Grand Cru Goldert.

Hertzog

Marcel Hertzog
6 place de la Marie,
68420 Gueberschwihr

Marcel Hertzog, who has for many years been the organist at Gueberschwihr church, owns just over two hectares of Grand Cru Goldert, from which he has made very good Gewurztraminer. Riesling and Muscat also grown.

Heydt

Excellent quality *sous marque* produced by F.E. Trimbach
See F.E. TRIMBACH

Heywang

Jean Heywang
7 rue Principale,
67140 Heiligenstein
Telephone: (88) 08.91.41

Established: 1954
Winemaker or *oenologist:* Jean and

Hubert Heywang
Production: 3,500 cases
Vineyards: 5.5 hectares (3ha Heiligenstein, 2.5ha Barr)
Grands crus: 0.9ha Kirchberg de Barr

One of the best producers of Klevener de Heiligenstein, although I find that variety more interesting than actually fulfilling and thus prefer Heywang's Gewurztraminer, especially his elegant, understated Grand Cru Kirchberg de Barr, which ages very gracefully.

Hoen

Baron de Hoen
Cooperative label for export markets, accounting for 25 per cent of CV Beblenheim's production.
See CV BEBLENHEIM

Hoen

Caves de Hoen
Cooperative label for traditional, on-site sales, accounting for 25 per cent of CV Beblenheim's production.
See CV BEBLENHEIM

Horcher

Ernest Horcher & Fils
6 rue due Vignoble,
68630 Mittelwihr
Telephone: (89) 47.93.26

Established: 1948
Winemaker or *oenologist:* Alfred Horcher
Production: 5,500 cases
Vineyards: 7 hectares (6ha

Mittelwihr, 1ha Riquewihr)
Grands crus: 0.3ha Mandelberg
(Mittelwihr)

I tasted a range of these wines for
the first time in 1990, but regret to
say that nothing stood out.

Horstein

J. Horstein
A *sous marque* used by CV
Pfaffenheim.
See CV PFAFFENHEIM

Hugel

Hugel & Fils
68430 Riquewihr
Telephone: (89) 47.92.15

Established: 1639 by H. U. Hugelin
Production: 100,000 cases
Vineyards: 25 hectares (0.4ha
Zellenberg, 24.6ha Riquewihr),
representing approximately 20 per
cent of total production, the
balance provided by more than 300
contracted growers owning 115
hectares
Grape varieties: 12ha Riesling,
1.2ha Tokay-Pinot Gris, 0.5ha
Pinot Noir, 11.2ha
Gewurztraminer, 0.1ha Muscat
Blanc à Petit Grains
Grands crus: 8ha Sporen
(Riquewihr), 3.8ha Schoenenbourg
(Riquewihr)

The most famous Alsace producer
in the world, Hugel has enormous
stocks in its vast cellars, which seem
to stretch further underground than
the actual village does on the
surface. The Hugel dynasty has

always provided some of Alsace's
greatest characters and it has not
failed us with 'Johnny' Hugel, the
twelfth generation to control the
vineyards and make the wines for
this great house since Hans Ulrich
Hugelin established the firm in
1639. The name Hugel means 'hill'
in Alsace dialect, which explains the
three hills or mounds on the family
crest (which itself dates from 1672).
Although Johnny still maintains a
very high-profile presence in the
firm, the business is gradually
passing into the hands of the
thirteenth generation, with the
quiet and composed Marc Hugel
taking over the winemaking role,
while Étienne tries manfully to
assume Johnny's marketing role.
Trying to fill his uncle's shoes on
the international scene is a hard
enough task anyway, but when
Johnny keeps stealing the limelight
it is almost impossible. The truth is
that Johnny will not stop talking
about Hugel until he is carried out
feet first and that, we all hope, will
not be for a long time.

Despite Hugel's well deserved
reputation, I have always found the
basic generics a bit lacking and
ordinary, although there is no
reason for this, especially as Johnny
has always insisted on minimum
ripeness levels well in excess of the
norm. The Gewurztraminer is an
exception to this disappointment,
but the one generic wine that has
risen above its previous standard
has been the Pinot 'Blanc de Blancs'
(labelled 'Les Amours' or 'Les
Vignards' on some markets), which
was not very special until the

splendid 1987 vintage, since when it has consistently been one of the region's most classic examples of this grape. For me, however, the real Hugel quality starts with its second range of Cuvée Tradition wines and gets really exciting with the third range of Jubilée Réserve Personnelle. The Tokay-Pinot Gris is an ideal example of this progression in quality, starting out with an ordinary generic that is never a poor wine but rarely excites, then assuming more richness and real style with the 'Cuvée Tradition' and then true class and finesse with the 'Jubilée Réserve Personnelle'. It should be noted that I do not say that the latter *cuvée* is even richer, as most of the time it is not weightier or fuller or sweeter. Its richness is exquisitely delicate and it is the refinement of style that gives the wine its undeniable class and finesse.

The Pinot Noir is a wine to watch here. The Jubilée Réserve Personnelle has not always been a first choice of mine, but in recent years this wine has developed in its structure and varietal character, building in the glass with an intensity that deepens with each vintage. While the generic Gewurztraminer is worth buying, I would miss the Cuvée Tradition and go for the Jubilée Réserve Personnelle, which has a fine, warm pungency of vanilla and banana spice. Hugel also produces one of the very greatest blended wines of Alsace, in a wine called Sporen Gentil until 'Gentil' was banned

1973 and then simply Sporen Hugel until Sporen was added to the list of *grands crus* and thus banned for blended wines. What this wine might be called in the future is not certain, but that its production will continue is (*see* Sporen entry under 'Blended Wines' in Chapter 7).

The Hugels are masters of several styles, but if they are supreme masters of anything, then it must surely be the art of late-harvest wine. Whereas most other producers are just coming to grips with Vendange Tardive and SGN wines, the Hugels have a cellar full of wonderful gems going back to the last century because it was they who essentially pioneered these styles of wine. Their Gewurztraminer, Tokay-Pinot Gris and Riesling Vendanges Tardives are special wines indeed, as are the Tokay-Pinot Gris and Riesling Sélections de Grains Nobles (*see* the 'In a totally different class' list of élite wines under the relevant entries in Chapter 7).

Humbrecht

Bernard Humbrecht
9 place de la Mairie,
68420 Gueberschwihr
Telephone: (89) 49.31.42

From a family of winegrowers dating back to 1620, Bernard Humbrecht's vineyards include two hectares of mostly Gewurztraminer (but also some Riesling and a little Muscat) on the Grand Cru Goldert. This grower is capable of very good wines indeed, especially Riesling.

Humbrecht

Marcel Humbrecht
18 rue Basse, 68420 Gueberschwihr
Telephone: (89) 49.31.47

This small grower makes superb village Riesling and owns just over two-thirds of a hectare on Grand Cru Goldert, where he grows Gewurztraminer, Riesling and Muscat, the last of which can be very fine indeed.

Hunaperle

Crémant d'Alsace label.
See CV HUNAWIHR

CV Hunawihr

Cave Coopérative Vinicole de Hunawihr et Environs
48 route de Ribeauvillé, Hunawihr, 68150 Ribeauvillé
Telephone: (89) 73.61.67

Established: 1955
Current membership: 96
Production: 160,000 cases (including 2 per cent sold to *négociants*)
Vineyards: 194 hectares
Grands crus: 9ha Rosacker (Hunawihr)
Labels: Calixte II (Crémant d'Alsace), Hunaperle (Crémant d'Alsace)

This cooperative produced an astonishing Tokay-Pinot Gris Réserve in 1988, with such fabulous acidity to back up its huge, intense fruit that it should have tremendous ageing potential.

Hunold

Bruno Hunold
29 rue aux Quatre-Vents, 68250 Rouffach
Telephone: (89) 49.60.57

Small grower with ten hectares of vineyards. Of the very few wines encountered, I have enjoyed a fruity Pinot Noir and a good Grand Cru Vorbourg.

Hurst

Auguste Hurst
5 rue Ste-Anne, 68230 Turckheim

This relatively unknown grower happens to be the largest owner of Grand Cru Brand, with just over five hectares (31 per cent Riesling, 30 per cent Gewurztraminer, 14 per cent Tokay-Pinot Gris, 14 per cent Pinot Noir and 11 per cent Muscat).

Huttard

Jean Huttard
10 route du Vin, 68340 Zellenberg
Telephone: (89) 47.90.49

Winemaker or *ocnologist:* Jean Claude Huttard
Production: 4,500 cases
Vineyards: 7 hectares (Bennwihr, Mittelwihr, Beblenheim, Riquewihr, Hunawihr, Ribeauvillé, Zellenberg), which account for this grower's total production
Grands crus: 0.1ha Sonnenglanz (Beblenheim), 0.1ha Marckrain (Bennwihr), 0.2ha Mandelberg (Mittelwihr)

Either I have been extremely unlucky or Monsieur Huttard has a big problem with his corks, which is a pity as some of his wines seemed to be very promising underneath their corky taint. With this qualification, the quality of his generic Gewurztraminer stood out.

Iltis

Jacques Iltis
1 rue Schlossreben, 68590 St-Hippolyte
Telephone: (89) 73.00.67

Very fruity Rouge de St-Hippolyte and a powerful Riesling Schlossreben.

CV Ingersheim

Cave Coopérative d'Ingersheim
1 rue Georges Clémenceau, Ingersheim, 68000 Colmar
Telephone: (89) 27.05.96

Established: 1926
Current membership: 181
Production: 250,000 cases
Vineyards: 259 hectares
(Ingersheim, Colmar, Katzenthal, Ammerschwihr, Niedermorschwihr)
Grands crus: 1.5ha (Florimont, Ingersheim and Sommerberg, Niedermorschwihr and Katzenthal)
Labels: Jean Geiler (20 per cent of sales), Weingartner (10 per cent), in addition to which the wines of Kuehn and Albert Schoech are separately accounted for in excess of the 250,000 cases indicated above

This cooperative excels at Riesling and Tokay-Pinot Gris. The best Riesling is, without doubt, the Grand Cru Sommerberg, which sometimes rivals Albert Boxler's brilliance, but the Steinweg is also a fine wine and one that probably requires more ageing. Although I have occasionally been disappointed by CV Ingersheim's generic Tokay-Pinot Gris, its Grande Cuvée is usually very good indeed and the Réserve Particulière is even better, in a richer, more upfront fashion. I have recently been impressed by this cooperative's big, smoky-rich Gewurztraminer Grand Cru Florimont and, occasionally, it can produce a fine Pinot Noir; the 1983 Grande Cave, for example, was a wine of tremendous delicacy for the year and one that has also aged gracefully.

Isenbourg

Château d'Isenbourg
See DOPFF & IRION

JosMeyer

JosMeyer
76 rue Clémenceau, Wintzenheim, 68000 Colmar
Telephone: (89) 27.01.57

Established: 1854 by Aloyse Meyer
Production: 33,000 cases
Vineyards: 12 hectares (4ha Wintzenheim, 8ha Turckheim), including 4ha rented, and representing about 40 per cent of total production, plus contracts

with 50 growers
Grape varieties: 1.2ha Sylvaner,
3.5ha Riesling, 2.1ha Pinot Blanc
and Auxerrois, 1.3ha Tokay-Pinot
Gris, 3.5ha Gewurztraminer, 0.2ha
Muscat Ottonel, 0.1ha Muscat
Blanc à Petit Grains, 0.1ha Muscat
Rosé à Petit Grains
Grands crus: 2ha Hengst
(Wintzenheim), 0.2ha Brand
(Turckheim)

This firm takes its name from the
son of its founder and was first used
by his son, Hubert Meyer, just after
the Second World War. The name
has gradually evolved from Joseph
Meyer & Fils, through Jos. Meyer
& Fils, to the current title of
JosMeyer, hence its alphabetical
position. Hubert Meyer's son is in
charge of the company today and
his responsibilities include making
the wines, which are large in
number and always attempt to be
very expressive, although some are
more successful than others.

Jean Meyer holds very passionate
views about Alsace, its quality and
future. One of his causes concerns
the effect that *grand cru* wines will
have on subsequent generations of
winemakers in his region. He
believes very strongly that *grand
cru* status should be available to all
varieties, not just the four classic
ones. His worry is that *grand cru*
sites, which naturally include most
of the best vineyards in Alsace, will
eventually be robbed of all
traditional vines that are not
perceived as noble varieties (e.g.,
Chasselas, Sylvaner, etc.). Meyer
recognizes that these varieties make

modest wines, but everything is
relative and, grown on the very best
sites, they obviously produce the
greatest possible examples of their
type. He thinks it is vital that such
yardsticks are kept alive, for
otherwise future generations will
have no inkling of the limits to
which these lowly varieties can be
stretched. There is nothing, of
course, to prevent growers from
continuing to grow these vines on
grand cru sites, provided they do
not commercialize the wines they
yield under the name of their
respective *crus*, but with the
premium paid for wines of *grand
cru* status, it is inevitable that all the
prized *grand cru* vineyards will one
day be planted exclusively with the
four money-making noble varieties.
It would not be possible, or right, to
redress the economic balance
completely, but a little financial
encouragement could be sufficient
to persuade some of the more
dedicated exponents of these
modest varieties to persevere. A
grand cru Chasselas would never
command the price received for a
Riesling, Gewurztraminer, Tokay-
Pinot Gris or Muscat *grand cru*, but
it could demand a premium over
other Chasselas and that premium
could be the difference required to
continue its cultivation. Meyer does
not see any reason why there should
not be such a thing as a *grand cru*
Chasselas and, frankly, neither do I,
but maybe a compromise could be
to commercialize the wines under
the name of the *grand cru* without
mentioning its status. I doubt that it
will ever happen because the

authorities have no interest in the survival of yardstick wines for such lowly vines as Chasselas *et al.*, even if the superior quality of such wines would enhance the reputation of Alsace. So what we have is dedicated people like Jean Meyer growing Chasselas on the Hengst and selling it as Chasselas 'H', which everyone knows means the Hengst anyway, while the authorities force the vast majority of these lesser vine varieties down on to the plain, where they can be cropped at the highest conceivable level, to make the cheapest possible generics or blend them into that wonderful flagship wine of Alsace called Edelzwicker. Perhaps somebody should make the point that as Pinot Blanc is the biggest growth area of Alsace, would it not be wise (or extremely profitable, if that is what it takes to move the powers that be) to encourage *grand cru* Pinot Blanc as the logical, upmarket target for new Alsace consumers to aim for?

Those interested in Chasselas should taste his fluffy-light 'H' Vieilles Vignes, although it is another modest variety that JosMeyer excels with on the Hengst: Auxerrois (Pinot Auxerrois 'H' Vieilles Vignes), which has a classic firm structure for such a weighty wine and is surprisingly complex. For more everyday drinking, the lighter, creamy Pinot Les Luttins is worth trying. Riesling is his most serious wine and JosMeyer Riesling Grand Cru Hengst can rival Domaine Zind Humbrecht's, given enough time in

bottle. The Gewurztraminer Les Archenets is consistently excellent, with beautiful spicy-banana finesse. Potentially higher in quality, but much less consistent, are the Gewurztraminers from the Grand Cru Hengst and the *lieu-dit* Herrenweg.

There are so many different *cuvées* here, that some brief explanation might be prudent: Mize du Printemps is used for Pinot Blanc that is bottled and sold in the spring (which *printemps* means in French) following the harvest; Le Kottabe is used for Riesling that is bottled and sold for drinking in the summer following the harvest; Cuvée des Folastries is used for Gewurztraminer that is bottled and sold in the late summer cum autumn following the harvest; Cuvée de la St-Martin is used for Hengst Riesling harvested on or about St Martin's Day, 11 November, which replaces the harvest-dated *cuvées* that are no longer allowed; Les Lutins is used for Pinot Blanc blended from several different locations, all of which have a similar soil (*lutin* means goblin or gnome, hence the roguish little chaps on the label); Les Pierrets is used for Riesling blended from several different locations, all of which have a similar soil; Les Archenets is used for Gewurztraminer blended from several different locations, all of which have a similar soil; Les Fleurons is used for Muscat blended from several different locations, all of which have a similar soil.

Since the late 1980s, the biggest

change in JosMeyer's vinification technique has been the abandonment of cultured yeast in favour of natural, indigenous yeast.

Jung

GAEC Roger Jung & Fils
23 rue de la 1ère Armée,
68340 Riquewihr
Telephone: (89) 47.92.17

This small, underrated producer owns vineyards in Riquewihr and Hunawihr, including plots on the *grands crus* of Schoenenbourg and Rosacker. Roger Jung has some lovely surprises for anyone who seeks out his range. The Pinot Blanc Les Préludes, for example, is a delightfully fresh and zesty wine that may have a slight spritz to lift the richness of its fruit. The Pinot Noir has lovely varietal aromas and almost sweet, redcurrant-pastille fruit, with just enough tannin to control development for a couple of years. I have also tasted attractive Muscat and in 1989 the Gewurztraminer Vendange Tardive had the botrytis expected in the better examples of that year, which gave the wine its velvety texture and mouth-filling concentration.

Jux

Domaine Jux
Chemin de la Fecht, 68000 Colmar
Telephone: (89) 79.13.76

Established: 1950
Production: 40,000 cases
Vineyards: 105 hectares, of which 85ha are planted, which account

for this domaine's entire production
Grape varieties: 2.5ha Sylvaner, 2.5ha Chasselas, 31.5ha Riesling, 8.9ha Pinot Blanc, 1.7ha Tokay-Pinot Gris, 16.2ha Pinot Noir, 18.3ha Gewurztraminer, 3.4ha Muscat (mixed), plus 20ha fallow

This domaine was established by Charles Jux, who was related to the owners of the Jux-Jacobert Distillery, founded in 1874 and purchased by Wolfberger in 1979 (now called Distillerie Wolfberger). It took Jux 28 years from 1945 to 1973 to build up the domaine to its present size, which is second only to Schlumberger, by purchasing over 200 different plots of lands. When completed, he had assembled the largest and most homogeneous domaine completely contained within an area known as the Hardt (*see* 'Colmar' entry, under 'Villages Profiles' in Chapter 4). At its height, Domaine Jux produced in excess of 83,000 cases, but most was of this was traded in bulk (Dopff & Irion had a contract to buy large quantities of grapes and wine) and only a small proportion was bottled and sold direct to tourists. Domaine Jux was taken over by Wolfberger in 1989 and when one weighs the potential production of this domain against the long-term task of building up sales, its survival depended on finding an organisation of the size and diversity of Eguisheim's cooperative simply to absorb the huge excess in production. Sales currently stand at just over 800 cases direct (i.e., at the domaine itself) and less than 1,500 cases wholesale.

The wines of the Hardt should be typically bright and rich, with plenty of flavour, but no great longevity. It is still early days for Wolfberger, but from the four major varieties of the 1989 vintage I have tasted, Gewurztraminer and Riesling fare the best, although there is a lot of room for development in both the quality of the product and its expressiveness. With Roland Guth in charge, this will happen, I am sure. That apart, I have just one criticism of Wolfberger's custodianship to date and two small suggestions. The criticism concerns the labelling. Although Wolfberger is to be congratulated for introducing a very elegant new label, which is identical to the one used for its own prestige *cuvée* (*grands crus*, Cuvées Armoriés, etc.), it should have put 'Hardt' on the label, as the success of this domaine will depend upon the reputation of this *lieu-dit*. The first of my two suggestions is to revive Chasselas and to do it as a prestige *cuvée*, not a bottom-line wine. Chasselas is already growing on this domaine, Hardt Chasselas was as good as Chasselas could get and if it were properly selected, vinified with skill and possibly bottled *sur lie*, would not only be a great success, but might encourage others to retain small amounts of this rapidly vanishing variety in their own locations, particularly if they have some historical reputation for it. My second suggestion is for the creation of a classic blended wine (not the

Edelzwicker already produced), again from a much restricted yield and perhaps even with just a hint of new oak.

See also WOLFBERGER

Karcher

Robert Karcher & Fils
11 rue de l'Ours, 68000 Colmar
Telephone: (89) 41.14.42

Coincidentally, the alphabetical order takes us to another Harth producer. If you are visiting Colmar and doing the sights, it is worth remembering that Robert Karcher's cellars are not very far from the city centre. He makes a good Gewurztraminer, but I have not been impressed with his other wines.

Kehren

Domaine Kehren
2 route du Vin,
68420 Voegtlinshoffen
Telephone: (89) 49.38.00

An old-established family of winegrowers, the Meyers have been resident in Voegtlinshoffen for more than 200 years. This domaine extends to seven hectares and includes a plot on Grand Cru Hatschbourg, although the best wine I have tasted here has been the Riesling Cuvée St-Ulrich. Also known as Denis Meyer.

Kieffer

Domaine Kieffer
76 route du Vin, 67140 Itterswiller

Telephone: (88) 85.50.22

Established: 1607
Winemaker or **oenologist:** Vincent
Kieffer
Production: 5,300 cases
Vineyards: 6 hectares (3ha
Itterswiller, 2ha Epfig, 1ha
Eichhoffen-Bernardvillé), which
account for this grower's total
production
Grands crus: None

An old family of *tonneliers* and
weinsticheren, I am in total
agreement with their philosophy in
the vineyards and cellars, but try as
I have, I cannot find wines of much
interest here, although they can cite
plenty of praise from the *Guide
Hachette* and the *Guide Dussert-
Gerber des Vins de France.* Also
known as François Kieffer & Fils.

Kientz

André Kientz
See René KIENTZ

Kientz

René Kientz
51 route du Vin,
67650 Blienschwiller
Telephone: (88) 92.40.94

Of a few wines encountered just
once, I enjoyed a nice, light fresh
and fruity Pinot Noir Réserve de la
Metzig, which was made in a rosé
style and, particularly, a Crémant
d'Alsace of no little finesse. Also
known as André Kientz.

CV Kientzheim-Kaysersberg

Cave Vinicole de Kientzheim-
Kaysersberg
Rue des Vieux Moulins,
Kientzheim, 68240 Kaysersberg
Telephone: (89) 47.13.19

Established: 1957
Current members: 119
Production: 160,000 cases (5 per
cent sold to *négociants*)
Vineyards: 170 hectares
Grands crus: Schlossberg
(Kaysersberg and Kientzheim),
Kaefferkopf (Ammerschwihr),
Altenberg de Bergheim

This cooperative's consistently
finest wine is its ripe and
harmonious Riesling Grand Cru
Schlossberg. The generic Muscat
(80 per cent Muscat Blanc à Petit
Grains and 20 per cent Muscat
Ottonel) is usually gently floral,
with delicate peachy fruit and good
acidity. I have also found the
Crémant d'Alsace to have plenty of
rich, ripe fruit, a mature and
biscuity bouquet and a fine mousse.

Kientzler

André Kientzler
50 route de Bergheim,
68150 Ribeauvillé
Telephone: (89) 73.67.10

Established: 1850
Production: 6,000 cases
Vineyards: 10 hectares (10ha
Ribeauvillé), which account for this
grower's total production
Grape varieties: 1ha Sylvaner,
0.8ha Chasselas, 2.4ha Riesling,
1.5ha Pinot Blanc, 1ha Tokay-Pinot

Gris, 2.5ha Gewurztraminer, 0.8ha
Muscat Ottonel
Grands crus: 1.4ha Geisberg
(Ribeauvillé), 1.2ha Kirchberg de
Ribeauvillé, 1.1ha Osterberg
(Ribeauvillé)

One of the most talented
winemakers in Alsace, André
Kientzler consistently produces the
region's finest Auxerrois and is
recognized for his Chasselas, which
can be surprisingly ripe and
weighty, but these are not his
greatest wines, of course. Elevating
such modest varieties to well above
their station is a tribute to his skill
and dedication, but he has Riesling
and Gewurztraminer growing in
prime sites and it is what he
manages to do with these that ranks
his wines as among the very best in
Alsace. Although his generic
Riesling has great class and finesse,
his Grand Cru Geisberg and Grand
Cru Osterberg are very much finer.
The Geisberg is the riper and more
opulent, with a wisp of smokiness
to the fruit, the Osterberg is more
classic and flinty, requiring longer
in bottle. Both make splendid
Vendanges Tardives and provide
SGNs that rank among the very
greatest in the region. He has twice
harvested a *vin de glace* from
Riesling on the Osterberg. His
Gewurztraminer is very aromatic
and expressive, especially from the
Grand Cru Kirchberg de
Ribeauvillé, where André Kientzler
regularly produces a wine that
ranks as the best of the *cru*. His
Riesling and Gewurztraminer are so
good that I tend to forget the

Tokay-Pinot Gris, but this variety
should not be overlooked. I often
prefer the basic generic to the
Réserve Particulière, but his
Vendange Tardive always shows
great banana finesse and potential,
assuming an almost SGN identity in
rich years like 1983 and 1989, yet
always elegant, never fat. His
deliciously delicate and fragrant
Muscat Grand Cru Kirchberg de
Ribeauvillé is another forgotten
Kientzler wine.

Klée

Henri Klée
11 Grand'rue, 68230 Katzenthal
Telephone: (89) 27.03.81

I know very little about this grower
except that he is from a family who
have been *vignerons* since 1624.

Klée

Victor Klée & Fils
18 Grand'rue, 68230 Katzenthal
Telephone: (89) 27.13.67

Another Klée, just down the road
and presumably related.

Klein

Georges Klein
10 route du Vin, 68590 St-
Hippolyte
Telephone: (89) 73.00.28

Only tasted once, a beautiful Rouge
de St-Hippolyte, easy to access, yet
with the structure to age and as
classic a Pinot Noir as can be found
in this region.

Klein

Jean-Pierre Klein
1 rue du Maréchal-Joffre,
67140 Andlau
Telephone: (88) 08.93.03

Fine Riesling Grand Cru
Wiebelsberg with elegant, racy fruit
and a touch of spice.

Klein

GAEC Joseph Klein & Fils
See Château WAGENBOURG

Klein

Raymond & Martin Klein
61 rue de la Vallée,
68570 Soultzmatt
Telephone: (89) 47.01.76

Klein is a ubiquitous winemaking
name in Alsace and of all the ones I
have come across I know the least
about this family enterprise.

Klein

Roger Klein
2 rue d'Aigle,
68770 Ammerschwihr

This grower owns Clos de
Meywihr, the smallest *clos* in
Alsace. It is south-facing, planted
entirely with Gewurztraminer and
its name alludes to the long lost
village of Meywihr.

Klein Aux Vieux Remparts

Route du Haut-Koenigsbourg,
68590 St-Hippolyte
Telephone: (89) 73.00.41

Established: 1981
Winemaker or *oenologist:* Jean-
Marie Klein
Production: 6,000 cases
Vineyards: 8 hectares (100 per cent
from St-Hippolyte), which account
for this grower's total production
Grands crus: None

While cooler years like 1987 can
have a tempering effect on fatter
varieties such as Gewurztraminer, I
nevertheless found Klein's 1987
Gewurztraminer Schlossreben a
most odd concoction, with crisp
Riesling-like characteristics, yet in a
way it was merely a cool vintage
exaggeration of this producer's
generic Gewurztraminer, which
always seems to have a very crisp
structure, but which remains true to
its varietal origins with a fine spicy
aroma and mellow fruit. The
Crémant d'Alsace contains 70 per
cent Chardonnay, but I have not yet
had the opportunity to taste it. Also
known as René Klein & Fils.

Kleinecht

Andre Kleinecht
45 rue Principale,
67140 Mittelbergheim

Small grower with vines on the
Grand Cru Kirchberg de Barr.

Klipfel

Domaine Klipfel
6 avenue de la Gare, 67140 Barr
Telephone: (88) 08.94.85

Established: 1824 by Martin Klipfel
Production: 100,000 cases

Vincyards: 35 hectares (27ha Barr, 5ha Rosheim, 3ha Andlau), representing 20 per cent of total production, plus some 15 contracted growers
Grape varieties: 1ha Sylvaner, 7ha Riesling, 2ha Pinot Blanc, 3ha Tokay-Pinot Gris, 5ha Pinot Noir, 15ha Gewurztraminer, 2ha Muscat Ottonel
Grands crus: 7.2ha Kirchberg de Barr (including 5.1ha Clos Zisser), 1.4ha Kastelberg (Andlau)
Labels: Eugène Klipfel ses Enfants et Petits-Enfants Successeurs (*négociant* wines), André Lorentz (*sous marque*)

This well-known house is also known as Lorentz-Klipfel, which gives a clue to the fact that the Klipfels are cousins of the Lorentz family of Gustave Lorentz in Bergheim. The Klipfels believe in very traditional vinification in large, old wooden *foudres*, no malolactic and no tartrate precipitation. When they get it right, Klipfel wines are among the longest-living in Alsace and they also keep significant quantities of old vintages maturing in their cellars. There is a big difference between the quality of Klipfel's own domaine wines, which represent no more than 20 per cent of the firm's production, and its *négociant* wines. If you are not sure, the easiest way to discern the difference is to look for the Domaine Klipfel Propriétaire Viticulteur declaration at the bottom of the label. Of these, the best certainly is the Gewurztraminer Clos Zisser, but I

have also had elegant, fruity Pinot Noir Rouge d'Alsace (but some pretty ropy ones too), and, in the biggest years, rich and beautifully balanced Tokay-Pinot Gris and Gewurztraminer from the Freiberg *lieu-dit*. An added bonus when visiting this firm is the Baeckaoffe that is served in its informal restaurant. Although not made on the premises, it does come from a splendid charcuterie close by and has proved to be one of the best examples of this classic Alsace dish I have encountered.

Klipfel

Eugène Klipfel ses Enfants et Petits-Enfants Successeurs
See Domaine KLIPFEL

Klug

Cooperative label accounting for 5 per cent of the sales of CV Bennwihr, for some of its best wines in selected markets.
See CV Bennwihr

Klur-Stoeckle

Klur-Stoecklé
9 Grand'rue, 68230 Katzenthal
Telephone: (89) 27.24.61

Fine Riesling Grand Cru Wineck-Schlossberg. Also has some reputation for Gewurztraminer from this *cru*.

Kobus

Fritz Kobus
See CV OBERNAI

Koeberlé-Kreyer

Koeberlé-Kreyer
28 rue du Pinot Noir,
68590 Rodern
Telephone: (89) 73.00.55

Winemaker or *oenologist:* Francis
Koeberlé
Production: 7,500 cases
Vineyards: 8.9 hectares (3.2ha
Rodern, 3.2ha Rorschwihr, 1.3ha
St-Hippolyte, 1.2ha Bergheim),
which account for this grower's
total production
Grands crus: 0.7ha Gloeckelberg
(Rodern)

This family enterprise has been in
existence since the seventeenth
century. The best wines here are the
very rich and succulent, Pinot Blanc
for everyday drinking and the
deeply flavoured Tokay-Pinot Gris
Grand Cru Gloeckelberg.

Koehly

Charles Koehly & Fils
36 rue du Pinot Noir,
68590 Rodern
Telephone: (89) 73.00.61

Established: 1930
Winemaker or *oenologist:*
Christian Koehly
Production: 4,200 cases
Vineyards: 7 hectares (3ha Rodern,
0.8ha Bergheim, 3.2ha St-
Hippolyte), which account for this
grower's total production

Grands crus: 2.3ha Gloeckelberg
(Rodern), 0.8ha Altenberg de
Bergheim

This small producer really ought to
be better known. His wines often
have a tremendous balance of
natural ripe acidity and richness of
extract. The Pinot Blanc, for
example, can be almost startling in
its acidity some years, which makes
the wine long-lived and provides a
welcome finesse in riper vintages.
The Tokay-Pinot Gris Grand Cru
Gloeckelberg is another wine with a
great natural capacity for acidity
and this grower also produces the
best Gewurztraminer from that
grand cru. Of Koehly's Vendanges
Tardives, which are of the sweeter
ilk, I have found the
Gewurztraminer from the *grands
crus* of both Gloeckelberg and
Altenberg de Bergheim to have
excellent richness and finesse.

Koehly

Jean-Marie Koehly
64 rue du Général de Gaulle,
67600 Kintzheim
Telephone: (88) 82.09.77

Not much known about this
Koehly, other than a superb, oak-
aged Pinot Noir tasted recently,
which had lovely colour and was
full of fruit-driven flavours.

Krossfelder

A cooperative label.
See CV DAMBACH-LA-VILLE

Kreutzfeld

Les Caves du Kreutzfeld
See Robert DIETRICH

Kreydenweiss

Marc Kreydenweiss
12 rue Deharbe, 67140 Andlau
Telephone: (88) 08.95.83

Established: seventeenth century by
Fernand Gresse
Production: 4,500 cases
Vineyards: 10.15 hectares (5.15ha
Andlau, 5ha Eichhoffen), which
account for this grower's total
production
Grape varieties: 3.3ha Riesling,
1.2ha Pinot Blanc, 2ha Tokay-Pinot
Gris, 0.75 Pinot Noir, 2ha
Gewurztraminer, 0.3ha Muscat
Ottonel, 0.6ha Chardonnay
Grands crus: 0.9ha Kastelberg
(Andlau), 1.1ha Wiebelsberg
(Andlau), 0.7ha Moenchberg
(Andlau and Eichhoffen)

Once described to me as 'the man
with the rude labels', Marc
Kreydenweiss has, however,
brought out far more controversial
labels than the one with a peculiarly
proportioned nude lady adorning it.
What about, for example, the one
with a head seemingly served up on
a platter? In any case, this quietly
spoken, introspective man is first
and foremost a talented winemaker
and should thus be judged on the
quality of his wines, rather than the
questionable calibre of the avant-
garde labels that sometimes
decorate his bottles. Until fairly
recently, these wines were sold

under the Domaine Fernand
Gresser label. Domaine Fernand
Gresser is a registered trademark
and has nothing to do with
Domaine André & Rémy Gresser,
although there is a family
connection. Mark's grandmother
was the sister of Rémy Gresser's
grandfather and her son, René
Kreydenweiss, married Fernand
Gresser's daughter. As Fernand
Gresser was a very prosperous
vigneron whose domaine was
extremely well known, Marc
Kreydenweiss kept that name alive
commercially while trying to
establish his own reputation.

Marc's first vintage was the
excellent 1971, which he harvested
at 23 years of age and anyone who
has recently had the privilege to
taste his 1971 Kastelberg Riesling,
which is still fabulously fresh and
racy with the petrol and honey only
just beginning to dominate the
wine, will realize what a
winemaking prodigy he must have
been. Since then he has made a
name for himself as one of the most
innovative growers in the region.
His revolutionary products have
included a bizarre but beautiful
barrique-aged Sylvaner from the
Kritt vineyard. This was
surprisingly good and great fun to
serve to blind-tasting freaks,
especially at a time when very few
Alsace wines were in fact oak-aged.
Those Sylvaner vines have now
been uprooted and, in 1988, Marc
planted Chardonnay, the intention
at the time being to produce
another *barrique*-aged Kritt wine,
even if it might have to be sold as a

vin de table, due to the AOC
regulations, which do not permit
Chardonnay varietals. He did in
fact vinify the first vintage (1991) in
oak and I thought it had very good
varietal character for such young
vines and some finesse too, but
Marc told me in May 1992 that it
would probably be blended into the
Pinot Blanc. It will be interesting to
see what happens with Marc
Kreydenweiss's Chardonnay. At
one time, I thought it might have
gone in his Crémant d'Alsace,
which had its followers, but
sometimes contained Auxerrois
that was too ripe for classic
méthode champenoise and gave the
wine an exotic, almost 'foxy' taste.

When he does it without bubbles,
Marc Kreydenweiss is an artist, as
far as Auxerrois is concerned, the
Kritt Klevner being one of the very
greatest Auxerrois wines available,
with its lush, honeyed, spicy-apricot
fruit floral hints and a touch of
tangerine-peel complexity on the
finish. His Kritt Gewurztraminer is
a wine of real strength and style,
although in the Vendange Tardive
style, it turns out better in good
rather than great years. He
regularly produces the finest Tokay-
Pinot Gris in the Grand Cru
Moenchberg and his Vendange
Tardive can be unbelievably
concentrated, yet retains
undeniable class, breed and finesse
and the SGN is in an altogether
different class again. His Riesling
Grand Cru Kastelberg is amazingly
fresh and racy in its youth and
capable of acquiring a fine petrolly
complexity, as the 1971 so

wonderfully demonstrates, and
makes superb Vendange Tardive
even in so-called poor years. Marc
Kreydenweiss's Riesling Grand Cru
Wiebelsberg has never really struck
me as special, except for the
exquisite 1985 (but that was from a
yield of just 35 hectolitres per
hectare), although his Vendange
Tardive from the same vineyard is
always outstanding. The Muscat
Clos Rebgarten probably qualifies
as his most underrated wine, with its
fine, floral aroma and deliciously
fragrant orange-flower fruit, and his
Clos du Val d'Eléon will probably be
one of his most talked about in years
to come. This *clos* was purchased by
Marc Kreydenweiss in 1986 and the
first wine was produced in 1990. It is
Marc's first classic blend – 70 per
cent Riesling and 30 per cent Tokay-
Pinot Gris – and shows tremendous
promise for young vines. Since 1991
all of Marc Kreydenweiss's wines
have been produced organically,
without the use of chemical
pesticide, herbicide or fungicide and
with the minimum use of SO_2
(although I have never noticed an
excess of this preservative in the past
vintages).

Krick

Hubert Krick
93-95 rue Clémenceau,
68000 Wintzenheim

Small grower with vineyards that
include 1.5 hectares of Grand Cru
Hengst (70 per cent
Gewurztraminer and 30 per cent
Riesling).

Kuehn

Vins d'Alsace Kuehn
3 Grand'rue, 68770 Ammerschwihr
Telephone: (89) 78.23.16

Established: 1675 by Jean Kuehn
Production: 40,000 cases
Vineyards: 8.1 hectares
Grape varieties: 0.4ha Sylvaner,
2.5ha Riesling, 1.3ha Pinot Blanc,
0.6ha Tokay-Pinot Gris, 0.3ha
Pinot Noir, 3ha Gewurztraminer
Grands crus: 2ha Sommerberg
(Katzenthal), 0.5ha Florimont
(Niedermorschwihr and
Katzenthal)
Labels: Albert Schoech (a merger
with this producer took place in
1978, since when this has evolved
into a second label and Kuehn itself
has been acquired by CV
Ingersheim)

This old house has never been one
of my top producers, but I have
some fond memories of
Gewurztraminer Cuvée St-Hubert
and Riesling Baron de Sciele, the
occasional, toasty-rich Pinot Blanc
Réserve and the odd Sigillé wine.
Nothing, however, stood out
during my last appraisal of this
range, which I cannot put down to
the influence, if any, of the CV
Ingersheim, as the cooperative was
in control of Kuehn when I enjoyed
those wines. The vinification is still
kept separate, the winemakers
remain different and, in any case,
the cooperative is a good producer
(*see* CV INGERSHEIM), so maybe
Kuehn is just going through a dull
patch?
See also Albert SCHOECH

Kuentz

Alphonse Kuentz
15 route du Vin, 68420 Husseren-
les-Châteaux
Telephone: (89) 49.31.60

I have tasted a few Grand Cru
Pfersigbergs from this grower, the
Gewurztraminer being really quite
good and certainly far better than
his Riesling. Also known as Jean-
Marc Kuentz.

Kuentz

Jean-Marc Kuentz
See Alphonse KUENTZ

Kuentz-Bas

Kuentz-Bas
14 route du Vin, Husseren-les-
Châteaux, 68420 Herrlisheim Près
Colmar
Telephone: (89) 49.30.24

Established: 1795 by Joseph Kuentz
Production: 25,000 cases
Vineyards: 12 hectares (2ha
Husseren-les-Châteaux, 8ha
Eguisheim, 2ha Obermorschwihr),
representing about 40 per cent of
total production, plus contracts
with more than 30 growers
Grape varieties: 0.2ha Sylvaner,
0.1ha Chasselas, 2ha Riesling, 3ha
Pinot Blanc, 1.6ha Tokay-Pinot
Gris, 1.5ha Pinot Noir, 2.5ha
Gewurztraminer, 0.6ha Muscat
Ottonel, 0.1ha Muscat à Petit
Grains (Blanc and Rosé), 0.4ha
Chardonnay
Grands crus: 0.6ha Eichberg
(Eguisheim), 1.6ha Pfirsigberg

(Eguisheim)

When André Bas married the daughter of Alfred Kuentz, the two families combined their vineyards and, in 1918, the name changed to Kuentz-Bas. By 1940 this small firm was enjoying considerable success, but when André Kuentz and his three sons returned after the war, they found the buildings and cellars destroyed, very little equipment and no stocks. Yet within five years, they had totally rebuilt the property, reclaimed the vineyards, extended and replenished the cellars, and re-established the brand on all markets. Quite some achievement, but only to be expected from such a hard-working family of perfectionists, and nowhere does this show through more than in the superb quality of the Kuentz-Bas wines. Cousins Christian Bas and Jacques Weber jointly run the firm today, with the immaculately dressed, jet-setting, ever-smiling Christian Bas spreading the Kuentz-Bas gospel abroad (smuggling fresh *foie gras* where fresh *foie gras* should not go, by all accounts), while the extremely knowledgeable, affable and gently spoken Jacques Weber is in charge of the vineyards and winemaking.

Every time I open a bottle of Kuentz-Bas, I always get the feeling I am broaching a wine of luscious flavour and luxuriant quality, which can only be the result of the number of times I have encountered such wines under this label. Kuentz-Bas is one of the few producers any

of whose Gewurztraminer or Tokay-Pinot Gris *cuvées* I can strongly recommend, although the Vendange Tardive versions are of a particularly high quality. Always harvested truly late (never before mid-November) the Vendanges Tardives of Kuentz-Bas are amongst the most expressive of their cool-weather or warm-weather *passerillage* style. The *grand cru* selections of Gewurztraminer are great wines indeed and the minuscule *cuvées* of Tokay-Pinot Gris Sélection de Grains Nobles Cuvée Jeremy are sublime and faultless. The Muscat is one of this producer's more underrated wines, yet both the basic generic and the Réserve Personnelle are beautifully discreet, fresh and floral wines (both 80 per cent Muscat Ottonel and 20 per cent old Muscat Rosé à Petit Grains). Kuentz-Bas still produce an attractively fragrant Crémant d'Alsace Réserve Personnelle, although the exceptionally fine Brut de Chardonnay is sadly no more. Jacques Weber is also beginning to carve out something of a reputation for his smooth and stylish Pinot Noir Réserve Personnelle. It should be noted that the Sigillé wines of Kuentz-Bas can be particularly outstanding.

Landmann

Gérard Landmann
124 route du Vin, 67680 Nothalten
Telephone: (88) 92.43.96

Established: 1960

415

Winemaker or *oenologist:* Gérard Landmann
Production: 3,300 cases
Vineyards: 4.5 hectares (2.5ha Nothalten, 1ha Epfig, 1ha Eichhoffen)
Grands crus: 1.5ha Muenchberg (Nothalten)

Gérard Landmann sells 90 per cent of his production under his own label and believes in the typicity of grape style, yet although I have tasted several of his wines, the only one that has stood out for me has been the Riesling Grand Cru Muenchberg, which was nice, fat and juicy, rather than classic.

Landmann

Seppi Landmann
20 rue de la Vallée,
68570 Soultzmatt
Telephone: (89) 47.09.33

Established: 1982
Winemaker or *oenologist:* Seppi Landmann
Production: 3,300 cases
Vineyards: 5 hectares (2ha Soultzmatt, 3ha Westhalten), which account for this grower's total production
Grands crus: 2ha Zinnkoepflé (Soultzmatt and Westhalten)

Seppi Landmann, or Landmann Seppi as he often styles himself, is obviously talented, but can be frustratingly inconsistent in quality and sometimes misleading in style. Selling his wines under the wide-ranging Vallée Noble denomination (*see* 'The *Lieux-Dits* of Alsace' in

Chapter 6), he regularly produces one of the region's few Sylvaners of real quality and consistently makes fine Riesling Vendange Tardive, yet his Riesling SGN should really be sold as a Vendange Tardive. The pity is that it is an excellent wine that disappoints too many people because it misses the mark. It might be very fine in quality, but it is not a full botrytis wine. As a Vendange Tardive, such a wine would excel and attract favourable comment about its perfumed, honeyed and slightly botrytis character, which might make some critics suggest that it is almost in the SGN class, but offered at that level (of sweetness, which does not necessarily mean a superior quality), it falls short of the sweetness and richness expected. This is not entirely due to Seppi Landmann's relatively dry and racy style, which will be applauded by many, as his 1988 SGN is really borderline at 117° Oeschle, which is just seven degrees above the minimum. No doubt he will get it right, especially when so many of his colleagues say the regulations are far too low as they are, although he also produced a strangely attenuated *vin de glace* in 1988. His regular renditions of Riesling and Gewurztraminer from the Grand Cru Zinnkoepflé have always been splendidly rich and lively and I have had fabulous generic Tokay-Pinot Gris, yet been disappointed by the Vendange Tardive wines of that variety. Seppi Landmann's Crémant d'Alsace Brut de Brut Vallée Noble is a fine and reliable wine that benefits from additional cellaring. At least his up-down-turn-around performance has me intrigued and I shall certainly be watching his wines in future, as it is such quirky producers who usually end up producing the most expressive wines. Also known as Landmann-Ostholt.

Landmann-Ostholt

See Seppi LANDMANN.

Laugel

Maison Michel Laugel
102 rue du Général de Gaulle,
67520 Marlenheim
Telephone: (88) 87.52.20

Established: 1889 by Michel Laugel
Production: 300,000 cases
Vineyards: 7 hectares (7ha Marlenheim), which account for barely 1 per cent of this grower's total production, the balance coming from 485 contracted growers
Grape varieties: All Pinot Noir

This very large Alsace producer was recently taken over by the vastly larger Loire-based firm of Rémy-Pannier. The wines are inexpensive, well packaged and usually maintain a fairly decent commercial quality, with the occasional *cuvée* capable of excelling in some years, which at these prices can be quite exciting. In good years, for example, the Gewurztraminer de Wangen can have an intense citrusy spice,

although I have not been impressed with most of this producer's village wines, even though they were among the very first to exploit this niche of the market with Pinot Noir de Marlenheim, Pinot Rouge de Marlenheim and Riesling de Wolxheim, in addition to the aforementioned Gewurztraminer, of course. I have had much better luck with the Cuvée Jubilaire range with the odd gem, such as a fine flowery Muscat with attractive peach-stone fruit, a real quality Tokay-Pinot Gris with excellent acidity to back up its fat, buttery fruit and even a brilliantly rich and honeyed Gewurztraminer Sélection de Grains Nobles on occasions. I must, however, re-emphasize that they are not consistently of such quality and, indeed, the last time I tasted several of these wines, not one of them stood out as the least bit special, although several fizzy ones did and Crémant d'Alsace is definitely Laugel's most dependable category. The Blancs de Blancs and Blanc de Noirs are both very stylish and regularly rank amongst the greatest sparkling wines of Alsace.

Lefèvre

Maréchal Lefèvre
A cooperative Crémant d'Alsace label.
See CV WESTHALTEN

Leiber

Domaine Edouard Leiber
5 rue Principale, 68420 Husseren-
les-Châteaux
Telephone: (89) 49.30.40

A small grower of some reputation
for Tokay-Pinot Gris, particularly
from the Grand Cru Eichberg.

Leininger

Gilbert Leininger
11 rue Sultzer, 67140 Barr

I know nothing about this grower,
except that he owns some vines on
the Grand Cru Altenberg de
Bergbieten.

Lentz

Cooperative label accounting for 10
per cent of the sales of CV Bennwihr.
See CV Bennwihr

Lichtlé

François Lichtlé
17 rue des Vignerons,
68420 Husseren-les-Châteaux
Telephone: (89) 49.31.34

Established in 1820, this small
family enterprise has something of a
reputation for its Crémant d'Alsace,
although I have not had the
opportunity to try it for myself.

Lichtlé

Fernand Lichtlé
28 rue des Forgerons,
68420 Gueberschwihr

This Lichtlé has one hectare of
Grand Cru Goldert (70 per cent
Gewurztraminer, 20 per cent
Muscat and 10 per cent Riesling).

Loberger

Domaine Joseph Loberger
10 rue de Bergholtz-Zell,
68500 Bergholtz
Telephone: (89) 76.88.03

A family of winegrowers since
1617, the Lobergers today own a
small six hectare domaine,
including a small plot of vines on
the Grand Cru Spiegel, the wines of
which I have not tasted, although I
have had a luscious, generic Tokay-
Pinot Gris on a couple of occasions.

Lorentz

André Lorentz
A *sous marque* of Klipfel.
See Domaine KLIPFEL

Lorentz

Gustave Lorentz
35 Grand'rue, 68750 Bergheim
Telephone: (89) 73.63.08

Established: 1836 by Gustave
Lorentz
Production: 170,000 cases
Vineyards: 27.8 hectares (all
Bergheim), representing about 10 to
15 per cent of total production, plus
contracts with some 50 growers

Grape varieties: 0.3ha Sylvaner, 9.3ha Riesling, 3.4ha Pinot Blanc, 1.7ha Tokay-Pinot Gris, 0.4ha Pinot Noir, 9.2ha Gewurztraminer, 0.9ha Muscat Ottonel, 0.3ha Muscat Rosé à Petit Grains, plus 2.3 fallow

Grands crus: 10.4ha Altenberg de Bergheim, 1.6ha Kanzlerberg (Bergheim)

Labels: Jérôme Lorentz (30 per cent of sales), J. Muller (10 per cent)

In beautiful Bergheim, behind the large, heavy wooden gates that fill a medieval archway and open into a cosy courtyard, you will find the friendly family firm of Gustave Lorentz. The production here is deceptively large, particularly if you are in the rustic little tasting room, chatting to young Georges Lorentz, who is the latest generation of his family to become involved in the business. Georges jet-sets around the world with the likes of Christian Bas, promoting wines at the same events, but whereas Christian seems at home in any city location, Georges always looks as if he belongs to a more rural environment, although both obviously went to the same school for smilers!

The best Gustave Lorentz wines are, without doubt, the Gewurztraminers. Even the basic Gewurztraminer Réserve is a consistently firm wine with a classic, almost stern, spiciness of fruit, which mellows and improves with age. Although the Grand Cru Altenberg de Bergheim is a magnificently full wine that ages

beautifully for ten years or more, Gustave Lorentz's most successful Gewurztraminer is in many ways its Cuvée Particulière, which is blended from the slopes beneath Altenberg de Bergheim and the *lieu-dit* of Rotenberg (not the one in Wintzenheim, which Domaine Zind-Humbrecht commercializes, but the one in Bergheim, to the south-west of the village, just on the border with Ribeauvillé, behind the Carola spa), as this is more an expression of the *négociant*'s art of blending a wine that is superior to its component parts. Pinot Blanc can be a delicious bargain, but the Tokay-Pinot Gris definitely has more style, with a rich Réserve, a Cuvée Particulière of some finesse and an intense yet classy Grand Cru Altenberg de Bergheim. The Rieslings are all capable of attaining some petrolly elegance, with the Cuvée Particulière the bargain for quality, but the Grand Cru Altenberg de Bergheim ages beautifully for such a big wine. The two most overlooked wines of Gustave Lorentz are the soft and tasty generic Pinot Blanc and the delicious Muscat Cuvée Particulière, which has a lovely orange-flower aroma, peachy-tangerine fruit and is preferable most years to this producer's Muscat from the Grand Cru Altenberg de Bergheim.

Lorentz

Jérôme Lorentz
A *sous marque* belonging to Gustave Lorentz, who established it in 1972.
See Gustave LORENTZ

Lorentz-Klipfel

See Domaine KLIPFEL

Lupfen

Domaine des Comtes de Lupfen
See Paul BLANCK

Madame Sans Gène

A cooperative Crémant d'Alsace
label.
See CV WESTHALTEN

Mader

Vins d'Alsace Mader
13 Grand'rue, 68150 Hunawihr
Telephone: (89) 73.80.32

Established: 1981
Winemaker or *oenologist:* Jean-Luc
Mader
Production: 3,300 cases
Vineyards: 5 hectares (3ha
Hunawihr, 1.5ha Ribeauvillé,
0.3ha Zellenberg, 0.2ha
Riquewihr), which account for this
grower's total production
Grands crus: 0.5ha Rosacker
(Hunawihr)

Jean-Luc Mader's family used to
sell their crop to CV Hunawihr
until 1980, when he returned from
Beaune with a degree in oenology
and was determined to do
something more rewarding than
selling grapes by the kilo. In a
relatively short time, he has built up
a range of wines that are noted for
their richness, even at generic level.
Mader's best wines to date have
been Riesling, especially the Grand

Cru Rosacker, but he also excels
with Muscat. This is a grower to
watch.

Mallo

Frédéric Mallo & Fils
2 rue St. Jacques, 68150 Hunawihr
Telephone: (89) 73.61.41

Established: 1885
Winemaker or *oenologist:* Jean
Jacques Mallo
Production: 5,500 cases
Vineyards: 7 hectares (5.5ha
Hunawihr, 1.2ha Mittelwihr, 0.3ha
Ribeauvillé)
Grape varieties: 2.1ha Riesling,
1.8ha Gewurztraminer, 3.1ha
Sylvaner, Pinot Blanc, Pinot Noir,
Tokay-Pinot Gris and Muscat
Grands crus: 1.5ha Rosacker
(Hunawihr), 0.5ha Mandelberg
(Mittelwihr)

Jean Jacques is the fourth
generation to run this small family
enterprise, which has been built on
the reputation of its Riesling.
Mallo's soft-styled Riesling Grand
Cru Rosacker has lots of finesse and
is easily his best wine, but fine and
delicate Gewurztraminer Grand
Cru Mandelberg is also of a high
calibre and, although he does not
have much Tokay-Pinot Gris in his
vineyards, his medal-winning
generic is a lovely, plump wine with
oodles of sweet, spicy fruit.

Mann

Albert Mann
13 rue du Château,
68320 Wettolsheim

Telephone: (89) 80.62.00

Established: eighteenth century
Winemaker or *oenologist:* Jacky
Barthelmé
Production: 6,000 cases
Vineyards: 12 hectares (5.5ha
Wettolsheim and Eguisheim, 4ha
Kientzheim & Kaysersberg, 2.5ha
Colmar & Sigolsheim), which
account for this grower's total
production
Grands crus: 1ha Schlossberg
(Kientzheim), 1.5ha Furstentum
(Kientzheim & Sigolsheim), 0.8ha
Hengst (Wintzenheim), 1ha
Steingrubler (Wettolsheim)

This producer of rich and well-
flavoured wines deserves to be
better known. Even the Pinot Blanc
Auxerrois is an intense wine that is
not without complexity and the
Pinot Noir is serious and deep
coloured, yet avoids the over-
extraction that spoils so many other
attempts to make a real red wine in
Alsace. Albert Mann's Riesling
Grand Cru Schlossberg is big, rich
and well balanced. The generic
Gewurztraminer is more medium-
dry than dry, but has a slight spritz,
which gives the wine a good, crisp
finish, while Grand Cru Hengst is a
much finer, even more luscious
wine. Although these
Gewurztraminers definitely fall into
the category of so-called dry wines
that have a certain residual
sweetness, Albert Mann's
Gewurztraminer SGN is merely
sweet, rather than intensely sweet,
yet it has the true opulence of a
botrytis wine. Another producer to
watch.

Mann

Wunsch & Mann
See WUNSCH & MANN

Marchal

A second label of Wolfberger used
on some export markets, which is
of little consequence in terms of this
cooperative's volume sales.
See WOLFBERGER

Maréchal

Maréchal Lefèvre
A cooperative Crémant d'Alsace
label.
See CV WESTHALTEN

Marronniers

Domaine des Marronniers
5 rue de la Commanderie, 67140
Andlau

Young grower with vineyards that
include just over half a hectare of
Riesling on Grand Cru Kastelberg.
Also known as Guy Wach.

Martinsbourg

Caves de la Martinsbourg and
Comtes de Martinsbourg
See A. GASCHY

Mattern

Domaine Mattern
10 cour de l'Abbaye, 67140 Andlau
Telephone: (88) 08.01.39

I know very little about this family
enterprise, except that it includes a

plot of vines on the Grand Cru Wiebelsberg, from which I once tasted a Riesling, and a *lieu-dit* called Klusterhof, which is commercialized by Domaine Matterne for Gewurztraminer, although I have never tasted it. Also known as Robert & Daniel Mattern.

Mattern

Robert & Daniel Mattern
See Domaine MATTERN

Mauler

GAEC André Mauler & Fils
3 rue Jean Macé,
68980 Beblenheim
Telephone: (89) 47.90.50

Nothing known about this small grower.

Mauler

Jean-Paul Mauler
3 place des Cigognes, 68630 Mittelwihr
Telephone: (89) 47.93.23

Established: 1958
Winemaker or *oenologist:* Jean-Paul Mauler
Production: 2,800 cases
Vineyards: 3.7 hectares (2.5ha Mittelwihr, 0.7ha Kientzheim, 0.5ha Riquewihr), which account for this grower's total production
Grands crus: 0.5ha Mandelberg (Mittelwihr)

Of the small range of wines tasted from this grower in 1990, it was his super-spicy Gewurztraminer Grand Cru Mandelberg that stood out.

Maurer

Albert Maurer
11 rue du Vignoble,
67140 Eichhoffen
Telephone: (88) 08.96.75

Nothing known about this small grower, except that he owns some ten hectares of vines.

Meierheim

Pierre Meierheim
A second label of Wolfberger used primarily for domestic supermarket sales and accounting for 15 per cent of the cooperative's volume turnover.
See WOLFBERGER

Mercklé

André Mercklé & Fils
1 place du Vieux Marché,
68770 Ammerschwihr
Telephone: (89) 78.28.82

Established: 1964
Winemaker or *oenologist:* Pierre Mercklé
Production: 4,500 cases
Vineyards: 7.5 hectares (5.7ha Ammerschwihr, 1ha Mittelwihr, 0.8ha Katzenthal), which account for this grower's total production
Grands crus: 0.9ha Kaefferkopf (Ammerschwihr)

Monsieur Mercklé selected six wines for me to taste in 1990, but nothing stood out, not even his

Crémant d'Alsace, even though it received a gold medal from Dijon.

Mersiol

Guy Mersiol
9 route du Vin, 67650 Dambach-la-Ville
Telephone: (88) 92.40.43

This small grower produces decent Gewurztraminer Grand Cru Frankstein.

Metz

Arthur Metz

This relatively unknown producer is the third-largest producer of Alsace wines, but its vast production is sold under many different labels, most of which bear no reference to Arthur Metz. In this way it is similar to Marne et Champagne, but whereas the success of that firm has enabled it to purchase several other producers, including a *Grande Marque*, the opposite happened to Arthur Metz, as it was itself recently taken over by Grands Chais de France. Which all goes to prove, I suppose, that there is a significant difference in the price and profitability of cheap Alsace wine and cheap Champagne.

Metz

Hubert Metz
57 route du Vin,
67650 Blienschwiller
Telephone: (88) 92.43.06

Winemaker or *oenologist:* Hubert Metz

Production: 5,500 cases
Vineyards: 9 hectares, which account for this grower's total production
Grands crus: 1ha Winzenberg (Blienschwiller)

Freshness is the hallmark of this small producer's most successful wines, which include a Pinot Noir Vieilles Vignes that has a nice edge of supple tannin, making it a fine food wine, the Gewurztraminer Grand Cru Winzenberg, which is a wine of some complexity and finesse, and the full-bodied, fine flavoured Crémant d'Alsace Réserve de la Dîme. Also known as Cave de la Dîme.

Metz

René & Hubert Metz
See Hubert METZ

Metz-Bleger

41 rue du Pinot Noir,
68590 Rodern

The oldest producer in Rodern, Metz-Bleger dates back to 1589 and today cultivates three hectares spread across 19 different parcels in this village and Orschwihr, including almost one hectare (42 per cent Gewurztraminer, 31 per cent Riesling and 27 per cent Pinot Noir) on Grand Cru Gloeckelberg.

Meyer

Denis Meyer
See Domaine KEHREN

Meyer

Eugène Meyer
21a rue de Bergholtz-Zell, 68500
Bergholtz

This producer, who has 1.2
hectares of Gewurztraminer,
Riesling and Tokay-Pinot Gris on
Grand Cru Spiegel, has been a
follower of biodynamic
winemaking principles since 1969
(introduced out of necessity, the
family having a history of asthma).

Meyer

JosMeyer
See JOSMEYER

Meyer

Domaine Julien Meyer
14 route du Vin, 67680 Nothalten
Telephone: (88) 92.60.15

I have heard good things about this
small grower, who owns some eight
hectares of vineyards, although I
have tasted only his excellent
Sylvaner from the *lieu-dit* of
Zellberg, which is always
flavoursome and, in warmer
vintages, is even capable of an
exotic richness. This is one
producer I shall be following up.

Meyer

Lucien Meyer
57 rue du Maréchal-Leclerc, 68420
Hattstatt

I know very little about this family
enterprise, other than that its
vineyards cover some eight hectares
and include a plot on the Grand
Cru Hatschbourg.

Meyer-Brauneiser

René Meyer-Brauneiser
83 rue Clémenceau, Wintzenheim,
68000 Colmar

Small grower that cultivates
Gewurztraminer, Riesling and
Tokay-Pinot Gris on the Grand Cru
Hengst.

Meywihr

Clos de Meywihr
See Roger KLEIN

Mittnacht

Domaine Mittnacht Frères
2 rue de l'Église, 68150 Hunawihr
Telephone: (89) 73.62.01

Established: 1958
Winemaker or *oenologist:* Louis
Mittnacht
Production: 10,000 cases
Vineyards: 16 hectares (11ha
Hunawihr, 5ha Ribeauvillé), which
account for this grower's total
production
Grands crus: 1.5ha Rosacker
(Hunawihr), 0.9ha Osterberg
(Ribeauvillé)

Not much experience of this family
enterprise, but I have had an
occasional Riesling Grand Cru
Rosacker of some note. Mittnacht
Frères owns the Clos des Gourmets
monopole in Hunawihr as well as a
small part of the Muehlforst *lieu-dit*.

Mittnacht-Klack

Mittnacht-Klack
8 rue des Tuileries,
68340 Riquewihr
Telephone: (89) 47.92.54

I have equally little knowledge of
this grower, although I have been
delighted by intense, petrolly-citrus
Riesling Grand Cru Schoenenbourg
and light, fine and fragrantly spicy
Gewurztraminer Grand Cru
Rosacker.

Mochel

Frédéric Mochel
56 rue Principale,
67310 Traenheim
Telephone: (88) 50.38.67

Winemaker or *oenologist:* Frédéric
Mochel
Production: 5,500 cases
Vineyards: 8 hectares (5 ha
Bergbieten, 3 ha Traenheim)
Grands crus: 5 ha Altenberg de
Bergbieten

Frédéric Mochel has always
produced the finest Grand Cru
Altenberg de Bergbieten, although
his Gewurztraminer has the sort of
tangy balance to its fruit that you
might expect to find in a Riesling,
while his Riesling has the sort of
spice you normally associate with
Gewurztraminer (vanilla, cloves
and cinnamon!). There is, however,
more to the sum total of a wine
than the mention of some of its
parts, as both these wines taste
most definitely of their actual
variety, the contrasting
characteristics merely being part of

their complexity. This producer's
generics should not be overlooked,
especially his elegant basic
Gewurztraminer, which shows a
fine sherbetty-banana finesse.

Mochel-Lorentz

GAEC Mochel-Lorentz
19 rue Principale,
67310 Traenheim

Fairly important grower on the
Grand Cru Altenberg de
Bergbieten, where he grows 2.3
hectares of Gewurztraminer and
Riesling.

Moritz

Charles Moritz & Fils
6 rue du Général-Koenig,
67140 Andlau

This producer's vineyards include
plots of Riesling vines in the *grands
crus* of Kastelberg and Wiebelsberg.

Moulin de Dusenbach

Domaine du Moulin de Dusenbach
See Bernard SCHWACH

Muhlberger

François Muhlberger
1 rue de Strasbourg,
67120 Wolxheim
Telephone: (88) 38.10.33

Established: 1777 by Joseph
Muhlberger
Winemaker or *oenologist:* Robert
Muhlberger
Production: 8,500 cases

Vineyards: 11 hectares
(Wolxheim), which account for this
grower's total production
Grands crus: Altenberg de
Wolxheim

This old-established producer
makes elegant, flowery Riesling and
Gewurztraminer, particularly from
Grand Cru Altenberg de Wolxheim.
His Gewurztraminer is flowery
rather than spicy. Muhlberger
makes an interesting 'Horn de
Wolxheim' blend of all three Pinots
(Pinot Blanc, Tokay-Pinot Gris and
Pinot Noir) grown on gravel and
flinty-limestone soil that dominates
this slope. Also exclusively owns
the Clos Philippe Grass in the *lieu-
dit* of Rothstein.

Mullenbach

Marcel Mullenbach
12 rue des Trois-Épis,
68230 Niedermorschwihr
Telephone: (89) 27.04.13

Established: 1950
Winemaker or *oenologist:* Marcel
& Jean-Marc Mullenbach
Production: 5,500 cases
Vineyards: 6.5 hectares (4.5ha
Niedermorschwihr, 1.2ha
Turckheim, 0.8ha Katzenthal),
which account for this grower's
total production
Grands crus: 2.5ha Sommerberg
(Niedermorschwihr)

This small grower is best known for
his Riesling Grand Cru
Sommerberg, but I prefer his
excellent generic Gewurztraminer.

Muller-Koeberle

Domaine Muller-Koeberle
22 route du Vin, 68590 St-
Hippolyte
Telephone: (89) 73.00.37

Established: 1962
Winemakers or *oenologists:* Jean
and Jacques Koeberle
Production: 22,000 cases
Vineyards: 22.9 hectares (19.6ha
St-Hippolyte, 1.5ha Orschwiller,
1.8ha Rorschwihr)
Grands crus: None

I have enjoyed a few wines from
this producer, particularly the
attractively fruity reds, which are
commercialized under two different
lieux-dits, Geissberg and
Burgreben, and have a fine, spicy-
cherry complexity. The intensely
flavoured, beautifully balanced
Tokay-Pinot Gris Vieilles Vignes
should not be ignored and, for the
Gewurztraminer, any mention of
cuvées 'David' or 'Ste-Cécile' will
indicate a late November harvest.

Muré

Clos St-Landelin, Route de Vin,
RN 83, 68250 Rouffach
Telephone: (89) 49.62.19

Established: 1630 by Michel Muré
Production: 60,000 cases
Vineyards: 21 hectares (all
Rouffach), representing about 25
per cent of total production, plus
contracts with 30 growers
Grape varieties: 1ha Sylvaner,
6.5ha Riesling, 0.5ha Pinot Blanc,
2.5ha Tokay-Pinot Gris, 2.5ha

Pinot Noir, 7ha Gewurztraminer,
1ha Muscat
Grands crus: 16ha *grand cru*
Vorbourg Clos St-Landelin
(Rouffach)

This important house used to be
run by eleventh-generation brother
and sister, René and Reine-Thérèse
Muré, until the unfortunate road
accident that deprived Alsace of
René's little dynamo of a sister.
Reine-Thérèse used her outgoing
personality and a non-stop work
ethic to market Muré so effectively
that the company was forced to
expand drastically and modernize
its production facilities, but fate
landed René with this higher profile
part of the job. From the memory of
my first couple of visits to Muré, I
am sure that this quiet and
introspective young man would
have preferred to have remained in
his underworld domain, where he
was happiest pottering around the
cellars, nurturing the wines that he
had every confidence Reine-Thérèse
would sell, but he is doing a fine job
of marketing Muré and his sister
would be proud.

Best known for its Clos St-
Landelin, which the Muré family
has owned since 1935 and which
now supplies most of their own-
domaine wines, this 16 hectare
estate is all classified as Grand Cru
Vorbourg. One of the special
characteristics of Vorbourg
generally and Clos St-Landelin
particularly, is its ability to ripen
fully the skins of Pinot Noir, which
supply more than enough pigment
for a well-coloured wine.

Unfortunately, the crafting of this
style of wine at Muré has
sometimes been too heavy-handed,
resulting in rather plodding,
foursquare wines. When Muré does
get it right, however, its Pinot Noir
Vielli en Pièce de Chêne is one of
the firmest, most serious and
intriguingly complex red wines in
Alsace. The Grand Cru Vorbourg
Clos St-Landelin Riesling is also a
big, blockbusting wine, but usually
has a much better balance and style
than its big brother the Pinot Noir.
Not all the Clos St-Landelin wines
are necessarily big, however. The
lightest and most refreshing is
Muscat, even in the hottest years
and, in 1990, Muré produced a rare
but voluptuous Vendange Tardive
from this variety.

This firm makes a speciality of
pure Riesling Crémant d'Alsace.
When it comes to sparkling wines,
the reader will realize by now that I
am adamant about aromatic
varieties like Riesling being totally
unsuitable for the classic dry style,
but there are always exceptions and
the Muré 1982 Crémant d'Alsace
disgorged in 1987 without dosage
to be sold as Brut 'o' was certainly
one, managing to retain an
exquisite Riesling aroma after five
years on its yeast. I have not tasted
it recently, nor did I taste any
follow-on *cuvée* on the last two
occasions I have tasted the Muré
range, but this firm is obviously
capable of producing a great wine
in this particular style.

Nartz

Michel Nartz
40 rue de la Paix,
67650 Dambach-la-Ville
Telephone: (88) 92.41.11

Family enterprise owning 5.5
hectares of vineyards, including a
plot on Grand Cru Frankstein, but
generic Gewurztraminer is the best
buy here.

Neumeyer

Gérard Neumeyer
29 rue Ettore-Bugatti,
67120 Molsheim
Telephone: (88) 38.12.45

Not much known about this
grower, except that he owns a plot
of vines on the Grand Cru
Bruderthal, from which I have had
a few wines, although none was
special.

North

Alain North
67520 Kuttolsheim

Small producer of Vin de Pays du
Bas-Rhin.

Oberhof

Domaine de l'Oberhof
See SALZMANN-THOMANN

Oberlin

Institut Oberlin
See Domain Viticole de la Ville de
COLMAR

CV Obernai

Cave Vinicole d'Obernai
30 rue du Général Leclerc,
67210 Obernai
Telephone: (88) 95.61.18

Established: 1959
Current membership: 10
Vineyards: 205 hectares
Grands crus: 2ha Wiebelsberg
Labels: Clos Ste-Odile, Divinal
Obernai, Fritz Kobus (Crémant
d'Alsace), Fischer (*vins de tables*)

The leading cooperative in the
Divinal group, CV Obernai's most
famous wines are those from the
Clos Ste-Odile, a vineyard
belonging to Michel Weiss, who is
also the owner of S.A. Ste-Odile, a
distillery and winery that, despite
the label on these wines, does not
actually make or bottle them. This
is accomplished by CV Obernai,
although the S.A. Ste-Odile winery
does receive the bottled products
back from the cooperative and
helps to market them. The best Clos
Ste-Odile is its Tokay-Pinot Gris,
followed closely by the
Gewurztraminer, with Riesling a
definite third. Under its own
cooperative label, which accounts
for 98 per cent of the total
production, CV Obernai currently
makes Gewurztraminer of some
finesse and has in the past been
quite successful with a very fruity
Riesling and a lively, floral Muscat.
Excess production is sold as *vin de
table* under the Fisher label.

Ollwiller

Château Ollwiller
Owned by J-H Gros & Fils, but the
wines are produced and marketed
by the cooperative at Soultz-
Wuenheim.
See CV VIEIL ARMAND

Orschwihr

Château d'Orschwihr
68500 Orschwihr
Telephone: (89) 74.25.00

This is owned by Hubert
Hartmann, whose château vineyard
extends from the Bollenberg to the
Grand Cru Pfingstberg, where he
makes a good Riesling. I have also
tasted Gewurztraminer and a Pinot
Noir under the Bollenberg *lieu-dit*,
but they are not as good. *See also*
the château entry in Chapter 6.

CV Orschwiller

Coopérative Vinicole d'Orschwiller
route du Vin, 67600 Orschwiller
Telephone: (89) 92.09.87

Current membership: 140
Vineyards: 123 hectares

I have very little experience of this
small cooperative, apart from an
occasional Riesling of no special
quality.

Ostertag

Domaine Ostertag
87 rue Finkwiller, 67680 Epfig
Telephone: (88) 85.51.34

Established: 1966 by Adolphe

Ostertag
Production: 6,000 cases
Vineyards: 9 hectares (6.2ha Epfig,
0.3ha Itterswiller, 2.5ha Nothalten)
Grape varieties: 1.5ha Sylvaner,
2.8ha Riesling, 0.5ha Pinot Blanc,
0.6ha Tokay-Pinot Gris, 0.6ha
Pinot Noir, 2.6ha Gewurztraminer,
0.3ha Muscat Ottonel, 0.1ha
Muscat à Petit Grains (both Blanc
and Rosé)
Grands crus: 1.3ha Muenchberg
(Nothalten)

Since young André Ostertag took
over his family's vineyards, he has
done everything except shoot the
director of CIVA. He is both
admired and avoided within Alsace
itself for his open-minded, green-
minded quality-conscious
philosophy, which results in wines
that range from sensational to
positively bizarre. I cannot
remember ever having an ordinary
or uninteresting wine from this
producer, although not a few have
shocked me, for even his failures are
extraordinary. I have never had an
Ostertag wine that lacked richness,
but in his search for the ultimate
style by using only the most natural
of means and through the severe
restriction of yield, his efforts have
occasionally created wines that
have been curiously balanced, over-
opulent or excessively oaky.

If, however, his failures fall apart
so spectacularly, his triumphs are
utterly beguiling, complete and
satisfying. André Ostertag is an
eccentric, a whacky winemaking
freak surrounded by the sanity and
boredom of Germanic commercial

order, but his off-beat attitude, outlandish approach and healthy disdain of petty bureaucracy are taking his customers on a voyage of discovery. Whether he eventually perfects his art hardly matters because we can reap the rewards of his experiments along the way, but if the mad apprentice does succeed, I wonder what awesome wines we can all look forward to from a mellowed master of Domaine Ostertag?

In the meantime, there are plenty of stunning successes to be had from the wayward lad, even from such a lowly and normally boring grape as Sylvaner. Try Ostertag's Vieilles Vignes, which he has been working on for quite a few years now, in which time he has managed to perfect a fine, floral intensity of unctuously ripe fruit. Tokay-Pinot Gris is probably his strongest variety and the beautifully rich and bedazzling Grand Cru Muenchberg vies with Riesling from the same site as his flagship wine. On the other hand, Riesling Fronholz is too fat to have real class, whereas Riesling Vignoble d'Epfig, which is obviously more generic than Fronholz (which is a *lieu-dit* within Epfig itself), shows obvious class from an early age. Fronholz is evidently better suited to Gewurztraminer because that variety from this *lieu-dit* is really splendid and benefits from a few years in bottle. This vineyard must also be good for Muscat in that although this is not one of Domaine Ostertag's most consistent varieties, Fronholz Muscat can be a truly beautiful and opulent wine. I would like to see André Ostertag attempt a *barrique* version of Muscat Fronholz in both the Vendange Tardive and SGN styles. He has experimented with oaked and unoaked versions of these late-harvest and botrytis wines from virtually every combination of variety and vineyard and many of these wines are among his most exciting achievements to date, so why not the Muscat?

Pape St-Léon IX

Cellier du Pape St-Léon IX
A second label of Wolfberger used primarily for the domestic market sales and accounting for 5 per cent of the cooperative's volume turnover.
See WOLFBERGER

CV Pfaffenheim

Cave Vinicole de Pfaffenheim-Gueberschwihr
5 rue du Chai, 68250 Pfaffenheim
Telephone: (89) 49.61.08

Established: 1957
Current members: 203
Production: 210,000 cases (including 5 per cent sold to *négociants*)
Vineyards: 190 hectares (Pfaffenheim, Gueberschwihr, Rouffach, Hattstatt, Herrlisheim, Obermorschwihr, Voegtlinshoffen)
Grands crus: 39ha Steinert, 35ha Goldert, 6ha Hatschbourg
Labels: Les Vignerons de Pfaffenheim (main label), Les

Producteurs Réunis d'Alsace (subsidiary organization), Hartenberger (Crémant d'Alsace, accounting for 10 per cent of total production), J. Hornstein (seldom seen *sous marque*), Ernest Wein (*sous marque* accounting for 10 per cent of total production)

One of the three best cooperatives in Alsace (CV Turckheim and Wolfberger being the other two), CV Pfaffenheim has a tremendous track record for its Hartenberger Crémant d'Alsace. This range is still good and strong, with plenty of excellent *cuvées*, but the very best of these, the Hartenberger Pinot Gris, is not as exceptional as it once was. Notwithstanding this small criticism, CV Pfaffenheim is very much a Pinot cooperative, excelling at each of the three varieties of this family permitted in Alsace. The Pinot Blanc from the Schneckenberg *lieu-dit*, for example, has deliciously fresh fruit, but all CV Pfaffenheim's *cuvées* of this variety are well worth buying, especially the gold medal and Sigillé wines, which last longer than the norm. Tokay-Pinot Gris is even richer and finer. Like the Pinot Blanc, medal-winning *cuvées* of this grape should be sought out. I well remember the generic from 1976, which won a Sigillé award and was extraordinarily rich and unbelievably fresh after 11 years and I have every confidence that it will be just as outstanding to drink in another 11. The Cuvée Rabelais is a Tokay-Pinot Gris to look out for: a wine of great finesse. The very greatest examples are, however, the *grand cru* wines of Goldert and Steinert. If anything, CV Pfaffenheim is even more successful at Pinot Noir, or it certainly is with its Cuvée des Dominicains, which is a superb selection from old vines.

The best Gewurztraminer here is the creamy-rich and wonderfully spicy Grand Cru Goldert. This cooperative used to produce one of the most delicious Chasselas, but it was always in tank and destined for Edelzwicker blends, which was a great pity. Since 1991, however, it has revived this variety by launching Chasselas Cuvée Lafayette, which gives me hopes about its future and also reminds me of another Cuvée Lafayette that CV Pfaffenheim used to market: Gentil d'Alsace Cuvée Lafayette, the last vintage of which I actually tasted (not necessarily the last one produced) was 1983, according to my notes, which describe the wine as typically rich and aromatic, and nothing at all to do with Edelzwicker. Gentil d'Alsace is in fact the designation I favour for a new category of classic blended wines in Alsace (*see* 'Blended Wines' entry in Chapter 7), although, even in 1983, this term had already been outlawed for ten years.

Pfister

Veuve Joseph Pfister
See Les Caves JB ADAM

Preiss

Victor Preiss
Cooperative label accounting for 5
per cent of the sales of CV
Bennwihr.
See CV BENNWIHR

Preiss-Henny

J-C Preiss-Henny
3 rue de Bouxhof, BP 8,
68630 Mittelwihr
Telephone: (89) 41.64.29

Established: 1535
Production: 30,000 cases
Vineyards: 15 hectares (7ha
Riquewihr, 8ha Mittelwihr)
Grands crus: 2ha Mandelberg
(Mittelwihr)

This address is just the old semi-
abandoned cellars of the once
famous firm of Preiss-Henny. Some
say that Preiss-Henny no longer
exists and that it is nothing more
than a *sous marque* of Léon Beyer.
True enough, Preiss-Henny has
been amalgamated with or
absorbed by Maison Beyer since
1981 and the wines are indeed
made there, but I have seen Hubert
Preiss working hard in Beyer's
cellars, so either he was so far down
on his luck that he could only get a
job swilling out somebody else's
cellars or he still actually makes the
Preiss-Henny wines himself, at
Maison Beyer, but separately and to
his own style. If not, why should he
bother to be there? Besides, it is all
in the family, as Hubert Preiss has
long been married to Marc Beyer's
sister.

In the days when things were
swinging, few producers could
boast a reputation like Preiss-
Henny's, although this fame has
been of a somewhat more recent
origin than the firm's 450 years of
existence might suggest. This house
was really created by a marriage
between the Preiss family, which
has always lived in Riquewihr, and
the Henny family, who have long
been residents of Mittelwihr. It was
from the marriage of Jean Adolphe
Camile Preiss to Berthe Henny (the
mother of Hubert's grandfather),
which took place on 6 July 1903,
that the fortunes of this house really
began, although personal tragedy
struck when Berthe died just five
years later. The families were,
however, determined to ensure the
survival of the newly formed Preiss-
Henny dynasty and Jean Adolphe
Camile Preiss married Berthe's
sister Marie-Hélène on 20 October
1910. Two wars came and went,
although no one will say whether it
was the last one that prompted the
name Adolphe to be dropped from
the title of the family firm. At its
height, Preiss-Henny produced one
of the best ranges of wines in
Alsace. I know this only because I
was determined to visit the
Mittelwihr premises, when I
happened to be living in the village
for a couple of months in 1987 and
I tried several old wines of
remarkable quality. Every time I
drove past the long wall with the
old painted name advertising the
tasting *caveau* of Preiss-Henny, I
would look to see whether anyone
was there, but never once did the

heavy double-doors open and from closer examination it was obvious that they had been firmly shut for years. I suppose it was curiosity, but I thought it ridiculous to go to Beyer to meet Hubert and taste his wines, when he still technically had premises in my temporarily adopted home town. So we agreed to meet at Mittelwihr. It was not exactly as I imagined it. In fact, the meeting was not exactly in the cellars, which Hubert told me were flooded. We conducted our meeting in a broken down caravan out the back. Now, I have had tastings in some queer places, but a caravan that would fall to pieces if towed on the open road was new to me. I just fitted inside, but Hubert had to bend in three. At that tasting, he was still making good generic Riesling, fine Riesling Cuvée Marcel Preiss, and a delicately rich Tokay-Pinot Gris, but it was the Gewurztraminer Cuvée Camile Preiss that was by far his best wine and this has remained perhaps his only fine wine. The old style of Preiss-Henny was soft, gentle with discreetly ripe aromas and as light as some of these wines seemed, they were capable of ageing truly gracefully. His finest wine used to be from the Mandelberg, from which he produced absolutely classic Gewurztraminer and one of the most graceful Rieslings in the region.

Preiss-Zimmer

Preiss-Zimmer
42 rue du Général de Gaulle,
68340 Riquewihr

Telephone: (89) 47.86.91

Established: 1848 by Jean Preiss
Production: 10,000 cases
Vineyards: 9.1 hectares
(Riquewihr: still owned by the Zimmers)
Grape varieties: 3ha Riesling, 1.2ha Pinot Blanc, 0.6ha Tokay-Pinot Gris, 4ha Gewurztraminer, 0.3ha Muscat Rosé à Petit Grains
Grands crus: 2.5ha Schoenenbourg (Riquewihr)

The winemaking and commercialization of these wines was taken over by the CV Turckheim in the late 1980s. Until then, it was run by Jean-Jacques Zimmer and his son Antoine, two of the most affable people you could meet. They were, however, more dedicated to hunting in the Vosges and this showed in the wines, none of which was anything to get excited about. Since Jean-Paul Ritzenthaler has managed the commercialization of this house and his cooperative has been in charge of the vinification, the production of these wines has been restricted to the Preiss-Zimmer vineyards only. Because their own domaine accounted for only 50 per cent of total production, the number of cases under the auspices of Monsieur Ritzenthaler has of course halved from the 20,000 cases Jean-Jacques last reported to me, to some 10,000 now. The quality has, however, more than doubled. They are much richer, livelier and far more expressive. It used to be advisable to stick to the Gewurztraminer, as it was the only

433

hope of flavour, but this has been
intensified under Ritzenthaler and
the Riesling Réserve Comte Jean de
Beaumont is now well worth trying
for its concentration of fruit and
complexity. The Zimmers still own
the vineyards listed above, which
are contracted to supply the grapes
for these wines. They also own the
Preiss-Zimmer property that fronts
as point of sale for these wines in
Riquewihr and, on the opposite side
of the street, the Tiré Bouchon
winstub, which is often the only
place open late at night (which
probably does not bother the
Zimmers, as they do not go hunting
until the wee hours) and can be
thoroughly recommended,
especially for Baeckaoffe (a sort of
Lancashire hotpot, made with pork,
beef and mutton, marinated in wine
and cooked all day).

Prélats

Domaine des Prélats
See Raymond ENGEL

Producteur

Producteur
A cooperative Crémant d'Alsace
label.
See CV WESTHALTEN

Producteurs Réunis d'Alsace

Les Producteurs Réunis d'Alsace
Subsidiary organization belonging
to the cooperative at Pfaffenheim.
See CV PFAFFENHEIM

Rabold

Raymond Rabold
6-8 rue du Val-du-Pâtre,
68500 Orschwihr
Telephone: (89) 74.10.18

A small family enterprise dating
back to 1734 and owning ten
hectares of vines today, including a
small plot on Grand Cru
Pfingstberg, where he produces a
good Riesling.

Rebgarten

Clos Rebgarten
See Marc KREYDENWEISS

Reinhart

Pierre Reinhart
See Vignobles REINHART

Reinhart

Vignobles Reinhart
7 rue du Printemps,
68500 Orschwihr
Telephone: (89) 76.95.12

Apart from tasting a splendid
Cuvée Charlotte Tokay-Pinot Gris
Vendange Tardive and receiving
plenty of information about the
famous, or perhaps infamous,
Bollenberg, I know very little about
this grower. Also known as Pierre
Reinhart.

Rempart

Domaine du Rempart
5 rue des Remparts,
67650 Dambach-la-Ville

Telephone: (88) 92.42.43

Established: 1985
Winemaker or *oenologist:* Gilbert
Beck
Production: 6,000 cases
Vineyards: 7.5 hectares (5.2ha
Dambach-la-Ville, 2.3ha Albé)
Grands crus: 1ha Frankstein
(Dambach-la-Ville)

Known variously as Gilbert Beck,
René Beck and René & Gilbert
Beck, these wines are in fact
marketed as Domaine du Rempart
(which should not be confused with
Vieux Remparts of René Klein &
Fils in St-Hippolyte). The
reputation of this family enterprise
is firmly based on its Riesling and
Pinot Noir wines and the best is the
Clos du Sonnenbach Pinot Rouge,
which is a well coloured wine with
vibrantly youthful and penetrating
fruit.

Rentz

Edmond Rentz
7 route du Vin, 68340 Zellenberg
Telephone: (89) 47.90.17

Some 17 hectares of vines, a decent
Pinot Noir tasted now and again,
but that is about it for this grower.

Réunis d'Alsace

Les Producteurs Réunis d'Alsace
See CV PFAFFENHEIM

CV Ribeauvillé

Cave Coopérative de Ribeauvillé et
Environs
2 route de Colmar,
68150 Ribeauvillé
Telephone: (89) 73.61.80

Established: 1895
Current members: 78
Production: 165,000 cases
(includes 5 per cent sold to
négociants)
Vineyards: 217 hectares
Grands crus: 3.5ha, comprising
Kirchberg de Ribeauvillé,
Gloeckelberg (Rodern & St-
Hippolyte), Osterberg (Ribeauvillé)
Labels: Giersberger (Crémant
d'Alsace), Traber (used for sales
through agents, accounts for 5 per
cent of total sales), Martin Zahn
(direct sales, accounts for 15 per
cent of total sales)

This cooperative produces fine,
firm, slow maturing Riesling from
the Grand Cru Kirchberg de
Ribeauvillé and fresh, zestful
Gewurztraminer from the Grand
Cru Gloeckelberg, but it is Clos du
Zahnacker, a classic blended wine,
that must take top honours here. It
comes from a triangular-shaped
clos that borders the Grand Cru
Osterberg on the Côte de
Ribeauvillé and has been planted
with vines since the ninth century.
Three different varieties have
traditionally been grown in equal
proportions in this vineyard since
the twelfth century, when it took its
name from the noble monk Martin
Zahn. The varieties planted today
are Tokay-Pinot Gris, Riesling and

Gewurztraminer and having tasted several vintages going back some 20 years, it is obvious to me that the wine made by the cooperative is very much a *vin de garde* and one of the greatest classic blends currently produced in Alsace. (*See* Clos du Zahnacker entry in both Chapter 6 and Chapter 7.)

Rieffel

André Rieffel & Fils
See Julien RIEFFEL & Fils

Rieffel

Julien Rieffel & Fils
11 rue Principale,
67140 Mittelbergheim
Telephone: (88) 08.95.48

Established: by André Rieffel
Winemaker or *oenologist:* André Rieffel
Production: 6,000 cases
Vineyards: 9 hectares (7ha Mittelbergheim, 1ha Andlau, 1ha Barr), which account for this grower's total production
Grands crus: 1ha Zotzenberg (Mittelbergheim), 0.5ha Kirchberg de Barr

This small producer has built its reputation on Klevner and Riesling Grand Cru Zotzenberg. I have not been impressed by the latter, but I can enthusiastically vouch for the former, particularly the Klevner Vieilles Vignes, which is super-rich and packed with tangy fruit and ripe acidity. Also known as André Rieffel & Fils.

Rieflé

Domaine Rieflé
11 place de la Mairie,
68250 Pfaffenheim
Telephone: (89) 49.62.82

Established: 1958
Winemaker or *oenologist:* Jean-Claude Rieflé
Production: 16,500 cases
Vineyards: 19.5ha hectares (Pfaffenheim, Gueberschwihr, Rouffach, Westhalten)
Grands crus: 0.8ha Steinert (Pfaffenheim)

Jean-Claude Rieflé emphatically stakes his reputation on the Tokay-Pinot Gris, which I have enjoyed for its fine, elegant style, but the best wine I have tasted from this domaine has been the Gewurztraminer Grand Cru Steinert, which has an excellent grapey-spicy aroma and some complexity. Jean-Claude Rieflé has been the prime mover in getting growers to adopt the all-encompassing designation Côte de Rouffach, under which any one of the appropriate *lieux-dits* can be utilized to avoid the confusion that is beginning to emerge in the mind of the consumer over the multiplicity of individual site names (*see* Côte de Rouffach entry in Chapter 6).

Rietsch

Pierre & Jean-Pierre Rietsch
32 rue Principale,
67140 Mittelbergheim
Telephone: (88) 08.00.64

I have not tasted the wines of this enterprise, but do know that it has a small plot on the Grand Cru Zotzenberg.

Ringenbach-Moser

Etablissements Ringenbach-Moser
12 rue du Vallon, 68240 Sigolsheim
Telephone: (89) 47.11.23

Established: 1936 by Guillaume Ringenbach
Winemaker or *oenologist:* François Ringenbach
Production: 19-20,000 cases
Vineyards: 5.3 hectares (2.8ha Sigolsheim, 1.1ha Bennwihr, 0.7ha Ammerschwihr, 0.1ha Kientzheim, 0.6ha Ingersheim), representing 20-25 per cent of total production, plus contracts with two growers for grapes and four other producers for wine in bulk
Grape varieties: 0.3ha Chasselas, 1.5ha Riesling, 1.1ha Pinot Blanc, 0.6ha Tokay-Pinot Gris, 0.3ha Pinot Noir, 1.3ha Gewurztraminer, 0.2ha Muscat Blanc à Petit Grains
Grands crus: 0.5ha Mambourg (Sigolsheim)

It's funny how some names sound or remind you of other words. I visited the Ringenbachs only once and that was after I postponed the original appointment because of urgent appointments in Rouffach and Hattstatt. It was just a bit of silliness at the time, but ever since I blurted out 'ring'em back tomorrow, we'll do the roof-rack and hat-stand today', the names have stuck and I am sure there are people in Alsace who think we cannot pronounce the names of these two important towns. The Ringenbachs are such charming people, I just wish I could be more enthusiastic about their wines. Not that there aren't some worthwhile buys here, simply that most of the rest are so boring. The generic Pinot Blanc is a very good opener that is easy to drink with plenty of off-dry creamy fruit. Tokay-Pinot Gris is even better, both as generic and Grand Cru Mambourg, just as delicious as the Pinot Blanc, but with more class and complexity. I have enjoyed some vintages of Ringenbach's Riesling Grand Cru Schlossberg, but not others. Of the different *cuvées* and vintages of Gewurztraminer, it is very difficult to pin down what I do and do not like, but there is obviously some potential. For everyday drinking, I prefer the generic Muscat to that from Grand Cru Mambourg, although in exceptional years the latter seemingly lives for ever, as the astonishing 1964 proves: it will still be a fine and beautifully honeyed wine in a decade or so from now.

Rolli-Edel

Willy Rolli-Edel
5 rue de l'Église, 68590 Rorschwihr
Telephone: (89) 73.63.26

This new, young grower with 12 hectares of vines is best for Tokay-Pinot Gris and Riesling.

Rolly Gassmann

Rolly Gassmann
1-2 rue de l'Église, Rorschwihr,
68590 St-Hippolyte
Telephone: (89) 73.63.28

Established: 1676
Production: 12,500 cases
Vineyards: 17 hectares (14.5ha
Rorschwihr, 1.5ha Bergheim, 1ha
Rodern), representing almost 90
per cent of total production, plus
2.4 hectares rented (0.3ha
Bergheim, 2.1 Rorschwihr)
Grape varieties: 2.8ha Sylvaner,
3.2ha Riesling, 3.1ha Pinot Blanc
(including 2.6ha Auxerrois), 2ha
Tokay-Pinot Gris, 1.3ha Pinot
Noir, 3.8ha Gewurztraminer, 0.6ha
Muscat Ottonel, 0.2ha Muscat
Rosé à Petit Grains
Grands crus: None

He *is* Gassmann, she *was* Rolly. I
have to say it because there are
evidently a lot of people who think
that Monsieur Gassmann's first
name is Rolly. It was, however, the
marriage of Marie-Thérèse Rolly to
Louis Gassmann that brought
about this small but successful
winemaking partnership.

Visiting Rolly Gassmann in
sleepy Rorschwihr can be a
problem if you have not been there
before. The first time I visited 1–2
rue de l'Église, it looked as if I
should be knocking on the side
door of the *mairie* or something.
With absolutely nobody about in
Rorschwihr, it was impossible to
ask if it really was the Rolly
Gassmann establishment, but I was
reassured when the door creaked

open and several feet below my
gaze two little heads popped out,
one almost on top of the other. The
Gassmanns are not the tallest
people, but they surely could not be
eighteen inches high? Slowly my
eyes adjusted to the inner gloom
and I noticed they were standing
almost at the bottom of the few
steep steps that lead up to the inside
of their double-door entry.

I soon discovered that the order
of the day at most Rolly Gassmann
tastings is for some twenty wines
from vat and bottle to be lined up
and, then, for every comment made
about a specific wine, Louis
Gassmann pops off for two or three
variations of the theme to illustrate
a point. Thus these events start off
reasonably enough, but end up
almost the size of a Paul Blanck
mega-tasting. Without the sight of
an endless row of wines, however,
the effect on an alcoholically hazed
mind is less daunting. Until, of
course, you climb those steep steps
to open the cellar doors and you
pop your own head out into the full
glare of strong sunlight, just
eighteen inches off the ground. By
then, of course, Rorschwihr is
bustling and several passers by look
down and wonder who the drunken
dwarf is.

Rolly Gassmann's wines are
typically rich, ripe and, let's face it,
a touch sweet. Their wines average
four grams per litre of residual
sugar and generally increase to
eight for better *cuvées*, such as
Réserve Rolly Gassmann or one of
the various *lieux-dits*, although it
can be as high as 10–11 grams for

some of the Tokay-Pinot Gris and Gewurztraminer wines. When well balanced with good acidity, this merely serves to enhance the natural richness and flavour of the wine. If over the top (for the wine – same level, different balance), it can make wines that range from fat to blowzy and distinctly overblown. Fortunately Rolly Gassmann get it right most of the time.

Take, for example, their Muscat Moenchreben. It is without doubt one of the two greatest Muscats in Alsace; an extravagantly rich and beautifully expressive wine with dazzling fruit and a welcome touch of sweetness (this Moenchreben is not the *grand cru* of Andlau and Eichhoffen, but a *lieu-dit* in the producer's home village of Rorschwihr). Also from Moenchreben is Rolly Gassmann's famous Auxerrois, which is fat, spicy and quickly becomes honeyed after bottling. Their reputation for this wine is well deserved when it is on cracking form, but out of all this producer's wines, it is probably the most prone to blowziness. On the other hand, Sylvaner is the least likely to get overblown and really profits from the Rolly Gassmann treatment, producing a far more generous, easier to enjoy version of this normally verdant variety.

Rominger

Eric Rominger
6 rue de l'Église, 68500 Bergholtz
Telephone: (89) 76.14.71

I have encountered a few of these wines on odd occasions and I was most impressed by a very refreshing Riesling Meissenberg, which had an opulent touch, and an excellent 1988 Crémant d'Alsace. Must find out more.

Rotgold

Pierre Rotgold
A second label of Wolfberger used primarily for domestic supermarket sales and accounting for 15 per cent of the cooperative's volume turnover.
See WOLFBERGER

Roth

A *sous marque* used by J. Hauller for Germany.
See J. HAULLER

Roth-Stein

Clos Roth-Stein
See Jean ARBOGAST

Rouffach

Lycée Agricole et Viticole de Rouffach
See Domaine de l'ÉCOLE

Ruhlmann

GAEC A. Ruhlmann
35 rue Mathias-Ringmann, 67140 Reichsfeld
Telephone: (88) 85.51.65

A beautiful 1988 Crémant d'Alsace tasted at the same time as Rominger's excellent 1988, otherwise nothing known about this producer.

Ruhlmann Dirringer

GAEC Ruhlmann-Dirringer
3 impasse Mullenheim,
67650 Dambach-la-Ville
Telephone: (88) 92.40.28

Nothing known about this producer.

Runner

François Runner
1 rue de la Liberté,
68250 Pfaffenheim
Telephone: (89) 49.62.89

Established: 1950
Winemaker or *oenologist:* François
Runner
Production: 11,000 cases
Vineyards: 11 hectares
(Pfaffenheim, Westhalten,
Rouffach)
Grands crus: 0.8ha Steinert
(Pfaffenheim)

François Runner believes that his Riesling is outstanding and that his Muscat is noted particularly for its aroma. I have not tasted many of Runner's wines, but those I have tasted were from very good vintages, yet I found nothing of particular note. Others have told me differently, so I will keep an eye on him.

St-Eloi

Cooperative label reserved for Crémant d'Alsace.
See CV TRAENHEIM

St-Imer

Clos St-Imer
See Maison Ernest BURN

St-Jacques

Clos St-Jacques
See Domaine Viticole de la Ville de COLMAR

St-Léon

Cellier du Pape St-Léon IX
A second label of Wolfberger, used primarily for domestic market sales, accounting for 5 per cent of the cooperative's turnover (in volume produced).
See WOLFBERGER

St-Landelin

Clos St-Landelin
See MURÉ

St-Urbain

Clos St-Urbain
See ZIND-HUMBRECHT

Ste-Hune

Clos Ste-Hune
See TRIMBACH

Ste-Odile

Clos Ste-Odile
See S.A. STE-ODILE and CV OBERNAI

Ste-Odile

S.A. Ste-Odile
15 rue de Boersch, 67210 Obernai

Run by Michel Weiss, who also
owns the *clos* of Ste-Odile, this is a
distillery and winery that, among
other operations, takes delivery of
Clos Ste-Odile wines, which have
been vinified from Weiss's own
grapes by CV Obernai, and then
markets them.
See CV OBERNAI

Salzmann

See SALZMANN-THOMANN

Salzmann-Thomann

Salzmann-Thomann
3 rue de l'Oberhof,
68240 Kaysersberg
Telephone: (89) 47.10.26

Winemaker or *oenologist:* Pierre
Thomann
Production: 5,800 cases
Vineyards: 8.7 hectares (4.6ha
Kientzheim, 2.8ha Kaysersberg,
1.3ha Ammerschwihr and
Sigolsheim), which account for this
grower's total production
Grands crus: 2.6ha Schlossberg
(Kientzheim)

The best wine here is the excellent,
rich and well balanced
Gewurztraminer Grand Cru
Schlossberg. Also known as
Salzmann and Domaine de
l'Oberhof.

Schaeffer-Woerly

Schaeffer-Woerly
3 place du Marché,
67650 Dambach-la-Ville
Telephone: (88) 92.40.81

Nothing known about this
enterprise, except that it owns a
small plot of vines on the Grand
Cru Frankstein.

Schaeflé

E. Schaeflé
4 rue de la Lauch,
68250 Pfaffenheim
Telephone: (89) 49.51.43

Nothing known about this grower,
except that he owns a small plot of
vines on the Grand Cru
Gloeckelberg. Also known as Vins
Schaeflé.

Schaeflé

Vins Schaeflé
See E. SCHAEFLÉ

Schaetzel

J. Schaetzel or Jean Schaetzel
See Domaine Martin SCHAETZEL

Schaetzel

Domaine Martin Schaetzel
3 rue de la 5ème Division Blindée,
68770 Ammerschwihr
Telephone: (89) 47.11.39

Winemaker or *oenologist:* Jean
Schaetzel
Production: 4,200 cases
Vineyards: 6 hectares

(Ammerschwihr), which account for this grower's total production
Grands crus: 1ha Kaefferkopf (Ammerschwihr)

Those who distrust expensive bottles and packaging should not be deterred from checking out this small grower, just because some of his wines are stylishly presented. He makes a fresh and lively Tokay-Pinot Gris Cuvée Réserve that shows real class and even succeeds with Sylvaner, the Vieilles Vignes of which tends to be quite rich and full, the touch of residual sweetness balancing nicely with the wine's naturally high acidity. Also known as J. Schaetzel or Jean Schaetzel.

Schaller

Edgard Schaller & Fils
1 rue des Châteaux,
68630 Mittelwihr
Telephone: (89) 47.90.28

Established: 1609
Production: 6,000 cases
Vineyards: 8 hectares (5ha Mittelwihr, 2ha Riquewihr, 1ha Zellenberg), which account for this grower's total production
Grape varieties: 1ha Sylvaner, 3ha Riesling, 1ha Pinot Blanc, 0.5ha Tokay-Pinot Gris, 1.5ha Gewurztraminer, 0.5ha Muscat Ottonel, 0.5ha Muscat Rosé à Petit Grains
Grands crus: 1ha Mandelberg (Mittelwihr)

An underrated producer of uncompromising style, Edgard Schaller's wines are not for the faint hearted. Current incumbent Patrick Schaller is a firm believer in never using malolactic and makes wines that are so inexorably dry that it takes a masochist to drink them when young. These are classics, but need to be tamed in bottle before they are let loose on the general public. Rumour has it that Patrick Schaller went to a little-known school of wine and discipline in old East Germany, where a very smart but severe looking *Frau* would rap students on the knuckles with the sharp end of a ruler every time they did anything wrong and twice when they got it right.

The Schaller style is unsurpassed when applied to razor-sharp Riesling, which can quickly show petrolly finesse on the nose, but has such ultra-dry steely fruit, high acidity and phenomenal extract that it requires many years to mellow in bottle. No wine displays this more emphatically than Schaller's superb Grand Cru Mandelberg Vieilles Vignes, although his Les Amandiers, which is made from young vines growing in the same vineyard, is relatively more accessible, but will still punish Schaller's more wimpish customers. His Crémant d'Alsace, which is also totally dry and unsuitable for beginners, is very fine and exceptionally expressive of Alsace (essentially 60 per cent Pinot Blanc, 35 per cent Riesling and 5 per cent Tokay-Pinot Gris, although he turns up the Tokay-Pinot Gris in acid years and increases the Riesling in fat ones), requiring a couple of years' extra ageing in bottle.

Schaller's Tokay-Pinot Gris has a very elegant richness and his unbending correctness of style applies to other grapes, including the Gewurztraminer, although you could be forgiven for thinking me totally mad if you try the luscious sweet Vendanges de la St-Nicolas, but that is made in true Vendange Tardive intensity, even if it does not claim the AOC designation. He sometimes makes a very good Muscat from a very heavy clay vineyard that retards ripening, increasing the acidity to sugar ratio, making it taste *vif* and fruity, although it is every bit as dry as the Riesling. To sum Schaller up, this is essentially a Riesling and Crémant producer, who also makes fine Gewurztraminer and damn good Tokay-Pinot Gris, but none of his wines can be ignored and most demand respect and plenty of age.

Scheidecker

Philippe Scheidecker
13 rue des Merles,
68630 Mittelwihr
Telephone: (89) 49.01.29

I have only just discovered this small grower, who owns just four hectares of vineyards, and have tasted only a few of his wines, but I have been suitably impressed. He produces an elegant Riesling Cuvée Prestige that is well worth seeking out, a more fruity and minerally complex Riesling Grand Cru Mandelberg, and a well flavoured generic Muscat.

Scherb

George Scherb & Fils
1 rue Haute, 68420 Gueberschwihr

Small but fine grower whose vineyards include just under half an hectare of Gewurztraminer on Grand Cru Goldert.

Scherb

Louis Scherb & Fils
68420 Gueberschwihr

Excellent small grower whose vineyards include 2.3 hectares (50 per cent Gewurztraminer, 25 per cent Riesling and 25 per cent Muscat) on Grand Cru Goldert.

Scherer

André Scherer
12 route du Vin, 68420 Husseren-les-Châteaux
Telephone: (89) 49.30.33

André Scherer is the eighth generation to work his family's vineyards, which include plots on the *grands crus* of Eichberg and Pfersigberg. From the Pfersigberg, Scherer produces a charming Riesling that is light in body, but not flavour. His Riesling Cuvée Jean Baptiste can be very good too. The vinification here is a combination of old tradition and new techniques.

Schillé

Pierre Schillé & Fils
14 rue du Stade, 68240 Sigolsheim
Telephone: (89) 47.10.67

Although I have not tasted this grower's full range, I have had the odd few wines, but only a recent Gewurztraminer from the Grand Cru Mambourg has stood out.

Schillinger

E. Schillinger
Rue des Forgerons,
68420 Gueberschwihr
Telephone: (89) 49.33.18

A light, fresh Pinot Noir tasted once, otherwise nothing known about this producer.

Schlegel-Boeglin

Jean-Paul Schlegel-Boeglin
22 rue d'Orschwihr, Westhalten,
68250 Rouffach
Telephone: (89) 47.00.93

The only wines I have encountered from this grower have been two quite good Rieslings from the Grand Cru Zinnkoepflé, of which the Vendange Tardive was the better.

Schleret

Charles Schleret
1-3 route d'Ingersheim, 68230 Turckheim
Telephone: (89) 27.06.09

Established: 1950 by Charles Schleret
Production: Confidential
Vineyards: 6 hectares, which account for this grower's total production
Grape varieties: 0.4ha Sylvaner,

1.2ha Riesling, 0.4ha Pinot Blanc, 0.3ha Tokay-Pinot Gris, 0.6ha Pinot Noir, 2.5ha Gewurztraminer, 0.6ha Muscat (Rosé à Petit Grains, Blanc à Petit Grains and Ottonel)

Known affectionately as the 'bachelor of Turckheim', Charles Schleret has a small but lucrative business that, it is rumoured, he does not want to share with anyone. If he is personally as rich as his wines are, it is little wonder that some of the ladies I met locally have been eyeing his assets. His Tokay-Pinot Gris can be fantastically rich and the Gewurztraminer, although soft and fragrant, is not lacking in intensity. My other favourite from Schleret is his beautifully dry Muscat, which has a delightful floral fragrance.

Schlossberg

Clos du Schlossberg
See Jean SIPP

Schlumberger

Domaines Schlumberger
100 rue Théodore Deck,
68500 Guebwiller
Telephone: (89) 74.27.00

Established: 1810 by Nicolas Schlumberger
Production: 85,000 cases
Vineyards: 140 hectares, of which 124.3 are in production (0.1ha Bergholtz, 101.2ha Guebwiller, 23ha Rouffach) and account for this grower's total production
Grape varieties: 19.2ha Sylvaner, 6ha Chasselas, 29.2ha Riesling,

16.1ha Pinot Blanc, 5.8ha Tokay-Pinot Gris, 5.3ha Pinot Noir, 39.3ha Gewurztraminer, 2.3ha Muscat Rosé à Petit Grains, 1.1ha other varieties
Grands crus: 18.1ha Kitterlé (Guebwiller), 20.1ha Saering (Guebwiller), 11.5ha Kessler (Guebwiller), 8.6ha Spiegel (Guebwiller)

This is the largest vineyard in Alsace and one of the most important in all of France. It was Nicolas Schlumberger who assembled more than 2,500 plots of land into the single most homogeneous viticultural estate in the region and the company remains in family hands today. Many of these vineyards, which extend 3.5 miles from Guebwiller to Rouffach, are so steep that they are terraced and still worked by horse; and Schlumberger claims to keep production strictly limited to a maximum of 47 hectolitres per hectare (but is in fact just over 61.5, if you take the trouble to work it out). If Schlumberger has one wine that has helped to build its considerable reputation over the years, it is Gewurztraminer, with the firm's most loyal customers having fond memories of the famous Cuvée Christine and the much rarer Cuvée Anne. These two *cuvées* are named after the daughters of Ernest Schlumberger, the great-great grandson of the founder, who ran this domaine from the turn of the century. Official designations now determine that Cuvée Christine is a

Vendange Tardive, while Cuvée Anne is a Sélection de Grains Nobles. I have always rated the Cuvée Christine very highly for its true late-harvest character, but find the Schlumberger style of making a drier, more alcoholic style of botrytis wine does not give it the degree of lusciousness expected in SGN wines. It is still a great wine, but it would make a far better super-Vendange Tardive. This is especially true now that so many wines of both designations are produced all over the region. The time when such wines were rarities that only the likes of Schlumberger could produce have long since gone and with it, I am afraid, the little bit of magic that made Cuvée Anne and even Cuvée Christine special. Still on the subject of Gewurztraminer, but back to the more traditional dry style, Schlumberger's Princes Abbés is an exceptionally fine generic that has a classic spicy aroma, beautifully rich fruit and an exquisite balance, but the *grands crus* of Kessler and Kitterlé are bigger, richer and far more complex.

Tokay-Pinot Gris has contributed nearly as much to Schlumberger's success as Gewurztraminer and recent vintages of the generic and the Réserve Spéciale have a noticeably increased creamy richness and show far more finesse than they did previously. With the advent of so many late-harvest wines, Schlumberger brought out in the 1989 vintage the first Cuvée Clarisse to be made since 1964. Again a great wine, but again this medium-sweet botrytis style would be far better categorized as a super-Vendange Tardive.

The generic Riesling is not one of Schlumberger's most consistent wines, but can be fine and floral. For classic Riesling, however, go for the two very different *grands crus*: either the crisp, petrolly Grand Cru Kitterlé, with its minerally ethereal complexity, or the elegant Saering, with its delicately ripe, peachy-floral fruit. Since the 1985 vintage, the Pinot Blanc has been quite fat and tasty. Even Schlumberger's Edelzwicker is a fresh and lively wine of some enjoyment, with its slightly aromatic character, but one step up and deliberately avoiding the Edelzwicker designation is Schlumberger Réserve, a much richer and more serious wine, with full body and lots of honey-laden, spicy-fruit.

The greatest strength of Schlumberger is, of course, its vast viticultural estate of immaculately groomed, prime vineyards. The hallmark of its most famous wines is the minerally *goût de terroir* that distinguishes these different growths. If Schlumberger has one great weakness, it is the disappointing quality of Sylvaner and Pinot Noir. When the Pinot Blanc was not quite so good as it is now, it was possible to start off a tasting here on the wrong foot, especially if you happened to get a stale Edelzwicker blend, which can easily happen anywhere. With perhaps a couple of different vintages of each of these wines, you could plough through six or more wines before finding anything interesting and, with all the wines coming exclusively from Schlumberger's own fabulous vineyards, that should never happen.

Schlosser

Marcel Schlosser
7 rue des Forgerons, 67140 Andlau

One hectare of Gewurztraminer on Grand Cru Moenchberg and a quarter of a hectare of Riesling on Grand Cru Wiebelsberg. Also known as Domaine du Vieux Pressoir.

Schmitt

Raymond Schmitt
92 rue du Mal-de-Lattre-de-Tassigny, 68360 Soultz
Telephone: (89) 76.43.44

Good but not great Riesling Grand Cru Ollwiller. Also produces Gewurztraminer, but I have not tasted it.

Schmitt

Roland Schmitt
35 rue des Vosges,
67310 Bergbieten
Telephone: (88) 38.20.72

Winemaker or *oenologist:* Roland Schmitt
Production: 5,800 cases
Vineyards: 7.5 hectares
(Bergbieten), which account for this grower's total production
Grands crus: 2.2ha Altenberg de Bergbieten

Out of 40 Rieslings tasted blind from the 1989 vintage, three of the very best came from Roland Schmitt, with his delicious Glintzberg *lieu-dit* showing almost as much class and finesse as his Grand Cru Altenberg de Bergbieten and Grand Cru Altenberg de Bergbieten Sélection de Vieilles Vignes. Obviously Monsieur Schmitt is one of the great Riesling makers of Alsace, but his ultra-fresh, delightfully pure Gewurztraminer should not be overlooked.

Schneider

Paul Schneider
1 rue de l'Hôpital,
68420 Eguisheim
Telephone: (89) 41.50.07

Well constructed Pinot Blanc and Tokay-Pinot Gris, but I have not been impressed with this producer's more aromatic varieties.

Schneider

René & Bernard Schneider
17 rue du Tir,
68770 Ammerschwihr
Telephone: (89) 78.23.86

Established: 1972
Winemakers or *oenologists:* René and Bernard Schneider
Production: 6,000 cases
Vineyards: 6.5 hectares (5.5ha Ammerschwihr, 0.2ha Katzenthal, 0.8ha Sigolsheim)
Grands crus: 1.1ha Kaefferkopf (Ammerschwihr)

This producer specializes in Kaefferkopf wines and can make good Riesling, but the Gewurztraminer does not stand out.

Schoech

Albert Schoech

Established in 1840 by Albert Schoech, who was mayor of Ammerschwihr from 1919 until 1945 and a founder-member of the revived Confrérie St-Étienne. In 1978 Schoech merged with Kuehn, since when it has become a second, but not second rate, label of that producer, which itself is now owned by CV Ingersheim.
See KUEHN

Schoech

Maurice Schoech
4 route de Kientzheim,
68770 Ammerschwihr
Telephone: (89) 78.25.78

This grower has a plot on the Kaefferkopf, but I have not tasted the wines.

Schoepfer

Jean-Louis Schoepfer
35 rue Herzog, 68920 Wettolsheim
Telephone: (89) 80.71.29

I have come across a Crémant d'Alsace from this grower, which was not at all bad, but I have no great experience of it and none of his other wines.

Schoepfer

Michel Schoepfer
43 Grand'rue, 68420 Eguisheim
Telephone: (89) 41.09.06

This grower's family have been winegrowers since 1656 and his vineyards comprise some eight hectares today. I do not know these wines very well, but I have had a very good generic Riesling and an excellent, full, well-coloured Pinot Noir.

Schoffit

Domaine Schoffit
27 rue des Aubépines,
68000 Colmar
Telephone: (89) 41.69.45

Bernard Schoffit is famous for his delicious, medal-winning Chasselas, which comes from 60-year-old vines in Colmar's Harth vineyard. His Harth Gewurztraminer is equally easy to drink. The secret of Schoffit's Harth wines is that he restricts production to around 50 hectolitres per hectare, which by today's standards is very modest for vines growing on the slopes, let alone the fertile soils of an alluvial plain. In 1986, the Schoffit family purchased Clos St-Théobold from Charles Hippler, President of the Syndicat du Viticole de Thann. Since this time Schoffit's wines have gone from very interesting to potentially great. Situated on the steep Grand Cru Rangen slope, Schoffit's Clos St-Théobold has already produced excellent Tokay-Pinot Gris (one

remarkable *cuvée* having been harvested at 216° Oechsle in 1989, which is the equivalent of 31 per cent alcohol) and the Gewurztraminer almost rivals it. Riesling, although very good, has quite a bit of catching up to do, if it is to reach the same starry heights as these other two varieties.

Schroedel

See Les Caves JB ADAM

Schueller

Gérard Schueller
1 rue des Trois Châteaux,
68420 Husseren-les-Châteaux
Telephone: (89) 49.31.54

Winemaker or *oenologist:* Gérard Schueller
Production: 4,200 cases
Vineyards: 5.5 hectares (0.5ha Husseren-les-Châteaux, 3.1ha Eguisheim, 1.9ha Obermorschwihr)
Grape varieties: 0.2ha Sylvaner, 1.1ha Riesling, 1.1ha Pinot Blanc, 0.8ha Tokay-Pinot Gris, 0.7ha Pinot Noir, 1.4ha Gewurztraminer, 0.2ha Muscat
Grands crus: 0.3ha Pfersigberg (Eguisheim), 0.2ha Eichberg (Eguisheim)

The Schuellers have been winegrowers, father and son, for more than two centuries and certainly excel at Gewurztraminer today, producing an amazingly expressive generic, with great spicy aroma and intense, well-balanced fruit and a finish full of tingling spice.

Schueller

Maurice Schueller
15 rue Basse, 68420 Gueberschwihr

Small family enterprise with vineyards that include just over two-thirds of a hectare of Grand Cru Goldert (50 per cent Gewurztraminer and 50 per cent Muscat).

Schwach

Bernard Schwach
25 route de Ste-Marie-aux-Mines, 68150 Hunawihr
Telephone: (89) 73.72.18

Very good Gewurztraminer Kaefferkopf and excellent Rouge d'Alsace, both under the Domaine du Moulin de Dusenbach label.

Schwach

François Schwach & Fils
28 route de Ribeauvillé, 68150 Hunawihr
Telephone: (89) 73.62.15

This small grower owns vines on the Kaefferkopf, where he produces Gewurztraminer, but I have not tasted it.

Schwach

Paul Schwach
30-32 route de Bergheim, 68150 Hunawihr
Telephone: (89) 73.62.73

I have had a good Pinot Noir from this grower; otherwise I know very little about his activities.

Schwartz

Émile Schwartz & Fils
3 rue Principale, 68420 Husseren-les-Châteaux
Telephone: (89) 49.30.61

This small family enterprise owns some six hectares of vineyards, which produce decent generic Gewurztraminer and Tokay-Pinot Gris. There is also a small plot of vines on the Grand Cru Pfersigberg, but I have not tasted the wine.

Schwartz

Jean-Luc Schwartz
70 route du Vin, 67140 Itterswiller
Telephone: (88) 85.51.59

I know nothing about this grower, except that his vineyards include a plot on Grand Cru Muenchberg, but I have not tasted the wine.

Schwartz

Justin Schwartz
16 route Romaine, 67140 Itterswiller
Telephone: (88) 85.51.59

Nothing known about this grower, except that he owns plots on the *lieu-dit* Fruehmes.

Schwartz

Oscar Schwartz Successeur
107 rue Principale, 67650 Blienschwiller
Telephone: (88) 92.41.73

Nothing known about this grower, except that he owns plots on the *lieu-dit* Oberberg.

Schwendemann-Haegelen

8 rue des Jardins, Wuenheim,
685000 Guebwiller

Small grower with Riesling on the
Grand Cru Ollwiller.

Seilly

GAEC Seilly
18 rue du Général-Gouraud,
67210 Obernai
Telephone: (88) 95.55.80

Winemaker or *oenologist:* Marc
Seilly
Production: 4,200 cases
Vineyards: 8 hectares (7ha
Obernai, 1ha Bernardswiller)
Grands crus: None

I have tasted only a handful of these
wines, but none stood out, even
though this family enterprise has
had enough experience, producing
wines, father and son, from some of
the best slopes of Obernai since
1865. Seilly places a lot of emphasis
on the 'Vin de Pistolet' story, which
is amusing in itself (*see* 'Blended
Wines' entry in Chapter 7), but the
wine is no better or worse than the
vast majority of Edelzwicker. As
Seilly produced this wine from a
plot of mixed vine varieties growing
in the *lieu-dit* Schenkenberg, they
should and could produce
something special.

Seltz

Albert Seltz
See Alsace SELTZ

Seltz

Alsace Seltz
21 rue Principale,
67140 Mittelbergheim
Telephone: (88) 08.91.77

Established: 1576
Winemaker or *oenologist:* Albert
Seltz
Vineyards: 10 hectares
(Mittelbergheim)
Grands crus: 2.5ha Zotzenberg
(Mittelbergheim)

Albert Seltz is one of the most
vociferous supporters of Sylvaner,
particularly when grown in
Mittelbergheim, where he is
convinced it assumes a classic status
equal to that of any Alsace varietal.
As if to prove his point, he managed
to produce a Sylvaner from his
Zotzenberg vineyard in 1989 that
had an astonishing 126° Oechsle,
which is 10° above the minimum
required for SGN. Unable to
mention either the vineyard or
botrytis designation, he called this
extraordinary wine 'Cuvée Z 126'.
Also known as Albert Seltz.

Sans Gène

Madame Sans Gène
A cooperative Crémant d'Alsace
label.
See CV WESTHALTEN

Sick-Dreyer

P. Sick-Dreyer
17 route de Kientzheim,
68770 Ammerschwihr
Telephone: (89) 47.11.31

Winemaker or *oenologist:* Pierre Dreyer
Production: 8,300 cases
Vineyards: 12.9 hectares (10ha Ammerschwihr, 0.3ha Katzenthal, 2ha Sigolsheim, 0.6ha Husseren-les-Châteaux), which account for this grower's total production
Grands crus: 2.5ha Kaefferkopf (Ammerschwihr), 0.3ha Mambourg (Sigolsheim)

This small, quality-conscious grower makes nice, fat, easy to please wines, although those from the Kaefferkopf are far more serious and concentrated. The Kaefferkopf Riesling is very intense and the Cuvée Joseph Dreyer is particularly successful. The Kaefferkopf Gewurztraminer SGN is a very powerful and well-constructed wine.

Siegler

J. Siegler Père & Fils
26-28 rue des Merles, 68630 Mittelwihr
Telephone: (89) 47.90.70

I know nothing about this family enterprise, except that they have been winegrowers since 1794.

Siffert

Domaine Siffert
16 route du Vin, 67600 Orschwiller
Telephone: (88) 92.02.77

Established: 1792
Winemaker or *oenologist:* Maurice Siffert
Production: 9,000 cases
Vineyards: 9.5 hectares (3.5ha Orschwiller, 3.8ha Kintzheim, 2.2ha St-Hippolyte and Rodern)
Grands crus: 1.5ha Praelatenberg (Orschwiller and Kintzheim)

Of the wines tasted here, it was the very fruity, varietally pure, Pinot Noir Coteaux du Haut-Koenigsbourg that has stood out.

Sigold

Comte de Sigold
Cooperative label for Crémant d'Alsace.
See CV SIGOLSHEIM

CV Sigolsheim

Cave Vinicole de Sigolsheim
12 rue St-Jacques,
68240 Sigolsheim
Telephone: (89) 47.12.55

Current membership: 140
Production: 250,000 cases
Vineyards: 285 hectares
Grands crus: 31.5ha Mambourg (Sigolsheim)
Labels: Comte de Sigold (Crémant d'Alsace)

I have seldom encountered the wines from this cooperative.

Simonis

Jean-Paul Simonis
1 rue du Chasseur Maurice-Besombes, 68770 Ammerschwihr
Telephone: (89) 47.13.51

Nothing known about this grower.

Sinne

Domaine de la Sinne
See Jérôme GESCHIKT & Fils

Sipp

Domaine Jean Sipp
60 rue de le Fraternité,
68150 Ribeauvillé
Telephone: (89) 73.60.02

Production: 13,000 cases
Vineyards: 18.6 hectares (2.3ha
Rodern, 2.3ha Bergheim, 14ha
Ribeauvillé), which account for this
grower's total production
Grape varieties: 1.5ha Sylvaner,
5ha Riesling, 1.5ha Pinot Blanc,
2ha Tokay-Pinot Gris, 2ha Pinot
Noir, 6ha Gewurztraminer, 0.3ha
Muscat Ottonel, 0.3ha Muscat
Blanc à Petit Grains
Grands crus: 2ha Kirchberg de
Ribeauvillé

An important grower with a large
domaine, yet quite small compared
to cousin Louis Sipp on the other
side of the village, although all Jean
Sipp's wines are entirely the
production of his own vineyards.
The difference between the two
Sipps is not, however, one of
quality but style. Both produce
long-lived wines, but Jean Sipp
makes wines that are easier to
access at an earlier stage and turn
honeyed with age, whereas the
Louis Sipp style is for a more crisp,
correct and absolutely dry wine that
requires time in bottle to mellow
into petrolly finesse. Jean Sipp
Tokay-Pinot Gris Trottacker is rich
and firm, capable of ageing very

well. His Riesling Grand Cru
Kirchberg de Ribeauvillé is classic
and long-lived. He also produces a
stylish generic Gewurztraminer
wine that is not quite dry, but has
some finesse, while the Réserve
Personnelle is richer and firmer. He
is capable of good Pinot Blanc,
particularly in years when the wines
have a little noble rot and have a
tendency towards exotic peach and
pineapple fruit flavours. Jean Sipp
also produces a classic blended
wine called Clos du Schlossberg
from a very steep vineyard. The
grapes are grown together (50 per
cent Riesling, 20 per cent
Gewurztraminer, 20 per cent
Tokay-Pinot Gris and 10 per cent
Muscat) and harvested at severely
restricted yields to produce a truly
classic *vin de garde.*

Sipp

Grands Vins d'Alsace Louis Sipp
5 Grand'rue, 68150 Ribeauvillé
Telephone: (89) 73.60.01

Established: 1925 by Louis Sipp
Production: 100,000 cases
Vineyards: 31 hectares (27.3ha
Ribeauvillé, 0.5ha Hunawihr,
3.2ha Bergheim), representing
25–30 per cent of total production,
plus 2.8 hectares rented (2.4ha
Ribeauvillé, 0.4ha Bergheim) and
has purchased from the same 80
growers owning 55 hectares in
Ribeauvillé for more than 60 years
Grape varieties: 2.1ha Sylvaner,
0.6ha Chasselas, 6.7ha Riesling,
7.6ha Pinot Blanc, 1.7ha Tokay-
Pinot Gris, 1.9ha Pinot Noir, 9.1ha
Gewurztraminer, 0.2ha Muscat

Ottonel, plus 1.1 fallow
Grands crus: 2.2ha Kirchberg de
Ribeauvillé, 1.8ha Osterberg
(Ribeauvillé)

I have followed the fortunes of
Louis Sipp for almost 20 years and
the quality of this firm's best *cuvées*
has always been top class. During
that time, I have learned that those
wines that may appear to be tight,
closed, even aggressive, in their
youth are the ones that turn into the
most beautiful and longest-lived of
the Louis Sipp range. Riesling first
and Gewurztraminer a close second
are the greatest wines here. All the
Riesling wines are typically firm
structured and austere in their
youth, but the severity of this style
increases as you climb further up
the scale, so that the more generic
cuvées, particularly those with
medals, appear to be the better
wines. They are, however, merely
more attractive earlier in their life
(though by no means as accessible
as those from cousin Jean Sipp up
the road) and it is the top *cuvées*,
particularly the Grand Cru
Kirchberg de Ribeauvillé, that
develop the most intense flavours
with time. Louis Sipp Rieslings gain
tremendous petrolly finesse and
complexity over a period of eight to
ten years. In the richest years, such
as 1983 and 1989, the naturally
austere Louis Sipp style will be
overwhelmed by the exuberant
character of such fabulously ripe
fruit, but the wines last just as long
and develop more along the lines of
honeyed-petrol complexity than
racy, petrolly finesse. Louis Sipp

Gewurztraminer is almost as great,
just as firm in its youth and
potentially every bit as long-lived.
Even the generic Gewurztraminer
ages beautifully, but it is, of course,
the intensely flavoured Grand Cru
Osterberg that evolves into the
most classic of Gewurztraminers. It
slowly cultivates a mellow
pungency of spice on the palate,
while the fruit remains quite crisp
and fresh. This is a wine that has
the grip to avoid any hint of
blowziness, no matter how much
spice it develops. I do not know the
source of Louis Sipp's sensational
1973 Gewurztraminer, Prix
d'Honneur Concours d'Alsace, but
I suspect there is more than a touch
of Osterberg in it. If you ever get the
chance to taste that wine, you will
know what I mean when discussing
the ultimate potential of the Louis
Sipp style. It is as fresh as a daisy.

Sipp-Mack

Domaine Sipp-Mack
1 rue des Vosges, 68150 Hunawihr
Telephone: (89) 73.61.88

Established: 1698
Winemaker or *oenologist:* Jacques
Sipp
Production: 13,500 cases
Vineyards: 16 hectares (3ha
Hunawihr, 7ha Ribeauvillé, 6ha
Bergheim), which account for this
grower's total production
Grands crus: 0.8ha Rosacker
(Hunawihr), 0.8ha Osterberg
(Ribeauvillé)

The best wines of this producer are
Rieslings. Sipp-Mack makes a

superior generic that is immediately attractive and often has a touch of spritz to lift the finish, but it is their Grand Cru Rosacker that stands out for its exceptional intensity of flavour.

Sorg

Bruno Sorg
8 rue Monseigneur Stumpf,
68420 Eguisheim
Telephone: (89) 41.80.85

Established: 1965
Winemaker or *oenologist:* Bruno Sorg
Production: 5,000 cases
Vineyards: 8.5ha hectares (3ha Eguisheim, 4ha Ingersheim, 1.5ha Turckheim-Niedermorschwihr), which account for this grower's total production
Grands crus: 0.9ha Florimont (Ingersheim), 0.8ha Pfersigberg (Eguisheim)

The rustic appearance of this grower's label accurately reflects his humble country origins, but does not give the slightest clue as to the fantastic quality of the wine inside the bottle. Bruno Sorg is a small grower whose wines are seldom seen locally, let alone on export markets, which is a great pity because either he is a natural winemaking genius or he accidentally makes classic wines from virtually every variety in all vintages. If anyone deserves to be much better known, it is Sorg. He makes luscious Auxerrois; firm, well-focused Tokay-Pinot Gris of great finesse; generic

Gewurztraminer of impeccable class; stunning, ultra-ripe Riesling from the Grand Cru Florimont, and simply the best Muscat in Alsace (Grand Cru Pfersigberg), which is where I would have left it had I not discovered quite late in my research for this book that his talent also extends to Crémant d'Alsace. His Blanc de Blancs might not be the very best in Alsace, but it has a super fruit-acidity balance and fine autolytic character, which in itself is quite astonishing for such basic winemaking facilities in the back of beyond.

Soultz-Wuenheim

CV Soultz-Wuenheim
See CV VIEIL ARMAND

Sparr

Pierre Sparr
2 rue de la Première Armée,
68240 Sigolsheim
Telephone: (89) 78.24.22

Established: 1680 by Jean Sparr
Production: 175,000 cases
Vineyards: 30 hectares (Sigolsheim and Turckheim), representing about 20 per cent of total production, plus contracts with more than 120 growers
Grands crus: 2.1ha Mambourg (Sigolsheim), 1.8ha Brand (Turckheim)

The overall impression I have of the wines produced by this friendly firm is one of extreme richness, often with a touch of sweetness in the Réserve of Cuvée Prestige. Perhaps the most massively rich wine of all is Sparr's Tokay-Pinot Gris Tête de Cuvée. The Riesling style is rich, but generally easy going, even in its best *cuvée* from the Grand Cru Schlossberg. The Gewurztraminer wines often have a touch of sweetness, even in the most basic generic *cuvées*, but there is always a genuine richness of fruit to back this up and the best wines can be very classy indeed. Grand Cru Mambourg Cuvée Centenaire and Grand Cru Brand Cuvée Réserve are finely balanced Gewurztraminers of true breed and show plenty of citrusy-spicy finesse. Continuation of the high-quality Kaefferkopf blend must be doubtful if the *grand cru* classification goes ahead, but it should be preserved, even if only as Cuvée K, for it was a perfect reflection of its 80 per cent Gewurztraminer and 20 per cent Tokay-Pinot Gris composition (*see* 'Blended Wines' in Chapter 7). This firm has, however, helped to keep the classic blended wine ball rolling with the introduction of a new *cuvée* called Symphonie, which is a high-quality blend of 35 per cent Riesling, 30 per cent Tokay-Pinot Gris, 25 per cent Pinot Blanc and 10 per cent Gewurztraminer. Sparr has been producing sparkling wine by the *méthode champenoise* here for nearly 20 years and this experience shows in its current releases of the non-vintage Sparr Brut Réserve, which is made from 50/50 Pinot Blanc and Auxerrois, shows fine autolysis and has the sort of richness that typifies most wines from this house.

Specht

Jean-Paul & Denis Specht
2 rue des Églises, 68630 Mittelwihr
Telephone: (89) 47.90.85

Established: 1955
Winemaker or *oenologist:* Jean-Paul & Denis Specht
Production: 5,500 cases
Vineyards: 6.5 hectares (3.5ha Mittelwihr, 2ha Ribeauvillé, 1ha Beblenheim), which account for this grower's total production
Grands crus: 0.1ha Sonnenglanz (Beblenheim), 0.4ha Mandelberg (Mittelwihr)

Of the few wines tasted recently from this small grower, none stood out.

Sperry

Pierre Sperry & Fils
3A route du Vin,
67650 Blienschwiller
Telephone: (88) 92.41.29

I have had only one wine from this grower, a Pinot Noir, but it was good and fruity.

Spielmann

Jean-Martin Spielmann
2 route de Thannenkirch,
68750 Bergheim
Telephone: (89) 73.63.18

Established: 1959
Winemaker or *oenologist:* Sylvie Spielmann
Production: 5,500 cases
Vineyards: 8 hectares (Bergheim), which account for this grower's

total production
Grands crus: 1.3ha Kanzlerberg
(Bergheim), 0.6ha Altenberg de
Bergheim

Although capable of producing the
odd wine that can disappoint from
a normally consistent *cuvée*, this
grower gets it right most of the time
and is well worth watching. His
Pinot Blanc is rich and flavoursome,
a touch aromatic and can have
splendid youthful honey. The
generic Gewurztraminer is full and
expansive with fine fruity spice that
may have a touch of spritz, but this
producer's best Gewurztraminers
and, indeed, his best two wines are
Grand Cru Altenberg de Bergheim
and Grand Cru Kanzlerberg, which
show a level of finesse not found in
any of his others. Spielmann's
Riesling Grand Cru Kanzlerberg is
less consistent, but can be very racy,
intense and exciting. Although I do
not have sufficient experience of
various vintages of this producer's
Muscat, it is worth keeping an eye
on if the deliciously rich and
honeyed 1988 Réserve is anything
to go by.

Spitz

Spitz & Fils
2 route du Vin,
67650 Blienschwiller
Telephone: (88) 92.40.33

Nothing known about this grower.

Staehle

Bernard Staehlé
15 rue Clémenceau,
68920 Wintzenheim
Telephone: (89) 27.39.02

Attractively fresh and floral
Riesling Cuvée Dame Blanche and
an excellent Crémant d'Alsace of
some finesse, but only tasted once.

Stentz

Domaine Aimé Stentz
37 rue Herzog, 68920 Wettolsheim
Telephone: (89) 80.63.77

Established: 1952
Winemaker or *oenologist:* Etienne
Stentz
Production: 10,000 cases
Vineyards: 13.5 hectares (2.7ha
Niedermorschwihr, 3.8ha
Wettolsheim, 5.9ha Wintzenheim,
1.1ha Colmar), which account for
this grower's total production
Grands crus: 0.5ha Steingrubler
(Wettolsheim), 1ha Hengst
(Wintzenheim), 0.4ha Sommerberg
(Niedermorschwihr)

The wine I prefer from this grower
is his fat and spicy Riesling Grand
Cru Sommerberg, but I have also
enjoyed his flavourful Pinot Noir.

Stentz

Fernand Stentz
40 route du Vin, Herrlisheim,
68420 Husseren-les-Châteaux
Telephone: (89) 49.30.04

Visited just once, on a whim and
without prior announcement. Like

many houses in the Husseren area, this grower's home has a veranda above the garage to exploit the fabulous view of the Alsace plain below and, as is customary for growers throughout France, the garage also doubles as a very hospitable *caveau* for receiving customers and tasting wines. I mentioned to Monsieur Stentz that his 1985 Pinot Noir was not very typical, however, having a strange almost Rioja-like oak, acidity and tannin, but he was not put out in the slightest (he even confessed that he had long since given up entering competitions because his wines were rejected for not tasting like Alsace!). His Gewurztraminer Cuvée Charles is another atypical Alsace wine, possessing unusually high acidity, which gives the wine remarkable freshness as it honeys with age.

Stinzi

Gérard Stinzi
29 rue Principale, 68420 Husseren-les-Châteaux

This small family enterprise, which owns four hectares of vines, including just over half a hectare of Gewurztraminer and Tokay-Pinot Gris on Grand Cru Eichberg, produces wines in wood by traditional methods.

Stoeffler

Charles Stoeffler
4 rue des Jardins, 67140 Barr
Telephone: (88) 08.02.64

Small grower with eight hectares of vineyards.

Straub

Joseph Straub & Fils
See Domaine de la TOUR

Stutzmann

Michel Stutzmann
67520 Kuttolsheim

Producer of Vin de Pays du Bas-Rhin.

Thomas

GAEC André Thomas & Fils
3 rue des Seigneurs,
68770 Ammerschwihr
Telephone: (89) 47.16.60

Established: 1960
Winemaker or *oenologist:* François Thomas
Production: 4,000 cases
Vineyards: 5 hectares (3.3ha Ammerschwihr, 1.4ha Kientzheim, 0.3ha Sigolsheim), which account for this grower's total production
Grands crus: 0.3ha Kaefferkopf (Ammerschwihr), 0.2ha Mambourg (Sigolsheim)

The wines of André Thomas are really quite good in general, but can go overboard on residual sweetness to fatten up supposedly dry wines. Consistently the finest wine in this range is the Gewurztraminer Grand Cru Mambourg Vendange Tardive, which is definitely sweet, rich and liquorous. In 1989 this wine had more botrytis than some SGN from other producers. The Riesling 1988 Cuvée Gilles was a one-off speciality, made by the *méthode vin de paille*, it is claimed, but tasting more like a superb SGN.

Tour

Domaine de la Tour
21 route du Vin,
67650 Blienschwiller
Telephone: (88) 92.48.72

Capable of very rich Vendanges Tardives, especially Tokay-Pinot Gris, which keeps a splendid freshness and balance. Also known as Joseph Straub & Fils.

Tourelle

Clos de la Tourelle
See CV VIEIL ARMAND

Traber

See CV RIBEAUVILLÉ
A cooperative label.

CV Traenheim

Cave Vinicole de Traenheim
Rue du Scharrach,
67310 Traenheim
Telephone: (88) 50.66.21

Established: 1952
Current membership: 270
Production: 330,000 cases (of which 60 per cent is sold directly by the cooperative, 30 per cent goes to Divinal and 10 per cent to *négociants*)
Vineyards: 305 hectares
Grands crus: 25ha (Altenberg de

Bergbieten, Altenberg de Wolxheim)
Labels: Les Vins du Roi Dagobert (main cooperative label), St-Eloi (Crémant d'Alsace)

Not tasted as often as other cooperatives, but those I have enjoyed include fresh, uncomplicated Sylvaner with a nice spritz; soft and creamy Klevner with excellent acidity; occasional Tokay-Pinot Gris of very good quality; good, orange-flower generic Muscat; and fine, expressive Gewurztraminer Altenberg de Bergbieten.
See also DIVINAL, CV ANDLAU and CV TRAENHEIM

Trimbach

F.E. Trimbach
15 route de Bergheim,
68150 Ribeauvillé
Telephone: (89) 73.60.30

Established: 1626 by Jean Trimbach
Production: 80,000 cases
Vineyards: 14 hectares (1.2ha Bergheim, 3.8ha Hunawihr, 9ha Ribeauvillé)
Grape varieties: 0.5ha Sylvaner, 0.2ha Chasselas, 6.5ha Riesling, 1.6ha Pinot Blanc, 0.6ha Tokay-Pinot Gris, 4.2ha Gewurztraminer, 0.3ha Muscat Ottonel, 0.1ha Muscat à Petit Grains
Grands crus: 0.6ha Geisberg (Ribeauvillé), 1.4ha Rosacker (Hunawihr), 2.3ha Osterberg (Ribeauvillé)
Labels: Heydt (not so much a *sous marque* as a special exclusivity)

The Trimbachs were originally winegrowers based in Riquewihr, where the son and grandson of founder Jean Trimbach were mayors in the seventeenth century. In the 1840s the family moved to Hunawihr, where Jean-Frédéric Trimbach was mayor for many years. It was not until the late nineteenth century, however, that his son, Frédéric-Emile Trimbach, really began to develop the activities of this house. Frédéric-Emile's initials still form the firm's title and his name is used for one of Trimbach's greatest wines, the Riesling Cuvée Frédéric-Emile. It was he who moved the business to Ribeauvillé, from where it operates today, its cellars having been recently renovated and extended. Since the Second World War and, in particular, since the early 1960s, the Trimbachs and Hugels have forged an amicable alliance in promoting Alsace wines all over the world. Rivals they may be, but friends they are too, as can be discerned when they are showing some rare old gems from their cellars, for nobody is more respectful of great Trimbach wines than Johnny Hugel and, equally, no one has publicly expressed greater compliments about classic Hugel wines than Hubert Trimbach.

Hubert and Bernard Trimbach (actually Heydt-Trimbach, hence the Heydt label, but they call themselves Trimbach plain and simple to avoid confusion among their customers) are brothers and, like many pairs of brothers, could not be more different. Hubert, who is blond and Nordic-looking, with an easy, outgoing character, lives out of a suitcase. He spreads the Trimbach gospel and is just as much at home in the world's finest hotels and restaurants than he is in Ribeauvillé. Bernard, on the other hand, is quieter, more intense, but jolly. He is the born winemaker and could not be happier than when he is sloshing around the cellars in his gumboots, hosing down everything in sight. Bernard likes to stay at home, entertaining friends there rather than in a restaurant. While rumour has it that Hubert even goes to bed in a shirt and tie, Bernard is more comfortable in jeans and a jumper. Hubert and Bernard still run the firm, but their sons, who represent the twelfth generation, are now firm fixtures. Hubert's son Jean probably travels as much as his father nowadays and Bernard's son Pierre is definitely in charge of winemaking, although if he does not watch where he is walking, he is likely to turn a corner and be hosed down by his father, who just will not take off those gumboots.

The Trimbachs make great Gewurztraminer, particularly the Seigneurs de Ribeaupierre, which from great years will assume awesome structure and pungency after ten or fifteen years. This is wine that can shock, even offend, but it is classic nonetheless. Tokay-Pinot Gris is probably this producer's most underrated wine, but take a Réserve Personnelle from a good vintage, tuck it away for a few years and you will have a wine of great finesse and complexity. I can normally take or leave the Sylvaner and Pinot Blanc, but would not rule either out in a really ripe year (*see* 'Sylvaner' entry in Chapter 7), but I do not know what they are doing with Pinot Noir, it just does not fit in with their house style. I suppose they *must* produce Edelzwicker, but I wish they did not. On the other hand, I would like to see a truly classic blended wine from this firm.

Above all else, however, the Trimbachs are producers of Riesling par excellence. Cuvée Frédéric-Emile, which comes from part of the Grand Cru Osterberg vineyard that overlooks their premises, is one of the greatest Rieslings in Alsace. It might even be the second greatest Riesling in Alsace, but Trimbach's Clos Ste-Hune is without question the very greatest. Although they have owned the tiny 1.3-hectare vineyard of Clos Ste-Hune for well over 200 years, the first vintage bearing its name was not produced until 1919. This treasured vineyard is situated within (but distinctly superior to) the 26-hectare Grand Cru Rosacker. For some stupid, bureaucratic reason the name of any solely owed vineyard in Alsace cannot be used as a *grand cru*, so the Trimbachs are expected to put the name Rosacker on their label, if they want to claim *grand cru* status, which they do not. They have no intention of using the Rosacker name and why should they? When they produce so little Clos Ste-Hune and sell it for the highest price of any dry Alsace wine, why bother

with a name and a classification claimed by wines that struggle to receive a third of the price? Without getting sidetracked by the occasional production of botrytis wines, Clos Ste-Hune is not just the best Riesling in Alsace, it is the region's greatest wine *per se* and as such deserves a classification of its own. If the authorities will not make it a *grand cru* in its own right, I will just have to elevate it to the unique classification of Premier Grand Cru d'Alsace.

The magical difference that turns Clos Ste-Hune into one of the world's greatest wines is the vineyard itself, as its wines are made in precisely the same fashion as all other Trimbach wines. They receive a standard vinification at 20–5°C and no malolactic. The vines average 22 years of age, grow in calcareous clay and yield 50 hectolitres per hectare, which is lowish but not so exceptional that it accounts for the special quality of this wine. Exactly what is in this little vineyard that makes its wines so outstanding, I have no idea, but the high price asked is not inflicted on Trimbach's loyal customers merely because of its intrinsically high quality. A 1.2 hectare plot of vines yielding 50 hectolitres per hectare means that no more than 700 cases can be produced each vintage. It is this rarity value that adds to the cost of Clos Ste-Hune.

You have to be a devotee to buy Clos Ste-Hune, not simply because of the cost, but because the wine does not immediately charm the consumer. It needs at least five years even to hint at the extent of its potential, although the youngest examples will unravel some of its future complexity if kept in the glass a while. Without doubt, Clos Ste-Hune is a magnificent wine. It is a wine that has a concentration that belies the deftness of its balance, a wine that is capable of extraordinary longevity and the epitome of finesse, grace and style. It is, as I say in Chapter 7, the quintessential Riesling.

It is not the aim of this book to provide tasting notes for each and every vintage of all the wines reviewed (*see* Explanatory note No.5 in Chapter 7), but the peerless position of this particular growth demands something more be said. Thus I proffer the following notes, most of which were made at Ribeauvillé in May 1990:

1989 Clos Ste-Hune Vendange Tardive, Hors Choix One of the greatest botrytis Rieslings I have ever tasted, this is so crisp and clean that it is like bottled fresh air. That is not sarcasm, it merely means that the noble fruit in this wine is unbelievably fresh and invigorating. Make no mistake, this is a beautiful wine, with a delicacy of fruit that is exquisite and elegant.

1988 Clos Ste-Hune Crisp, fine and elegant, this is a Riesling of great finesse that will take a decade to show its full potential.

1987 Clos Ste-Hune Fresh, aromatic, citrusy appeal; initial glimpse of richness cut off by the austerity of its youth.

1986 Clos Ste-Hune Wonderfully precocious, petrolly nose – complex and full of finesse; huge concentration of fruit, but tight with youth and a massive amount of ripe acidity promising extraordinary longevity even for Clos Ste-Hune; complex minerally extract dominates the finish. An astonishing wine, considering 1986 was merely a good, not special, vintage, it promises to develop like the 1970.

1985 Clos Ste-Hune Hints of a classy Riesling bouquet developing; rich mid-palate flavour full of deliciously ripe, white-peach fruit; plenty of refreshing, ripe acidity on the finish. It will be interesting to see how the 1986 and 1985 develop, the former being so exceptional and the latter having the pedigree of vintage. Which will be the deciding factor?

1983 Clos Ste-Hune Fat for Clos Ste-Hune, but then it is a 1983. Succulent strawberry aroma filtering through on to the palate; a big wine with a lemony-spicy tang, lots of extract and very fine acidity for the year.

1983 Clos Ste-Hune Vendange Tardive Scintillating, lemon-zest aroma, which is more reminiscent of a seven-month than a seven-year wine; lovely, lemony fruit – tangy rather than sweet. An absolutely stunning wine, so fresh and vital.

1983 Clos Ste-Hune Sélection de Grains Nobles Deep, full and powerful nose, but does not have the sweetness and botrytis I expect from this style of wine. It is such a big and ponderous wine that I would not like to predict how it will develop over the next 20 years. The mere discussion of a 27-year life-span must mean it is a fine, possibly great wine, but the Vendange Tardive is the better wine in terms of pure quality.

1982 Clos Ste-Hune Attractive nose and nice, citrusy fruit on mid-palate, but not the finesse Clos Ste-Hune consumers are accustomed to, although the flowery, almost Muscaty, aftertaste is most appealing. A very good Riesling, but not the class expected of Clos Ste-Hune.

1981 Clos Ste-Hune Fine, rich, petrolly bouquet; steely-rich Riesling fruit on the palate, firm and with finesse. Infinitely better than the 1982 and a wine of real class, even by Clos Ste-Hune's stringent standards.

1979 Clos Ste-Hune If I liked the 1981, I simply adored the 1979, easily the best wine of the tasting so far. A fine Riesling bouquet with a touch of spice and exceptional finesse; rich, succulent, petrolly fruit on the palate, again with great finesse and absolutely superb, honeyed complexity and finesse on the finish. Finesse, finesse, finesse! A great Clos Ste-Hune.

1978 Clos Ste-Hune The nose is spoilt by a touch of fixed sulphur, which filters through on the palate, making the fruit dull, almost unclean, with a toasty-vegetal aftertaste. Two half-bottles tasted since were very similar, making this the only truly disappointing Clos Ste-Hune I have come across.

1977 Clos Ste-Hune If any vintage should be a disappointment, it is the 1977 and, true enough, it is not a classic Clos Ste-Hune, but it is a very enjoyable Riesling, with a screeching petrolly aroma leading to steely-petrolly fruit, firm acidity and fine, honeyed complexity on the finish. Although several orders beneath the 1979, it is a fine Riesling and far superior to the 1978 Clos Ste-Hune.

1976 Clos Ste-Hune Intensely aromatic nose of fine, spicy-petrolly complexity; a great concentration of fresh, zippy fruit on the palate. A mouth-watering wine of unbelievable youth, still a long way from developing the honeyed finesse that comes with maturity. A wine to compare with the 1979. At the moment they are equal in quality, both definitely among the world's greatest wines, though totally different in style. If I had to put my money on one or the other, I think the 1976 will eventually outlive the 1979, but I doubt that I will be around to collect my winnings.

1975 Clos Ste-Hune When I tasted this immediately after the 1976, I thanked goodness that I was not scoring the wines because I would be on 21 out of 20 by now. Magnificent petrolly nose of great finesse; exquisitely rich, astonishing acidity, huge extract and such a long finish that I though I was suspended in a black hole! The balance of this wine is nothing short of amazing. Equally great and just as young as the 1976, this will be another fascinating pair to follow, but unlike the 1979 and 1981, I would not know which to put my money on.

1973 Clos Ste-Hune Providing this wine is not tasted after the 1975 and 1976 Clos Ste-Hune, most devotees of the Riesling would probably not be able to imagine a greater example of this variety. A lusciously rich and honeyed bouquet, the wine has delicately rich fruit, an elegant balance and a graceful finish that I judge will develop a little honey to balance the nose by the mid-1990s. The 1973 vintage was underrated in the Rhine, both in Germany and Alsace, as this wine vividly demonstrates.

1971 Clos Ste-Hune The sample tasted was not as good as others I have tasted of this vintage. It showed the youthful fruit I was expecting on the palate, but was a little tired on the nose and a bit *passé* on the finish. At its best, this is wine to rival the 1975, 1976 and 1979.

1970 Clos Ste-Hune This vintage generally does not compare with the likes of 1971, or even 1973, but from the remarkable Clos Ste-Hune vineyard and given the ideal cellaring at Ribeauvillé, the 1970 was better than both on the day: an opulently honeyed nose, deliciously rich, vanilla-scented fruit and great, honeyed complexity on the finish. This perfectly preserved example was probably *à pointe* in 1990, but a 20-year-old wine that is *à pointe* could keep on a plateau for a long time.

1969 Clos Ste-Hune Another astonishingly youthful, fine, honeyed Riesling of great complexity and finesse, I initially marked it a tad lower (in my mind, not as a score) than the 1970, but it built in the glass and I subsequently upgraded it as on a par. Certainly the vintage as a whole was intrinsically superior.

1967 Clos Ste-Hune A year that was technically superior to 1969 for Alsace as a whole, this has always been one of Clos Ste-Hune's famed vintages. I rate it very highly indeed, but on the day it was two tads below both the 1969 and 1970, although from its wonderfully rich and honeyed bouquet I thought it would be their equal. Acidity was, however, the deciding factor. I could not say that the 1967 lacked acidity, but it did lack a certain exuberance of acidity that is always noticeable in the very best vintages of Clos Ste-Hune. Again, I am being super-critical, as I think I should be for a wine I consider to be the world's greatest Riesling. It is relatively a tad or two below the very best Clos Ste-Hune, yet nevertheless a truly great Riesling.

1967 Clos Ste-Hune Vendange Tardive A quite deep-coloured wine with a rich, profound nose and an extraordinary balance between depth of flavour and elegance of style. Should continue to improve for a decade so. A *grand vin* indeed.

1966 Clos Ste-Hune A fabulous honey-rich bouquet of great finesse and charm; exquisitely rich fruit with a lovely balance of acidity, much longer and finer on the palate than the basic (if one can use such a term) Clos Ste-Hune 1967, due to a better balance of acidity. Classic Clos Ste-Hune.

CV Turckheim

Cave Vinicole de Turckheim
Rue des Tuileries,
68230 Turckheim
Telephone: (89) 27.06.25

Established: 1955
Current membership: 261
Production: 26,000 cases
Vineyards: 302 hectares
Grands crus: 10ha Brand (Turckheim), 1ha Hengst (Wintzenheim), 1ha Sommerberg (Niedermorschwihr), 0.5ha Wineck-Schlossberg (Katzenthal), 2ha Ollwiller (Wuenheim), 1ha Schoenenbourg (Riquewihr), 1ha Sporen (Riquewihr)
Labels: Mayerling (Crémant d'Alsace), Preiss-Zimmer (this cooperative now makes and markets the wines of Preiss-Zimmer. *See* that entry for more details)

With CV Pfaffenheim and Wolfberger, this is one of the three best cooperatives in Alsace. It is a Pinot producer of very high order. At the bottom of the Pinot ladder, there are the unpretentious and delightfully fruity Pinot Blanc and the richer Val St-Grégoire, both of which are 50/50 Pinot Blanc and Auxerrois. The wines sold as Klevner have up to 80 per cent Auxerrois in the blend and are thus much riper and more mellow, but have good fruit-acidity balance, particularly in good, though not great, years. Tokay-Pinot Gris is obviously a step-up in quality and the generic here is truly excellent, but their top *cuvées* can be sensational. Some of CV Turckheim's most successful Sigillé-winning Tokay-Pinot Gris have come from the Brand, even if they sometimes did not mention this on the label (1976 and 1983, for example), but I have not seen this wine lately, although the cooperative has been gradually fashioning a splendidly rich Grand Cru Hengst of exquisite finesse. The third and final Pinot is at least as successful, as the Cuvée à l'Ancienne is consistently one of the best Pinot Noirs produced in the red wine style, albeit in a delicately light and fruity rendition. Having witnessed the deft touch with which CV Turckheim craft their red wines, it will come as no surprise to discover that this cooperative makes a very fine rosé. Its Rosé de Turckheim is as sumptuous as this style comes and a wine of outstanding class for such an unpretentious wine.

The Sylvaner here is at least drinkable and can rise above its station in some vintages, whereas I have often found the generic Muscat preferable to the supposedly higher-quality *cuvées*. Riesling can be excellent, but is not consistent. The Riesling Décapole, Grand Cru Brand and Vendange Tardive can be stunningly rich and racy, but sometimes they disappoint. Grand Cru Sommerberg is the best Riesling at the moment, but Grand Cru Schoenenbourg can be too fat and lacks finesse. Most houses that excel with Tokay-Pinot Gris are also very good with Gewurztraminer and CV Turckheim is no exception, particularly if it comes from the Grand Cru Brand or is a Vendange Tardive. Last but not least, the non-vintage Crémant d'Alsace Brut sold under the cooperative's Mayerling label has exceptional richness and acidity, with fine autolytic character.

Clos du Val d'Eléon

See Marc KREYDENWEISS

CV Vieil Armand

Cave du Vieil Armand
1 route de Cernay, Wuenheim,
68360 Soultz

Telephone: (89) 76.73.75

Established: 1958
Current membership: 125
Production: 86,000 cases (only about 9,000 cases sold)
Vineyards: 116 hectares
Grape varieties: 9ha Sylvaner, 30ha Riesling, 31ha Pinot Blanc, 8ha Tokay-Pinot Gris, 20ha Pinot Noir, 16ha Gewurztraminer, 2ha Muscat (mixed)
Grands crus: Ollwiller (Wuenheim)
Labels: Also known as CV Soultz-Wuenheim, this cooperative makes and markets the wines of Clos de la Tourelle and Château Ollwiller, both of which are owned by J-H Gros & Fils.

Part of the Wolfberger group since 1982, most of this cooperative's production ends up in Wolfberger blends, although some 9,000 cases are sold under the CV Vieil Armand label, either by mail order or direct retail sales to visitors. I have not visited this cooperative, have rarely tasted its wines and cannot therefore make a sensible overall judgement, although Château Ollwiller is capable of producing a polished Riesling.
See also WOLFBERGER

Vierling

Joseph Vierling
67117 Fessenheim-le-Bas

Small producer of Auxerrois, Sylvaner and Pinot Noir under the Vin de Pays du Bas-Rhin denomination.

Vierling

Lucie Vierling
67370 Neugartheim

Small producer of Pinot Blanc
under the Vin de Pays du Bas-Rhin
denomination.

Vieux Pressoir

Domaine du Vieux Pressoir
See Marcel SCHLOSSER

Vignerons De Pfaffenheim

Les Vignerons de Pfaffenheim
Main label for the cooperative at
Pfaffenheim.
See CV PFAFFENHEIM

Ville de Colmar

See Domaine Viticole de la Ville de
COLMAR

Viticole de la Ville de Colmar

See Domaine Viticole de la Ville de
COLMAR

Vogt

Laurent Vogt
4 rue des Vignerons, 67120
Wolxheim
Telephone: (88) 38.50.41

Nothing known about this small
grower.

Wach

Guy Wach
See Domaine des MARRONNIERS

Wach

Jean Wach
16A rue du Maréchal Foch,
67140 Andlau
Telephone: (88) 08.09.73

Very little known about this small
grower, except that he owns 7.5
hectares.

Wackenthaler

André Wackenthaler
8 rue du Kaefferkopf,
68770 Ammerschwihr
Telephone: (89) 78.23.76

I have had one or two excellent
Gewurztraminers from this grower,
particularly from the Kaefferkopf,
where he also makes Riesling that is
good, but not in the same class.

Wagenbourg

GAEC Joseph Klein & Fils
Château Wagenbourg,
68570 Soultzmatt
Telephone: (89) 47.01.41

The Klein family, who have been
winegrowers since 1605, acquired
this property in 1905. Gentle rosé,
decent Gewurztraminer and
restrained Riesling.

Wagner

Gérard Wagner
6 rue de la Chaîne, 67140 Andlau
Telephone: (88) 08.02.89

Nothing known about this grower.

Wantz

André Wantz
1 rue Neuve, 67140 Mittelbergheim
Telephone: (88) 08.00.41

Little known about this grower, other than that he comes from a line of *vignerons* stretching back to 1575 and owns some seven hectares today, including a plot on the *lieu-dit* Brandluft, where he grows Sylvaner.

Wantz

Ch. Wantz
36 rue St-Marc, 67140 Barr
Telephone: (88) 08.90.44

Established: Since 1945 by Charles Wantz
Production: 150,000 cases
Vineyards: 3.6 hectares (0.7ha Barr, 1.5ha Mittelbergheim, 1.4ha Heiligenstein), representing just 3 per cent of total production, plus contracts with more than 250 growers
Grape varieties: 0.6ha Sylvaner, 0.8ha Riesling, 0.6ha Pinot Blanc, 0.2ha Tokay-Pinot Gris, 0.4ha Pinot Noir, 0.7ha Gewurztraminer, 0.2ha Muscat Ottonel, 0.1ha Klevener de Heiligenstein
Labels: Goldlinger (non-AOC *vin mousseux*)

A very large producer, whose generic wines can be disappointing, but who does produce good fruity Rouge d'Ottrott, is capable of extremely fine Riesling from the Grand Cru Wiebelsberg and, of course, makes some good Klevener de Heiligenstein. I have also tasted various Riesling, Tokay-Pinot Gris and Gewurztraminer bearing Sigillé awards. As the wines of Ch. Wantz are competitively priced, there seems little sense buying the cheaper lacklustre products when for only a small premium the *cuvées* at the top of this producer's list are immeasurably better.

Weber

Bernard Weber
49 rue de Saverne, 67120 Molsheim
Telephone: (88) 38.52.67

Established: eighteenth century
Winemaker or *oenologist:* Bernard Weber
Production: 4,000 cases
Vineyards: 5.3 hectares (5.3ha Molsheim), which account for this grower's total production
Grands crus: 3.5ha Bruderthal (Molsheim)

Of the wines tasted from this producer, I am afraid the only one that has stood out was a strangely exotic Crémant d'Alsace Blanc de Blancs, which had an almost botrytized character of tropical fruits and vanilla. I tasted it only once and I do not know what to make of it.

Weck

Clément Weck
2 place de la Marie,
68420 Gueberschwihr

Owns just over one hectare (80 per cent Gewurztraminer and 20 per cent Muscat) of Grand Cru Goldert.

Wein

Ernest Wein
Also known as E. Wein, this *sous marque* is used by CV Pfaffenheim.
See CV PFAFFENHEIM

Weinbach

Domaine Weinbach
Clos des Capucins, 68240
Kaysersberg
Telephone: (89) 47.13.21

Established: 1898 by Théodore and
Jean-Baptiste Faller
Production: 13,000 cases
Vineyards: 25 hectares
(Kientzheim, Kaysersberg), which
account for this grower's total
production
Grape varieties: 1.4ha Sylvaner,
0.9ha Chasselas, 9.5ha Riesling,
1.1ha Pinot Blanc, 2.4ha Tokay-
Pinot Gris, 1.3ha Pinot Noir, 6.8ha
Gewurztraminer, 0.3ha Muscat
Ottonel, 0.3ha Muscat Rosé à Petit
Grains, plus 1.0ha fallow
Grands crus: 2ha Schlossberg
(Kientzheim)

Until the Revolution, Domaine
Weinbach was a monastery
belonging to an independent branch
of Franciscans called the Order of
Friars Minor Capuchins (or
Capucins in French) and both the
house and garden were known as
Clos des Capucins.
  Life in this residence today is I
suspect far more hectic than the
tranquillity of the Capucins'
ordered life. A visit to the Fallers
can easily turn into a French farce.
More than once I have turned up

with my wife for an apéritif-cum-
tasting prior to going out to dinner
with the Fallers, only to be
interrupted by a casual caller
requiring a tasting before buying a
case or two of wine. We are usually
seated in the middle reception
room, which has doors in all three
interior walls, one on the right,
which leads to the main entrance,
one in the middle, which leads to
the kitchen and one on the left,
which leads to another reception
room. Madame Colette Faller
excuses herself while she attends to
the unexpected caller, leaving her
daughter Cathérine to show us a
few wines that she has just brought
up from the cellar. Madame Faller
exits right to greet the new guests
outside, as we taste the first wine.
Cathy asks what we think of the
wine, but before we can answer, a
minibus full of Japanese (there is a
local Japanese school) pulls into the
drive, so Cathy excuses herself and
exits right. Meanwhile Madame
Faller comes through the kitchen
door, asks how we are doing, pours
a different wine and takes the first
bottle with her as she returns
through the kitchen to her guests in
the cellars. After a minute or two,
Cathy enters from the other
reception room, where she has
deposited a rather noisy gaggle of
Japanese tourists. Not realizing that
we were on the second wine, she
pours an over-generous quantity
into our glasses (no doubt to keep
us alcoholically anaesthetized while
they process the new arrivals) and
says that she will be back shortly to
see what we think of it forgetting

that she had not given us the opportunity to answer her enquiry about the first wine. Cathy exits left with the second bottle as Madame Faller enters right with the first bottle, sees that our glasses are still full (in fact they must have been even more full than when she last left us), tut-tuts and tells us to drink up, then realizes that the second bottle is missing. Where is it? she asks. Cathy took it, we say and Madame Faller exits left, still clasping the first bottle, in search of Cathy and the second. Cathy comes in through the kitchen and asks where her mother is. In the other reception room, we say, looking for you. Me? she asks. Yes. Where's the second bottle? She took it with her. Cathy exits left as we hear Madame Faller outside and realize she is escorting Cathy's Japanese visitors to the cellars. Cathy enters left, asking where her guests are; we say they're outside with her mother. Cathy exits right, the middle door opens and an elderly lady gestures at two complete strangers who have just walked into her kitchen. Who are they? she asks. We don't know. Where's Colette? With Cathy's guests, in the cellars I think. Where's Cathy? Looking for her mother – no, sorry, she's gone after her mother because she's looking for her guests. Whose guests? Her guests, Cathy's that is. Where are Colette's guests? Don't know, we haven't seen them. Could these be them, she inquires, gesturing once again at the couple in the kitchen. We don't know. The old lady mutters something and returns to the kitchen and in almost the same instant, the kitchen door swings open, Madame Faller flies through with the couple in tow, looks at our glasses in bewilderment and asks if there's anything wrong with the wine because we don't appear to be drinking it.

This goes on and on, coming in through one door, exiting through another, opening different bottles, pouring some wines twice, others not at all. On one occasion, the telephone rang at the height of all this madness and Madame Faller dropped the instrument, screamed, picked up a gun and ran out of the house. A neighbour had telephoned to say that a van was parked outside Clos des Capucins and its occupants were at that very moment harvesting Madame Faller's roses. Apparently it is a common occurrence, which is why she keeps the gun, an antique incapable of discharging, next to the telephone.

A day in the life of the Fallers may seem like a French farce to outsiders, but the stars of the cast take their task very seriously, producing some of the most stunning wines in Alsace.

Clos des Capucins, the jewel in this domaine's crown, is the rose-bordered, wall-enclosed, vineyard immediately in front of Madame Faller's charming house, but although all Domaine Weinbach's wines carry a Clos des Capucins label, very few of them are the exclusive product of that 5.2-hectare vineyard. In fact, only three wines are pure Clos des Capucins:

Riesling Cuvée Théo,
Gewurztraminer Cuvée Théo and
Tokay-Pinot Gris Ste-Cathérine,
although this *clos* also supplies
Domaine Weinbach with 80 per
cent of its Muscat and 50 per cent
of its Pinot Noir. As Madame Faller
bottles and sells each cask
separately, it is perfectly possible
that other wines are pure Clos des
Capucins, but it is impossible to
discern which they are in the
marketplace.

As I wax lyrical about these
wines under the various wine styles
and the *grands crus*, it would be
prudent to sort out the relevance of
Domaine Weinbach's various
cuvées here: Riesling Cuvée Théo
and Gewurztraminer Cuvée Théo
are both named after Madame
Faller's late husband, pure Clos des
Capucins and usually harvested at
the end of October.
Gewurztraminer Cuvée Laurence is
named after one of Madame
Faller's two daughters, pure Grand
Cru Furstentum and usually
harvested at the beginning or
middle of November. Riesling Ste-
Cathérine was so named because
one of Madame Faller's daughters
is named Cathérine and as Ste
Cathérine's Day is 25 November,
she thought it would be interesting
to harvest a wine on or about that
day every year; this wine is from the
Grand Cru Schlossberg. Tokay-
Pinot Gris Ste-Cathérine is so
named for the same reason; it is
pure Clos des Capucins and also
harvested on 25 November or
thereabouts.

Weingarten

Domaine Weingarten
See BERNHARD-REIBEL

Weingartner

Cooperative label accounting for 10
per cent of CV Ingersheim's sales.
See CV INGERSHEIM

Weiss

Michel Weiss
See STE-ODILE

Welty

Jean-Michel Welty
22-24 Grand'rue, 68500 Orschwihr
Telephone: (89) 76.09.03

I know very little about this grower,
other than that he produces a
decent generic Reisling that I have
tasted twice only, but on both
occasions it was soft and easy to
drink with a simple, yet appealing,
flowery aroma.

CV Westhalten

Cave Vinicole de Westhalten,
2 route de Soultzmatt,
68250 Westhalten
Telephone: (89) 47.01.27

Established: 1955
Current membership: 135
Production: 240,000 cases (70 per
cent sold under the cooperative
label, including the Heim brand, 30
per cent sold in bottle to
négociants)
Vineyards: 230 hectares

(Westhalten, Soultzmatt, Rouffach, Soultz, Steinbach)
Grands crus: 7ha (Zinnkoepflé and Vorbourg, Rouffach)
Labels: Heim (40 per cent of sales, i.e., 28 per cent of total production), Producteur (Crémant d'Alsace), Maréchal Lefèvre (Crémant d'Alsace), Madame Sans Gène (Crémant d'Alsace),

I have had good Tokay-Pinot Gris Cuvée Réserve and some fine Crémant d'Alsace. The Cuvée Producteur (50/50 Pinot Blanc and Auxerrois) is fat, creamy and commercial, Maréchal Lefèvre (50 per cent Pinot Blanc, 30 per cent Auxerrois and 20 per cent Tokay-Pinot Gris) has much finer acidity and structure, and Madame Sans Gène (100 per cent Pinot Noir) is a rosé that usually shows delightful, strawberry fruit. The Sans Gène Tradition, without any mention of gender, is white and the least interesting fizz produced here. Heim, which was purchased in the early 1980s, has not been a separate entity since 1984, since when all of its wines have been produced by the cooperative, in the cooperative.

Wiederhirn

Maison Wiederhirn
7 rue du Cheval, 68340 Riquewihr
Telephone: (89) 47.92.10

Established: 1915 by Julie Wiederhirn-Maurer
Production: 4,000 cases
Vineyards: 5.5 hectares (0.4ha Bennwihr, 0.5ha Kientzheim, 2ha Mittelwihr, 2.6ha Riquewihr),

which account for this grower's total production
Grape varieties: 0.1ha Sylvaner, 0.1ha Chasselas, 1.7ha Riesling, 0.8ha Pinot Blanc, 0.8ha Tokay-Pinot Gris, 0.3ha Pinot Noir, 1.4ha Gewurztraminer, 0.1ha Muscat Ottonel, 0.2ha Muscat Rosé à Petit Grains
Grands crus: 0.9ha Schoenenbourg (Riquewihr), 0.3ha Sporen (Riquewihr), 0.3ha Mandelberg (Mittelwihr)

Tucked down a little medieval alleyway, underneath this producer's charming town house are cellars that include part of Riquewihr's old *remparts* dating back to 1291. Like many Alsace growers, the owner's home is his business and tastings are conducted in the drawing room. Daniel Wiederhirn has a tendency to make his Rieslings in a somewhat sweet style, especially in very ripe years such as 1989, but the pure quality and genuine richness of wines such as his Réserve come whistling through. His Riesling Grand Cru Schoenenbourg Vieilles Vignes has been inexplicably inconsistent of late, but is capable of elegant peachy fruit and breathtaking finesse (1983 and 1985 were the last such gems). I also have fonder memories of past vintages of Tokay-Pinot Gris and Gewurztraminer than I do of more recent ones, but the potential of both vineyard and winemaker remains, so I shall keep a watchful eye on these wines.

Willm

Alsace Willm
32 rue du Dr Sultzer, BP 13,
67140 Barr
Telephone: (88) 08.19.11

Established: 1896 by Émile Willm
Production: 42,000 cases
Vineyards: 7.2 hectares (Barr),
representing about 20 per cent of
total production, the balance coming
from the vast cellars of Wolfberger
Grape varieties: 1.5ha Sylvaner,
1.3ha Riesling, 0.2ha Tokay-Pinot
Gris, 4.2ha Gewurztraminer
Grands crus: 7.2ha Kirchberg de
Barr (including 6ha of Clos
Gaensbroennel)

Wolfberger purchased Alsace Willm
in 1984 and acquired Domaine
Willm, which includes the famous
6-hectare Clos Gaensbroennel
vineyard, situated on the lower
slopes of the Kirchberg de Barr.
Although the wines are no longer
made on the domaine, they do retain
their own style and Clos
Gaensbroennel, particularly the
Gewurztraminer Clos
Gaensbroennel, is unquestionably
as massively rich and egocentric as it
always has been. Indeed it is almost
impossible to pin the style of this last
wine down, yet somehow it is
always, uniquely, Clos
Gaensbroennel, whether it tastes fat
and spicy in its more traditional
guise or like an alcoholic fruit salad
topped with butterscotch ice cream
in one of its more way-out moods.
Of the rest of the range, Riesling is
the most consistent. At generic level,
the spritz on the finish might remind

you that it has been made by
Wolfberger, but it is slightly fuller,
softer and sweeter in style. The
Grand Cru Kirchberg de Barr
Réserve Exceptionnelle is
consistently fine wine that is made
to lay down (except, I think, for the
'iffy' 1988). I have also had
excellent, powerful Riesling
Vendange Tardive. My only real
complaint here is that some Willm
wines have occasionally had off-
putting vegetal aromas.

Willman

A *sous marque* used by J. Hauller
for selected markets.
See J. HAULLER

Windsbuhl

Clos du Windsbuhl
See ZIND HUMBRECHT

Wischlen

A. Wischlen
4 rue de Soultzmatt,
68111 Westhalten
Telephone: (89) 47.01.24

Nothing known about this grower.

Wittmann

André Wittmann
7-9 rue Principale,
67140 Mittelbergheim
Telephone: (88) 08.95.79

Good Riesling Grand Cru
Zotzenberg, otherwise nothing
known about this grower.

Wolfberger

Cave Vinicole Eguisheim
6 Grand'rue, 68420 Eguisheim
Telephone: (89) 41.11.06

Established: 1902
Current membership: 453
Production: 1 million cases
Vineyards: Group total of just over
1157 hectares, of which
Wolfberger-Eguisheim actually
accounts for 638ha (Wintzenheim,
Wettolsheim, Eguisheim, Husseren-
les-Châteaux, Voegtlinshoffen,
Obermorschwihr, Hattstatt,
Herrlisheim, Bergholtz, Bergholtz-
Zell, Orschwihr). The membership
of two subsidiary cooperatives own
519ha (CV Dambach-la-Ville
403ha and CV Soultz-Wuenheim,
otherwise known as CV Vieil
Armand, 116ha). Within all the
above statistics, Wolfberger
actually owns in its own right the
105ha at Domaine Jux in Colmar
and 7.2ha at Willm in Barr,
including 6ha of the prised Clos
Gaensbroennel.
Grape varieties: 75ha Sylvaner,
45ha Chasselas, 98ha Riesling,
154ha Pinot Blanc, 54ha Tokay-
Pinot Gris, 48ha Pinot Noir, 152ha
Gewurztraminer, 12ha Muscat
(mixed)
Grands crus: 50ha (Hengst,
Pfirsigberg, Eichberg, Steingrubler,
Spiegel, Hatschbourg, Florimont,
Steinert and, through CV Soultz-
Wuenheim, Grand Cru Ollwiller
and, through CV Dambach-la-Ville,
Grand Cru Frankstein)
Labels: Wolfberger (the premier
brand accounts for about 65 per
cent of total production), Pierre

Rotgold and Pierre Meierheim
(both domestic supermarket brands
totalling 30 per cent of sales),
Cellier du Pape St-Léon IX (roughly
5 per cent), Aussay (secondary
export brand that represents no
more than 0.05 per cent), Marchal
(tertiary export brand of minimal
importance), Clos Jean-Philippe
Sturm (single-vineyard exclusivity),
Clos de la Tourelle (single-vineyard
Crémant d'Alsace), Château
Ollwiller (single vineyard
exclusivity), Domaine Jux
(domaine-bottled wines from the
largest vineyard in Colmar's
Hardt), Willm (*négociant* taken
over by Wolfberger in the early
1980s, these wines are now made at
Eguisheim, but marketed
separately)

Founded by 17 *Darlehnskassen*, or
private bankers, who also
established the CV Dambach-la-
Ville and the Cave Centrale de
Schiltingheim at the same time.
These were not exactly cooperatives
as we know them today, but simply
pressing, vinification, storage and
marketing facilities that were put at
the disposal of growers who lacked
the capacity to make and sell the
wines themselves. The cooperative
at Schiltingheim, which is a
northern suburb of Strasbourg, no
longer exists, but Dambach does
and, although it went its own way,
eventually joined the Wolfberger
group in 1976.

Large producers in every wine
region of the world set themselves
up as targets for critics who think
that everything small must be

beautiful and everything large is, by definition, bad. Wolfberger has been no exception; it represents almost 9 per cent of the total output of Alsace wine and, worse, it's a cooperative! But small growers are quite capable of producing some of the most atrocious wines and the one advantage every large winery has (whether it decides to utilize it or not) is that with so much raw material coming in, it can select a relatively large number of truly exceptional wines compared to producers of a lesser size in the same area. The truth is that you can get good and bad producers of all sizes and the main factor that determines which they will be is the philosophy of the winemaker. Wolfberger has Roland Guth, who is probably the most underrated winemaker in Alsace and is definitely one of the most talented in France. If you do not believe me, pick a winemaker you know and respect and ask him. They will all tell you that Guth is a genius and a hard-working one at that. He is every bit as passionate about wine as the most quality-minded and expressive of small growers and he has the advantage of having 9 per cent of the entire region's production to play around with. He will take technology to its very limits or go back to basics, whatever it requires, and he sometimes does both with the same wine.

It has been said that cooperatives cannot produce top-quality wines because the growers keep the best grapes for themselves and deliver only what they do not want. This could, of course, also apply to any large *négociant,* but the point to remember about Wolfberger is that all of its members are compelled to deliver their entire harvest (in grapes, not wine) to the cooperative. This would be intolerable to some growers and it obviously was when the rule was introduced in 1956, as this cooperative's membership plummeted from over 700 to just 140! But there are several thousand growers in Alsace who have other occupations or are more viticulturally than oenologically minded and many of these have inherited excellent vineyards. For such people, this cooperative's policy is not only tolerable, it is preferable, especially with prices of between 10 and 15 per cent above the norm. Instituting such a policy was a terrible gamble, but one that has paid off, as Wolfberger has not merely survived, it has thrived to the point of becoming far and away the region's largest producer. Equally important, however, is that no wine may be returned to the growers, so there are no own-labelled co-op clones. This applies to all cooperatives in Alsace, as far as I can make out – certainly, that is what they claim.

There is nothing special about the cheapest Wolfberger wines, but there is nothing wrong with them either; they are no worse or better than the generic ranges of some very famous houses and do in any case represent very good value. The basic Riesling is perhaps the most disappointing generic, but Pinot Blanc, Tokay-Pinot Gris and Muscat are usually quite good and one, in fact, is consistently the best of its type. I refer to the cheapest Pinot Noir (the one with the funny little Noak cartoon on the label), which I prefer not just to Wolfberger's, but to most other more expensive versions of this variety (although Wolfberger's 1983 Rouge Armorié was not bad). You have only to trade up to the next two ranges (Grande Réserve and Sigillé) to find wines of the most exciting quality and value across the board. Value is not, however, the only accolade that can be afforded Wolfberger's wines, as its range of Armorié (specially selected wines from exceptional vintages) and *grand cru* wines does offer some of the region's great classic wine bargains.

Wolfberger's reputation has to a large extent been built on its range of Crémant d'Alsace and the cooperative has just built an enormous sparkling wine facility on some of the non-AOC land belonging to Domaine Jux in the Hardt area of Colmar. Called 'L'Espace' by Wolfberger and a 'palais de science fiction' by French newspapers, it is the ultimate fizz factory and filled to overflowing with state-of-the-art equipment that first came into use for the 1991 vintage. The Wolfberger Brut and Brut Millésimé are both pure, good Pinot Blanc wines that rapidly develop toasty aromas in bottle. The pure Riesling Crémant d'Alsace is fine for those seeking to upgrade from *sekt*, but this style is too aromatic for me. However, the addition of a small amount of Riesling to the Brut Prestige, which also contains Pinot Blanc, Pinot Noir and Tokay-Pinot Gris, gives the wine a certain floral finesse and raciness, which help to ensure the wine remains fresh as it gets toasty. Magnums of Prestige Brut rate as Wolfberger's best Crémant and have aged gracefully in my cellar for up to seven years after purchase. The Crémant Rosé, a delightful wine full of soft, red fruit flavours lifted by a fine mousse, is Wolfberger's second best fizz. *See* also CV DAMBACH-LA-VILLE, Domaine JUX, Alsace WILLM and CV VIEIL ARMAND

Wunsch & Mann

Wunsch & Mann
2 rue des Clefs, 68920 Wettolsheim
Telephone: (89) 80.79.63

Some excellent wines from Grand Cru Steingrubler under the Collection Joseph Mann label, particularly the Riesling, but fine Tokay-Pinot Gris too, although the generic Cuvée St-Rémy is just as good.

Wurtz

Bernard Wurtz
12 rue du Château,
68630 Mittelwihr
Telephone: (89) 47.93.24

Although tasted infrequently, the generic Tokay-Pinot Gris has always been fabulous.

Wurtz

W. Wurtz
6 rue du Bouxhof,
68630 Mittelwihr
Telephone: (89) 47.93.16

Excellent generic Tokay-Pinot Gris.
Also known as GAEC Willy Wurtz.

Zahn

Martin Zahn
A cooperative label.
See CV RIBEAUVILLÉ

Zahnacker

Clos du Zahnacker
See CV RIBEAUVILLÉ

Zeyssolff

G. Zeyssolff
156 route de Strasbourg,
67140 Gertwiller
Telephone: (88) 08.90.08

I have had one light, but nicely
structured Pinot Noir from this
grower, whose family have been
*vigneron*s since 1778.

Ziegler-Mauler

J-J Ziegler-Mauler
2 rue des Merles, 68630 Mittelwihr
Telephone: (89) 47.90.37

I know nothing about this grower,
except that he owns some four
hectares of vines.

Zimmermann

A. Zimmermann
3 Grand'rue, 67600 Orschwiller
Telephone: (88) 92.08.49

Truly exceptional, luxuriantly rich
Tokay-Pinot Gris Réserve
Exceptionnelle.

Zimmermann

Jules & Rémy Zimmermann
13 rue des Prêtres,
68570 Soultzmatt
Telephone: (89) 47.02.69

A family enterprise with five
hectares in the Vallé Noble, but I
have not tasted their wines.

Zind Humbrecht

Domaine Zind Humbrecht
34 rue Maréchal-Joffre,
68000 Wintzenheim
Telephone: (89) 27.02.05

Established: 1620 by the
Humbrecht family
Production: 17-18,000 cases
Vineyards: 30 hectares (4.2ha
Thann, 15ha Turckheim, 7.6ha
Wintzenheim, 3.2ha
Gueberschwihr–Hattstatt–
Pfaffenheim), which account for
this grower's total production
Grape varieties: 1.8ha Sylvaner,
9ha Riesling, 2.7ha Pinot Blanc,
2.7ha Tokay-Pinot Gris, 1.8ha
Pinot Noir, 10.2ha
Gewurztraminer, 1.4ha Muscat
Ottonel, 0.4ha Muscat à Petit
Grains (mixture of Blanc and Rosé)
Grands crus: 4.2ha Rangen
(Thann), 0.6ha Goldert

(Gueberschwihr), 1.4ha Brand
(Turckheim), 1.4ha Hengst
(Wintzenheim)

Few people command the respect
that Léonard Humbrecht does. He
is a legend throughout Alsace, not
just among other growers, but
merchants too. There is not one
négociant too large or too lofty to
acknowledge his tireless enthusiasm
and almost evangelical crusade for
lower yields, particularly in the
grands crus, where he passionately
believes the maximum must be 35
hectolitres per hectare, rather than
70, which is the current limit. You
have only to taste Zind
Humbrecht's rich and expressive
wines to realize how right he is. The
effects of *terroir* are elusive and the
higher the yield, the more diluted it
becomes. At 70 hectolitres there is
little chance that any discernible
character can be captured. It is
because of the greed or ignorance of
those producers who squeeze every
last drop of wine out of their
vineyards that Léonard Humbrecht
has waged his campaign and the
fact that many Alsace *grand cru*
wines have improved with each
vintage is no small tribute to his
efforts.

There are numerous reasons for
the stunning quality of Domaine
Zind Humbrecht wines, but first
and foremost it is the superb
situation of its various vineyards,
which comprise 30 hectares and
stretch across 24 miles of the
region's most southerly vineyards.
This supreme estate includes the
grands crus of Hengst, Brand,

Goldert and Rangen, not to
mention the exceptional *crus* of
Herrenweg (close to Brand) and
Clos Hauserer (close to Hengst) and
the recent addition of Clos
Windsbuhl, which is in Hunawihr
and threatens to carve out a
reputation approaching Trimbach's
nearby Clos Ste-Hune. The next
reason for Domaine Zind
Humbrecht's exceptional
performance is the way in which
Léonard cultivates these
intrinsically superior sites, planting
the vines in high density and being
severe in his pruning to provide
very low yields per vine. Then there
are the principles applied in the
vinification of the wines, never
over-processing the product and
always opting for natural methods
over high-tech ones. There are also
many different reasons for the style
(as opposed to the quality) of
Domaine Zind Humbrecht, but I
suppose the most basic ones must
include the fact that the wines do
not go through malolactic and are
also traditionally vinified in oak
foudres.

Perhaps the hardest thing to
grasp about Domaine Zind
Humbrecht is that it has been in
existence only since 1959, when
Léonard Humbrecht married
Geneviève Zind, thus uniting the
two families' vineyards. It seems
preposterous to think that they
actually contemplated selling up
and moving away from Alsace
shortly after their marriage, but we
can all say thank goodness they
changed their minds. Léonard
Humbrecht is a shy man who

prefers working in the vineyard to travelling the world and telling people how wonderful his wines are. His wife is almost as knowledgeable and just as charming, although more outgoing, and their son Olivier, who has written a thesis about the influence of soil on the aromatics of wine and now makes the wines, while his father looks after the viticultural side of the business, has the unique distinction of being the first Frenchman to qualify as a Master of Wine. He is just as committed to quality and *terroir* as Léonard Humbrecht, but perhaps presents this knowledge in a slightly more technical way (which is not to deny Léonard's profound technical expertise).

When we first met, Olivier let me taste some of the *vin de paille* he had just produced. It took an awful lot of shrivelled grapes to produce just over a demijohn's worth, but the nectar was so precious that the balance was bubbling away in a cider bottle, attached to the mother fermenter by some sort of oenological umbilical cord. When one burped, so did the other. As we sipped the *vin de paille*, Olivier began to explain his Heath

Robinson device, but was rudely interrupted as a rat ran across the floor and disappeared behind a barrel. This surprised Olivier more than it surprised me. I am used to seeing the odd rat flitting about cellars that may be several centuries old, but we were in the new extension to his cellars and it was apparently the first one Olivier had seen. He took care, however, to collect our glasses and diligently pour their precious dregs back into the quietly gurgling demijohn before taking a stick to the intruding rodent. With such priorities, the future of Zind Humbrecht seems assured.

Zink

Pierre-Paul Zink
27 rue de la Lauch,
68250 Pfaffenheim
Telephone: (89) 49.60.87

A small family enterprise of 3.5 hectares.

Zisser

Clos Zisser
See Domaine KLIPFEL

Appendices

Appendix 1
Vintage Assessments

───

The following notes provide a summary of principal factors, climatic and viticultural, affecting the quality of Alsace wines vinified since 1969, beyond which the assessments are progressively more brief, as the records become less comprehensive and our interest more academic. Every vintage back to 1900 is covered, beyond which there is commentary of sorts on various vintages going back as far as AD585 and, of course, the existence of such esoteric information from many diverse sources is for historical interest or even amusement, rather than of any practical use.

> *Notes*
> 1. In addition to the 'Surface area planted', there will be on average a further 5 per cent 'first leaf' and 5 per cent 'second leaf', which will not be in production, of course.
> 2. Under 'Grape prices', the 'Oechsle base' is what the price per kilo was based on (and thus reflected the relative must weights of every variety in each year), thus a variety that achieves a price of, say, 7.00F/kg (70° Oechsle) would be 7.50F for grapes of 75° Oeschle, 8.20F for grapes of 82° Oeschle and so on.

1992

Quality overview: Soft, early drinking vintage, similar to 1982.
Surface area planted: 13,650 hectares (estimated)
Total production: 1,275,000 hectolitres (estimated)
Average yield: 93.4 hectolitres per hectare (estimated)

A mild winter forced the vines to undergo bud-break ten days earlier than normal and the warm spring that followed encouraged an extremely precocious flowering, which caused anxiety, but was completed without problem. The summer was hot and dry, with August temperatures beating all records since 1921. Due to the protective influence of the Vosges mountains, Alsace was spared the torrential rain that played havoc on the rest of France and southern Europe in general, blessing the region with the earliest harvest since 1976. In some areas of Alsace, the harvest was in fact earlier.

Schlumberger, for example, reported picking its Pinot Blanc two days earlier in 1992 than it did in 1976. The earliest official starting dates for the harvest were 21 September (or 17 September by special request) for Crémant d'Alsace; 30 September (or 21 September by special request) for AOC Alsace and AOC Alsace Grand Cru; although growers were *strongly advised* to wait until at least 5 October in the case of Riesling and Gewurztraminer. CIVA also issued an official date of 15 October for the commencement of picking Vendange Tardive and SGN wines, but as this was just ten days after its own recommended starting date for picking of normally harvested wines from two of the four varieties permitted, this cannot be regarded as a strict implementation of authentic late-harvest regulations. With ideal weather from the start of the Crémant crop until the November rains, all grape varieties were harvested in pristine condition. A potential defect of the 1992 grapes is their low acidity, which will limit their longevity. Although this was a huge vintage, potentially it was even larger and summer pruning (crop thinning) was considered a necessity by all growers who wished to avoid making attenuated wines. No one could be more low-yield-minded than Léonard Humbrecht, yet despite a strict policy of short-pruning and the use of a low-nitrogen biological fertilizer, he was amazed by the rampant fertility of the different grape varieties that was evident by late June. 'Where we normally found two clusters, there were four and clusters that normally produce 80 grapes, yielded 200 or more,' he told me. Humbrecht's team worked continuously from the end of June until mid-August, cutting off unwanted bunches. Some vineyards had to be worked through twice. After all this effort, the average yield of Domaine Zind Humbrecht was kept to 66 hectolitres per hectare, which illustrates just how vast the total Alsace crop could have been. It is impossible to say with any accuracy, but several well-informed producers have estimated that it could have topped two million hectolitres! Those quality-conscious growers who were strict in their summer pruning made some remarkable wines that should be well worth digging out. Hugel, for example, cut off almost 25 per cent of the bunches in its own vineyards in July, making some very concentrated wines, including a basic dry Riesling of 11.6 per cent alcohol, compared to an average of just 10 per cent for Riesling in general. When Domaine Zind Humbrecht's steep Clos St-Urbain vineyard on the Rangen in Thann was struck by an isolated summer hailstorm, it was considered very unfortunate indeed, but it reduced yields to 35 hectolitres per hectare for Tokay-Pinot Gris and 25 hectolitres per hectare for Riesling, resulting in wines so influenced by the soil that it was impossible to identify which varieties were which amid the powerful aromatic components of *terroir* in early 1993. Due to the lack of rain, no botrytis developed, or at least none was reported to the author at the time of writing, although SGNs were certainly produced and Hugel even managed to make a Tokay-Pinot Gris SGN with a potential alcoholic strength of more than 19 per cent. In general, though, the late-harvest wines of 1992 are Vendange Tardive, not SGN, and it is very much a *passerillé* year.

GRAPE PRICES

Chasselas	@	6.17F/kg (69° Oechsle base)
Sylvaner	@	6.17F/kg (73° Oechsle base)
Pinot Blanc	@	6.43F/kg (79° Oechsle base)
Riesling	@	8.41F/kg (74° Oechsle base)
Tokay-Pinot Gris	@	8.91F/kg (89° Oechsle base)
Muscat	@	7.50F/kg (73° Oechsle base)
Gewurztraminer	@	10.74F/kg (87° Oechsle base)
Pinot Noir	@	8.93F/kg (84° Oechsle base)

Note The grape prices for 1992 are the *prix indicatif* (official suggested price before any premiums agreed between grower and buyer) rather than the *prix effective* (the actual price paid).

1991

Quality overview: Good to average, similar to 1986.
Surface area planted: 13,487 hectares
Total production: 1,114,654 hectolitres
Average yield: 82.6 hectolitres per hectare

Lucky Alsace was almost untouched by the severe frosts that devastated large parts of most other French wine regions. The flowering was late, but after a lovely summer the vines had caught up and promised yet another exceptional vintage. This seemed to be what would happen when the harvest for Crémant began on 25 September, because what little rain there was had been only since 20 September and could, at that time, be seen as beneficial. By 9 October, however, when picking commenced for the main crop, heavy rain had settled in and an excellent vintage turned into merely a good to average one. There is a silver lining to every black cloud and for Alsace it was probably the rot damage done to Riesling and Pinot Blanc grapes, which began in late-September and reduced an embarrassingly large yield (particularly when some areas of France ravaged by the early frosts were reporting up to 100 per cent crop loss) to a relatively modest one. There were some surprises, such as the two-year-old Riesling vines in Hugel's 350ème Anniversaire vineyard on the Schoenenbourg providing grape bunches, albeit a small number, with a potential alcohol of 14.8 per cent, which may be used only for *vin de table* (I look forward to tasting such an extraordinary *vin ordinaire*). Overall, however, the quality is light and fresh, appealing more to Muscat and Gewurztraminer, with pure Auxerrois or Auxerrois-dominated wines preferable to pure Pinot Blanc. If any classic wine has been produced, it might well be Crémant d'Alsace.

GRAPE PRICES

Chasselas	@ 6.58F/kg	(70° Oechsle base)
Sylvaner	@ 6.58F/kg	(73° Oechsle base)
Pinot Blanc	@ 7.34F/kg	(81° Oechsle base)
Riesling	@ 9.35F/kg	(72° Oechsle base)
Tokay-Pinot Gris	@ 11.31F/kg	(81° Oechsle base)
Muscat	@ 8.94F/kg	(74° Oechsle base)
Gewurztraminer	@ 13.74F/kg	(89° Oechsle base)
Pinot Noir	@ 11.12F/kg	(77° Oechsle base)

1990

Quality overview: Between 1988 and 1983 in quality and style.
Surface area planted: 13,353 hectares
Total production: 1,084,854 hectolitres
Average yield: 81.2 hectolitres per hectare

Bud-break was two weeks in advance of 1989, but a cold and rainy June settled down to provide ideal conditions for coulure, which reduced potential yield, particularly for Gewurztraminer and Muscat. A very hot summer with a nice sprinkling of rain in late-August, which primed the ripening process beautifully, gave a well sized crop of beautifully ripe and healthy grapes. The harvest began on 24 September for Crémant and 4 October for the rest. This is a quicker developing vintage than 1989 and more generous than 1988, but still classic, dry and long-lived in style, with all varieties performing exceptionally well. The late-harvest crop in 1990 was the second largest produced in Alsace, but the wines do not generally have the same botrytis character as those of 1989, which was the largest late-harvest vintage on record. It is definitely a warm *passerillé* year and, although with such a vast crop there will be many exceptions, this is the sort of vintage where it normally pays to buy expensive Vendanges Tardives, rather than market price SGN.

GRAPE PRICES

Chasselas	@ 6.20F/kg	(80° Oechsle base)
Sylvaner	@ 6.20F/kg	(81° Oechsle base)
Pinot Blanc	@ 6.63F/kg	(85° Oechsle base)
Riesling	@ 8.48F/kg	(84° Oechsle base)

Tokay-Pinot Gris   @ 10.77F/kg (96° Oechsle base)
Muscat   @ 8.49F/kg (85° Oechsle base)
Gewurztraminer   @ 13.62F/kg (102° Oechsle base)
Pinot Noir   @ 10.01F/kg (91° Oechsle base)

1989

Quality overview: Great vintage, more expressive of vintage than soil and comparable to 1983 and 1976.
Surface area planted: 13,162 hectares
Total production: 1,226,242 hectolitres
Average yield: 93.2 hectolitres per hectare

After 1988, the Alsace vintage that was diluted from its heralded 'great' to merely 'very good' by rain during the harvest, you might think Alsace producers would not want to jump the gun, but before the first grape was picked 1989 was already declared the vintage of the century. The weather held, for once, so it did turn out to be the vintage of the century. Or one of them, to be precise. Muré stated, 'Never in our memories have we measured such high sugar densities', and Léonard Humbrecht, normally a modest man of few words, was so impressed by the Tokay-Pinot Gris he harvested from his Rotenberg vineyard that he declared 1989 to be 'the best vintage in our history'. This was perhaps understandable, given that his Rotenberg Tokay-Pinot Gris had an astonishing potential alcoholic degree of 26 per cent by volume! Viticulturally, it was one of those years when nothing could go wrong; the flowering was early and took place under ideal conditions, the summer was magnificent (except for hailstorms in mid-July) and the grapes ripened early and in perfect condition, with absolutely no rot, except for the noble stuff, which was quite rampant in those vineyards where grapes had been left for late harvest. The only major drawback was for young vines affected by drought. The harvest began on 14 September for Crémant and 27 September for the rest of the crop. This is a great Riesling vintage with few bad wines, although due to the high must levels the style has a tendency to be a bit sweet, which might be better than over-alcoholic. One or two have a bitterness and the unbalanced feel of a 'stuck' fermentation that has been restarted and, although there are a number of really scintillating Rieslings, some of the best 1988s will prove to be even better. The next best variety is Tokay-Pinot Gris and there are some great pure Pinot Blanc (as opposed to the Auxerrois, many of which were simply too fat). Most other varieties were successful, with the exception of Muscat, much of which is dull and some downright catty. Generally, the 1989 vintage produced ultra-ripe generic wines that assumed a Vendanges Tardives character and Vendanges Tardives that were so rich in botrytis that they were more like SGN.

GRAPE PRICES

Chasselas	@ 5.42F/kg (71° Oechsle base)
Sylvaner	@ 5.42F/kg (73° Oechsle base)
Pinot Blanc	@ 5.59F/kg (82° Oechsle base)
Riesling	@ 6.91F/kg (75° Oechsle base)
Tokay-Pinot Gris	@ 7.81F/kg (91° Oechsle base)
Muscat	@ 6.92F/kg (76° Oechsle base)
Gewurztraminer	@ 8.58F/kg (90° Oechsle base)
Pinot Noir	@ 7.95F/kg (90° Oechsle base)

1988

Quality overview: Wines more expressive of the soil than the vintage.
Surface area planted: 12,998 hectares
Total production: 1,055,445 hectolitres
Average yield: 81.2 hectolitres per hectare

Flowering was two weeks earlier than normal, the summer was ideal and the grapes maintained their advanced state right up until the harvest, which began on 21 September for Crémant and 5 October for the rest of the crop. The fruit was slightly diluted by some rain during the picking, but this was only relative, reducing a potentially great vintage to one that was 'merely' very good. This vintage is marked by very high must levels, some of which surpassed those of 1983. These wines are firm, sturdy and intensely flavoured, with high extract levels, and capable of great longevity, reminding me very much of the 1981s. Without a light hand in the winery, some have turned out a bit four-square, but many producers made great wines, particularly Pinot Blanc, Auxerrois, Tokay-Pinot Gris, Gewurztraminer and Riesling, the best of which will eventually outperform the top 1989s.

GRAPE PRICES

Chasselas	@ 4.83F/kg (76° Oechsle base)
Sylvaner	@ 4.83F/kg (76° Oechsle base)
Pinot Blanc	@ 4.95F/kg (84° Oechsle base)
Riesling	@ 5.82F/kg (77° Oechsle base)
Tokay-Pinot Gris	@ 6.41F/kg (91° Oechsle base)
Muscat	@ 5.98F/kg (76° Oechsle base)
Gewurztraminer	@ 7.15F/kg (91° Oechsle base)
Pinot Noir	@ 6.84F/kg (88° Oechsle base)

1987

Quality overview: Below average in quality, but some elegant
Gewurztraminers produced.
Surface area planted: 12,862 hectares
Total production: 1,068,202 hectolitres
Average yield: 83.1 hectolitres per hectare

After a good bud-break, everything went downhill, with a late flowering
(July), the vines entered a cold summer almost two weeks behind their
normal vegetative cycle and never caught up. The harvest began on 7
October for Crémant, 9 October for Muscat and Pinot Noir and 16
October for the rest of the crop. This was a poor year in particular for
Tokay-Pinot Gris, some awful wines having been produced (the successful
ones stand out: Marcel Deiss Bergheim, Mittnacht Frères Cuvée Ste-
Cathérine and Hugel & Fils Jubilée). Much better for Gewurztraminer,
with many elegant wines produced.

GRAPE PRICES

Chasselas	@ 4.73F/kg (65° Oechsle base)
Sylvaner	@ 4.73F/kg (67° Oechsle base)
Pinot Blanc	@ 4.82F/kg (74° Oechsle base)
Riesling	@ 5.44F/kg (71° Oechsle base)
Tokay-Pinot Gris	@ 5.93F/kg (81° Oechsle base)
Muscat	@ 5.87F/kg (68° Oechsle base)
Gewurztraminer	@ 6.59F/kg (83° Oechsle base)
Pinot Noir	@ 6.46F/kg (79° Oechsle base)

1986

Quality overview: A medium-weight, goodish vintage, but initial hopes
were over-optimistic.
Surface area planted: 12,773 hectares
Total production: 1,188,579 hectolitres
Average yield: 93.1 hectolitres per hectare

Perfect flowering followed by excellent, sunny weather gave growers great
hopes, but these were dashed by the unseasonably cold and damp weather
in late August and early September. A potentially excellent vintage was
thus downgraded to just plain good, then average and finally below average, before being raised again by four weeks of sunny conditions starting
20 September. The harvest began on 30 September for Crémant, on 13
October for all Pinot varieties (including Auxerrois) and 9 October for the

rest of the crop. Must levels were slightly below the norm, but the best wines were those generic wines that were made for easy, everyday drinking and actually drunk early. These included some particularly refreshing and delicious Muscats, but the comment also applies across the board. Some of the so-called better *cuvées* have not lasted well, however, with time in bottle merely enhancing a taste of rot in some wines, even though there was no hint of such an off-taste in most wines consumed immediately after the vintage. There are always exceptions, of course, and I cannot think of a greater one than Domaine Zind Humbrecht's Rotenberg Tokay-Pinot Gris SGN, which was harvested with the equivalent of 425g/l of sugar.

GRAPE PRICES

Chasselas	@ 4.79F/kg (67° Oechsle base)
Sylvaner	@ 4.79F/kg (66° Oechsle base)
Pinot Blanc	@ 4.90F/kg (77° Oechsle base)
Riesling	@ 5.43F/kg (70° Oechsle base)
Tokay-Pinot Gris	@ 5.94F/kg (82° Oechsle base)
Muscat	@ 5.82F/kg (69° Oechsle base)
Gewurztraminer	@ 6.48F/kg (83° Oechsle base)
Pinot Noir	@ 6.32F/kg (79° Oechsle base)

1985

Quality overview: An excellent vintage overshadowed by 1983 before and the trio of 1988, 1989 and 1990 after.
Surface area planted: 12,598 hectares
Total production: 895,392 hectolitres
Average yield: 71.1 hectolitres per hectare

The harvest in 1985, which began on 30 September for Crémant and 7 October for the rest of the generic crop (14 October for Reisling *grands crus*), will always be remembered for its two months of solid autumn sunshine. Combined with the relatively low regional yield (caused in part by severe winter damage), this gave nicely concentrated, well-balanced wines that were attractive from the start. Unlike the 1986s, the best wines from this vintage have aged very gracefully and will continue to do so. Generally the must weights were above average and some Gewurztraminer and Pinot Noir had very high sugar levels indeed. This is an elegant, gently rich vintage of generally medium-term longevity, but with some long-term surprises. More Vendanges Tardives than 1983, but less SGN due to insufficient botrytis.

GRAPE PRICES

Chasselas	@ 4.86F/kg (71° Oechsle base)
Sylvaner	@ 4.86F/kg (77° Oechsle base)
Pinot Blanc	@ 4.92F/kg (81° Oechsle base)
Riesling	@ 5.45F/kg (73° Oechsle base)
Tokay-Pinot Gris	@ 5.83F/kg (87° Oechsle base)
Muscat	@ 5.79F/kg (80° Oechsle base)
Gewurztraminer	@ 6.57F/kg (92° Oechsle base)
Pinot Noir	@ 6.33F/kg (86° Oechsle base)

1984

Quality overview: Best forgotten, except for some Muscat at the time.
Surface area planted: 12,449 hectares
Total production: 807,798 hectolitres
Average yield: 64.9 hectolitres per hectare

In a poor growing season throughout France, Alsace was relatively better off than other regions, but only relatively. The harvest began on 18 October for all varieties except the Riesling, which began picking on 24 October and only one Vendange Tardive was officially certified (Gustave Lorentz). Most wines were adequate, all things considered, but there were some truly exceptional Muscats produced, albeit for immediate consumption.

GRAPE PRICES

Chasselas	@ 4.22F/kg (69° Oechsle base)
Sylvaner	@ 4.22F/kg (65° Oechsle base)
Pinot Blanc	@ 4.28F/kg (72° Oechsle base)
Riesling	@ 4.83F/kg (66° Oechsle base)
Tokay-Pinot Gris	@ 5.07F/kg (80° Oechsle base)
Muscat	@ 5.00F/kg (72° Oechsle base)
Gewurztraminer	@ 5.75F/kg (82° Oechsle base)
Pinot Noir	@ 5.49F/kg (76° Oechsle base)

1983

Quality overview: Voluptuous.
Surface area planted: 12,308 hectares
Total production: 988,604 hectolitres
Average yield: 80.3 hectolitres per hectare

An early bud-break and flowering, followed by a gloriously hot and sunny summer and a long, balmy autumn, broken by just a little cloud mid-October. The harvest began on 26 September for Crémant and 6 October for the rest of the crop, with the exception of Riesling, for which picking commenced on 10 October. What can be said about one of the truly great vintages? Although it was tailor-made for the noble varieties, perhaps we should not forget that it was the beautifully ripe and opulent Pinot Blanc (including Auxerrois) of this vintage that first showed a Chardonnay-mad market that Alsace had its own answer to the current demand. Prior to 1983, far too many Pinot Blanc wines were neutral, lacking and too downright boring to grasp any self-respecting wine-drinker's attention. Then, all of a sudden, this varietal took off and growers could not plant enough of the stuff. The explanation is that until 1983, most Pinot Blanc was overcropped and underripe, which was fine for Crémant, but too feeble and pathetic for a still varietal wine. But 1983 will be remembered for its noble varieties, the lush, concentrated, complex Riesling, Tokay-Pinot Gris and Gewurztraminer (it was not a Muscat year and the Pinot Noir in 1985 was better) in a multitude of special *cuvées*, the sources of which would soon gravitate into Vendange Tardive and *grand cru*, although these were around at the time, especially the late-harvest wines, for which 1983 was a record year, of course. The outstanding quality of this vintage was such that it was being compared by the Grandes Maisons to 1976, 1971, 1959 and even 1934 (which illustrates how good 1988 and, particularly, 1989 are and how few and far between the truly great vintages are).

GRAPE PRICES

Chasselas	@ 2.97F/kg (71° Oechsle base)
Sylvaner	@ 2.97F/kg (79° Oechsle base)
Pinot Blanc	@ 3.08F/kg (83° Oechsle base)
Riesling	@ 3.67F/kg (75° Oechsle base)
Tokay-Pinot Gris	@ 4.25F/kg (88° Oechsle base)
Muscat	@ 4.08F/kg (74° Oechsle base)
Gewurztraminer	@ 5.00F/kg (96° Oechsle base)
Pinot Noir	@ 4.67F/kg (85° Oechsle base)

1982

Quality overview: Huge vintage, but surprisingly not bad!
Surface area planted: 12,052 hectares
Total production: 1,452,662 hectolitres
Average yield: 120.5 hectolitres per hectare

The 1982 vintage must go down in history for several reasons. Until the beginning of May the vines were two weeks behind. Between 12 May and 1 June, temperatures soared to 30°C and the flowering took place ten days early, which effectively meant the vines went through 62 days of growth in one month! A few days of cold dampened spirits in June and the hot summer weeks, which were interspersed with rain and hailstorms, had everyone biting nails wondering what the autumn would bring. It was brilliant. Well, the start in September was, anyway. When the harvest began on 7 October for Muscat and Pinot varieties, the weather had turned wet and miserable. Picking started on 11 October for Sylvaner and 13 October for Riesling. As the rain caused the grapes to swell and burst, many wines were obviously diluted, but how much of this record-busting vintage was actually rainwater clinging to the outside of the bunches, rather than absorbed inside the fruit, no one will ever know. It is, however, a testament to the inherent quality of Alsace and the expertise of its winemakers that so much of it was actually drinkable. And I mean that literally. Not adequate like 1984, but drinkable in the sense that if you had a glass, you wanted to drink it. Mind you, it was all *vin de consommation courante* in quality, whatever the AOC status suggested, as most of the wines deteriorated rapidly in bottle (some amazing exceptions survive). Brussels got in on the act by officially rebuking the region for going *so far* above its maximum permitted yield, but I think they should have been congratulated, although goodness knows what volumes they would be pumping out today, had they been.

GRAPE PRICES

Chasselas	@ 2.92F/kg (66° Oechsle base)
Sylvaner	@ 2.92F/kg (66° Oechsle base)
Pinot Blanc	@ 3.04F/kg (71° Oechsle base)
Riesling	@ 3.62F/kg (68° Oechsle base)
Tokay-Pinot Gris	@ 4.10F/kg (79° Oechsle base)
Muscat	@ 4.10F/kg (72° Oechsle base)
Gewurztraminer	@ 4.92F/kg (79° Oechsle base)
Pinot Noir	@ 4.60F/kg (76° Oechsle base)

1981

Quality overview: Spotty, but underrated and capable of some splendid long-lived wines.
Surface area planted: 11,749 hectares
Total production: 903,749 hectolitres
Average yield: 76.9 hectolitres per hectare

Hail destroyed more than 500 hectares in the Bas-Rhin, but a sunny flowering all round and an alternation of sun and rain throughout July and August speeded up the vine cycle without causing much rot, with the harvest beginning 2–5 October (the later date always for Riesling). Not a consistent vintage, lots of ups and downs, some typically refreshing Muscat, but it was the firm, well-concentrated Gewurztraminers and Rieslings that stood out. This was particularly remarkable for the Riesling, the must weights for which were not that high (generally lower than in 1980 and 1984), but many had high extract and developed a fine, minerally intensity.

GRAPE PRICES

Chasselas	@ 3.74F/kg (69° Oechsle base)
Sylvaner	@ 3.74F/kg (71° Oechsle base)
Pinot Blanc	@ 3.90F/kg (73° Oechsle base)
Riesling	@ 4.72F/kg (70° Oechsle base)
Tokay-Pinot Gris	@ 4.99F/kg (79° Oechsle base)
Muscat	@ 5.42F/kg (67° Oechsle base)
Gewurztraminer	@ 6.23F/kg (83° Oechsle base)
Pinot Noir	@ 5.73F/kg (77° Oechsle base)

1980

Quality overview: Minor in size and quality.
Surface area planted: 11,600 hectares
Total production: 599,304 hectolitres
Average yield: 51.7 hectolitres per hectare

Very small and very late harvest due to bad flowering, with Muscat and Gewurztraminer worst hit. Picking began 23–25 October. Most wines were light and lacking, the best had a certain delicate fruitiness best appreciated at the time, but many were nervous and fragile, with very few improving for more than a year or two.

GRAPE PRICES

Chasselas	@ 3.65F/kg (71° Oechsle base)
Sylvaner	@ 3.61F/kg (64° Oechsle base)
Pinot Blanc	@ 3.77F/kg (73° Oechsle base)
Riesling	@ 4.57F/kg (65° Oechsle base)
Tokay-Pinot Gris	@ 4.96F/kg (82° Oechsle base)
Muscat	@ 5.56F/kg (73° Oechsle base)
Gewurztraminer	@ 7.22F/kg (85° Oechsle base)
Pinot Noir	@ 5.71F/kg (79° Oechsle base)

1979

Quality overview: Good quality, medium weight.
Surface area planted: 11,439 hectares
Total production: 1,074,039 hectolitres
Average yield: 93.9 hectolitres per hectare

A good flowering, followed by a sunny July, a warm August with good humidity and a hot and very sunny September. The harvest began 11–15 October, yielding a large crop of good quality. Many wines have lasted much longer than initially expected, but Rieslings stand out, some of which have evolved with great elegance.

GRAPE PRICES

Chasselas	@ 3.24F/kg (69° Oechsle base)
Sylvaner	@ 3.20F/kg (68° Oechsle base)
Pinot Blanc	@ 3.35F/kg (74° Oechsle base)
Riesling	@ 3.79F/kg (71° Oechsle base)
Tokay-Pinot Gris	@ 4.06F/kg (82° Oechsle base)
Muscat	@ 4.25F/kg (68° Oechsle base)
Gewurztraminer	@ 5.30F/kg (83° Oechsle base)
Pinot Noir	@ 4.50F/kg (79° Oechsle base)

1978

Quality overview: Generally disappointing, but some of the best *cuvées* of Gewurztraminer and Tokay-Pinot Gris have been unfairly overlooked.
Surface area planted: 11,313 hectares
Total production: 692,575 hectolitres
Average yield: 61.2 hectolitres per hectare

The vines were retarded due to a poor spring and a dull summer, but grape ripening advanced rapidly in September and early-October, when it was sunny and very hot. The harvest began on 19 October (23 October for Riesling) and, as always in such years, Gewurztraminer and Muscat were worst hit (down 40 per cent and 80 per cent respectively), although this probably helped the quality and intensity of the former. Certainly it was the Gewurztraminer wines, together with those of the Tokay-Pinot Gris, that were the unsung heroes of this vintage.

GRAPE PRICES

Chasselas	@ 3.84F/kg (73° Oechsle base)
Sylvaner	@ 3.88F/kg (67° Oechsle base)
Pinot Blanc	@ 3.90F/kg (74° Oechsle base)
Riesling	@ 4.20F/kg (65° Oechsle base)
Tokay-Pinot Gris	@ 4.79F/kg (74° Oechsle base)
Muscat	@ 5.57F/kg (70° Oechsle base)
Gewurztraminer	@ 7.12F/kg (89° Oechsle base)
Pinot Noir	@ 5.15F/kg (81° Oechsle base)

1977

Quality overview: Any vintage would suffer hot on the heels of 1976, and 1977 was indisputably poor, but not as bad as this year was for other French regions.
Surface area planted: 11,222 hectares
Total production: 951,814 hectolitres
Average yield: 84.8 hectolitres per hectare

Alsace did not suffer quite as severely from the March frosts as other regions and, although it did have to endure the same mediocre summer, the vineyards were saved to some extent by a sunny September. The harvest began on 17 October and most wines were light, thin and quite acidic.

GRAPE PRICES

Chasselas	@ 2.86F/kg (61° Oechsle base)
Sylvaner	@ 2.86F/kg (63° Oechsle base)
Pinot Blanc	@ 2.91F/kg (67° Oechsle base)
Riesling	@ 4.32F/kg (65° Oechsle base)
Tokay-Pinot Gris	@ 3.71F/kg (74° Oechsle base)
Muscat	@ 3.76F/kg (63° Oechsle base)
Gewurztraminer	@ 4.67F/kg (80° Oechsle base)
Pinot Noir	@ 4.60F/kg (74° Oechsle base)

1976

Quality overview: The greatest vintage since 1959.
Surface area planted: 10,834 hectares
Total production: 880,832 hectolitres
Average yield: 81.3 hectolitres per hectare

Like the rest of France, Alsace enjoyed an exceptionally precocious vintage, but benefited from short, sharp rainstorms denied to most other regions, which helped the ripening process and were a mark of the region's semi-continental climate. The harvest, which began on 20 September, took place in ideal, sunny conditions. This is, without doubt, a great vintage for noble varieties, particularly Riesling, Gewurztraminer and Tokay-Pinot Gris. Some stupendous Rieslings were produced. It was this vintage that saw the first late-harvest wines made on a regional basis. The best 1976 wines will last another 20 years or more.

GRAPE PRICES

Chasselas	@ 2.02F/kg (75° Oechsle base)
Sylvaner	@ 2.02F/kg (76° Oechsle base)
Pinot Blanc	@ 2.11F/kg (84° Oechsle base)
Riesling	@ 3.42F/kg (80° Oechsle base)
Tokay-Pinot Gris	@ 2.80F/kg (90° Oechsle base)
Muscat	@ 2.77F/kg (79° Oechsle base)
Gewurztraminer	@ 3.24F/kg (93° Oechsle base)
Pinot Noir	@ 3.31F/kg (87° Oechsle base)

1975

Quality overview: Good, but not exceptional.
Surface area planted: 10,275 hectares
Total production: 792,647 hectolitres
Average yield: 77.1 hectolitres per hectare

The product of a long, dry summer, an unstable early autumn, but an October that had some fine and sunny days, the 1975 harvest began on 6 October and produced wines of medium weight and a quality somewhere between 1985 and 1986. Pinot Noir and Muscat were perhaps the most outstanding varieties, but generally all wines were for relatively early consumption, with just the odd exceptional long-lived Riesling.

GRAPE PRICES

Chasselas	@ 1.44F/kg (69° Oechsle base)
Sylvaner	@ 1.46F/kg (67° Oechsle base)
Pinot Blanc	@ 1.52F/kg (77° Oechsle base)
Riesling	@ 2.42F/kg (75° Oechsle base)
Tokay-Pinot Gris	@ 2.12F/kg (85° Oechsle base)
Muscat	@ 2.18F/kg (76° Oechsle base)
Gewurztraminer	@ 2.46F/kg (83° Oechsle base)
Pinot Noir	@ 2.34F/kg (83° Oechsle base)

1974

Quality overview: Generally dull and boring, but dotted with the odd surprise.
Surface area planted: 10,186 hectares
Total production: 616,459 hectolitres
Average yield: 60.5 hectolitres per hectare

Early bud-break and a good flowering, followed by an exceptionally dry and hot July, then an unusually wet and cool autumn. The harvest began on 10 October and produced wines that were generally light, fresh and well balanced for early drinking, but prone to ageing rather than improving in bottle, with the exception of Gewurztraminer, which was rare, but very high in must weight (Hugel averaged 91°C Oechsle from its contracted growers, which was just one degree less than 1976!). There were also some exceptional Rieslings, such as Léon Beyer's Riesling Cuvée Particulière, which had a lovely, honeyed-petrolly aroma and fresh, zesty fruit at about ten years of age.

GRAPE PRICES

Chasselas	@ 1.09F/kg (73° Oechsle base)
Sylvaner	@ 1.12F/kg (69° Oechsle base)
Pinot Blanc	@ 1.22F/kg (77° Oechsle base)
Riesling	@ 1.95F/kg (74° Oechsle base)
Tokay-Pinot Gris	@ 1.75F/kg (85° Oechsle base)
Muscat	@ 1.88F/kg (73° Oechsle base)
Gewurztraminer	@ 2.20F/kg (91° Oechsle base)
Pinot Noir	@ 1.90F/kg (83° Oechsle base)

1973

Quality overview: The most underrated post-war vintage.
Surface area planted: 10,230 hectares
Total production: 1,096,856 hectolitres
Average yield: 107.2 hectolitres per hectare

No spring frosts, an abundant flowering, lovely summer and a long, sunny autumn provided a very large crop of exceptionally fine grapes, when the harvest began 10–15 October. Excellent performances across the varieties, but particularly beautiful Riesling, Tokay-Pinot Gris and Gewurztraminer, and all surviving wines have matured exquisitely.

GRAPE PRICES

Chasselas	@ 1.40F/kg (71° Oechsle base)
Sylvaner	@ 1.41F/kg (70° Oechsle base)
Pinot Blanc	@ 1.46F/kg (78° Oechsle base)
Riesling	@ 1.80F/kg (73° Oechsle base)
Tokay-Pinot Gris	@ 1.64F/kg (84° Oechsle base)
Muscat	@ 1.81F/kg (70° Oechsle base)
Gewurztraminer	@ 1.88F/kg (86° Oechsle base)
Pinot Noir	@ 1.86F/kg (82° Oechsle base)

1972

Quality overview: Worse than 1977!
Surface area planted: 9,643 hectares
Total production: 813,127 hectolitres
Average yield: 84.3 hectolitres per hectare

Only a late, dry and sunny summer prevented the harvesting of green pea-like grapes, when picking began on 19 October. Even so, this vintage yielded the lowest must weights in the last 30-odd years.

GRAPE PRICES

Chasselas	@ 1.86F/kg (62° Oechsle base)
Sylvaner	@ 1.88F/kg (61° Oechsle base)
Pinot Blanc	@ 1.94F/kg (68° Oechsle base)
Riesling	@ 2.40F/kg (60° Oechsle base)
Tokay-Pinot Gris	@ 2.19F/kg (77° Oechsle base)
Muscat	@ 2.41F/kg (62° Oechsle base)
Gewurztraminer	@ 2.67F/kg (77° Oechsle base)
Pinot Noir	@ 2.48F/kg (74° Oechsle base)

1971

Quality overview: A truly great vintage.
Surface area planted: 9,509 hectares
Total production: 524,723 hectolitres
Average yield: 55.2 hectolitres per hectare

A long, hard winter had damaged some vineyards, but growth was advanced by an exceptionally hot and dry March, only to bring forward the flowering to coincide with the worst possible conditions. Thus the potential quantity was slashed, particularly for Gewurztraminer and Muscat, but with a dry and hot summer interspersed by beneficial, short rainstorms, followed by a sunny September, a reduced crop of exceptional quality was ready for harvesting from 4 October. Gewurztraminer was stunning, Riesling almost rivalled it and there were some fabulous Tokay-Pinot Gris, but all varieties excelled to one degree or another and gave wines that have always shown a remarkable balance of generosity and strength. It is now fascinating to compare the same varieties of 1971 and 1973.

GRAPE PRICES

Chasselas	@ 1.10F/kg (83° Oechsle base)
Sylvaner	@ 1.12F/kg (81° Oechsle base)
Pinot Blanc	@ 1.21F/kg (90° Oechsle base)
Riesling	@ 1.47F/kg (82° Oechsle base)
Tokay-Pinot Gris	@ 1.48F/kg (99° Oechsle base)
Muscat	@ 1.82F/kg (91° Oechsle base)
Gewurztraminer	@ 2.21F/kg (104° Oechsle base)
Pinot Noir	@ 1.90F/kg (97° Oechsle base)

1970

Quality overview: Overlooked at the time and now passé.
Surface area planted: 9,625 hectares
Total production: 951,688 hectolitres
Average yield: 98.9 hectolitres per hectare

This huge harvest began picking on 15 October and produced many surprisingly good wines, but was unfortunate to be squeezed between two obviously great vintages. Gewurztraminer particularly aromatic, Tokay-Pinot Gris rich and full, Riesling showed lovely racy character capable of medium-term maturity and Muscat was an early-drinking delight.

GRAPE PRICES

Chasselas	@ 0.78F/kg (74° Oechsle base)
Sylvaner	@ 0.79F/kg (71° Oechsle base)
Pinot Blanc	@ 0.92F/kg (75° Oechsle base)
Riesling	@ 1.05F/kg (75° Oechsle base)
Tokay-Pinot Gris	@ 1.11F/kg (82° Oechsle base)
Muscat	@ 1.33F/kg (73° Oechsle base)
Gewurztraminer	@ 1.51F/kg (84° Oechsle base)
Pinot Noir	@ 1.42F/kg (79° Oechsle base)

1969

Quality overview: Tremendous acidity and extract, exceptionally long-lived.
Surface area planted: 9,441 hectares
Total production: 636,511 hectolitres
Average yield: 67.4 hectolitres per hectare

A splendid late summer and magnificent autumn transformed a potentially disastrous vintage into a miraculous one, by the time that picking commenced on 13 October. An atypical year, 1969 has more in common with the same vintage in Champagne than any Alsace vintage either before or since. Each variety developed differently, the only common denominator being the high acidity that marked the 1969 Champagnes and has kept all these wines so fresh for so long. Initially, many of the wines appeared to be too hard, the proportion of malic to tartaric being exceptionally high due to climatic conditions. Surviving bottles of the best Tokay-Pinot Gris, Rieslings and Gewurztraminers will happily live until the next millennium.

GRAPE PRICES

Chasselas	@ 0.85F/kg (71° Oechsle base)
Sylvaner	@ 0.92F/kg (71° Oechsle base)
Pinot Blanc	@ 1.02F/kg (80° Oechsle base)
Riesling	@ 1.09F/kg (73° Oechsle base)
Tokay-Pinot Gris	@ 1.15F/kg (84° Oechsle base)
Muscat	@ 1.58F/kg (75° Oechsle base)
Gewurztraminer	@ 1.74F/kg (86° Oechsle base)
Pinot Noir	@ 1.51F/kg (85° Oechsle base)

1968

Quality overview: Awful.
Surface area planted: 9,706 hectares
Total production: 848,231 hectolitres
Average yield: 87.4 hectolitres per hectare

The harvest began on 14 October for what was one of the most awful vintages in memory. Oechsle levels were generally higher than either 1972 or 1977, but wines were probably a shade worse! Dehydrating Sylvaner and disgustingly pungent cat's-pee Muscat.

GRAPE PRICES

Chasselas	@ 0.74F/kg (66° Oechsle base)
Sylvaner	@ 0.81F/kg (66° Oechsle base)
Pinot Blanc	@ 0.96F/kg (70° Oechsle base)
Riesling	@ 1.08F/kg (70° Oechsle base)
Tokay-Pinot Gris	@ 1.11F/kg (77° Oechsle base)
Muscat	@ 1.41F/kg (68° Oechsle base)
Gewurztraminer	@ 1.68F/kg (80° Oechsle base)
Pinot Noir	@ 1.43F/kg (74° Oechsle base)

1967

Quality overview: Great and bad.
Surface area planted: 9,344 hectares
Total production: 764,594 hectolitres
Average yield: 81.8 hectolitres per hectare

The 1967 harvest, which began on 9 October, produced an uneven quality, with some wines that were as bad as 1977 and others that were truly exceptional. Of the best wines, Gewurztraminer was greatest, showing tremendous power and aroma, but Riesling and Tokay-Pinot Gris wines were also fabulous.

GRAPE PRICES

Chasselas	@ 0.84F/kg (73° Oechsle base)
Sylvaner	@ 0.87F/kg (72° Oechsle base)
Pinot Blanc	@ 0.90F/kg (83° Oechsle base)
Riesling	@ 1.05F/kg (79° Oechsle base)
Tokay-Pinot Gris	@ 1.18F/kg (90° Oechsle base)
Muscat	@ 1.58F/kg (77° Oechsle base)
Gewurztraminer	@ 1.63F/kg (94° Oechsle base)
Pinot Noir	@ 1.56F/kg (85° Oechsle base)

1966

Quality overview: Stylish, long-lived.
Surface area planted: 9,205 hectares
Total production: 651,943 hectolitres
Average yield: 70.8 hectolitres per hectare

Picking began on 10 October, producing turbocharged Gewurztraminer and beautifully proportioned Tokay-Pinot Gris. Riesling did not generally perform well, but some specific *cuvées* of great style and finesse could be found. The one pity is that they were not very skilled at red wine making in Alsace, as some fantastic Pinot Noirs were harvested.

GRAPE PRICES

Chasselas	@ 0.83F/kg (76° Oechsle base)
Sylvaner	@ 0.87F/kg (74° Oechsle base)
Pinot Blanc	@ 1.00F/kg (84° Oechsle base)
Riesling	@ 1.08F/kg (77° Oechsle base)
Tokay-Pinot Gris	@ 1.22F/kg (93° Oechsle base)
Muscat	@ 1.60F/kg (76° Oechsle base)
Gewurztraminer	@ 1.62F/kg (95° Oechsle base)
Pinot Noir	@ 1.82F/kg (90° Oechsle base)

1965

Quality overview: Believed to be the lousiest vintage of the century!
Surface area planted: 8,902 hectares
Total production: 610,873 hectolitres
Average yield: 68.6 hectolitres per hectare

Harvest began on 16 October. A year of lousy weather produced lousy grapes and lousy wines.

GRAPE PRICES

Chasselas	@ 0.67F/kg (70° Oechsle base)
Sylvaner	@ 0.71F/kg (70° Oechsle base)
Pinot Blanc	@ 0.84F/kg (70° Oechsle base)
Riesling	@ 1.03F/kg (70° Oechsle base)
Tokay-Pinot Gris	@ 1.03F/kg (80° Oechsle base)
Muscat	@ 1.24F/kg (70° Oechsle base)
Gewurztraminer	@ 1.22F/kg (80° Oechsle base)
Pinot Noir	@ 1.56F/kg (80° Oechsle base)

1964

Quality overview: Excellent, very ripe and long-lived.
Surface area planted: 9,246 hectares
Surface area planted: 833,346 hectolitres
Average yield: 90.1 hectolitres per hectare

The harvest began on 5 October and favoured bigger wines, from the naturally richer varieties, such as Gewurztraminer and Tokay-Pinot Gris, but also Riesling Vendange Tardive. Most of these wines have the edge over the 1966s, but comparisons between the best wines of the two vintages will continue to fascinate for many years to come.

1963

Quality overview: Bad.
Surface area planted: 9,380 hectares
Total production: 939,434 hectolitres
Average yield: 100.2 hectolitres per hectare

Harvest began on 14 October. As bad as 1968, but not quite comparable to 1965.

1962

Quality overview: Good.
Surface area planted: 8,793 hectares
Total production: 741,101 hectolitres
Average yield: 84.3 hectolitres per hectare

A good, but early-drinking vintage, the harvest for which began on 18 October.

1961
Harvest began on 9 October (8,377 hectares; 563,181 hectolitres; 67.2 hectolitres per hectare). Great vintage, comparable to something between 1988 and 1989.

1960
Harvest began on 10 October (7,643 hectares; 618,171 hectolitres; 80.9 hectolitres per hectare). Light-bodied, easy drinking wines.

1959
Harvest began on 1 October (7,934 hectares; 516,360 hectolitres; 65.1 hectolitres per hectare). Great vintage, comparable to 1976.

1958
Harvest began on 6 October (7,982 hectares; 685,430 hectolitres; 85.9 hectolitres per hectare). Light, average quality.

1957
Harvest began on 12 October (7,388 hectares; 383,356 hectolitres; 51.9 hectolitres per hectare). Stronger in construction than 1958, but only a touch above average in quality.

1956
Harvest began on 20 October (7,242 hectares; 191,311 hectolitres; 26.4 hectolitres per hectare). The year of the frost. Average quality.

1955
Harvest began on 17 October (7,653 hectares; 572,470 hectolitres; 74.8 hectolitres per hectare). Exceptionally aromatic, very good in quality.

1954
Harvest began on 15 October (7,499 hectares; 551,353 hectolitres; 73.5 hectolitres per hectare). Good quality.

1953
Harvest began on 3 October (7,290 hectares; 563,017 hectolitres; 77.2 hectolitres per hectare). Excellent quality, attractive to drink from the start.

1952
Harvest began on 29 September (6,931 hectares; 360,479 hectolitres; 52 hectolitres per hectare). Very good quality, harmonious and easy to drink.

1951
Harvest began on 15 October (6,601 hectares; 474,883 hectolitres; 71.9 hectolitres per hectare). A poor year, on a par with the likes of 1963 or 1968.

1950
Good quantity and good quality, far better than in other French regions. Some place it on a par with 1952.

1949
Precocious harvest and excellent quality, but not as good as either 1945 or 1947.

1948
Good quality, but often forgotten due to the exceptional vintages immediately before and after.

1947
Greatest vintage since 1934.

1946
Goodish quality.

1945
A great year, but not quite the class of 1947.

1944
Average quality, but the battle of the Colmar Pocket destroyed entire villages in Alsace during the winter of 1944/5, including vast amounts of fermenting wine residing in many cellars.

1943
Large volume, very good quality.

1942
Large volume, good quality.

1941
Large volume and despite widespread rot, not bad quality.

1940
Rampant rot, small volume, poor quality.

1939
Large volume, above average quality.

1938
April frosts greatly reduced the potential size of the harvest, which was very small in quantity, but very good in quality.

1937
Similar volume to 1936, but very good to excellent in quality.

1936
Medium quantity of above average quality.

1935
Large crop of average quality.

1934
Very large volume of truly great quality, surviving bottles of the best of which are still pure magic.

1933
Due to April frost, the quantity was small. The quality was generally average to poor, but with a few pleasant surprises.

1932
Medium-sized harvest of above average quality.

1931
A wet and miserable summer gave a fairly large harvest of unripe, acidic wines.

1930
Important-sized harvest of below average quality.

1929
Large crop of excellent to great wines that were fat, rich and complex, but not quite the longevity of the 1928s.

1928
Small to medium-sized harvest of great wines.

1927
Very small crop of very poor quality.

1926
Tiny crop of good, easy drinking wines.

1925
Very small crop of uneven quality.

1924
Alsace was still troubled with phylloxera, but managed to produce a medium-sized crop of good quality.

1923
Alsace was again troubled with phylloxera, but even more so than in 1922, consequently the harvest was tiny and not quite as good.

1922
The first of three consecutive years in which Alsace was particularly troubled with phylloxera; the wines were quite good, but many were acidic.

1921
Despite a cold summer, truly excellent wines were produced, although not quite as great as in other French regions.

1920
Small crop of below average quality.

1919
An important volume of generally good, occasionally very good to excellent, wines produced.

1918
Mediocre to poor quality.

1917
With most men fighting on one side or the other, these good quality wines were harvested by women, children and the old.

1916
Again harvested by women, children and the old. The year was dry, the

grapes failed to achieve good ripeness, but no sugar was available or allowed for chaptalization.

1915
The first vintage fully affected by the war. Good-quality wines.

1914
The first vintage of 'the war to end all wars', it was very uneven in quality, with some good, very good and very poor wines made.

1913
Very poor vintage.

1912
After a winter of almost Arctic proportions, particularly in February, when many vines were frozen to death, thin, acid wines were produced.

1911
An incredibly hot summer produced wines of very good to excellent quality.

1910
Poor quality.

1909
Frost and hail in the spring followed by a stormy summer produced miserably poor wines.

1908
Fair to good quality.

1907
Cold spring and a poor flowering, but fairly good wines.

1906
Widespread attacks of downy mildew again reduced the volume. Mediocre quality.

1905
Very dry summer followed by attacks of downy mildew reduced the quantity, but good to passable wines were produced.

1904
Large volume of good to very good quality.

1903
Although very humid conditions encouraged the spread of oidium and greatly reduced the yield, this was an above average quality vintage, with some wines that verged on good to very good.

1902
Spring frosts and oidium prevalent at harvest time. Small crop of very poor quality.

1901
Cold year produced thin, acid wines.

1900
Despite the rain and the rot, this vintage has an excellent reputation.

Note *Only selected vintages are featured from here.*

1895
The last great vintage of the nineteenth century.

1894
One of the worst vintages of the century.

1893
Excellent quality.

1888
Undrinkable!

1884
Very good quality.

1876
Very good quality.

1875
One of the greatest vintages of the century.

1874
A great year and the first of three consecutive vintages of truly remarkable quality.

1870
Excellent to great year.

1859
Poor year.

1857
Very hot summer, excellent wines.

1852, 1851 and 1850
Three of the worst vintages of the century. After this trio of vintages, winemakers would have been forgiven had they stopped going to church and sought help by sacrifice on the Bollenberg!

1848
Excellent to great.

1847
Great frost on the plains, but excellent wines produced on the slopes.

1846
Great vintage.

1842
Very hot and dry, excellent quality.

1834
Great quality wines produced everywhere.

1831
Very cold year, lousy wines.

1825
Very dry year, very good quality.

1822
Very early harvest of excellent quality.

1821, 1820, 1818, 1817, 1816 and *1814*
With six out of eight vintages yielding tiny crops of very poor quality wines, burning bishops on the Bollenberg must have become *de rigueur*!

1811
The first great vintage of the nineteenth century.

1801
The first worst vintage of the nineteenth century.

1793
Minus 20° Celsius on 30 June!

1779
Small crop, great quality.

1771
The smallest harvest of the eighteenth century and one of the worst.

1770 and *1767*
Almost as tiny in volume as *1771* and even worse quality!

1764
Frost in September, very poor quantity and quality.

1763
Very cold year, poor quality.

1762
One of the greatest vintages of the eighteenth century.

1760
Very hot year, excellent quality.

1753
Generally believed to be the greatest vintage of the eighteenth century.

1750 and *1749*
Terrible conditions, no wines produced at all!

1740
Freezing cold year, very acidic wines.

1718
Huge volume and the first great vintage of the eighteenth century.

1683
The last great vintage of the seventeenth century.

1682
Two harvests in one year and both were good!

1666
The second 'vintage of the century' for the seventeenth century (well, Alsace was French by this time!).

1632–1638
Six years of war and famine, three without any harvest whatsoever and the other three were lousy in quality and amongst the smallest on record.

1631
The greatest vintage of the seventeenth century.

1608
Siberian conditions totally destroyed the vintage and froze the previous year's wine in the cellars.

1604
Huge crop of great quality.

1602
Vines frozen, no wine produced.

1575
First good crop for 15 years!

1573
Snow in April!

1572
Snow in June!

1557
Frosts in August, wine undrinkable!

1556
Great vintage.

1544
Crop destroyed by hail, no wine produced.

1537
Great vintage.

1530
Snow in April.

1516
Great vintage.

1511
Crop destroyed by frost, no wine produced.

1505
The greatest vintage of the sixteenth century.

1503
Crop destroyed by drought, no wine produced.

1494
Crop destroyed by frost, no wine produced.

1487
Crop destroyed by hail, no wine produced.

1486
Crop destroyed by rot after continuous rain, no wine produced.

1484
The harvest was so large that 50 litres of wine cost the same as one egg!

1471
Great vintage.

1470
Crop destroyed by hail, no wine produced.

1468
Tiny crop, but great quality.

1458
Grapes ripe by 21 May!

1457
Crop destroyed by hail, no wine produced.

1446, *1443* and *1442*
Crops destroyed by frost, no wine produced.

1439, *1438* and *1437*
Famine, no wine produced.

1436
Continuous rain, crop destroyed by rot, no wine produced.

1431
Another crop that was so large the wine had to be used for mixing mortar
(*see* 1255).

1430
Crop destroyed by frost, no wine produced.

1428
Very cold spring, heavy snows, very little wine produced.

1425
Crop destroyed by frost, no wine produced.

1420
Harvest in July!

1392
Crop destroyed by frost, no wine produced.

1380
Very hot year, wines of exceptional quality produced.

1364
Crop destroyed by a plague of grasshoppers, no wine produced.

1353
Great vintage.

1349
Bubonic plague.

1347
Very severe late frosts, most of the crop destroyed and the remainder was undrinkable!

1341
Crop destroyed by frost, no wine produced.

1339
Crop destroyed by a plague of grasshoppers, no wine produced.

1334
Crop destroyed by frost, no wine produced.

1315
Continuous rain between May and November (but try telling the younger generation today and they just won't believe you!), no wines produced.

1314
Famine, no wine produced.

1300
Great vintage.

1298
Too much wine produced!

1297
Huge crop of great quality.

1289
Crop destroyed by frost, no wine produced.

1278
Crop destroyed by frost, no wine produced.

1275
Crop destroyed by August storms, no wine produced.

1274
Picking started in November, good quality.

1272
Most of the crop eaten by wolves!

1268
Crop destroyed by frost, no wine produced.

1258
Crop destroyed by frost, no wine produced.

1255
The crop was so large that, after filling up all the casks, the excess wine had to be used for mixing mortar!

1253
Crop destroyed by hail, no wine produced.

1246
Crop eaten by caterpillars, no wine produced.

1234
Crop destroyed by hail, no wine produced. Wines in the cellar frozen to their casks.

1232
So hot it was possible to fry eggs on paving stones. Wines of great quality produced. Best for 50 years.

1231
Famine, no wine produced.

1205
July storms destroyed vineyards, no wine produced.

1194
Famine, no wine produced.

1189
Crop destroyed by frost, no wine produced.

1186
Huge crop harvested early in August, good quality wines.

1146 and *1143*
Crop destroyed by frost, no wine produced.

1136
Excessive rain followed by drought, very little wine produced.

1129 and *1126*
Crop destroyed by frost, no wine produced.

1100 and *1096*
Famine, no wine produced.

882
Good quantity of good-quality wines.

805
Poor quality wines.

792
Famine, no wine produced.

763
Severely cold winter.

585
Poor vintage.

Appendix 2
Earlier Classifications

STOLTZ

In 1828, J. L. Stoltz cited 17 *lieux-dits* as the best vineyards in Alsace, in his *Notizen aus dem Elässichen Weinbau.* Condensed from 25 pages, they are listed below in alphabetical order of the villages in which they are (or were, as the case may be) located:

ANDLAU *Kastelberg, Wiebelsberg, Mönchberg* (shared with Eichhoffen)

BERGHEIM *Tempelhof* (formerly the property of the Templars, now part of Grand Cru Kanzlerberg)

CERNAY *Hube oder Haube* (no longer in existence, with Cernay itself possessing only one hectare of vines today)

DIEFFENTHAL *Neubruch* (no longer utilized)

GUEBWILLER *Wanne* (no longer utilized, 'Gewann' literally means 'big *lieu-dit*', which is apt for a town possessing four *grands crus*)

JUNGHOLTZ *Schauenberg* (no longer utilized)

MOLSHEIM *Finkenberg* (now part of Grand Cru Bruderthal, but also used as a *lieu-dit* by Bernard Becht and Bernard Weber)

ORSCHWIHR *Côtes au-dessus d'Orschwihr* (now part of Grand Cru Praelatenberg)

RIBEAUVILLÉ *Zahnacker* (utilized by CV Ribeauvillé)

RIQUEWIHR *Schoenenbourg*

SCHERWILLER *Ortenbourg* (presumably close to or part of Rittersberg, which is located beneath the ruins of Ortenbourg castle)

SIGOLSHEIM *Côtes au-dessus Sigolsheim* (now part of *grands crus* Mambourg and Furstentum)

THANN *Rangen*

TURCKHEIM *Brand*

WOLXHEIM *Altenberg*

Stoltz also ranked five villages and two *lieux-dits* as the finest producers of red wine:

VILLAGES Ammerschwihr, Kientzheim, Ribeauvillé, Rodern and Turckheim
LIEUX-DITS *Steinberg* (Kaysersberg) and *Côtes d'Ottrott*

SITTLER AND MAROCKE

The following vineyards were singled out by Claude Sittler and Robert
Marocke in their exhaustive study *Terroirs et Vins d'Alsace*, which was
published by the Louis Pasteur University, Strasbourg (3rd Edition, 1988).
Sittler and Marocke state that these growths are limited in number and
size, have previously well-established reputations and are mostly restricted
to the same geological substratum.

Haut-Rhin

AMMERSCHWIHR *Kaefferkopf, Meywihr*
BLEBENHEIM *Sonnenglanz*
BENNWIHR *Rebgarten, Markrain*
BERGHEIM *Altenberg, Buerlenberg, Kanzlerberg, Rotenberg*
BERGHOLTZ *Spiegel*
CERNAY *Huben*
COLMAR *Hardt*
EGUISHEIM *Pfirsichberg* (sic), *Eichberg*
GUEBERSCHWIHR *Goldert, Rebgarten, Clos St-Immer* (sic)
GUEBWILLER *Schimberg, Kessler, Saering, Kitterlé, Wanne, Heissenstein*
HATTSTATT *Brandstatt, Hatschbourg, Eisbourg*
HERRLISHEIM *Elsbourg*
HUNAWIHR *Rosacker, Muehlforst, Clos Ste-Hune, Heitzloch*
INGERSHEIM *Florimont*
KATZENTHAL *Schlossberg, Wineck*
KAYSERSBERG *Schlossberg, Geisbourg*
KIENTZHEIM *Schlossberg, Furstentum, Kirrenburg, Clos des Capucins,
Altenburg*
MITTELWIHR *Mandelberg*
NIEDERMORSCHWIHR *Sommerberg*
ORSCHWIHR *Lippelsberg, Bollenberg, Affenberg, Pfingstberg*
PFAFFENHEIM *Schneckenberg, Bergweingarten, Steinert*
RIBEAUVILLÉ *Kirchberg, Girsberg, Osterberg, Trottacker, Zahnacker,
Geisberg, Hagel, Steinacker*
RIQUEWIHR *Schoenenbourg, Sporen*
RODERN *Rouge de Rodern* (speciality), *Gloeckelberg*
ROUFFACH *Clos St-Landelin, Bollenberg, Lerchenberg, Vorbourg*
ST-HIPPOLYTE *Geisberg, Schlossreben*

SIGOLSHEIM *Mamburg* (sic), *Vogelgarten, Altenburg, Furstentum*
SOULTZMATT *Zinnkoepflé*
THANN *Rangen*
TURCKHEIM *Brand, Schneckelsbourg, Eichberg*
VOEGTLINSHOFFEN *Hatschbourg, Hagelberg*
WALBACH *Côtes du Val St-Grégoire*
WESTHALTEN *Zinnkoepflé, Bollenberg, Strangenberg, Vorbourg*
WETTOLSHEIM *Steingrubler*
WINTZENHEIM *Hengst, Wartstein*
WUENHEIM *Ollwiller (Château)*
ZELLENBERG *Hagenschlauf, Schlossreben, Mantelkragen, Schoenenbourg, Froehn*

Bas-Rhin

ANDLAU *Kastelberg, Wiebelsberg, Moenchberg*
AVOLSHEIM *Finkenberg*
BARR *Kirchberg, Freiberg, Goensbroennel, Zisser*
BERGBIETEN *Altenberg*
BERNARDVILLÉ *Eichelberg*
BLIENSCHWILLER *Oberberg, Wintzenberg*
CHÂTENOIS *Hahnenberg, Rittersberg*
CLÉEBOURG *Reifenberg, Hausberg*
DAHLENHEIM *Engelberg, Silberberg*
DAMBACH *Bernstein, Blettig, Frankstein*
DORLISHEIM *Katzenburg*
EICHHOFFEN *Moenchberg*
EPFIG *Fronholtz, Pflanzer*
HEILIGENSTEIN *Klevner de Heiligenstein* (speciality)
ITTERSWILLER *Kirchberg*
KINTZHEIM *Hahnenberg*
MARLENHEIM *Steinklotz* or *Côtes de Marlenheim, Rouge de Marlenheim* (speciality)
MITTELBERGHEIM *Zotzenberg, Hagel, Stein, Brandluft, Pfoeller*
MOLSHEIM *Bruderthal, Finkenberg*
MUTZIG *Stierkopf*
NORDHEIM *Sonnenberg*
NOTHALTEN *Munchberg* (sic)
OBERNAI *Clos Ste-Odile, Schenckenberg* (sic)
ORSCHWILLER *Hahnenberg, Praelatenberg, Kirchberg*
OTTROTT *Rouge d'Ottrott* (speciality)
SCHERWILLER/DIEFFENTHAL *Rittersberg*
WOLXHEIM *Altenberg, Horn*

Appendix 3
Production Analysis

SERIES I

TABLE 1   Evolution of surface area cultivated for
AOC Alsace 1981–91 in total and for each vine variety

	1981	1982	1983	1984	1985
Mixed Vines	539	529	475	694	495
Chasselas	417	403	389	347	315
Sylvaner	2,500	2,497	2,527	2,537	2,523
Pinot Blanc	2,004	2,118	2,236	2,265	2,358
Riesling	2,247	2,364	2,449	2,519	2,606
Tokay-PG	547	559	585	558	618
Muscat	423	417	427	392	378
Gewurztraminer	2,433	2,453	2,477	2,381	2,496
Pinot Noir	639	712	743	756	809
Total	11,749	12,052	12,308	12,449	12,598

Note: The difference 1981–91 refers to the increase or decrease on 1981, thus
the 1981 Gewurztraminer base of 2,433 hectares represents 100 per cent and the

TABLE 2   Evolution of Alsace grape varieties 1981–91

	1981	1982	1983	1984	1985
Mixed Vines	4.6	4.4	3.9	5.6	3.9
Chasselas	3.5	3.3	3.2	2.8	2.5
Sylvaner	21.3	20.7	20.4	20.3	20.1
Pinot Blanc	17.1	17.6	18.2	18.2	18.7
Riesling	19.1	19.6	19.9	20.3	20.7
Tokay-PG	4.7	4.6	4.8	4.5	4.9
Muscat	3.6	3.5	3.5	3.1	3.0
Gewurztraminer	20.7	20.4	20.1	19.2	19.8
Pinot Noir	5.4	5.9	6.0	6.0	6.4
Total	100.0	100.0	100.0	100.0	100.0

Note: The difference 1981–91 is not the percentage increase or decrease on
base, but merely the variation between the proportions recorded in these ten
years, thus, although Gewurztraminer vines increased from 2,433 hectares in

(Expressed in hectares)

1986	1987	1988	1989	1990	1991	Difference 1981–91
513	488	406	420	441	402	−25%
315	291	279	267	240	230	−45%
2,513	2,492	2,472	2,440	2,411	2,367	−05%
2,430	2,475	2,523	2,585	2,644	2,699	+35%
2,651	2,704	2,797	2,871	2,958	3,015	+34%
648	681	726	773	828	884	+54%
396	376	387	376	357	371	−12%
2,459	2,485	2,496	2,491	2,485	2,503	+03%
848	870	912	939	989	1,016	+59%
12,773	12,862	12,998	13,162	13,353	13,487	+15%

1991 total of 2,503 hectares is therefore the equivalent of 103 per cent, consequently there has been an increase of 3 per cent.

(Expressed as a percentage of AOC Alsace in total)

1986	1987	1988	1989	1990	1991	Difference 1981–91
4.0	3.8	3.1	3.2	3.3	3.0	−1.6
2.5	2.3	2.2	2.0	1.8	1.7	−1.8
19.7	19.4	19.0	18.5	18.1	17.5	−3.8
19.0	19.2	19.4	19.7	19.8	20.0	+2.9
20.7	21.0	21.5	21.8	22.1	22.3	+3.2
5.1	5.3	5.6	5.9	6.2	6.6	−1.9
3.1	2.9	3.0	2.9	2.7	2.8	−0.8
19.3	19.3	19.2	18.9	18.6	18.6	−2.1
6.6	6.8	7.0	7.1	7.4	7.5	−2.1
100.0	100.0	100.0	100.0	100.0	100.0	0.0

1981 to 2,503 hectares in 1991, the proportion of the entire vineyards of AOC Alsace they represented actually decreased from 20.7% to 18.6%, due to the overall increase in yards over this period.

CHART 1 **Mixed Vines** Evolution in hectares 1981–91

Year	Hectares
1991	402
90	441
89	420
88	406
87	488
86	513
85	495
84	694
83	475
82	529
1981	539

CHART 2 **Chasselas** Evolution in hectares 1981–91

Year	Hectares
1991	230
90	240
89	267
88	279
87	291
86	315
85	315
84	347
83	389
82	403
1981	417

CHART 3 **Sylvaner** Evolution in hectares 1981–91

Year	Hectares
1991	2,367
90	2,411
89	2,440
88	2,472
87	2,492
86	2,513
85	2,523
84	2,537
83	2,527
82	2,497
1981	2,500

CHART 4 **Pinot Blanc** Evolution in hectares 1981–91

Year	Hectares
1991	2,699
90	2,644
89	2,585
88	2,523
87	2,475
86	2,430
85	2,358
84	2,265
83	2,236
82	2,118
1981	2,004

CHART 5 **Riesling** Evolution in hectares 1981–91

Year	Hectares
1991	3,015
90	2,958
89	2,871
88	2,797
87	2,704
86	2,651
85	2,606
84	2,519
83	2,449
82	2,364
1981	2,247

CHART 6 **Tokay-Pinot Gris** Evolution in hectares 1981–91

Year	Hectares
1991	884
90	828
89	773
88	726
87	681
86	648
85	618
84	558
83	585
82	559
1981	547

CHART 7 **Muscat** Evolution in hectares 1981–91

1991	371
90	357
89	376
88	387
87	376
86	396
85	378
84	392
83	427
82	417
1981	423

CHART 8 **Gewurztraminer** Evolution in hectares 1981–91

1991	2,503
90	2,485
89	2,491
88	2,496
87	2,485
86	2,459
85	2,496
84	2,381
83	2,477
82	2,453
1981	2,433

CHART 9 **Pinot Noir** Evolution in hectares 1981–91

1991	1,016
90	989
89	939
88	912
87	870
86	848
85	809
84	756
83	743
82	712
1981	639

PRODUCTION ANALYSIS

CHART 10 **Production of AOC Crémant d'Alsace 1981–91**
(Expressed in Hectolitres)

Year	Value
1991	104,700
90	108,583
89	116,268
88	80,582
87	83,637
86	46,859
85	25,039
84	27,232
83	47,350
82	67,024
1981	34,979

CHART 11 **Production of AOC Alsace Grands Crus 1984–91**
(Expressed in Hectolitres)

Year	Value
1991	38,518
90	37,987
89	38,432
88	37,291
87	27,121
86	29,386
85	17,738
1984	7,800

CHART 12 **Production of Vendanges Tardives 1981–91**
(Expressed in Hectolitres)

Year	Value
1991	2,280
90	19,950
89	23,840
88	6,100
87	945
86	2,500
85	9,395
84	400
83	7,600
82	1,200
1981	700

CHART 13 **Production of Selection de Grains Nobles 1981–91**
(Expressed in Hectolitres)

Year	Hectolitres
1991	281
90	5,336
89	12,275
88	3,440
87	20
86	440
85	225
84	15
83	750
82	40
1981	20

SERIES II

TABLE 3   Performance of Grape Prices Relative to Size of Harvest 1975–90
(Prices in French francs; Annual Production in Hectolitres)

	1975	1976	1977	1978	1979	1980	1981	1982	1983	1984	1985	1986	1987	1988	1989	1990
Chasselas	1.44	2.02	2.86	3.94	3.34	3.68	3.74	2.92	2.97	4.22	4.86	4.79	4.73	4.83	5.42	6.20
Sylvaner	1.46	2.02	2.86	3.98	3.30	3.64	3.74	2.92	2.97	4.22	4.86	4.79	4.73	4.83	5.42	6.20
Pinot Blanc	1.52	2.11	2.91	4.00	3.45	3.80	3.90	3.04	3.08	4.28	4.92	4.90	4.82	4.95	5.59	6.63
Riesling	2.42	3.42	4.32	4.35	3.94	4.62	4.72	3.62	3.67	4.83	5.45	5.43	5.44	5.82	6.91	8.48
Tokay-PG	2.12	2.80	3.71	4.89	4.16	5.01	4.99	4.10	4.25	5.07	5.83	5.94	5.93	6.41	7.81	10.77
Muscat	2.18	2.77	3.76	5.67	4.35	5.61	5.42	4.10	4.08	5.00	5.79	5.82	5.87	5.98	6.92	8.49
Gewurztraminer	2.46	3.24	4.67	7.32	5.50	7.27	6.23	4.92	5.00	5.75	5.75	6.48	6.59	7.15	8.58	13.62
Pinot Noir	2.34	3.31	4.60	5.30	4.65	5.76	5.73	4.60	4.67	5.49	6.33	6.32	6.46	6.84	7.95	10.01
Annual Production	792K	881K	952K	693K	1074K	599K	904K	1453K	989K	808K	895K	1189K	1068K	1055K	1226K	1084K

527

Note
It is interesting to note that the larger the harvest the lower the price, a very German trait indeed, as in most French regions, the growers can usually find a reason why prices should increase, but seldom agree to lower them, even in the most prolific of crop when the best that buyers can hope for will be a certain stability in prices. The contrast of peaks and troughs in prices and the size of harvest in Alsace is not 100 per cent, as other market forces can come into play, but it is more than sufficient to show a definite underlying trend.

GRAPH I
Performance of Grape Prices Relative to Size of Harvest 1975–90
Vertical scale represents French francs and, for Annual Production, Hectolitres: 1FF = 100,000 h/l)

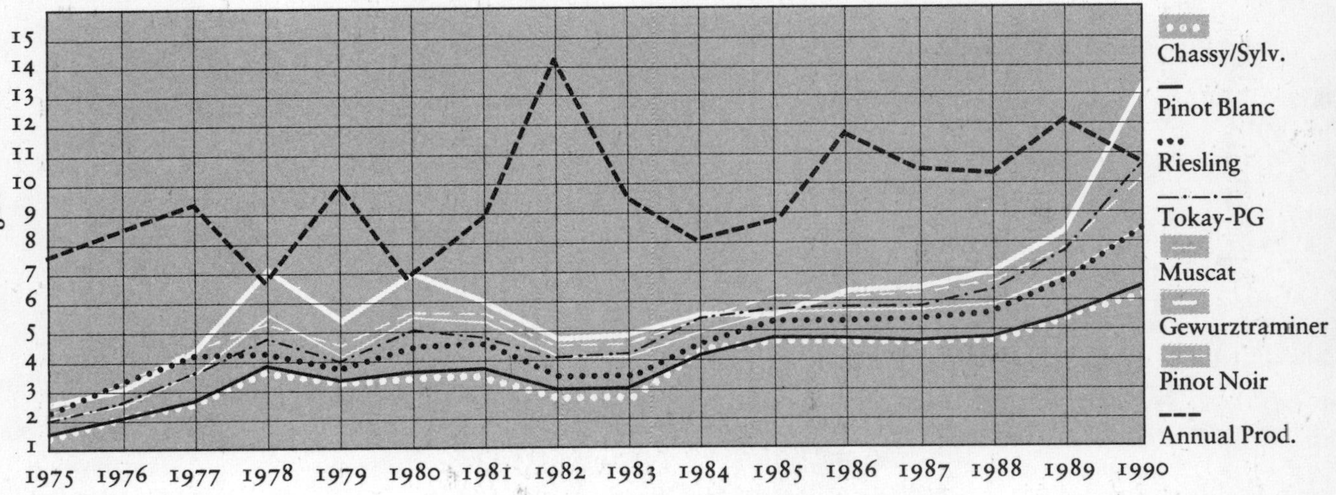

Chassy/Sylv.
Pinot Blanc
Riesling
Tokay-PG
Muscat
Gewurztraminer
Pinot Noir
Annual Prod.

528

Appendix 4
Sales and Export Statistics

Overproducing or underselling?

From the figures above, it can be seen that over the 15 years Alsace has produced the equivalent of more than one year's crop in excess of that which it has managed to sell. This is, in fact, a good equilibrium between sales and production, as a glimpse at the graph will show the gently rising line of sales cutting right through the middle of production, which can never be accurately projected or controlled. If the 15-year span is broken down into three five-year periods (table above), it becomes clear that the greatest excess production was between 1981/82 and 1985/86, with just one year (1982) to blame. Remove this anomaly and we can see that Alsace typically produces just 5 per cent more than it sells. My only concern is where does it go? Few firms can be like Hugel & Fils, who deliberately build up stocks of mature wine, but if there was not a single drop of wine in Alsace prior to the 1976 harvest, then there must be on average more than a year's stocks sloshing round in everyone's cellars. The fact is that there was 768,855 hectolitres in stock on 31 August of that year, which by simple arithmetic means there must have been 2,104,222 hectolitres on 31 August 1991, but the official stock figures show only 1,034,574 hectolitres!

SERIES III

TABLE 4 Total Sales and Total Production Breakdown of AOC Alsace 1967/77 to 1990/91 over three 5-year periods
(Expressed in Hectolitres)

	Total Sales	Totals	Annual Production	Difference
90/91	1,093,459		1,226,242	
89/90	1,119,579	5,146,393 Sales	1,055,445	
88/89	1,034,573	5,433,860 Production	1,068,202	
87/88	956,897		1,188,579	+287,467
86/87	941,885		895,392	
85/86	927,476	Sales	895,392	
84/85	980,976		807,798	
83/84	897,715	4,393,626	988,604	
82/83	834,150	5,048,205 Production	1,452,662	
81/82	753,309		903,749	+654,579
80/81	730,554		599,304	
79/80	706,277	Sales	1,074,039	
78/79	681,449	3,805,230	692,575	
77/78	828,814	4,198,551 Production	951,814	
76/77	858,136		880,819	+393,321
	Total Sales 13,345,249			
	Total Production 14,680,616		Total Difference +1,335,367	

530

Note: Annual production figures above relate to the first of the two years indicated (thus the Annual Production for campaign year 76/77 refers to the 1976 harvest).

GRAPH 2   Comparison of Total Sales & Production of AOC Alsace Wines 1976/77 to 1990/91 (Expressed in Hectolitres)

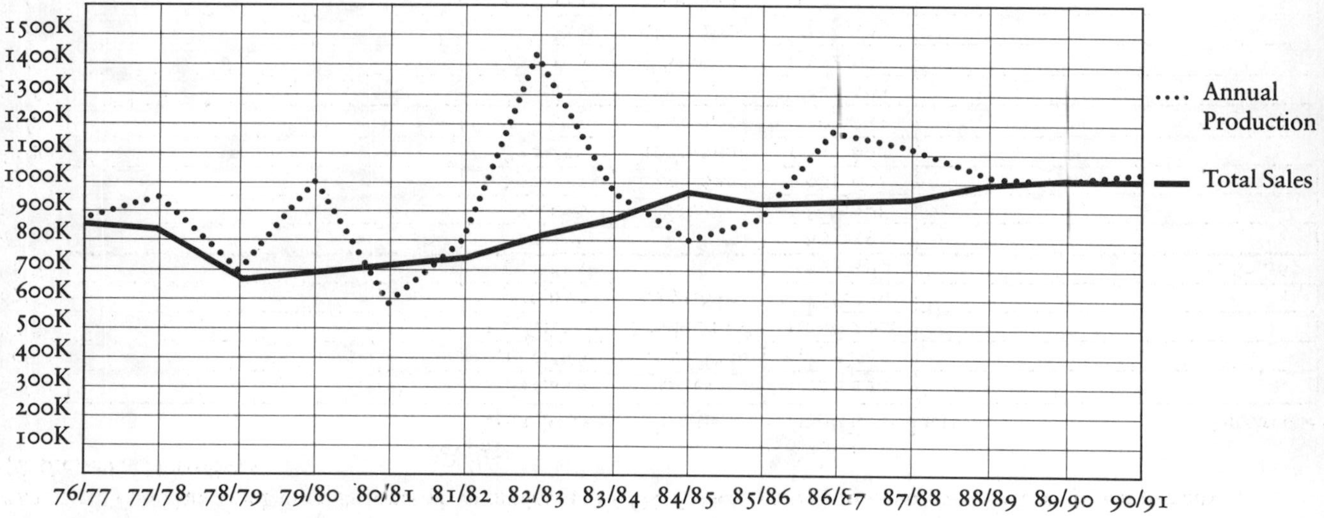

Annual Production

Total Sales

1500K
1400K
1300K
1200K
1100K
1000K
900K
800K
700K
600K
500K
400K
300K
200K
100K

76/77 77/78 78/79 79/80 80/81 81/82 82/83 83/84 84/85 85/86 86/87 87/88 88/89 89/90 90/91

TABLE 5   Export, Home Market & Total Sales of AOC Alsace 1976/77 to 1990/91
(Expressed in Hectolitres)

	France (Hectos)	Per cent	Total Sales (Hectos)	Export (Hectos)	Per cent
90/91	771.295	70.5	1,093,459	322,164	29.5
89/90	769,739	68.8	1,119,579	349,840	31.2
88/89	711,361	68.8	1,034,573	323,212	31.2
87/88	657,612	68.7	956,897	299,285	31.3
86/87	666,568	70.8	941,885	275,317	29.2
85/86	641,093	69.1	927,476	286,383	30.9
84/85	670,860	68.4	980,976	310,116	31.6
83/84	641,411	71.4	897,715	256,304	28.6
82/83	602,184	72.3	834,150	230,966	27.7
81/82	569,823	75.6	753,309	183,486	24.4
80/81	558,627	76.5	730,554	171,927	23.5
79/80	552,083	78.2	706,277	154,194	21.8
78/79	540,592	79.3	681,449	140,857	20.7
77/78	652,820	78.8	828,814	175,994	21.2

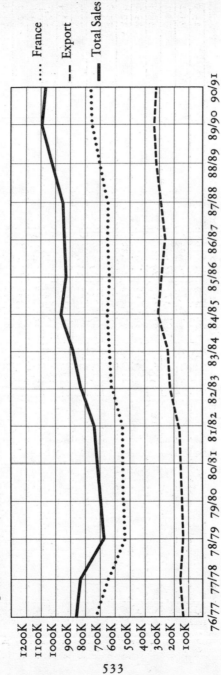

GRAPH 3   Export, Home Market & Total Sales of AOC Alsace Wines 1976–77 to 1990–91 (Expressed in Hectolitres)

TABLE 6 Evolution of Production & Sales of AOC Crémant d'Alsace
(Expressed in Hectolitres)

	Production	Total Sales	Exports
1991	104,700	87,672	8,928
90	108,583	81,231	6,819
89	116,268	68,546	5,321
88	80,582	57,576	4,598
87	83,637	47,742	3,887
86	46,859	40,391	3,363
85	25,039	33,286	2,435
84	27,232	28,672	1,456
83	47,350	23,171	1,661
82	67,024	16,428	707
1981	34,979	4,000	170
11-year Totals	742,253	237,449	39,345

GRAPH 4   Evolution of Production & Sales of AOC Crémant d'Alsace 1981–91
(Expressed in Hectolitres)

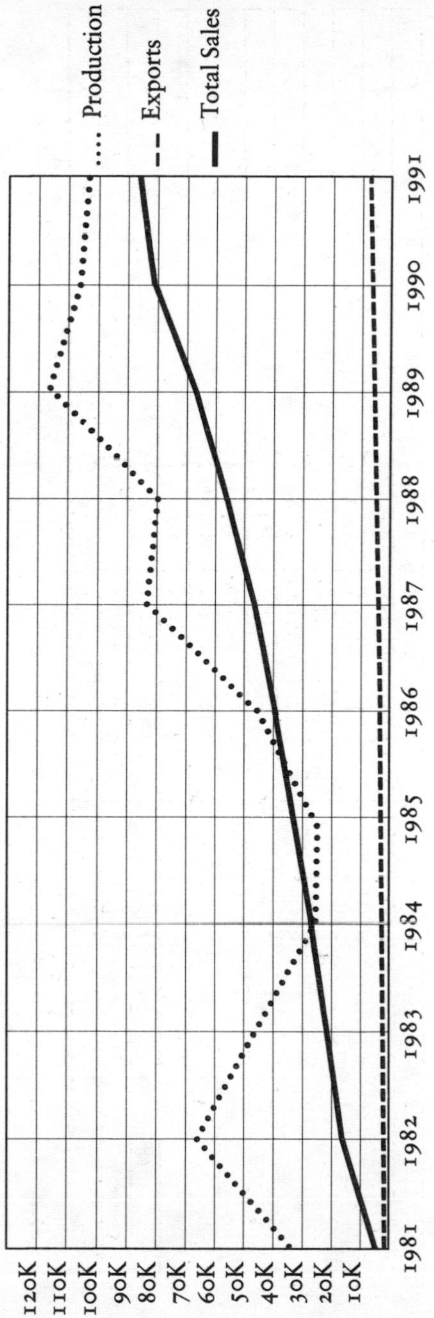

Production ......
Exports – –
Total Sales ——

TABLE 7 Top Export Countries AOC Alsace (without Crémant) 1982–91 comparison

	1982				1991				% Difference	
	HI	%	1,000FF	%	HI	%	1,000FF	%	HI	Value
Germany	129,799	68.2	147,323	58.2	150,815	49.5	249,111	40.1	+16	+69
Holland	11,391	6.0	17,341	6.9	43,506	14.3	88,142	14.2	+282	+408
Benelux	14,685	7.7	26,518	10.5	36,600	12.0	94,904	15.3	+149	+258
Denmark	2,753	1.5	4,638	1.8	26,828	8.8	53,273	8.6	+875	+1049
Great Britain	7,288	3.8	13,748	5.4	16,610	5.5	44,119	7.1	+128	+221
Italy	283	0.2	507	0.2	949	0.3	2,886	0.4	+235	+469
Ireland	241	0.1	444	0.2	557	0.2	1,719	0.3	+131	+287
Spain	–	–	–	–	196	0.1	606	0.1	N/A	N/A
Greece	–	–	–	–	57	0.0	158	0.0	N/A	N/A
Portugal	–	–	–	–	9	0.0	31	0.0	N/A	N/A
Total EEC	166,440	87.5	210,519	83.2	276,127	90.7	534,949	86.1	+66	+154
USA	4,397	2.3	9,320	3.7	6,542	2.1	24,560	4.0	+49	+164
Canada	4,703	2.5	8,407	3.3	6,149	2.0	15,844	2.6	+31	+88
Switzerland	8,470	4.4	13,203	5.2	3,877	1.3	10,149	1.6	–54	–23
Sweden	505	0.3	1,148	0.4	3,551	1.2	8,860	1.4	+603	+672
Japan	180	0.1	423	0.2	1,883	0.6	8,163	1.3	+946	+1830
Finland	–	–	–	–	1,004	0.3	2,461	0.4	N/A	N/A
Norway	150	0.1	373	0.1	918	0.3	2,910	0.5	+512	+680
S/Total	184,845	97.2	243,393	96.1	300,051	98.5	607,896	97.9	+62	+150
Other Countries	5,361	2.8	9,749	3.9	4,445	1.5	12,915	2.1	–17	+32
Export Totals	190,215	100.0	253,142	100.0	304,496	100.0	620,811	100.0	+60	+145

CHART 14   **Total Exports of AOC Alsace 1969–91** (excluding Crémant)

	Hectolitres (×1,000)	French Francs (millions)
91	304	621
90	345	614
89	326	549
88	299	501
87	281	469
86	279	449
85	297	422
84	277	336
83	255	309
82	190	253
81	170	212
80	166	192
79	138	169
78	172	171
77	157	129
76	129	88
75	99	63
74	73	52
73	76	63
72	92	47
71	69	32
70	55	25
69	42	18

CHART 15
Exports of AOC Alsace to Germany 1969–91 (excluding Crémant)

	Hectolitres	French Francs (×1,000)
91	150,815	249,111
90	184,720	263,008
89	186,568	253,510
88	182,550	253,083
87	178,489	246,987
86	181,220	242,514
85	197,589	223,822
84	193,029	190,191
83	189,014	187,948
82	129,799	147,323
81	113,063	121,426
80	112,429	111,198
79	87,197	90,129
78	114,181	97,372
77	100,847	71,135
76	79,185	45,713
75	57,397	29,380
74	37,347	21,836
73	33,364	26,241
72	51,518	20,281
71	33,922	12,574
70	25,393	9,129
69	17,656	5,572

CHART 16
Exports of AOC Alsace to Holland 1969–91 (excluding Crémant)

	Hectolitres	French Francs (×1,000)	
91	43,506	88,142	
90	43,093	77,585	
89	38,768	67,665	
88	31,238	56,686	
87	26,060	46,804	
86	24,882	44,042	
85	24,285	38,469	
84	21,819	30,473	
83	15,735	25,077	
82	11,391	17,341	
81	9,484	14,008	
80	12,131	16,673	
79	9,588	13,604	
78	10,430	11,883	
77	9,193	9,017	
76	6,991	5,841	
75	4,701	3,841	
74	3,336	2,783	
73	3,372	2,736	
72	2,936	1,935	
71	2,440	1,451	
70	1,911	1,061	
69	1,522	745	

CHART 17
Exports of AOC Alsace to Benelux 1969–91 (excluding Crémant)

	Hectolitres	French Francs (×1,000)	
91	36,600	94,904	
90	35,305	83,235	
89	29,918	66,303	
88	23,767	55,750	
87	22,083	48,527	
86	18,133	39,671	
85	17,708	36,954	
84	17,489	31,972	
83	16,886	29,661	
82	14,685	26,518	
81	14,515	24,190	
80	15,735	23,521	
79	14,722	22,815	
78	15,237	19,923	
77	16,484	17,372	
76	16,792	14,278	
75	13,569	10,724	
74	10,936	9,115	
73	10,529	8,446	
72	10,664	6,701	
71	9,958	5,021	
70	7,679	3,550	
69	6,547	2,642	

CHART 18
Exports of AOC Alsace to Denmark 1991–91 (excluding Crémant)

	Hectolitres	French Francs (×1,000)
91	26,828	53,273
90	25,407	45,759
89	21,662	39,270
88	18,577	33,899
87	15,024	28,256
86	14,963	26,506
85	13,027	20,796
84	9,239	13,579
83	4,661	7,394
82	2,753	4,638
81	1,909	2,824
80	1,535	2,371
79	1,078	1,789
78	921	1,227
77	967	931
76	1,334	1,288
75	300	290
74	302	287
73	503	435
72	154	104
71	233	133
70	230	134
69	118	69

CHART 19
Exports of AOC Alsace to Great Britain 1969–91 (excluding Crémant)

	Hectolitres	French Francs (×1,000)
91	16,610	44,119
90	20,344	47,313
89	15,567	36,950
88	16,039	36,024
87	12,970	30,809
86	12,268	28,879
85	14,432	33,689
84	9,874	20,269
83	8,841	17,413
82	7,288	13,748
81	6,166	10,753
80	6,131	9,468
79	7,633	12,421
78	8,248	10,473
77	7,476	7,393
76	6,211	5,020
75	5,688	4,581
74	5,306	4,639
73	8,046	7,122
72	6,693	4,139
71	6,521	3,295
70	4,709	2,324
69	3,006	1,446

CHART 20
Exports of AOC Alsace to Canada 1969–91 (excluding Crémant)

	Hectolitres	French Francs (×1,000)
91	6,149	15,884
90	8,085	19,751
89	7,811	18,310
88	5,960	12,779
87	6,879	18,018
86	7,792	17,143
85	8,106	16,417
84	8,582	15,094
83	5,134	9,372
82	4,703	8,407
81	4,294	7,059
80	3,291	5,214
79	2,599	4,204
78	5,855	7,246
77	6,209	6,158
76	4,632	4,320
75	4,285	3,770
74	2,140	1,872
73	3,411	2,984
72	3,590	2,754
71	2,102	1,491
70	2,142	1,440
69	2,016	1,328

CHART 21
Exports of AOC Alsace to USA 1969–91 (excluding Crémant)

	Hectolitres	French Francs (×1,000)
91	6,542	24,560
90	7,449	22,958
89	5,826	17,281
88	4,867	13,157
87	5,089	14,857
86	6,292	17,366
85	11,380	28,132
84	6,200	13,999
83	5,650	12,539
82	4,397	9,320
81	3,022	5,575
80	3,333	5,163
79	3,860	5,995
78	5,843	7,472
77	4,733	5,256
76	3,413	3,180
75	2,199	1,854
74	2,946	2,818
73	4,948	4,491
72	4,173	3,105
71	3,252	2,095
70	2,380	1,499
69	1,865	1,288

CHART 22
Exports of AOC Alsace to Switzerland 1969–91 (excluding Crémant)

	Hectolitres	French Francs (×1,000)
91	3,877	10,149
90	4,493	10,614
89	5,148	10,946
88	4,609	10,135
87	4,326	9,245
86	4,507	9,558
85	3,447	6,941
84	3,605	6,346
83	3,719	6,840
82	8,470	13,203
81	8,580	12,669
80	6,083	8,601
79	4,737	6,809
78	4,759	5,470
77	4,875	4,406
76	4,839	3,489
75	6,408	4,105
74	5,182	3,729
73	5,134	4,762
72	5,401	3,120
71	3,883	2,057
70	3,786	1,971
69	3,087	1,406

CHART 23
Exports of AOC Alsace to Sweden 1969–91 (excluding Crémant)

	Hectolitres	French Francs (×1,000)
91	3,551	8,860
90	5,102	11,270
89	4,370	9,835
88	2,936	6,837
87	2,239	5,525
86	2,109	4,863
85	1,528	3,384
84	841	1,878
83	466	1,045
82	505	1,148
81	304	592
80	239	400
79	226	376
78	195	263
77	218	239
76	318	316
75	216	204
74	205	206
73	341	299
72	294	196
71	342	194
70	366	196
69	355	168

CHART 24
Exports of AOC Alsace to Japan 1975–91 (excluding Crémant)

	Hectolitres	French Francs (×1,000)
91	1,883	8,163
90	2,000	7,832
89	2,398	7,951
88	1,867	5,440
87	1,300	3,851
86	980	2,809
85	589	1,404
84	500	1,251
83	440	1,802
82	180	423
81	382	698
80	211	373
79	178	319
78	118	180
77	102	125
76	82	101
75	44	38

Appendix 5
AOC and EC Regulations

All wines produced in Common Market countries must comply with EC regulations unless national or local ones are stricter. Although this region did not assume *appellation contrôlée* status until 1962, most of the regulations controlling the production of AOC Alsace wines actually date from the Ordinance of 2 November 1945.

BASIC YIELD

Ordonnance du 2 novembre 1945
The maximum yield for all grape varieties is set at 100 hectolitres per hectare for the *appellation* of Alsace or Vin d'Alsace. On top of this there is a 20 per cent PLC (*Plafond Limité de Classement*), which effectively raises the maximum to 120 hectolitres per hectare, provided the grower applying for PLC submits every one of his wines for a special tasting test, which they must pass, otherwise they all go for distillation. The maximum yield before PLC can be amended up or down on an annual basis upon the recommendation of the Regional Committee of Experts and has in fact been set at 80 hectolitres per hectare every year since 1987.

Comment: The PLC concept is not specific to Alsace; it is universal to all AOCs. On first examination, the threat of distillation (if not the yield itself) seems very stiff and should thus discourage growers from going after the higher production level. However, no AOC tasting attempts to test the actual quality of a wine. All that is required is that they should be fault-free and show a certain typicity. The tastings are blind, of course, but as the judges are the producers, who obviously have the most to lose, the degree of typicity demanded is often very basic indeed. The yield is, without doubt, ridiculously high for any quality wine, even at its annually amended level.

Basic alcoholic strength

Ordonnance du 2 novembre 1945
To claim the *appellation* of Alsace or Vin d'Alsace, a wine must have a minimum natural strength of 8.5 per cent alcohol by volume (otherwise known as ABV). This is before any chaptalization (if permitted for the year in question), thus the grapes harvested must contain at least 144 g/l of natural sugar. Chaptalization, or the supplementing of grape juice with sugar, may only be authorized by the Minister of Agriculture on an annual basis upon the recommendation of a local committee of experts.

Comment: Départemental vins de pays *in northern France must be at least 9 per cent!*

Bottling regulations

Decret 55.673 du 20 mars 1955; Arrête du 13 mai 1959; Decret du 19 mars 1963.
Since 1972 all Alsace wines have to be bottled in the region (thus no export in bulk) and, since 1959, three years prior to full AOC recognition, the only bottle permitted has been its famous *flûte d'Alsace* (although the bottling of cheap Edelzwicker in bulbous litre bottles is tolerated).

Comment: The decision to bottle everything in the region is, from the producer's point of view, a very healthy move, for once bulk-wine leaves the region, he has no control over it and cannot be responsible for shady importers who might fraudulently blend his product. It must therefore be applauded. While all lovers of Alsace probably have a soft spot for the tall, elegant flûte d'Alsace, *it has certainly hampered the sale of these wines to the broad spectrum of consumers, especially in English-speaking countries, who mistake its contents for German wine. Additionally, the fact that everyone is obliged to use a certain type of bottle is considered by some to be too restrictive.*

Vintage and varietal content

Ordonnance du 2 novembre 1945, modifié et complété par Decret du 30 juin 1971
If a specific vintage or grape is indicated on the label, all wines must be 100 per cent of the year and grape in question, whereas most other regions enforce only the EC minimum of 85 per cent.

Use of Clairet and Schillerwein

Ordonnance du 2 novembre 1945, modifié et complété par Decret du 30 juin 1971
Permitted for Pinot Noir vinified in the rosé style.

Klevener de Heiligenstein

Articles 1 and 2, Loi du 2 janvier 1970
Unique village *appellation* permitted for wines produced from the Savagnin Rosé.

Comment: *Whether these vines actually are Savagnin Rosé is doubtful, but they are different (more discreet) than the Gewurztraminer vine found throughout Alsace.*

Vendange Tardive and Sélection de Grains Nobles

Decret du 1 mars 1984
Late-harvested wines must be declared prior to harvest to enable their certification by INAO officials at the time of pressing. Wines must also be subjected to stiffer (than basic AOC) tasting and analysis. For varieties and technical specification, *see* appropriate section in Chapter 7.

Comment: *The Vendange Tardive regulations are in desperate need of additional controls to ensure that the actual date of harvest is late (rather than the grapes merely reaching the ripeness levels required) and to force producers to explain on the label whether the wines are dry, sweet or in between.*

Alsace Grand Cru

Decret du 20 novembre 1975, modifié par Decret du 23 novembre 1983
This *appellation* covers pure varietal wines from four noble varieties only (Gewurztraminer, Tokay-Pinot Gris, Riesling & Muscat) grown in specific sites and replaces the original 'expression' of *grand cru*, which could be blended from various different vineyards and also applied to Pinot Noir. The maximum yield is set at 70 hectolitres per hectare, but has been amended to 65 hectolitres per hectare each year since 1987. For technical specifications *see* appropriate section in Chapter 7.

Comment: *Ridiculously high yield, even at amended level, for wines claiming grand cru status.*

Crémant d'Alsace

Decret du 24 août 1976
White and rosé *méthode champenoise appellation* for Riesling, Pinot
Blanc, Pinot Noir, Tokay-Pinot Gris, Auxerrois and Chardonnay. The rosé
style must be 100 per cent Pinot Noir. Maximum yield of 100 hectolitres
per hectare (reduced to 80 hectolitres per hectare on an annual basis since
1990), maximum pressing limit of 100 litres from every 150 kilos of
grapes, with a minimum alcoholic strength of 8.5 per cent ABV. The
strength of mousse should be four atmospheres, which is less than most
Champagnes (which average 5.5–6 atmospheres), but not quite as low as
the Crémant traditionally produced by the champenois (3.6). EC dosage
levels apply, thus *brut* styles of Crémant d'Alsace must be less than 15g/l of
sugar. All Crémant d'Alsace wines must have a minimum of nine months
sur lie.

Appendix 6
Linguistic Analysis

They say that when an Englishman walks into a small Welsh pub, everyone starts talking Welsh, yet very few Welsh can actually speak their mother tongue. If you judge the nationality of a country by the language it speaks, the Celtic nations surrounding England have long since disappeared, although they have their own distinct identity and very strong nationalist passions. What, linguistically, is the nationality of Alsace, which has endured four changes of sovereignty in this century alone? The changing emphasis in the teaching of languages at school at each of these four junctures has complicated the already complex speech pattern of Alsace, providing marked differences according to age and location within the two *départements*.

Replicate the Englishman in a Welsh pub test and sit down at a table in any café in Alsace. If you eavesdrop, they will not withdraw into their own dialect, but you will hear both French and German and the odd smattering of something quite different, which will be snippets from the Alsace dialect. The conversation can drift from one language to another, sometimes changing in mid-sentence.

The last official census was 1979, which gives a very precise overview of the linguistic pattern, albeit one that has shifted slightly with time. An opinion poll was taken in 1986, but its statistics are obviously less accurate than an official survey of the entire population and it is not sufficiently up-to-date to make it worth muddying the waters with another set of figures.

In 1979, 75 per cent of the population spoke and understood the Alsace .dialect, 8 per cent understood it but could not speak it, while 17 per cent could neither speak nor understand it. In the Bas-Rhin, the figures were 77 per cent, 7 per cent and 16 per cent and in the Haut-Rhin, they were 73 per cent, 9 per cent and 18 per cent respectively. The dialect is more widespread in rural areas (88 per cent) than urban (60 per cent), with the highest concentrations in the very north of Bas-Rhin and the very south of Haut-Rhin. It is least spoken in Strasbourg, Colmar and Mulhouse, where the migrant population from other parts of France has had an effect.

547

All the above figures relate to people of 15 years or over; for those under 15, the percentages are obviously reduced as Alsace has been increasingly Gallicized in the post-war era, but the dialect does remain surprisingly strong, due to parental influence, with 67 per cent of children capable of both speaking and understanding it in the Bas-Rhin and 59 per cent in the Haut-Rhin. Do not forget that these figures are based on 1979 statistics, thus, in 1992, the 'children' under 15 would in fact be between 13 and 28 years of age, with no percentages known for those under this lower limit, although you could guestimate that they would show merely a very slight whittling down of the old figures.

The following is a region-wide comparison of the Alsace dialect and the German and French languages for population over 15 (over 28 in 1992). Figures are percentages:

	Alsace	German	French
Speak and understand	75	63	100*
Understand but do not speak/write	8	17	–
Do not understand/speak/write	17	20	–

Note * It is 'assumed' that the entire population of Alsace write and speak French, but it is well known that some very old citizens cannot write French and a number of these have difficulty even understanding it.

Welsch

There are scattered settlements, particularly deep within the Vosges mountains, that speak only a specific dialect called Welsch or Walsch (or Walch or Walcha). This has no connection with Wales, although it is indeed a Celtic dialect (or Gallic, Gallic merely being Roman for Celtic). The word Welsch or its several derivatives have come to mean anything westward, where Alsace is not spoken, and originates from the original Celtic inhabitants who were forced up into the higher Vosges by barbarians before the Romans arrived.

Although only Welsch is spoken in the isolated settlements of the Vosges, its linguistic border is not the crest of the Vosges, as often reported, but much further down on the Alsace side. Thus in Riquewihr, the Alsace dialect prevails, but a few kilometres up the road in Fréland, not a word is spoken and Welsch takes over. Similarly, in Kaysersberg the Alsace dialect predominates, yet at Hachimette it is Welsch and the river Weiss becomes La Blanche, separating the two dialects.

Glossary

This attempts to be a comprehensively cross-referenced glossary to most of the technical and tasting terms found in this book. Some of the more straightforward terms may simply be used in a way that assumes a certain level of knowledge that might not exist for some readers, whereas other more involved, technical or possibly contentious terms are not explained in the main body of the book because they would interrupt the flow of the text. You can go for a ride around the glossary if one definition utilizes a word or words you do not fully comprehend. They should all be there. I hope you do not have a wasted journey!

AC   Commonly used abbreviation of *appellation d'origine contrôlée*.
ACETAL   Believed to give mature sparkling wines their biscuity, nutty complexity, acetal is the product of autolysis and is created by a biological condensation of alcohol, acetaldehyde and various esters (chiefly ethyl acetate).
ACETALDEHYDE   The principal aldehyde in all wines, but found in much greater quantities in sherry. In light, unfortified table wines a small amount of acetaldehyde enhances the bouquet, but an excess is undesirable, unstable, half-way to complete oxidation and evokes a sherry-like smell.
ACETIC ACID   With the exception of carbonic gas, this is the most important volatile acid found in wine. Small amounts contribute positively to the attractive flavour of a wine, but larger quantities taste vinegary.
ACIDITY   Essential for the life and vitality of a wine. Too little natural fruit acidity makes a wine dull, flat and short; too much and it is sharp and raw. With just the right balance, the fruit is refreshing and its flavour lingers in the mouth. See **Total acidity** and **pH**.
AFTERTASTE   The flavour and aroma left in the mouth after the wine has been swallowed.
AGES GRACEFULLY   A wine that retains, sometimes even increases, finesse as it ages.
AGGRESSIVE   The opposite of soft and smooth. Young wines can seem aggressive, but may round out with a little time in bottle.

ALDEHYDE   The intermediate stage between an alcohol and an acid, formed during the oxidation of an alcohol. Acetaldehyde is the most important of common wine aldehydes.

ALSACE   The old province of Alsace, which corresponds roughly to the *départements* of the Haut-Rhin and Bas-Rhin.

ALSATIAN   Despite the assertion of André Simon that an Alsatian is a dog (Pierre-Étienne Dopff barks like one if you call him Alsatian) and the preference of authors such as Pamela Vandyke Price for using the French *Alsacien* (sic), Alsatian is correct and does not offend French authors or translators, who freely use the term. For an English author, the use of some French terms can be legitimate, but the constant use of *alsacien* (or *alsacienne*, as the gender of the case may be) in a book such as this would be as affected as insisting on *parisien* or *parisienne*, when Parisian would do nicely. Alsatian should no more offend Alsatians than German shepherds, which is the dog's correct title, anyway. What about Dalmatians and Eskimos? Life would become complicated if we should not refer to certain people because dogs are named after them. Don't mention Afghans (because of the hound), Belgians (sheepdog), Irish (terrier and wolfhound), Scottish (terrier and deerhound), Welsh (terrier and corgi). The list goes on and, of course, you know what toy spaniels the English are!

AMPELOGRAPHER   Somebody who studies, records and identifies the vine.

AMYLIC   Refers to amyl or isoamyl acetate, which is produced naturally during the vinification process and in proportionately greater quantities the lower the fermentation temperature. In its pure form, amyl acetate is commercially known as 'banana oil' or 'pear oil'.

ANTIOXIDANT   Substance used for counteracting oxidation (e.g. sulphur-dioxide, ascorbic acid).

AOC   Commonly used abbreviation of *appellation d'origine contrôlée*.

AOC ALSACE   An area of 20,244.84 hectares (13,487 of which are under vine), spread over the *départements* of the Haut-Rhin and Bas-Rhin.

APPELLATION D'ORIGINE CONTRÔLÉE   The first national wine regime ever implemented, it is a guarantee of origin system with rudimentary quality controls that accounts for 20–25 per cent of French wine production.

AROMA   This should really be confined to the fresh and fruity smells reminiscent of grapes, rather than the more winey or bottle-mature complexities of bouquet; but is not always possible to use the word in its purest form, hence aroma and bouquet may be read as synonymous. An aroma can also be a single smell, in which case a bouquet would be a combination of aromas. See also **primary aroma**, **secondary aroma** and **tertiary aroma**.

AROMATIC GRAPE VARIETIES   The most aromatic classic grapes are

Gewurztraminer, Muscat, Riesling and Sauvignon Blanc.

ASCORBIC ACID   This acid, otherwise known as vitamin C, is used as an antioxidant in winemaking.

ASEPTIC   Free from micro-organisms that could be harmful to wine.

ASSEMBLAGE   A French term for the operation of putting together a blend, usually of base wines for a sparkling wine, but could be legitimately applied to the blending of any wine.

ATMOSPHERES   A measure of atmospheric pressure: 1 atmosphere = 15 pounds per square inch. The average internal pressure of a bottle of Crémant is four atmospheres.

ATTACK   A wine with good attack suggests one that is complete, and readily presents its full armament of taste characteristics to the palate. The wine is likely to be youthful rather than mature and its attack augurs well for its future.

AUSLESE   A category of German QmP wine above Spätlese, but below Beerenauslese, it is very sweet and made from late-picked grapes that may be botrytis affected. Depending which German region the wine is made in, an Auslese will have a minimum must weight of between 83 and 105° Oechsle.

AUTOLYSIS   The autolytic effect of ageing a wine on its lees is not desired in most wines, the two exceptions being those bottled *sur lie* and sparkling wines. Yeast autolysis occurs after the yeast has completed its primary function of fermentation. The expended cells collect as sediment where they undergo an enzymatic breakdown known as autolysis. This contributes to the 'champagny' character of a sparkling wine and, in a much lesser form, adds a creamy fullness to the fruit of a wine bottled *sur lie* (the extra freshness such wines are noted for comes from the fact that to bottle *sur lie*, the wine cannot be racked or filtered, and thus contains significantly more CO_2). Autolysis creates acetal, which helps to develop the biscuity complexity of a sparkling wine. It also releases reducing enzymes, which inhibit oxidation, thus sparkling wines need significantly less SO_2 than ordinary still ones. Autolysis also absorbs certain yeast nutrients that are essential for fermentation, which is one reason that sparkling wines do not referment when the final dosage of sugar is added.

BALANCE   The harmonious relationship between acid, alcohol, fruit, tannin and other natural elements.

BANANA   Although banana is an amylic aroma most commonly found in many white wines that have been cool-fermented, there is a certain banana characteristic that is specific to the youthful character of fine quality Gewurztraminer and Tokay-Pinot Gris. This banana is distinguished from the cool-fermented amylic aroma by a discernible degree of finesse, which varies according to the intrinsic quality of the wine. The amount of banana aroma and its relative finesse are a good guide to the degree and complexity of spice that will eventually build up with bottle-age.

BARREL-FERMENTED New barrels impart a distinctly oaky character, whereas the older the barrel, the less oaky and more oxidative the wine will be. Whether new or old, barrel-fermented wines have more complex aromas than wines that have simply been matured in wood.

BARRIQUE A term used to indicate a wine that has been fermented or matured in small oak barrels. Although French, it is a word that is increasingly used on labels in Germany, thus an obvious choice for Alsace.

BAS-RHIN One of the two *départements* that comprise the former province of Alsace.

BEERENAUSLESE A category of German QmP wine above Auslese, but below Trockenbeerenauslese, it is intensely sweet and made from late-picked, botrytized grapes. Depending which German region the wine is made in, a Beerenauslese will have a minimum must weight of between 110 and 128° Oechsle.

BENTONITE A fine clay containing a volcanic ash derivative otherwise called montromillonite. It is hydrated silicate of magnesium and activates a precipitation in wine when used as a fining agent. It is negatively charged and therefore used to fine out positive charged suspensions such as protein. Bentonite fining is commonly applied before fermentation, but may also be utilized afterwards to clear any remaining suspensions (e.g. protein haze).

BIG VINTAGE YEAR Terms usually applied to great years, because the exceptional weather conditions produce bigger (i.e. fuller, richer) wines than normal. May also be used literally to describe a year with a big crop.

BIG WINE A full-bodied wine with an exceptionally rich flavour.

BIODYNAMIC Wines produced biodynamically are grown without the aid of chemical or synthetic sprays or fertilizers and vinified with natural yeast and the minimum use of filtration, SO_2 and chaptalization.

BISCUITY A desirable aspect of bouquet found in some quality sparkling wines and thought to be due to acetal or, if coarser in character, could be derived from a certain preponderance of acetaldehyde.

BITE A very definite qualification of grip. Usually a desirable characteristic, but an unpleasant 'bite' is possible.

BITTERNESS (1) An unpleasant aspect of a poorly made wine. (2) An expected characteristic in some Italian wines. (3) The result of an as yet undeveloped concentration of flavours that should, with maturity, become rich and delicious. An edge of bitterness may result from raw tannin.

BLIND, BLIND TASTING An objective tasting where the identity of wines is unknown to the taster until after he or she has made notes and given scores. All competitive tastings are blind.

BLOWZY An overblown and exaggerated fruity aroma and smell, often attributed to basic Californian wines. It is something that experts feel is vulgar, while many consumers find it flattering.

BODY The extract of fruit and alcoholic strength that together give an impression of weight in the mouth.

BOTRYTIS   Literally rot, which is usually an unwanted disorder of the vine, but *Botrytis cinerea* or noble rot is necessary for the production of the finest quality of sweet wines and, perhaps confusingly, it is commonly contracted to botrytis or botrytized grapes, when discussing such wines.

BOTRYTIS CINEREA   The technically correct name for noble rot, the only rot that is not simply welcome by winemakers, but quite emphatically longed for in the sweet wines areas.

BOTRYTIZED GRAPES   Literally 'rotten grapes', but commonly used for grapes that have been affected by *Botrytis cinerea*.

BOTTLE-AGE   The length of time a wine spends in bottle before it is consumed. A wine that has good bottle-age is one that has sufficient time to mature properly. The development in bottle is more reductive than oxidative.

BOUQUET   This should really be applied to the combination of smells directly attributable to a wine's maturity in bottle – thus aroma for grape and bouquet for bottle. But it is not always possible to use these words in their purest form, hence aroma and bouquet may be read as synonymous.

BREED   The finesse of a wine that is due to the intrinsic quality of grape and *terroir* combined with the irrefutable skill and experience of a great winemaker.

BRUT   Normally reserved for sparkling wines, *brut* literally means raw or bone dry, but in practice there is always some sweetness and so it can at the most only be termed dry. It is the necessarily high acidity of sparkling wines (to carry the flavour through the bubbles on to the palate) that demands that a *brut* wine be sweetened with up to 15 grams per litre of sugar. Only a sparkling wine described as Extra Brut will contain no added sugar, but most Crémant d'Alsace wines are made in the *brut* style.

BUTTERY   A rich, fat and positively delicious character found in many white wines, particularly if produced in a great vintage or warm country. Many Tokay-Pinot Gris can be described as buttery.

CARBON DIOXIDE   This is naturally produced in the fermentation process, when the sugar is converted into almost equal parts of alcohol and carbon dioxide or CO_2. The CO_2 is normally allowed to escape as a gas, although a tiny amount will always be present in its dissolved form (H_2CO_3) in any wine, even a still one, otherwise it would taste dull, flat and lifeless. If the gas is prevented from escaping, the wine becomes sparkling.

CARBONIC ACID   This is the correct term for carbon dioxide (or CO_2) when dissolved in water (H_2O), which is the main ingredient of wine, and carbonic acid is thus expressed as H_2CO_3. It is sometimes referred to as a volatile acid, although the acid is held in equilibrium with the gas in its dissolved state and cannot be isolated in its pure form.

CARBONIC GAS   Synonymous with carbon dioxide.

CASEIN   A milk protein sometimes used for fining.

CASK-FERMENTED   Synonymous with barrel-fermented.

CEDARWOOD   Purely a subjective word applied to a particular bouquet associated with the bottle maturity of a wine previously stored or fermented in wood, usually oak.

CENTRIFUGAL FILTRATION   Not filtration in the pure sense, but a process whereby unwanted matter is separated from wine or grape juice by so-called centrifugal force.

CHAPTALIZATION   The practice of adding sugar to fresh grape juice to raise a wine's alcoholic potential. Theoretically it takes 1.7 kilograms of sugar per hectolitre of wine to raise the alcoholic strength by one percentage point, but red wines actually require 2 kilograms to allow for evaporation during the remontage. The term chaptalization is named after Antoine Chaptal, a brilliant chemist and technocrat who served Napoleon as minister of the interior from 1800 to 1805 and instructed winegrowers on the advantages of adding sugar at the time of pressing.

CHARM   Another subjective term: if a wine charms, it appeals without blatantly attracting in an obvious fashion.

CHÂTEAU   This French term literally means a castle or stately home. Whereas many château-bottled wines do actually come from magnificent edifices that could truly be described as châteaux in every sense of the word, many may be modest one-storey villas and some are no more than purpose-built cuveries, while a few are merely tin sheds!

CHEWY   An extreme qualification of meaty.

CHLOROSIS   A vine disorder caused by mineral imbalance (too much lime, not enough iron or magnesium), which is often called green sickness.

CHOCOLATE   Often used to describe the odour and flavour of Pinot Noir wines. It is not as esoteric as it sounds because chocolate is used in Spanish cookery to give a winey taste to stews and casseroles when no wine is available. The fruity character of a wine can become chocolatey in wines with a pH above 3.6.

CITRUS, CITRUSY   A subjective term for a tangy fruit flavour found in some white wines that is more racy than lemony and suggests a certain finesse. It is closely associated with the petrol character of a fine, mature Riesling.

CLASSIC, CLASSY   Both subjective words to convey an obvious impression of quality. These terms are applied to wines that not only portray the correct characteristics for their type and origin, but possess the finesse and style indicative of top quality wines.

CLEAN   A straightforward term applied to a wine devoid of any unwanted or unnatural undertones of aroma and flavour.

CLONE   A variety of vine that has developed differently due to a process of selection, either natural, as in the case of a vine adapting to local conditions, or by man.

CLOSED   Refers to the nose or palate of a wine not showing very much at all and implies that some of these qualities are 'hidden' and should develop with time in bottle.

CLOYING The sickly and sticky character of a poor sweet wine, where the finish is heavy and often unclean.

CO_2 The chemical symbol for carbon dioxide.

COARSE A term that should be applied to a rough and ready wine, not necessarily unpleasant, but certainly not fine.

COCHYLIS A parasitic moth that usually lays its eggs on the buds of a vine in the spring or summer and, depending when the eggs hatch, the larvae will feed on tender shoots, flowers or fruit.

COMPACT FRUIT This term suggests a good weight of fruit with a correct balance of tannin (if red) and acidity that is presented on the nose and palate in a manner that is opposite to open-knit.

COMPLETE Refers to a satisfaction in the mouth indicating that the wine has everything: fruit, tannin, acidity, depth, length, etc.

COMPLEXITY Refers to many different nuances of smell or taste. Great wines in their youth may have a certain complexity, but it is only with maturity in bottle that a wine will eventually achieve its potential in terms of complexity.

COOL-FERMENTED Term commonly used (and misused) for white wines fermented at between 10 and 15° C and maintained at that temperature through various cooling devices.

CORRECT A wine with all the correct characteristics for its type and origin. Not necessarily an exciting wine, but one that cannot be faulted.

CORKED Correctly used, the term applies to the cause, a penicillin infection inside the cork, at one time an infrequent occurrence, rather than anything inherently wrong with the wine. Sadly, infected corks are turning up quite regularly these days and can be recognized by an almost green, musty-woody aspect of smell and flavour.

COULURE A physiological disorder of the vine that occurs as a result of alternating periods of warm and cold, dry and wet conditions after the bud-break. If this culminates in a flowering during which the weather is too sunny, the sap rushes past the embryo bunches to the shoot-tips, causing vigorous growth of foliage, but denying the clusters an adequate supply of essential nutrients and the barely formed berries dry up and drop to the ground. While no grower likes imperfect flowering, its yield-reducing effect has had its positive effects. It was coulure combined with a crop-cutting spring-frost and a long, hot, dry summer that created the legendary 1961 vintage in Bordeaux – without the coulure it would have been excellent, with it, it was one of the three greatest vintages of all time.

CREAMY A subjective term used to convey the impression of a creamy flavour that may be indicative of the variety of grape or method of vinification. Sweet botrytis wines are often very creamy.

CREAMY-OAK A more subtle, lower-key version of the vanilla-oak character that is most probably derived from wood lactones during maturation in small oak barrels.

CROSS   A cross is a vine that has been propagated by crossing two or more varieties within the same species (*Vitis vinifera*, for example), while a hybrid is a cross between two or more varieties from more than one species.

CRYPTOGAMIC   Refers to fungoid or fungus-based disease like grey rot.

CRISP   A clean wine, with good acidity showing on the finish, yielding a fresh and positive aftertaste.

CRU   French term meaning a 'growth' that may be used in some official classifications, such as *grand cru*, or simply as synonymous with *lieu-dit*.

CUT   There are two common uses for this term: (1) In blending, a wine of a specific character may be used to cut a wine dominated by an opposite quality. This can range from a bland wine that is cut by a small quantity of very acidic wine, through a white wine that is cut with a little red wine to make a rosé (allowed only in Champagne), to the illegal practice of diluting wine with water. (2) In matching food and wine, a wine with high acidity may be used to cut the organoleptic effect of grease from a grilled or fried dish, or an oily fish, just as the effervescence of a fine sparkling wine cuts the creamy texture of certain sauces and soups.

CUVAISON   The French term for that part of the fermentation period of a red wine when the juice is kept in contact with its skins.

CUVÉE   A French term meaning a specific blend, such as Cuvée Frédéric-Émile (F.E. Trimbach).

CUVERIE, CUVIER   The French name for a room or building housing the fermenting vats.

DEFINITION   A wine with good definition is one that is clean, with a correct balance of acidity, tannin and fruit and a positive expression of varietal character.

DÉGORGEMENT   The French for disgorgement.

DELICATE   Describes the quieter characteristics of quality that give a wine charm.

DEMETER   An organization to which some biodynamic producers belong.

DEPTH   Refers first to a wine's depth of flavour and, second, to its depth of interest.

DIRTY   Applies to any wine with an unpleasant off-taste or off-smell, probably the result of poor vinification or bad bottling.

DISGORGEMENT   The sediment created during the second fermentation of sparkling wines made by the *méthode champenoise* is disgorged prior to sale.

DISTINCTIVE   A wine with a positive character. All fine wines are distinctive to one degree or another, but not all distinctive wines are necessarily fine.

DOWNY MILDEW   A cryptogamic disorder of the vine, also referred to variously as false mildew, peronospora and plasmopara.

DRYING UP   A wine that has lost some of its freshness and fruit through age in the bottle. It may still be enjoyable, but all remaining bottles should be drunk up quickly.

DUSTY   Akin to peppery in a red wine or a blurring of varietal definition in a white wine.

EARTHY   A drying impression in the mouth. Some wines can be enjoyably earthy, but finest quality wines should be as clean as a whistle.

EASY   A simple, enjoyable quality in a wine, probably soft and cheap.

EDGE   Almost, but not quite, synonymous with grip, a wine can have an edge of bitterness or tannin. Edge usually implies that a wine has the capacity to develop, while grip may be applied to a wine in various stages of development, including fully mature.

EDGY   Synonymous with nervous.

EISWEIN   Originally a German concept, this rare wine resulted from the tradition of leaving grapes on the vine in the hope of attracting noble rot. If frost or snow freezes the grapes and they are harvested and pressed in their frozen state, an Eiswein may be produced, but only if the ice that rises to the top of the vat is scraped off to leave the concentrated juice for fermentation. When grapes freeze, it is the water that freezes first; thus, when it is removed, a remarkably rich wine with a unique balance of sweetness, acidity and extract can result. In Germany, an Eiswein is technically in the same ripeness category as Beerenauslese, which is above Auslese, but below Trockenbeerenauslese, with a minimum must weight of between 110 and 128° Oechsle, the variation depending on the German region in which the wine is made.

ELEGANT   A subjective term applied to wines with a certain style and finesse.

EMBRYO BUNCHES   In spring, the vine develops little clusters of miniature green berries that will bloom a few weeks later. If a berry successfully flowers, it is capable of developing into a grape and the embryo bunch is thus an indication of the potential size of the crop.

ESTERS   Sweet-smelling compounds, contributing to the aroma and bouquet of a wine, formed during fermentation and throughout the process of maturation.

ETHANOIC ACID   Synonymous with acetic acid.

ETHANOL   Synonymous with ethyl alcohol.

ETHYL ALCOHOL   The main alcohol in wine is so important in quantitative terms that to speak of a wine's alcohol is to refer purely to its ethyl alcohol content.

EUDEMIS   A parasitic moth that usually lays its eggs on the buds of a vine in the spring or summer and, depending when the eggs hatch, the larvae will feed on tender shoots, flowers or fruit.

EVERYDAY WINES   Inexpensive, easy drinking wines.

EXPRESSIVE   A wine that is expressive is true to its grape variety and *terroir*.

EXTRACT   Sugar-free soluble solids that give body to a wine. The term covers everything from proteins and vitamins to tannins, calcium and iron.

FALSE MILDEW   A cryptogamic disorder of the vine, also referred to variously as downy mildew, peronospora and plasmopara.

FAN-LEAF   Called *court-noué* in France, this viral disease is spread by the Xiphinema index and causes stunted shoots, leaf deformity and poor fruit set.

FARMYARDY   A term used by many people to describe a wine, quite often from a Pinot variety, that has matured through its initial freshness of fruit, past the desired stage of roundness and the pleasing phase when it acquires certain vegetal undertones. The wine is still healthy and drinkable – for some, it is at the very peak of perfection.

FAT   A wine full in body and extract.

FATTY ACIDS   A term sometimes used for volatile acids.

FERMENTATION   The biochemical process by which enzymes secreted by yeast cells convert sugar molecules into almost equal parts of alcohol and carbonic gas.

FILTER, FILTRATION   There are various methods of filtration that entail passing the wine or juice through a medium that prevents particles of a certain size from passing.

FINE WINES   Quality wines, representing only a small percentage of all wines produced. Great wines are the very élite of this section.

FINESSE   That elusive, indescribable quality separating a fine wine from those of slightly lesser quality.

FINING   The clarification of fresh grape juice or wine is often speeded up by the use of various fining agents, such as tannin, gelatine, egg white, bentonite, etc. Fining agents operate by an electrolytic reaction to fine out oppositely charged matter.

FINISH   The quality and enjoyment of a wine's aftertaste and the length of time it continues.

FIRM   Refers to a certain amount of grip. A firm wine is a wine of good constitution, held up with a certain amount of tannin or acidity.

FIRST LEAF   The first twelve months in the life of a vine after its grafting is often called its first leaf, referring to its first vegetative cycle. Such vines rarely produce fruit and even if they do, the grapes do not qualify for AOC; thus it is in the interest of the grower to cut off any clusters that may appear, to encourage the young vine to concentrate its limited resources on building the overall plant structure.

FIRST PRESSING   The first pressing yields the sweetest, cleanest, clearest juice.

FIXED ACIDITY   This is the total acidity less the volatile acidity.

FIXED SULPHUR   The principal reason SO_2 is added to grape juice and wine is to prevent oxidation, but only free sulphur can do this. Upon contact with wine, some SO_2 immediately combines with oxygen and other elements, such as sugars and acids, and what remains is free sulphur, capable of combining with molecules of oxygen at some future date. That which is combined is known as fixed or bound sulphur.

FLABBY   The opposite of crisp, referring to a wine lacking in acidity and consequently dull, weak and short.

FLESHY   A wine with plenty of fruit and extract.

FOUDRE   A large wooden cask or vat.

FOXY   The very distinctive, highly perfumed character of certain indigenous American grape varieties that can be sickly sweet and cloying to unconditioned European or antipodean palates.

FREE-RUN JUICE   The juice that runs free from the press, under the pressure of its own weight, before the pressing operations begin, in the case of white wine, and the fermented red wine that is drained off from the *manta*. It is the richest wine in both cases.

FREE SULPHUR   The active element of SO_2 in wine, free sulphur combines with intruding molecules of oxygen.

FRESH, FRESHNESS   Wines that are clean and still vital with youth.

FRUIT   Wine is made from grapes and must therefore be 100 per cent fruit, yet it will not have a fruity flavour unless the grapes used have the correct combination of ripeness and acidity.

FULL   Usually refers to body, e.g. full-bodied. But a wine can be light in body yet full in flavour.

FULLY FERMENTED   A wine that is allowed to complete its natural course of fermentation and thus yield a totally dry wine.

GELATINE   A positively charged fining agent used for removing negatively charged suspended matter, especially an excess of tannin, in wines.

GENERIC   A wine, usually blended, of a general *appellation*.

GENEROUS   A generous wine gives its fruit freely on the palate, while an ungenerous wine is likely to have little or no fruit and, probably, an excess of tannin. All wines should have some degree of generosity.

GOOD GRIP   A healthy structure of tannin supporting the fruit in a wine.

GOÛT DE TERROIR   A French term for an earthy taste.

GRAFT   The joint between the rootstock and the scion of the producer vine.

GRAPEY   Can be applied to the aroma and flavour of a wine that is reminiscent of grapes rather than wine. This is not as common as might be imagined, unless the wine is from Muscat or Gewurztraminer.

GREEN   Young and tart, as in Vinho Verde. It can be either a derogatory term, or simply an indication of youthful wine that might well improve.

GREEN SICKNESS   A common name for chlorosis, a vine disorder caused by mineral imbalance (too much lime, not enough iron or magnesium).

GRIP   A term applied to a firm wine with a positive finish. A wine showing grip on the finish indicates a certain bite of acidity and, if red, tannin.

GROWTH   Literally a translation of *cru*, it is commonly used to describe one specific vineyard as in, for example, a *grand cru*.

GUTSY   A wine full in body, fruit, extract and, usually, alcohol. Normally applied to ordinary quality wines.

GYROPALETTE   Metal cage capable of holding approximately 500 bottles, which can easily be mounted on to motorized frames that rotate and tilt the cage, usually by way of a computerized program, some of which can be adapted to suit the user, while others have two or three set programs.

HARSH   A more derogatory form of coarse.

HAUT-RHIN   One of the two *départements* that comprise the former province of Alsace.

HERBAL, HERBAL-OAK   Herbal-oak is applied to certain wines that are matured in cask, but unlike vanilla-oak, creamy-oak, smoky-oak and spicy-oak, the probable cause is unknown. A herbal character devoid of oak is usually derived from the varietal character of a grape and is common to many varieties.

HOLLOW   A wine that appears to lack any real flavour in the mouth compared with the promise shown on the nose.

HONEST   Applied to any wine, usually of a fairly basic quality, that is true in character to its type and origin and does not give any indication of being souped-up or blended in any unlawful way. 'Honest' is more honest than 'typical'.

HYDROGEN SULPHIDE   When hydrogen combines with sulphur, the result is a smell of bad eggs. If this occurs prior to bottling and is dealt with immediately it can be rectified by the winemaker but, if allowed to progress, the hydrogen sulphide can develop into mercaptans and ruin the wine.

IRON   Found as a trace element in fresh grapes grown in soils where relatively substantial ferrous deposits are located. Therefore wines from such sites may naturally contain a tiny amount of iron barely perceptible on the palate. If there is too much, the flavour becomes medicinal. Above 7 mg/litre for white, 10 mg/litre for red, there is a danger of the wine going cloudy.

ISINGLASS   A gelatinous fining agent obtained from the swim-bladder of freshwater fish and used to clear hazy, low-tannin wines.

JAMMY   Commonly used to describe a fat and eminently drinkable red wine, rich in fruit if perhaps a bit contrived and lacking a certain elegance.

LACTIC ACID   The 'milk-acid', so-called because it is the acid that develops in sour milk, is created during the malolactic fermentation.

LEACHING   A term sometimes used when referring to the deliberate removal of tannin from new oak by steaming, or when discussing certain aspects of soil, such as pH, that can be affected when carbonates are leached by rainwater.

LEES The sediment deposited during fermentation, lees consist mostly of dead yeast cells, which undergo autolysis, a decaying process that is a possible source of bacterial infection, thus most wines are racked several times prior to bottling. A wine described on the label as *sur lie* has been kept on its lees until bottling.

LEMONY Many dry and medium-sweet white wines have a tangy, fruity acidity that is suggestive of lemons.

LENGTH Refers to a wine where the flavour lingers in the mouth a long time after swallowing.

LIE The French for lees.

LIEU-DIT The French for a named site and commonly used in Alsace for specific growths that do not have *grand cru* status, although it could as easily apply to those that do.

LIGHT VINTAGE, YEAR A year that produces relatively light wines. Not a great vintage, but not necessarily a bad one either.

LINGERING Normally applied to the finish of a wine – an aftertaste that literally lingers.

LIQUOROUS Literally liqueur-like, this term is often applied to dessert wines of an unctuous and viscous quality.

LIQUORICE A characteristic concentration of flavours from heat-shrivelled, rather than botrytis-shrivelled, grapes.

LIVELINESS A term that usually implies a certain youthful freshness of fruit due to good acidity and an above average carbonic gas content.

MACERATION A term that is usually applied to the period during the cuvaison when the fermenting juice is in contact with its skins. This traditionally involves red winemaking, but it is on the increase for white wines utilizing prefermentation maceration techniques.

MALIC A tasting term that describes the green apple aroma and flavour found in some young wines, due to the presence of malic acid, the dominant acid found in apples.

MALIC ACID A very strong-tasting acid that is reduced during the fruit's ripening process, but a quantity persists in ripe grapes and, though reduced by fermentation, in wine too. The quantity of malic acid present in a wine may be considered too much, particularly for a red wine, and the smoothing effect of replacing it with just two-thirds the quantity of the much weaker lactic acid is often desirable.

MALOLACTIC The so-called malolactic fermentation is sometimes referred to as a secondary fermentation, but both 'secondary' and fermentation are inappropriate. The malolactic, or malo, as it may simply be called, is a biochemical process that converts the hard malic acid of unripe grapes into soft lactic or 'milk-acid' (so-called because it is the acid of sour milk) and carbonic gas. To ensure that this can take place, it is essential that specific bacteria be present. These are found naturally on grape skins among the yeasts and other micro-organisms and to undertake their task, they require a medium that consists of a certain warmth, a low level of sulphur, a pH between 3 and 4 and a supply of various nutrients found naturally in grape juice. This is easily achieved with today's technology, although it was often hit or miss in the past.

MANTA   The cap of skins that rises to the top of a vat during the cuvaison.

MARC   The residue of skins, pips and stalks after pressing.

MARQUE   A brand or make.

MATURE, MATURITY   Refer to a wine's development in bottle, as opposed to ripe, which is a state of maturity of the grape itself.

MEAN   An extreme qualification of ungenerous.

MELLOW   Round and at its peak of maturity.

MERCAPTANS   Methyl and ethyl alcohols can react with hydrogen sulphide to form mercaptans, foul-smelling compounds that are often impossible to remove and can thus ruin a wine. Mercaptans can smell of garlic, onion, burnt rubber or stale cabbage.

MILDEW   Generic name used for cryptogamic diseases of powdery mildew and downy mildew.

MILLERANDAGE   A physiological disorder of the vine that occurs after cold or wet weather at the time of the flowering. This makes fertilization very difficult, consequently many berries fail to develop and remain small and seedless even when the rest of bunch is full-sized and ripe.

MINERAL   Some wines can have a minerally aftertaste that can range from pleasant to unpleasant. Riesling grown on granite soil often has a perceivable mineral complexity.

MOUSSE   The effervescence of a sparkling wine, which is deceiving in a glass and can best be judged in the mouth. (The same wine may appear to be flat in one glass and vigorous in another due to the different surfaces, which could in turn be due to either manufacture or the washing up!) The bubbles should be small and persistent, with the strength of effervescence dependent on the style of wine.

MOUSSEUX   French for sparkling wine.

NEMATODE   Tiny, threadlike, parasitic or ectoparasitic worm that can transmit various viral diseases to the vine.

NERVY, NERVOUS   A subjective term usually applied to a dry white wine that is firm and vigorous, but not quite settled down.

NOBLE ROT   The fungus *Botrytis cinerea* responsible for the world's greatest sweet wines and the term often used to describe the fascinating complexity of aroma and flavour found intrinsically in all such wines. Also known as Edelfäule in Germany and Edelkeur in South Africa.

NOSE   The smell or odour of a wine, encompassing both aroma and bouquet.

OAK, OAKY, OAK-AGED, OAK-MATURED   Oak casks are often used for the maturation of wines and, less frequently, for their fermentation. Such wines often display a positively vanilla odour from the aldehyde vanillin found naturally in oak, but it is not simply a matter of whether a wine is aged in oak or not, nor is it as simple as how oaky it is. The type, degree, subtlety and complexity of oak on the bouquet and flavour of a wine are affected by many contributing factors: the type of oak (Limousin, Nevers, etc.), whether it was kiln-dried or weathered (and how long it was weathered), if it was sawn or split (and how it was sawn or split), the degree to which the barrel was toasted during its manufacture, the size of the barrel, whether it was new or had been used (and, if so, how many times), if the wine was barrel-fermented in addition to oak-aged, the length of time the wine was kept in wood. And wines react differently to the same barrel-fermentation and oak-ageing conditions according to their levels of acidity, tannin and alcohol. The sum of the effect of all these factors determines not only the degree of oak encountered in a wine, but also the type of oak character detected. There are in my vocabulary five basic oak-influenced aromas and flavours: vanilla-oak, creamy-oak, smoky-oak, spicy-oak and herbal-oak. A wine may be predominantly of one category or a combination of two, three, four or all five and the result can induce the use of many subjective words, including cedarwood, cigar-box and, in higher pH wines, chocolate-box. Relatively little new wood is used in Alsace, even though there has been something of a trend towards it for the odd *cuvée* by some of the younger winemakers in the region. What does exist has been weathered and split, as is the norm in France, with just light or medium toast. Ironically, while I have encountered many New World winemakers who have gone to great expense to ship Vosges wood half-way around the world, most oak used in Alsace has originated from the centre of France and been coopered in Burgundy.

OECHSLE   A Germanic system for measuring the sugar in grape juice based on its density: thus 1° Oechsle is the equivalent of a specific gravity (SG) of 1.001, 50° Oechsle equals 1.050 SG, 75° Oechsle 1.075, etc.

OENOLOGY, OENOLOGIST   The scientific study of wine is a branch of chemistry and a wine chemist is known as an oenologist or, in France, an *oenologue*. The 'o' is not pronounced in English and Americans even spell these words as enology and enologist.

OFF VINTAGE, YEAR   A year in which many poor wines are produced due to adverse climatic conditions, such as very little sunshine during the summer, which can result in unripe grapes, or rain or humid heat at the harvest, which can result in rot. Generally a vintage to be avoided, but approach any opportunity to taste the wines with an open mind because there are always good wines made in every vintage, however poor, and they have to be sold at bargain prices due to its widespread bad reputation.

OIDIUM   A cryptogamic disease of the vine that is recognized by a white powdery deposit on the shoots, upper surfaces of the leaves and young berries (it seldom attacks ripe grapes). Also known as powdery mildew, true mildew or *Uncinula necator*.

OPENKNIT   An open and enjoyable nose or palate; usually a modest wine that is not capable of very much development.

OPULENT   Suggestive of a rather luxurious varietal aroma, very rich, but not quite blowzy.

ORGANIC WINES   A generic term covering wines that are produced with the minimum amount of SO_2, from grapes that have been grown without chemical fertilizers, pesticides or herbicides. There are many terms on a label that can reveal the organically produced origin of a wine: 'Produit de l'Agriculture Biologique', 'Culture Biologique', 'Production de la Méthode Agrobiologique', 'Nature & Progrès', 'Ce vin provient de vignes cultivées sans engrais, sans herbicide, sans insecticide'.

ORGANOLEPTIC   Affecting a bodily organ or sense, usually taste and smell.

OSMOTIC PRESSURE   When two solutions are separated by a semi-permeable membrane, water will leave the weaker solution for the other in an endeavour to create an equilibrium. In winemaking terms this is most usually encountered when yeast cells are expected to work in grape juice with an exceptionally high sugar content. Since water accounts for 65 per cent of a yeast cell, osmotic pressure causes the water to escape through its semi-permeable exterior. The cell caves in, a phenomenon called plasmolysis, and the yeast dries up, eventually dying, after which autolysis may occur.

OVERTONE   A dominating element of nose or palate and usually one that is not directly attributable to the grape or wine, e.g. oak.

OXIDATION, OXIDIZED   These terms are ambiguous. From the moment grapes are pressed or crushed, oxidation sets in and the juice or wine at every stage of its development is oxidized to one extent or another. Oxidation is an essential and unavoidable element of fermentation and, combined with reduction, it is the process by which wine matures in bottle. All wine is therefore oxidized to a certain extent and it is really the rate and degree of oxidation that matter. These terms have been generally misused as a form of condemnation for so long that it would seem pedantic to describe a wine as too oxidized.

OXIDATIVE   Wine matures by an interaction of reductive and oxidative processes, the latter being recognized by characteristics that range from being so subtle that they merely bridge the divide between the smell of fermentation and the aroma of young wine, through various complexities to absolute vinegar.

PALATE   The flavour or taste of a wine.

PASSERILLAGE   Grapes without noble rot that are left on the vine are cut off from the plant's metabolic system as its sap withdraws into its roots. In the warmth of the day, followed by the cold of the night, the grapes dehydrate and concentrate in a process known as passerillage and the sweet wine produced from it is prized in certain areas. A passerillage wine from a hot autumn will be totally different to one from a cold autumn.

PEAK The so-called peak in the maturity of a wine is subject to the consumer's point of appreciation. Those liking fresher, crisper wines will perceive an earlier peak (in the same wine) than 'golden-oldy' drinkers. As a rule of thumb a wine will remain at its peak for as long as it took to reach it.

PERONOSPORA A cryptogamic disorder of the vine, also referred to variously as downy mildew, false mildew and plasmopara.

PÉTILLANT A wine with enough residual carbonic gas to create a light sparkle.

PETROL, PETROLLY With some bottle-age, the finest Rieslings have a vivid and zesty bouquet that the cognoscenti refer to as petrolly. To any stranded motorist who has had the misfortune to swallow the tiniest amount of petrol while siphoning fuel from one car to another, it is obvious that the smell of even the most petrolly Riesling has nothing to do with the stuff put into petrol tanks. The petrolly character has, in fact, more affinity with various zesty and citrusy odours, but there are so many lemony, limy, citrusy, zesty smells that are totally different from one another and the Riesling's petrolly character is both singular and unmistakable. Objectively, its use is baffling and misleading, yet, from a practical point of view, it is one of the few words of wine vocabulary that actually communicates quickly and accurately a specific characteristic from one taster to another.

PH A measure of active acidity or alkalinity. It does not give any indication of the total acidity of a wine, but neither does the palate. When we perceive the acidity in wine, it is more closely associated with the pH than the total acidity. Also used for measuring the active acidity or alkalinity of soil. A pH of 7 is neutral; above 7 is increasingly alkaline, below 7 increasingly acid, thus in terms of acidity, it is a reverse ratio, the lower the pH, the higher the acidity. This is, however, active acidity, not total. Wines of different total acidity can have the same pH and wines of the same total acidity can have different pH levels. Most wines have a pH of between 3.1 and 3.4, although some can range from 2.7 to 3.9 and white wines are naturally lower than red wines.

PHYLLOXERA Full name *Phylloxera vastatrix*, this is a vine louse that spread from America in the late nineteenth century to virtually every viticultural region in the world. New vines had (and still have) to be grafted to phylloxera-resistant American rootstocks.

PIQUANT Usually applied to a pleasing white wine with a positive underlying fruit and acidity.

PLASMOPARA A cryptogamic disorder of the vine, also referred to variously as downy mildew, false mildew and peronospora.

POWDERY MILDEW   A cryptogamic disorder of the vine, also referred to variously as true mildew, oidium and *Uncinula necator*.

PREFERMENTATION MACERATION   A much in vogue practice of macerating the juice of white grapes on their skins prior to fermentation. As the skins contain most of the aromatic properties of a grape, this enhances the varietal character.

PRICKLE   Indicates a wine with residual carbonic gas, but with less than the light sparkle of a pétillant, noticeable by a slight prickling effect on the sides and tip of the tongue, pin-prick-sized bubbles forming on the bowl of the glass and, if strong enough, a collection of minuscule bubbles round the rim. It can be desirable in some fresh white and rosé wines, particularly if the wine would otherwise be flabby, as its tactile impression can convince the consumer that he or she is feeling the sharp chemical pinch of acidity. It lifts and enlivens, but is not suitable for *vins de garde* and is usually taken as a sign of an unwanted secondary fermentation in a red wine.

PRIMARY AROMA   One of three fundamental aroma categories; a primary aroma comes from the grape and is not the product of fermentation (secondary), or of bottle or cask development (tertiary).

PRODUCER VINE   Vines are grafted on to a rootstock for resistance against phylloxera, but the grapes produced are characteristic of the above-ground producer vine, which is normally a variety of *Vitis vinifera* and may also be called the scion.

PROTEIN HAZE   Protein is present in all animal and vegetable cells and therefore in all wines. Too much protein can react with tannin and cause a haze in some wine, in which case bentonite is usually used as a fining agent to remove it.

QMP   Commonly abbreviated form of *Qualitätswein mit Prädikat,* which literally means a 'quality wine with predication', the levels of predication starting at Kabinett and going upwards through Spätlese, Auslese, Beerenauslese and Eiswein to Trockenbeerenauslese. The use of these Prädikaten is determined by increasing levels of ripeness, expressed in degrees Oechsle.

RACKED   To rack a wine entails draining it off its lees into a fresh cask or vat and the term derives from the different levels (or racks) from which the wine is run from one container to another. Racking usually involves an aeration of the wine, particularly if it is transferred by pumping. In some wines this is desirable, but in others it is not and can be avoided or reduced by using gravity or by employing an enclosed pumping system that utilizes an inert gas such as nitrogen.

RACY   Often applied to wines of the Riesling grape. It accurately suggests the liveliness, vitality and acidity of this grape.

REDOX   The ageing of wine was originally conceived as purely oxidative, but it was discovered that when one substance in wine oxidized, another reduced, thus it is a *reductive-oxidative* process.

REDUCTION Wine matures by an interaction of reductive and oxidative processes. Organoleptically, however, wines reveal either oxidative or reductive characters.

REDUCTIVE All bottle-fermented wines (e.g. Crémant d'Alsace) are slightly more reductive than oxidative.

REMONTAGE French term for the operation whereby fermenting wine is pumped over the cap or *manta* of skins during the cuvaison.

RETICENT Suggests that the wine is holding back on its nose or palate, perhaps through youth, and may well develop with a little more maturity.

RICH, RICHNESS A balanced wealth of fruit and a good depth on the palate and finish.

RIPE A wine with the richness that only ripe grapes can give. It is the ripeness of grapes, rather than the maturity of wine.

RIPE ACIDITY Ripe grape acidity is tartaric acid, as opposed to malic or unripe acidity.

ROBUST A milder form of 'aggressive', which may often be applied to a mature product, i.e. the wine is robust by nature, not aggressive through youth.

ROOTSTOCK Since the spread of phylloxera in the nineteenth century, the majority of vines in most commercial vineyards have been grafted on to phylloxera-resistant rootstock.

ROUND A wine that, through maturity in bottle, has rounded off all its edges of tannin, acidity, extract, etc.

ROUTE DU VIN In each famous wine area of France there is a well sign-posted *Route du vin* that takes in all the most important wine centres plus ancillary sites of historic interest, and can be followed using a map obtained from the local tourist office.

SCION That part of the graft that belongs to the fruit-and leaf-bearing producer vine, as opposed to the stock, which belongs to the root-producing rootstock.

SEC The French for dry.

SECOND, SECONDARY FERMENTATION Strictly speaking this is the fermentation that occurs in bottle during the *méthode champenoise*, but the term is sometimes mistakenly used to refer to the malolactic fermentation or a continuation of the first or main alcoholic fermentation that can occur with the warmth of spring, after having been stopped by the cold of winter.

SECONDARY AROMA One of three fundamental aroma categories; a secondary aroma is the product of fermentation, not the fruit (primary), or the bottle or cask (tertiary).

SECOND LEAF The second year in the life of a vine, so called because it yields its first leaf in its first year and so on. A vine will not produce much fruit, if any, in its second year and cannot, in any case, be harvested for AOC wines until its third leaf or year.

SHARP This applies to acidity, whereas bitterness applies to tannin. An immature wine might be sharp, but, if used by professional tasters, this term is usually a derogatory one.

SHERRY-LIKE The odour of a wine in an advanced state of oxidation and undesirable in anything other than sherry.

SHORT A wine that may have a good nose and flavour, but which falls short of the finish, the taste quickly disappearing after the wine has been swallowed.

SMOKINESS, SMOKY, SMOKY-COMPLEXITY, SMOKY-OAK Some grapes have a smokiness and a similar character can come from well-toasted oak casks or unfiltered wine.

SMOOTH The opposite of aggressive and more extreme than round.

SO₂ Sulphur dioxide.

SOFT Interchangeable with smooth, although it usually refers to the fruit on the palate, whereas smooth is more often applied to the finish. Soft is very desirable, but 'too soft' is derogatory, implying a weak and flabby wine.

SOLID Interchangeable with firm.

SOUPED-UP Implies a wine has been blended with something richer or more robust. A wine may well be legitimately souped-up, or it could mean that the wine has been played around with. The wine might not be correct, but it could still be very enjoyable.

SOUS MARQUE Another marque under which wines, usually second rate in quality, are offloaded.

SPÄTLESE A category of German QmP wine above Kabinett, but below Auslese; it is quite sweet and made from late-picked grapes that occasionally may be botrytis-affected. Depending which German region the wine is made in, a Spätlese will have a minimum must weight of between 76 and 95° Oechsle.

SPICY A varietal characteristic of certain grapes such as Gewurztraminer. The Tokay-Pinot Gris and Auxerrois definitely also have some spiciness.

SPRITZ, or SPRITZIG Synonymous with *pétillant*.

STUCK FERMENTATION A stuck fermentation is always difficult to rekindle and, even when successful, the wine can taste strangely bitter. The most common causes are high temperature (when the heat rises to 35° C or above), nutrient deficiency (yeast cells die if denied an adequate supply of nutrients) and high sugar content (when yeast cells may die from osmotic pressure).

STYLISH Wines possessing all the subjective qualities of charm, elegance and finesse. A wine might have the 'style' of a certain region or type, but a wine is either stylish or it is not.

SUBTLE Although this should mean a significant yet understated characteristic, it is often used by wine snobs who taste a wine with a famous label, but are unable to detect anything exceptional and need a word to get out of difficulty.

SULPHUR DIOXIDE   An antioxidant with aseptic qualities used in the production of wine. It should not be noticeable in the finished product, but for various reasons a whiff may be detected on recently bottled wines, which a good swirl in the glass or a vigorous decanting should remove. With a few months in bottle this whiff ought to disappear. The acrid odour of sulphur in a wine should, if detected, be akin to the smell of a recently extinguished match. If it has a rotten egg aroma then the wine should be returned to the retailer, as this means the sulphur has reduced to hydrogen sulphide and the wine may well have formed mercaptans that you will not be able to remove.

SUPPLE   Indicates a wine easy to drink, not necessarily soft, but suggesting more ease than simply 'round' does. With age (or in certain wines, Californian, etc.) the tannin in wine becomes supple.

SUPPLE TANNIN   Wine tannin has a characteristically hard tactile effect in the mouth, but it may be described as supple in a mature wine where the tannin has been rounded, but only ripe, hydrolysed tannins can soften. Unripe grape tannins and stalk and pip tannins will never round and soften.

SUR LIE   A term most commonly seen on the label of Muscadet, although few such wines are *sur lie* in the true sense of a wine that has not been racked or filtered prior to bottling. The authentic *sur lie* process can be a gamble because it increases the possibility of bacterial infection, but the risk is worth it when it enhances the quality of wines made from neutral grape varieties. If carried out properly, it adds a creamy-yeasty fullness that gives an extra dimension of depth and, retaining more of the carbonic gas created during fermentation, it also imparts a certain liveliness and freshness.

TABLE WINE   A term that often implies a modest, even poor, quality of wine because it is the literal translation of *vin de table*, the lowest level of French wine. It is not necessarily, however, a derogatory term in English, as it has been traditionally used to distinguish between a light (or table wine) and a fortified wine.

TANNIC, TANNIN   Generic terms that refer to various different polyphenols found naturally in wine from the grape skin (which are the most supple), the pips and stalks (the harshest, but may be deliberately included by leaving some of the stalks on or through the judicious addition of *vin de presse*), but can also come from non-grape sources, such as wood tannins (from new casks, where the type of oak used will determine the relative hardness of the tannins), liquid tannin (which is sometimes added during fining) and even cork tannin (from the cork after bottling).

TART   Refers to a noticeable acidity, coming somewhere between sharp and piquant.

TARTARIC ACID   The ripe acid of grapes, this increases slightly when the grapes increase in sugar during the véraison.

TARTRATES, TARTRATE CRYSTALS   These are sometimes precipitated when wines have experienced low temperatures and look like sugar crystals at the bottom of a bottle. A fine deposit of glittering crystals can be deposited on the base of a cork, if it has been soaked in a sterilizing solution of metabisulphite prior to bottling. Both are harmless.

TÊTE DE *CUVÉE*   The first flow of juice during the pressing, the cream of the *cuvée*. It is the easiest to extract and the highest in quality with the best balance of acids, sugars and minerals.

TERTIARY AROMA   One of three fundamental aroma categories; a tertiary aroma is the product of fermentation, not the fruit (primary), or the fermentation (secondary). As such, the tertiary aroma is technically part of the bouquet.

THIN   A wine lacking in body, fruit and other properties.

THIRD LEAF   The third year in the life of a vine, so called because it yields its first leaf in its first year and so on. This is the very first year that a vine may produce grapes for the production of AOC wines.

TOTAL ACIDITY   The total amount of acidity in a wine is usually measured in grams per litre and, because each acid is of a different strength, expressed either as sulphuric or tartaric acid. To convert from sulphuric to tartaric divide by 0.65, to convert from tartaric to sulphuric multiply by 0.65.

TRIES   Consecutive manual sweeps through a vineyard during which the pickers select individual berries of botrytized grapes.

TROCKENBEERENAUSLESE   The highest category of German QmP wine, Trockenbeerenauslese is an intensely sweet wine made from late-picked, heavily botrytized grapes. Depending which German region the wine is made in a Trockenbeerenauslese will have a minimum must weight of between 150 and 154° Oechsle.

TRUE MILDEW   A cryptogamic disorder of the vine, also referred to variously as powdery mildew, oidium and *Uncinula necator*.

TYPICAL   An over-used and less than honest form of honest.

UNCINULA NECATOR   A cryptogamic disorder of the vine, also referred to variously as true mildew, powdery mildew and oidium.

UNDERTONE   Subtle, supporting and not dominating like an overtone. In a fine wine the oak-ageing character, for example, will be a relatively strong and simple overtone during its formative years and a delicate undertone when the wine is mature, adding to a vast array of other nuances that give it complexity.

UNGENEROUS   A wine that lacks generosity will probably have little or no fruit and far too much tannin and acidity.

UNRIPE ACIDITY   Unripe grape acidity is malic acid, as opposed to tartaric or ripe acidity.

UPFRONT   Suggests an attractive, simple quality immediately recognized, which says it all. The wine may initially be interesting, but there would be no further characteristics developing and the last glass would be just the same as the first. Inexpensive Californian wines are often upfront and laid-back.

VANILLA, VANILLA-OAK   Often used to describe the nose and sometimes the palate of an oak-aged wine, especially Rioja. It is the most basic and obvious of oak-induced characteristics and comes from an aldehyde called vanillin that is found naturally in oak and picked up by wine matured in cask.

VANILLIN   An aldehyde found naturally in both oak and vanilla pods.

VARIETAL, VARIETAL CHARACTER   The characteristics portrayed in a wine that are directly attributable to and indicative of the variety of grape from which it is made.

VDQS   A commonly used abbreviation of *Vin délimité de qualité supérieur*, which is an official classification one step above *Vin de pays*, but one below AOC.

VEGETAL   A term applied to wines of a certain maturity, often Chardonnay or Pinot wines that are well rounded and have taken on a bouquet pleasingly reminiscent of vegetation, rather than fruit. It comes after rounded and before farmyardy.

VENDANGEUR   The French for a picker or harvester.

VÉRAISON   This is the ripening period, when the grapes do not change much in size, but gain in colour, if black, and increase in sugar and tartaric acid, while decreasing in unripe malic acid.

VIGNERON   A French term for a vineyard worker.

VIN DE GARDE   A wine capable of significant improvement if allowed to age.

VIN DE GLACE   The French equivalent of Eiswein.

VIN DE GOUTTE   Wine made from the free-run juice.

VIN DE PAILLE   Once the preserve of the Jura, this famous wine is now also produced in Alsace. Literally meaning 'straw wine', the term is derived from its traditional method of production in which late-picked grapes are left to dry and shrivel in the sun on straw mats. In Alsace, this evolved by the eighteenth century into hanging the grapes in huge barns. They can be the most complex and sweetest of dessert wines.

VIN DE PAYS   A French *vin de table* from a geographical area that is usually much larger than a quality wine area, although many in Languedoc-Roussillon are in fact from much smaller areas. It is a rustic style of country wine that is one step above *vin de table* plain and simple, but one beneath VDQS.

VIN DE PRESSE   Very dark, tannic red wine pressed out of the *manta*, after the vin de goutte has been drained off.

VIN DE TABLE   Literally table wine, although not necessarily a direct translation of it (*see* TABLE WINE). It is the lowest level of wine in France and not allowed to show either the grape variety used or the area of origin. In practice it is likely to be a blend of various varieties from numerous areas that has been blended in bulk to produce a wine of consistent character, or lack of it, as the case may be.

VIN ORDINAIRE   Literally a very ordinary wine, this term is usually applied to a French *vin de table*, although as a severe criticism it may be used for anything up to and including an AOC wine.

VINIFICATION   Far more than simply fermentation, this involves the entire process of making wine, from the moment the grapes are picked to the point it is bottled.

VINIMATIC   An enclosed, rotating fermentation tank with blades fixed to the inner surface, a Vinimatic works on the cement-mixer principle. Used initially to extract the maximum colour with the minimum oxidation, it is now being utilized for prefermentation maceration.

VIN JAUNE   The famous 'yellow wine' of the Jura derives its name from the honey-gold colour that results from a deliberate oxidation beneath a sherry-like flor. The result is similar to an aged fino sherry, although it is not fortified, nor is the grape used, the Savagnin, similar to the Palomino of Jerez.

VINTAGE   A vintage wine is merely the wine of one year only (or at least 85 per cent according to the EC) and the year may be anything from poor to great. It is a misnomer to use vintage to indicate a wine of special quality, although the origin of such misuse is understandable, as the finest wines used only to be declared in good vintages.

VIVID   The fruit in some wines can be so fresh, ripe, clean-cut and expressive, that it quickly gives a vivid impression of complete character in the mouth.

VOLATILE ACIDITY   Sometimes called fatty acids, these acids are capable of evaporating at low temperatures. Too much volatile acidity is a sign of instability, but small amounts play a significant role in the taste and aroma of a wine. Formic, butyric and proprionic are all volatile acids found in wine, but acetic and carbonic are the most important.

WEIGHT, WEIGHTY   This term usually, though not necessarily, refers to the body of a wine. It is possible to use weight in contrast to body, stating, for example, that a particular example has 'a good weight of fruit for such a light-bodied wine'.

WET FEET   The vine does not like poorly drained soils, thus the 'wet feet' capacity or resistance of a specific variety may be referred to.

WOOD LACTONES   Various esters that are picked up from new oak and may be the source of certain creamy-oak characteristics.

WOOD-MATURED   Normally refers to a wine that has been aged, not fermented, in new oak, not old.

XIPHINEMA INDEX   An ectoparasitic nematode.

YEAST   Yeast is vital for all winemaking. Its cells excrete a number of enzymes, some 22 of which are necessary to complete the chain reaction known as fermentation.

YEAST ENZYMES   Each enzyme acts as a catalyst for one activity and is specific for that task and no other in the fermentation process.

YEAST NUTRIENT   Just as we need various nutrients to function, so does yeast. For winemaking purposes yeast nutrients are required in the most minute of quantities. These nutrients are: amino acids, vitamins (thiamine) and minerals (potassium, sulphate, phosphate and magnesium). Trace elements of iron, copper, zinc, boron and manganese are also responsible for stimulating yeast growth, but calcium, although it activates enzymes, is not essential.

YEASTY   Not a complimentary term for most wines, but can be desirable in a good quality sparkling wine, especially when young.

ZESTY   A lively characteristic that suggests a zippy tactile impression combined, maybe, with a hint of citrusy aroma.

ZING, ZINGY, ZIP, ZIPPY   Terms all indicative of something refreshing, lively and vital, resulting from a high balance of fruit and acidity or, perhaps, from a prickle or *pétillance*.

Bibliography

Berry, Liz: *The Wines of Alsace* (Bodley Head, 1989)

Boesch, Maurice: *800 Ans de Viticulture en Haute-Alsace* (Imprimerie Art'Real, 1983)

Burn, Bernadette and Gilles Schmidt: *Alsace Clos et Grands Crus* (Jacques Legrand, 1989)

Duijker, Hubrecht: *Loire, Alsace and Champagne* (Mitchell Beazley, 1983)

Gaertner, Pierre and Robert Frédérick: *The Cuisine of Alsace* (Barron's, 1981)

Hallgarten, Fritz: *Alsace: its Wine Gardens, Cellars and Cuisine* (Wine and Spirit Publications, 1978)

Heck, Michèle-Caroline: *All Alsace* (Bonechi, 1984)

Heck, Michèle-Caroline: *Colmar and the Route du Vin* (Bonechi, 1980)

Layton, Tommy: *Wines and People of Alsace* (Cassell, 1970)

Ortlieb, Jean-Michel: *Plan and instruction based on experience, in order to improve the products of the land, in particular the vineyards, dictated by patriotic instinct, its sole purpose being to promote the welfare of mankind* (originally published in 1789, translated and reprinted by Hugel & Fils, 1989)

Pomerol, Charles (editor): *The Wines and Winelands of France: Geological Journeys* (Robertson McCarta, 1989)

Price, Pamela Vandyke: *Alsace Wines* (Sotheby Publications, 1984)

Renvoize, Guy: *Guide des Vins d'Alsace* (Solarama, 1983)

Robinson, Jancis: *Vines, Grapes and Wines* (Mitchell Beazley, 1986)

Sittler, Claude and Robert Marocke: *Terroirs et Vins d'Alsace* (Louis Pasteur University, Strasbourg, Third Edition 1989)

Spetz, Georges: *Légendes d'Alsace* (Paris, 1912)

Stoltz, J. L: *Notizen aus dem Elässichen Weinbau* (Strasbourg, 1828)

Style, Sue: *A Taste of Alsace* (Pavillion Books, 1990)

Thiebaut, A: *Alsace* (SAEP, 1986)

Willan, Anne: *French Regional Cookery* (Hutchinson, 1981)

Map Credits

The map of Alsace (facing page 1) was drawn by John Flower, based on the map of Alsace in *Sotheby's World Wine Encyclopedia*, courtesy of Dorling Kindersley. The maps between pages 157 and 224 are reproduced by permission of the Institut Geographique National (IGN authorization no. 90.3032). The reference sources on which the individual maps are based are as follows:

Altenberg de Bergbieten: IGN Map No. 3716 East (1/25000).
Altenberg de Bergheim: IGN Map No. 3718 West (1/25000).
Altenberg de Wolxheim: IGN Map No. 3716 East (1/25000).
Brand: IGN Map No. 3718 West (1/25000).
Bruderthal: IGN Map No. 3716 East (1/25000).
Eichberg: IGN Map No. 3719 West (1/25000).
Engelberg: IGN Map No. 3716 East (1/25000).
Florimont: IGN Map No. 3718 West (1/25000).
Frankstein: IGN Map Mont Sainte-Odile Obernai (1/25000).
Froehn: IGN Map No. 3718 West (1/25000).
Furstentum: IGN Map No. 3718 West (1/25000).
Geisberg: IGN Map No. 3718 West (1/25000).
Gloeckelberg: IGN Map No. 3718 West (1/25000).
Goldert: IGN Map No. 3719 West (1/25000).
Hatschbourg: IGN Map No. 3719 West (1/25000).
Hengst: IGN Map No. 3718 West & 3719 West (1/25000).
Kaefferkopf: IGN Map No. 3718 West (1/25000).
Kanzlerberg: IGN Map No. 3718 West (1/25000).
Kastelberg: IGN Map No. 3717 East (1/25000).
Kessler: IGN Map No. 3719 West (1/25000).
Kirchberg de Barr: IGN Map No. 3717 East (1/25000).
Kirchberg de Ribeauvillé: IGN Map No. 3718 West (1/25000).
Kitterlé: IGN Map No. 3719 West (1/25000).
Mambourg: IGN Map No. 3718 West (1/25000).
Mandelberg: IGN Map No. 3718 West (1/25000).

575

Marckrain: IGN Map No. 3718 West (1/25000).
Moenchber: IGN Map No. 3717 East (1/25000).
Muenchberg: IGN Map Mont Sainte-Odile Obernai (1/25000).
Ollwiller: IGN Map No. 3719 West (1/25000).
Osterberg: IGN Map No. 3718 West (1/25000).
Pfersigberg: IGN Map No. 3719 West (1/25000).
Pfingstberg: IGN Map No. 3719 West (1/25000).
Praelatenberg: IGN Map Taennchel-Dambach (1/25000).
Rangen: IGN Map Grand Ballon Thann (1/25000).
Rosacker: IGN Map No. 3718 West (1/25000).
Saering: IGN Map No. 3719 West (1/25000).
Schlossberg: IGN Map No. 3718 West (1/25000).
Schoenenbourg: IGN Map No. 3718 West (1/25000).
Sommerberg: IGN Map No. 3718 West (1/25000).
Sonnenglanz: IGN Map No. 3718 West (1/25000).
Spiegel: IGN Map No. 3719 West (1/25000).
Sporen: IGN Map No. 3718 West (1/25000).
Steinert: IGN Map No. 3719 West (1/25000).
Steingrubler: IGN Map No. 3719 West (1/25000).
Steinklotz: IGN Map No. 3715 East (1/25000).
Vorgbourg: IGN Map No. 3719 West (1/25000).
Wiebelsberg: IGN Map No. 3717 East (1/25000).
Wineck-Schlossberg: IGN Map No. 3718 West (1/25000).
Winzenberg: IGN Map Mont Sainte-Odile Obernai (1/25000).
Zinnkoepflé: IGN Map No. 3719 West (1/25000).
Zotzenberg: IGN Map Mont Sainte-Odile Obernai (1/25000).

Index

Main references are in **bold**. Alternative names are listed where it is likely that the reader may look up one rather than the other. Each grape variety has its own individual reference and is also listed under **Grape varieties**, Clos Ste-Hune may be found under both **Clos** and **Ste-Hune**, etc. The abbreviation (*syn*) indicates that the entry is a grape synonym.

A360P 242
Abbeys
  6th century 2
  14th century 3, 64
  Baumgarten 192
  Ebersmunster 200
  Haut Seille 201
  Masmunster 201
  Murbach 115, 164, 176
  Muri 213, 243
  Schwarze 84
  Ste-Richarde 68
  Wissembourg 80
Abbots
  Braun 243
  Masmunster 201
  Murbach 176
Abondante grape 11
Acids
  decanoic 42
  gluconic 31
  lactic 39
  malic 28, 39
  octanoic 42
  primary grape 28
  tartaric 28

Adalric 114
Adam, Caves JB 67, 100, 180, 269,
  281, 286, 310, 316, 325–6, 352
Adam, Domaine Pierre 180, 291, 352
Adam the Monk 3
Aedui tribe 13
Aeolian soil 57
Affenberg lieu-dit 518
Agaisheim 86
Agilo-marneux 58
Agrilo-limoneuse 58
Albé village 65
Albrecht, Domaine Lucien 116, 199,
  230, 276, 291, 318, 332, 339, 352
Aldaric 92
Alemanni 1, 13
Alemannia 13
Allemagne, etymological origin 13
Allimant-Laugner 281, 353
Alluvium 56–7
Almond tree hill 188
Alsace
  Dukes of 114
  first wines 3
  linguistic analysis 547
  original name 3
  trade structure 345
  varietal concept and origin 262
  vineyard ownership 349–50
Alsace plains 56
  soil 55
  vineyards 49
Alsace producers
  cooperatives 346
  cooperatives table 347
  grandes maisons 348–9
  growers 349
  négociants 347–8

ten most important 345
types 345
Alsace Seltz 244, 300, 450
Alsace Willm 70–71, 184, 227, 229,
    288, 291–2, 395, 472, 473
Altenberg de Bergbieten grand cru 2,
    157, 239, 247, 519
Altenberg de Bergheim grand cru 2,
    158, 159, 518
Altenberg de Wolxheim grand cru 2,
    143, 160, 239, 250–51, 517,
    519
Altenbourg lieu-dit 243
Altenburg de Kientzheim 518
Altenburg de Sigolsheim 519
Altwaesch lieu-dit 254
Amalricivilare 66
Amberg, Yves 88, 353
Ammerschwihr village 2, 4, 49, 66,
    518
Amylic character 39
Andlau village 1–2, 68, 517, 519
Anstotz & Fils, GAEC 70, 259, 353
Anthocyanins 40
Antipope, St-Hippolytus 127
AOC Alsace
    alcoholic strength regulations 544
    area classified 64, 261
    area in production 64, 261
    average production 261
    average yield 261
    bottling regulation 544
    clairet regulation 545
    Crémant d'Alsace percentage 261
    Crémant d'Alsace regulation 546
    grand cru area classified 261
    grand cru percentage 261
    grand cru production 261
    grand cru regulation 545
    hectares in production 49
    Klevener de Heiligenstein
        regulation 545
    origins 261
    production & yield 262
    red and rosé percentage 261
    regulations 148, 543
    schillerwein regulation 545
    SGN regulation 545
    varietal appellation 263–5
    varietal content regulation 544
    Vendange Tardive regulation 545
    vintage content regulation 544
    white wine percentage 261

yield regulation 543
AOC system 11
    raison d'être 271
Aqueous rocks 57
Arbogast, Jean 231, 354
Archbishop, Strasbourg 258
Arenaceous rocks 57
Argillaceous soils 58
Argille 58
Ariovistus 13
Armagnacs
    raid on Guebwiller 92
    scaling-ladders 93
Arnold, Pierre 169, 354
Assemblage of Crémant d'Alsace 43
Association des Viticulteurs 10–11
Augustus Caesar 13
Autolysis 44
Auvernat Gris grape (syn) 33
Auxerrois grape 32, 266–7, 270–71,
    302
Avolsheim village 69, 519

Baeckaoffe 434
Balbronn village 64, 70
Ballandean Winery 298
Ballon
    Grand 222, 258
    Petit 222, 258
Baltenweck, Jean-Pierre 173, 354
Bannwarth & Fils, Laurent 243, 354
Barbier, Roger 354
Bärenstein, House of 83
Barmès-Buecher, Domaine 41–2, 177,
    215, 250, 252, 276, 286, 292, 303,
    355
Barr village 70, 519
Barr, lords of 96
Barth, Monseigneur Médard 3, 64
Bas, Christian 415
Basalt 58
Bas-Rhin
    AOC Alsace area 64
    hectares in production 64
    Vin de Pays du 306, 334–5, 365, 428
Baumann & Fils, J-J 123, 208, 243,
    286, 355
Baumann-Zirgel 189, 355
Baumgarten Abbey 192
Baur, Charles 86, 164, 197, 292, 355
Baur, Maison Léon 180, 239, 281, 286,
    356
Baur Petit-Fils, François 162, 292, 355

Beblenheim village 71, 518
Becht, Bernard 69, 85, 246, 517, 356
Becht, Pierre 357
Bechtold, Domaine Jean-Pierre 83,
   129, 166, 357, 357
Beck, Jean-Claude 89, 169, 246, 357
Beck, René & Gilbert 65, 235, 247,
   281, 434
Beck Hartweg, Yvette & Michel 169,
   360
Beck succ, Paul 255, 357
Becker, Maison Jean 106, 145, 170,
   201, 248, 252, 255, 281, 286, 292,
   297, 299, 319, 327, 358
   Martine Becker 359
   Philippe Becker 170, 281, 297, 327,
      358–9
Bench grafting 20
Bennwihr village 72, 518
Bentonite 38, 40
Bergbieten village 73, 519
Berger, Frédéric 211, 361
Bergheim village 14, 73, 267, 517–8
Bergholtz village 74, 518
Bergholtz-Zell village 64, 75
Bergweingarten lieu-dit 2, 243, 518
Bernardswiller village 76
Bernardvillé village 76, 519
Bernhard, Jean-Marc 361
Bernhard-Reibel, Cécile 80, 239, 258,
   361
Bernstein lieu-dit 519
Berrwiller village 77
Berstett village 77
Beyer, Maison Léon 86, 147, 152–5,
   165, 189, 197, 269, 276, 286, 292,
   323, 348, 361, 362, 378, 432, 496
   Marc Beyer 152–3, 362, 432
Beyer, Luc 362
Beyer, Patrick 88, 362
Biecher & Fils, Jean 345, 362, 387
Bildstoeckle lieu-dit 243
Birgele lieu-dit 243
Bischenberg 77
Bischoffsheim village 77
Bishops
   burning of 510
   Richwin 89
   Strasbourg 3, 217
   St-Gregory 107
Bixkoepflé 103
Black arts 243
Blanck, André 207, 286, 363

Blanck & Fils, GAEC Paul 105, 130,
   171, 206–7, 243, 248, 253, 269,
   286, 292, 318, 323, 339–40, 375,
   438
   GAEC Paul 363
   Frédéric Blanck 363
   Marcel Blanck 171, 363
   Philippe Blanck 375
Blauburgunder grape (syn) 34
Blauer Klevner grape (syn) 34
Blauer Spätburgunder grape (syn) 34
Bléger, Claude 364
Blettig lieu-dit 519
Blienschwiller village 77, 519
Bock, Jérôme 6
Bodenacker 255
Boeckel, Vins Fins d'Alsace E. 185,
   191, 219, 224, 286, 302, 316, 339,
   364
Boehler, Georges 334, 365
Boersch-St-Léonard village 78
Boesch, Léon 223, 258, 365
Bollenberg lieu-dit 116, 126, 243,
   509–10, 518–9
Bordeaux 258, 260, 263
Botrycine 31
Botrytis cinerea 30
Bott Frères, Maison 286, 292, 365
Bottling
   cold sterile 41
   times 41
Bott-Geyl, Maison 72, 189, 211, 276,
   292, 366
Bouquettraube grape 11
Bourgheim village 78
Boxler, Albert 111, 136, 162, 209,
   286–7, 323, 325, 366, 367, 402
Boxler, Justin 367
Brand grand cru 135, 161, 517, 519
   dragon of 161–2
   original size 161
Brand, Lucien 89, 180, 251, 292, 367
Brandhof lieu-dit 244
Brandluft lieu-dit 244, 519
Brandstatt lieu-dit 518
Brant, Sebastian 202
Braun, Abbot 243
Braun, Camille & Fils 116, 269, 292,
   367
Braun, François 116, 199, 286, 292,
   367
Brauneisen-Fink, Monique &
   Gérard 177, 368

Breitstein lieu-dit 245
Bronner, Ernest 368
Brown Muscat grape (syn) 35
Bruche canal 256
Bruche Valley 110
Bruderthal grand cru 2, 517, 519, 163
Bud-break 25
Buecher & Fils, Paul 270, 281, 303, 368
Buehl lieu-dit 255
Buerlenberg lieu-dit 518
Buhl village 79
Burdin grape 11
Burg lieu-dit 245
Burger grape 8
Burgreben lieu-dit 245
Burgundy 6–7, 263
Burlenberg lieu-dit 245
Burn, Maison Ernest 92, 174, 231, 275, 297, 319, 327, 368

Cabernet Sauvignon grape 372
Cadillac grafting 20
Caesar, Julius 13
Caesaris Mons 103
Caesar's Peak 103
Caïdenthalo 102
Calcareous clay 58
Calcareous soil 56, 58
Calcaro-gréseux 58
Calcium 55
Capucins, Clos des 104, 227, 228, 286, 322, 468–70, 518
Carbonaceous soil 58
Carbonates 62
Carola mineral water 120
Casein 40
Castles
    Eberhard's 86
    Eguisheim 86
    Giersberg 120
    Haut-Koenigsbourg 239
    Haut-Ribeaupierre 120
    Husseren 99
    Kientzheim 104
    les trois châteaux 99
    Lupfen 104
    Mittelwihr 109
    Ortenbourg 129, 255, 517
    Ramstein 129
    St-Ulrich 120
    Wineck 102
Caterpillars, plague of 515

Cattin, Joseph 95, 138, 176, 281, 292, 297, 316, 318, 339, 369, 370, 383, 386
Cattin, Théo 95, 138, 176, 244, 270, 276, 286, 292, 369
Cave du Vieil Armand 465
Caves JB Adam 67, 100, 180, 269, 281, 286, 310, 316, 325–6, 352
Celtic dialect 548
Centrifuge 38
Cernay village 79, 517–8
Chalk 58
Champ du Mensonge 130
Champagne, comparison of standards with 43
Chapelle St-André 68
Chardonnay grape 37, 237, 268, 302, 338
Charlemagne 130
Charles the Bald 14
Charles the Fat 68, 106
Chasselas grape 7–8, 36, 300–301
Château de Kientzheim 67
Château de Riquewihr 227, 377
Château du Moulin 226
Château d'Isenbourg 126, 225, 377–8
Château d'Orschwihr 115, 199, 226, 244, 429
Château Ollwiller 144, 194, 226, 236, 287, 465, 519
Château Wagenbourg 227, 466
Châtenois village 80, 519
Childebert II 107, 216
Chlorides 62
Chlorosis 22, 54–5
Chrétien, Oberlin 372
Chrodoldes villa 124
Chrodoldesvilare 124
CIVA 271, 388–9
Clairet 303
Clay 58
Clay-loam 59
Cléebourg village 80, 267, 519
Clevner grape (syn) 32, 35, 303
Climate 49
Clos de la Tourelle 144, 226, 236, 465
Clos de Meywihr 231, 409
Clos des Aubépines 127, 228
Clos des Capucins 104, 227, 228, 286, 322, 468–70, 518
Clos des Gourmets 229, 424
Clos du Jardin 230
Clos du Schlossberg 2, 120, 234, 310,

452
Clos du Sonnenbach 65, 235, 281, 435
Clos du Val d'Eléon 68, 236, 311, 413
Clos du Vicus Romain 236
Clos du Windsbuhl 98
Clos du Zahnacker 120–21, 237–8, 258, 307, 312, 435
Clos Gaensbroennel 70, 152, 184, 227, 229, 238, 291–2, 472–3, 519
Clos Hauserer 141–2, 229, 286, 318, 325, 477
Clos Himmelreich 115, 230
Clos Jean-Philippe Sturm 85, 235
Clos Jebsal 135, 230, 275, 317–8
Clos Meywihr 66
Clos Philippe Grass 143, 229, 256, 426
Clos Rebgarten 68, 297, 231, 413
Clos Rothstein 354
Clos Roth-Stein 143, 231
Clos Ste-Hune 52, 97–9, 152, 204, 227, 233, 283, 285–6, 460–64, 477, 518
Clos Ste-Odile 113–14, 234, 428, 519
Clos St-Imer 91–92, 174, 231, 275, 297, 368–9
Clos St-Immer (sic) 518
Clos St-Jacques 232, 372
Clos St-Landelin 126, 218, 232, 282, 287, 297, 319, 426–7, 518
Clos St-Théobold 133, 233, 288, 448
Clos St-Urbain 133, 233, 275, 318, 482
Clos Windsbuhl 99, 237, 303, 317–18, 326
Clos Zisser 70–71, 184, 238, 292, 410
Clovis 1, 13
Coates, Clive 234
Cobble 59
Cochylis 219
Code du Vin 11
Cold stabilisation 40
Colluvial deposits 59
Colmar village 3–4, 47, 65–6, 68, 81, 518
Colmar, Domaine Viticole de la Ville de 372
Colmar Pocket, Battle for the 81, 109, 504
Colmar Tribunal 67, 179, 210
Colombain, Lucie 99, 373
Comité de Délimitation des Grands Crus 149
Comtes de Lupfen, Domaine des 105, 130, 171, 206–7, 243, 248, 253,
269, 286, 292, 318, 323, 339–40, 363
Cönesheim 104
Confrérie St-Etienne 4, 67, 104, 343, 447
Convent, Ettenheim 217
Côte de Ribeauvillé 238, 312, 435
Côte de Rouffach 126, 139, 240, 436
Côte des Amandiers 108, 189, 239, 393
Côte Val St-Grégoire 394
Coteau de Pfaffenheim 257
Coteaux du Haut-Koenigsbourg 104, 116, 127, 239, 282, 451
Coteaux du Mossig 50, 83–4, 106–7, 115, 128–9, 131, 134, 239
Coteaux d'Eguisheim 85, 239
Côtes du Val St-Grégoire 246
Côtes au-dessus d'Orschwihr 517
Côtes au-dessus Sigolsheim 517
Côtes de Barr 239
Côtes de Marlenheim 519
Côtes de Ribeauvillé 120, 240, 309–10
Côtes du Val St-Grégoire 135, 138, 141, 146, 241, 519
Côtes d'Ottrott 518
Couderc rootstock 23
Count Ruthaud 84
Counts of Ribeaupierre 120
Crax 108
Crémant d'Alsace 43, 119, 216, 232, 236, 302
  appropriate grapes 44
  autolysis 44
  dégorgement 45
  dosage 45
  future 43
  gyropalettes 45
  remuage 45
  secondary fermentation 44
  yields 43
Crops
  analysis by size 527
  destroyed by caterpillars 515
  destroyed by drought 512
  destroyed by frost 511–16
  destroyed by grasshoppers 513–14
  destroyed by hail 512–13, 515
  destroyed by rain 514
  destroyed by rot 512–13
  destroyed by storms 514–15
  destroyed by wolves 514
  first in 15 years 511

Cro-magnon man 86
Crushing 38, 41
Crystalline 59
Custer, Mathias 388
CV Andlau 96, 334, 353, 376
CV Beblenheim 159, 286, 339, 345, 356
CV Bennwihr 190, 254–5, 340, 345, 360
CV Cléebourg 80–81, 113, 125, 133, 244, 250–51, 254, 270, 281, 370
CV Dambach-la-Ville 169, 373, 473
CV Eguisheim 165, 176, 197, 211, 215, 279, 373
CV Hunawihr 237, 253, 276, 281, 287, 292, 340, 345, 401, 420
CV Ingersheim 111, 167, 209, 245, 252, 257, 287, 292, 339, 345, 402, 414, 447
CV Kientzheim 345
CV Kientzheim-Kaysersberg 180, 207, 248, 253, 287, 339, 407
CV Obernai 114–15, 219, 234, 293, 339, 345, 376, 428
CV Orschwiller 429
CV Pfaffenheim 175–6, 214, 243, 247, 254, 257, 270, 276, 281, 293, 339–40, 345, 348, 430, 464
CV Ribeauvillé 121, 173, 186, 189, 195, 211, 213, 237–8, 287, 293, 307, 312, 339, 345, 435, 517
CV Sigolsheim 451
CV Traenheim 73, 158, 160, 240, 270, 294, 297, 376, 458
CV Turckheim 136, 162, 177, 194, 209, 241, 249, 270, 277, 281–2, 288, 293–4, 316, 340, 345, 431, 464, 433, 517, 519
CV Vieil Armand 144, 194, 226, 236, 287, 465, 473
CV Westhalten 132, 218, 223, 241, 258, 339, 470
CV Sigolsheim 258

Dagobert 106, 134
    Les Vins du Roi 73, 158, 160, 240, 270, 294, 297, 376, 458
Dahlenheim village 2, 82, 519
Dambach-la-Ville village 83
Dangolsheim village 84
Decanoic acid 42
Decapolis 103
Dégorgement 45

Deiss, Domaine Marcel 74, 122, 127, 159, 208, 245–6, 248, 270, 276, 280, 285–6, 288, 292, 321, 324, 326, 328–9, 331, 374, 386, 487
    Jean-Michel Deiss 159, 280, 328, 374
Deodatus, Dr Claudius 202
Dextrin 31
De-stemming 38, 41
Dieffenthal village 84, 517, 519
Dietrich, Claude 243, 258, 276, 292, 374
    Elizabeth Dietrich 375
Dietrich, Robert 276, 339–40, 375
Dietrich & Fils, Laurent 375
Dinghofrecht 87
Diringer, GAEC 375
Dirler, Vins 75, 94, 183, 206, 211, 286, 297, 324, 335, 375
Dirringer, Domaine J-L 376
Dischler, Charles 144, 160, 376
Divinal 376
Dolder, Christian 244, 300, 376
Dolomite 59
Domaine Aimé Stentz 111, 177, 209, 236, 255, 282, 288, 303, 456
Domaine André & Rémy Gresser 69, 87–8, 191, 219, 244, 251, 276, 287, 393, 412
Domaine Barmès-Buecher 141–2, 177, 215, 250, 252, 276, 286, 292, 303, 355
Domaine de la Sinne 390
Domaine de la Tour 78, 458
Domaine de l'Ecole 382
Domaine des Comtes de Lupfen 105, 130, 171, 206–7, 243, 248, 253, 269, 286, 292, 318, 323, 339–40, 363, 375, 438
Domaine des Marronniers 182, 191, 421
Domaine du Rempart 66, 281, 434
Domaine Edouard Leiber 99, 165, 418
Domaine Hering 184, 229, 287, 397
Domaine Jean Sipp 258, 270, 277, 288, 293, 307, 310, 452
Domaine Jean-Pierre Bechtold 83, 129, 166, 357
Domaine Joseph Loberger 418
Domaine Julien Meyer 112, 249, 259, 300, 424
Domaine Jux 82, 248, 405, 473, 475
Domaine J-L Dirringer 376

Domaine Kehren 176, 406
Domaine Kieffer 89, 101, 247, 406
Domaine Klipfel 71, 125, 182, 184,
    238–9, 246, 292, 299, 409
Domaine Lucien Albrecht 116, 199,
    230, 276, 291, 318, 332, 339, 352
Domaine Marcel Deiss 74, 122, 127,
    159, 208, 245–6, 248, 270, 276,
    280, 285–6, 288, 292, 321, 324,
    326, 328–9, 331, 374, 386, 487
Domaine Martin Schaetzel 180, 276,
    300, 441
Domaine Mattern 251, 421
Domaine Mittnacht Frères 205, 229,
    253, 276, 424, 487
Domaine Muller-Koeberle 127, 228,
    245, 247, 257, 276, 282, 333, 426
Domaine Ostertag 89, 112, 193, 242,
    246, 249, 269, 276, 287, 291, 297,
    300, 316, 318, 325–6, 328–9, 429
Domaine Pierre Adam 180, 291, 352
Domaine Rieflé 119, 214, 240–41,
    243, 247, 256, 276, 293, 436
Domaine Schlumberger 75, 94, 126,
    183, 186–7, 205, 276, 287–8, 293,
    309, 348, 405, 444, 482
Domaine Schoffit 82, 134, 203, 233,
    249, 277, 288, 300, 302, 448
Domaine Siffert 201, 239, 282, 451
Domaine Sipp-Mack 99, 205, 288, 453
Domaine Viticole de la Ville de
    Colmar 82, 232, 372
Domaine Weinbach 105, 206–7, 228,
    277, 286, 288, 291, 316, 319,
    322–6, 384, 468
Domaine Zind Humbrecht 92, 99, 119,
    136, 142, 162, 174, 177, 203,
    229–30, 233, 237, 249–50, 255,
    270, 275, 277, 286–7, 291, 294,
    297, 300, 303, 316–18, 321, 323,
    325–6, 328–9, 331, 404, 476, 482,
    488
  Bernard Humbrecht 92, 175
  Léonard Humbrecht 134, 202–3,
      359, 477–8, 482, 485
  Marcel Humbrecht 92, 149, 175,
      287, 297
  Olivier Humbrecht 202–3, 359, 478
  Geneviève Zind 477
Dompeter 69
Domus Petri 69
Dontenville, Gilbert 248, 377
Dopff, Guy 348, 378

Dopff, Pierre-Etienne 344, 380, 550
Dopff & Irion 123, 126, 208, 213,
    225–7, 276, 287, 292, 296–7, 340,
    344–5, 348, 377, 405
Dopff au Moulin 82, 122, 136, 162,
    208, 213, 226, 287, 292, 300, 316,
    335, 339–40, 344–5, 348, 376,
    380
Dorfburg lieu-dit 245
Dorin grape (syn) 36
Dorlisheim village 85, 239, 519
Dosage 45
Drainage 52
Drouhin Clos des Mouches 148
Duijker, Hubrecht 81, 161
Dukes of Alsace 114
Durrmann, André 182, 219, 381
Dussourt, André 88, 382

Eberhard 86, 115
Eberhard's castle 86
Eberhardo 92
Ebersmunster Abbey 200
EC wine regulations 543
Echevins des Strasbourg 96
Ecklé, Jean-Paul 102, 220, 382
Ecole, Domaine 382
Ecole d'Alsace 348
Edelwein 4, 9, 305
Edelzwicker 10, 212, 298, 301, 305,
    306, 307–8, 383, 446
Edesberg 84
EEC wine regime 148
Eguisheim village 2, 85, 518
Eguisheim castle 86
Ehenheim 114, 256
Ehinhaim 114
Ehrhart, André 142, 180, 382
Ehrhart & Fils, François 174, 382
Ehrhart, Henri 177, 180, 276, 287,
    307, 383
Eichberg grand cru 2, 519, 164
Eichelberg lieu-dit 519
Eichhoffen village 87, 517, 519
Einhart 124, 259, 276, 383
Einsden village 201
Eisbourg lieu-dit 518
Elbling grape 7–9, 11
Elsbourg lieu-dit 518
Emperor Ferdinand 114
Empress Maria Theresa 202
Engel, Raymond 201, 276, 384
Engel & Fils, Fernand 159, 383

Engelberg grand cru 2, 239, 519, 166
Engelgarten lieu-dit 246
Entenlachbuehl lieu-dit 255
Enzymes, secretion during
   fermentation 38
Epfig village 87, 519
Ergersheim village 89
Ermel, David 205, 384
Espace, Wolfberger's 475
Etablissements Ringenbach-Moser 437
Ettenheim, convent of 217
Eudémis moth 219, 272

Fahrer, Armand 384
Falernium, ancient wine of 3, 64, 130
Faller (*see also* Domaine Weinbach)
   Cathy 468–9
   Mme Colette 105, 227, 286, 321,
      468–70
Faller & Fils, Robert 121, 173, 186,
      281, 292, 297, 384
Fauna and flora
   Caspian found in Alsace 222
   Mediterranean found in Alsace 167,
      222, 258
Faust, Liliane 335, 385
Feherburgundi 32
Feldspar 59
Felsen lieu-dit 246
Felspar 59
Fendant grape (*syn*) 36, 301
Fermentation 38–43
   cool 39
   malolactic 39, 42
   non-alcoholic 39
   red wine 41–2, 278
   secondary 39, 44
   sparkling wines 43
   temperatures 42
   types of vessel 38
   white wine 38–40
Ferruginous clay 59
Field grafting 20–21
Field of Deceit 130
Filtration 38
Fining 38
   colloidal groups 40
   electrolytic attraction 40
   negative charge 40
   positive charge 40
Finkenberg 239, 246, 517, 519
Fischart, Johann 102
Fleith, René 100, 281, 287, 292, 316,

385
Flesch, François 385
Flexbourg village 90
Florentius, Georgius 107
Florimont grand cru 167, 518
Florival 93
Flowering of the vine 27
Flûte d'Alsace 149, 278
Forst lieu-dit 108
Francia Media 14
Francia Occidentalis 14
Francia Orientalis 14
Franconia 299
Franco-Prussian War 8–9
Frankish lords
   Kazo 102
   Richo 122
Franks 12-13
Frankstein grand cru 168, 519
Frederick III 69
Freiberg 519
French Revolutionary government 8
French-German divide, embryonic 12
Freudenreich, Pierre 86, 97, 197, 287,
      292, 385–6
Freudenreich & Fils, Pierre 385
Frey, Charles 386
Freyburger, Marcel 180, 386
Freyburger & Fils, Louis 159, 245, 386
Freyermuth, Lucien 345, 386
Frick, Pierre 119, 214, 243, 248, 256,
      272, 276, 287, 297, 387
Frieberg lieu-dit 246
Frisians 3
Fritsch, Romain 107, 216, 387
Froehn grand cru 169, 519
Fromentot grape (*syn*) 33
Fronholz lieu-dit 246, 519
Frontignac grape (*syn*) 35
Frost, vulnerability of vines to 25, 27
Fruehmess lieu-dit 247
Fruit set 28
Fulrade 5–6, 127
Furdenheim village 90
Furmint grape 6
Furstentum grand cru 2, 49, 171,
      517–19

GAEC André Mauler & Fils 422
GAEC André Thomas & Fils 457
GAEC Anstotz & Fils 259, 353
GAEC A. Ruhlmann 439
GAEC Bernard & Daniel Haegi 244,

394
GAEC Diringer 375
GAEC Greiner-Schleret 189, 239, 393
GAEC Joseph Klein & Fils 466
GAEC Mochel-Lorentz 158, 425
GAEC Roger Young & Fils 213, 252,
    270, 281, 316, 405
GAEC Seilly 450
Gaensbroennel, Clos 70, 152, 184,
    227, 229, 238, 291–2, 472–3, 519
Gaensweide lieu-dit 254
Gaentzbrunnen lieu-dit 247
Gaessel lieu-dit 254
Galet, Pierre 271
Galgenrain lieu-dit 247
Gantzer, Lucien 175, 388
Gaschy, Antoine 389
Gaschy, A. 388
Gaschy, Bernard 389
Gaschy, Jean-Antoine 389
Gassmann, Louis 438
Gauls 12
Geiler, Jean 100
Geisberg grand cru 2, 172, 518
Geisberg lieu-dit 247
Geisbourg lieu-dit 518
Geissberg lieu-dit 247
Gelatine 40
Gelber Muskateller grape (syn) 35
Gentil 10, 212, 305, 330–31
    banned in 1973 400
    d'Alsace 308
    Gaensbroennel 229
    Sporen 212, 400
German vineyards in Alsace 143
Germania Inferior 13
Germania Superior 13
Germanic language, earliest 12
Gertwiller village 90
Geschickt & Fils, Jérôme 180, 221,
    287, 319, 390
Gewann 517
Gewurztraminer grape 21, 35, 289–90
Geyer, Roger & Roland 193, 219, 390
Giersberg castle 120
Gilg, Armand 223, 390
Gimbrett-Berstett village 91
Ginglinger, Paul 86, 164, 197, 287,
    390
Ginglinger, Pierre-Henri 165, 390
Ginglinger-Fix 176, 391
Girsberg lieu-dit 518
Gisselbrecht, Louis 169, 392, 391

Gisselbrecht & Fils, Willy 169, 193,
    292, 339–40, 392
Glacial moraine 59
Glintzberg lieu-dit 239, 247
Gloeckelberg grand cru 123, 173, 518
Gluconic acid 31
Gneiss 59
Gocker, Philippe 205, 392
Goldert grand cru 2, 174, 518
Goldriesling grape 11
Gourmand and gourmet, origin and
    meaning of terms 7
Gourmets, Clos des 229, 424
Goxwiller village 91
Grad, Charles 253
Graf von Eguisheim und Dagsburg 86
Graf von Horbourg 71
Grafreben lieu-dit 247
Grafting 19 21
    bench 20
    Cadillac type 20
    field 20–21
    Hengl type 20
    Jupiter type 20
    Mayorquine type 20
    Omega type 20
    prohibition of by German
        authorities 10
    Saw-type 20
Grand Ballon 47
Grandes Maisons d'Alsace 348
Grands Chais de France 423
Grands Crus
    alternative classification 153
    anti-crus 151–3
    argument for other varieties 54–5
    blended wine argument 153–4
    Crémant d'Alsace 154
    first law 148
    hectares classified 155
    hectares in production 155
    soil argument 150–51
    technical specification 155–6
    volume of production 155
Grands Vins d'Alsace Louis Sipp 186,
    195, 240, 288, 293, 309–10, 452
Granite 59
Granite Belt, Queensland-Sylvaner
    of 298
Grape crosses 10–11, 18, 21, 262
Grape cultivation
    all evolution by hectares 520–21
    mixed evolution by hectares 522

Grape hybrids 10–11, 21, 23, 79–80, 90, 139, 146, 262
Grape prices 527–8
Grape varieties (*see also* Wines)
  Abondante 11
  Auvernat Gris (*syn*) 33
  Auxerrois 32, 266–7, 270–71, 302
  Blauburgunder (*syn*) 34
  Blauer Klevner (*syn*) 34
  Blauer Spätburgunder (*syn*) 34
  Bouquettraube 11
  Brown Muscat (*syn*) 35
  Burdin 11
  Burger 8
  Cabernet Sauvignon 372
  Chardonnay 37, 268, 302
  Chasselas 7, 36, 300–1
  Chasselas evolution 522
  Clevner (*syn*) 32, 303
  Dorin (*syn*) 36
  Elbling 7, 11
  Feherburgundi (*syn*) 32
  Fendant (*syn*) 36, 301
  Fromentot (*syn*) 33
  Frontignac (*syn*) 35
  Furmint 6
  Gelber Muskateller (*syn*) 35
  Gentil 330–31
  Gewurztraminer 35, 289–90
  Gewurztraminer evolution 524
  Goldriesling 11
  Grauer Burgunder (*syn*) 33
  Grauer Mönch (*syn*) 33
  Grauklevner (*syn*) 33
  Gutedel (*syn*) 36, 303
  Hárslevelu 6
  Huxelrebe 143
  Johannisberg Riesling (*syn*) 34
  Kleiner Rauschling 330–31
  Kliener Riesling grape 9
  Klevanka (*syn*) 33
  Klevener 7, 95–6, 333–4, 353, 398, 467, 545
  Klevner (*syn*) 32, 34, 303
  Knipperlé 11, 330–1
  Landot 11
  Léon Millot 11
  Malvoisie (*syn*) 33
  Maréchal Foch 11
  Moscato Bianco (*syn*) 35
  Moscato di Canelli (*syn*) 35
  Moscato d'Asti (*syn*) 35
  Müller-Thurgau 11, 143

Muscadel Ottonel (*syn*) 35
Muscat 6, 35
Muscat à Petit Grains 294–5
Muscat Blanc à Petit Grains 35
Muscat Canelli (*syn*) 35
Muscat de Frontignan (*syn*) 35
Muscat d'Alsace 35, 294–5
Muscat evolution 524
Muscat Ottonel 35, 294–5
Muscat Rosé à Petit Grains 35
Muscatel Branco (*syn*) 35
Muskadel (*syn*) 35
Muskateller (*syn*) 35
Muskateller Ottonel (*syn*) 35
Muskat-Ottonel (*syn*) 35
Muskotoly (*syn*) 35
Ortlieber 330–31
Perlan (*syn*) 36
Pinot Auxerrois 303
Pinot Auxerrois (*syn*) 32
Pinot Beurot (*syn*) 33
Pinot Bianco (*syn*) 32
Pinot Blanc 6, 32, 37, 266–7, 271, 289
Pinot Blanc evolution 523
Pinot Chardonnay (*syn*) 37
Pinot Grigio (*syn*) 33
Pinot Gris 303
Pinot Gris (*syn*) 33
Pinot Meunier 11
Pinot Nero (*syn*) 34
Pinot Noir 5–6, 34, 41, 266–7, 277–8
Pinot Noir evolution 524
Portugieser 143
Rajinski Rizling (*syn*) 34
Rajnai Rizling (*syn*) 34
Red Gentil 330–31
Rheinriesling (*syn*) 34
Riesling 6, 34, 282–3, 289
Riesling evolution 523
Riesling Renano (*syn*) 34
Riesling Reno (*syn*) 34
Roter Muskateller (*syn*) 35
Rulanda (*syn*) 33
Ruländer (*syn*) 33
Savagnin 304
Scheurebe 143
Seibel 11
Seyval Villard 11
Spätburgunder (*syn*) 34
Sylvaner 36, 7, 298
Sylvaner evolution 522

Syrah 372
Szürkerbarat (*syn*) 33
Tokay-Pinot Gris 6, 33, 266–7, 271, 273–4
Tokay-Pinot Gris evolution 523
Traminer (*syn*) 6, 304
Valais (*syn*) 36
Viognier 372
Weissburgunder (*syn*) 32
Weisse Muscketraube (*syn*) 35
Weisse Muskateller (*syn*) 35
Weisser Burgunder grape (*syn*) 32
Weisser Riesling (*syn*) 34
White Muscat (*syn*) 35
White Riesling (*syn*) 34
Grapes
  acid conversion 28
  botrytis cinerea 30–31
  embryo bunches 26
  hydrolysed tannins 28
  late harvest 30
  metabolism 28
  noble rot 30–31
  order of ripening 29
  pourriture noble 30–31
Grasberg lieu-dit 248
Grass, Clos Philippe 143, 229, 256, 426
Grasshoppers, plague of 513–14
Grauer Burgunder grape (*syn*) 33
Grauer Mönch grape (*syn*) 33
Grauklevner grape (*syn*) 33, 274
Gravel 59
Greiner, Jean 189, 239, 393
Greiner, Paul 11
Greiner-Schleret, GAEC 189, 239 393
Grès or Gréseux 59
Gresser, Domaine André & Rémy 69, 87–8, 191, 219, 244, 251, 276, 287, 393, 412
Gros Rhin grape (*syn*) 36
Grosshardt lieu-dit 248
Grosstein lieu-dit 248
Gruss & Fils, Joseph 394
Gsell, Joseph 394
Gueberschwihr village 2, 91, 518
Guebwiller village 92, 47, 92, 517–18
Gueth & Fils, A. 241, 246, 253, 394
Guide Dussert-Gerber des Vins de France 407
Guide Hachette 407
Gutedel grape (*syn*) 36, 301, 303
Guth, Roland 95, 176, 406, 474

Gypsiferous marl 60
Gypsum 60
Gyropalette 45

Haegelin, Matterne 116, 252, 276, 394
Haegi, GAEC Bernard & Daniel 244, 394
Hagel lieu-dit 518–19
Hagelberg lieu-dit 519
Hagenschlauf lieu-dit 245, 248, 519
Hahnenberg lieu-dit 80, 248, 519
Hailengenftein (*sic*) 95
Halbeisen, Jean 159, 394
Halde lieu-dit 2, 234
Hapsburg princes 103
Hapsburgs, fief of 116
Hardt lieu-dit 82, 248, 475, 518
  Grosshardt 248
  Mittelhardt 248
  Oberhardt 248
Hárslevelu grape 6
Harth lieu-dit 82, 248, 448
Hartmann, André 138, 176, 287, 394
Hartmann, Gérard & Serge 138, 176, 395
Hartmannswiller village 94
Hartmannswillerkopf 94
Hartweg, Jean-Paul 211, 395
Harvesting 29
  in July 513
  in May 512
  mechanical 29
  proclamation 84
  SGN 30, 38
  twice in one year 511
  Vendange Tardive 30, 38
Hasenhaut lieu-dit 254
Hatschbourg grand cru 94–5, 175, 518–19
Hattstatt village 94, 518
Hauller, Louis 83, 88–9, 169, 396
Hauller & Fils, J. 83, 129, 169, 248, 255, 292, 300, 345, 395
Hausberg lieu-dit 519
Hauserer, Clos 141–2, 229, 286, 318, 325, 477
Haute Seille Abbey 201
Haut-Koenigsbourg castle 239
Haut-Koenigsbourg, Coteaux de 245
Haut-Rhin
  AOC Alsace area 64
  hectares in production 64
  Vin de Pays du 306, 334–5, 354

Haut-Ribeaupierre castle 120
Hebinger & Fils, Jean-Victor 396
Heidehaus 125
Heidelberg Man 12
Heiligenstein village 7, 95, 519
Heim, Jean-Paul 335, 396
Heim, SA 241, 471
Heimbourg lieu-dit 249
Heissenberg 249
Heissenstein lieu-dit 93, 112, 249, 518
Heitzloch lieu-dit 518
Heitzmann & Fils, H. & J. 396
Helgenstein 95
Hell-Cadé, Léon 396
Hengl grafting 20
Hengst grand cru 2, 176, 519
Henry V 126
Herade de Landsberg 89
Hercules 202
Hering, Domaine 184, 229, 287, 397
Herrenstubengesellschaft 4, 67
Herrenweg lieu-dit 250
Herrlisheim village 64, 96, 518
Hertz, Albert 165, 280, 287, 292, 303, 397
Hertz, Bruno 203, 292, 397
Hertzog, Gérard 175, 398
Hertzog, Marcel 175, 398
Heydt-Trimbach family 459
Heyligenstein (sic) 95
Heywang, Jean 96, 292, 334, 398
Higerst lieu-dit 255
Hill of flowers 167
Himmelreich, Clos 115, 230
Hippler, Charles 448
Hippolytus, Saint 5
Hohenbourg lieu-dit 89
Holtzberg 117
Holy Roman Emperors
    Charlemagne 130
    Charles the Fat (and king of
        Swabia) 106
    Ferdinand I 114
    Frederick III (and king of
        Germany) 69
    Henry V (and king of Bohemia/
        Hungary) 126
    Louis the Pious 130
    Maximilian I (and king of
        Germany) 103
Holy Roman Empress, Maria
    Theresa 202
Homo errectus 12

Horcher & Fils, Ernest 398
Horn de Wolxheim lieu-dit 239, 250, 519
Hornblende 60
Houssen village 97
Hube oder Haube lieu-dit 517
Huben lieu-dit 518
Huettgasse lieu-dit 250
Hugel & Fils 38, 122, 147, 155, 212, 270, 276, 281, 292, 310–11, 313, 316–18, 320–21, 324, 326, 328–9, 348, 369, 395, 399, 459, 482–3, 487, 529
Hans Ulrich Hugel 399
Johnny Hugel 4, 11, 14, 147–51, 212, 311, 320, 329, 344, 459
Jean Hugel 313
Marc Hugel 399
Humbrecht, Bernard (firm) 92, 175, 400
Humbrecht, Léonard (see also Zind
    Humbrecht) 134, 202–3, 359, 477–8, 482, 485
Humbrecht, Marcel (firm) 92, 149, 175, 287, 297, 401
Humbrecht, Olivier (see also Zind
    Humbrecht) 202–3, 359, 478
Humus 60
Huna 98
Hunawihr village 2, 97, 518
Hunold, Bruno 218, 401
Hunon 98
Hüntsch 4
Hurst, Auguste 162, 401
Husseren castles of 99
Husseren-les-Châteaux village 99
Huttard, Jean 245, 401
Huxelrebe grape 143
Hydroponics 52

Igneous rock 60
Iltis, Jacques 257, 281, 287, 333, 402
Immerschenberg 77
INAO 75, 147–8, 154, 179
Ingersheim village 100, 518
INRA 149, 219–20
Irish monks 75
Irish prince 232
Irmstett village 100
Iron 54
Isinglass 40
Itterswiller village 96, 100

'Jardin, Clos du 230
Jebsal, Clos 135, 230, 275, 317–18
Johannisberg Riesling grape (syn) 34
Johnson, Hugh 299
JosMeyer 136, 142, 155, 162, 177,
    250, 270, 272, 287, 293, 302, 402
Jean Meyer 177, 403
Jung & Fils, GAEC 213, 252, 270, 281,
    316, 405
Jungholtz village 101, 517
Jupiter grafting 20
Jura 304
Jux, Domaine 82, 248, 405, 473, 475

Kaefferkopf lieu-dit 66–7, 72, 153–4,
    178, 210, 309, 518
Kanzlerberg grand cru 73, 159, 181,
    517–18
Kapelweg 250
Karcher, Robert 249
Karcher & Fils, Robert 406
Karchweg 250
Kastelberg grand cru 1–2, 182, 517,
    519
Kastelthal 102
Katharinenthal 102
Katzenburg 519
Katzenthal village 2, 49, 101, 518
Kaufstueckel lieu-dit 254
Kaysersberg village 2, 66, 102, 518
Kazo, Lord 102
Kefferberg lieu-dit 239, 251
Kehren, Domaine 176, 406
Keimberg lieu-dit 251
Kessler grand cru 2, 183, 518
Keuper 60
Kieffer, Domaine 89, 101, 247, 406
Kienheim village 104
Kientz, René 407
Kientzheim castle 104
Kientzheim village 2, 49, 104, 518
Kientzler, André 186, 195, 272, 276,
    287, 292, 297, 301, 316, 318, 326,
    332, 385, 407
Kings
    Charles the Bald (France) 14
    Charles the Fat (Swabia & Holy
        Roman Emperor) 68, 106
    Childebert II (France) 107, 216
    Dagobert (France) 106, 134
    Ferdinand I (and Holy Roman
        Emperors) 114
    Frederick III (Germany and Holy
        Roman Emperor) 69
    Henry V (Bohemia/Hungary) 126
    Lothair II (Lorraine) 14
    Louis the German (Bavaria) 14
    Louis XIV (France) 7, 8, 14, 238
    Maximilian I (Germany and Holy
        Roman Emperor) 103
Kintzheim village 2, 105, 519
Kirchberg de Barr grand cru 70, 184,
    519
Kirchberg de Ribeauvillé grand cru 2,
    120–21, 185, 240, 518
Kirchberg d'Itterswiller lieu-dit 519
Kirchberg d'Orschwiller lieu-dit 519
Kirchheim village 106
Kirrenburg lieu-dit 518
Kirsch country 137
Kitterlé grand cru 2, 186, 518
Klavner grape (syn) 35
Kléc, Henri 408
Klée & Fils, Victor 102, 408
Klein, Georges 281, 333, 408
Klein, Jean-Pierre 409
Klein, Raymond & Martin 409
Klein, Roger 409
Klein & Fils, Joseph 227
Klein & Fils, René 245, 247, 302, 409
Klein Aux Vieux Remparts 245, 247,
    292, 302–3, 409
Kleinknecht, André 185, 409
Klevanka grape (syn) 33
Klevener 7, 95–6
Klevener de Heiligenstein 7, 95–6,
    333–4, 353, 398, 467, 545
    villages in appellation 333
Klevner grape (syn) 32, 34, 303
Klevner de Heiligenstein (sic) 519
Kliener Rauschling grape 330–31
Kliener Riesling grape 9
Klipfel, Domaine 71, 96, 125, 182,
    184, 238–9, 246, 292, 299, 334,
    345, 409
Klipfel, Eugène 96, 334, 345
Klur-Stoecklé 220, 287, 410
Klusterhof lieu-dit 251
Knipperlé grape 9, 11, 330–31
Kober rootstock, Selection 5BB 22
Koeberlé-Kreyer 124, 174, 270, 276,
    411
Koehly, Jean-Marie 105, 411
Koehly & Fils, Charles 159, 173, 270,
    276, 292, 316, 411
Kreydenweiss, Marc 69, 87, 182, 191,

219, 231, 236, 251–2, 272, 276,
  287, 292, 297, 299, 303, 311, 318,
  324, 339, 412
Krick, Hubert 177, 413
Kritt lieu-dit 251
Kronenbourg 252
Kuehn, Vins d'Alsace 414
Kuentz, Alphonse 86, 165, 197, 292,
  414
Kuentz-Bas 86, 99, 164, 197, 276, 281,
  291, 293, 297, 302, 316–17,
  323–4, 337–40, 348, 414
  Christian Bas 415
  Jacques Weber 415
Kugelsberg 192
Kuttolsheim village 334

Landmann, Gérard 89, 112, 193, 287,
  415
Landmann Seppi 132, 223, 276, 287,
  293, 300, 332, 340, 416
Landmann-Ostholt 223, 272, 276,
  281, 293
Landot grape 11
Landsberg, Herade de 89
Language of Alsace 547
Laugel Maison Michel 107, 216,
  339–40, 345, 417
Leg breakers 94
Lehm 60
Leiber, Domaine Edouard 99, 165, 418
Leimbach village 106
Leimenthal 252
Leininger, Gilbert 158, 418
Leo IX 86, 157
Léon Millot grape 11
Lerchenberg lieu-dit 68, 252, 518
Letzenberg lieu-dit 252
Lichtlé, Fernand 175, 418
Lichtlé, François 418
Lieux-dits, chronology of 2
Limestone 60
Limon 60
Lippelsberg lieu-dit 115–16, 252, 518
Liqueur d'expédition 45
Loam 60
Loberger, Domaine Joseph 418
Loess 60
Lorberger-Hell, Joseph 211
Lord's mountain 255
Lord's vines 248
Lorentz, Gustave 74, 159, 181, 270,
  276, 287, 293, 345, 348, 418, 489

Lothair II 14
Louis the German 14
Louis the Pious 130
Louis XIV 7, 14, 238
  royal edicts 7–8
Lupfen, castle of the counts of 104
Lupfen, Domaine des Comtes de 105,
  130, 171, 206–7, 243, 248, 253,
  269, 286, 292, 318, 323, 339–40,
  363

Mader 99, 121, 204, 287, 297, 420
Magnesium 54–5
Maison Becker 106, 145, 170, 201,
  248, 252, 255, 281, 286, 292, 297,
  299, 319, 327, 358
Maison Bott Frères 286, 292, 365
Maison Bott-Geyl 189, 211, 276, 292,
  366
Maison Burn 92, 174, 231, 275, 297,
  319, 327, 368
Maison du Val de Villé 65
Maison Léon Baur 180, 239, 281, 286,
  356
Maison Léon Beyer 86, 147, 152–5,
  165, 189, 197, 269, 276, 286, 292,
  323, 348, 361, 496
Maison Michel Laugel 216, 339–40,
  345, 417
Maison Wiederhirn 189, 208, 213,
  288, 471
Malic acid 28
Mallo & Fils 99, 121, 189, 204, 276,
  287, 293, 420
Malolactic fermentation 39
  requirements 39–40
Malvoisie grape (syn) 33
Mambourg grand cru 2, 187, 517
Mamburg (sic) 519
Mandelberg grand cru 1–2, 188, 518
Mann, Albert 141–2, 177, 207, 249,
  254, 270, 282, 287, 293, 324, 332,
  420
Mantelkragen lieu-dit 519
Marble 57
Marckrain grand cru 190
Maréchal Foch grape 11
Markrain (sic) 518
Marl 60
Marlenheim village 2, 107, 280, 519
Marlstone 61
Marne 61
Marne & Champagne 88, 423

Marno-calcaire 61
Marocke, Robert 149, 518
Marronniers, Domaine des 421
Masmunster, abbot and Abbey of 201
Mattern, Domaine 219, 251, 421
Mauer (Germany) 12
Mauler, Jean-Paul 189, 293, 422
Mauler & Fils, GAEC André 422
Mauler Jean-Paul 109
Maurer, Albert 422
Maximilian I 103
Mayorquine grafting 20
Mechanical harvesting 29
Meissenberg 252
Mercklé & Fils, André 422
Merovingian kings
    Childebert II 107, 216
    Dagobert 106, 134
Merovingian lords
    Adalric 114
Mersiol, Guy 169, 423
Metamorphic rocks 61
Méthode Champenoise 43
Metz, Arthur 88, 345, 423
Metz, Hubert 221, 245, 282, 293, 340,
    423
Metzig 110
Metz-Bleger 174, 423
Meyer, Domaine Julien 112, 249, 259,
    300, 424
Meyer, Eugène 211, 424
Meyer, François 221
Meyer, Jean 177, 403
Meyer, Lucien 176, 424
Meyer-Brauneiser, René 424
Meywihr lieu-dit 518
Meywihr, Clos de la 231, 409
Mica 61
Mildew 9, 17
    downy 5, 34, 36–7, 507–8
    powdery 5, 34–7, 63
Millardet et de Grasset 41B
    rootstock 22
Millstone 61
Mittelbergheim village 2, 107, 519
Mittelhardt lieu-dit 248
Mittelwihr castle 109
Mittelwihr village 1–2, 11, 108, 518
Mittnacht Frères, Domaine 205, 229,
    253, 276, 424, 487
Mittnacht-Klack 208, 287, 293, 425
Mochel, Frédéric 134, 157, 287, 293,
    425

Mochel-Lorentz, GAEC 158, 425
Moenchberg grand cru 1–2, 191, 519
Moenchreben 252
Molsheim village 2, 110, 517, 519
Mönchberg 517
Monkeys' Mountain 105
Monk's hill 192, 252
Mont de Sigolsheim 105
Mont Ste-Odile 76, 89, 91, 114, 118,
    128
Montagne des Singes 105
Moritz & Fils, Charles 182, 191, 219,
    425
Moscato Bianco grape (syn) 35
Moscato di Canelli grape (syn) 35
Moscato d'Asti grape (syn) 35
Muehlforst lieu-dit 253, 518
Muenchberg grand cru 2, 192
Muhlberger, François 149, 160, 229,
    250, 256, 287, 293, 425
Mulching 28
Mulhouse 3–4, 64
Mullenbach, Marcel 111, 426
Muller-Koeberle, Domaine 127, 228,
    245, 247, 257, 276, 282, 333, 426
Müller-Thurgau grape 11, 143
Munchberg (sic) 519
Murbach Abbey 115, 164, 176
Murbach abbot 176
Muré 282, 287, 297, 426
    Reine-Thérèse Muré 427
    René Muré 427
Muri Abbey 213, 243
Muscadel Ottonel grape (syn) 35
Muscat grape 6, 35
Muscat à Petit Grains grape 294–5
Muscat Blanc à Petit Grains grape 35
Muscat Canelli grape (syn) 35
Muscat de Beaumes de Venise 295
Muscat de Frontignan grape (syn) 35
Muscat d'Alsace grape 35, 294–5
Muscat Ottonel grape 35, 294–5
Muscat Rosé à Petit Grains grape 35
Muscatel Branco grape (syn) 35
Muschelkalk 61
Muskadel grape (syn) 35
Muskateller grape (syn) 35
Muskateller Ottonel grape (syn) 35
Muskat-Ottonel grape (syn) 35
Muskotoly grape (syn) 35
Mutzig village 110, 519
Mutzig beer 110

Named sites, chronology 2
Napoléon 144, 160
Nartz, Michel 428
Nematodes 22
Neolithic period 12
Neolithic remains 132
Neubruch 517
Neubrunnen 254
Neumeyer, Gérard 163, 428
Nibelungenlied, epic poem 134
Niedermorschwihr village 2, 49, 111, 518
Nigellus, Ermoldus 3, 64, 130
Nitrogen 54
Noak 279, 281, 475
Noble rot 30
Nordheim village 111, 334, 519
North, Alain 335, 428
Nothalten village 2, 112, 519

Ober Ehenheim 114
Ober Rebgarten 254
Oberberg lieu-dit 77, 253, 519
Oberer-Weingarten lieu-dit 253
Oberhardt lieu-dit 248
Oberhoffen village 112
Oberlin, Chrétien 71
Obermorshwihr village 113
Obernai village 2, 113, 519
Octanoic acid 42
Odours
  amylic or cool fermentation 39
  primary 39
  secondary 39
Odratzheim village 115
Oidium 9, 17, 508
Ollwiller grand cru 2, 194
Omega grafting 20
ONIVINS 75
Oolite 61
Oolith 61
Order of Friars Minor Capuchins 468
Orschwihr village 2, 115, 517-8
Orschwihr, Château of 429
Orschwiller village 2, 116, 519
Ortenbourg castle 129, 255, 517
Ortlieber grape 330-31
Osenbach village 64, 117
Osterberg grand cru 120, 195, 518
Ostertag, André 89, 112, 193, 242, 246, 249, 269, 276, 287, 291, 297, 300, 316, 318, 325-6, 328-9, 429
Osthoffen village 117

Otaleswilre 115
Ottrott village 118, 519
Oxides 62

Pagan House 125
Pantheum Hygisticum 202
Particle size 61
Passerillage 30, 314
Patergarten 253
Perchaim 74
Perlan grape (syn) 36
Perlite 61
Perpignan 258
Petite Chronique de Thann 134
Pfaffenheim village 2, 118, 518
Pfaffenheim, Coteaux of 243
Pfersigberg grand cru 2, 196
Pfingstberg grand cru 2, 198, 518
Pfirsichberg (sic) 518
Pfirsigberg 86
Pflaenzerreben lieu-dit 253
Pflanzer 519
Pfleck 254
Pfoeller 519
Phosphate 54
Phosphates 62
Photosynthesis 54
Phylloxera 5, 9-10, 16-19, 21-4, 506
  etymological origin 18
  leaf-form 18
  life-cycle 18-19
  origin of European outbreak 17
  pre-phylloxera vines 16
  root-forms 18
  sexual-form 18
  Tyroglyphus 17
  winged-form 19
Phylloxera-free vines 62
Pinot Auxerrois grape (syn) 32, 303
Pinot Beurot grape (syn) 33
Pinot Bianco grape (syn) 32
Pinot Blanc grape 6, 32, 266-7, 271, 289
Pinot Chardonnay grape (syn) 37, 302
Pinot Grigio grape (syn) 33
Pinot Gris grape 6, 33, 274, 303
Pinot Meunier grape 11
Pinot Nero grape (syn) 34
Pinot Noir grape 5-6, 34, 41, 266-7, 277-8
  clones 41
  colour extraction 41-2
  origins 5

soft tannin extraction 41–2
Plagues
    bubonic 513
    caterpillars 515
    grasshoppers 513–14
Pliny 6, 127
Pope Leo IX 86, 157, 226
Portugieser grape 143
Potassium 54
Praelatenberg grand cru 2, 200, 517, 519
Precipitated salts 61
Preiss, Hubert 432
Preiss, Jean Adolphe Camile 432
Preiss-Henny, J-C 189, 432
Preiss-Zimmer 287, 293, 348, 433, 464
Press-house operations 38, 41–2
Protein haze 40
Protocelts 12
Proto-Germanics 12
Proto-Indo-Europeans 12
Pruning 24
Puglisi, Angelo 298

Quartz 62
Queensland's Granite Belt 298
Quintessence SGN 321

Rabold, Raymond 199, 434
Rainfall 47
    precipitation map 48
Rajinski Rizling grape (syn) 34
Rajnai Rizling grape (syn) 34
Ramstein castle 129
Rangen grand cru 27, 201, 517, 519
Ratbertovilare 120
Ratberto's villa 120
Rebgarten, Clos 231, 297, 413
Rebgarten lieu-dit 68, 91, 254, 518
Red Gentil grape 330–31
Red hill 255
Red Traminer grape (syn) 35
Reichsfeld village 119
Reifenberg lieu-dit 254, 519
Reinhart, Vignobles 244, 434
Religious cults 243
Rempart, Domaine du 281, 434
Remuage 45
Rémy-Pannier 417
Rentz, Edmond 435
Rheinfalz 299
Rheinriesling grape (syn) 34
Rhine, viticultural influence 50

Ribeauvillé village 2, 119, 517–18
Richard d'Epfig 198
Richo, Lord 122
Richovilare 122
Richter 110
    rootstock 23
Riedseltz village 121
Rieffel & Fils, Julien 224, 244, 273, 436
Rieflé, Domaine 119, 214, 240–41, 243, 247, 256, 276, 293, 436
Riesling grape 6, 10, 34, 282–3, 289
Riesling Renano grape (syn) 34
Riesling Reno grape (syn) 34
Rietsch, Pierre & Jean-Pierre 224, 436
Rimelsberg 255
Ringenbach-Moser, Etablissements 437
Riquewihr village 2, 6–7, 14, 121, 517–18
Rissling 282
Rittersberg lieu-dit 129, 255, 517, 519
Ritzenthaler, Jean-Paul 433
Rivers
    Bruche 50
    Fecht 51
    Giessen 51
    Ill 4
    Lauch 51
    Mosel 9
    Mossig 50
    Ombach 140
    Rhine 3, 9, 12–13, 50
    Rhône 12
    Saône 12
    Thur 51
    Weiss 51
    Weissbach 51
Rodern village 123, 518
Roemerberg 255
Rolli-Edel, Willy 124, 437
Rolly, Thérèse 438
Rolly Gassmann 124, 250, 253–4, 257, 270, 273, 288, 293, 297, 300, 324, 438
Romans 1, 6, 13
Rominger, Eric 75, 206, 252, 439
Rootstock 21–3
    110 Richter 23
    161–9 Couderc 23
    3309 Couderc 23
    41B Millardet et de Grasset 22
    5BB Selection Kober 22

5C Teleki 23
SO4 22
Rorschwihr village 123
Rosacker grand cru 2, 152, 204, 518
Rosé de Marlenheim 95, 107
Rosé de Turckheim 281
Rosé d'Alsace 277–8
Rosenberg 255
Rosenwiller village 124
Rosheim village 124
Rotenberg lieu-dit 141, 255, 518
Roter Muskateller grape (syn) 35
Roter Traminer grape (syn) 35
Rotgold, Pierre 439
Rothmuerlé 256
Rothmüerle 256
Rothstein Clos 354
Roth-Stein Clos 143, 231
Rothstein lieu-dit 239, 256
Rott village 125
Rot-Murlé 256
Rouffach village 125, 518
Rouffach, feminists of 126
Rouge de Marlenheim 519
Rouge de Rodern 95, 277, 518
Rouge de St-Hippolyte 247, 281
Rouge d'Alsace 41–2, 277–9, 303–4
Rouge d'Ottrott 95, 277, 519
Route des Crêtes 79
Rubeaquam 126
Ruhlmann, GAEC A. 119, 439
Ruhlmann Dirringer 440
Rulanda grape (syn) 33
Ruländer grape (syn) 33
Runner, François 214, 243, 440
Rupp, Georges 80, 371
Ruthaud, Count 84

SA Heim 471
Sable 62
Sableuse 62
Saering grand cru 2, 205, 518
St-Gregory of Tours 107
St-Hippolyte village 126, 518
St-Hippolytus 5, 127
St-Imer, Clos 91–2, 174, 231, 275, 297, 368–9
St-Immer (sic), Clos 518
St-Jacques, Clos 232, 372
St-Jorgom 89
St-Landelin, Clos 126, 218, 232, 282, 287, 297, 319, 426–7, 518
St-Nabor village 127

St-Pierre village 128
St-Théobold 202
St-Théobold, Clos 133, 233, 288, 448
St-Ulrich castle 120
St-Urbain, Clos 133, 233, 275, 318, 482
Ste-Hune 98
Ste-Hune, Clos 52, 97–9, 152, 204, 227, 233, 283, 285–6, 460–4, 477, 518
Ste-Odile 114, 131, 234
Ste-Odile, Clos 13–14, 234, 428, 519
Ste-Odile, Mont 76, 89, 91, 114, 118, 128
Ste-Richard Abbey 68
Salt-water meadow 132
Salzmann-Thomann 207, 293, 441
Sand 62
Sandstone 62
Sandy-loam 62
Satanists 243
Sauternes 321
Savagnin grape 304
Saw-type grafting 20
Schaeffer-Woerly 169, 441
Schaeflé, E. 441
Schaetzel, Domaine Martin 180, 276, 300, 441
Schaller & Fils, Edgard 109, 189, 276, 288, 293, 339, 442
    Patrick Schaller 442
Scharrach 128
Scharrachbergheim-Irmstett village 128
Schauenberg 517
Scheidecker, Philippe 288, 443
Schenckenberg (sic) 519
Schenk d'Ehenheim lieu-dit 256
Schenkenberg lieu-dit 2, 256
Scherb & Fils, Georges 175, 443
Scherb & Fils, Louis 175, 443
Scherer, André 99, 165, 197, 443
Scherwiller village 129, 517, 519
Scheurebe grape 143
Schick, Brigitte 93
Schillé & Fils, Pierre 188, 443
Schillerwein 304
Schillinger, E. 444
Schimberg lieu-dit 93, 518
Schist 62
Schlegel-Boeglin, Jean-Paul 223, 444
Schleret, Charles 136, 276, 293, 297, 444
Schlossberg grand cru 2, 206, 518

Schlossberg, Clos du 2, 120, 234, 310, 452
Schlosser, Marcel 191, 219, 293, 446
Schlossreben lieu-dit 127, 257, 518–19
Schlumberger, Domaine 75, 94, 126, 183, 186–7, 205, 276, 287–8, 293, 309, 348, 405, 444, 482
Nicolas Schlumberger 445
Schmidt, René 208
Schmitt, Raymond 144, 194, 446
Schmitt, Roland 247, 288, 293, 446
Schmitt, R. & G. 88
Schneckelsbourg lieu-dit 161, 519
Schneckenberg lieu-dit 118, 161, 213, 243, 257, 518
Schneider, Paul 447
Schneider, René & Bernard 180, 447
Schoech, Albert 402, 447
Schoech, Maurice 180, 447
Schoenenbourg grand cru 111, 121–2, 208, 517–19
Schoepfer, Jean-Louis 447
Schoepfer, Michel 448
Schoffit, Domaine 82, 134, 203, 233, 249, 277, 288, 300, 302, 448
Schongauer, Martin 79
Schueller, Gérard 197, 293, 448
Schueller, Maurice 175, 449
Schwach, Bernard 180, 212, 288, 294, 449
Schwach, Paul 449
Schwach & Fils, François 180, 449
Schwartz, Jean-Luc 193, 449
Schwartz, Justin 101, 247, 449
Schwartz & Fils, Emile 197, 449
Schwartz Successeur, Oscar 253, 449
Schwarze Abbey 84
Schweitzer, Albert 103
Schwendemann-Haegelen 194, 450
Schwendi, Baron Lazare de 6, 103, 105, 142, 167, 274
Scree 62
Sedimentary rock 62
Seibel grape 11
Seilly, GAEC 450
Sélection de Grains Nobles 30
Selection Kober 5BB rootstock 22
Seltz, Albert or Alsace 244, 299–300, 450
Sendel 254
Seppi Landmann 132, 223, 276, 287, 293, 300, 332, 340, 416
Sequani tribe 12–13

Seyval Villard grape 11
Shale 63
Shingle 63
Sick-Dreyer 67, 99, 102, 130, 180, 288, 324, 450
Siegler Père & Fils, P. 451
Siffert, Domaine 201, 239, 282, 451
Sigillé de Qualité, Confrérie St-Etienne 284, 343, 386
Sigolsheim village 2–3, 49, 64, 129, 517, 519
Sigolsheim Union 258, 345
Sigolttesberg 187
Sigwalt 130
Silberberg lieu-dit 124, 257, 519
Siliceous soil 55, 63
Silt 63
Silvaner grape (syn) 36
Simonis, Jean-Paul 451
Sinne, Domaine de la 221, 390
Sinne, origin and meaning of the term 390
Sipp, Domaine Jean 186, 234, 258, 270, 277, 288, 293, 307, 310, 452
Sipp, Grands Vins d'Alsace Louis 186, 195, 240, 288, 293, 309-310, 452
Sipp-Mack, Domaine 99, 205, 288, 453
Sittler, Claude 49, 149, 518
Slate 63
SO4 rootstock 22
Soil, general 52–63
active-lime in 22
general influence 53
high lime content 22
influence by type 55
in the plains 55
in the Vosges foothills 55
in the Vosges mountains 55
minerals required
more than a medium 53
particle size 61
pH 54
temperature 53
topsoil and subsoil 54
water-retention 53
Soil types
active-lime in 22
aeolian 57
alluvial 56–7
aqueous 57
arenaceous 57
argillaceous 58

basalt 58
calcareous 56–8
calcareous clay 58
carbonaceous 58
chalk 58
clay 58
clay-loam 59
colluvial 59
crystalline 59
dolomite 59
feldspar or felspar 59
ferruginous clay 59
glacial moraine 59
gneiss 59
granite 59
gravel 59
gypsiferous marl 60
gypsum 60
hornblende 60
humus 60
igneous rock 60
keuper 60
limestone 60
loam 60
loess 60
marl 60
marlstone 61
metamorphic 61
mica 61
millstone 61
muschelkalk 61
oolite 61
oolith 61
perlite 61
quartz 62
sand 62
sandstone 62
sandy-loam 62
schist 62
scree 62
sedimentary rock 62
shale 63
shingle 63
siliceous 55, 63
silt 63
slate 63
steige 63
stratified rock 63
tufa 63
villé 63
volcanic 63
Soil characteristics found in wine 55
Sommerberg grand cru 2, 49, 209, 518

Sonnenbach, Clos du 65, 235, 281, 435
Sonnenberg lieu-dit 519
Sonnenglanz grand cru 67, 71, 210, 518
Sophie d'Andlau 69
Sorg, Bruno 86, 100, 167, 197, 273, 277, 288, 293, 296–7, 340, 454
Soultz village 130
Soultzmatt village 49, 131, 519
Soultz-les-Bains village 131
Spa baths 131
Sparr, Pierre 130, 136, 162, 180, 188, 207, 277, 288, 293, 310–11, 324, 339–40, 454
Spätburgunder grape (syn) 34
Specht, Jean-Paul & Denis 455
Sperry & Fils, Pierre 78, 455
Spiegel grand cru 74–5, 92, 211, 518
Spielmann, Jean-Martin 159, 181, 270, 294, 297, 319, 455
Spitz & Fils 456
Sporen grand cru 2, 212, 518
Sporen Gentil 310, 400
Staehlé, Bernard 288, 456
Steige 63
Stein 519
Steinacker lieu-dit 518
Steinbach village 132
Steinberg lieu-dit 518
Steiner (sic) 213
Steinert grand cru 2, 213, 518
Steingrubler grand cru 2, 215, 519
Steinklotz grand cru 2, 216, 239, 519
Steinseltz village 132
Steinweg 257
Stentz, Domaine Aimé 111, 177, 209, 236, 255, 282, 288, 303, 456
Stentz, Fernand 456
Stichgeld 4
Stichwein 4
Stierkopf 519
Stintzi, Gérard 165, 457
Stoeffler, Charles 457
Stoltz, J. L. 85, 93, 101, 129, 244, 246, 517
Stone 63
Stork and Glass Club 348
Stotzheim village 133
Strangenberg lieu-dit 139, 258, 519
Strasbourg 4, 50
Stratified rock 63
Straub & Fils, Joseph 78
Stripicher 356

Sturm, Clos Jean-Philippe 85, 235
Stutzmann, Michel 335, 457
Suebi tribe 13
Sulphates 62
Sulphur dioxide 40
Super-SGN 321
Sylvaner grape 7, 36, 224, 298
Syndicat pour le Défense des Vins de
    Pays du Bas-Rhin 365
Syrah grape 372
Szürkerbarat grape (syn) 33

Tannin 40
Tartaric acid 28
Tartrate deposits 40
Teleki 5C rootstock 23
Tempelhof 517
Templars 181, 517
Teutonic heroes of Nibelungenlied 134
Thann village 133, 517, 519
Thirty Years War 3, 7, 14, 99, 128
Thomas, André 130, 180, 188, 316,
    319, 328
Thomas & Fils, GAEC André 457
Tiré Bouchon, Winstub 434
Tokay d'Alsace or Tokay-Pinot Gris
    grape 6, 33, 266–7, 271, 273–4
Topography 46
Tour, Domaine de la 458
Tourelle, Clos de la 144, 226, 236, 465
Tours d'Eguisheim 99
Traenheim village 134
Traminer grape (syn) 6, 35, 305
Traminer Aromatico grape (syn) 35
Traminer Rose grape (syn) 35
Tramini grape (syn) 35
Trichogramma minutum 220
Trimbach, F.E. 98–9, 120, 147, 152,
    154–5, 173, 195, 204, 227, 233–4,
    283–5, 291, 299–300, 321, 323,
    325–6, 348, 458
    Bernard Trimbach 344, 459
    Hubert Trimbach 344, 459
    Jean Trimbach 459
    Jean-Frédéric Trimbach 459
    Pierre Trimbach 459
Trois châteaux 99
Trois-Epis 209
Trottacker lieu-dit 258, 518
Trottehuse ze Hagenach lieu-dit 258
Tufa 63
Turckheim village 135, 518
Turks 6

Turks' Blood 135, 162
Tyroglyphus phylloxera 17

Uffolz village 136
Undersberg 112, 192
Ungersberg 119
Union, Sigolsheim 258, 345

Val d'Eléon, Clos du 68, 236, 311, 413
Valais grape (syn) 36
Vallée Noble 139, 258
Varietal wines, first in Alsace 5
Vendange Tardive 30
Vendredi, mystery of the lieu-dit 368
Véraison 28
Verdun, Treaty of 14
Vicus Romain, Clos du 236
Viel Armand 94
Vierling, Joseph 335, 465
Vierling, Lucie 335, 466
Vieux-Thann village 64, 136
Vignobles Reinhart 244, 434
Vila Eberhardo 92
Villa Columbaria 81
Villé village 63, 137
Vin de glace 223, 408, 416
Vin de paille 67, 96, 103, 105, 118,
    121, 123, 127, 136, 144, 478
Vin de Pays du Bas-Rhin 306, 334–5,
    365, 428
Vin de Pays du Haut-Rhin 306, 334–5,
    354
Vin de Pistolet 114
Vin gris 280
Vin jaune 304
Vin Mousseux d'Alsace 335
Vin noble 4, 9
Vine training, raison d'être 24
Vines
    active-lime resistance 22
    botrytis cinerea 30–31
    bud-break 25
    cane training 24
    chemical fumigation 17
    chlorosis 22
    coulure 26–7
    crosses 9–11, 18, 21, 262
    dormancy 25
    embryo bunches 26
    en foule 16, 24
    fan-leaf 22
    flooding 17
    flowering 27

fruit set 28
grafting 16, 18
harvesting 29
hybrids 9–11, 21, 23, 79–80, 90,
    139, 146, 262
iron deficiency 22
late-harvest 30
life of grafted 16
life of pre-phylloxera 16
lord's 248
metabolism of grape 28
millerandage 26–7
mineral requirements 54
mulching 28
nematode resistance 22
noble rot 30–31
overproduction 9, 490–91, 513–15
overproduction or underselling 529
phylloxera-resistant species 21
pourriture noble 30–31
pre-phylloxera 16
pruning 24–5
rootstock 9, 16–18, 21–4, 32–7
root-knot 22
sap rising 25
spraying 26, 28–9
spur training 24
ungrafted 24
véraison 28
vulnerability to frost 25, 27
weeding 28
weeping 25
Vineyard names, chronology 2
Vineyards
    Alsace vins de pays 50
    Alsace vins de tables 50
    altitude temperature 49
    AOC Alsace area 49
    Bas-Rhin 49
    chemical purification 10
    drainage 52
    foothills 49
    Haut-Rhin 49
    highest 49
    mountain 49
    non-AOC 50
    plains 49
Vinification 38–45
    bottling 41
    cold stabilisation 40
    filtration 38, 40–42
    fining 38, 40, 42
    free-run juice 42

malolactic 42
prefermentation maceration 278
press wine 42
pre-fermentation filtration 38
protein haze 40
racking 40, 42
red wine 41–2, 278
red wine over-extraction 279
sparkling wines 43
sulphur dioxide 40
Vinimatic 42, 278
    white wine 38–40
Vinimatic 42, 278
Vins de pailles 144
Vins Dirler 75, 94, 183, 206, 211, 286,
    297, 324, 335, 376, 375
Vins d'Alsace, Mader 420
Vins d'Alsace Kuehn 414
Vins Fins d'Alsace E. Boeckel 185, 191,
    219, 224, 286, 302, 316, 339, 364
Vintages of the century 509–15
Vinum nobile 4
Viognier grape 372
Viticultural cycle 24–31
Viticultural Institute in Colmar 71
Vitis allobrogica 6, 127
Vitis vinifera 5, 22
Voegtlinshoffen village 137, 519
Vogelgarten lieu-dit 130, 258, 519
Vogt, Laurent 466
Volcanic soils 63
Volerie des Aigles 105
Voltaire 208
Vorbourg grand cru 125–6, 139, 217,
    518–19
Vorlauf 107, 280
Vosges foothills
    slopes 56
    soil 55
    vineyards 49
Vosges mountains
    slopes 56
    ballons 47
    influence 47
    soil 55
    vineyards 49

Wach, Guy 182, 191
Wach, Jean 466
Wackenthaler, André 180, 288, 466
Wade, Bob 236
Wagner, Gérard 466
Walbach village 138, 519

Walch 548
Walcha 548
Walsch 548
Wangen village 138
Wangenbourg 138
Wanne lieu-dit 517–18
Wantz, André 244, 467
Wantz, Ch. 96, 118, 219, 282, 288,
    332–4, 467
Wantz, Ehrhardt 95–6
Wartstein 519
Watchman of Turckheim 135
Wattwiller village 139
Weber, Bernard 110, 163, 246, 319,
    517, 467
Weber, Jacques 415
Weck, Clément 467
Weeding 28
Week, Clément 175
Weinbach, Domaine 105, 206–7, 228,
    277, 286, 288, 291, 316, 319,
    322–6, 384, 468
Weingarten, Domaine 258
Weinsticher 4
Weinsticheren 7, 69, 407
Weiss valley 105
Weissburgunder 32
Weisse Muscketraube grape (syn) 35
Weisse Muskateller grape (syn) 35
Weisser Burgunder grape (syn) 32
Weisser Riesling grape (syn) 34
Welsch, language of 548
Welsh, of the Vosges mountains 547
Welty, Jean-Michel 470
Westerberg lieu-dit 259
Westerweingarten lieu-dit 239, 259
Westhalten village 49, 139, 519
Westhaulda 139
Westhoffen village 140
Westphalia, Treaty of 14
Wettolsheim village 2, 140 519
White Muscat grape (syn) 35
White Riesling grape (syn) 34
Wiebelsberg grand cru 68, 182, 219,
    517, 519
Wiederhirn, Maison Daniel 189, 208,
    213, 288, 471
Wihr-au-Val village 141
Willm, Alsace 70–71, 184, 227, 229,
    288, 291–2, 395, 472
Windsbuhl, Clos 98, 99, 237, 303,
    317–18, 326
Wineck castle 102

Wineck lieu-dit 518
Wineck-Schlossberg grand cru 2, 49,
    220
Wines
  acid conversion of 39
  AOC Grand Cru 340–42
  Auxerrois and new oak 272, 270–73
  Bereich Südliche Weinstrasse 143
  blended 264, 305–12
  breakdown by variety 264
  Chasselas 264, 300–302
  Chasselas and new oak 301
  cheapest 512
  Clairet 303
  Clairet regulation 545
  classic blends 307, 308–12
  common bottle-aged descriptors 266
  common youthful descriptors 266
  competition wines 342 3
  Crémant d'Alsace 43, 119, 216, 232,
    236, 264, 302, 335–40
  Crémant d'Alsace production 525
  Crémant d'Alsace regulation 546
  Crémant d'Alsace sales and
    production 534–5
  Edelwein 305–6
  Edelzwicker 10, 305–6, 306–7
  export statistics Benelux 538
  export statistics Canada 540
  export statistics Denmark 539
  export statistics Germany 537
  export statistics global 537
  export statistics Great Britain 539
  export statistics Holland 538
  export statistics Japan 542
  export statistics Sweden 541
  export statistics Switzerland 541
  export statistics USA 540
  export, home market and total
    sales 532–3
  frozen to casks 515
  Gentil 10, 305–6
  Gentil d'Alsace 308
  Gewurztraminer 264, 289–94
  Gewurztraminer and new oak 290
  Gewurztraminer SGN 322–4
  Gewurztraminer Vendange
    Tardive 315–16
  Grand Cru production 525
  grand cru regulation 545
  Klevener de Heiligenstein 7, 95–6,
    333–4, 545
  Klevener de Heiligenstein

regulation 545
Klevner de Heiligenstein (*sic*) 519
Muscat 264, 294–7
Muscat and new oak 296
Muscat SGN 327–8
Muscat Vendange Tardive 319
none produced 510–16
overproduction 9, 490–91, 513–15
overproduction or underselling? 529
passerillé 314
pH level 40
Pinot 264, 266–70
Pinot and new oak 269
Pinot Noir 264, 277–82
Pinot Noir (red) and new oak 279
Pinot Noir (rosé) and new oak 280
Quintessence SGN 321
Riesling 264, 282–8
Riesling and new oak 285
Riesling SGN 325–6
Riesling Vendange Tardive 318–19
Riesling-Zwicker 10
Rosé 280
Rosé de Marlenheim 95
Rosé de Turckheim 281
Rouge de Marlenheim 519
Rouge de Rodern 95, 277, 332, 518
Rouge de St-Hippolyte 247, 281–2,
    333
Rouge d'Alsace 41–2, 277, 279,
    303–4
Rouge d'Ottrott 277, 282, 332–3
Rouge d'Ottrott 95
sales and production 530–31
Schillerwein 304
schillerwein regulation 545
SGN, general 319, 320–27
SGN and new oak 322
SGN production 526
SGN regulation 545
super-SGN 321
Sylvaner grape 264, 298–300
Sylvaner grape and new oak 299
Tokay-Pinot Gris 264, 273–7
Tokay-Pinot Gris and new oak 275
Tokay-Pinot Gris EC legislation 274
Tokay-Pinot Gris SGN 324–5
Tokay-Pinot Gris sweetness
    issue 274
Tokay-Pinot Gris Vendange
    Tardive 317, 318
top export countries 536
Traminer-Zwicker 10

undrinkable 508, 511, 514
used to mix mortar 513, 515
Vendange Tardive, general 312–20
Vendange Tardive production 525
Vendange Tardive regulation 545
Vendange Tardive – dry or
    sweet? 314
Vendanges Tardives and new
    oak 315
vin de glace 195, 223, 408, 331–2
vin de paille ancient recipe 329–31
vin de paille, general 67, 96, 103,
    105, 118, 121, 123, 127, 136, 144,
    328–31
Vin de Pays du Bas-Rhin 306, 334–5,
    365, 428
Vin de Pays du Haut-Rhin 306,
    334–5, 354
vin de pistolet 114, 256
vin gris 280
vin jaune 304
vins de pays 334–5
vintage of the century 512
vorlauf 107, 280
youthful descriptors 266
Zwicker 9, 10, 72, 79, 82, 305–7,
    342
Wines Rouge d'Ottrott 519
Wingisheim 142
Winstub le Sommelier 74
Winstub Tiré Bouchon 434
Wintzenberg 519
Wintzenheim village 2, 141, 519
Winzenberg grand cru 77–8, 221
Wischlen, A. 472
Wissembourg Abbey 80
Wissembourg village 3, 13, 64, 142
Witches 243
Wittmann, André 224, 472
Wolfberger 38, 71, 82, 86–7, 95, 138,
    141–42, 165, 176–7, 184, 194,
    197, 211, 215, 226, 235–6, 248,
    277, 279, 281, 288, 294, 340, 345,
    347, 373, 405–6, 431, 439, 464–5,
    473
Wolfberger's L'Espace Crémant
    d'Alsace winery 475
Wolxheim village 6, 143, 517, 519
Wuenheim village 2, 144, 519
Wunsch & Mann 141, 177, 215, 288,
    475
Württemberg, dukes 71
Wurtz, Bernard 475

Wurtz, W. 277, 476

Yeast
  alcoholic levels 38
  dried or cultured 38
  indigenous 38
  nutrients 42

Zahlberg 111
Zahn, Martin 238, 435
Zahnacker, Clos du 120–21, 237–8,
  258, 307, 312, 435
Zahnacker lieu-dit 2, 517–18
Zell 145
Zellberg lieu-dit 259
Zellenberg village 144, 519
Zellwiller village 145
Zeyssolff, G. 90, 476
Ziegler-Mauler, J-J 476
Zimmer, Antoine 433–4
Zimmer, Jean-Jacques 433–4
Zimmerbach village 146
Zimmermann, A. 277, 476

Zimmermann, Jules & Rémy 476
Zind, Geneviève 477
Zind Humbrecht
  Domaine 92, 99, 119, 136, 142, 162,
    174, 177, 203, 229–30, 233, 237,
    249–50, 255, 270, 275, 277,
    286–7, 291, 294, 297, 300, 303,
    316–18, 321, 323, 325–6, 328–9,
    331, 404, 476, 482, 488
  Léonard Humbrecht 134, 202–3,
    359, 477–8, 482, 485
  Marcel Humbrecht 92, 149, 175,
    287, 297
  Olivier Humbrecht 202–3, 359, 478
  Geneviève Zind 477
Zink, Pierre-Paul 478
Zinnkoepflé grand cru 49, 222, 519
Zisser lieu-dit 519
Zisser, Clos 70–71, 184, 238, 292, 410
Zotzenberg grand cru 2, 224, 519
Zwicker 9–10, 79, 82
  Riesling-Zwicker 10
  Traminer-Zwicker 10